A TEXT BOOK OF

NETWORK ANALYSIS AND SYNTHESIS

For
Semester II

SECOND YEAR DEGREE COURSES IN ELECTRONICS/ ELECTRONICS AND TELECOMMUNICATION ENGINEERING

As Per New Revised Syllabus of
North Maharashtra University, Jalgaon,
June 2013-2014

Dr. Sachin D. Ruikar
Associate Professor, E&TC Department
Sinhgad Academy of Engineering
Kondhwa (Bk.) Pune

Advancement of knowledge

N3094

NETWORK ANALYSIS AND SYNTHESIS ISBN 978-93-83971-32-9

First Edition : January 2014

© : Author

The text of this publication, or any part thereof, should not be reproduced or transmitted in any form or stored in any computer storage system or device for distribution including photocopy, recording, taping or information retrieval system or reproduced on any disc, tape, perforated media or other information storage device etc., without the written permission of Author with whom the rights are reserved. Breach of this condition is liable for legal action.

Every effort has been made to avoid errors or omissions in this publication. In spite of this, errors may have crept in. Any mistake, error or discrepancy so noted and shall be brought to our notice shall be taken care of in the next edition. It is notified that neither the publisher nor the author or seller shall be responsible for any damage or loss of action to any one, of any kind, in any manner, therefrom.

Published By :
NIRALI PRAKASHAN
Abhyudaya Pragati, 1312, Shivaji Nagar,
Off J.M. Road, PUNE – 411005
Tel - (020) 25512336/37/39, Fax - (020) 25511379
Email : niralipune@pragationline.com

Printed at
Repro Knowledgecast Limited
India

DISTRIBUTION CENTRES
PUNE

Nirali Prakashan
119, Budhwar Peth, Jogeshwari Mandir Lane
Pune 411002, Maharashtra
Tel : (020) 2445 2044, 66022708, Fax : (020) 2445 1538
Email : bookorder@pragationline.com

Nirali Prakashan
S. No. 28/25, Dhyari,
Near Pari Company, Pune 411041
Tel : (022) 24690204 Fax : (020) 24690316
Email : dhyari@pragationline.com
bookorder@pragationline.com

MUMBAI
Nirali Prakashan
385, S.V.P. Road, Rasdhara Co-op. Hsg. Society Ltd.,
Girgaum, Mumbai 400004, Maharashtra
Tel : (022) 2385 6339 / 2386 9976, Fax : (022) 2386 9976
Email : niralimumbai@pragationline.com

DISTRIBUTION BRANCHES

NAGPUR
Pratibha Book Distributors
Above Maratha Mandir, Shop No. 3, First Floor,
Rani Jhanshi Square, Sitabuldi, Nagpur 440012,
Maharashtra, Tel : (0712) 254 7129

BENGALURU
Pragati Book House
House No. 1, Sanjeevappa Lane, Avenue Road Cross,
Opp. Rice Church, Bengaluru – 560002.
Tel : (080) 64513344, 64513355,
Mob : 9880582331, 9845021552
Email:bharatsavla@yahoo.com

JALGAON
Nirali Prakashan
34, V. V. Golani Market, Navi Peth, Jalgaon 425001,
Maharashtra, Tel : (0257) 222 0395
Mob : 9423491860

KOLHAPUR
Nirali Prakashan
New Mahadvar Road,
Kedar Plaza, 1st Floor Opp. IDBI Bank
Kolhapur 416 012, Maharashtra. Mob : 9855046155

CHENNAI
Pragati Books
9/1, Montieth Road, Behind Taas Mahal, Egmore,
Chennai 600008 Tamil Nadu, Tel : (044) 6518 3535,
Mob : 94440 01782 / 98450 21552 / 98805 82331, Email : bharatsavla@yahoo.com

---

RETAIL OUTLETS
PUNE

Pragati Book Centre
157, Budhwar Peth, Opp. Ratan Talkies,
Pune 411002, Maharashtra
Tel : (020) 2445 8887 / 6602 2707, Fax : (020) 2445 8887
Pragati Book Centre
Amber Chamber, 28/A, Budhwar Peth,
Appa Balwant Chowk, Pune : 411002, Maharashtra,
Tel : (020) 20240335 / 66281669
Email : pbcpune@pragationline.com

Pragati Book Centre
676/B, Budhwar Peth, Opp. Jogeshwari Mandir,
Pune 411002, Maharashtra
Tel : (020) 6601 7784 / 6602 0855
PBC Book Sellers & Stationers
152, Budhwar Peth, Pune 411002, Maharashtra
Tel : (020) 2445 2254 / 6609 2463

MUMBAI
Pragati Book Corner
Indira Niwas, 111 - A, Bhavani Shankar Road, Dadar (W), Mumbai 400028, Maharashtra
Tel : (022) 2422 3526 / 6662 5254, Email : pbcmumbai@pragationline.com

---

www.pragationline.com   info@pragationline.com

PREFACE

It gives me immense pleasure to present this book on **"Network Analysis and Synthesis"**.

The book is written mainly for the second year students of Electronics/Electronics and Telecommunication Engineering courses of North Maharashtra University for the subject **"Network Analysis and Synthesis"**. It is written as per the revised syllabus of North Maharashtra University, Jalgaon (w.e.f. 2012).

In recent years communication has become an important part of our life. It has become essential to understand basic concept of Network Analysis almost for every engineer.

This text includes information about Network Analysis and Synthesis. Mathematical treatment of various concepts are given wherever necessary. Number of Solved Problems and Exercises are included in each unit.

Unit I provides the Concepts of System and Network Functions.

Unit II provides the Concepts of Frequency Selective Networks.

Unit III provides the Concepts of Two Port Networks Parameters.

Unit IV provides the Concepts of Attenuators and Filters.

Unit V provides the Concepts of Synthesis of Networks.

Nirali Prakashan put the book, what we thought into reality. Our sincere thanks to Shri. Dineshbhai Furia, Shri, Jignesh Furia and Shri. M. P. Munde. The books could be completed in time, due to sincere and hard work of Nirali Prakashan's staff namely Mr. Akbar Shaikh, Mrs. Sonal Pokharkar, Mrs. Prajakta Shrimandikar and Miss Chaitali Takale. I thank them all.

I also thankful to **Mr. Pruthviraj M. More**, Branch Manager, Jalgaon office for his valuable help and efforts for promotion of my books.

Valuable suggestions from my esteemed readers to improve the text will be most welcome and highly appreciated.

January 2014 **Author**

Pune

SYLLABUS

Unit I: System and Network Functions　　　　　　　　(09 Lectures, 16 marks)

(a) Definition and Types of Network Function with their Numericals.

(b) Concept of Complex frequency and Characteristics of Standard Signals.

(c) Concept of Laplace Transform and Laplace Transform of basic R, L and C Component.

(d) Network Analysis using Laplace Transform with initial condition, Numericals.

(e) Concept of Pole and Zero, Time-domain behaviour from Pole-zero Plot, Concept of residues.

Unit II: Frequency Selective Networks　　　　　　　　(08 Lectures, 16 marks)

(a) Concept Resonance, Types of Resonance, Q-factor and their significance.

(b) Series Resonance, Resonance frequency with Derivation, Variation of Impedance, Current with Frequency, Bandwidth and Selectivity, Examples.

(c) Parallel Resonance, Resonance Frequency, Bandwidth and Selectivity, Examples.

Unit III: Two Port Networks Parameters　　　　　　　　(08 Lectures, 16 marks)

(a) Introduction to Two Port Network and their different parameters such as Z, Y, h, ABCD Parameter with Equivalent Circuit.

(b) Concept of Reciprocity and Symmetry condition for Two Port Network Parameters.

(c) Inter-connection of Two Port Networks in Series, Parallel, Cascade Connection and Series-Parallel Connection.

(d) Inter-conversion of the Parameters, Examples of finding the different Two Port Network Parameters.

Unit IV: Attenuators and Filters　　　　　　　　(08 Lectures, 16 marks)

(a) Concept of Neper and Decibel (dB).

(b) Introduction of Attenuator, Types of Attenuator, Design of Symmetrical 'T' and 'π' Attenuator, Examples.

(c) Filter Fundamentals and Design of different types of Filters such as constant K-type Low Pass and High Pass Filter, Examples.

(d) Design of m-Derived Low Pass and High Pass filter, Examples. Concept of Band Pass, Band Stop Filter, Terminating Half Section and Concept of Composite Filter.

Unit V: Synthesis of Networks　　　　　　　　(09 Lectures, 16 marks)

(a) Hurwitz Polynomial and its properties, Check Hurwitz Criteria by Routh array or Continued Fraction expansion method, Examples.

(b) Positive Real Function and its Properties, Procedure for Testing of Positive Real Function, Examples.

(c) Synthesis of One Port Network such as LC, RC, RL with their properties.

(d) Synthesis of L-C, R-C and R-L networks using Foster and Cauer forms, Examples.

CONTENTS

UNIT I: SYSTEM AND NETWORK FUNCTIONS — 1.1 – 1.106

UNIT II: FREQUENCY SELECTIVE NETWORKS — 2.1 – 2.82

UNIT III: TWO PORT NETWORKS PARAMETERS — 3.1 – 3.30

UNIT IV: ATTENUATORS AND FILTERS — 4.1 – 4.138

UNIT V: SYNTHESIS OF NETWORKS — 5.1 – 5.116

Unit I

SYSTEM AND NETWORK FUNCTIONS

Contents ...

1.1 System Function or Network Functions
1.2 Laplace Transform
    1.2.1 Method of Transformation
    1.2.2 The Concept of Complex Frequency
    1.2.3 Definition of Laplace Transform
    1.2.4 Properties of Laplace Transform
        1.2.4.1 Linearity
        1.2.4.2 Real Differentiation (Differentiation with respect to Time)
        1.2.4.3 Real Integration (Integration with respect to Time)
        1.2.4.4 Differentiation by s (In the Frequency Domain)
        1.2.4.5 Complex Translation
        1.2.4.6 Real Translation (Shifting Theorem)
        1.2.4.7 Scaling
1.3 Poles and Zeros
1.4 Necessary Condition for Transfer Function and Driving Point Function
1.5 Time Domain behaviour from Pole-Zero Plot
1.6 Magnitude and Phase (Frequency Domain) Response from Pole-Zero Plot
1.7 Pole Position and Stability
    Exercise

1.1 SYSTEM FUNCTION OR NETWORK FUNCTIONS

A network function F (s) is a function of 's' relating transform of voltage and currents. The network may contain passive component dependent sources, **but must not contain any independence energy sources and initial conditions**.

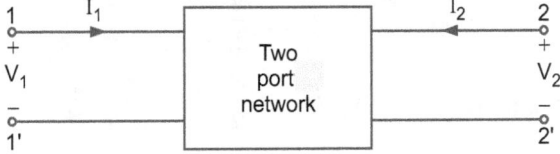

Fig. 1.1

In a linear network (system), excitation e (t) and response r (t) are related by linear differential equations. But when Laplace transform is used, then relation between E (s) and R (s) is algebraic.

Thus, $\quad\quad\quad R(s) = F(s) E(s)$ ... (1.1)

F (s) is called system function. It assume many forms depending on whether excitation E (s) is voltage or current and response (R) is voltage or current.

Driving Point Functions: If excitation and response are measured at same pair of terminals, then it is called driving point function.

$$Z_{11}(s) = \frac{V_1(s)}{I_1(s)} \quad\quad \ldots (a)$$

is a driving point impedance function.

$$Z_{22}(s) = \frac{V_2(s)}{I_2(s)} \quad\quad \ldots (b)$$

is also driving point impedance function.

Thus, $Z_{11}(s)$, $Z_{22}(s)$ are transform impedances which are ratio of voltage transform to current transform at a port.

Similarly, $\quad\quad Y_{22}(s) = \dfrac{I_2(s)}{V_2(s)}$

and $\quad\quad Y_{11}(s) = \dfrac{I_1(s)}{V_1(s)}$

are transform admittances. Here they are called driving point admittance function.

Transfer Functions: If excitation and response are measured at separate terminal pairs, then it is called transfer function. For two port network, there are four types of transfer function.

Voltage transfer function, $\quad G_{21}(s) = \dfrac{V_2(s)}{V_1(s)}$ ... (c)

Current transfer function, $\quad \alpha_{21}(s) = \dfrac{I_2(s)}{I_1(s)}$ ... (d)

Transfer impedance function, $\quad Z_{21}(s) = \dfrac{V_2(s)}{I_1(s)}$ ... (e)

Transfer admittance function, $\quad Y_{21}(s) = \dfrac{I_2(s)}{V_1(s)}$ ... (f)

Following examples explain various types of network functions.

This is series R–L–C circuit which has only one port. Driving point impedance function for this is

$$Z(s) = R_1 + L_1 s + \frac{1}{C_1 s}$$

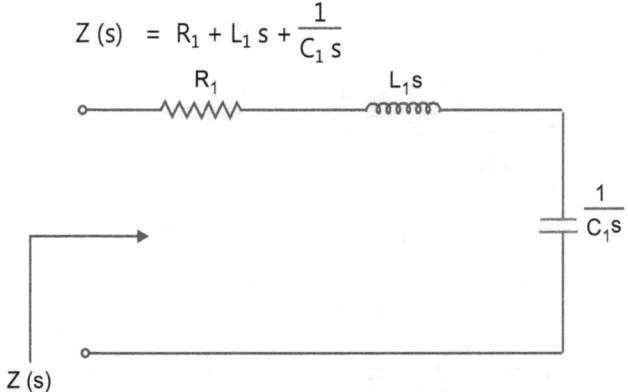

Fig. 1.2: One-port network

For this network, driving point admittance function is

$$Y(s) = Cs + \frac{1}{(R + sL)}$$

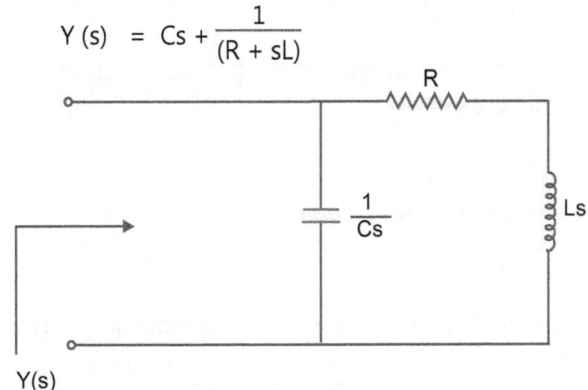

Fig. 1.3: One-port network

Thus for one port network only driving point impedance and admittance functions are define. Also $Z(s) = \frac{1}{Y(s)}$. But transfer functions are not defined.

Now consider two port network shown in Fig. 1.4.

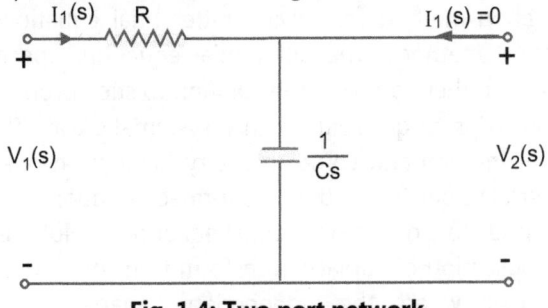

Fig. 1.4: Two port network

Driving point impedance function is

$$Z_{11}(s) = \frac{V_1(s)}{I_1(s)} = R + \frac{1}{sC}$$

Transfer impedance function

$$Z_{21}(s) = \frac{V_2(s)}{I_1(s)} = \frac{1}{sC}$$

Voltage ratio transfer function,

$$G_{21}(s) = \frac{\frac{1}{Cs} \cdot I_1(s)}{\left(R + \frac{1}{Cs}\right) I_1(s)}$$

i.e.
$$G_{21}(s) = \frac{1}{1 + RCS}$$

Current ratio transfer function,

$$\alpha_{21}(s) = \frac{I_2(s)}{I_1(s)} = 0$$

Impedance functions and admittance functions together are called as immittance functions. For one port networks,

$$Z(s) = \frac{1}{Y(s)},$$

While for two port networks, usually,

$$Z_{12}(s) \neq \frac{1}{Y_{12}(s)}$$

In general, all network functions are the ratio of polynomial in s. The general form is

$$F(s) = \frac{p(s)}{q(s)} = \frac{a_0 s^n + a_1 s^{n-1} + \ldots + a_n}{b_0 s^m + b_1 s^{m-1} + \ldots + b_m} \qquad \ldots (1.2)$$

where 'n' is the degree of numerator polynomial and 'm' is the degree of denominator polynomial.

1.2 LAPLACE TRANSFORM

Laplace Transformation method for solving differential equations offers a number of advantages over classical methods. The differential equations specifying performance of complicated networks are rather complex. The solution to such problems is time consuming. Laplace Transformation helps to get solution in a systematic way. This method gives total solution - the particular integral and complementary function in one operation. The initial conditions are automatically specified in the transformed equations.

In the classical methods for solving differential equations, solutions are obtained directly in the time domain. Application of Laplace Transform transforms the differential equations to the frequency domain where the independent variable is complex frequency 's'.

Differentiation and integration in the time domain are transformed into algebraic operations. Thus, the solution is obtained by simple algebraic operations in the frequency domain.

1.2.1 Method of Transformation

Fig. 1.5 shows the philosophy of transform methods. It shows the procedure to obtain Sol. of differential equation.

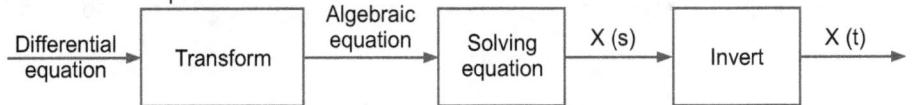

Fig. 1.5: Transform method to solve integro-differential equation

Step I: Consider the linear differential equation

$$y(x(t)) = f(t) \qquad \ldots (a)$$

where
$f(t)$ = Forcing function
$x(t)$ = Unknown variable
$y(x(t))$ = Differential equation

Step II: Transforming both sides of equation (a),

$$T[y(x(t))] = T[f(t)] \qquad \ldots (b)$$
$$Y(X(s), s) = F(s) \qquad \ldots (c)$$

where,
$X(s) = T[x(t)]$
$F(s) = T[f(t)]$
$Y(X(s), s)$ = Algebraic equation in s.

Thus, by process of transformation differential equation in time domain are changed to algebraic equations in frequency domain.

Step III: Solve equation (c) algebraically to obtain $X(s)$.
Step IV: Take inverse transformation to obtain

$$x(t) = T^{-1}[X(s)] \qquad \ldots (d)$$

1.2.2 The Concept of Complex Frequency

The Sol. of the differential equations for networks gives rise to time domain function in the form

$$K_n e^{S_n t} \qquad \ldots (a)$$

where,
$$S_n = \sigma_n + j\omega_n \qquad \ldots (1.3)$$

is the complex number defined as the complex frequency,

ω_n is imaginary part of complex frequency interpreted as radian frequency (radians/sec.),
σ_n is real part of complex frequency defined as neper frequency (nepers/sec.).

The radian frequency ω_n appears in time domain equations in the forms $\sin \omega_n t$ or $\cos \omega_n t$.

σ_n appears as an exponential factor $I = I_0 e^{\sigma_n t}$ such that

$$\sigma_n = \frac{1}{t} \ln \frac{I}{I_0} \qquad \ldots (1.4)$$

Case I: Let $\quad s_n = \sigma_n + j0$

The exponential function of equation (a) becomes $K_n e^{\sigma_n t}$. It is an exponential function which increases exponentially for $\sigma_n > 0$ and decays exponentially for $\sigma_n < 0$.

When $\sigma_n = 0$; $K_n e^{\sigma_n t} = K_n e^{0t} = K_n$ ... (b)

A time invariant quantity which in terms of current and voltage is described as "direct current".

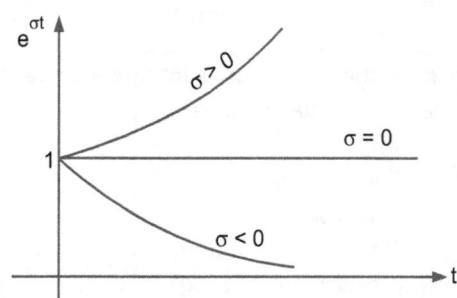

Fig. 1.6: Plot of $e^{\sigma t}$ for positive, negative and zero value of σ

Case II: Let $\quad s_n = 0 \pm j\omega_n$ (radian frequency only)

$\therefore \quad K_n e^{\pm j\omega_n t} = K_n (\cos \omega_n t \pm j \sin \omega_n t)$ ... (c)

Case III: Let $\quad s_n = \sigma_n + j\omega_n$

$$K_n e^{(\sigma_n + j\omega_n) t} = K_n e^{\sigma_n t} e^{j\omega_n t}$$

$$= K_n e^{\sigma_n t} (\cos \omega_n t + j \sin \omega_n t) \quad \text{... (d)}$$

$$\text{Re}\left(e^{s_n t}\right) = e^{\sigma_n t} \cos \omega_n t$$

$$\text{Im}\left(e^{s_n t}\right) = e^{\sigma_n t} \sin \omega_n t$$

For $\sigma_n < 0$, waveform is damped sinusoid.

For $\sigma_n > 0$, oscillations increase exponentially.

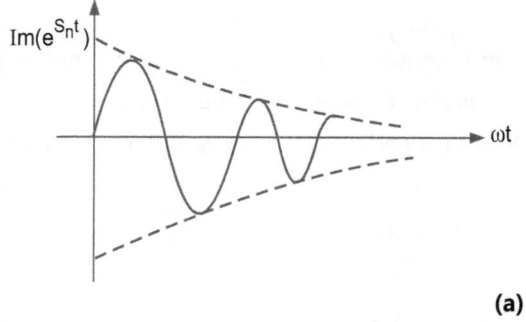 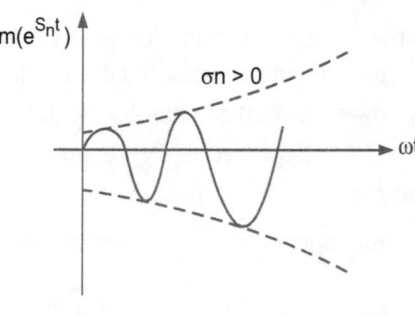

(a)

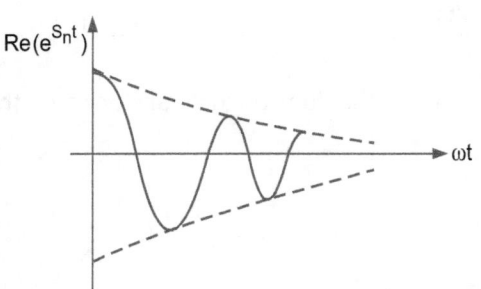 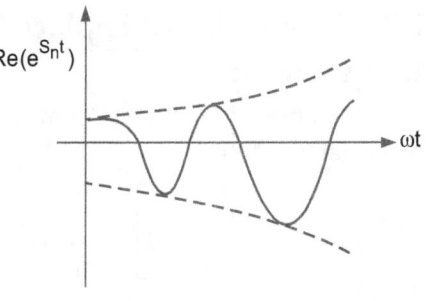

(b)
Fig. 1.7: Real and imaginary projections of rotating phasors ωt

1.2.3 Definition of Laplace Transform

The Laplace Transform of a function of time f (t) is defined as,

$$L[f(t)] = F(s) = \int_0^\infty f(t)\, e^{-st}\, dt \qquad \ldots (1.5)$$

where, s is the complex frequency variable $s = \sigma + j\omega$

Thus, Laplace Transform converts general time domain function f (t) into a corresponding frequency domain representation F (s).

Ex. 1.1: Find Laplace Transform of unit step function defined as,

$$u(t) = 1;\ t \geq 0$$
$$ = 0;\ t < 0$$

Sol.: $f(t) = u(t)$

∴ By definition of Laplace Transform,

$$F(s) = \int_0^\infty u(t)\, e^{-st}\, dt = \int_0^\infty 1 \cdot e^{-st}\, dt = \left.\frac{e^{-st}}{-s}\right|_0^\infty$$

$$= 0 - \left(-\frac{1}{s}\right) = \frac{1}{s}$$

∴ $$L\, u(t) = \frac{1}{s}$$

Ex. 1.2: Find Laplace Transform of $f(t) = e^{at}$.

Sol.: $f(t) e^{at} u(t)$

By definition of Laplace Transform,

$$F(s) = \int_0^\infty e^{at}\, e^{-st}\, dt = \left.-\frac{e^{-(s-a)t}}{s-a}\right|_0^\infty = \frac{1}{s-a}$$

∴ $$L\, e^{at} u(t) = \frac{1}{s-a}$$

1.2.4 Properties of Laplace Transform

1.2.4.1 Linearity

The transform of a finite sum of time functions is the sum of the transforms of the individual transforms.

i.e. $\quad L\left[\sum_i f_i(t)\right] = \sum_i L[f_i(t)]$

If $f_1(t)$ and $f_2(t)$ are two functions of time and a and b are constants.

Then, $L[a f_1(t) + b f_2(t)] = a F_1(s) + b F_2(s)$ ... (1.6)

where, $\quad L f_1(t) = F_1(s)$

and $\quad L f_2(t) = F_2(s)$

1.2.4.2 Real Differentiation (Differentiation with Respect to Time)

If $\quad L f(t) = F(s)$

then, $\quad L\left[\dfrac{d}{dt} f(t)\right] = s F(s) - f(0-)$ ... (1.7)

where, $f(0-)$ is the value of $f(t)$ at $t = 0-$ ($t = 0-$ is the time just before $t = 0$).

Similarly for transform of second derivative,

i.e.
$$L\left[\dfrac{d^2}{dt^2} f(t)\right] = L\left[\dfrac{d}{dt} \cdot \dfrac{d}{dt} f(t)\right]$$

$$= s\left[L \dfrac{d}{dt} f(t)\right] - \dfrac{df}{dt}(0-)$$

$$= s[s F(s) - f(0-)] - \dfrac{df}{dt}(0-)$$

$$= s^2 F(s) - s f(0-) - \dfrac{df}{dt}(0-) \quad\quad\quad ... (1.8)$$

Hence, general expression for n^{th} derivative is,

$$L \dfrac{d^n}{dt^n} f(t) = s^n F(s) - s^{n-1} f(0-) - s^{n-2} f'(0-) - \ldots - f^{n-1}(0-) \quad ... (1.9)$$

where, $\quad f'(0-) = \dfrac{d}{dt} f(0-); \quad f^{n-1}(0-) = \dfrac{d^{n-1} f(0-)}{dt^{n-1}}$

This property transforms differential equations in time domain to algebraic equations in the frequency domain.

1.2.4.3 Real Integration (Integration with respect to Time)

If $L f(t) = F(s)$, then the Laplace Transform of the integral of f (t) is F (s) divided by s that is,

$$L\left[\int_0^t f(t)\, dt\right] = \frac{F(s)}{s} \qquad \ldots (1.10)$$

1.2.4.4 Differentiation by s (In the Frequency Domain)

Differentiation by s in the complex frequency domain corresponds to multiplication by t in the time domain that is,

$$L[t\, f(t)] = -\frac{d\, F(s)}{ds} \qquad \ldots (1.11)$$

1.2.4.5 Complex Translation

By the complex translation property if

$$F(s) = L f(t)$$

then, $\qquad F(s-a) = L[e^{at} f(t)] \qquad \ldots (1.12)$

where, a is a complex number.

1.2.4.6 Real Translation (Shifting Theorem)

This theorem transforms a delayed or shifted function of time.

i.e. $\qquad F(t) = f(t-a)\,;\ t > a$

$\qquad\qquad\quad = 0\,;\qquad t < a$

Let $\qquad L[f(t)] = F(s)$

then, the transform of the function delayed by time a is,

$$L[f(t-a)\, u(t-a)] = e^{-as} F(s) \qquad \ldots (1.13)$$

1.2.4.7 Scaling

If $\qquad L f(t) = F(s)$

then, $\qquad L[f(at)] = \dfrac{1}{a} F\left(\dfrac{s}{a}\right)$ where, $a > 0 \qquad \ldots (1.14)$

1.2.4.8 Scalar Multiplication

If $\qquad L f(t) = F(s)$

then, $\qquad L k f(t) = k F(s) \qquad \ldots (1.15)$

1.2.4.9 Convolution in Time Domain

If $f_1(t)$ and $f_2(t)$ are two functions which are zero for $t < 0$, the convolution theorem states that if the transform of $f_1(t)$ is $F_1(s)$ and transform of $f_2(t)$ is $F_2(s)$, then the transform of the convolution of $f_1(t)$ and $f_2(t)$ is the product of the individual transforms $F_1(s) F_2(s)$ that is,

$$L\left[\int_0^t f_1(t-u) f_2(u)\, du\right] = F_1(s) F_2(s) \qquad \ldots (1.16)$$

The integral $\int_0^t f_1(t-u) f_2(u)\, du$ is the convolution integral or folding integral and is denoted operationally as

$$\int_0^t f_1(t-u) f_2(u)\, du = f_1(t) * f_2(t) \qquad \ldots (1.17)$$

This theorem is used to find the inverse transformation.

1.2.4.10 Applications of Properties of Laplace Transform to Find Laplace Transforms of Typical Functions

Ex. 1.3:
$$f(t) = \sin \omega t = \frac{e^{j\omega t} - e^{-j\omega t}}{2j}$$

Sol.: Using property of linearity,

$$L \sin \omega t = \frac{1}{2j}\left[L\, e^{j\omega t} - L\, e^{-j\omega t}\right]$$

$$= \frac{1}{2j}\left[\frac{1}{s-j\omega} - \frac{1}{s+j\omega}\right]$$

$$= \frac{\omega}{s^2 + \omega^2}$$

Ex. 1.4:
$$f(t) = \cos \omega t = \frac{e^{j\omega t} + e^{-j\omega t}}{2}$$

Sol.:
$$L[\cos \omega t] = \frac{1}{2}\left[L\, e^{j\omega t} + L\, e^{-j\omega t}\right]$$

$$= \frac{1}{2}\left[\frac{1}{s-j\omega} + \frac{1}{s+j\omega}\right]$$

$$= \frac{s}{s^2 + \omega^2}$$

Ex. 1.5: The unit ramp function

$$f(t) = t; \quad t > 0$$
$$= 0; \quad t < 0$$

Sol.: By property of Laplace Transform,

$$L[t\,f(t)] = -\frac{dF(s)}{ds}$$

Let
$$f(t) = u(t)$$

$\therefore$
$$F(s) = L\,\omega(t) = \frac{1}{s}$$

Hence,
$$L[t\,f(t)] = -\frac{d}{ds}\left(\frac{1}{s}\right)$$

$$= \frac{1}{s^2}$$

Ex. 1.6: The unit impulse function is given by

$$\delta(t) = 1; \quad t = 0$$
$$= 0; \quad \text{for all other values of } t$$

Sol.: Unit impulse function is first derivative of a unit step function.

$$\frac{d}{dt}\omega(t) = \delta(t)$$

By property of Laplace Transform,

$$L\left[\frac{d}{dt}\omega(t)\right] = s\,F(s) - f(0-)$$

$$= s \cdot \frac{1}{s} - 0$$

$$= 1$$

Ex. 1.7: Find Laplace Transform of te^{-at}.

Sol.: By property of complex translation,

$$L\,e^{at}\,f(t) = F(s-a)$$

Let
$$f(t) = t$$

$\therefore$
$$F(s) = \frac{1}{s^2}$$

$\therefore$
$$L\,t\,e^{-at} = \frac{1}{(s+a)^2}$$

Ex. 1.8: $f(t) = t^n$

Sol.: $L(t^n) = \int_0^\infty e^{-st} t^n \, dt$

Put $st = x$

$\therefore \quad L\, t^n = \int_0^\infty e^{-x} \frac{x^n}{s^n} \cdot \frac{dx}{s}$

$= \frac{1}{s^{n+1}} \int_0^\infty e^{-x} x^n \, dx$

$= \frac{\Gamma(n+1)}{s^{n+1}}$

If n is positive integer, $\Gamma(n+1) = n!$

$\therefore \quad L(t^n) = \frac{n!}{s^{n+1}}$ \quad if n is positive integer

---

Ex. 1.9: Find Laplace Transform of $e^{-at} \cos \omega t$.

Sol.: Let $f(t) = \cos \omega t$

$\therefore \quad F(s) = \frac{s}{s^2 + \omega^2}$

By property of complex translation,

$$L\, e^{-at} \cos at = \frac{s+a}{(s+a)^2 + \omega^2}$$

Ex. 1.10: Verify the convolution theorem for the pair of functions $f_1(t) = t$, $f_2(t) = e^{at}$.

Sol.: Since, $f_1(t) = t$ and $f_2(t) = e^{at}$

$F_1(s) = \frac{1}{s^2}$ and $F_2(s) = \frac{1}{s-a}$

Convolution theorem states that,

$$L\left[\int_0^t f_1(u) f_2(t-u) \, du\right] = L\left[\int_0^t f_1(t-u) \cdot f_2(u) \, du\right] = F_1(s) F_2(s)$$

Now,
$$\int_0^t f_1(u) f_2(t-u)\, du = \int_0^t u \cdot e^{a(t-u)}\, du$$

$$= \left[\frac{u}{-a} e^{a(t-u)} - \int_0^t \frac{e^{a(t-u)}}{-a} \cdot 1\, du\right] \quad \text{(Integrating by part)}$$

$$= \left[\frac{u}{-a} e^{a(t-u)} - \frac{1}{a^2} e^{a(t-u)}\right]_0^t$$

$$= \frac{1}{a^2}\left[e^{at} - at - 1\right]$$

Hence,
$$L\left\{\int_0^t f_1(u) \cdot f_2(t-u)\, du\right\} = L\left\{\frac{1}{a^2}(e^{at} - at - 1)\right\}$$

$$= \frac{1}{a^2}\left[\frac{1}{s-a} - \frac{a}{s^2} - \frac{1}{s}\right]$$

$$= \frac{1}{s^2(s-a)}$$

$$= F_1(s) \cdot F_2(s)$$

Hence, the convolution theorem for given pair of functions is verified.

1.2.4.11 The Initial-Value and Final-Value Theorems

The initial value theorem states that the initial value of the time domain function f(t) can be obtained from its Laplace transform F(s) by first multiplying the transform by s and then letting s approach infinity.

$$f(0+) = \lim_{t \to 0+} f(t) = \lim_{s \to \infty} sF(s) \qquad \ldots (1.18)$$

The above equation is valid for continuous function or at most having a step discontinuity at t = 0.

The final value theorem states that

$$\lim_{t \to \infty} f(t) = \lim_{s \to 0} sF(s) \qquad \ldots (1.19)$$

provided the poles of F(s) must not be in right half of complex frequency plane.

Table 1.2: Laplace Transforms of some typical functions

f (t)	F (s)
$\delta(t)$	1
u (t)	$\dfrac{1}{s}$
t u (t)	$\dfrac{1}{s^2}$
t^n	$\dfrac{n!}{s^{n+1}}$
e^{-at}	$\dfrac{1}{s+a}$
$t\,e^{-at}$	$\dfrac{1}{(s+a)^2}$
$\dfrac{t^{n-1}}{(n-1)!}\,e^{-at}$	$\dfrac{1}{(s+a)^n}$
$\sin \omega t$	$\dfrac{\omega}{s^2+\omega^2}$
$\cos \omega t$	$\dfrac{s}{s^2+\omega^2}$
$e^{-at} \sin \omega t$	$\dfrac{\omega}{(s+a)^2+\omega^2}$
$e^{-at} \cos \omega t$	$\dfrac{s+a}{(s+a)^2+\omega^2}$
$\cosh \alpha t$	$\dfrac{s}{s^2-\alpha^2}$
$\sinh \alpha t$	$\dfrac{\alpha}{s^2-\alpha^2}$

Table 1.3: Properties of Laplace Transform

Operation	Property
Addition	$L[a f_1(t) + b f_2(t)] = a F_1(s) + b F_2(s)$
Scalar multiplication	$L[k f(t)] = k F(s)$
Time differentiation	$L\left\{\dfrac{d f(t)}{dt}\right\} = s F(s) - f(0-)$
	$L\left\{\dfrac{d^2 f(t)}{dt^2}\right\} = s^2 F(s) - s f(0-) - f'(0-)$
	$L\left\{\dfrac{d^n f(t)}{dt^n}\right\} = s^n F(s) - s^{n-1} f(0-) - s^{n-2} f'(0-) \ldots - f^{n-1}(0-)$
Time integration	$\displaystyle\int_{0-}^{t} f(u)\, du = \dfrac{F(s)}{s}$
Complex translation	$L\, e^{at} f(t) = F(s-a)$
Shifting theorem	$L[f(t-a)\, u(t-a)] = e^{-as} F(s)$
Convolution theorem	$L\, f_1(t) * f_2(t) = F_1(s) F_2(s)$
Initial value theorem	$f(0+) = \displaystyle\lim_{s \to \infty} s F(s)$
Final value theorem	$F(\infty) = \displaystyle\lim_{s \to 0} s F(s)$

1.2.5 Inverse Laplace Transform

If $\{f(t)\} = F(s)$, then $f(t)$ is called the inverse Laplace Transform of $F(s)$. This relation is denoted by

$$L^{-1}\{F(s)\} = f(t) \qquad \ldots (1.20)$$

Following are some of the methods to find inverse Laplace Transform by using known Laplace transforms of elementary functions.

1.2.5.1 Shifting Theorem

If $\qquad L^{-1}[F(s)] = f(t)$

then, $\qquad L^{-1}\{F(s-a)\} = e^{at} f(t) \qquad \ldots (1.21)$

1.2.5.2 Frequency Multiplication Theorem

If standard transform $F(s)$ is multiplied by s, then the inverse transform is the differentiation of $f(t)$.

If $\quad L^{-1}\{F(s)\} = f(t)$ and $f(0) = 0$,

Then, $\quad L^{-1}\{s F(s)\} = \dfrac{d}{dt} f(t)$ ... (1.22)

This can be generalized as,

$$L^{-1}\{s^n F(s)\} = \dfrac{d^n}{dt^n}\{f(t)\}$$ ... (1.23)

with conditions $f(0) = f'(0) = \ldots = f^{n-1}(0) = 0$.

Ex. 1.11: Find inverse Laplace transform of the following:

(a) $\quad F(s) = \dfrac{1}{s+5}$

$\therefore \quad L^{-1} \dfrac{1}{s+5} = e^{-5t} \qquad\qquad \left[\because L^{-1} \dfrac{1}{s+a} = e^{at}\right]$

(b) $\quad F(s) = \dfrac{2s+6}{s^2+4}$

$L^{-1} \dfrac{2s+6}{s^2+4} = L^{-1}\left[2 \cdot \dfrac{s}{s^2+4} + 3 \cdot \dfrac{2}{s^2+4}\right]$

$\qquad = 2\cos 2t + 3\sin 2t$

(c) $\quad F(s) = \dfrac{s+7}{s^2+2s+5}$

Sol.: First complete a square in the denominator.

Thus, $\quad s^2 + 2s + 5 = (s+1)^2 + (2)^2$

Hence, $\quad F(s) = \dfrac{s+7}{(s+1)^2 + (2)^2} = \dfrac{s+1}{(s+1)^2 + (2)^2} + 3 \dfrac{2}{(s+1)^2 + (2)^2}$

But $\quad L[\cos 2t] = \dfrac{s}{s^2 + 2^2}$ and $L[\sin 2t] = \dfrac{2}{s^2 + (2)^2}$

By shifting theorem,

$L^{-1}\left\{\dfrac{s+1}{(s+1)^2 + (2)^2}\right\} = e^{-t}\cos 2t$

$L^{-1}\left\{\dfrac{2}{(s+1)^2 + (2)^2}\right\} = e^{-t}\sin 2t$

Thus, $L^{-1} \dfrac{s+7}{s^2+2s+5} = e^{-t}\cos 2t + 3e^{-t}\sin 2t$

1.2.5.3 Partial Fraction Expansion

When a network is analyzed using Laplace Transform, the final form of Sol. is a quotient of polynomial in s. Let the numerator and denominator polynomials be designated as P (s) and Q (s) respectively as,

$$I(s) = \frac{P(s)}{Q(s)} \qquad \ldots (1.24)$$

where, Q (s) = 0 is the characteristic equation.

To find out i (t) inverse Laplace Transform of I (s) should be found. For this, the transform expression for I (s) must be written as addition of simple terms.

The first step in the expansion of the quotient $\frac{P(s)}{Q(s)}$ is to check that the order of P (s) should be less than that of Q (s). If this condition is not fulfilled, P (s) should be divided by Q (s) to obtain equation of the form,

$$\frac{P(s)}{Q(s)} = A_0 + A_1 s + A_2 s^2 + \ldots\ldots B_{m-n} s^{m-n} + \frac{P_1(s)}{Q(s)} \qquad \ldots (a)$$

where,
- m = Order of P (s)
- n = Order of Q (s)

The second step is to factorize denominator polynomial Q (s).

$$Q(s) = a_0 s^n + a_1 s^{n-1} + \ldots\ldots + a_n \qquad \ldots (b)$$
$$= a_0 (s - s_1) \ldots\ldots (s - s_n)$$

where, $s_1, s_2, \ldots\ldots, s_n$ are n roots of the characteristic equation Q (s) = 0.

There are following three main possibilities of the roots of Q (s).

1. All the roots of Q (s) = 0 are simple and real. Then the partial fraction expansion is

$$\frac{P_1(s)}{(s-s_1)(s-s_2)\ldots\ldots(s-s_n)} = \frac{k_1}{s-s_1} + \frac{k_2}{s-s_2} + \ldots\ldots + \frac{k_n}{s-s_n} \qquad \ldots (c)$$

where, $k_1, k_2, \ldots\ldots, k_n$ are real constants called residues.

2. If the root of Q (s) = 0 is of multiplicity r, that is repeated. Then the partial function expansion for the repeated root is,

$$\frac{P_1(s)}{(s-s_1)^r} = \frac{k_{11}}{s-s_1} + \frac{k_{12}}{(s-s_1)^2} + \ldots\ldots + \frac{k_{1r}}{(s-s_1)^r} \qquad \ldots (d)$$

and there will be similar terms for every other repeated roots.

3. If two roots of Q (s) = 0 form a complex conjugate pair. Then partial fraction expansion is

$$\frac{P_1(s)}{Q_1(s)(s+\alpha+j\omega)(s+\alpha-j\omega)} = \frac{k_1}{(s+\alpha+j\omega)} + \frac{k_1^*}{(s+\alpha-j\omega)} + \ldots\ldots \qquad \ldots (e)$$

where k_1^* is complex conjugate of k_1.

Ex. 1.12: Determine the partial fraction expansion of given polynomial and determine its inverse transform.

(a) $$F(s) = \frac{7s + 2}{s^3 + 3s^2 + 2s}$$

The order of numerator polynomial is less than denominator polynomial, hence condition is satisfied.

Step I: Factorize denominator polynomial.

Hence,
$$F(s) = \frac{7s + 2}{s(s^2 + 3s + 2)}$$

$$= \frac{7s + 2}{s(s + 1)(s + 2)}$$

$$= \frac{k_1}{s} + \frac{k_2}{s + 2} + \frac{k_3}{s + 1}$$

Step II: All roots are real and simple.

$$k_1 = \left.\frac{7s + 2}{(s + 1)(s + 2)}\right|_{s = 0}$$

i.e. Multiply $F(s)$ by s and evaluate value for $s = 0$.

$$= \frac{2}{2}$$

$$= 1$$

$$k_2 = \left.\frac{7s + 2}{s(s + 1)}\right|_{s = -2}$$

i.e. Multiply $F(s)$ by $(s + 2)$ and evaluate value for $s = -2$.

$$= \frac{-12}{2}$$

$$= -6$$

$$k_3 = \left.\frac{7s + 2}{s(s + 2)}\right|_{s = -1}$$

i.e. Multiply $F(s)$ by $(s + 1)$ and evaluate value for $s = -1$.

$$= \frac{-7 + 2}{-1}$$

$$= 5$$

Hence,
$$F(s) = \frac{7s + 2}{s(s^2 + 3s + 2)}$$

$$= \frac{1}{s} - \frac{6}{s + 2} + \frac{5}{s + 1}$$

Step III: Take Inverse Laplace Transform of individual terms.

$$\therefore \quad f(t) = L^{-1} F(s)$$

$$= L^{-1} \frac{1}{s} + L^{-1} \frac{(-6)}{s+2} + L^{-1} \left(\frac{5}{s+1}\right)$$

$$= t - 6e^{-2t} + 5e^{-t}$$

(b)
$$F(s) = \frac{2s+1}{s(s+1)^2(s+2)}$$

$$= \frac{k_1}{s} + \frac{k_2}{(s+2)} + \frac{k_{31}}{(s+1)} + \frac{k_{32}}{(s+1)^2}$$

$$k_1 = \left.\frac{2s+1}{(s+1)^2 + (s+1)}\right|_{s=0}$$

$$= \frac{1}{2}$$

$$k_2 = \left.\frac{2s+1}{s(s+1)^2}\right|_{s=-2}$$

$$= \frac{-3}{-2}$$

$$= \frac{3}{2}$$

$$k_{31} = \left.\frac{d}{ds}\left[\frac{(s+1)^2(2s+1)}{s(s+1)^2(s+2)}\right]\right|_{s=-1}$$

$$\left[\because k_{ir-1} = \frac{d}{ds}(s+si)^r \frac{P_1(s)}{Q(s)}\right]_{s=si}$$

$$= \frac{d}{ds}\left[\frac{2s+1}{s(s+2)}\right]$$

$$= \left.\frac{s(s+2) \cdot 2 - (2s+1)(2s+2)}{s^2(s+2)^2}\right|_{s=-1}$$

$$= -2$$

$$k_{32} = \left.\frac{2s+1}{s(s+2)}\right|_{s=-1}$$

$$= 1$$

$$\therefore \quad F(s) = \frac{1}{2s} + \frac{3}{2(s+2)} - \frac{2}{(s+1)} + \frac{1}{(s+1)^2}$$

Taking inverse Laplace Transform,

$$f(t) = \frac{1}{2} + \frac{3}{2} e^{-2t} - 2e^{-t} + te^{-t}$$

(c) Determine partial fraction expansion for

$$F(s) = \frac{(2s + 1)}{(s^2 + 2s + 5)(s + 1)}$$

The roots of polynomial $(s^2 + 2s + 5)$ are

$$s_1, s_2 = \frac{-b \pm \sqrt{b^2 - 4ac}}{2a}$$

$$= \frac{-2 \pm \sqrt{4 - 20}}{2}$$

$$= -1 \pm j2$$

Hence,
$$F(s) = \frac{k_1}{(s + 1)} + \frac{k_2}{(s + 1 - j2)} + \frac{k_2^*}{(s + 1 + j2)}$$

where,
$$k_1 = \left.\frac{(2s + 1)}{(s^2 + 2s + 5)}\right|_{s = -1}$$

$$= \frac{-2 + 1}{1 - 2 + 5} = -\frac{1}{4}$$

$$k_2 = \left.\frac{(2s + 1)}{(s + 1)(s + 1 + j2)}\right|_{s = -1 + j2}$$

$$= \frac{2(-1 + j2) + 1}{(-1 + j2 + 1)(-1 + j2 + 1 + j2)}$$

$$= \frac{1}{8} - j\frac{1}{2}$$

$$k_2^* = \frac{1}{8} + j\frac{1}{2}$$

∴ Partial fraction expansion of $F(s)$ is,

$$F(s) = \frac{\left(-\frac{1}{4}\right)}{s + 1} + \frac{\frac{1}{8} - j\frac{1}{2}}{s + 1 - j2} + \frac{\frac{1}{8} + j\frac{1}{2}}{s + 1 + j2}$$

1.2.5.4 Use of Convolution Theorem

If the function $F(s)$ whose inverse transform is required can be expressed as product of $F_1(s) \cdot F_2(s)$, where inverse transforms of $F_1(s)$ and $F_2(s)$ are known, then convolution theorem can be used to find inverse transform.

If
$$L^{-1} F_1(s) = f_1(t)$$
$$L^{-1} F_2(s) = f_2(t)$$
and
$$F(s) = F_1(s) \cdot F_2(s)$$
Then,
$$L^{-1} F(s) = L^{-1} F_1(s) F_2(s)$$
$$= \int_0^t f_1(t-u) f_2(u) \, du \qquad \ldots (1.25)$$

(Note: $f_1(t)$ and $f_2(t)$ are interchangeable.)

Corollary: Since $L^{-1}\left(\dfrac{1}{s}\right) = 1 \cdot u(t)$

$$L^{-1} F(s) = f(t)$$

Let $F_1(s) = \dfrac{1}{s}, \quad F_2(s) = F(s)$

Hence, $L^{-1}\left[\dfrac{F(s)}{s}\right] = \int_0^t 1 \cdot f(u) \, du$

Ex. 1.13: Obtain the inverse Laplace Transform of the following using convolution theorem.

(a) $\quad F(s) = \dfrac{1}{s^2 (s+1)^2}$

Sol.: $\quad F(s) = \dfrac{1}{s^2 (s+1)^2}$

$$= \dfrac{1}{s^2} \cdot \dfrac{1}{(s+1)^2}$$

Let $\quad F_1(s) = \dfrac{1}{s^2}$ $\qquad \therefore$

$$L^{-1} \dfrac{1}{s^2} = t$$

$$F_2(s) = \dfrac{1}{(s+1)^2}$$

$$L^{-1} \dfrac{1}{(s+1)^2} = t e^{-t}$$

$$= f_1(t)$$
$$= f_2(t)$$

Using convolution theorem (equation 1.25),

$$L^{-1}\left\{\frac{1}{s^2(s+1)^2}\right\} = \int_0^t (t-u) \cdot u e^{-u}\, du$$

Now integrating by parts,

$$\int_0^t (t-u)\, u e^{-u}\, du = \int_0^t u(t-u) e^{-u}\, du$$

$$= \left[-(ut - u^2) e^{-u} - \int_0^t -(t - 2u) e^{-u}\, du\right]_0^t$$

$$= \left\{-(ut - u^2) e^{-u} - \left[(t - 2u) e^{-u} + \int e^{-u}(-2)\, du\right]\right\}_0^t$$

$$= \left[-(ut - u^2) e^{-u} - (t - 2u) e^{-u} - (-2) e^{-u}\right]_0^t$$

$$= t e^{-t} + 2 e^{-t} - t - 2$$

(b) $\qquad F(s) = \dfrac{1}{s(s+1)}$

Sol.: $\qquad F(s) = \dfrac{1}{s(s+1)}$

Let $\qquad F_1(s) = \dfrac{1}{s} \qquad \therefore \qquad f_1(t) = u(t)$

$\qquad F_2(s) = \dfrac{1}{s+1} \qquad \therefore \qquad f_2(t) = e^t u(t)$

By convolution theorem,

$$L^{-1} F(s) = \int_0^t f_1(u) f_2(t-u)\, du$$

$$= \int_0^t f_1(t-u) f_2(u)\, du = \int_0^t 1 \cdot e^{-u}\, du$$

$$= \left.\frac{e^{-u}}{-1}\right|_0^t$$

$$= -[e^{-t} - 1]$$

$$= 1 - e^{-t}$$

1.2.6 Laplace Transform of Basic R.L.C. Components

(A) Resistance: Voltage and current through the resistor are related in time domain by expression

$$v_R(t) = R\, i_R(t) \qquad \ldots (a)$$

or

$$i_R(t) = G\, v_R(t) \qquad \ldots (b)$$

The corresponding transform equations are,

$$V_R(s) = R\, I_R(s) \qquad \ldots (c)$$
$$I_R(s) = G\, V_R(s) \qquad \ldots (d)$$

Thus,

$$\frac{V_R(s)}{I_R(s)} = Z_R(s) = R \qquad \ldots (1.26)$$

is the transformed impedance of resistor.

$$\frac{I_R(s)}{V_R(s)} = Y_R(s) = G \qquad \ldots (1.27)$$

is the transformed admittance of resistor.

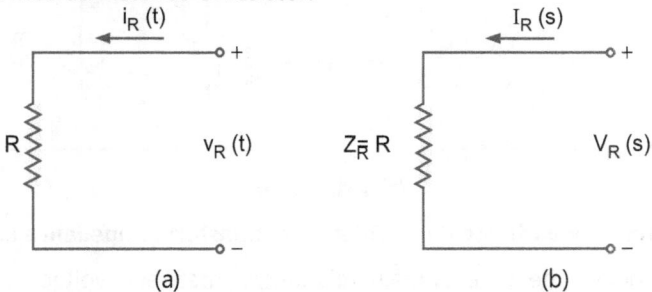

(a)   (b)

Fig. 1.8: The resistor and its transformed impedance

(B) Inductance: The time domain relationship between voltage and current in an inductor is expressed as,

$$v_L(t) = L\,\frac{di_L(t)}{dt} \qquad \ldots (1.28)$$

Transforming equation (1.42) in s domain,

$$V_L(s) = L\left[s\, I_L(s) - i_L(0-)\right] \qquad \ldots (1.29)$$

where, $i_L(0-)$ is the initial current in the inductor.

Therefore,

$$I_L(s) = \frac{1}{sL} V(s) + \frac{i_L(0-)}{s} \qquad \ldots (1.30)$$

$$I_L(s) - \frac{i_L(0-)}{s} = I_1(s) = \frac{1}{sL} V(s)$$

∴

$$\frac{I_1(s)}{V(s)} = \frac{1}{sL} = \text{Transformed admittance}$$

$$= Y_L(s) \qquad \ldots (1.31)$$

and transformed impedance is

$$Z_L(s) = \frac{1}{Y_L(s)} = sL \qquad \ldots (1.32)$$

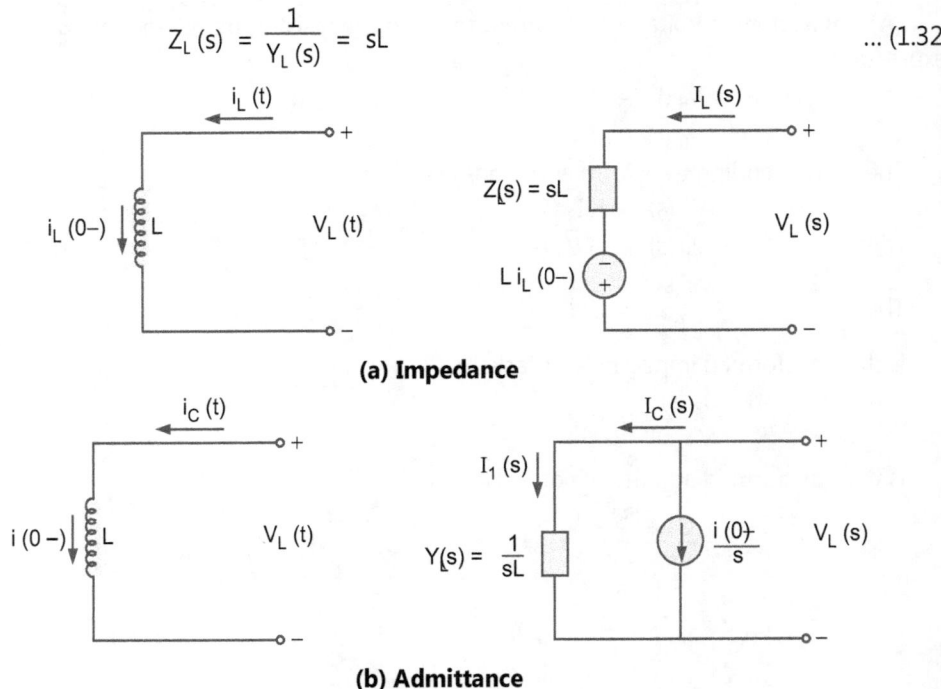

(a) Impedance

(b) Admittance

Fig. 1.9: The inductor with initial current and its transform impedance and admittance

(C) Capacitance: The time domain relationship between voltage and current for a capacitor is given by,

$$i_C(t) = C \frac{dV_C(t)}{dt}$$

$$V_C(t) = \frac{1}{C} \int_{-\infty}^{t} i_C(t)\, dt \qquad \ldots (1.33)$$

The equivalent transform equation for voltage is

$$V_C(s) = \frac{1}{C}\left[\frac{I_C(s)}{s} - \frac{q(0-)}{s}\right] \qquad \ldots (1.34)$$

where, $\dfrac{q(0-)}{C}$ (Initial voltage on the capacitor)

$$\therefore \quad \frac{1}{sC} I_C(s) = V_C(s) + \frac{V_C(0-)}{s} \qquad \ldots (e)$$

Let $V_C(s) + \dfrac{V_C(0-)}{s} = V_1(s)$

$\therefore \quad Z_C(s) = \dfrac{V_1(s)}{I_1(s)} = \dfrac{1}{sC}$ ... (1.35)

Thus, capacitor with an initial charge has an equivalent transform circuit with an impedance $\dfrac{1}{sC}$ in series with a voltage source having transform $\dfrac{-V_C(0-)}{s}$.

Similarly from equation (1.48),

$$I_C(s) = C\left[s\,V_C(s) - V_C(0-)\right]$$

$$sC\,V_C(s) = I_C(s) + C\,V_C(0-) \quad ...(f)$$

Let transform current in $Y_C(s)$ be,

$$I_1(s) = I_C(s) - C\,V_C(0-)$$

$\therefore \quad Y_C(s) = \dfrac{I_1(s)}{V_C(s)} = sC$ ... (1.36)

Thus, capacitor with an initial charge has an equivalent transform representation as an admittance sC in parallel with transform current source of value $C\,v_C(0-)$.

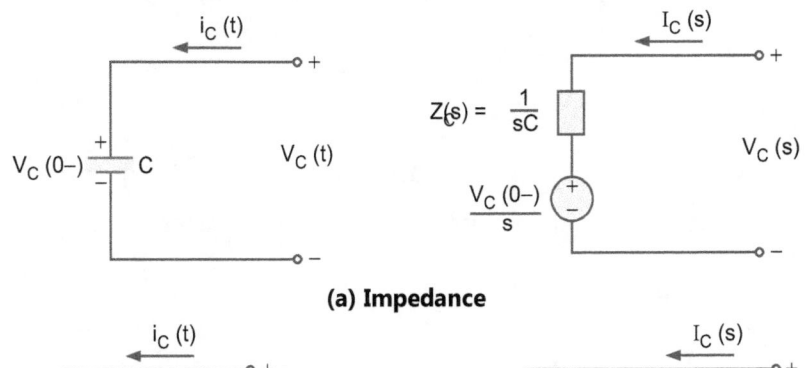

(a) Impedance

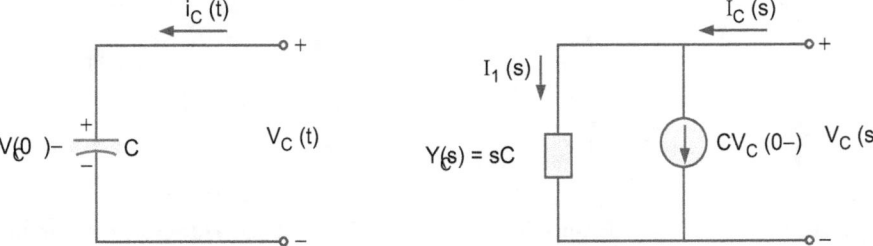

(b) Admittance

Fig. 1.10: The capacitor with initial voltage and its transform impedance and admittance

SOLVED EXAMPLES

Ex. 1.14: In the network shown in the Fig. 1.20, the switch K is moved from position a to position b at t = 0, a steady state having previously been established at position a. Solve for the current i (t) using the Laplace transformation method.

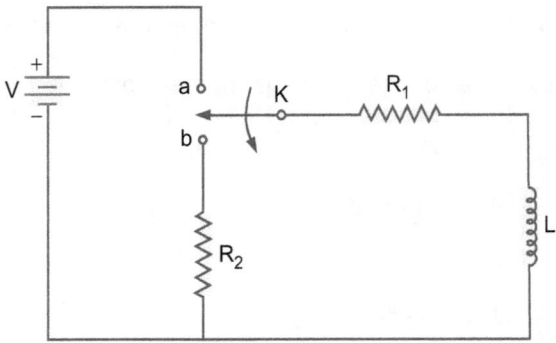

Fig. 1.11

Sol.: When switch is in position 'a', steady state is achieved and inductor L acts as S.C. in the steady state as shown in Fig. 1.11 (a).

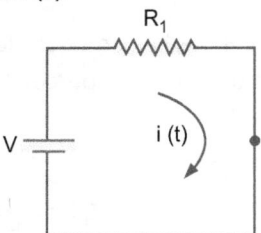

Fig. 1.11 (a)

When the switch is moved to position 'b', the circuit takes the form as shown in Fig. 1.11 (b).

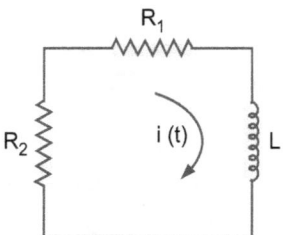   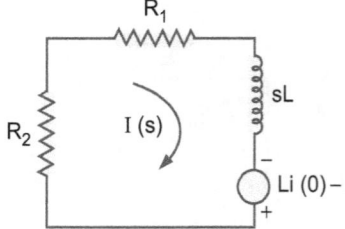

Fig. 1.11 (b): Circuit in position 'b'   **Fig. 1.11 (c): Transformed circuit**

Applying KVL to circuit in Fig. 1.11 (b),

$$(R_1 + R_2) i(t) + L \frac{d}{dt} i(t) = 0$$

Taking Laplace Transform,

$$L[sI(s) - i_L(0-)] + (R_1 + R_2) I(s) = 0$$

$$\therefore \quad L\left[sI(s) - \frac{V}{R_1}\right] + (R_1 + R_2) I(s) = 0$$

Collecting terms of I (s),

$$[sL + R_1 + R_2] I(s) = \frac{LV}{R_1}$$

$$\therefore \quad I(s) = \frac{LV}{R_1}\left(\frac{1}{sL + R_1 + R_2}\right)$$

$$= \frac{V}{R_1}\left[\frac{1}{s + \frac{(R_1 + R_2)}{L}}\right]$$

Taking Inverse Laplace Transform,

$$i(t) = \frac{V}{R_1} e^{-\left(\frac{R_1 + R_2}{L}\right)t} \quad \text{for } t \geq 0$$

Ex. 1.15: In the network shown as in Fig. 1.12 the switch K is moved from position a to position b at t = 0. A steady state current being previously established, derive the expression for current i (t).

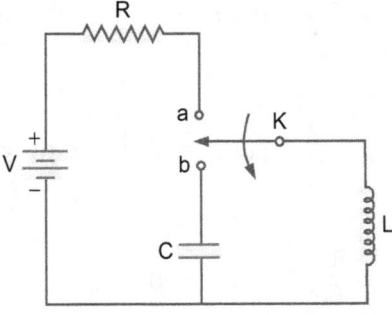

Fig. 1.12

Sol.: When switch is in position 'a', steady state is established. The inductor L acts as S.C. in the steady state.

$$i_a(t) = \frac{V}{R}$$

$$i_L(0-) = \frac{V}{R} \text{ Amp.}$$

$$V_C(0-) = 0 \text{ volts}$$

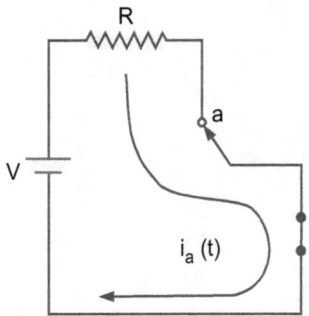

Fig. 1.12 (a)

In position 'b' circuit becomes as shown in Fig. 1.12 (b).

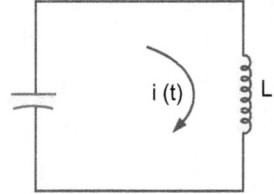   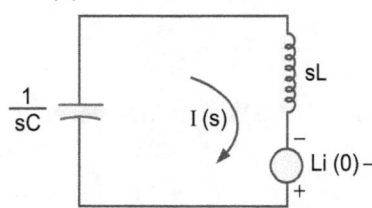

Fig. 1.12 (b)   **Fig. 1.12 (c)**

Applying KVL to circuit in Fig. 1.12 (b),

$$L\frac{di(t)}{dt} + \frac{1}{C}\int_{-\infty}^{t} i(t)\, dt = 0$$

But

$$V_C(0-) = \frac{1}{C}\int_{-\infty}^{0} i(t)\, dt = 0$$

∴

$$L\frac{di(t)}{dt} + \frac{1}{C}\int_{0}^{t} i(t)\, dt = 0$$

Taking Laplace Transform,

$$L[sI(s) - i_L(0-)] + \frac{1}{sC} I(s) = 0$$

$$I(s)\left[sL + \frac{1}{sC}\right] - L\frac{V}{R} = 0$$

$$I(s)\left(\frac{1 + s^2 LC}{sC}\right) = \frac{VL}{R}$$

Unit I | 1.28

$$\therefore \quad I(s) = \frac{VL}{R} \cdot \frac{sC}{1 + s^2 LC}$$

$$= \left(\frac{V}{R}\right) \cdot \frac{s}{s^2 + \frac{1}{LC}}$$

Taking Inverse Laplace Transform,

$$i(t) = \left(\frac{V}{R}\right) \cos\left(\frac{t}{\sqrt{LC}}\right) \text{ Amp}$$

Ex. 1.16: The circuit shown in Fig. 1.13 is in steady state with switch on position 1. At t = 0, it is moved to position 2. Find i (t) using Laplace Transform.

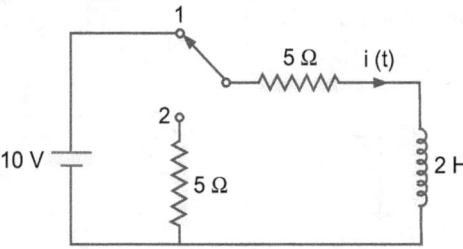

Fig. 1.13

Sol.:

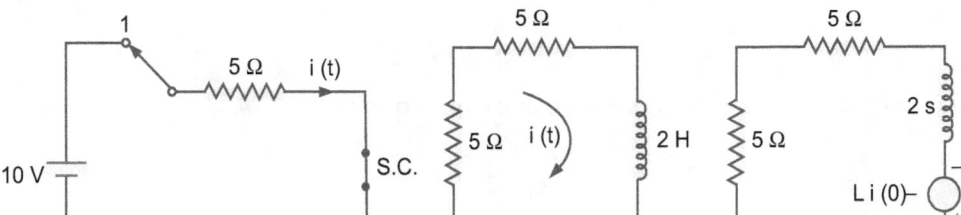

Fig. 1.13 (a): SW in position 1, steady state condition   **Fig. 1.13 (b): SW in position 2**   **Fig. 1.13 (c): Transformed circuit**

In position 1, steady state is reached, the inductor acts as short circuit as shown in Fig. 1.13 (a).

$$\therefore \quad i_L(0-) = i_L(0+) = \frac{10}{5} = 2 \text{ A}$$

In position 2, the circuit appears as shown in Fig. 1.13 (c).

Applying KVL to the circuit,

$$5\, i(t) + 5\, i(t) + 2 \frac{di(t)}{dt} = 0$$

Transforming the equation,

$$5 I(s) + 5 I(s) + 2[s I(s) - i_L(0-)] = 0$$

$$10 I(s) + 2s I(s) - 4 = 0 \qquad [\because i_L(0-) = 2A]$$

$$\therefore \quad I(s) = \frac{4}{10 + 2s}$$

$$= \frac{2}{s+5}$$

Taking Inverse Laplace Transform of I (s),

$$i(t) = 2e^{-5t} \text{ Amp.}$$

Ex. 1.17: In the circuit shown in Fig. 1.14, find $v_a(t)$ using Laplace Transform. Assume $i_L(0-) = 2A$.

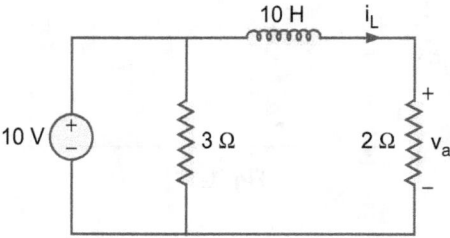

Fig. 1.14

Sol.: Applying KVL to the outer loop of circuit shown in Fig. 1.14,

$$10 = 10 \cdot \frac{di_L(t)}{dt} + 2i_L(t) \qquad \ldots (a)$$

Transform equation (a) using Laplace Transform.

Hence, transformed circuit appears as shown in Fig. 1.14 (a).

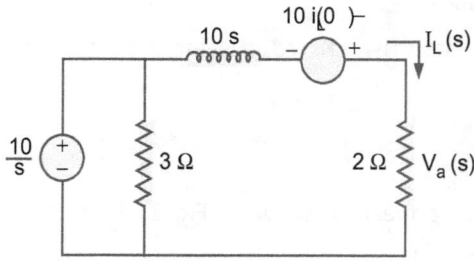

Fig. 1.14 (a)

Thus,
$$\frac{10}{s} = 10\left[s\,I_L(s) - 2\right] + 2I_L(s)$$

$$\frac{10}{s} + 20 = (10s + 2)\,I_L(s)$$

$$I_L(s) = \frac{\frac{10}{s} + 20}{10s + 2} = \frac{10 + 20s}{10s + 2}$$

$$= \frac{2s + 1}{s + 0.2} = \frac{5}{s} + \frac{3}{s + 0.2}$$

$$V_a(s) = 2\,I_L(s)$$

$$= \frac{10}{s} + \frac{6}{s + 0.2}$$

Taking Inverse Laplace Transform of $V_a(s)$,

$$V_a(t) = 10 + 6e^{-0.2t} \text{ volts}$$

Ex. 1.18: For the circuit shown in Fig. 1.15, solve for i(t) using Laplace Transform with switch 'K' closed at t = 0. Assume zero initial conditions.

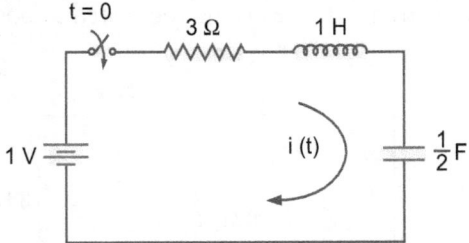

Fig. 1.15

Sol.: Applying KVL,

$$1\,u(t) = R\,i(t) + L\frac{di(t)}{dt} + \frac{1}{C}\int_{-\infty}^{t} i(t)\,dt \qquad \ldots (a)$$

Taking Laplace Transform of equation (a),

$$\frac{1}{s} = R\,I(s) + sL\,I(s) + \frac{1}{sC}\,I(s)$$

$$\frac{1}{s} = 3\,I(s) + s\,I(s) + \frac{2}{s}\,I(s)$$

$$1 = (s^2 + 3s + 2)\,I(s)$$

$$\therefore \quad I(s) = \frac{1}{s^2 + 3s + 2}$$

$$= \frac{1}{(s+2)(s+1)}$$

$$= \frac{A}{s+2} + \frac{B}{s+1}$$

$$A = \frac{(s+2)}{(s+1)(s+2)}\bigg|_{s=-2} = -1$$

$$B = \frac{(s+1)}{(s+1)(s+2)}\bigg|_{s=-1} = 1$$

$$I(s) = \frac{1}{(s+1)} - \frac{1}{(s+2)}$$

Taking Inverse Laplace Transform,

$$i(t) = e^{-t} - e^{-2t} \quad \text{Amp.}; \ t > 0$$

Ex. 1.19: For the circuit shown in Fig. 1.16, the switch S is kept in position 1 for long period to establish steady state conditions. The switch is then shifted to position 2 at t = 0. Find out the expression for current after switching the switch to position 2.

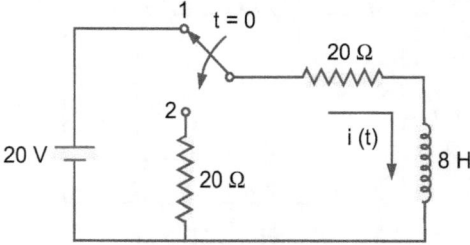

Fig. 1.16

Sol.:

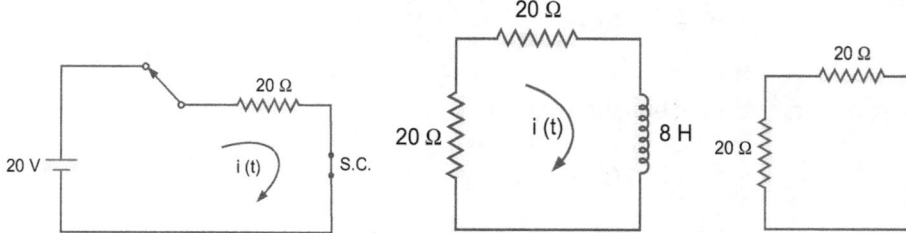

Fig. 1.16 (a): Steady state condition after SW in position 1 for long period

Fig. 1.16 (b): Circuit with SW in position 2

Fig. 1.16 (c): Transformed circuit

After the SW in position 1 for long period, steady state condition is established. The inductor acts as short circuit.

$$\therefore \quad i_L(0-) = \frac{20}{20} = 1 \text{ Amp.}$$

Applying KVL to circuit shown in Fig. 1.16 (b),

$$20\, i(t) + 20\, i(t) + 8 \frac{di(t)}{dt} = 0$$

Taking Laplace Transform,

$$20\, I(s) + 20\, I(s) + 8\, [s\, I(s) - i_L(0-)] = 0$$

$$\therefore \quad 40\, I(s) + 8s\, I(s) - 8(1) = 0$$

$$\therefore \quad I(s) = \frac{8}{[8s + 40]}$$

$$= \frac{1}{s+5}$$

Taking Inverse Laplace Transform,

$$i(t) = e^{-5t} \text{ Amp.}$$

Ex. 1.20: Let $V_C(0-) = 2$ V with the polarities as shown in Fig. 1.17. Write a suitable differential equation and using Laplace Transform find $V_C(t)$.

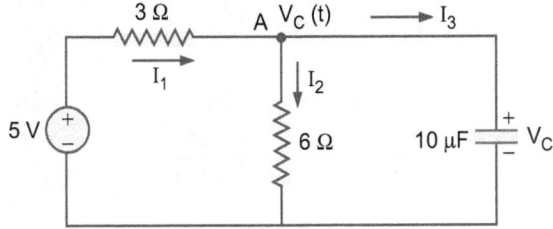

Fig. 1.17

Sol.: The node voltage at node A be $V_C(t)$. Applying KCL at node A,

$$I_1 = I_2 + I_3$$

$$\frac{5 - V_C(t)}{3} = \frac{V_C(t)}{6} + C \frac{dV_C}{dt}$$

i.e. $$\frac{5 - V_C(t)}{3} = \frac{V_C(t)}{6} + 10 \times 10^{-6} \frac{dV_C(t)}{dt}$$

$$\frac{5}{3} - V_C(t) \left[\frac{1}{3} + \frac{1}{6}\right] = 10 \times 10^{-6} \frac{dV_C(t)}{dt}$$

Taking Laplace Transform of the above differential equation,

$$\left(\frac{5}{3s} - \frac{1}{2}\right) V_C(s) = 10 \times 10^{-6} [s V_C(s) - 2] \qquad [\because V_C(0-) = 2V]$$

$$\frac{5}{3s} + 20 \times 10^{-6} = V_C(s) \left[10 \times 10^{-6} s + \frac{1}{2}\right]$$

$$\frac{5 + 60 s \times 10^{-6}}{3s} = V_C(s) \left[\frac{20 \times 10^{-6} s + 1}{2}\right]$$

$$\therefore \quad V_C(s) = \frac{10 + 120 s \times 10^{-6}}{3s [1 + 20 \times 10^{-6} s]}$$

$$= \frac{\frac{10}{3} + 40 s \times 10^{-6}}{(20 \times 10^{-6}) \cdot s \cdot \left[s + \frac{1}{20 \times 10^{-6}}\right]}$$

$$= \frac{K_1}{s} + \frac{K_2}{s + \frac{1}{20 \times 10^{-6}}}$$

where,

$$K_1 = \left.\frac{\frac{10}{3} + 40s \times 10^{-6}}{20 \times 10^{-6} \left(s + \frac{1}{20 \times 10^{-6}}\right)}\right|_{s=0} = \frac{10}{3}$$

$$K_2 = \left.\frac{\frac{10}{3} + 40s \times 10^{-6}}{(20 \times 10^{-6}) s}\right|_{s = -\frac{1}{20 \times 10^{-6}}}$$

$$= -\frac{4}{3}$$

$$\therefore \quad V_C(s) = \frac{(10/3)}{s} + \frac{(-4/3)}{\left(s + \frac{1}{20 \times 10^{-6}}\right)}$$

Taking Inverse Laplace Transform of $V_C(s)$,

$$V_C(t) = \frac{10}{3} - \frac{4}{3}(e)^{-\frac{t}{20 \times 10^{-6}}} \text{ volts}$$

Ex. 1.21: After being on position 'A' for long time the switch is thrown on position 'B' at t = 0 in the circuit shown in Fig. 1.18. Find $i_L(t)$ using Laplace Transform.

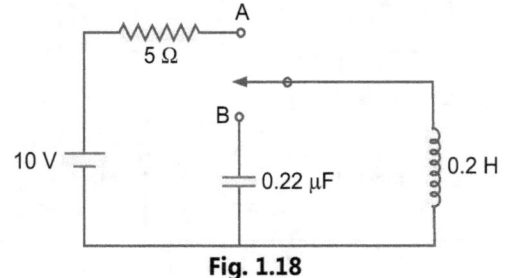

Fig. 1.18

Sol.:

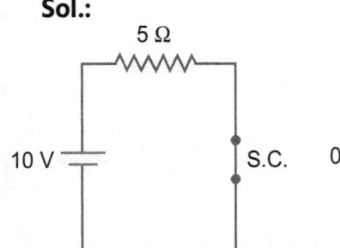

Fig. 1.18 (a): SW position A, steady state established

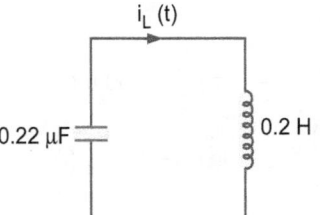

Fig. 1.18 (b): SW in position B

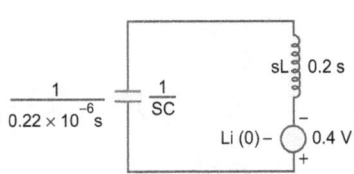

Fig. 1.18 (c): Transformed circuit

When SW is in position 'A' for a long time, steady state is achieved. The inductor acts as short circuit. Equivalent circuit appears as shown in Fig. 1.18 (a).

$$\therefore \quad i_L(0-) = \frac{10}{5} = 2 \text{ A}$$

When SW is thrown to position B [Fig. 1.18 (b)], at t = 0, applying KVL,

$$L\frac{di_L}{dt} + \frac{1}{C}\int i_L \, dt = 0$$

Transforming equation in s domain,

$$L[s I_L(s) - i_L(0-)] + \frac{1}{sC} I_L(s) = 0$$

i.e. $\quad 0.2 [s I_L(s) - 2] + \dfrac{1}{0.22 \times 10^{-6} \, s} I_L(s) = 0$

$$I_L(s)\,[0.044 \times 10^{-6}\, s^2 + 1] = 0.088 \times 10^{-6}\, s$$

$$I_L(s) = \frac{0.088 \times 10^{-6}\, s}{0.044 \times 10^{-6}\left(s^2 + \dfrac{1}{0.044 \times 10^{-6}}\right)} = 2 \cdot \frac{s}{s^2 + \dfrac{1}{0.044 \times 10^{-6}}}$$

Taking Inverse Laplace Transform,

$$i_L(t) = 2 \cos \frac{t}{0.209 \times 10^{-3}} \text{ Amp.}$$

Ex. 1.22: In the network as shown in Fig. 1.19, the switch is closed at t = 0. If the network is unenergized before the switch is closed, find expressions for $i_1(t)$ and $i_2(t)$.

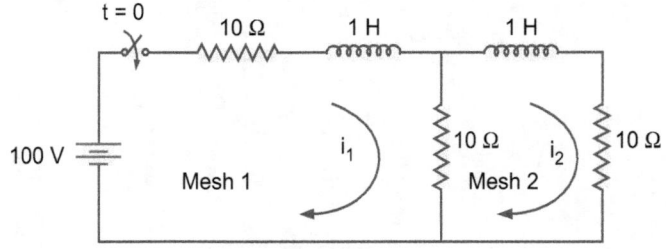

Fig. 1.19

Sol.: At t = 0, switch is closed.
Apply KVL to mesh 1 and mesh 2.

$$10\, i_1(t) + \frac{di_1(t)}{dt} + 10\,[i_1(t) - i_2(t)] = 100\, u(t)$$

$$\therefore \quad 20\, i_1(t) + \frac{di_1(t)}{dt} - 10\, i_2(t) = 100\, u(t) \quad \ldots (a)$$

$$\frac{di_2(t)}{dt} + 10\, i_2(t) + 10\,[i_2(t) - i_1(t)] = 0$$

$$\therefore \quad 20\, i_2(t) + \frac{di_2(t)}{dt} - 10\, i_1(t) = 0 \quad \ldots (b)$$

Transforming equations (a) and (b),

$$20\, I_1(s) - 10\, I_2(s) + s\, I_1(s) = \frac{100}{s}$$

$$-10\, I_1(s) + 20\, I_2(s) + s\, I_2(s) = 0$$

$$\therefore \quad (s + 20)\, I_1(s) - 10\, I_2(s) = \frac{100}{s} \quad \ldots (c)$$

$$-10\, I_1(s) + (s + 20)\, I_2(s) = 0 \quad \ldots (d)$$

Solve equations (c) and (d) simultaneously. By Cramer's rule,

$$I_1(s) = \frac{\begin{vmatrix} 100/s & -10 \\ 0 & (s+20) \end{vmatrix}}{\begin{vmatrix} s+20 & -10 \\ -10 & s+20 \end{vmatrix}} = \frac{\frac{100}{s}(s+20)}{(s^2 + 40s + 300)}$$

$$= \frac{100\,(s+20)}{s\,(s^2 + 40s + 300)}$$

$$= \frac{100\,(s+20)}{s\,(s+10)\,(s+30)}$$

By partial fraction expansion,

$$I_1(s) = \frac{A}{s} + \frac{B}{(s+10)} + \frac{C}{(s+30)}$$

where,
$$A = \left.\frac{100(s+20)s}{s(s+10)(s+30)}\right|_{s=0}$$

$$= \frac{100(20)}{10 \times 30} = \frac{20}{3} = 6.667$$

$$B = \left.\frac{100(s+20)(s+10)}{s(s+10)(s+30)}\right|_{s=-10}$$

$$= \frac{100 \times 10}{-10(20)} = -5$$

$$C = \left.\frac{100(s+20)(s+30)}{s(s+10)(s+30)}\right|_{s=-30}$$

$$= \frac{100(-10)}{-30(-20)} = -\frac{5}{3} = -1.667$$

$$\therefore \quad I_1(s) = \frac{6.667}{s} - \frac{5}{s+10} - \frac{1.667}{s+30}$$

Taking Inverse Laplace Transform,

$$i_1(t) = 6.667 - 5e^{-10t} - 1.667\, e^{-30t} \text{ Amp.}$$

Similarly,
$$I_2(s) = \frac{\begin{vmatrix} s+20 & 100/s \\ -10 & 0 \end{vmatrix}}{s^2 + 40s + 300}$$

$$= \frac{1000}{s(s+10)(s+30)}$$

The partial fraction expansion of this equation is

$$I_2(s) = \frac{K_1}{s} + \frac{K_2}{(s+10)} + \frac{K_3}{(s+30)}$$

where,
$$K_1 = \left.\frac{1000 \times s}{s(s+10)(s+30)}\right|_{s=0}$$

$$= \frac{1000}{300} = 3.333$$

$$K_2 = \frac{1000(s+10)}{s(s+10)(s+30)}\bigg|_{s=-10}$$

$$= \frac{1000}{-10(20)} = -5$$

$$K_3 = \frac{1000(s+30)}{s(s+10)(s+30)}\bigg|_{s=-30}$$

$$= \frac{1000}{-30(-20)} = 1.667$$

$$\therefore \quad I_2(s) = \frac{3.333}{s} - \frac{5}{s+10} + \frac{1.667}{s+30}$$

Taking Inverse Laplace Transform,

$$i_2(t) = 3.333 - 5e^{-10t} + 1.667\, e^{-30t}, \; t > 0 \text{ Amp.}$$

Ex. 1.23: For the circuit shown in Fig. 1.20 solve for $i_1(t)$ and $i_2(t)$ using Laplace transform with switch closed at t = 0.

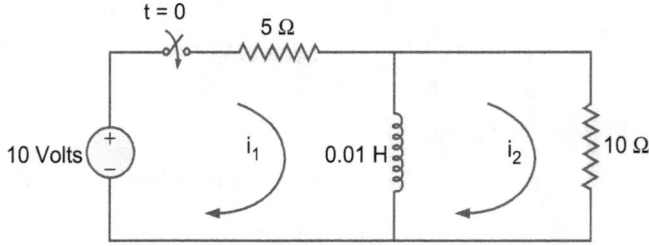

Fig. 1.20

Sol.: Assume initial values of $i_1(t)$ and $i_2(t)$ to be zero.
Applying KVL to the two loops in the circuit,

$$10\, u(t) = 5i_1(t) + 0.01\frac{d}{dt}[i_1(t) - i_2(t)]$$

$$0 = 10\, i_2(t) + 0.01\frac{d}{dt}[i_2(t) - i_1(t)]$$

Taking Laplace Transform of above set of equations.

$$\frac{10}{s} = 5I_1(s) + 0.01\, s\, [I_1(s) - I_2(s)]$$

$$\frac{10}{s} = [5 + 0.01\, s]\, I_1(s) - 0.01\, s\, I_2(s) \qquad \ldots (a)$$

$$0 = 10\, I_2(s) + 0.01\, s\, [I_2(s) - I_1(s)]$$

$$= -0.01\, s\, I_1(s) + (10 + 0.01\, s)\, I_2(s) \qquad \ldots (b)$$

By Cramer's rule,

$$I_1(s) = \frac{\begin{vmatrix} 10/s & -0.01\,s \\ 0 & 10 + 0.01\,s \end{vmatrix}}{\begin{vmatrix} 5 + 0.01\,s & -0.01\,s \\ -0.01\,s & 10 + 0.01\,s \end{vmatrix}}$$

$$= \frac{\dfrac{10}{s}(10 + 0.01\,s)}{(50 + 0.15\,s)} = \frac{\dfrac{10}{s} \times 0.01(1000 + s)}{0.15\left(s + \dfrac{50}{0.15}\right)}$$

$$= \frac{2}{3} \cdot \frac{(1000 + s)}{s\,(s + 333.33)} = \frac{A}{s} + \frac{B}{(s + 333.33)}$$

where,

$$A = \frac{2}{3} \times \frac{1000}{333.33} = 2$$

$$B = \frac{2}{3} \times \frac{(1000 - 333.33)}{-333.33} = -\frac{4}{3}$$

Thus,

$$I_1(s) = \frac{2}{s} - \frac{(4/3)}{(s + 333.33)}$$

Taking Inverse Laplace Transform,

$$i_1(t) = 2 - \frac{4}{3}\,e^{-333.33\,t} \text{ Amp.}; \ t > 0 \text{ Amp.}$$

Similarly,

$$I_2(s) = \frac{\begin{vmatrix} 5 + 0.01\,s & 10/s \\ -0.01\,s & 0 \end{vmatrix}}{\begin{vmatrix} 5 + 0.01\,s & -0.01\,s \\ -0.01\,s & 10 + 0.01\,s \end{vmatrix}} = \frac{0.1}{50 + 0.15\,s} = \frac{2}{3} \cdot \frac{1}{s + 333.33}$$

$$\therefore \quad i_2(t) = L^{-1} I_2(s) = \frac{2}{3}\,e^{-333.33\,t} \text{ Amp.}; \ t > 0$$

Ex. 1.24: The switch in the Fig. 1.21 is in position 1 for a long time; it is moved to position 2 at t = 0, obtain the expression for i (t).

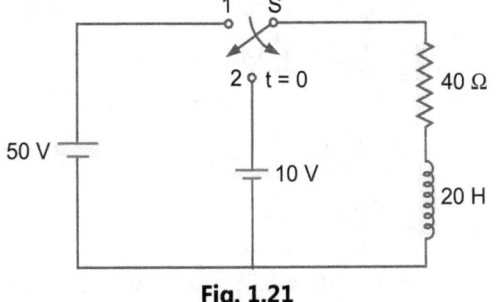

Fig. 1.21

Sol.: When switch is in position 1 for a long time, inductor acts as short circuit. [Fig. 1.21 (a)].

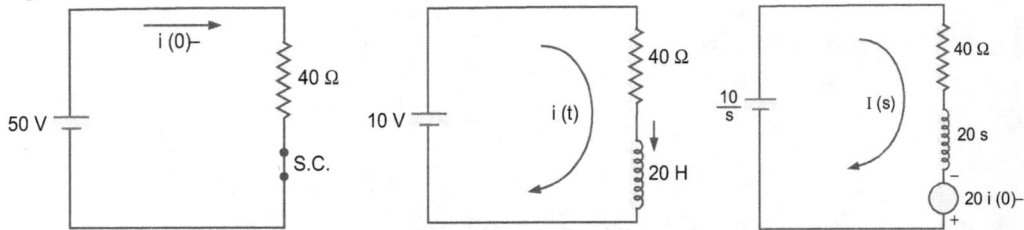

Fig. 1.21 (a): SW in position 1, steady state reached   Fig. 1.21 (b): SW in position 2   Fig. 1.21 (c): Transformed circuit

$$\therefore \quad i(0-) = \frac{50}{40} = 1.25 \text{ Amp.}$$

When SW is changed to position 2, circuit acts as shown in Fig. 1.21 (b).
Applying KVL to circuit in Fig. 1.21 (b),

$$10\, u(t) = 40\, i(t) + 20\frac{di(t)}{dt}$$

Taking Laplace Transform,

$$\frac{10}{s} = 40\, I(s) + 20\,[s\, I(s) - i(0-)]$$

$$= (40 + 20s)\, I(s) - 25$$

$$I(s) = \frac{\frac{10}{s} + 25}{40 + 20s} = \frac{(10 + 25s)}{s\, 20\,(s+2)}$$

$$= \frac{25\left(s + \frac{10}{25}\right)}{20s(s+2)} = \frac{1.25\,(s + 0.4)}{s\,(s+2)}$$

$$= \frac{A}{s} + \frac{B}{s+2}$$

where,

$$A = \left.\frac{1.25\,(s + 0.4)}{(s+2)}\right|_{s=0}$$

$$= 0.25$$

$$B = \left.\frac{1.25\,(s + 0.4)}{s}\right|_{s=-2}$$

$$= \frac{1.25\,(-1.6)}{(-2)} = 1$$

$$\therefore \quad I(s) = \frac{0.25}{s} + \frac{1}{s+2}$$

$$\therefore \quad i(t) = L^{-1} I(s) = 0.25 + e^{-2t} \text{ Amp.}\,;\; t > 0$$

Ex. 1.25: For the circuit shown in Fig. 1.22, determine the current i (t) for t > 0. The switch S has been closed for a long time and is opened at t = 0.

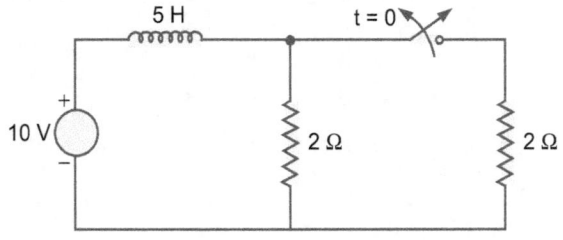

Fig. 1.22

Sol.:

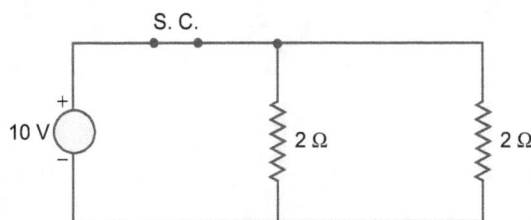

Fig. 1.22 (a): SW closed, steady state reached

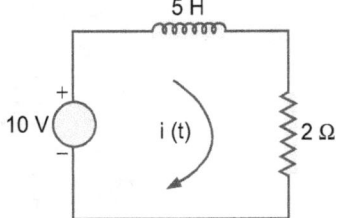

Fig. 1.22 (b): SW opened at t = 0

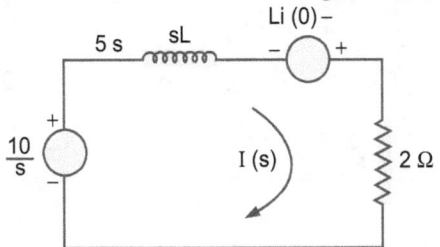

Fig. 1.22 (c): Transformed circuit

The switch has been in closed position for a long time, hence steady state has reached and inductor acts as short circuit. Hence, current through inductor.

$$\therefore \quad i(0-) = \frac{10}{2 \parallel 12} = \frac{10}{1} = 10 \text{ Amp.}$$

At t = 0, the SW is opened. Hence, circuit appears as shown in Fig. 1.22 (b).
Applying KVL to the circuit shown in Fig. 1.22 (b),

$$10 \, u(t) = 5\left[\frac{di(t)}{dt}\right] + 2\, i(t)$$

Transforming equation in s domain,

$$\frac{10}{s} = 5[s\, I(s) - i(0-)] + 2\, I(s)$$

$$= 5[s\, I(s) - 10] + 2\, I(s)$$

$$= (2 + 5s)\, I(s) - 50$$

Unit I | 1.41

∴ $I(s) = \dfrac{\dfrac{10}{s} + 50}{2 + 5s} = \dfrac{10 + 50s}{s(2 + 5s)}$

$= \dfrac{2 + 10s}{s(s + 0.4)} = \dfrac{A}{s} + \dfrac{B}{(s + 0.4)}$

where, $A = \dfrac{2 + 10s}{(s + 0.4)}\bigg|_{s=0}$

$= \dfrac{2}{0.4} = 5$

$B = \dfrac{2 + 10s}{s}\bigg|_{s = -2/5 = -0.4}$

$= \dfrac{2 - 4}{-0.4} = 5$

Thus, $I(s) = \dfrac{5}{s} + \dfrac{5}{s + 0.4}$

∴ $i(t) = L^{-1} I(s)$

$= 5 + 5e^{-0.4t}$ Amp.

Ex. 1.26: Find i(t) for t > 0 in the circuit shown in the Fig. 1.23 if the switch is opened at t = 0.

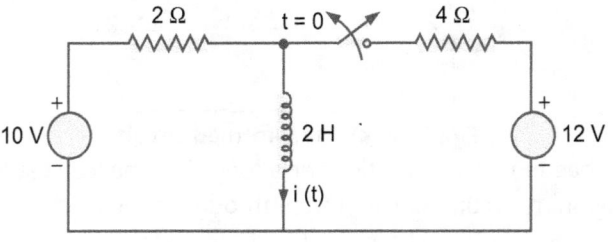

Fig. 1.23

Sol.:

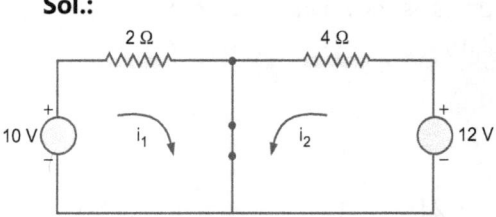

Fig. 1.23 (a): SW in closed position steady state reached

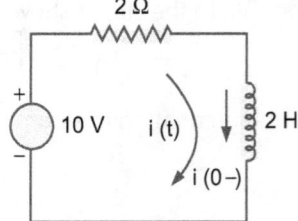

Fig. 1.23 (b): SW opened

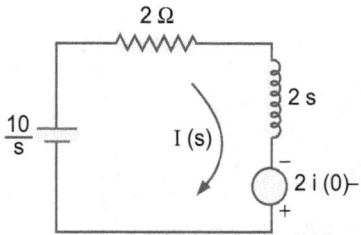

Fig. 1.23 (c): Transformed circuit

The steady state current in the inductor is

$$i(0-) = i_1(0-) + i_2(0-)$$

$$i(0-) = \frac{10}{2} + \frac{12}{4} = 8 \text{ Amp.}$$

Applying KVL to circuit in Fig. 1.32 (b),

$$10 = 2i(t) + 2\frac{di(t)}{dt}$$

Taking Laplace Transform,

$$\frac{10}{s} = 2I(s) + 2[sI(s) - i(0-)]$$

$$= [2 + 2s]I(s) - 16$$

$$\therefore \quad I(s) = \frac{\frac{10}{s} + 16}{2(s+1)} = \frac{5 + 8s}{s(s+1)}$$

$$= \frac{A}{s} + \frac{B}{s+1} = \frac{5}{s} + \frac{3}{(s+1)}$$

Taking Laplace Inverse,

$$i(t) = 5 + 3e^{-t} \text{ Amp.}; \ t > 0 \text{ Amp.}$$

Ex. 1.27: The network shown in Fig. 1.24 reaches steady state with the switch K closed. At t = 0, the switch is opened. Find i(t) for t > 0.

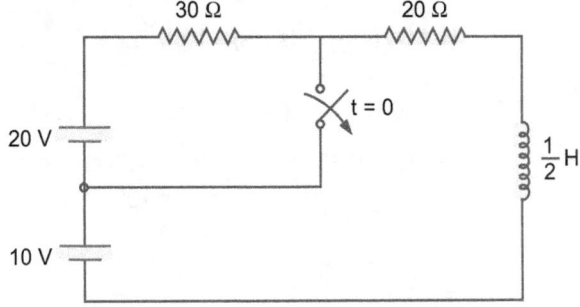

Fig. 1.24

Sol.:

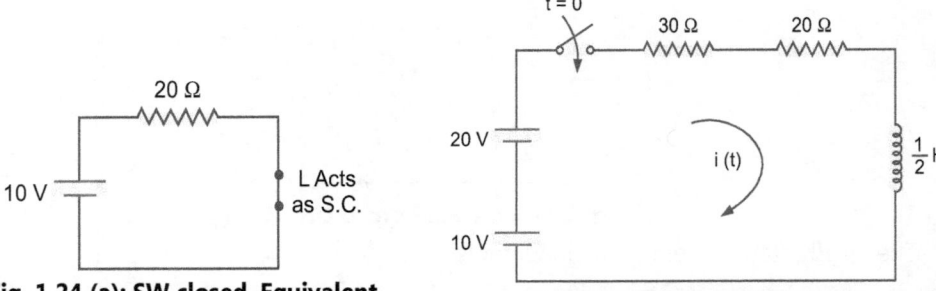

Fig. 1.24 (a): SW closed. Equivalent circuit is steady state

Fig. 1.24 (b): Equivalent circuit when SW is open

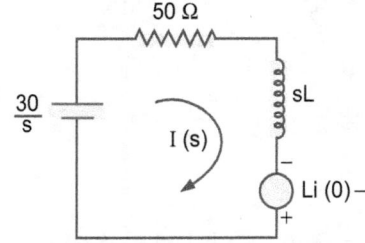

Fig. 1.24 (c): Transformed circuit

When the circuit is in closed state, before t = 0, the steady state is reached. Hence, the inductor acts as short circuit.

$$\therefore \quad i(0-) = \frac{10}{20} = 0.5 \text{ A}$$

When the switch is opened, the circuit takes the form as shown in Fig. 1.24 (b).
Applying KVL,

$$30 \, u(t) = 30 \, i(t) + 20 \, i(t) + \frac{1}{2} \cdot \frac{di(t)}{dt}$$

Taking Laplace Transform,

$$\frac{30}{s} = 50 \, I(s) + \frac{1}{2} [(s \, I(s) - i(0-)]$$

$$= 50 \, I(s) + \frac{1}{2} [s \, I(s) - 0.5]$$

$$\therefore \quad \frac{30}{s} + 0.25 = \left[50 + \frac{1}{2}s\right] I(s)$$

$$\therefore \quad I(s) = \frac{(30 + 0.25 \, s)}{s \left[50 + \frac{1}{2}s\right]} = \frac{2(30 + 0.25 \, s)}{s(s + 100)}$$

$$= \frac{A}{s} + \frac{B}{s + 100}$$

where,

$$A = \left.\frac{2(30 + 0.25s)s}{s(s+100)}\right|_{s=0}$$

$$= \frac{60}{100} = 0.6$$

$$B = \left.\frac{20(30 + 0.25s)(s+100)}{s(s+100)}\right|_{s=-100}$$

$$= \frac{60 - 50}{-100} = -0.1$$

$$\therefore \quad I(s) = \frac{0.6}{s} - \frac{0.1}{s+100}$$

$$= 0.6 - 0.1\, e^{-100t} \text{ Amp.} \,;\, t > 0$$

Ex. 1.28: After being on position 1 for a long time the switch is thrown on position 2 at $t = 0$ in the circuit shown in Fig. 1.25. Find $i_L(t)$ using Laplace Transform and sketch the waveform of $i_L(t)$.

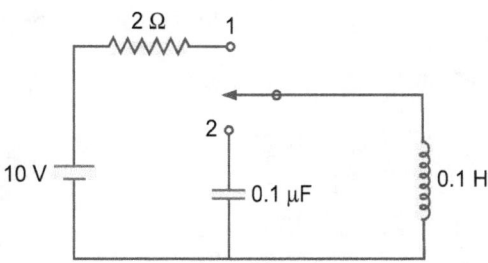

Fig. 1.25

Sol.: Circuit at time $t = 0-$ is as shown in Fig. 1.25 (a).

$$\therefore \quad i_L(0-) = \frac{10}{2}$$

$$= 5 \text{ Amp.}$$

Fig. 1.25 (a)

When the switch is changed to position 2, circuit takes the form as shown in Fig. 1.25 (b).

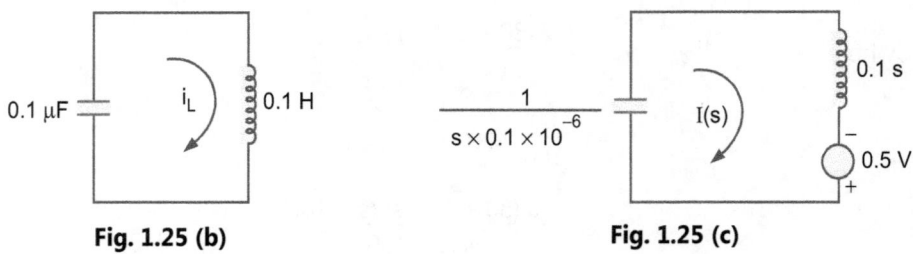

Fig. 1.25 (b) **Fig. 1.25 (c)**

Applying KVL,

$$\frac{1}{C}\int_{-\infty}^{t} i(t)\,dt + L\frac{di}{dt} = 0$$

i.e.

$$\frac{1}{C}\int_{0}^{t} i(t)\,dt + L\frac{di}{dt} = 0$$

(Since, initial voltage across capacitor is zero)

Transforming the equation,

$$\frac{1}{sC} I(s) + L[sI(s) - i(0-)] = 0$$

∴ $I(s) \times \left[\dfrac{1}{0.1 \times 10^{-6}\, s} + 0.1\, s\right] - 0.5 = 0$

∴ $I(s) = \dfrac{0.5}{\left[\dfrac{1 + 0.01 \times 10^{-6}\, s^2}{0.1 \times 10^{-6}\, s}\right]}$

$= \dfrac{0.05 \times 10^{-6}\, s}{1 + 0.01 \times 10^{-6}\, s^2}$

$= \dfrac{0.05 \times 10^{-6}\, s}{0.01 \times 10^{-6}\left(s^2 + \dfrac{1}{0.01 \times 10^{-6}}\right)}$

$= 5 \times \dfrac{s}{s^2 + 10^8}$

∴ $i(t) = L^{-1} I(s)$

$= 5 \cos(10^4)\, t$ Amp.

Ex. 1.29: In the circuit shown in Fig. 1.26, the switch K is thrown from position a to b at t = 0. Just before the switch is thrown to be the initial conditions are i (0–) = 2 A and V_C (0–) = 2 V. Find the current i (t). Assume L = 1 H, R = 3 Ω, C = 0.5 µF, V_1 = 5 V.

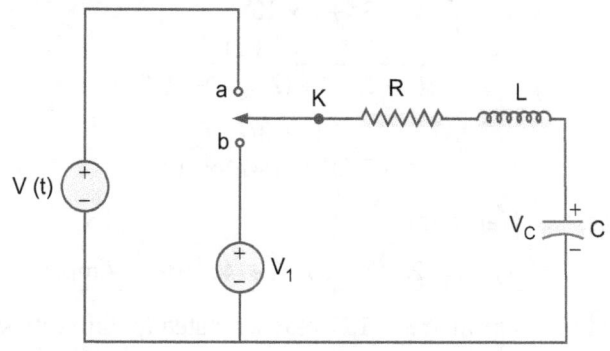

Fig. 1.26

Sol.:

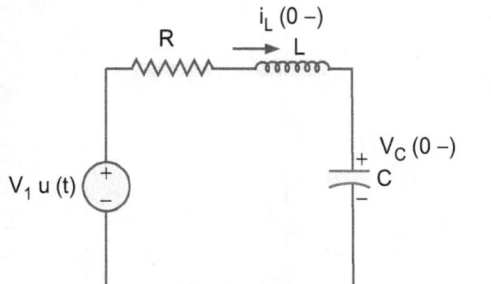

Fig. 1.26 (a): Switch in position 'b'

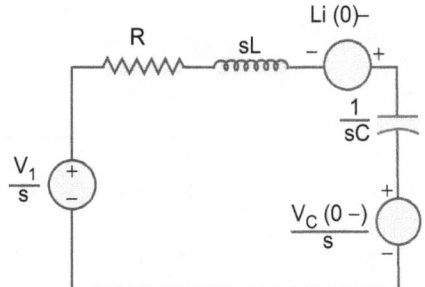

Fig. 1.26 (b): Transformed circuit

Applying KVL to circuit in Fig. 1.26 (a),

$$V_1 \, u(t) = R \, i(t) + L \frac{di(t)}{dt} + \frac{1}{C} \int_{-\infty}^{t} i(t) \, dt$$

Taking Laplace Transform,

$$\frac{V_1}{s} = R I(s) + L [s I(s) - i(0-)] + \frac{1}{sC} I(s) + \frac{V_C(0-)}{s}$$

$$\frac{5}{s} = 3I(s) + s I(s) - 2 + \frac{1}{s(0.5 \times 10^{-6})} + \frac{2}{s}$$

$$\therefore \quad I(s) \left[3 + s + \frac{2 \times 10^6}{s} \right] = \frac{5}{s} - \frac{2}{s} + 2 = \frac{3}{s} + 2$$

$$I(s) = \frac{(3+2s)/s}{(s^2+3s+2\times 10^6)/s}$$

$$= \frac{3+2s}{s^2+3s+2\times 10^6}$$

$$= \frac{2(s+3/2)}{(s+3/2)^2+(2\times 10^6 - 9/4)}$$

$$= \frac{2(s+3/2)}{(s+3/2)^2+(1.414\times 10^3)^2}$$

Taking Inverse Laplace Transform,

$$i(t) = 2e^{-(3/2)t}\cos(1.414\times 10^3)t \text{ Amp.}; \ t>0$$

Ex. 1.30: The network shown in Fig. 1.27 reaches a steady state with switch K opened. At t = 0, the switch is closed. Find i(t) for t > 0.

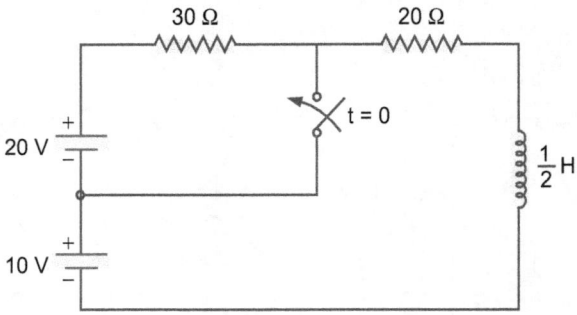

Fig. 1.27

Sol.:

$$i(0-) = \frac{30}{50} = 0.6 \text{ A}$$

Fig. 1.27 (a): Switch K opened, steady state reached

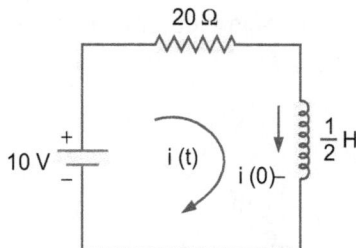

Fig. 1.27 (b): Equivalent circuit
SW K closed at t = 0

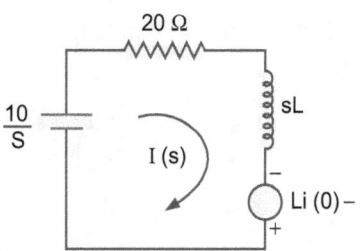

Fig. 1.27 (c): Transformed circuit

Applying KVL to circuit in Fig. 1.36 (b),

$$10 = 20\,i(t) + \frac{1}{2}\frac{di(t)}{dt}$$

Taking Laplace Transform,

$$\frac{10}{s} = 20\,I(s) + \frac{1}{2}[s\,I(s) - 0.6]$$

∴ $$\frac{10}{s} + 0.3 = I(s)\left[20 + \frac{s}{2}\right]$$

∴ $$I(s) = \frac{10 + 0.3\,s}{s(40 + s)/2}$$

$$= \frac{2(10 + 0.3\,s)}{s(40 + s)}$$

$$= \frac{A}{s} + \frac{B}{s+40}$$

$$= \frac{0.5}{s} + \frac{0.1}{s+40}$$

∴ $$i(t) = L^{-1} I(s) = 0.5 + 0.1\,e^{-40t} \text{ Amp.}$$

Ex. 1.31: As shown in Fig. 1.28, 10 V battery is connected to the circuit by closing the SW at t = 0. Assume that initial voltage on the capacitor is zero. Determine the expression for $V_C(t)$ and $i_C(t)$. Sketch waveforms.

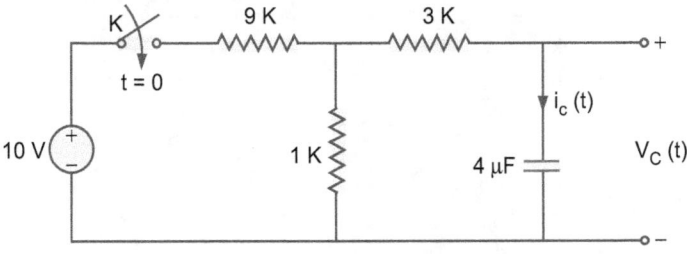

Fig. 1.28

Sol.: Convert the circuit shown in Fig. 1.28 into Thevenin's equivalent circuit as in Fig. 1.28 (a).

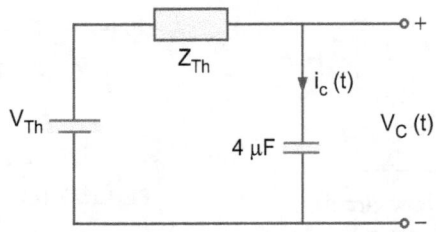

Fig. 1.28 (a): Thevenin's equivalent circuit

To find V_{Th} remove capacitor C and determine A.C. voltage between points A and B in Fig. 1.28 (b).

$$V_{Th} = V_{AB} = 10 \times \frac{1\,K}{9\,K + 1\,K} = 1 \text{ volt}$$

Fig. 1.28 (b): At t > 0

To find Z_{Th}, consider Fig. 1.28 (c)

∴ $Z_{Th} = Z_{AB}$
   $= 3\,K + (1\,K \parallel 9\,K)$
   $= 3\,K + \left(\frac{1 \times 9}{1 + 9}\right) K$
   $= 3.9 \text{ k}\Omega$

Fig. 1.28 (c)

Reconnect capacitor of 4 µF to Thevenin's equivalent circuit.

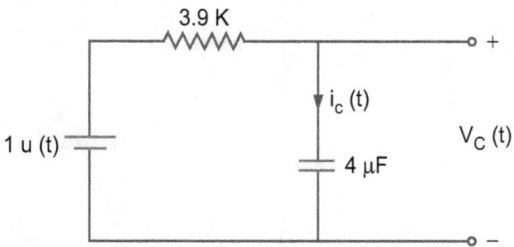

Fig. 1.28 (d)

Applying KCL to equivalent circuit in Fig. 1.28 (d),

$$1\, u(t) = 3.9\,K\, i_C(t) + \frac{1}{C}\int_{-\infty}^{t} i(t)\, dt \quad \ldots (1)$$

Since, initial voltage across capacitor is zero,

$$V_C(0-) = \frac{1}{C}\int_{-\infty}^{0} i(t)\, dt = 0$$

Transforming equation (1),

$$\frac{1}{s} = 3.9 \times 10^3\, I_C(s) + \frac{1}{sC} I_C(s) = I_C(s)\left[3.9 \times 10^3 + \frac{1}{4 \times 10^{-6}\, s}\right]$$

$$\therefore \quad I_C(s) = \frac{1/s}{\left[3.9 \times 10^3 + \frac{25 \times 10^4}{s}\right]} = \frac{1}{3.9 \times 10^3\left[s + \frac{25 \times 10^4}{3.9 \times 10^3}\right]}$$

$$= 2.564 \times 10^{-4} \times \frac{1}{(s + 64.1)}$$

$$\therefore \quad i_C(t) = 2.564 \times 10^{-4} \times e^{-64.1\, t}\ \text{Amp.}$$

Similarly, $\quad V_C(s) = \frac{1}{sC} I(s)$

$$\therefore \quad V_C(s) = \frac{2.564 \times 10^{-4}}{4 \times 10^{-6}\, s} \times \frac{1}{(s + 64.1)}$$

$$= \frac{64.1}{s\,(s + 64.1)} = \frac{A}{s} + \frac{B}{(s + 64.1)} = \frac{1}{s} + \frac{(-1)}{s + 64.1}$$

$$\therefore \quad V_C(t) = L^{-1}\, V_C(s)$$

$$= 1 - e^{64.1\, t}\ \text{volts}$$

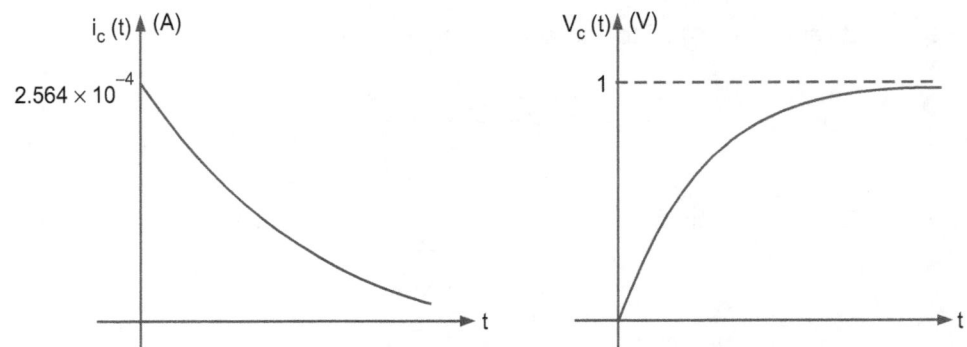

Fig. 1.28 (e): Response curves for $i_C(t)$ and $v_C(t)$

1.3 POLES AND ZEROS

As said above, in general network function F (s) is ratio of two polynomials of 's' and is written as

$$F(s) = \frac{p(s)}{q(s)} = \frac{a_0 s^n + a_1 s^{n-1} + \ldots + a_n}{b_0 s^m + b_1 s^{m-1} + \ldots + b_m} \quad \ldots (1.37)$$

where a, b are coefficients with real positive value with p (s) having 'n' roots, q (s) having 'm' roots.

Hence F (s) is rewritten as

$$F(s) = H \cdot \frac{(s - Z_1)(s - Z_2) \ldots (s - Z_n)}{(s - P_1)(s - P_2) \ldots (s - P_m)} \quad \ldots (1.38)$$

where $H = \dfrac{a_0}{b_0}$ is a constant.

Zeros: When $s = Z_1, Z_2, Z_3, \ldots, Z_n$ then network function F (s) = 0. **Hence complex frequencies, at which network function F (s) vanishes, are called as zeros of network function**. Roots of numerator polynomial p (s) are zeros of network functions.

Poles: When $s = P_1, P_2, \ldots, P_m$, then network function F (s) = ∞. **Hence complex frequencies at which value of network function F (s) becomes infinite are called as poles of network function**. Roots of denominator polynomial q (s) are poles of network functions.

Significance of Poles and Zeros:

Poles and zeros together with scale factor (H) completely specifies a network function. When two or more poles or zeros have same value then those poles or zeros are said to be repeated. Poles or zeros which are not at s = 0 or ∞ are said to be finite poles or zeros. For any rational network function, if poles and zeros at 0 and at ∞ are taken into account in addition to finite poles and zeros. Then,

Total number of poles = Total number of zeros

Poles and zeros are critical frequencies because at poles network function becomes '∞' while at zero network function becomes 0. At any other frequency network function has finite non-zero value. For example, if

$$Z_{11}(s) = \frac{V_1(s)}{I_1(s)}$$

then a pole of $Z_{11}(s)$ implies zero current for finite value of driving voltage i.e. it signifies a open circuit. While zeros of $Z_{11}(s)$ implies zero voltage $V_1(s)$ for finite value of driving point current i.e. it signifies a short circuit.

Representation of Poles and Zeros:

Poles and zeros are represented on a complex 's' plane. Poles are marked 'X' while zeros are marked as '0'.

For example, if
$$F(s) = \frac{s^2(s+4)}{(s+1)(s^2+4s+5)}$$

then,
$$F(s) = \frac{s^2(s+4)}{(s+1)(s+2+j1)(s+2-j1)}$$

This is represented as

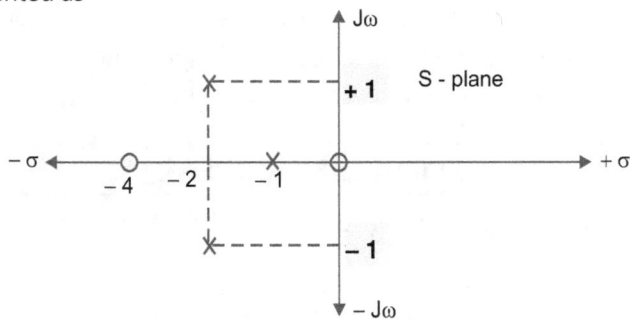

Fig. 1.29: Pole - zero locations

Note that there are two zeros at origin. Also complex poles and zeros always occur in conjugate.

1.4 NECESSARY CONDITIONS FOR TRANSFER FUNCTION AND DRIVING POINT FUNCTION

When given network is dissipationless (loss less) then network has only imaginary poles and zeros.

A network function having poles and zeros, which are real or complex, is stable if real part of poles and zeros are negative i.e. poles and zeros are lying in left half of s-plane.

Necessary condition for driving point function:

1. Coefficient in polynomial $p(s)$ and $q(s)$ of $F(s) = \frac{p(s)}{q(s)}$ must be real and positive.
2. Complex and imaginary poles and zeros occur in conjugate.

3. Polynomial p (s), q (s) must not have missing terms between highest and lowest degree unless all even or odd terms missing.
4. Real part of all poles and zeros must be negative and not positive. If real part is zero, then pole and zero must be simple.
5. p (s) and q (s) must differ at most by one in highest or lowest degree.

Necessary condition for transfer function:

For a given network function F (s) to be a transfer function,
1. Coefficients in polynomials p (s) and q (s) must be real and those of q (s) must be positive.
2. Imaginary or complex poles and zeros are conjugate.
3. Real part of poles must be negative. If it is zero, then it must be simple pole.
4. Polynomial q (s) must not have any missing term between highest and lowest degree unless all even or odd terms missing.
5. Polynomial p (s) may have terms missing between highest and lowest degree and some coefficient may be negative.
6. Degree of p (s) may be as small as zero independent of degree of q (s).
7. For G_{21} and α_{12}, p (s) and q (s) must have same highest degree.
8. For Z_{21} and Y_{21} highest degree of p (s) is greater than q (s) by unity.

SOLVED EXAMPLES

Ex. 1.32: Poles and zeros plot of a voltage transfer function is as shown. D.C. gain is 10. Find transfer function.

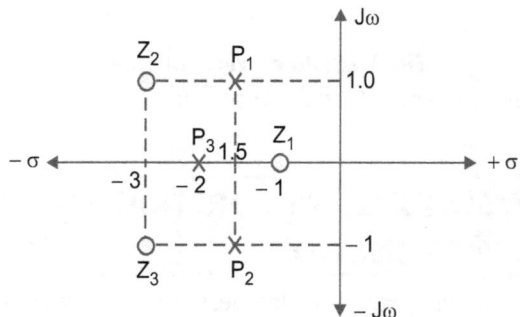

Fig. 1.30: Pole-zero plot for Ex. 1.32

Sol.: Zeros are at $Z_1 = -1$
$Z_2 = -3 + j1$
$Z_3 = -3 - j1$

Poles are at $P_1 = -1.5 + j1$
$P_2 = -1.5 - j1$
$P_3 = -2$

Hence transfer function is

$$T(s) = K\frac{(s+1)(s+3+j1)(s+3-j1)}{(s+2)(s+1.5+j1)(s+1.5-j1)} = K\frac{(s+1)(s^2+6s+10)}{(s+2)(s^2+3s+3.25)}$$

Since d.c. gain is 10, i.e. $T(s) = 10$ for d.c. ($s = 0$),

$$\therefore \quad 10 = \frac{K \times 1 \times 10}{2 \times 3.25}$$

$$\therefore \quad K = 6.5$$

Hence required transfer function is

$$T(s) = \frac{6.5(s+1)(s^2+6s+10)}{(s+2)(s^2+3s+3.25)}$$

Ex. 1.33: For the network shown determine transfer function $Y_{21}(s)$ and plot the pole-zeros of $Y_{21}(s)$.

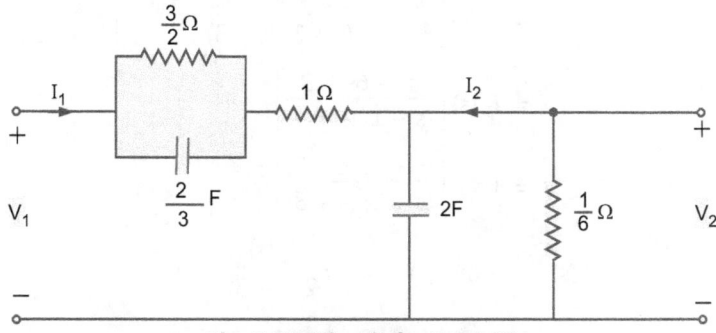

Fig. 1.31: Circuit for Ex. 1.33

Sol.: Transformed circuit of the network given is

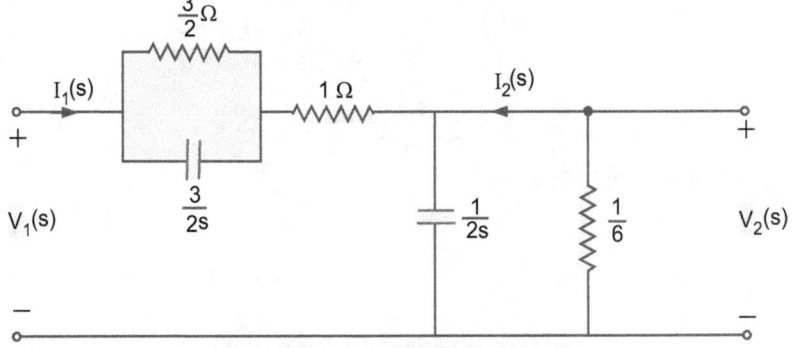

Fig. 1.31 (a): Transformed circuit

Now,
$$Y_{21}(s) = \frac{I_2(s)}{V_1(s)}$$

$$V_2(s) = \frac{\frac{1}{2s} \times \frac{1}{6}}{\frac{1}{2s} + \frac{1}{6}} \times I_1(s) = \frac{1}{6+2s} \times I_1(s)$$

$$V_1(s) = \frac{I_1(s)}{6+2s} + \left(\frac{\frac{3}{2} \times \frac{3}{2s}}{\frac{3}{2}+\frac{3}{2s}} + 1\right) I_1(s)$$

$$= \frac{I_1(s)}{6+2s} + \left(\frac{9}{6s+6} + 1\right) I_1(s)$$

$$= \frac{I_1(s)}{6+2s} + \frac{s+2.5}{(s+1)} I_1(s)$$

$$= \frac{I_1(s)}{1}\left[\frac{0.5}{(s+3)} + \frac{s+2.5}{(s+1)}\right]$$

$$= I_1(s)\left[\frac{0.5 + 0.5s + s^2 + 5.5s + 7.5}{(s+1)(s+3)}\right]$$

$$= I_1(s)\left[\frac{s^2 + 6s + 8}{(s+1)(s+3)}\right]$$

$$= I_1(s)\left[\frac{(s+4)(s+2)}{(s+1)(s+3)}\right]$$

Also, $\quad I_2(s) = -6V_2(s) = -6 \times \dfrac{I_1(s)}{2(s+3)}$

$$= -3 \times \frac{I_1(s)}{(s+3)}$$

$$Y_{21}(s) = \frac{I_2(s)}{V_1(s)} = -\frac{3}{(s+3)} \times \frac{(s+1)(s+3)}{(s+4)(s+2)}$$

$$= -3 \times \frac{(s+1)}{(s+4)(s+2)}$$

Pole-zero plot is shown below.

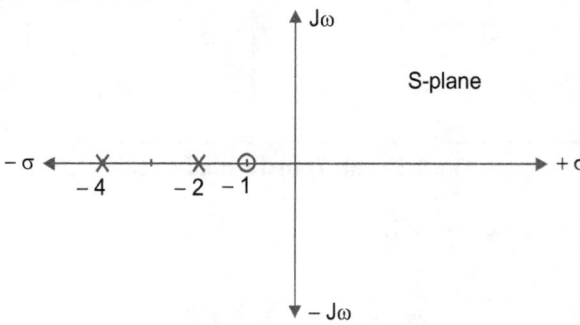

Fig. 1.31 (b): Pole-zero plot

Ex. 1.34: For the network determine voltage ratio $\frac{V_2}{V_1}$, current ratio $\frac{I_2}{I_1}$ and transfer impedance $\frac{V_2}{I_1}$.

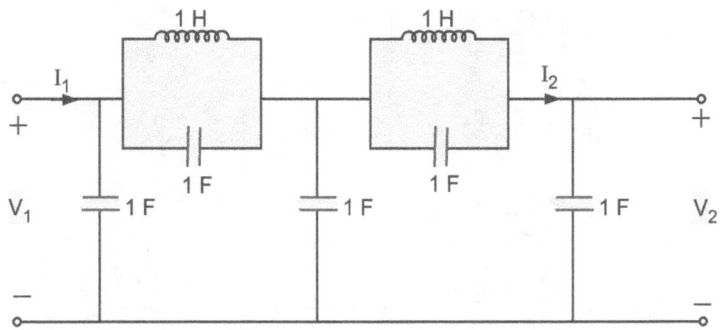

Fig. 1.32: Circuit for Ex. 1.34

Sol.: Transformed circuit is as shown below.

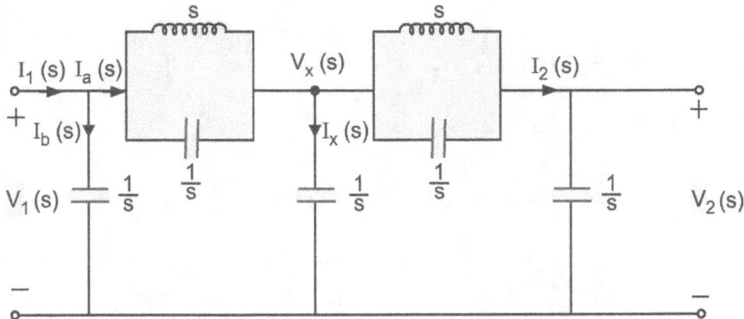

Fig. 1.32 (a): Transformed circuit

We have, $V_2(s) \times s = I_2(s)$

$$V_x(s) = V_2(s) + \left[\frac{s \times \frac{1}{s}}{s + \frac{1}{s}}\right] I_2(s)$$

$$= V_2(s) + \frac{s}{s^2 + 1} \times s \cdot V_2(s)$$

$$= V_2(s)\left[1 + \frac{s^2}{s^2 + 1}\right]$$

$$= V_2(s)\left[\frac{1 + 2s^2}{1 + s^2}\right]$$

$$I_x(s) = sV_x(s) = s\left[\frac{1+2s^2}{1+s^2}\right]V_2(s)$$

$$I_a(s) = I_x(s) + I_2(s)$$

$$= \left[\frac{s(1+2s^2)}{1+s^2} + s\right]V_2(s)$$

$$= \left[\frac{s^3 + s + s + 2s^3}{(1+s^2)}\right]V_2(s)$$

$$= \frac{3s^3 + 2s}{(1+s^2)} \times V_2(s)$$

$$\therefore \quad I_a(s) = \frac{s(2+3s^2)}{(1+s^2)} \times V_2(s)$$

$$V_1(s) = V_x(s) + \left[\frac{s}{s^2+1}\right] \times I_a(s)$$

$$V_1(s) = V_2(s)\left[\frac{(1+2s^2)}{(1+s^2)} + \frac{s^2(3s^2+2)}{(1+s^2)^2}\right] \qquad \ldots (2)$$

$$I_1(s) = I_a(s) + I_b(s)$$

$$= V_2(s)\left[\frac{s(3s^2+2)}{1+s^2}\right] + sV_1(s)$$

$$= V_2(s)\left[\frac{s(3s^2+2)}{(1+s^2)} + \frac{s(1+2s^2)}{(a+s^2)} + \frac{s^3(2+3s^2)}{(1+s^2)^2}\right]$$

$$I_1(s) = V_2(s)\left[\frac{s(3s^2+2)(1+s^2) + s(1+2s^2)(1+s^2) + s^3(2+3s^2)}{(1+s^2)^2}\right]$$

$$I_1(s) = V_2(s)\left[\frac{3s^5 + 5s^3 + 2s + 2s^5 + 3s^3 + s + 3s^5 + 2s^3}{(1+s^2)^2}\right] \qquad \ldots (3)$$

Hence by (1), (2) and (3), we have,

$$\frac{V_2(s)}{V_1(s)} = \frac{(1+s^2)^2}{3s^4 + 2s^2 + 2s^4 + 3s^2 + 1} = \frac{(1+s^2)^2}{5s^4 + 5s^2 + 1}$$

$$\frac{I_2(s)}{I_1(s)} = \frac{s(1+s^2)^2}{8s^5 + 10s^3 + 3s}$$

$$\frac{V_2(s)}{I_1(s)} = \frac{(1+s^2)^2}{(8s^5 + 10s^3 + 3s)}$$

Ex. 1.35: Find ratio $\dfrac{V_2}{V_1}$ for the circuit shown in Fig. 1.33.

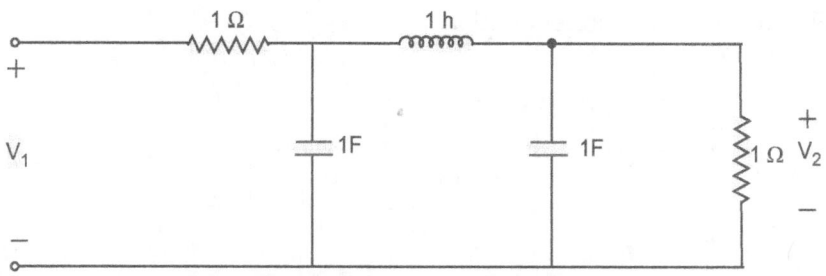

Fig. 1.33: Circuit for Ex. 1.35

Sol.: Transformed circuit is shown below.

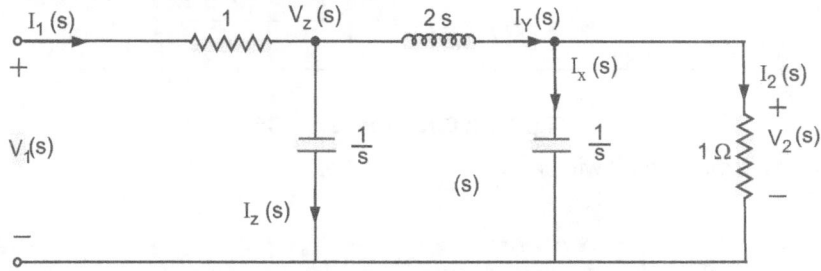

Fig. 1.33 (a): Transformed circuit

Now,
$$I_2(s) = V_2(s)$$
$$I_x(s) = sV_2(s)$$
$$I_y(s) = I_x(s) + I_2(s) = V_2(s)[1+s]$$
$$V_z(s) = V_2(s) + 2s \times I_y(s) = V_2(s)[1+2s(s+1)]$$
$$I_z(s) = sV_z(s) = V_2(s) \cdot s[1+2s(s+1)]$$
$$I_1(s) = I_z(s) + I_y(s)$$
$$= V_2(s)\left[1+s+s[1+2s(s+1)]\right]$$
$$= V_2(s)[1+s+s+2s^3+2s^2]$$
$$= V_2(s)[2s^3+2s^2+2s+1]$$
$$V_1(s) = V_z(s) + V_2(s)[2s^3+2s^2+2s+1]$$
$$= V_2(s)[1+2s^2+2s+2s^3+2s^2+2s+1]$$
$$= V_2(s)[2s^3+4s^2+4s+2]$$
$$\dfrac{V_2(s)}{V_1(s)} = \dfrac{1}{2s^3+4s^2+4s+2}$$

Ex. 1.36: (1) For the network shown with port 2 open, show that input impedance at port '1' is 1 Ω.

(2) Find voltage ratio transfer function.

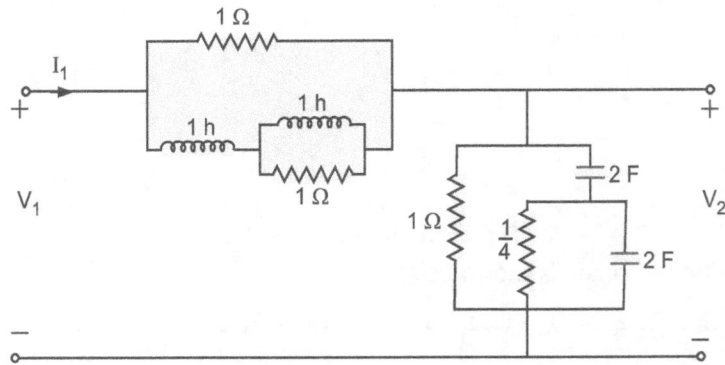

Fig. 1.34: Circuit for Ex. 1.36

Sol.: Transformed circuit will be

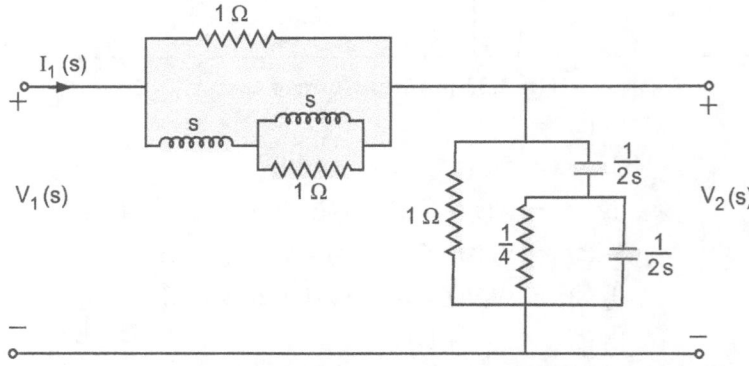

Fig. 1.34 (a): Transformed circuit

The circuit can be written as

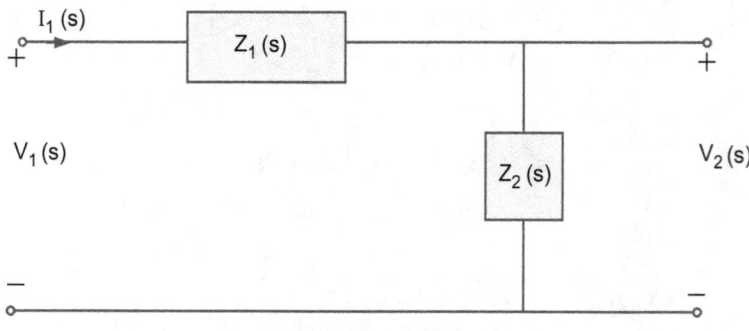

Fig. 1.34 (b): Simplified circuit

$$Z_1(s) = 1 \parallel s + \frac{s}{s+1} = 1 \parallel \left(\frac{s^2 + 2s}{s+1}\right)$$

$$= \frac{\left(\frac{s^2+2s}{s+1}\right)}{\left(\frac{s^2+2s}{s+1}\right)+1} = \frac{s^2+2s}{s^2+3s+1}$$

$$Z_2(s) = 1 \parallel \left(\frac{1}{2s} + \frac{1}{2s+4}\right) = 1 \parallel \left(\frac{4s+4}{2s \times (2s+4)}\right)$$

$$= \frac{1 \times \frac{(s+1) \times 2}{(2s^2+4s)}}{1 + \frac{2(s+1)}{2s^2+4s}} = \frac{(s+1)\,2}{(2s^2+4s)+2(s+1)}$$

$$= \frac{2(s+1)}{2(s^2+3s+1)} = \frac{s+1}{(s^2+3s+1)}$$

(1) Hence input impedance at port '1' is

$$Z_{in} = Z_1(s) + Z_2(s)$$

$$= \frac{s^2+2s}{s^2+3s+1} + \frac{(s+1)}{(s^2+3s+1)}$$

$$= \frac{s^2+3s+1}{s^2+3s+1} = 1\,\Omega$$

(2) Voltage ratio transfer function

$$= \frac{V_2(s)}{V_1(s)} = \frac{Z_2(s)}{Z_2(s)+Z_1(s)} = \frac{Z_2(s)}{1} = \frac{(s+1)}{(s^2+3s+1)}$$

Ex. 1.37: Show that with $Z_a \times Z_b = R_o^2$ in the bridged 'T' network,

$$\frac{V_2}{V_1} = \frac{1}{1 + \frac{Z_a}{R_o}}$$

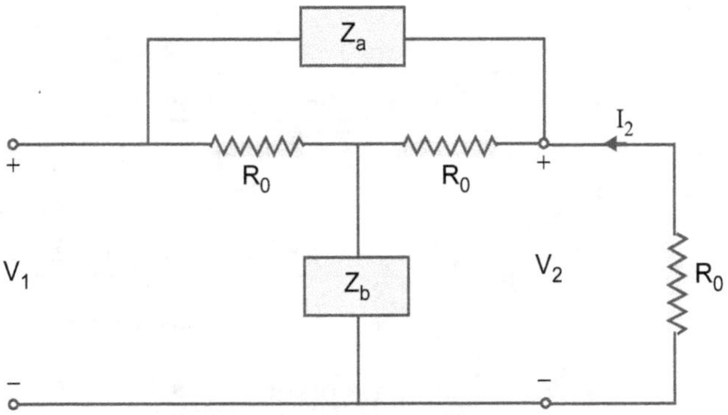

Fig. 1.35: Circuit for Ex. 1.37

Sol.: Converting 'T' network into π network, the given circuit can be written as

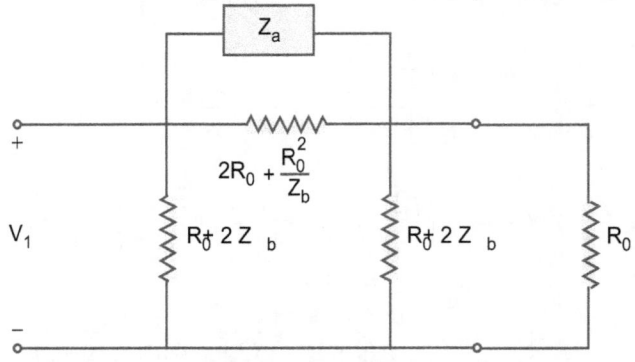

Fig. 1.35 (a): Equivalent circuit

Let
$$Z_2 = R_0 \parallel (R_0 + 2Z_b)$$
$$= \frac{R_0(R_0 + 2Z_b)}{2(Z_b + R_0)}$$

$$Z_1 = Z_a \parallel (2R_0 + Z_a)$$
$$= \frac{Z_a(2R_0 + Z_a)}{(2R_0 + 2Z_a)}$$
$$= \frac{Z_a(Z_a + 2R_0)}{2(R_0 + Z_a)} \qquad \text{where } Z_a = \frac{R_0^2}{Z_b}$$

∴ $$V_2(s) = \frac{Z_2}{Z_1 + Z_2} V_1(s)$$

∴ $$\frac{V_2(s)}{V_1(s)} = \frac{Z_2}{Z_1 + Z_2}$$

∴ $$\frac{V_2(s)}{V_1(s)} = \frac{1}{1 + \frac{Z_1}{Z_2}}$$

$$= \frac{1}{1 + \frac{Z_a(Z_a + 2R_0)(Z_b + R_0)}{R_0(R_0 + Z_a)(R_0 + 2Z_b)}}$$

$$= \frac{1}{1 + \frac{Z_a}{Z_0} \cdot \frac{(Z_a \times Z_b + 2R_0^2 + R_0 Z_a + 2Z_b R_0)}{(R_0^2 + 2Z_a Z_b + R_0 Z_a + 2Z_b R_0)}} \qquad (\because Z_a Z_b = R_0^2)$$

$$= \frac{1}{1 + \frac{Z_a}{Z_0}} \quad \text{hence proof.}$$

Ex. 1.38: For the bridge 'T' network shown calculate following network functions.
(1) $Z_{11}(s)$, (2) $Z_{22}(s)$, (3) $Z_{12}(s)$, (4) $G_{21}(s)$, (5) $\alpha_{21}(s)$

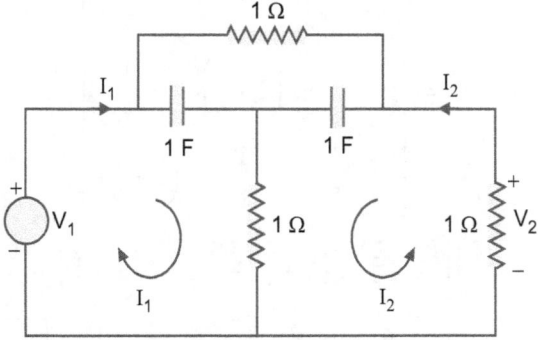

Fig. 1.36: Circuit for Ex. 1.38

Sol.: Transformed circuit is as shown in Fig. 1.78.

KVL across $I_1(s)$ is

$$\left(1 + \frac{1}{s}\right) \times I_1(s) + 1 \cdot I_2(s) - \frac{1}{s} I_3(s) = V_1(s)$$

KVL across $I_2(s)$ is

$$I_1(s) + \left(2 + \frac{1}{s}\right) I_2(s) + \frac{1}{s} I_3(s) = 0$$

KVL across $I_3(s)$ is

$$-\frac{1}{s} I_1(s) + \frac{1}{s} I_2(s) + \left(1 + \frac{2}{s}\right) I_3(s) = 0$$

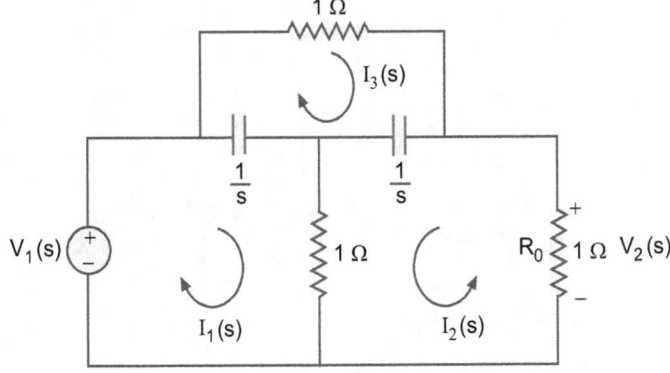

Fig. 1.36 (a): Transformed circuit

Solving for $I_2(s)$ and $I_1(s)$

$$\Delta = \begin{vmatrix} \left(1+\dfrac{1}{s}\right) & 1 & -\dfrac{1}{s} \\ 1 & \left(2+\dfrac{1}{s}\right) & +\dfrac{1}{s} \\ -\dfrac{1}{s} & \dfrac{1}{s} & \left(1+\dfrac{2}{s}\right) \end{vmatrix}$$

$$\Delta = \left(1+\dfrac{1}{s}\right)\left[\left(2+\dfrac{1}{s}\right)+\left(1+\dfrac{2}{s}\right)-\dfrac{1}{s^2}\right] - 1\left(1+\dfrac{2}{s}\right) - \dfrac{1}{s^2} - \dfrac{1}{s^2}\left(2+\dfrac{1}{s}\right) - \dfrac{1}{s^2}$$

$$= \left(1+\dfrac{1}{s}\right)\left[2+\dfrac{4}{s}+\dfrac{1}{s}+\dfrac{2}{s^2}-\dfrac{1}{s^2}\right] - 1 - \dfrac{2}{s} - \dfrac{1}{s^2} - \dfrac{1}{s^3} - \dfrac{2}{s^2} - \dfrac{1}{s^2}$$

$$= \dfrac{2}{1}+\dfrac{5}{s}+\dfrac{1}{s^2}+\dfrac{2}{s}+\dfrac{5}{s^2}+\dfrac{1}{s^3} - 1 - \dfrac{1}{s^3} - \dfrac{2}{s^2} - \dfrac{2}{s} - \dfrac{2}{s^2}$$

$$= 1 + \dfrac{2}{s^2} + \dfrac{5}{s}$$

$$= \dfrac{(s^2+5s+2)}{s^2}$$

$$\Delta_1 = \begin{vmatrix} 2+\dfrac{1}{s} & \dfrac{1}{s} \\ \dfrac{1}{s} & \left(1+\dfrac{2}{s}\right) \end{vmatrix}$$

$$= \left(2+\dfrac{1}{s}\right)\left(1+\dfrac{2}{s}\right) - \dfrac{1}{s^2} = \dfrac{2s^2+5s+1}{s^2}$$

$$\Delta_2 = \begin{vmatrix} 1 & \dfrac{1}{s} \\ -\dfrac{1}{s} & \left(1+\dfrac{2}{s}\right) \end{vmatrix}$$

$$= 1 + \dfrac{2}{s} + \dfrac{1}{s^2} = \dfrac{s^2+2s+1}{s^2}$$

$\therefore \qquad I_1(s) = \dfrac{\Delta_1}{\Delta} V_1(s)$

Hence,
$$Z_{11}(s) = \frac{V_1(s)}{I_1(s)} = \frac{\Delta}{\Delta_1} = \frac{s^2 + 5s + 2}{2s^2 + 5s + 1}$$

$$V_2(s) = -R_0 I_2(s) \qquad \text{But } R_0 = 1$$

$$= -1 \cdot \frac{\Delta_2}{\Delta} V_1(s)$$

Hence,
$$G_{21}(s) = \frac{V_2(s)}{V_1(s)} = -\frac{s^2 + 2s + 1}{s^2 + 5s + 2} \qquad \text{... Ans.}$$

$$\alpha_{21}(s) = \frac{I_2(s)}{I_1(s)} = \frac{\Delta_2}{\Delta_1} = \frac{s^2 + 2s + 1}{2s^2 + 5s + 1}$$

$$Z_{12}(s) = \frac{V_1(s)}{I_2(s)} = \frac{\Delta}{\Delta_2} = \frac{s^2 + 5s + 2}{s^2 + 2s + 1} = Z_{12}(s)$$

Ex. 1.39: Find impedance function $\dfrac{V(s)}{I(s)}$ of the network.

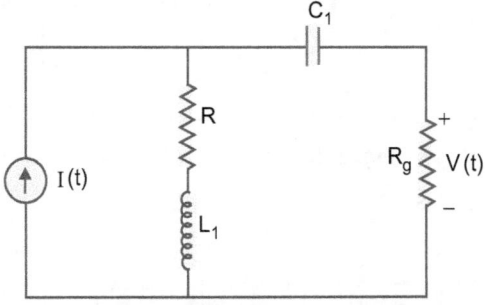

Fig. 1.37: Circuit for Ex. 1.39

Sol.: Transformed circuit is

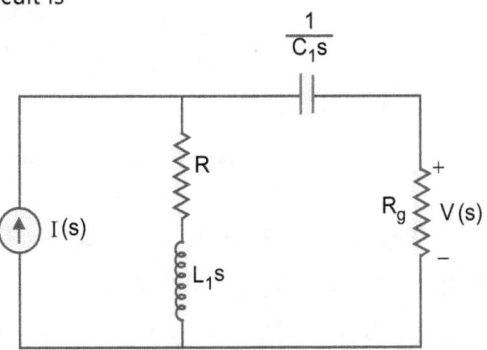

Fig. 1.37 (a): Transformed circuit

Using current divider current through resistor R_g is given by

$$\frac{I(s) \times (R + sL_1)}{(R + R_g) + L_1 s + \dfrac{1}{C_1 s}}$$

Hence, voltage, $V(s) = \dfrac{R_g (R + sL_1) I(s)}{(R + R_g) + \left(sL_1 + \dfrac{1}{C_1 s}\right)}$

∴ Impedance function $\dfrac{V(s)}{I(s)} = \dfrac{R_g (R + sL_1)}{(R + R_g) + \left[L_1 s + \dfrac{1}{C_1 s}\right]}$

Ex. 1.40: Write nodal equation for R.C. ladder network and determine function $\dfrac{V_o}{V_i}$.

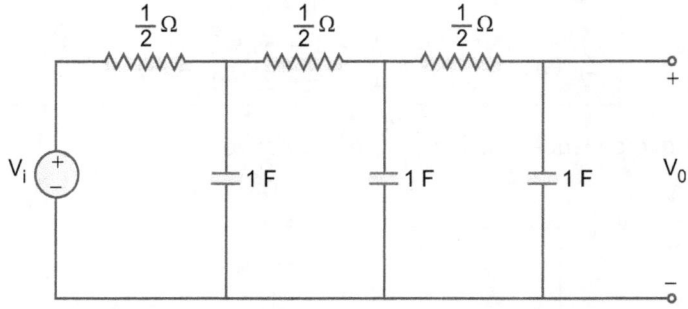

Fig. 1.38: Circuit for Ex. 1.40

Sol.: Transformed circuit is

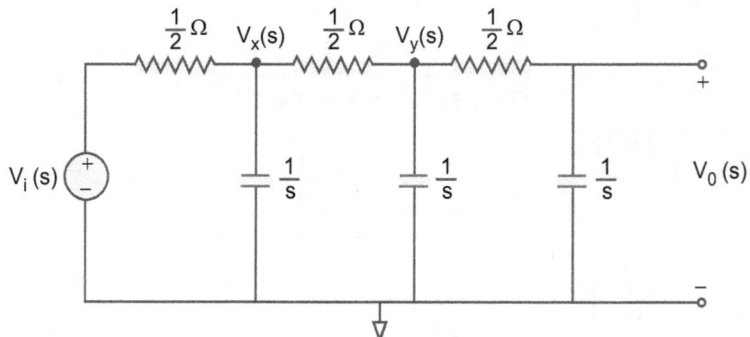

Fig. 1.38 (a): Transformed circuit

Let $V_x(s)$, $V_y(s)$ be unknown node voltages. KCL at $V_x(s)$ gives

$$\dfrac{V_i(s) - V_x(s)}{\dfrac{1}{2}} = \dfrac{V_s(s)}{\dfrac{1}{s}} + \dfrac{V_x(s) - V_y(s)}{\dfrac{1}{2}}$$

or
$2V_i(s) = 2V_x(s) + sV_x(s) + 2V_x(s) - 2V_y(s)$

$2V_i(s) = V_x(s)(4 + s) - 2V_y(s)$ ... (1)

KCL at $V_y(s)$ gives

$$2[V_y(s) - V_x(s)] + sV_y(s) + \frac{2s V_y(s)}{s+2} = 0$$

$$\Rightarrow V_y(s)\left[2 + s + \frac{2s}{s+2}\right] = 2V_x(s) \qquad \ldots (2)$$

Substitute $V_x(s)$ from (2) in equation (1),

$$2V_i(s) = (4+s)\left[1 + \frac{s}{2} + \frac{s}{s+2}\right]V_y(s) - 2V_y(s)$$

$$= V_y(s)\left[(4+s)\left(1 + \frac{s}{2} + \frac{s}{s+2}\right) - 2\right]$$

$$\Rightarrow 2V_i(s) = V_y(s)\left[4 + 2s + \frac{4s}{s+2} + s + \frac{s^2}{2} + \frac{s^2}{s+2} - 2\right]$$

$$= V_y(s)\left[\frac{4(s+2) + 6s(s+2) + 2(s^2 + 4s) + s^2(s+2)}{2(s+2)}\right]$$

$$= V_y(s)\left[\frac{4s + 8 + 6s^2 + 12s + 2s^2 + 8s + s^3 + 2s}{(s+2)2}\right] = V_y(s)\left[\frac{s^3 + 8s^2 + 26s + 8}{(s+2)2}\right]$$

$$\therefore V_y(s) = \frac{4(s+2)}{(s^3 + 8s^2 + 26s + 8)} \times V_i(s)$$

Now using voltage divider relation,

$$V_o(s) = \frac{\frac{1}{s} V_y(s)}{\frac{1}{s} + \frac{1}{2}} = \frac{2V_y(s)}{(s+2)} = \frac{8V_i(s)}{s^3 + 8s^2 + 26s + 8}$$

Hence, $\dfrac{V_o(s)}{V_i(s)} = \dfrac{8}{s^3 + 8s^2 + 26s + 8}$ ... Ans.

Ex. 1.41: For the circuit find voltage ratio $\dfrac{V_o}{V_i}$ and plot pole-zero on S-plane.

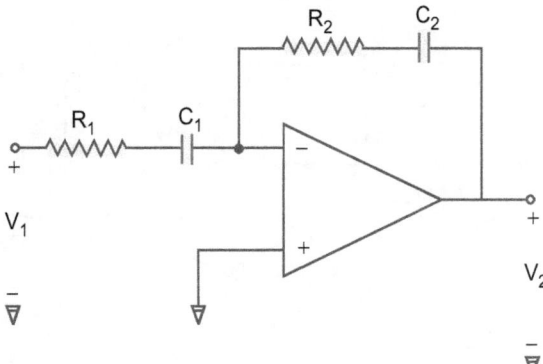

Fig. 1.39: Circuit for Ex. 1.41

Sol.: If
$$Z_1(s) = R_1 + \frac{1}{C_1 s} = \frac{1 + R_1 C_1 s}{C_1 s}$$

and
$$Z_2(s) = R_2 + \frac{1}{C_2 s} = \frac{1 + R_2 C_2 s}{C_2 s}$$

Pole-zero plot if $R_1 C_1 > R_2 C_2$ is shown in Fig. 1.82 (a).

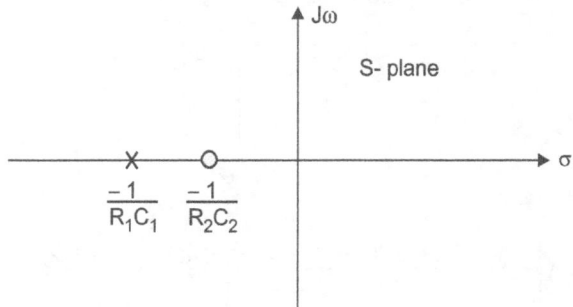

Fig. 1.39 (a) Pole-zero plot

Then,
$$\frac{V_2(s)}{V_1(s)} = -\frac{Z_2(s)}{Z_1(s)}$$

$$= -\frac{C_1}{C_2} \cdot \frac{(1 + R_2 C_2 s)}{(1 + R_1 C_1 s)}$$

There is zero at $s = -\dfrac{1}{R_2 C_2}$

Plot at $s = -\dfrac{1}{R_1 C_1}$

Ex. 1.42: Find transfer function $\dfrac{V_2(s)}{V_1(s)}$ and plot pole-zero.

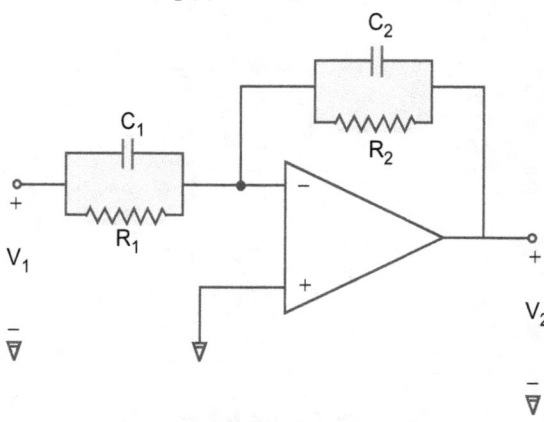

Fig. 1.40: Circuit for Ex. 1.42

Sol.: Here $Z_1(s) = R_1 \| \dfrac{1}{C_1 s} = \dfrac{R_1 \times \dfrac{1}{C_1 s}}{R_1 + \dfrac{1}{C_1 s}} = \dfrac{R_1}{1 + R_1 C_1 s}$

$$Z_2(s) = R_2 \| \dfrac{1}{C_2 s} = \dfrac{R_2}{1 + R_2 C_2 s}$$

Hence, $\dfrac{V_2(s)}{V_1(s)} = \dfrac{Z_2(s)}{Z_1(s)} = \dfrac{-R_2}{R_1} \cdot \dfrac{(1 + R_1 C_1 s)}{(1 + R_2 C_2 s)}$

the zero is at $s = -\dfrac{1}{R_1 C_1}$

Pole is at $s = -\dfrac{1}{R_2 C_2}$

Pole-zero plot if $R_1 C_1 > R_2 C_2$ is

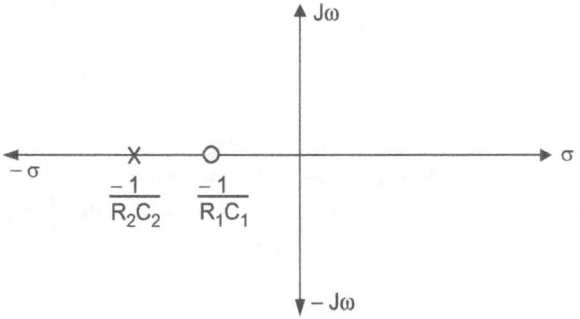

Fig. 1.40 (a)

Ex. 1.43: Find transfer function $T(s) = \dfrac{V_2(s)}{V_1(s)}$ and plot pole-zero diagram.

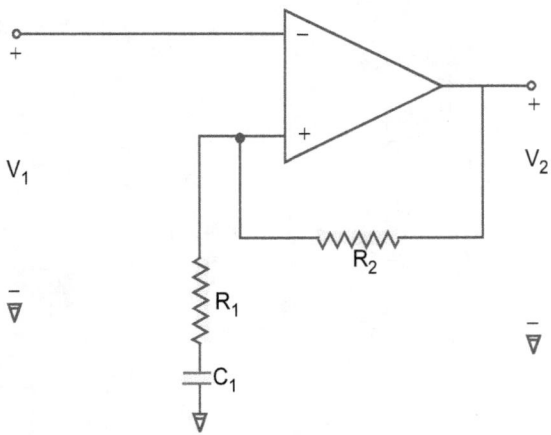

Fig. 1.41: Circuit for Ex. 1.43

Sol.: If $Z_1(s) = R_1 + \dfrac{1}{C_1 s} = \dfrac{1 + R_1 C_1 s}{C_1 s}$

Then since this is non-inverting amplifier,

$$T(s) = \dfrac{V_2(s)}{V_1(s)} = 1 + \dfrac{R_2}{Z_1(s)} = 1 + \dfrac{R_2 C_1 s}{(1 + R_1 C_1 s)} = \dfrac{1 + (R_1 C_1 + R_2 C_1) s}{1 + R_1 C_1 s}$$

Zero is at $s = -\dfrac{1}{R_1 C_1 + R_2 C_1}$

Pole is at $s = -\dfrac{1}{R_1 C_1}$

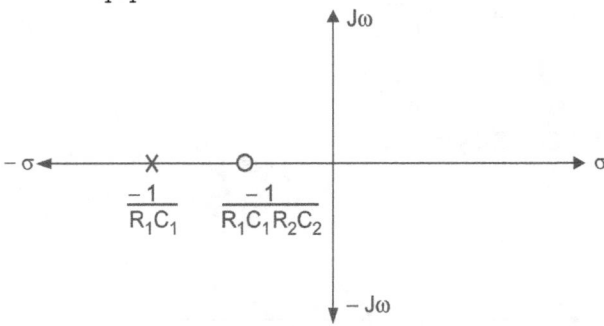

Fig. 1.41 (a): Pole-zero plot

Since input impedance of OP-AMP is ideally infinite and output impedance is zero, there is absolutely no loading from one stage to other stage when OP-AMPs are cascaded. Hence for cascaded OP-AMPs overall transfer function is multiplication transfer function of individual stage.

Following example explains this.

Ex. 1.44: For the cascaded OP-AMP find overall transfer function

$$T(s) = \dfrac{V_2(s)}{V_1(s)}$$

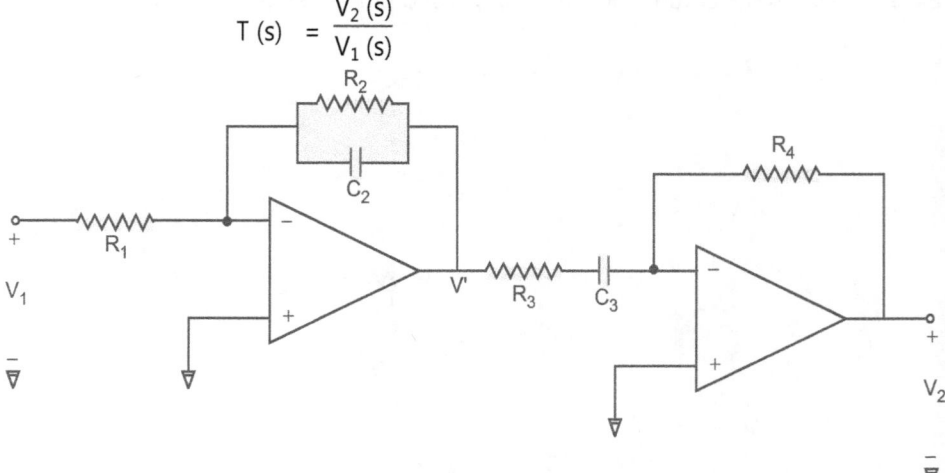

Fig. 1.42: Circuit for Ex. 1.44

Sol.: Let $T_1(s)$ be transfer function of first OP-AMP.

i.e.
$$T_1(s) = \frac{V'(s)}{V_1(s)}$$

$$= \frac{-\left(\dfrac{R_2 \times \dfrac{1}{C_2 s}}{R_2 + \dfrac{1}{C_2 s}}\right)}{R_1}$$

$$= \frac{-R_2/R_1}{1 + R_2 C_2 s}$$

Let $T_2(s)$ be transfer function of second OP-AMP.

$$T_2(s) = \frac{V_2(s)}{V'(s)}$$

$$= -\frac{R_4}{R_3 + \dfrac{1}{C_3 s}} = -\frac{R_4 C_3 s}{1 + R_3 C_3 s}$$

Hence overall transfer function $T(s)$ is

$$T(s) = T_1(s) \times T_2(s)$$

$$= \frac{R_2}{R_1} \cdot \frac{R_4 C_3 s}{(1 + R_2 C_2 s)(1 + R_3 C_3 s)}$$

1.5 TIME DOMAIN BEHAVIOUR FROM POLE-ZERO PLOT

Time domain behaviour of a system can be determined from pole-zero plot of the system function on S-plane.

For example, let a driving voltage $V(s)$ be applied to a network having a impedance $Z(s)$ then,

Current,
$$I(s) = \frac{V(s)}{Z(s)} = \frac{P(s)}{q(s)} = F(s)$$

where
$$\frac{P(s)}{q(s)} = \frac{H(s - Z_1)(s - Z_2) \dots (s - Z_n)}{(s - P_1)(s - P_2) \dots (s - P_m)} \quad \dots m > n$$

$$= \frac{K_1}{(s - P_1)} + \frac{K_2}{(s - P_2)} + \dots$$

K_1 and K_2 etc. are called residue at P_1 and P_2 etc.

The poles determine the time domain behaviour of $i(t)$. Scale factor H and zeros together with poles determine magnitude of each term of $i(t)$.

Graphical method for determination of residue:

Let
$$F(s) = \frac{K_1}{(s-P_1)} + \frac{K_2}{(s-P_2)} + \ldots + \frac{K_m}{(s-P_m)} \quad \ldots (1)$$

Then residue K_i is given by

$$K_i = [(s-P_i)F(s)]_{s \to P_i} = H\frac{(P_i-Z_1)(P_i-Z_2)\ldots(P_i-Z_n)}{(P_i-P_1)(P_i-P_2)\ldots(P_i-P_m)} \quad \ldots (2)$$

From complex plane (s) point of view, equation (2) interprets that "Each term $(P_i - Z_i)$ represents a vector drawn from Z_i to pole in question i.e. P_i.

Also each term $(P_i - P_k)$, $i \neq k$, represents vector drawn from other poles to pole in question i.e. P_i.

Hence,
$$K_i = \frac{\text{Product of vectors from each zero to } P_i}{\text{Product of vectors from other poles to } P_i} \times H$$

For example: Given pole-zero diagram as below:

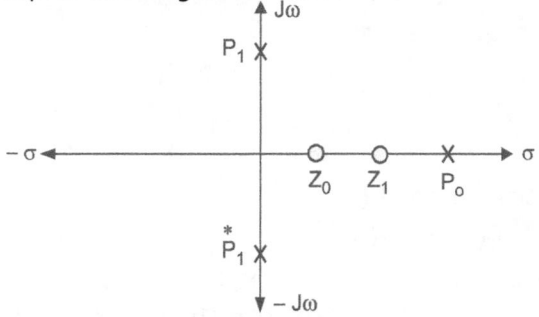

Fig. 1.43: Pole-zero plot

Now function representing above pole-zero plot is

$$F(s) = \frac{H(s+Z_0)(s+Z_1)}{(s+P_0)(s-P_1)(s-P_1^*)}$$

$$= \frac{K_0}{(s+P_0)} + \frac{K_1}{(s-P_1)} + \frac{K_1^*}{P_1^*}$$

Now to find residue at P_1:

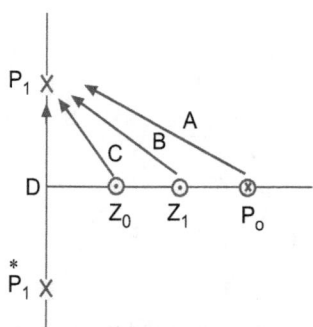

Fig. 1.43 (a): Residue at P_1

$$K_1 = \frac{CB}{AD} \times H$$

i.e. $K_1 = \frac{\text{(Vector from } Z_0 \text{ to } P_1\text{)} \text{(Vector from } Z_1 \text{ to } P_1\text{)}}{\text{(Vector from } P_0 \text{ to } P_1\text{)} \text{(Vector from } P_1^* \text{ to } P_1\text{)}} \times H$

Note: Graphical method can be used if poles are simple and complex. But it cannot be used when there are multiple (repeated) poles.

Ex. 1.45: Voltage transform V (s) of a network is given by

$$V(s) = \frac{4s}{(s+2)(s^2+2s+2)}$$

Plot its poles and zeros. Calculate residue at poles graphically, Hence find V (t).

Sol.: Pole-zero plot is as shown in Fig. 1.44 below.

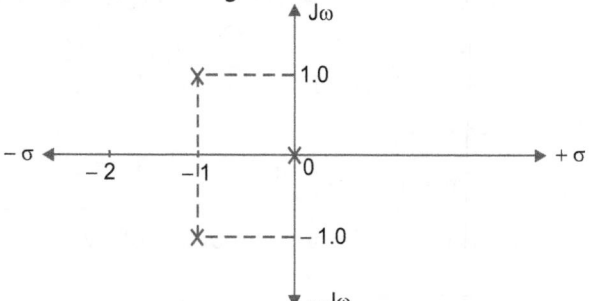

Fig. 1.44: Pole-zero plot

$$V(s) = \frac{4s}{(s+2)(s+1+j1)(s+1-j1)}$$

$$= \frac{K_0}{(s+2)} + \frac{K_1}{(s+1+j1)} + \frac{K_1^*}{(s+1-j1)}$$

(a) Residue at s = – 2 is K_0

$$K_0 = \frac{4 \times 2 \angle -180°}{\sqrt{2} \angle -135° \times \sqrt{2} \angle +135°}$$

$$= \frac{4 \times 2}{2} \angle -180° = -4$$

Fig. 1.44 (a): Residue at s = – 2

(b) Residue at s = – 1 – j1 is K_1

$$K_1 = \frac{4 \times \sqrt{2} \angle 135°}{\sqrt{2} \angle 45° \times 2 \angle +90°} = 2\angle 0° = 2$$

(c) Residue at s = – 1 – 1 + j1 is K_1^*

$$K_1^* = \frac{4 \times \sqrt{2} \angle -135°}{\sqrt{2} \angle 45° \times 2 \angle -90°} = \frac{4}{2} \angle 0° = 2$$

Hence given function is

$$V(s) = \frac{-4}{(s+2)} + \frac{2}{(s+1+j1)} + \frac{2}{s+1-j1}$$

$$= \frac{-4}{s+2} + 2\left[\frac{2s+2}{(s+1)^2+1}\right] = \frac{-4}{(s+2)} + \frac{4(s+1)}{(s+1)^2+1}$$

Hence, $V(t) = -4e^{-2t} + 4e^{-t}\sin t$

$= 4\left[e^{-t}\sin t - e^{-2t}\right]$

Ex. 1.46: Graphically determine residue at poles of the following function

$$F(s) = \frac{s^2+4}{(s+2)(s^2+9)}$$

Sol.: Given F(s) can be written as

$$F(s) = \frac{s^2+4}{(s+2)(s+j3)(s-j3)} = \frac{(s+j2)(s-j2)}{(s+2)(s+j3)(s-j3)}$$

$$= \frac{K_0}{s+2} + \frac{K_1}{(s+j3)} + \frac{K_1^*}{(s-j3)}$$

(a) To find residue at s = – 2, plot is

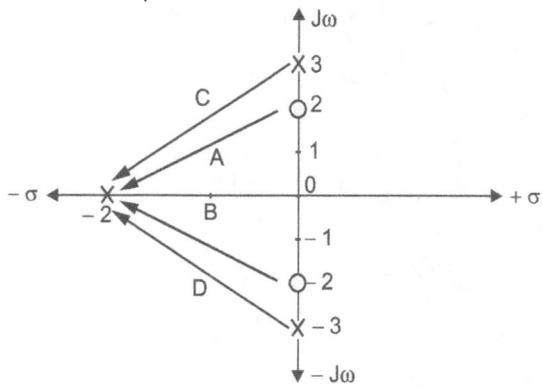

Fig. 1.45: Residue K_0

$$K_0 = \frac{AB}{CD}$$

$$A = \sqrt{8} \angle 225°$$
$$B = \sqrt{8} \angle 135°$$
$$C = \sqrt{13} \angle 236.4°$$
$$D = \sqrt{13} \angle 123.7°$$

$$\therefore \quad K_0 = \frac{\sqrt{8} \angle 225° \times \sqrt{8} \angle 135°}{\sqrt{13} \angle 236.4° \times \sqrt{13} \angle 123.7°}$$

$$= \frac{8}{13} \angle 360° - 360°$$

$$= \frac{8}{13}$$

(b) To find residue at s = j3.

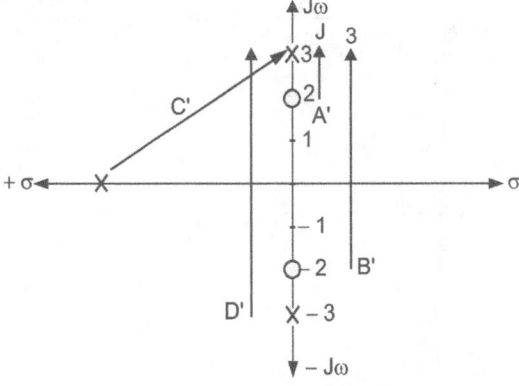

Fig. 1.45 (a): Residue K_1

$$K_1 = \frac{A'B'}{C'D'}$$

$$= \frac{1 \angle 90° \times 5 \angle 90°}{\sqrt{13} \angle 56.31° \times 6 \angle 90°}$$

$$= \frac{5}{\sqrt{13} \times 6} \angle 33.69°$$

$$= 0.231 \angle 33.7°$$

$$= 0.192 + j\,0.128$$

(c) Similarly residue at s = − j3 can be found out which is complex conjugate of K_1.

i.e. $\quad K_1^* = 0.231 \angle -33.7°$

$$= 0.192 - j\,0.128$$

Ex. 1.47: Find residue of the pole frequency using pole-zero plot of following function:

$$F(s) = \frac{(s+1)(s+4)}{(s+2)(s+5)}$$

Sol.: Given: $F(s) = \dfrac{s^2+5s+4}{s^2+7s+10}$

Since numerator degree is equal to denominator degree, divide by numerator by denominator before PEE carried out.

$$F(s) = 1 - \frac{(2s+6)}{(s+2)(s+5)}$$

$$= 1 - \left[\frac{K_0}{(s+2)} + \frac{K_1}{(s+5)}\right] 2$$

Pole-zero plot of function

$$F_1(s) = \frac{s+3}{(s+2)(s+5)} \text{ is as shown below.}$$

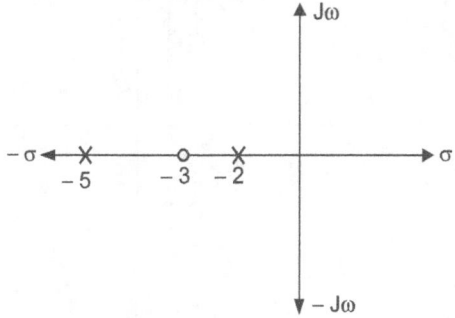

Fig. 1.46: Pole-zero plot

Residue at pole $s = -2$ is

$$K_0 = 2 \cdot \frac{A}{B} = \frac{2\angle 0}{3\angle 0} = \frac{2}{3}$$

Fig. 1.46 (a): Residue K_0

Residue at pole s = – 5 is

$$K_1 = 2 \cdot \frac{A'}{B'} = \frac{2 \times 2 \angle 180°}{3 \angle 180°} = \frac{4}{3}$$

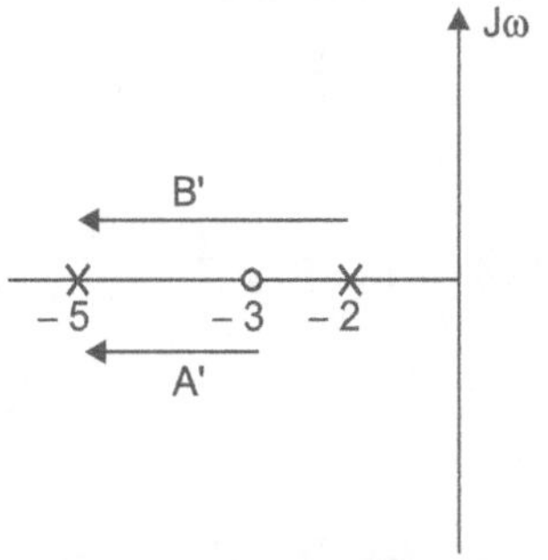

Fig. 1.46 (b): Residue K_1

Hence given function is

$$F(s) = 1 - \left[\frac{2}{3(s+2)} + \frac{4}{3(s+5)}\right]$$

$$= 1 - \frac{2}{3(s+2)} - \frac{4}{3(s+5)}$$

Taking inverse L-T gives,

$$f(t) = U(t) - \frac{2}{3} e^{-2t} - \frac{4}{3} e^{-5t}$$

1.6 MAGNITUDE AND PHASE (FREQUENCY DOMAIN) RESPONSE FROM POLE-ZERO PLOT

Let $F(s) = \dfrac{P(s)}{q(s)}$ be any network function.

F(s) can be written as

$$F(s) = \frac{H(s - Z_1)(s - Z_2) \ldots (s - Z_n)}{(s - P_1)(s - P_2) \ldots (s - P_m)}$$

At $s = j\omega$, we have,

$$F(j\omega) = \frac{P(j\omega)}{q(j\omega)}$$

$$= H \frac{(j\omega - Z_1)(j\omega - Z_2) \ldots (j\omega - Z_n)}{(j\omega - P_1)(j\omega - P_2) \ldots (j\omega - P_m)}$$

is the frequency response of the network. This consists of two parts.

(a) $|F(j\omega)|$ versus 'ω' is magnitude (amplitude) response.

(b) $e^{j\phi(\omega)} = \angle \phi(\omega)$ versus 'ω' gives phase response.

For various values of 'ω' phase response and amplitude response can be plotted as a graph. If this plot is straight line (Asymptotic), then this plot is called as Bodes plot.

Ex. 1.48: For function $F(s) = \dfrac{s}{s+10}$, find phase and magnitude response.

Sol.: We have, $\quad F(j\omega) = \dfrac{j\omega}{j\omega + 10}$

(a) Magnitude plot:

$$|F(j\omega)| = \dfrac{\omega}{\sqrt{100 + \omega^2}}$$

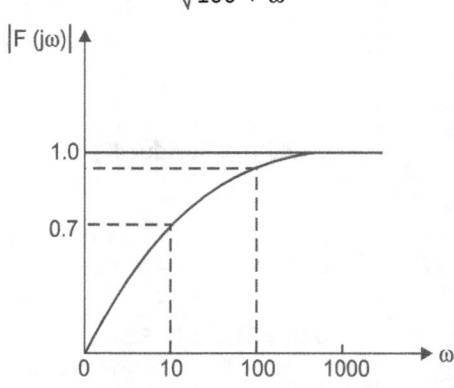

Fig. 1.47: Magnitude plot

At $\omega = 0$, $\quad |F(j\omega)| = 0$

At $\omega = 10$, $\quad |F(j\omega)| = 0.707$

At $\omega = 100$, $\quad |F(j\omega)| = 0.995$

At $\omega = 1000$, $\quad |F(j\omega)| = 1.0$

(b) Phase plot: $\quad F(j\omega) = \phi(j\omega)$ versus 'ω'

gives phase plot.

We have, $\quad \phi(j\omega) = \tan^{-1}\left(\dfrac{\omega}{0}\right) - \tan^{-1}\left(\dfrac{\omega}{10}\right)$

$$= 90° - \tan^{-1}\left(\dfrac{\omega}{10}\right)$$

For $\omega = 0$, $\quad \phi(j0) = 90°$

$\omega = 10$, $\quad \phi(j10) = 45°$

$\omega = 100$, $\quad \phi(j100) = 5.7°$

$\omega = 1000$, $\quad \phi(j1000) = 0°$

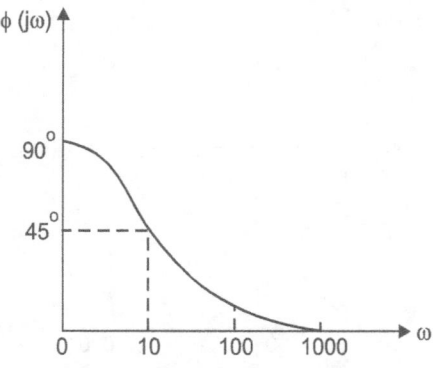

Fig. 1.47 (a): Phase plot

Ex. 1.49: Find magnitude of phase response for

$$F(s) = \frac{s+10}{s-10}$$

Sol.:

$$F(j\omega) = \frac{10+j\omega}{j\omega-10}$$

(a) Magnitude of F (jω) is given by

$$|F(j\omega)| = \frac{\sqrt{100+\omega^2}}{\sqrt{100+\omega^2}}$$

For all 'ω' magnitude is unity, hence its plot is

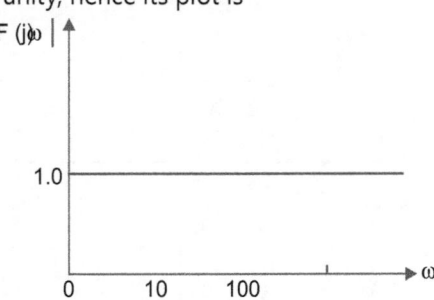

Fig. 1.48: Magnitude plot

(b) Phase response of F (jω):

$$\phi(j\omega) = \tan^{-1}\left(-\frac{\omega}{10}\right) + \tan^{-1}\left(-\frac{\omega}{10}\right)$$

$$= 2\tan^{-1}\left(-\frac{\omega}{10}\right)$$

For ω = 0, $\phi(j0)$ = 0°
      ω = 10, $\phi(j10)$ = 90°
      ω = 100, $\phi(j100)$ = 168.6°
      ω = 1000, $\phi(1000)$ = 178.9°

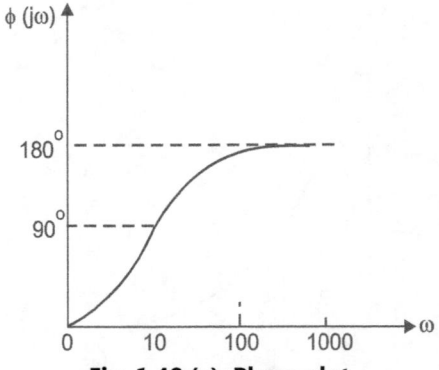

Fig. 1.48 (a): Phase plot

When amplitude and phase of a system function is to be calculated at a particular frequency then pole-zero plot can be used. Following two examples illustrate how to find this.

Ex. 1.50: Evaluate amplitude and phase of the network function $F(s) = \dfrac{4s}{s^2 + 2s + 2}$ from pole-zero plots at $s = j0$, $s = j2$.

Sol.: Pole-zero plot is as shown below in Fig. 1.49.

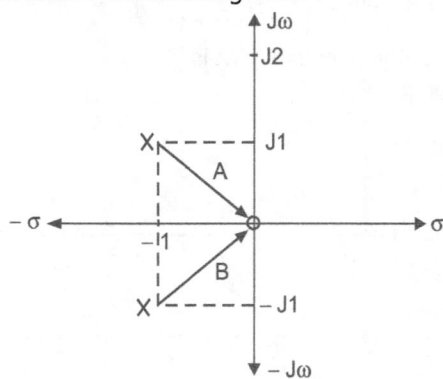

Fig. 1.49: Pole-zero plot

$$F(s) = \frac{4s}{(s + 1 + j1)(s + 1 - j1)}$$

(a) At $s = j0$, $F(j0) = 4 \times \dfrac{\text{Product of vectors from all zeros to } j0}{\text{Product of vectors from all poles to } j0}$

$$= \frac{4 \times 0 \angle 0°}{A \times B} = \frac{4 \times 0 \angle 0°}{\sqrt{2} \angle -45° \times \sqrt{2} \angle +45°}$$

$$= 0 \angle 0°$$

Hence at $s = j0$, magnitude and phase are '0'.

(b) At $s = j2$, $F(j2) = \dfrac{\text{Product of vectors from all zeros to j2}}{\text{Product of vectors from all poles to j2}}$

$$= \dfrac{2 \angle 90°}{\sqrt{2} \angle 45° \times \sqrt{10} \angle \tan^{-1}(3)} = 0.447 \angle -26.56°$$

Hence, at $s = j2$, Magnitude = 0.447, Phase = $-26.56°$

Ex. 1.51: Using pole-zero plot, find magnitude and phase of the function

$$F(s) = \dfrac{(s+1)(s+3)}{s(s+2)}$$

at $s = -4$ and $s = j4$.

Sol.: Pole-zero plot is as shown besides in Fig. 1.50.

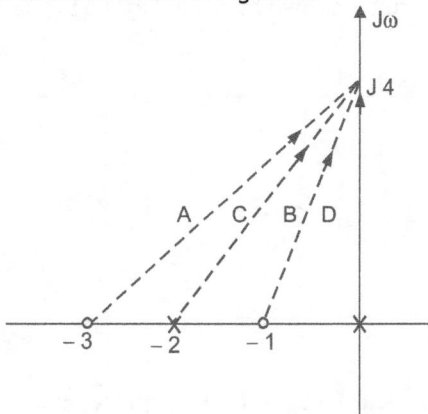

Fig. 1.50: Pole-zero plot

(a) At $s = j4$, we have,

$$F(j4) = \dfrac{\text{Product of vectors from all zeros to j4}}{\text{Product of vectors from all poles to j4}}$$

$$= \dfrac{A \cdot B}{C \cdot D} = \dfrac{5 \angle 53.13° \times \sqrt{17} \angle 76°}{\sqrt{20} \angle 63.4° \times 4 \angle 90°}$$

$$= 1.15 \angle -24.3°$$

Hence at $s = j4$, Magnitude = 1.15, Phase = $-24.3°$.

(b) At $s = -4$, we have,

$$F(-4) = \dfrac{1 \angle 180° \times 3 \angle 180°}{4 \angle 180° \times 2 \angle 180°}$$

$$= \dfrac{3}{8} \angle 0°$$

Hence at = $s = -j4$, Magnitude = $\dfrac{3}{8}$, Phase = $0°$.

Ex. 1.52: For the network shown, find the driving point function Z (s). Plot the poles and zeros of Z (s) on S-plane.

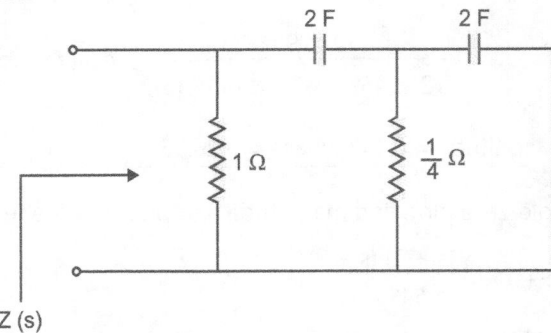

Z (s)

Fig. 1.51: Circuit for Ex. 1.52

Sol.: The transformed circuit is shown below in Fig. 1.51 (a).

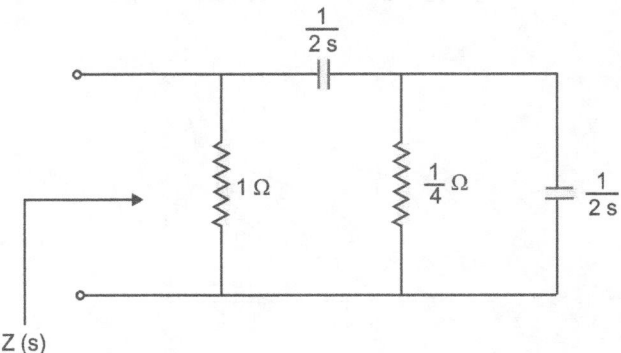

Z (s)

Fig. 1.51 (a): Transformed circuit

$$Z(s) = 1\,\Omega \parallel \left[\frac{1}{2s} + \frac{1}{2s} \parallel \frac{1}{4} \right]$$

$$= 1\,\Omega \parallel \left[\frac{1}{2s} + \frac{1/8s}{\frac{1}{2s} + \frac{1}{4}} \right] = 1\,\Omega \parallel \left[\frac{1}{2s} + \frac{1}{2s+4} \right]$$

$$= 1\,\Omega \parallel \left[\frac{2s+4+2s}{2s(2s+4)} \right] = 1\,\Omega \parallel \left[\frac{4s+4}{2s(2s+4)} \right]$$

$$= 1\,\Omega \parallel \frac{s+1}{(s^2+2s)} = \frac{1 \times \dfrac{s+1}{s^2+2s}}{1 + \dfrac{s+1}{s^2+2s}} = \frac{s+1}{(s^2+3s+1)}$$

Thus, $\quad Z(s) = \dfrac{P(s)}{q(s)} = \dfrac{s+1}{(s^2+3s+1)}$

The zeros are given by P (s) = 0 i.e. s = – 1.
Poles are given by equation q (s) = $s^2 + 3s + 1 = 0$

Thus using quadratic equation formula, we get,

$$s = \frac{-3 \pm \sqrt{9-4}}{2} = \frac{-3 \pm \sqrt{5}}{2}$$

Thus poles at $s_1 = 2.618$ and $s_2 = -0.3819$.

The pole-zero plot is shown below.

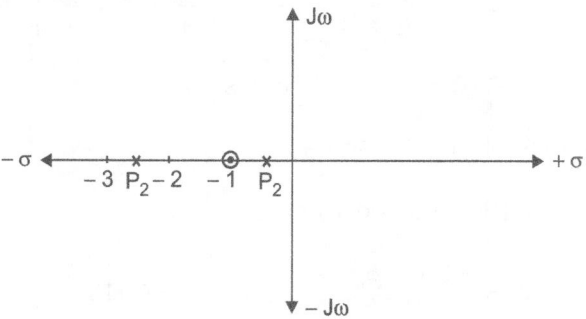

Fig. 1.51 (b): Pole-zero plot

Ex. 1.53: Find input impedance $Z_{in}(s)$ and plot its poles and zeros of the circuit.

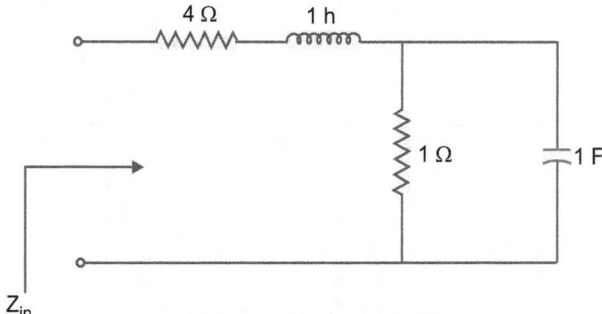

Fig. 1.52: Circuit for Ex. 1.53

Sol.: The transformed circuit is shown below.

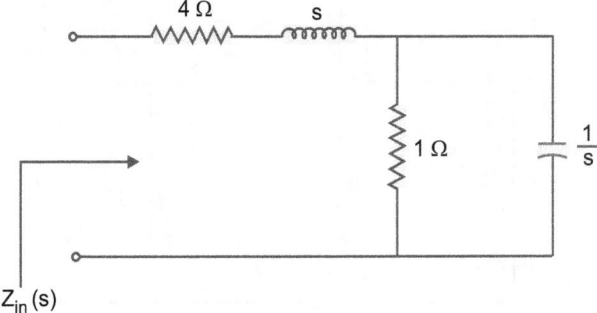

Fig. 1.52 (a): Transformed circuit

$$Z_{in}(s) = 4 + s + \left[(1\,\Omega) \| \left(\frac{1}{s}\right)\right] = (s+4) + \left[\frac{1 \times \frac{1}{s}}{1 + \frac{1}{s}}\right] = (s+4) + \frac{1}{(s+1)}$$

$$= \frac{(s+4)(s+1) + 1}{(s+1)} = \frac{s^2 + 5s + 5}{(s+1)} = \frac{N(s)}{D(s)}$$

The poles are given by $D(s) = (s+1) = 0$ i.e. at $s_1 = -1$.

The zeros are given by $N(s) = s^2 + 5s + 5 = 0$

This is a quadratic equation. The roots are

$$s = \frac{-5 \pm \sqrt{(5)^2 - 4 \times 5}}{2 \times 1} = -2.5 \pm 1.118$$

Thus zeros are at $s_1 = -1.38$ and $s_2 = -3.618$.

The pole-zero plot is shown below in Fig. 1.52 (b).

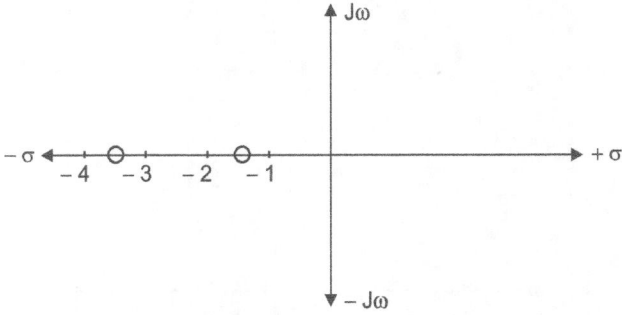

Fig. 1.52 (b): Pole-zero plot

Ex. 1.54: Find $Z(s) = \frac{V_1}{I_1}$ and $T(s) = \frac{V_2}{V_1}$ for the network shown in the Fig. 1.53.

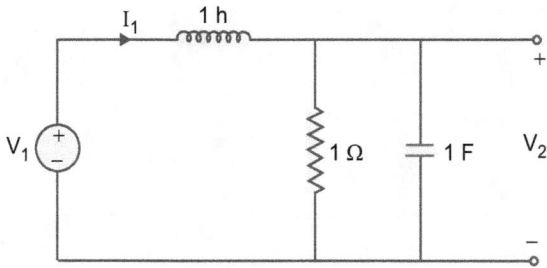

Fig. 1.53: Circuit for Ex. 1.54

Sol.: The transformed circuit is shown below in Fig. 1.53 (a).

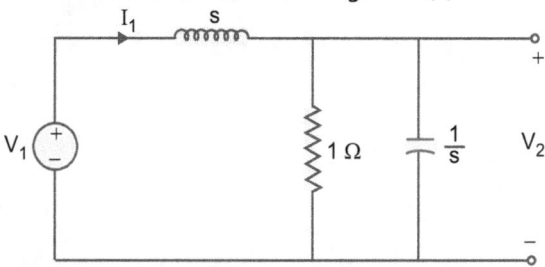

Fig. 1.53 (a): Transformed circuit

Let $\quad Z_1(s) = 1\,\Omega \,\|\, \dfrac{1}{s} = \dfrac{1 \times \dfrac{1}{s}}{1 + \dfrac{1}{s}} = \dfrac{1}{(s+1)}$

Then, $\quad I_1 = \dfrac{V_1}{s + Z(s)} = \dfrac{V_1}{s + \dfrac{1}{(s+1)}} = \dfrac{(s+1)\,V_1}{(s^2 + s + 1)}$

Thus, $\quad Z(s) = \dfrac{V_1}{I_1} = \dfrac{s^2 + s + 1}{(s+1)}$

Also by voltage divider relation, we get,

$$V_2 = \dfrac{Z_1(s) \cdot V_1}{Z_1(s) + s} = \dfrac{\dfrac{1}{s+1} \cdot V_1}{\left(\dfrac{1}{s+1}\right) + s} = \dfrac{V_1}{(s^2 + s + 1)}$$

Thus, $\quad T(s) = \dfrac{V_2}{V_1} = \dfrac{1}{(s^2 + s + 1)}$

Ex. 1.55: For the circuit shown, find input admittance $Y_{in}(s)$ and hence obtain equivalent inductance of the circuit.

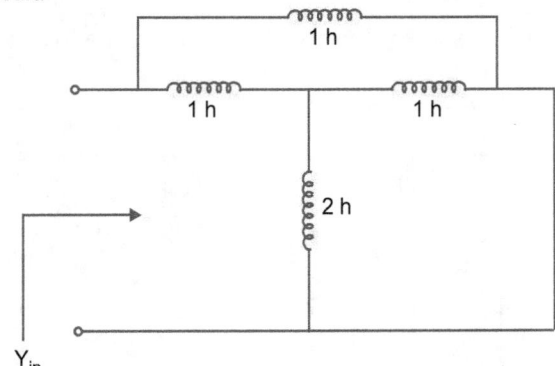

Fig. 1.54: Circuit for Ex. 1.55

Sol.: The transformed circuit is shown below in Fig. 1.54 (a).

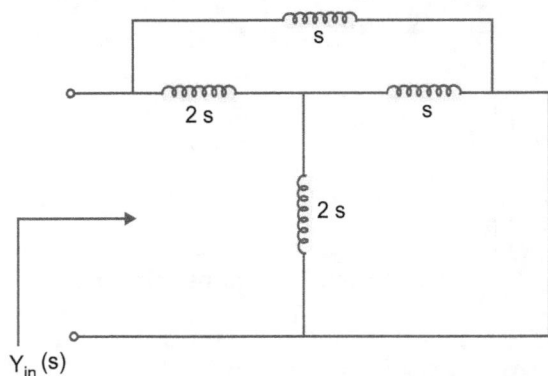

Fig. 1.54 (a): Transformed circuit

The equivalent circuits are as shown below in Fig. 1.54 (b).

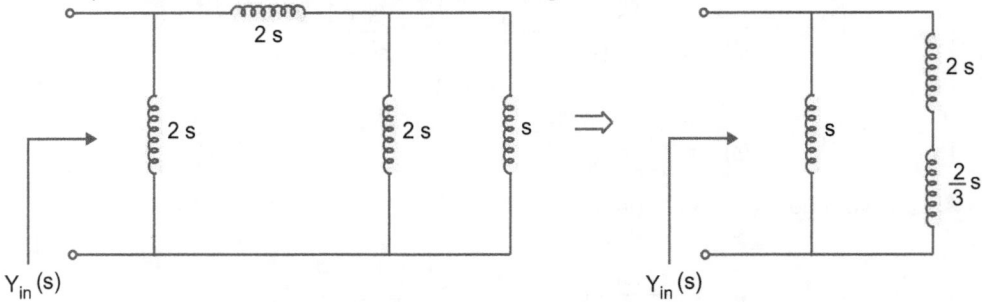

Fig. 1.54 (b): Equivalent circuits

Thus the resultant admittance will be

$$Y_{in}(s) = \frac{1}{s} + \left(2s + \frac{2s}{3}\right) = \frac{1}{s} + \frac{3}{8s} = \frac{8+3}{8s} = \frac{11}{8s} \text{ mho}$$

Hence, $L_{eq} = \frac{8}{11}$ Henry, is the equivalent inductance.

Ex. 1.56: For the network shown, find the expression for the following network functions $\frac{V_2}{V_1}, \frac{I_2}{I_1}, \frac{V_2}{I_1}$ and $\frac{I_2}{V_1}$.

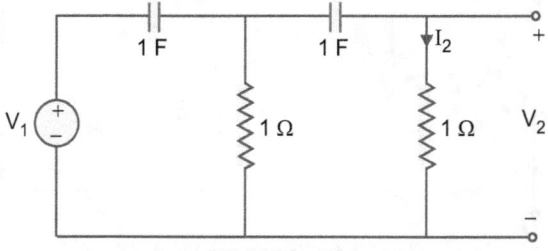

Fig. 1.55: Circuit for Ex. 1.56

Sol.: The transformed circuit is shown below in Fig. 1.55 (a).

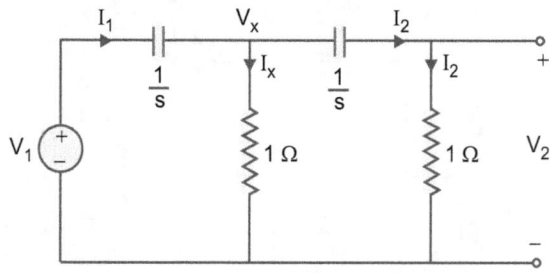

Fig. 1.55 (a): Transformed circuit

$$I_2 = \frac{V_2}{1} = V_2 \qquad \ldots \text{(a)}$$

$$V_x = V_2 + \frac{1}{s} I_2 = V_2 + \frac{V_2}{s}$$

$$= \left(\frac{s+1}{s}\right) V_2 \qquad \ldots \text{(b)}$$

$$I_x = \frac{V_x}{1} = \left(\frac{s+1}{s}\right) V_2$$

Thus, $\quad I_1 = I_x + I_2 = V_2 \left(\frac{s+1}{s}\right) + V_2$

$$= \left(\frac{2s+1}{s}\right) V_2 \qquad \ldots \text{(c)}$$

Hence, $\quad V_1 = \dfrac{I_1}{s} + V_x = \left(\dfrac{2s+1}{s^2}\right) V_2 + \left(\dfrac{s+1}{s}\right) V_2$

$$V_1 = V_2 \left[\frac{(2s+1) + s(s+1)}{s^2}\right]$$

$$= \left[\frac{s^2 + 3s + 1}{s^2}\right] V_2 \qquad \ldots \text{(d)}$$

Thus, $\quad \dfrac{V_2}{V_1} = \dfrac{s^2}{s^2 + 3s + 1}, \quad \dfrac{V_2}{I_2} = \dfrac{s}{(2s+1)}$

$$\frac{I_2}{V_1} = \frac{V_2}{\left(\dfrac{s^2 + 3s + 1}{s^2}\right) V_2} = \frac{s^2}{(s^2 + 3s + 1)}$$

$$\frac{I_2}{I_1} = \frac{V_2}{\left(\dfrac{2s+1}{s}\right) V_2} = \frac{s}{(2s+1)}$$

Ex. 1.57: Find driving point impedance and driving point admittance of the circuit shown.

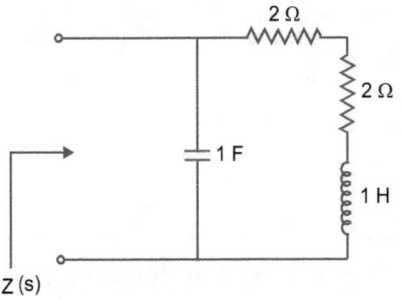

Fig. 1.56: Circuit for Ex. 1.57

Sol.: The transformed circuit is shown below in Fig. 1.56 (a).

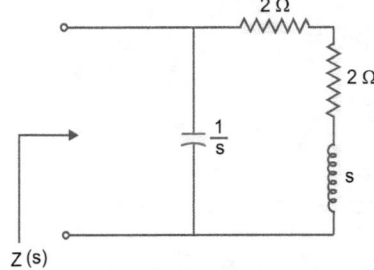

Fig. 1.56 (a): Transformed circuit

Let $\quad Z_1(s) = (2 + 2 + s) = (4 + s)$

Then, $\quad Z(s) = \dfrac{1}{s} \parallel Z_1(s) = \dfrac{1}{s} \parallel (4 + s)$

$$Z(s) = \dfrac{\dfrac{1}{s} \times (s+4)}{(s+4) + \dfrac{1}{s}} = \dfrac{s+4}{(s^2 + 4s + 1)} = \text{Driving point impedance.}$$

Hence, $\quad Y(s) = \dfrac{s^2 + 4s + 1}{(s+4)} = \text{Driving point admittance}$

Ex. 1.58: Determine $\dfrac{V_2}{I_1}$ and $\dfrac{V_2}{V_1}$ for the circuit shown in Fig. 1.57.

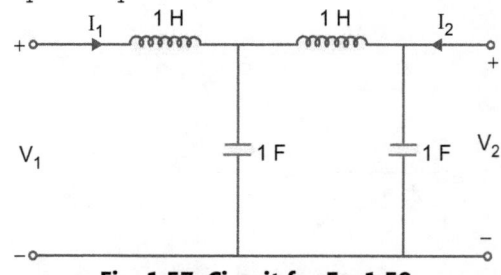

Fig. 1.57: Circuit for Ex. 1.58

Sol.: The transformed circuit is shown below in Fig. 1.57 (a).

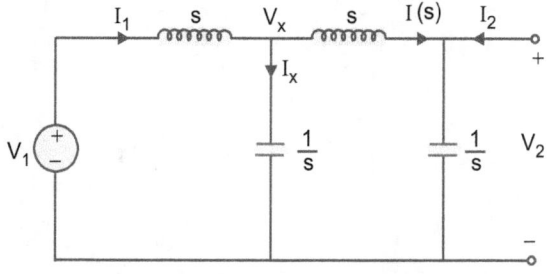

Fig. 1.57 (a): Transformed circuit

With output open ($I_2 = 0$), we have,

$$I(s) = \frac{V_2}{1/s} = sV_2$$

$$V_x = sI(s) + V_2 = s^2 V_2 + V_2 = V_2(s^2 + 1)$$

$$I_x = sV_x = s(s^2 + 1)V_2 = (s^3 + s)V_2$$

$$I_1 = I_x + I(s) = (s^3 + s)V_2 + sV_2 = V_2(s^3 + 2s)$$

$$V_1 = sI_1 + V_x = s(s^3 + 2s)V_2 + (s^2 + 1)V_2$$

$$= V_2(s^4 + 2s^2 + s^2 + 1) = V_2(s^4 + 3s^2 + 1)$$

Thus,
$$\frac{V_2}{V_1} = \frac{1}{(s^4 + 3s^2 + 1)}$$

$$\frac{V_2}{I_1} = \frac{V_2}{V_2(s^3 + 2s)} = \frac{1}{(s^3 + 2s)} = \frac{1}{s(s^2 + 2)}$$

Ex. 1.59: Find the input impedance and plot its poles and zeros of the circuit shown below in Fig. 1.58.

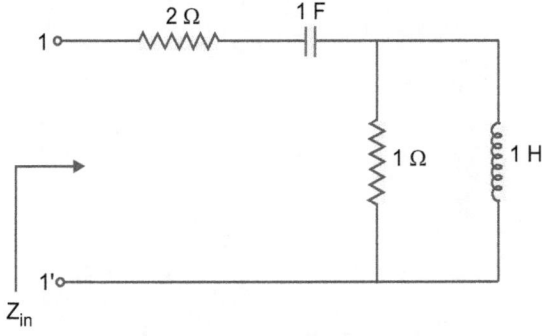

Fig. 1.58: Circuit for Ex. 1.59

Sol.: The transformed circuit is shown below in Fig. 1.58 (a).

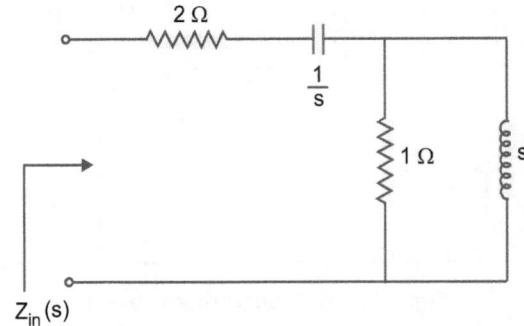

Fig. 1.58 (a): Transformed circuit

$$Z_{in}(s) = \left[2 + \frac{1}{s}\right] + 1 \parallel s = 2 + \frac{1}{s} + \frac{s}{(s+1)}$$

$$= \frac{2s(s+1)(s+1) + s^2}{s(s+1)}$$

$$= \frac{3s^2 + 2s + s + s^2}{s(s+1)} = \frac{3s^2 + 3s + 1}{s(s+1)}$$

The pole is at $s = -1$ and $s = 0$.

Zeros are given by equation $3s^2 + 3s + 1 = 0$. This is an quadratic equation, the roots of which are

$$s = \frac{-3 \pm \sqrt{9 - 4 \times 3}}{6} = \frac{-3 \pm j\sqrt{3}}{6} = -\frac{1}{2} \pm j\frac{\sqrt{3}}{6}$$

Thus, $s_1 = -\frac{1}{2} + j\frac{\sqrt{3}}{6}$ and $s_2 = -\frac{1}{2} - j\frac{\sqrt{3}}{6}$

The pole-zero plot is shown below.

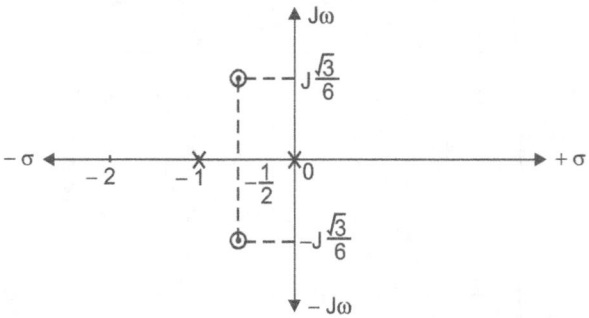

Fig. 1.58 (b): Pole-zero plot

Ex. 1.60: Find the input impedance $Z_{in}(s)$ and plot its poles and zeros for the circuit shown in Fig. 1.59.

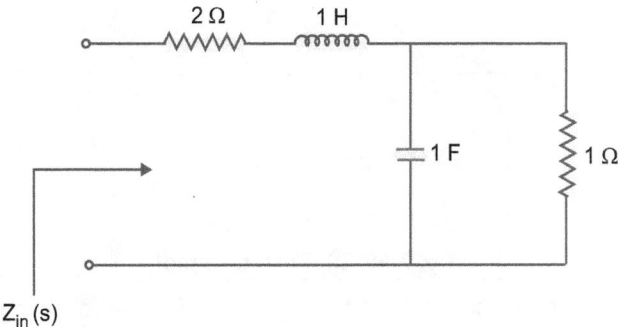

Fig. 1.59: Circuit for Ex. 1.60

Sol.: The transformed circuit is shown below in Fig. 1.102 (a).

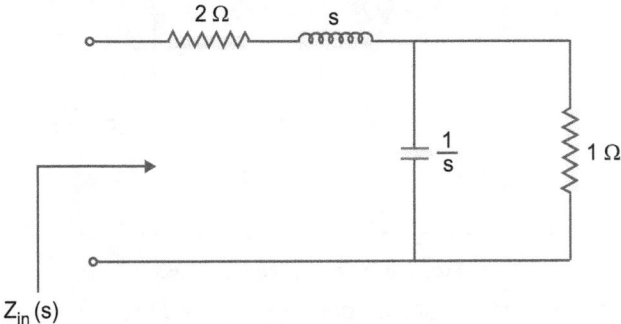

Fig. 1.59 (a): Transformed circuit

Now, $\quad 1 \parallel \dfrac{1}{s} = \dfrac{1/s}{1 + \dfrac{1}{s}} = \dfrac{1}{(s+1)}$

$$Z_{in}(s) = 2 + s + \dfrac{1}{(s+1)} = \dfrac{2(s+1) + s(s+1) + 1}{(s+1)} = \dfrac{s^2 + 3s + 3}{(s+1)}$$

Thus pole is at $s = -1$.

The zeros are obtained from equation $s^2 + 3s + 3 = 0$

Solving this quadratic equation gives

$$s = \dfrac{-3 \pm \sqrt{9 - 4 \times 3}}{2 \times 1} = \dfrac{-3 \pm \sqrt{-3}}{2} = -\dfrac{3}{2} \pm j\dfrac{\sqrt{3}}{2}$$

Thus poles are at $s_1 = -\dfrac{3}{2} + j\dfrac{\sqrt{3}}{2}$ and $s_2 = -\dfrac{3}{2} - j\dfrac{\sqrt{3}}{2}$.

The plot is as shown below in Fig. 1.59 (b).

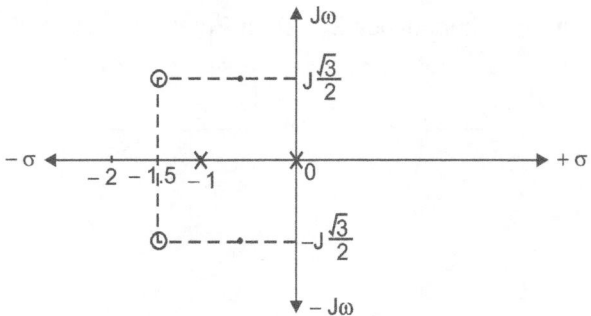

Fig. 1.59 (b): Pole-zero plot

Ex. 1.61: For the network shown, find the expression for the following network functions $\frac{V_2}{V_1}$, $\frac{I_2}{I_1}$ and $\frac{V_2}{I_1}$.

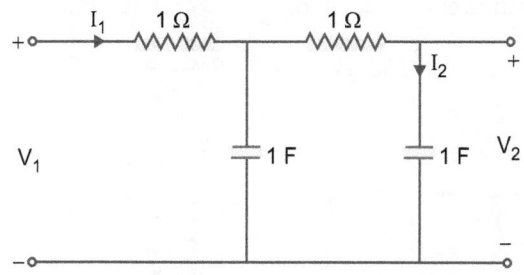

Fig. 1.60: Circuit for Ex. 1.61

Sol.: The transformed circuit is shown below in Fig. 1.60 (a).

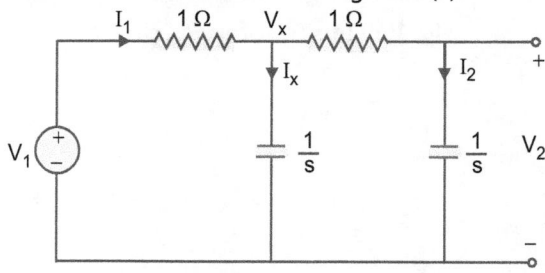

Fig. 1.60 (a): Transformed circuit

We have,
$$I_2 = \frac{V_2}{1/s} = sV_2$$

$$V_x = 1 \times I_2 + V_2 = sV_2 + V_2 = (s+1)V_2$$

$$I_x = \frac{V_x}{1/s} = sV_x = s(s+1)V_2$$

$$I_1 = I_x + I_2 = s(s+1)V_2 + V_2 = V_2(s^2 + 2s)$$

$$V_1 = I_1 \times 1 + V_x = V_2(s^2 + 2s) + (s+1)V_2 = V_2(s^2 + 3s + 1)$$

Thus,
$$\frac{V_2}{V_1} = \frac{1}{s^2 + 3s + 1}$$

$$\frac{I_2}{I_1} = \frac{sV_2}{V_2(s^2 + 2s)} = \frac{s}{(s^2 + 2s)} = \frac{1}{(s+2)}$$

$$\frac{V_2}{I_1} = \frac{V_2}{V_2(s^2 + 2s)} = \frac{1}{s(s+2)}$$

Ex. 1.62: Find the driving point impedance of the circuit shown below in Fig. 1.61.

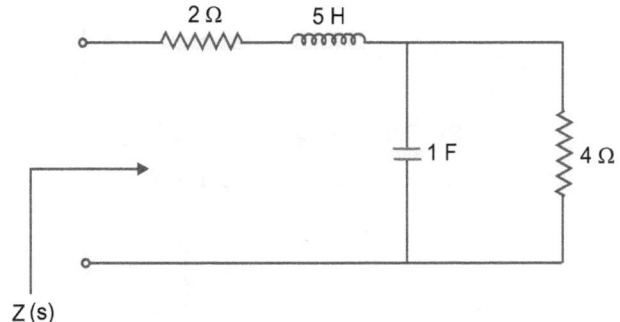

Fig. 1.61: Circuit for Ex. 1.62

Sol.: The transformed circuit is shown below in Fig. 1.61 (a).

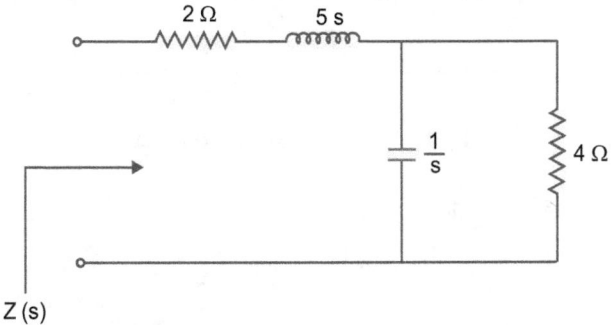

Fig. 1.61 (a): Transformed circuit

We have,
$$Z_1(s) = \frac{1}{s} \parallel 4 = \frac{4/s}{\left(4 + \frac{1}{s}\right)} = \frac{4}{(4s + 1)}$$

$$Z(s) = \text{Driving point impedance} = 2 + 5s + Z_1(s)$$

$$= 2 + 5s + \frac{4}{(4s+1)} = \frac{(2 + 5s)(4s+1) + 4}{(4s+1)}$$

$$= \frac{20s^2 + 8s + 5s + 2 + 4}{(4s+1)} = \frac{20s^2 + 13s + 6}{(4s+1)}$$

Ex. 1.63: Write driving point impedance Z (s) of the circuit shown in Fig. 1.62. Locate the poles and zeros of Z (s) on S-plane.

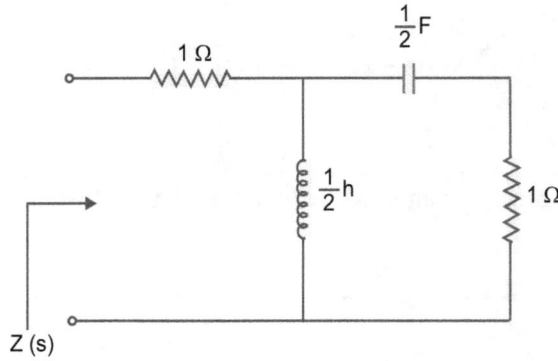

Fig. 1.62: Circuit for Ex. 1.63

Sol.: The transformed circuit is shown below in Fig. 1.62 (a).

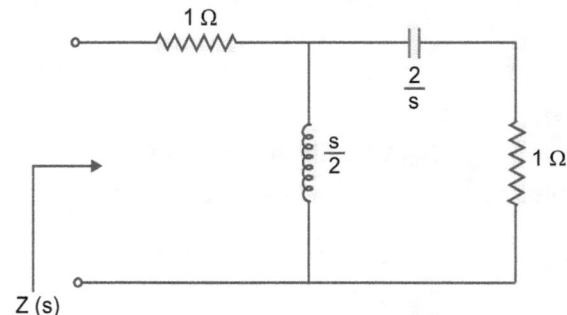

Fig. 1.62 (a): Transformed circuit

Now, let $Z_1(s) = \dfrac{s}{2} \parallel \left(1 + \dfrac{2}{s}\right) = \dfrac{s}{2} \parallel \dfrac{2+s}{s}$

$$= \dfrac{\dfrac{s}{2} \times \dfrac{(s+2)}{s}}{\dfrac{s}{2} + \dfrac{s+2}{s}} = \dfrac{\dfrac{s(s+2)}{2s}}{\dfrac{s^2+2s+4}{2s}} = \dfrac{s(s+2)}{(s^2+2s+4)}$$

Then driving point impedance,

$$Z(s) = 1 + Z_1(s) = 1 + \dfrac{s(s+2)}{s^2+2s+4}$$

$$= \dfrac{(s^2+2s+4) + s^2 + 2s}{(s^2+2s+4)}$$

Thus, $Z(s) = \dfrac{P(s)}{q(s)} = s\left[\dfrac{s^2 + 2s + 2}{s^2 + 2s + 4}\right]$

$= 2\left[\dfrac{(s+1+j1)(s+1-j1)}{(s+1+j\sqrt{3})(s+1-j\sqrt{3})}\right]$

Thus poles are at $s_1 = -1 + j\sqrt{3}$ and $s_2 = -1 - j\sqrt{3}$
Zeros are at $s_3 = -1 + j1$ and $s_4 = -1 - j1$

The pole-zero plot of $Z(s)$ is shown below in Fig. 1.62 (b). It consists of two complex poles and zeros each.

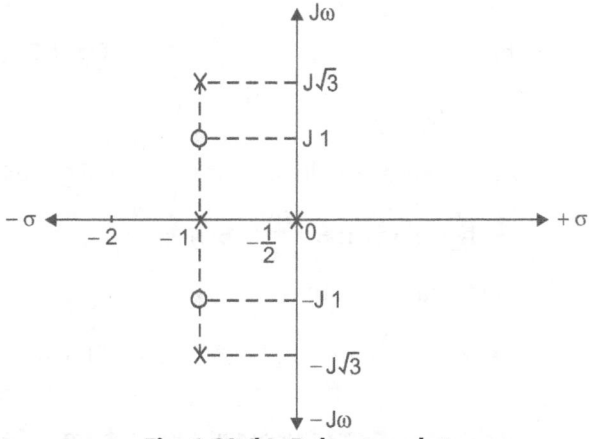

Fig. 1.62 (b): Pole-zero plot

Ex. 1.64: Find $V_2(s)$ in the circuit shown. Use Superposition theorem and Laplace transform method.

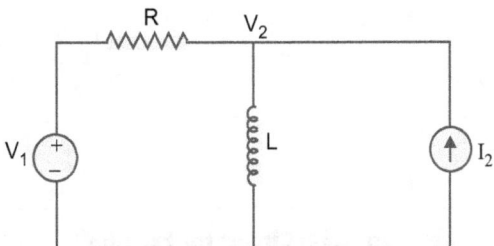

Fig. 1.63: Circuit for Ex. 1.64

Sol.: The transformed circuit is shown below in Fig. 1.63 (a).

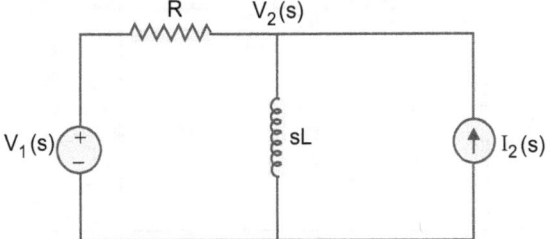

Fig. 1.63 (a): Transformed circuit

Step I: With $V_1(s)$ only considered, circuit is as shown in Fig. 1.63 (b).

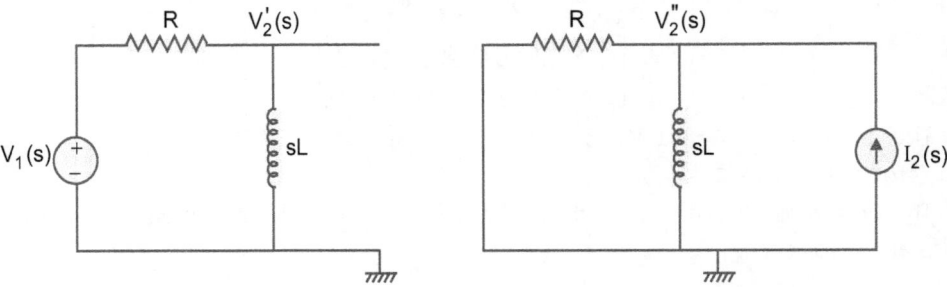

Fig. 1.63 (b) Fig. 1.63 (c)

$$V_2'(s) = V_1(s) \times \frac{sL}{sL + R} = \frac{sL}{R + sL} \times V_1(s) \quad \ldots (a)$$

Step II: With only $I_2(s)$ considered, the circuit is as shown in Fig. 1.63 (c).

$$V_2''(s) = I_2(s) \times sL \parallel R = \frac{sRL}{sL + R} \times I_2(s) \quad \ldots (b)$$

Step III: By superposition theorem, we have,

$$V_2(s) = V_2'(s) + V_2''(s) = \frac{sL}{R + sL}[V_1(s) + RI_2(s)]$$

Ex. 1.65: Find $Z = \dfrac{V_1}{I_1}$ and $T(s) = \dfrac{V_2}{V_1}$ for the circuit shown in Fig. 1.64.

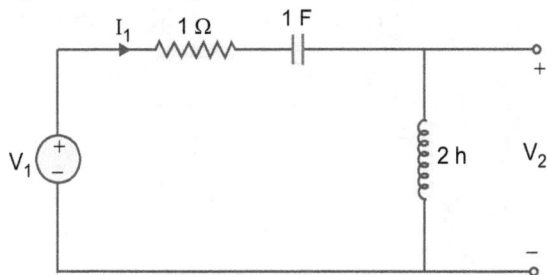

Fig. 1.64: Circuit for Ex. 1.65

Sol.: The transformed circuit is shown below in Fig. 1.64 (a).

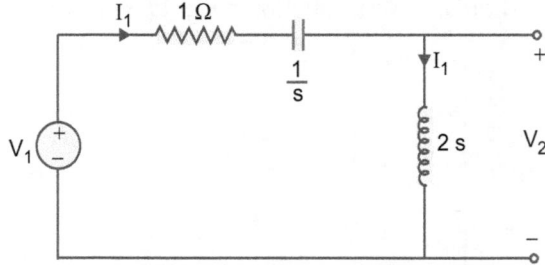

Fig. 1.64 (a): Transformed circuit

We have, $$I_1 = \frac{V_1}{1 + \frac{1}{s} + 2s} = \frac{sV_1}{(2s^2 + s + 1)}$$

Thus, $$\frac{V_1}{I_1} = \frac{(2s^2 + s + 1)}{s}$$

$$V_2 = 2s\, I_1 = 2s^2 \times \frac{V_1}{(2s^2 + s + 1)}$$

Thus, $$T(s) = \frac{V_2}{V_1} = \frac{2s^2}{(2s^2 + s + 1)}$$

Ex. 1.66: Determine V (s) in the circuit shown. Assume zero initial conditions. Use Laplace transform method.

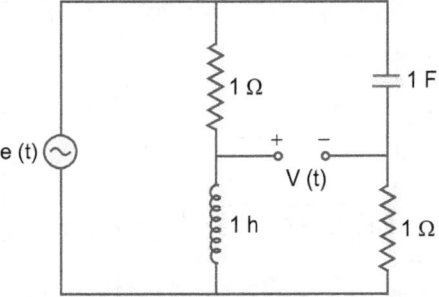

Fig. 1.65: Circuit for Ex. 1.66

Sol.: The transformed circuit is shown below in Fig. 1.65 (a).

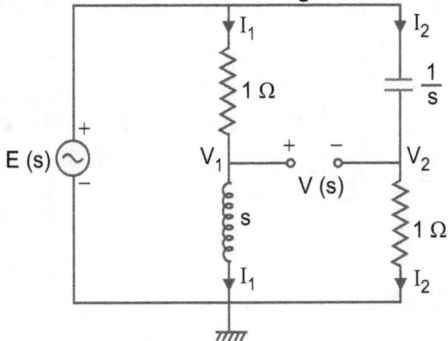

Fig. 1.65 (a): Transformed circuit

$$I_1 = \frac{E(s)}{(1 + s)} \qquad \text{Thus,} \quad V_1 = sI_1 = \frac{sE(s)}{(s + 1)}$$

$$I_2 = \frac{E(s)}{\left(1 + \frac{1}{s}\right)} = \frac{sE(s)}{s + 1} \qquad \text{Thus,} \quad V_2 = 1 \times I_2 = \frac{sE(s)}{(s + 1)}$$

Hence, $$V(s) = V_1 - V_2 = \frac{sE(s)}{(s + 1)} - \frac{sE(s)}{(s + 1)} = 0$$

Ex. 1.67: Find driving point impedance and driving point admittance for the circuit shown in Fig. 1.66.

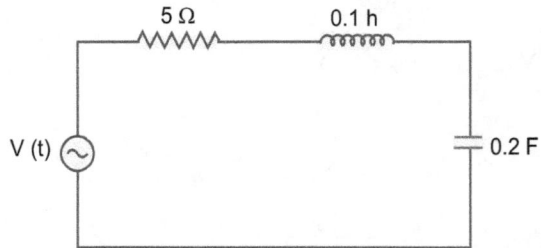

Fig. 1.66: Circuit for Ex. 1.67

Sol.: The transformed circuit is shown below in Fig. 1.66 (a).

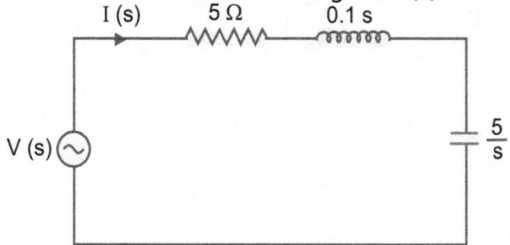

Fig. 1.66 (a): Transformed circuit

Driving point impedance,

$$[Z(s)] = \frac{V(s)}{I(s)} = 5 + 0.2s + \frac{5}{s} = \frac{s^2 + 50s + 50}{10s}$$

Driving point admittance,

$$[Y(s)] = \frac{I(s)}{V(s)} = \frac{10s}{s^2 + 50s + 50}$$

Ex. 1.68: For the network function draw pole-zero plot and obtain time response i(t).

$$I(s) = \frac{2s}{(s+1)(s+2)}$$

Sol.: The zero is at s = 0.
Poles are at s = – 1 and s = – 2.
The pole-zero plot is shown below in Fig. 1.67.

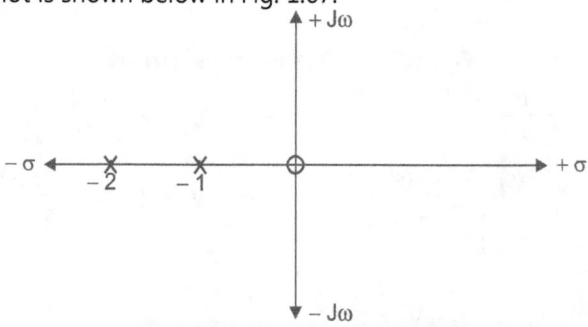

Fig. 1.67: Pole-zero plot of I (s)

$$I(s) = \frac{2s}{(s+1)(s+2)} = \frac{K_1}{(s+1)} + \frac{K_2}{(s+2)}$$

$$K_1 = [(s+1)I(s)]_{s \to -1} = \left[\frac{2s}{(s+2)}\right]_{s \to -1} = \frac{-2}{(-1+2)} = -2$$

$$K_2 = [(s+2)I(s)]_{s \to -2} = \left[\frac{2s}{(s+1)}\right]_{s \to -2} = \frac{-4}{(-2+1)} = 4$$

Thus,
$$I(s) = \frac{-2}{(s+1)} + \frac{4}{(s+2)}$$

$$i(t) = L^{-1}[I(s)] = -2e^{-t} + 4e^{-2t}$$

Ex. 1.69: Draw the pole-zero plot of following function:

$$H(s) = \frac{s^2 + 4}{s^2 + 6s + 4}$$

Sol.: The function can be written as

$$H(s) = \frac{(s + J2)(s - j2)}{(s + 0.764)(s + 5.236)}$$

The zeros are at $s_1 = j2$ and $s_2 = j2$.
The poles are at $s_3 = -0.764$ and $s_4 = -5.236$.
The pole-zero plot is shown below.

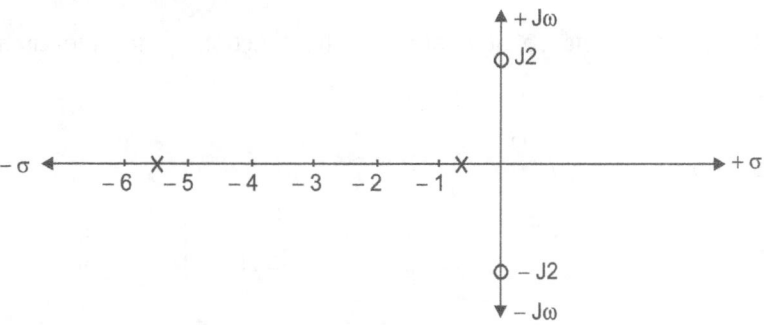

Fig. 1.68: Pole-zero plot

Ex. 1.70: For the given network function, draw the pole-zero plot and hence obtain the time domain response.

$$V(s) = \frac{5(s+5)}{(s+2)(s+7)}$$

Sol.: The zero is at $s = -5$.
The poles are at $s_1 = -2$ and $s_2 = -7$.
The pole-zero plot is shown below in Fig. 1.69.

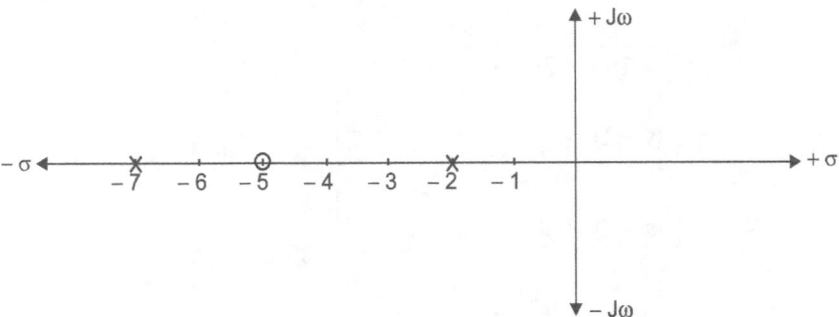

Fig. 1.69: Pole-zero plot

We have, $V(s) = \dfrac{5(s+5)}{(s+2)(s+7)} = \dfrac{k_0}{(s+2)} + \dfrac{k_1}{(s+7)}$

$K_0 = [(s+2)V(s)]_{s \to -2} = \left[\dfrac{5(s+5)}{(s+7)}\right]_{s \to -2} = 5\left(\dfrac{3}{5}\right) = 3$

$K_1 = [(s+7)V(s)]_{s \to -7} = \left[\dfrac{5(s+5)}{(s+2)}\right]_{s \to -7} = \dfrac{5 \times -2}{-5} = 2$

Thus, $V(s) = \dfrac{3}{(s+2)} + \dfrac{2}{(s+7)}$

$V(t) = 3e^{-2t} + 2e^{-7t}$

Ex. 1.71: Determine the voltage ratio transfer function $\dfrac{V_2}{V_1}$ for the circuit shown in Fig. 1.70.

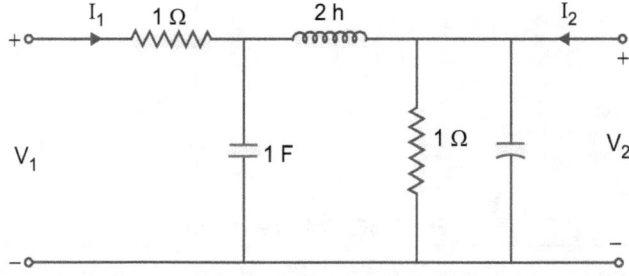

Fig. 1.70: Circuit for Ex. 1.71

Sol.: With an output open i.e. $I_2 = 0$, the voltage ratio transfer function is given by

$T(s) = \dfrac{V_2}{V_1}$

$= \dfrac{1}{2s^3 + 4s^2 + 4s + 2}$

1.7 POLE POSITION AND STABILITY

Most important requirement of any system is stability. An unstable system usually is considered as a useless system.

Stability of the system can be classified as absolute stability and relative stability. **Absolute stability** is the condition where the system is stable or unstable. It is like yes or no type answer. Once a system is confirmed to be stable, then **relative stability** of the system determines degree of the stability.

As defined earlier, a system is said to be stable if bounded input excitation the output (response) does not go on increasing indefinitely.

Impulse response of the system can be used to determine the system stability.

A stable system is one in which impulse response will approach zero for sufficiently large time.

An unstable system is one in which impulse response grows without bound. i.e. it approaches to infinity for sufficient large time.

In marginally stable system, impulse response approaches a constant non-zero value or a constant amplitude oscillation for a sufficient large time.

The pole position and system stability is very closely related. The necessary and sufficient condition for the system to be stable is that the roots of the characteristic equation of the system must lie on negative half of the S-plane. Thus, if $T(s) = \dfrac{N(s)}{D(s)}$ is the transfer function, then roots of $D(s) = 0$ must lie on the negative half of S-plane. For any root (pole) on right half of S-plane the system will be unstable.

Let us now consider the relationship between pole positions and the corresponding impulse responses.

(a) **Poles on the negative real axis:** Consider a simple pole on negative real axis.

i.e. $$F(s) = \dfrac{K}{(s+a)}$$

The corresponding impulse response is given by
$$f(t) = L^{-1}[F(s)] = Ke^{-at}$$

For large t, f (t) approaches to zero as shown in the Fig. 1.71. Thus it is a stable system. Suppose we have multiple poles in the system. For example, consider
$$F(s) = \dfrac{K}{(s+a)^r}$$

Then the response will be
$$f(t) = K\, t^r\, e^{-at}$$

This also approaches to zero as $t \to \infty$. Hence this is a stable system.

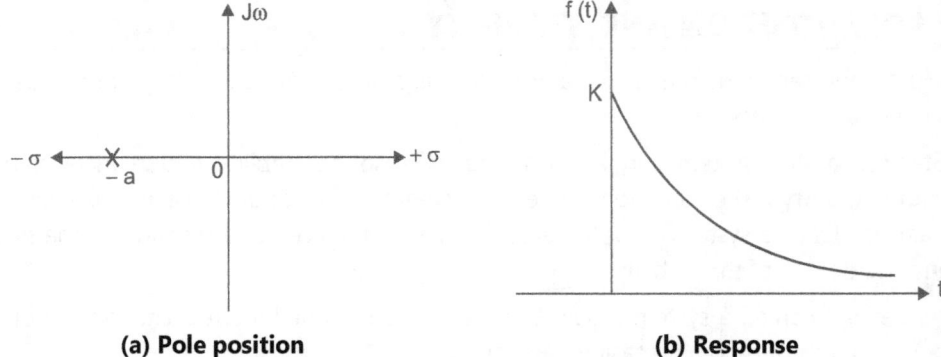

(a) Pole position (b) Response

Fig. 1.71: Poles on negative real axis and its response

Thus for all poles lying on the negative real axis, the system is stable.

(b) Complex poles on left half of S-plane: Consider an F (s) with poles at $s = -\sigma_1 \pm j\beta_1$ as in Fig. 1.72.

$$F(s) = \frac{K_1}{(s + \sigma_1 - j\beta_1)} \pm \frac{K_2}{(s + \sigma_1 + j\beta_1)}$$

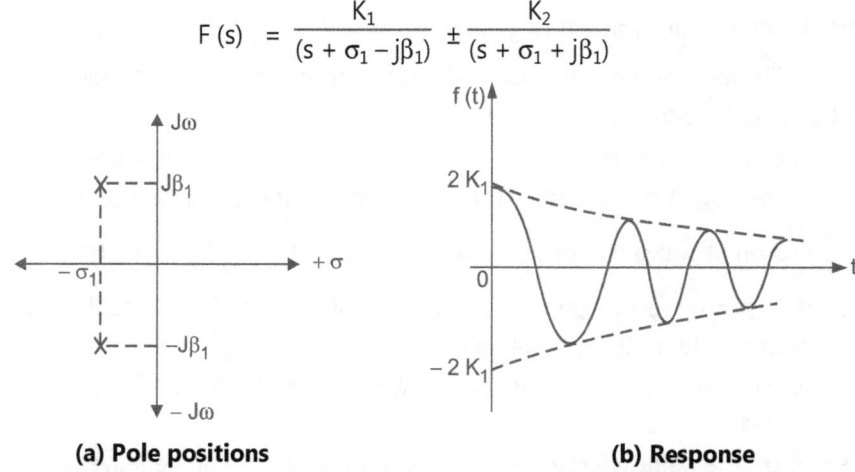

(a) Pole positions (b) Response

Fig. 1.72: Complex poles on left half of S-plane and its response

The corresponding time response is given by

$$f(t) = L^{-1}[F(s)] = L^{-1}\left[\frac{2K_1(s + \alpha_1)}{(s + \alpha_1)^2 + \beta_1^2}\right]$$

As t approaches infinity f (t) becomes zero. Thus the system becomes stable.

For multiple order of poles on left half of the S-plan, the response will be of the form

$$f(t) = 2t_1 t^r e^{-\alpha_1 t} \cos \beta_1 t$$

This also approaches to zero as $t \to \infty$.

Thus **"For all complex poles lying on left half of S-plane, the system is stable"**.

(c) Poles on positive real axis: Consider a function in which pole is on right half of S-plane i.e.

$$F(s) = \frac{K}{(s-a)}$$

Then response will be

$$f(t) = Ke^{+at}$$

This response increases exponentially to infinity as $t \to \infty$. Thus the system is unstable. If there are multiple order of poles on +ve real axis, the system becomes more unstable.

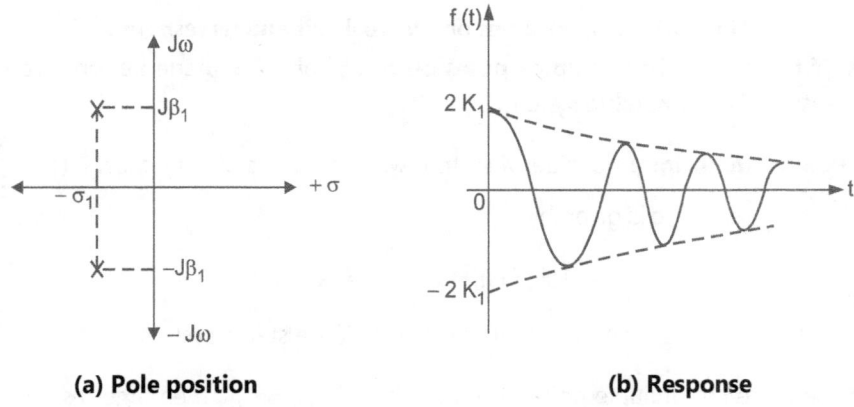

(a) Pole position   (b) Response

Fig. 1.73: Simple pole on positive real axis and its response

Thus "If the system has any pole on right half of S-plane then it is an unstable system".

(d) Complex poles on the right half of S-plane: Consider a system with complex poles at $s = \alpha_1 + j\beta_1$. i.e.

$$F(s) = \frac{K_1}{(s - \alpha_1 + j\beta_1)} + \frac{K_1}{(s - \alpha_1 - j\beta_1)}$$

The time response is given by

$$f(t) = L^{-1}[F(s)] = L^{-1}\left[\frac{2K_1(s - \alpha_1)}{(s - \alpha_1)^2 + \beta_1^2}\right] = 2K_1 e^{\alpha_1 t} \cos \beta_1 t$$

Thus, $f(t)$ increases exponentially with damped oscillations as $t \to \infty$ as shown in Fig. 1.74.

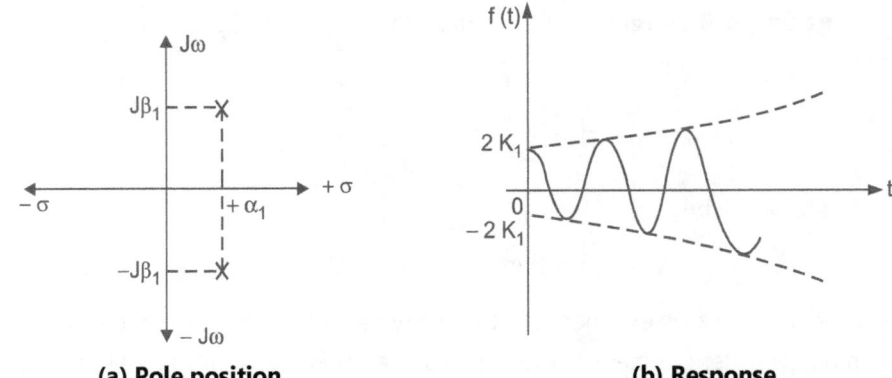

(a) Pole position (b) Response

Fig. 1.74: Complex poles on +ve real axis and its response

Thus "**If the system has complex poles on right half of S-plane i.e. on +ve real axis then the system is an unstable system**".

(e) Pole at the origin: Consider a system with the poles at origin. i.e. $F(s) = \dfrac{K}{s}$. Now the time domain response is given by

$$f(t) = L^{-1}[F(s)] = L^{-1}\left[\dfrac{K}{s}\right] = K\,u(t)$$

Thus, as $t \to \infty$, f (t) remains constant at K. Hence it is a stable system.

Suppose there are multiple poles at the origin. If $F_1(s) = \dfrac{K}{s^2}$, then time response will be given by

$$f_1(t) = K\,t\,u(t)$$

This shows that if $t \to \infty$, then f (t) $\to \infty$ and hence it is a unstable system.

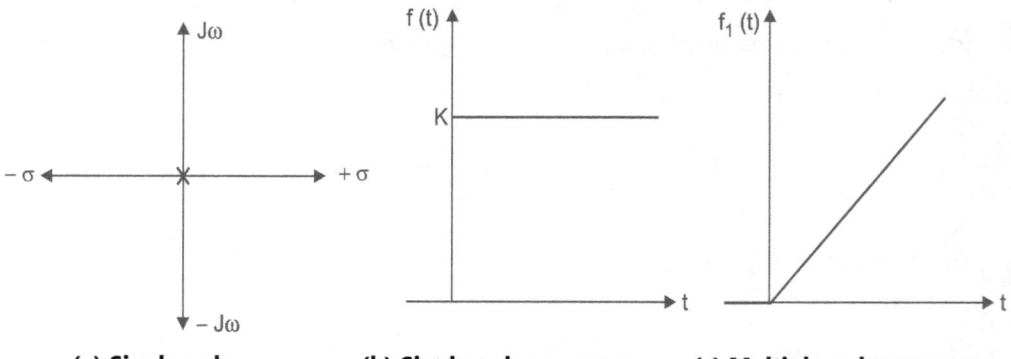

(a) Single pole (b) Single pole response (c) Multiple pole response

Fig. 1.75: Single and multiple pole at origin and its response

Thus "**If there is single pole at origin, then the system is stable. If there are multiple poles at origin, then the system is unstable**".

EXERCISE

1. Define poles and zeros of a network functions. What are the significance of a pole and zero in a network function?
2. Give the essential properties of driving point function.
3. Give the essential properties of transfer function.
4. Give the essential properties of an driving point function.
5. Explain how time domain behaviour can be obtained from pole-zero plot.
6. Explain how frequency domain behaviour (magnitude plot and phase plot) can be obtained from the pole-zero plot.
7. Explain what is meant by stable and unstable system. Explain how location of pole-zero on S-plane affect the system stability.
8. For the LC ladder network shown obtain the voltage ratio transfer function in the form

$$K\left[\frac{(s^2 + a)(s^2 + b)}{(s^2 + c)(s^2 + d)}\right]$$

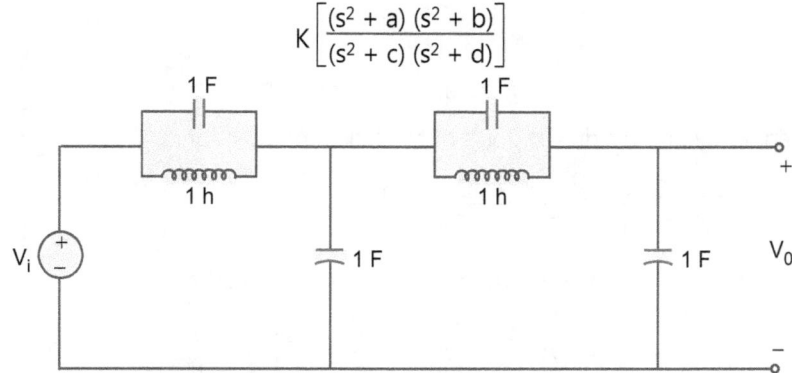

Fig. 1.76: Circuit for Q.8

9. For the Twin T network show that the transfer function is given by

$$\frac{V_o(s)}{V_i(s)} = \frac{s^2 + 1/R^2C^2}{s^2 + \left(\frac{4}{RC}\right)s + \frac{1}{R^2C^2}}$$

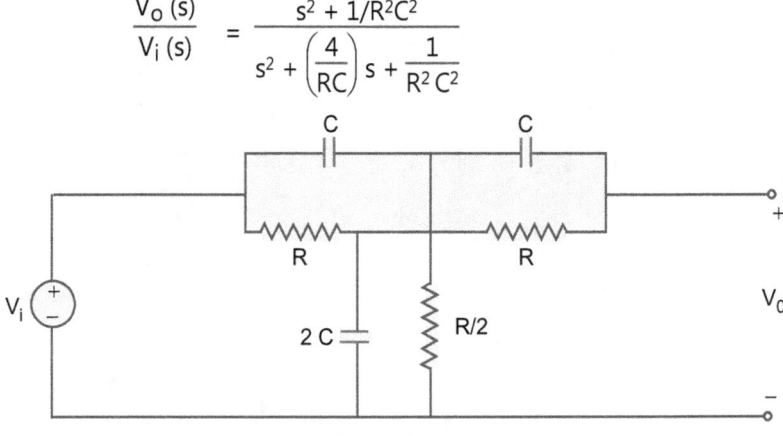

Fig. 1.77: Circuit for Q.9

10. For the symmetrical lattice network show that

$$\frac{V_o(s)}{V_1(s)} = \frac{s^2 - s + 1}{s^2 + s + 1}$$

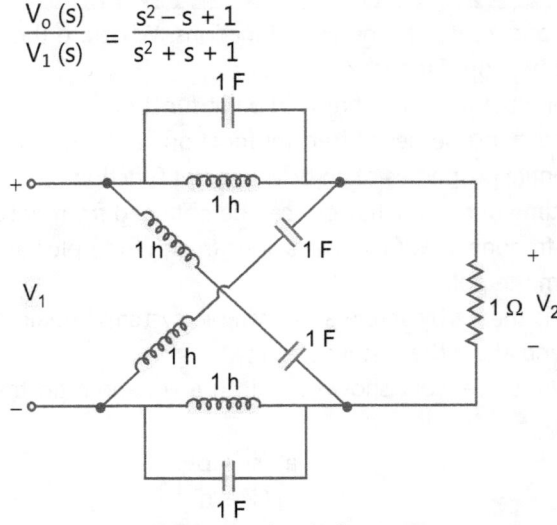

Fig. 1.78: Circuit for Q.10

11. Graphically find residue at poles of the following functions:

   (1) $\dfrac{2s + 5}{(s + 2)(s + 3)}$ (2) $\dfrac{s^2 + 10s + 16}{s^2 + 8s + 7}$

12. Draw the magnitude and phase plot of following functions:

   (1) $\dfrac{s}{(s + 10)^2}$ (2) $\dfrac{s + 10}{(s + 100)}$ (3) $\dfrac{(s + 10)(s + 50)}{(s + 200)}$

Unit II
FREQUENCY SELECTIVE NETWORKS

Contents ...
2.1 Introduction
2.2 Quality Factor Q
    2.2.1 Q of an Inductor
    2.2.2 Q of a Capacitor
2.3 Resonating Circuits
    2.3.1 General Rules for Finding the Condition of Resonance
2.4 Series Resonating Circuit
    2.4.1 Resonating Frequency
    2.4.2 Quality Factor
    2.4.3 Reactance Curve
    2.4.4 Phasor Diagrams
    2.4.5 Impedance
    2.4.6 Current at Resonance
    2.4.7 Voltage across L and C at f_r
    2.4.8 Variation of Z, Y and ϕ with f
    2.4.9 Variation of V_L and V_C with f
    2.4.10 Bandwidth of Series RLC Circuit
    2.4.11 Selectivity
    2.4.12 Effect of R_g on Bandwidth and Selectivity
    2.4.13 Applications of Series RLC Circuit
    2.4.14 Summary of Series RLC Circuit
    2.4.15 Important Formulae
2.5 Numericals on Series Resonating Circuits
2.6 Parallel Resonating Circuit
    2.6.1 Antiresonating Frequency
    2.6.2 Reactance Curve
    2.6.3 Impedance of Parallel RLC Circuit

2.6.4   Currents in Antiresonant Circuit
2.6.5   Bandwidth and Selectivity of Parallel RLC Circuit
2.6.6   General Case: Resistance in Both Branches
2.6.7   Applications of Parallel RLC Circuit
2.6.8   Summary of Parallel RLC Circuit
2.6.9   Important Formulae
2.7 Numericals on Parallel Resonating Circuits
2.8 Comparison of Series and Parallel Resonating Circuits
Exercise

2.1 INTRODUCTION

- Frequency response of any system is the measure of system's output spectrum in response to the input signal. [Output spectrum is output voltage or gain of system].
- The concept of frequency response also called as frequency curve is extremely important in all the fields of science and engineering, forming the foundation for understanding factors that determine various important parameters of the particular system like its accuracy, stability etc.
- This is applicable to any type of system, be it a electrical, mechanical, chemical, biological etc.
- As seen in Fig. 2.1 (a) of the systems or components are ideally expected to have a flat frequency response (e.g. OP-AMP) i.e. a system or component must reproduce all the desired input signals at all the frequencies with no emphasis or attenuation of a particular frequency band.
- But in some cases, the frequency response of the system may be chosen deliberately to reject some frequency components of the forcing function or to emphasize on others.
- The networks designed to impart such a behaviour are called as frequency selective networks.
- Tuned circuits or resonant circuits, Twin T networks and wein bridge networks are all some of the most popular examples of a frequency selective networks.
- Even the hottest means of entertainment today, Radio Mirchi ... Radio city ... are also nothing but examples of frequency selective networks, where we select only one frequency (i.e. one individual radio station) in the complete available band.

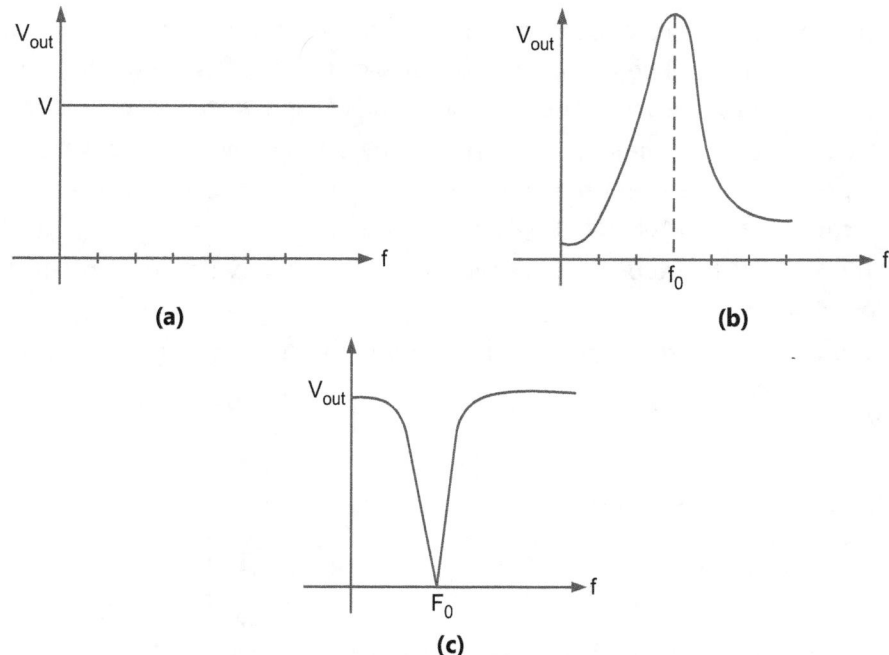

**Fig. 2.1: Ideal frequency response or frequency curve:
(a) An amplifier, (b), (c) Frequency selective network**

- Fig. 2.1 (a) shows flat frequency curve say for an ideal amplifier wherein the input at all the frequencies is equally amplified, thus giving a constant output voltage V at any frequency f. Fig. 2.1 (b) shows the frequency curve of a frequency selective network. Observe that output voltage of the circuit at frequency f_0 is appreciably high, thus making f_0 easily and prominently distinguishable or separable from rest of the other frequencies at which the output is very less.
- The other possibility as shown in Fig. 2.1 (c) is also very much possible in some frequency selective networks (like notch filters) i.e. having zero output voltage at f_0 and thus making it similarly distinguishable and separable from rest of the frequencies.
- We will discuss few such frequency selective networks in this unit.
- Inductors and capacitors are used along with resistors in the frequency selective networks.

2.2 QUALITY FACTOR Q

- We have seen that the frequency selective networks are made up of R, L and C components.
- The frequency responses of these frequency selective networks are not flat but are of a nature which makes one frequency prominently distinguishable from others. The frequency curves thus have a particular height and a width.

- The height of the curve depends only upon the value of R for constant – amplitude excitation [This will be very clear in further section 2.4.6]. But the width of the curve, or steepness of the sides depends upon the other two element values i.e. L and C.
- Inductors and capacitors are basically energy storing devices. Various inductors or capacitors can be compared in the terms of efficiency of energy storage. Figure of merit or quality factor Q is such a measure of efficiency.
- The width of the response curve thus depends on a very important parameter, the quality factor i.e. Q.
- The higher the value of the Q, the narrower and the sharper is the peak of the response curve.

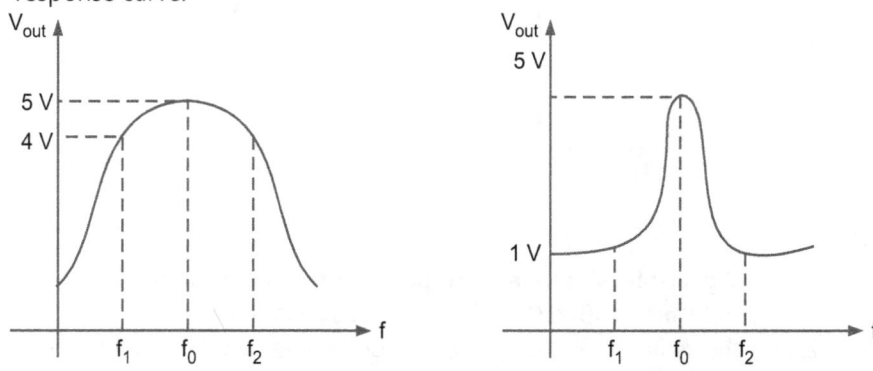

Fig. 2.2: An example of frequency response of a frequency selective network having (a) Very low Q, (b) Very high Q

- Fig. 2.2 (a) shows the frequency response curve of a selective circuit having low value of Q. Observe that in this case it is very difficult to separate f from the band of frequencies between f_1 and f_2 because all these frequencies have more or less the same voltage less. So it is hard to identify only one frequency.
- Fig. 2.2 (b) on the other hand shows the frequency response curve of the same circuit but now having a very higher value of Q. In this case, selecting f_0 is very easy because it is almost the only frequency with very high output. So it can be easily distinguished from others.
- It is very difficult to find the tallest boy in a group of 5 students where each of the boy has a height of 5.4", 5.3", 5.5", 5.35", 5.45" individually. The same task can be very easily done at a glance in a group of boys where the boys have the height of 5.2", 5.1", 7.1", 5.1", 5.3".
- Note that height of both the curves in Fig. 2.2 (a) and (b) is same. But curve in Fig. 2.2 (b) is more selective than curve in Fig. 2.2 (a).
- Thus, any frequency selective network must always have a narrow and a sharp peak.

- This quality factor Q, can be defined in two ways:
  - Generally Q is defined in terms of the ratio of the peak energy stored in the circuit to that of the energy being lost in one cycle such that

$$Q = 2\pi \times \frac{\text{Peak energy stored}}{\text{Energy dissipated per cycle}}$$

The factor of 2π is used to keep this definition of Q consistent with the second definition.

$$Q = \frac{f_r}{\Delta f} = \frac{\omega_r}{\Delta \omega} \ldots \text{[This will be more clear in section 2.4.10]}$$

where,
- f_r : Resonant frequency
- Δf : Bandwidth
- ω_r : Angular resonant frequency
- $\Delta \omega$: Angular bandwidth

Let us now define the Q of a (coil) inductor and a capacitor.

2.2.1 Q of a Inductor or a Coil

Inductor is always associated with a series resistance (R_S) as shown in Fig. 2.3. Energy stored in the inductor is maximum when the current is maximum i.e. I_m.

Thus, Maximum energy stored $= \frac{1}{2} L I_m^2$

Average power dissipated in the inductor $= I_{rms}^2 R_S = \left(\frac{I_m}{\sqrt{2}}\right)^2 R_S = \frac{1}{2} I_m^2 R_S$

Energy dissipated per cycle $= \dfrac{I_m^2 R_S}{2f}$

Thus, $\therefore \quad Q_L = 2\pi \times \dfrac{\frac{1}{2} L I_m^2}{\dfrac{I_m^2 R_S}{2f}}$

$$Q_L = 2\pi \times \frac{L I_m^2}{2} \times \frac{2f}{I_m^2 R_S}$$

$$\boxed{Q_L = \frac{\omega L}{R_S}}$$

where,
- Q_L = Quality factor of an inductor
- R_S = Series resistance
- I_m = Peak or maximum value of current in the circuit
- f = Frequency of operation
- L = Value of the inductor

Comments on Q of the coil:

- Resistance and inductance of the coil and hence Q is effected by the length of the coil, its shape, number of turns and also the core on which the coil is wounded.
- At low frequencies, value of Q must obviously be low because Q of a coil is directly proportional to the frequency (ω).
- As the frequency increases, the Q of the coil also rises. But then, because of the skin effect and dielectric losses, at high frequency, the resistance R of the coil also increases and its comparatively increases more rapidly.
- Quality factor Q of the coil is inversely proportional to the resistance R. So as a net effect, eventually Q drops off.
- In general, Q versus frequency graph is as shown in Fig. 2.4.

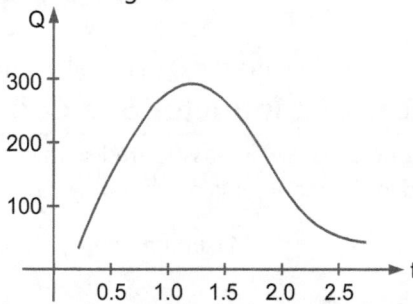

Fig. 2.3: A practical inductor   **Fig. 2.4: Variation of Q as a function of frequency**

- Q of a form coil be raised by adding a core of a magnetic material usually in compressed powdered form. Inductance and hence Q increases by using the core material of low eddy current and hysteresis losses.
- Q of the coil controls the effective Q of the circuit and is thus the controlling factor.

2.2.2 Quality Factor of a Capacitor

Capacitor is always associated with a resistor R_P as shown in Fig. 2.5. This is called as a leakage resistance. If E_m is the maximum voltage across the capacitor, then

$$\text{Maximum energy stored} = \frac{1}{2} C E_m^2 = \frac{1}{2} C \left[\frac{I_m}{C\omega}\right]^2$$

Average power lost in resistor

$$P_D = \left(\frac{I_m}{\sqrt{2}}\right)^2 R_P$$

$$= \frac{I_m^2}{2} R_P$$

$$\text{Energy lost per cycle} = \frac{I_m^2 R_P}{2f}$$

Thus,
$$Q_C = 2\pi \frac{\frac{1}{2}C\left[\frac{I_m}{C\omega}\right]^2}{\frac{I_m^2 R}{2f}}$$

$$Q = \frac{1}{2}C\left[\frac{I_m}{C\omega}\right]^2 \times \frac{2f}{I_m^2 R_P} = \frac{I_m^2 \cdot 2f \cdot C}{2C^2 \omega^2 I_m^2 R_P}$$

$$\boxed{Q_C = \frac{1}{\omega C R_P}}$$

where,
- Q_C = Quality factor of a capacitor
- ω = Frequency of operation
- R_P = Leakage resistance
- E_m = Maximum voltage across capacitor
- C = Capacitor

Comments on Q of the capacitor:
- The leakage resistance R_P in case of capacitor is very large so the losses in a capacitor are usually very small and hence Q of the capacitor is large.
- Even if losses are small, they are still affected by the type of dielectric material used.
- Air has the lowest losses of the various materials frequently used and then followed by polystyrene, mica and paper.

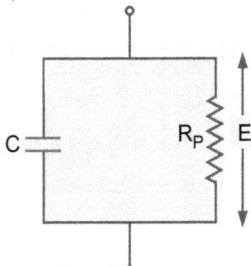

Fig. 2.5: A practical capacitor

2.3 RESONATING CIRCUITS

- Whenever, the natural frequency of oscillation of a system (would be electrical, mechanical or a civil structure) coincides with the frequency of the driving force (a voltage source in an electric circuit or a wind force in a civil structure) the two system resonate with respect to each other and the system has maximum response to a fixed magnitude of driving force. This phenomenon is known as Resonance.

- This phenomenon may be useful under certain conditions and sometimes it may prove to be disastrous for the system.
- There are many engineering applications of resonance. And so it is a very phenomenon, which must be taken into consideration when designing a system.
- For example: A suspension bridge in Washington showed tendencies to oscillate up and down during the construction and only a few months after construction, it began to build up oscillations under a moderate wind and within a hour the multibillion dollar bridge was reduced to pieces. This is a typical example of designing a bridge ignoring the possibility of phenomenon of resonance on the bridges.
- Thus in general resonance is defined as a phenomenon, in which
    - applied voltage and resulting current are in phase.
    - circuit exhibits unity power factor condition [$\cos \phi = 1$].
    - the reactance in an A.C. circuit gets cancelled if the inductive and capacitive reactances are in series or the susceptances get cancelled if the inductive and capacitive reactances are in parallel.
    - Complex impedance of the A.C. circuit consists of only the real resistive part.
- Resonance in series circuit i.e. when R, L and C are all connected in series is referred as series resonance or simply resonance. Similarly resonance in parallel circuits is referred as parallel resonance or antiresonance. In this unit, we will study series and parallel resonance in detail.

2.3.1 General Rules for Finding the Condition for Resonance

To find the condition for resonance, it is necessary to simplify and write down the impedance Z and to state the condition that the z will be resistive (i.e. only real part). This can be done in many ways depending upon the nature of z.

(a) If z is in the form of (r, ϕ), the resonant condition is $\phi = 0$.

(b) If z is in the form of $R + jX$, the resonant condition is $X = 0$.

(c) If z is in the form of $G + jB$, the resonant condition is $B = 0$.

(d) If z is in the form of term $\dfrac{A + JB}{C + JD}$, then resonant conditions is $\dfrac{B}{A} = \dfrac{C}{D}$.

(e) This condition is equivalent to saying the numerator and denominator have equal angle and hence the angle of z is 0.

It may be noted that we will be using condition (b) to find the resonant frequency of a series R-L-C circuit and condition (c) to find condition of resonance for a parallel R-L-C circuit.

2.4 SERIES RESONANCE

- A series circuit of R, L and C is shown in Fig. 2.6, driven by a generator of V volts.
- The resistance R, which is connected in series with Inductor and Capacitor actually includes:
  - Generator Resistance – R_g.
  - Series Resistance R_S of an inductor.
  - Leakage Resistance R_P of a capacitor.
  - Any other resistance introduced into the circuit as load.

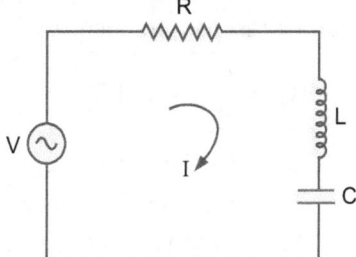

Fig. 2.6: Series R, L, C circuit

2.4.1 Resonating Frequency

Applying KVL to the series RLC circuit in Fig. 2.6,

$$V = R - I + I j\omega L - \frac{jI}{\omega C}$$

$$V = I\left[R + j\left(\omega L - \frac{1}{\omega C}\right)\right]$$

Since, the resonance has been defined as a unity power factor, then at resonant frequency, f_r the reactive term must be zero.

∴ At resonance

$$\omega_o L - \frac{1}{\omega_r C} = 0$$

ω is replaced by ω_r in the above equation is satisfied only and only at $\omega = \omega_r$.

$$\omega_r L = \frac{1}{\omega_R C}$$

$$\omega_r^2 LC = 1$$

$$\omega_r^2 = \frac{1}{LC}$$

$$\boxed{f_r = \frac{1}{2\pi\sqrt{LC}}} \quad \ldots (2.1)$$

where, f_r is the resonating frequency of the series RLC circuit.

2.4.2 Quality Factor

- Quality factor depends on the energy stored by the elements.
- In series RLC circuit, inductor and capacitor are connected in series, so the same current will flow through them and the same energy will be stored by both the elements.
- Value of Q depends on frequency when Q of a resonant circuit is stated or specified value is by default the value of Q at the resonant frequency f_r.
- So the Q factor of a series resonant circuit is nothing but the Q factor of the used inductor or of capacitor at the resonant frequency.

$$\boxed{Q = \frac{\omega_r L}{R} = \omega_r RC} \quad \ldots(2.2)$$

where, Q = Quality factor of the series RLC circuit at the resonant frequency
ω_0 = Resonant frequency
L = Inductor
C = Capacitor

Q in terms of circuit elements.
We have,

$$Q = \frac{\omega_r L}{R} = \frac{1}{\omega_r RC}$$

Substituting $\omega_0 = \frac{1}{\sqrt{LC}}$ in this equation

$$Q = \frac{L}{\sqrt{LC}\, R}$$

$$= \frac{\sqrt{LC}}{RC}$$

$$\boxed{Q = \frac{1}{R}\sqrt{\frac{L}{C}}} \quad \ldots(2.3)$$

where, R, L and C are the components of the series resonant circuit
Q is Quality factor of resonant circuit

2.4.3 Reactance Curves

- The graph of reactance of a reactive components versus the frequency is called as the reactance curve.
- Inductor and the capacitor are the reactive elements in series RLC circuit.

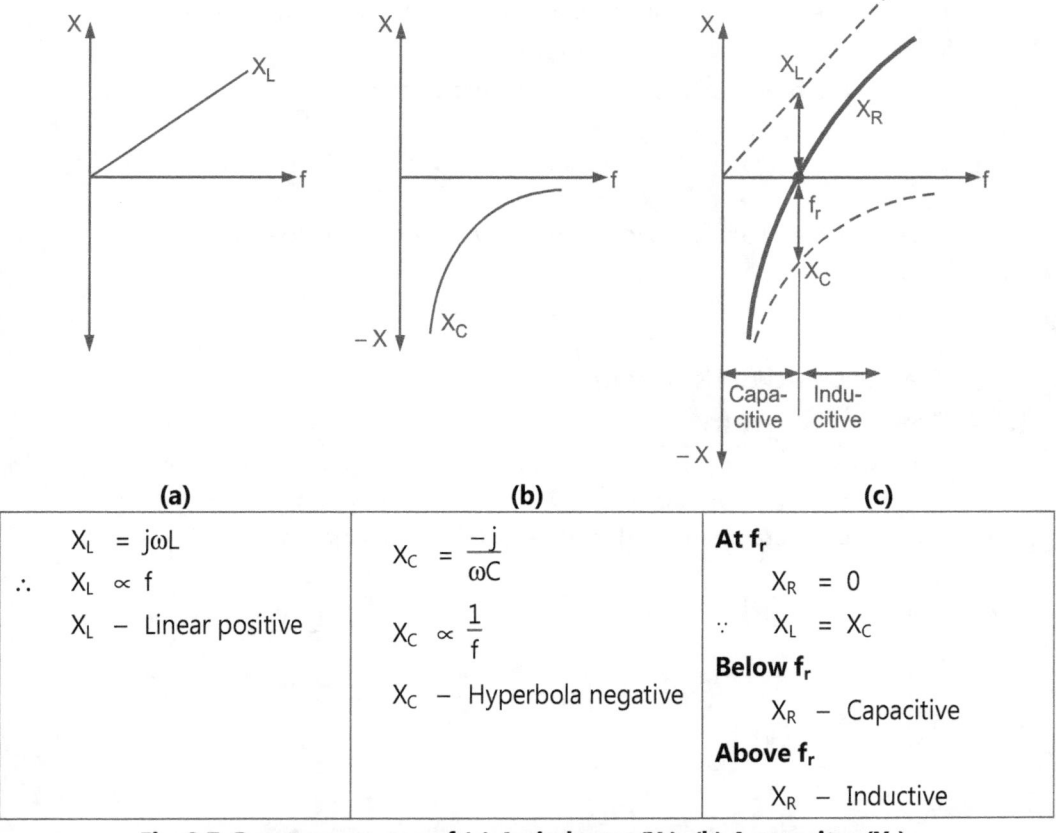

Fig. 2.7: Reactance curves of (a) An inductor (X_L), (b) A capacitor (X_C), (c) Total reactance plot of series RLC circuit indicating f_r

- It can be seen from definition
$$jX_L = j\,2\pi f_L$$
that inductive reactance X_L is a linear positive function of frequency which plots as a straight line through the origin.
- Similarly from the definition,
$$jX_C = \frac{-j}{2\pi f_C}$$
that the capacitive reactance, X_C appears as a negative hyperbola, asymptotic to the reactance and the frequency axes.
- Curves X_L and X_C are added algebrically, as would be the case in a series resonant circuit, to give the resultant curve X_R which indicates the resonating frequency f_r.
- As seen in Fig. 2.7 (c) at f_r, $X_L = X_C$ and thus canceling each other to give zero reactance or a purely resistive circuit.

- The series resonating circuit is capacitive below the resonating frequency f_r and it is inductive above the resonating frequency.
- This can also be logically justified. At low frequencies,

$$\omega L < \frac{1}{\omega C}$$

i.e. $\quad X_L < X_C$

Therefore, the circuit is capacitive. Similarly at high frequencies,

$$\omega L > \frac{1}{\omega C}$$

$\therefore \quad X_L > X_C$

Therefore, the circuit is inductive.

2.4.4 Phasor Diagrams

- A sinusoidal current and a given frequency is characterized by two parameters, an amplitude and a phase angle.
- The phasor diagrams are used to represent these parameters.

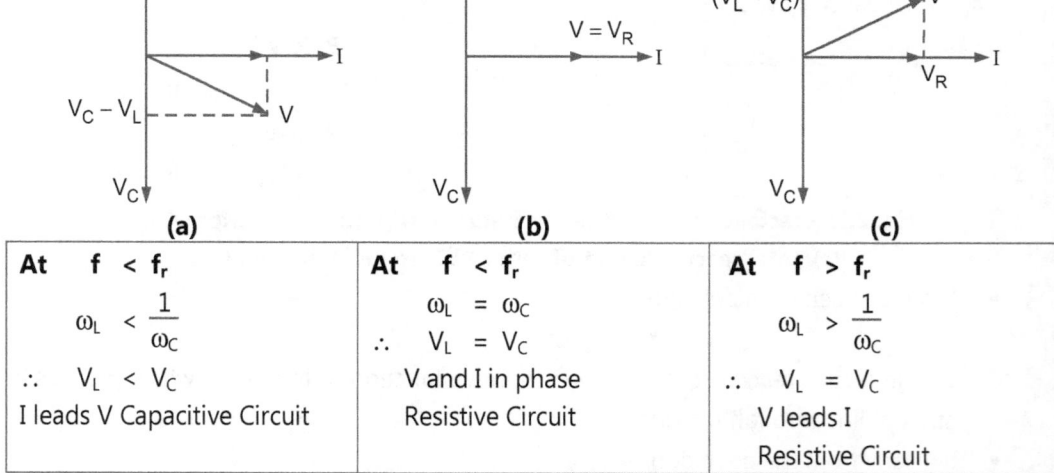

At $\quad f < f_r$	At $\quad f < f_r$	At $\quad f > f_r$
$\omega L < \dfrac{1}{\omega C}$	$\omega L = \omega C$	$\omega L > \dfrac{1}{\omega C}$
$\therefore \quad V_L < V_C$	$\therefore \quad V_L = V_C$	$\therefore \quad V_L = V_C$
I leads V Capacitive Circuit	V and I in phase Resistive Circuit	V leads I Resistive Circuit

**Fig. 2.8: Phasor diagrams of a series RLC circuit at frequency
(a) Below resonating frequency, (b) At resonating frequency, (c) Above resonating frequency**

- For any frequency f, lower than resonant frequency f_r as already explained in reactance curves, the circuit is capacitive having X_C as the dominating reactance. The current leads the resultant supply voltage V.
- Similarly at f_r, X_L is equal to X_C and therefore when connected in series V_L is also equal to V_C. Thus, canceling each other. Current and the supply voltage are in phase and circuit behaves as a resistive circuit.

- For any frequency f, higher than the resonant frequency f_r, the inductive reactance is dominating with X_L greater than X_C and thus V_L greater than V_C. The current leads the supply voltage and circuit behaves as inductive.

2.4.5 Impedance of Series RLC Circuit

The impedance of series RLC circuit is given by

$$Z = R + j\left(\omega L - \frac{1}{\omega C}\right)$$

Hence, the magnitude of impedance is given by

$$|Z| = \frac{\sqrt{Z^2 + X^2}}{\sqrt{R^2 + \left(\omega L - \frac{1}{\omega C}\right)^2}} \quad \ldots X = X_L - X_C$$

Thus, total impedance it any frequency

$$\boxed{|Z| = \sqrt{R^2 + \left(\omega L - \frac{1}{\omega C}\right)^2}} \quad \ldots(2.4)$$

(a) Impedance of series RLC circuit at resonance:

At resonance $\omega L = \frac{1}{\omega C}$.

∴ Impedance at frequency f_r is

$$\boxed{Z = R} \quad \ldots(2.5)$$

$$\ldots \text{At resonating frequency } f_r$$

(b) Impedance of series RLC circuit in the terms of Quality factor Q_0.

$$Z = R + j\left(\omega L - \frac{1}{\omega C}\right)$$

$$Z = R\left[1 + j\left(\frac{\omega L}{R} - \frac{1}{\omega CR}\right)\right]$$

$$Z = R\left[1 + j\left(\frac{\omega_r L}{R} \cdot \frac{\omega}{\omega_r} - \frac{1}{\omega_r CR} \cdot \frac{\omega_r}{\omega}\right)\right]$$

$$Z = R\left[1 + j\left(Q \cdot \frac{\omega}{\omega_r} - Q \frac{\omega_r}{\omega}\right)\right]$$

$$Z = R\left[1 + jQ\left(\frac{\omega}{\omega_r} - \frac{\omega_r}{\omega}\right)\right]$$

Thus, impedance at any frequency f in terms of quality factor Q is

$$\boxed{Z = R\left[1 + jQ\left(\frac{\omega}{\omega_r} - \frac{\omega_r}{\omega}\right)\right]} \quad \ldots(2.6)$$

(c) Impedance of series RLC circuit just near resonance: Let δ be the fractional deviation of the actual frequency from the resonant frequency, such that this new variable δ may be defined as

$$\delta = \frac{f - f_r}{f_r}$$

$$= \frac{\omega - \omega_r}{\omega_r} = \frac{\omega}{\omega_r} - 1$$

Thus giving, $\quad \dfrac{\omega}{\omega_r} = 1 + \delta$

Substituting in equation 2.6,

$$Z = R\left[1 + jQ\left(1 + \delta - \frac{1}{1 + \delta}\right)\right]$$

$$Z = R\left[1 + jQ\left(1 + \delta - (1 + \delta)^{-1}\right)\right]$$

Using binomial theorem

$$(1 + \delta)^{-1} \tilde{=} 1 - \delta + \delta^2$$

Thus, finally impedance of a series resonant circuit for small deviations from the resonant frequency, is given as

$$\boxed{Z = R\,[1 + jQ\,\delta\,(2 - \delta)]} \qquad \ldots(2.7)$$

To summarise,

$$|Z| = \sqrt{R^2 + \left(\omega L - \frac{1}{\omega C}\right)^2}$$

$$Z = R \qquad \ldots \text{at resonance}$$

$$Z = R\left[1 + jQ\left(\frac{\omega}{\omega_r} - \frac{\omega_r}{\omega}\right)\right] \qquad \ldots \text{in terms of Q}$$

$$Z = R\,[1 + jQ\,\delta\,(2 - \delta)] \qquad \ldots \text{just near } F_r$$

2.4.6 Current at Resonance

At resonant frequency, f_r

$$Z = R$$

$\therefore \qquad \boxed{I_r = \dfrac{V}{R}} \qquad \ldots(2.8)$

where,
$\quad I_r$ = Current at the resonating frequency f_r
$\quad V$ = Supply voltage
$\quad R$ = Resistance in the series RLC circuit

- This current I_r, at resonating frequency f_r will be the maximum current flowing through it.

- This is because the impedance of series RLC circuit is minimum at the resonance and it is equal to R.
- The value of the I_r and thus the nature of the frequency curve will be completely decided by R.
- Larger the value of R, small will be the current and so, steep slope with narrow and a sharp peak in the curve will not be achieved. Instead if the resistance is small, then the current at resonance rises sharply to a very high value. This is indicated in Fig. 2.9.

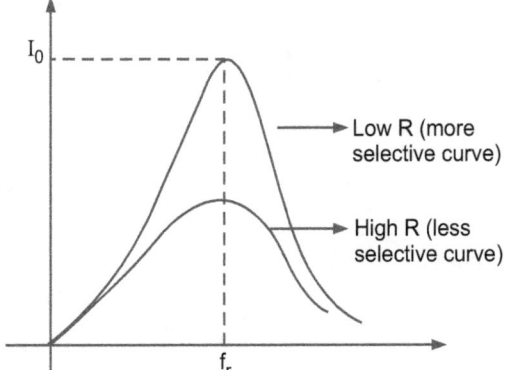

Fig. 2.9: Variation of current with frequency

- In earlier section when discussing about the quality factor Q, a statement was mentioned saying.

  "Height of the frequency curve depends only upon the value of R for constant amplitude excitation".
- This statement must now be clear. The steepness of the curve can be varied by varying the resistance R.
- When value of R is low, I_0 is high thus increasing the height of the frequency curve and making it more selective and vice versa.
- So, when the input is of a constant amplitude, R in the series RLC circuit decides the height of the curve.
- It must be noted that current in RLC circuit at $\omega = 0$ is always zero, as the capacitor reactance is ∞. Therefore, the graph starts from origin and has some finite value at $f = \infty$.

2.4.7 Voltage Across R, L and C at Resonance

At resonance, current $I_r = \dfrac{V}{R}$.

Inductor, resistor and capacitor are all connected in series so the same current will be flowing through them.

∴ Voltage across inductor $V_L = I_r \cdot X_L$

$$= I_r (\omega_r L)$$
$$= I_r \cdot \omega_r L$$
$$= \frac{V}{R} \cdot \omega_r L$$

$$\boxed{V_L = Q \cdot V} \qquad \ldots(2.9)$$

Similarly, voltage cross capacitor

$$V_C = I_r \cdot X_C$$
$$= \frac{V}{R} \left(\frac{1}{\omega_r C}\right)$$

$$\boxed{V_C = Q \cdot V} \qquad \ldots(2.10)$$

Recollect equation (2.2) as per which

$$Q = \frac{\omega_r L}{R} = \frac{1}{\omega_r C R_P}$$

- Thus, V_L and V_C i.e. voltage across inductor and a capacitor is Q times the input voltage V.
- Q is always greater than one so the voltages developed across L and C are more than the applied voltage and are thus said to be amplified or magnified by a factor of Q.
- At resonance, series RLC circuit acts as a voltage amplifier and hence Q_0 is also referred as the magnification factor of the circuit.
- Through at resonance the voltages developed V_L and V_C are more than the applied voltage they actually cancel each other because they are equal in magnitude and opposite in phase.

2.4.8 Variation of Impedance, Admittance and Phase with Frequency

- At resonance, impedance is minimum and is equal to R. For Z at any other frequency will always be greater than R. This is indicated in Fig. 2.10 (a).
- Admittance is reciprocal of impedance so obviously if Z is minimum at f_r then at f_r Y will be maximum. So Fig. 2.10 (b) shows exact opposite nature of Y with respect to frequency.
- We have already seen, that below resonating frequency, the circuit is capacitive in nature (I leads V). Therefore, phase angle is negative. Above the resonant frequency circuit imparts inductive characteristics. Therefore, the phase angle tends to be positive (I lags V).

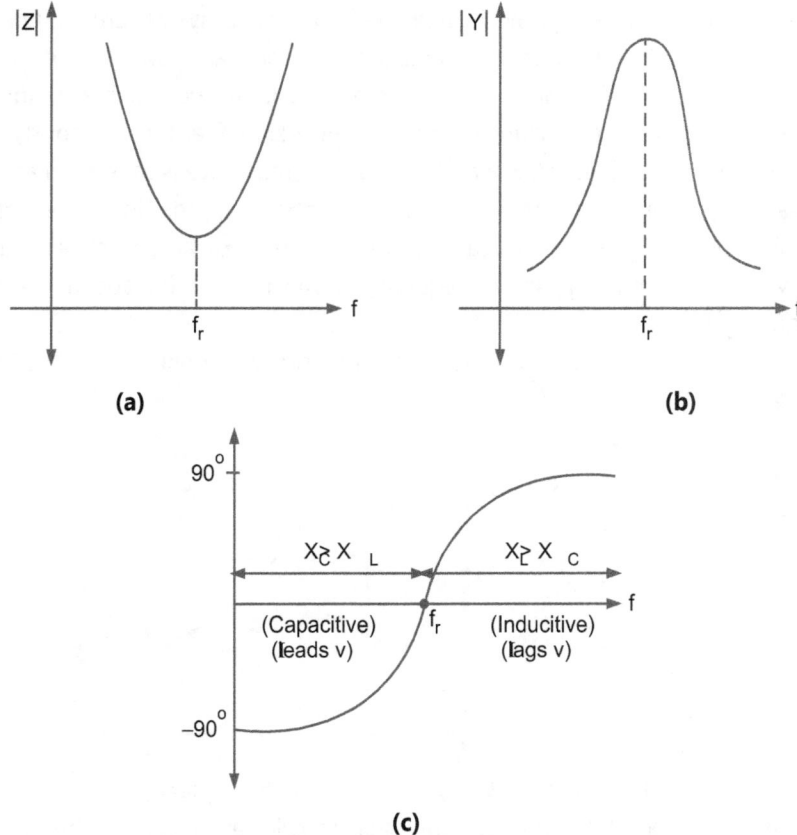

Fig. 2.10: Variation of (a) Z impedance, (b) Y admittance, (c) ϕ phase angle with frequency in a series resonating

- At the resonant frequency f_r, the circuit is purely resistive. So the phase angle ϕ is zero at resonance ($\cos \phi = 1$).
- This is indicated in Fig. 2.10 (c). However, it must be noted that the phase relations between the voltage and current in the individual elements R, L and C are not same. The current is inductor lags voltage by 90° and in the capacitor it leads the voltage by 90°.

2.4.9 Variation of V_L and V_C with Frequency

- We have seen that at resonance frequency ω_r, voltages across inductor and capacitor are equal but are of opposite signs and thus cancel each other. But these voltages are not the maximum voltages that can be appeared across them.
- Thus, the maximum voltage across inductor and capacitor appear the some other frequency and not the resonant frequency so the maximum values of V_L and V_C appear at some other frequency say f_L and f_C and not at f_r.

- This point can also be logically justified. Voltage will always depend on impedance. In this case, V_L and V_C will depend on reactance, X_L and X_C. Now at resonance, $X_L = X_C$. But this reactance of capacitor and inductor is definitely not the maximum reactance. In fact, the capacitive reactance is dominating below f_r and so obviously it must be some frequency f_C, below f_r where the capacitive reactance is maximum and therefore voltage V_C should be maximum. Similarly above f_r, the inductive reactance is dominating and circuit is inductive with higher value of X_L. So naturally, the voltage V_L will be maximum at some frequency f_L which must be above the resonating frequency f_r.
- This variation of V_L and V_C with frequency in a series resonating circuit is indicated in Fig. 2.11.

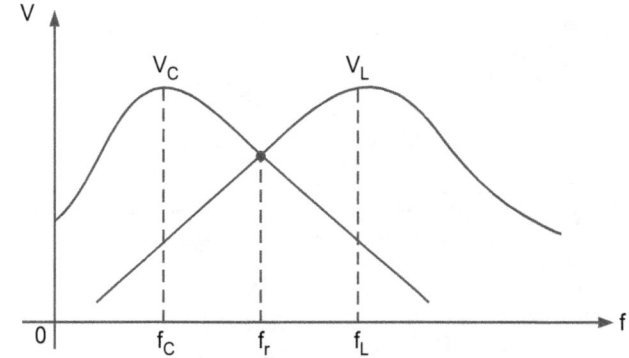

Fig. 2.11: Variation of V_C and V_L with frequency

- Let us now attempt to find the expression to calculate f_C and f_L, the frequencies at which maximum voltage appears across a capacitor and an inductor.

(a) To calculate f_C: Voltage across capacitor

$$V_C = I \cdot X_C$$

$$V_C = I \cdot \left(\frac{1}{\omega C}\right)$$

$$V_C = \left(\frac{V}{Z}\right)\left(\frac{1}{\omega C}\right)$$

$$V_C = \frac{V}{\sqrt{R^2 + \left(\omega L - \frac{1}{\omega C}\right)^2}} \times \frac{1}{\omega C}$$

$$V_C = \frac{V}{\omega C \sqrt{R^2 + \left(\omega L - \frac{1}{\omega C}\right)^2}}$$

To find the frequency f_C, at which V_C is maximum, differentiate V_C with respect to ω, and equate it to zero.

We have,

$$V_C^2 = \frac{V^2}{\omega^2 C^2 \left[R^2 + \left(\omega L - \frac{1}{\omega C}\right)^2\right]}$$

$$\frac{d}{d\omega}[V_C^2] = \frac{d}{d\omega}\left[\frac{V^2}{\omega^2 C^2 \left(R^2 + \left(\frac{\omega^2 LC - 1}{\omega C}\right)^2\right)}\right]$$

$$= \frac{d}{d\omega}\left[\frac{V^2}{R^2\omega^2 C^2 + (\omega^2 LC - 1)^2}\right]$$

$$\frac{d}{d\omega}[V_C^2] = \frac{-V^2[2\omega R^2 C^2 + 2(\omega^2 LC - 1)\cdot 2\omega LC]}{[R^2\omega^2 C^2 + (\omega^2 LC - 1)^2]^2}$$

Since $V \neq 0$

$$2\omega C^2 R^2 + 2(\omega^2 LC - 1)\cdot 2\omega LC = 0$$
$$2\omega C^2 R^2 + (2\omega^2 LC - 2)\, 2\omega LC = 0$$
$$CR^2 + 2\omega^2 L^2 C\, 2L = 0$$
$$2\omega^2 L^2 C = 2L - CR^2$$
$$\omega^2 = \frac{1}{LC} - \frac{R^2}{2L^2}$$

Thus, frequency f_C at which V_C is maximum is given by,

$$\boxed{f_C = \frac{1}{2\pi}\sqrt{\frac{1}{LC} - \frac{R^2}{2L^2}}} = \boxed{f_r\sqrt{1 - \frac{R^2 C}{2L}}} \quad \ldots (2.11)$$

$\therefore \quad f_r = \frac{1}{2\pi}\sqrt{\frac{1}{LC}}$, f_C is always less than [lower] f_r

(b) To calculate f_L: Voltage across inductor

$$V_L = I \cdot X_L$$
$$V_L = \frac{V}{Z} \cdot \omega L$$
$$V_L = \frac{V}{\sqrt{R^2 \rightarrow \left(\omega L - \frac{1}{\omega C}\right)^2}} \cdot \omega L$$
$$V_L = \frac{V \cdot \omega L}{\sqrt{R^2 + \left(\omega L - \frac{1}{\omega C}\right)^2}}$$

To find the frequency f_L at which V_L is maximum, differentiate V_L with respect to ω and equate it to zero.

We have,

$$V_L^2 = \frac{\omega^2 L^2 V^2}{R^2 + \frac{(\omega^2 LC - 1)^2}{\omega^2 C^2}}$$

$$V_L^2 = \frac{\omega^4 L^2 V^2 C^2}{R^2 \omega^2 C^2 + (\omega^2 LC - 1)^2}$$

$\frac{d}{d\omega}(V_L^2)$ and equating it to zero gives,

$$2\omega^2 LC - \omega^2 R^2 C^2 - 2 = 0$$
$$\omega^2 (2LC - R^2 C^2) = 2$$
$$\omega^2 = \frac{2}{2LC - R^2 C^2}$$
$$\omega^2 = \frac{1}{LC - \frac{R^2 C^2}{2}}$$
$$f_L = \frac{1}{2\pi \sqrt{LC - \frac{R^2 C^2}{2}}}$$
$$f_L = \frac{1}{2\pi\sqrt{LC} \times \sqrt{1 - \frac{R^2 C^2}{2L}}}$$

$$\boxed{f_L = \frac{f_r}{\sqrt{1 - \frac{R^2 C}{2L}}}} \qquad \ldots(2.12)$$

Thus, frequency f_L at which V_L is maximum is always higher than resonating frequency f_r. To summarise maximum V_C at

$$f_C = f_r \sqrt{1 - \frac{R^2 C}{2L}} \qquad f_C < f_r$$

Maximum V_L at

$$f_L = \frac{f_r}{\sqrt{1 - \frac{R^2 C}{2L}}} \qquad f_L > f_r$$

2.4.10 Bandwidth of a Series Resonant Circuit

- Bandwidth is the measure of effectiveness with which a series resonant circuit selects given frequency and rejects all other frequencies.
- Bandwidth or frequency discrimination of a resonant circuit is defined as the width of a resonant wave in cycles at the frequency at which the power in the circuit is the half of the maximum power.

- Bandwidth requirement will depend upon the type of applications. It is about 400 Hz for telephone signals and about 6 MHz for the video (or television) signal. Example, in case of an op-amp, bandwidth should ideally be infinite and practically as large as possible where as contradictory to this in resonant circuit, this bandwidth must be as small as possible, which will make the circuit more and more selective. [Recall the example in Section 2.2].
- The bandwidth of series RLC circuit is defined as the band of frequencies over which the power in the circuit is half of its maximum value.

$$\text{Maximum power} = I_r^2 R \qquad \because I_r \text{ is maximum current}$$

At f_1,
$$\text{Half power} = \frac{1}{2} I_r^2 R = \left(\frac{I_r}{\sqrt{2}}\right)^2 R$$
$$= 0.707\, I_r^2 R$$

- Thus, at half power frequencies current becomes 0.707 times the maximum value as seen in Fig. 2.12.

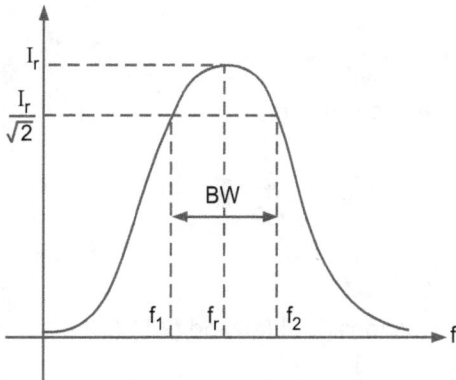

Fig. 2.12: Frequency response of series RLC Circuit

- These half power frequencies are also referred are also referred as 3 dB frequencies. Let us determine these frequencies.

Thus, we have,

Current in series RLC Circuit at f_1 and f_2 = 0.707 or $= \frac{1}{\sqrt{2}} I_r$

(half power frequencies)

$$\frac{V}{\sqrt{R^2 + \left(\omega L - \frac{1}{\omega C}\right)^2}} = \frac{1}{\sqrt{2}} \frac{V}{R}$$

$$\therefore \sqrt{R^2 + \left(\omega L - \frac{1}{\omega C}\right)^2} = \sqrt{2}\, R$$

Squaring both the sides.

$$R^2 + \left(\omega L - \frac{1}{\omega C}\right)^2 = 2R^2$$

$$\left(\omega L - \frac{1}{\omega C}\right)^2 = R^2$$

Taking square roots

$$\boxed{\left(\omega L - \frac{1}{\omega C}\right) = \pm R} \quad \ldots(2.13)$$

Thus, at half power frequencies f_1 and f_2 in series RLC circuit,

$$\boxed{\text{Reactive part of impedance} = \text{Resistive part of impedance}}$$

At f_1 and ω_1 (Below resonance)

$$X_C > X_L$$

i.e.

$$\frac{1}{\omega C} > \omega L$$

∴

$$\omega_1 L - \frac{1}{\omega_1 C} = -R \quad \ldots(2.14\,(a))$$

Similarly at f_2 or ω_2 (Above resonance)

$$X_L > X_C$$

i.e.

$$\omega L > \frac{1}{\omega C}$$

∵

$$\omega_2 L - \frac{1}{\omega_2 C} = +R \quad \ldots(2.14\,(b))$$

Adding the above two equations (2.14 (a)) and (2.14 (b)).

$$\omega_1 L - \frac{1}{\omega_1 C} + \omega_2 L - \frac{1}{\omega_2 C} = 0$$

$$(\omega_1 + \omega_2) L - \left(\frac{1}{\omega_2} + \frac{1}{\omega_1}\right)\frac{1}{C} = 0$$

$$(\omega_1 + \omega_2) L - \left(\frac{\omega_1 + \omega_2}{\omega_1 \omega_2}\right)\frac{1}{C} = 0$$

$$(\omega_1 + \omega_2) L = \left(\frac{\omega_1 + \omega_2}{\omega_1 \omega_2}\right)\frac{1}{C}$$

$$\omega_1 + \omega_2 = \frac{1}{LC} \quad \ldots(2.14\,(c))$$

$$\omega_1 + \omega_2 = \omega_r^2$$

$$\omega_r = \frac{1}{\sqrt{LC}}$$

$$\therefore \boxed{\omega_r = \sqrt{\omega_1 \omega_2}} \qquad \ldots (2.14\,(d))$$

or

$$\boxed{f_r = \sqrt{f_1 f_2}}$$

Thus, resonating frequency f_r is geometric means of two half power frequencies f_1 and f_2. Subtracting 2.14 (a) from 2.14 (b).

$$(\omega_2 + \omega_1) L - \left(\frac{1}{\omega_1} - \frac{1}{\omega_2}\right)\frac{1}{C} = 2R$$

$$(\omega_2 + \omega_1) L + \left(\frac{\omega_2 - \omega_1}{\omega_1 \omega_2}\right)\frac{1}{C} = 2R$$

From C we have $\omega_1 \omega_2 = \dfrac{1}{LC}$

$$\therefore \quad (\omega_2 + \omega_1) L + (\omega_2 - \omega_1) L = 2R$$

$$\omega_2 - \omega_1 = \frac{R}{L}$$

$$\boxed{BW = f_2 - f_1 = \frac{R}{2\pi L}} \qquad \ldots (2.15)$$

$$\boxed{\text{Bandwidth} = (f_2 - f_1) = \frac{R}{2\pi L}}$$

$$BW = \frac{R \cdot f_r}{2\pi L \; f_r}$$

$$BW = \frac{f_r}{\dfrac{\omega_r L}{R}}$$

$$\boxed{BW = \frac{f_r}{Q}} \qquad \ldots (2.16)$$

where, $Q = \dfrac{\omega_r L}{R}$ i.e. the quality factor at the resonance of the circuit including generator, inductor, capacitor resistances and any load connected.

- Observe the BW is inversely proportional to the quality factor 'Q'. Q must be of a large value for the circuit to be very frequency selective. So if the circuit is frequency selective it will naturally have less bandwidth and vice versa.
- So, bandwidth is sometimes so also defined as means of comparing the selectivity of various designs.

2.4.11 Selectivity

- Frequency selective networks are designed to distinguish or select one particular frequency from the other frequencies in the given band.

- So 'selectivity' is one of the most important properties of any frequency selective network.
- Selectivity of any frequency selective network is defined as the ability of the circuit to discriminate or distinguish between the desired and the undesired frequencies.
- Selectivity is also, very often defined as the ratio of resonant frequency to the bandwidth of the resonant circuit.

$$\text{Selectivity} = \frac{\text{Resonant frequency}}{\text{Bandwidth}}$$

$$= \frac{f_r}{BW} = \frac{f_r}{(f_2 - f_1)}$$

$$\text{Selectivity} = \frac{f_r}{\frac{f_r}{Q}}$$

$$= Q$$

$$\boxed{\text{Selectivity} = Q} \quad \ldots (2.17)$$

Thus, selectivity of a series resonant circuit is directly proportional to the quality factor of a circuit. [This quality factor is always defined at f_r]. If quality factor Q is very high, the selectivity is high and the response curve becomes sharper and the bandwidth decreases.

A smaller value of Q tends to make the curve flatter. This is indicated in Fig. 2.13.

Thus, to summarize in series RLC circuit.

$$\boxed{\text{Selectivity} \propto \frac{1}{\text{Bandwidth}} \propto Q}$$

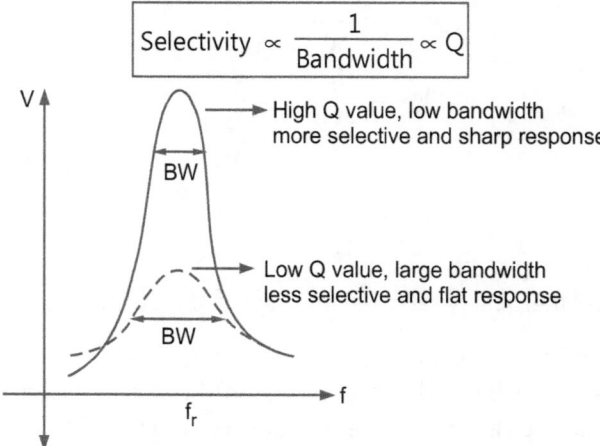

Fig. 2.13: Frequency response of a series RLC circuit for a high and low value of Q

2.4.12 Effect of R_g on Bandwidth and Selectivity

- An ideal current or a voltage source is non-existent in the real world. A practical current or a voltage source always has an internal resistance R_P or R_S in parallel or in series with the source, respectively. This resistance affects the behaviour of the circuit.

- This internal resistance is also referred to as generator resistance R_g'. Taking this into the series RLC circuit can be redrawn as:

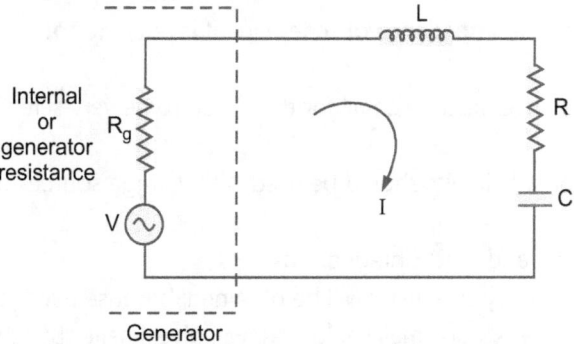

Fig. 2.14: Series RLC circuit with R_g

- We have earlier defined bandwidth as

$$BW = \frac{f_r}{Q} = \left(\frac{R}{\omega L}\right) f_r$$

where, Q is that of the complete circuit including:
- Generator resistance R_g
- Inductor and capacitor resistances
- Resistance of any connected load

So, in order to study the effect of the generator resistance R_g, let us separate this resistance from 'R'. Thus,

$$R = R_g + R'$$

where,
R = Total circuit resistance
R_g = Generator resistance
R' = Resistance of capacitor, inductor and any connected load

Thus, rewriting the equation of BW in terms of R_g and R', we have,

$$BW = f_r \left(\frac{R}{\omega L}\right)$$

$$BW = f_r \left(\frac{R_g + R'}{\omega L}\right)$$

$$BW = f_r \left(\frac{R_g}{\omega L} + \frac{R'}{\omega L}\right)$$

$$\boxed{BW = f_r \left(\frac{R_g}{\omega L} + \frac{1}{Q_{circuit}}\right)} \quad \ldots (2.18)$$

$$Q_{circuit} = \frac{\omega L}{R'}$$

We have already studied that, the

1. $\qquad Z = R \qquad$ ... at resonating frequency f_r

   i.e. At resonance impedance of series circuit is equal to total resistance of the circuit

2. And the resistance must be small for the circuit to be very selective and have less bandwidth.

- So series resonant circuits should be used with voltage sources of low internal resistance.
- This is desirable and is advantageous as:
    1. Good frequency selectivity will be obtained, because BW is directly proportional to R i.e. (R_g + R'). So small value of R_g will give smaller Bandwidth and thus higher selectivity.
    2. The impedances can be matched to obtain maximum power transfer. This can be obtained by making

$$R_g = R'$$

i.e. Generator resistance = Circuit resistance

Thus, in matched condition

$$BW = \left(\frac{R_g}{\omega L} + \frac{R'}{\omega L}\right) f_r$$

$$\boxed{BW = \frac{2}{Q} f_r} \qquad \ldots (2.19)$$

$$Q = \frac{\omega L}{R}$$

$$\boxed{\text{Selectivity} = \frac{Q}{2}} \qquad \ldots (2.20)$$

- Thus, to summarise the effect of generator resistance on the bandwidth and selectivity it is clear that the generator resistance must be very low when a selective circuit is desired. A voltage source with higher value of R_g will increase the bandwidth making the frequency response curve flat and comparatively less selective.

2.4.13 Applications of Series RLC Circuit

- Series resonating circuit is used as an voltage amplifier.
- Series resonating circuits are used in m derived filters (to be discussed in next unit) because of their property of very low impedance at resonance. They are used to instantly increase the attenuation in filters to infinity.
- Series resonating circuits are also used in resonant converters.
- They are used to obtain high power output at specific frequency.

2.4.14 Summary of Series Resonating Circuit

The characteristics of series resonance circuit are:
1. At series resonating circuit, the input impedance is minimum or the admittance is maximum at resonating frequency f_r.
2. At resonance, circuit is purely resistive and hence the power factor is unity.
3. At f_{ar}, current in the circuit is maximum.
4. The circuit is capacitive for the frequencies below f_{ar} and it is inductive for the frequency below f_{ar}.
5. At reasonable, series RLC circuit acts as a voltage amplifier.
$$V_C = V \cdot Q$$
and
$$V_L = Q \cdot V$$
They are equal in magnitude and opposite to each other.
6. Quality factor is given as,
$$Q = \frac{R}{\omega_r L} = \frac{1}{\omega_r CR}$$
7. The resonant frequency f_r is given as,
$$f_r = \frac{1}{2\pi\sqrt{LC}}$$
9. R_g, generator resistance must be as small as possible for achieving high selectivity in series RLC circuit,
$$\text{Bandwidth} = \frac{f_r}{Q}$$
10. $f_r = \sqrt{f_1 f_2}$, where f_1 and f_2 are half power frequencies, f_r is geometric mean of f_1 and f_2.
11. At half power frequencies the resistive and reactive impedance are equal.

2.4.15 Important Formulae

Important Formulae of series resonating circuit

	Series RLC Circuit
1. Diagram	(circuit diagram showing V source with R, L, C in series)
2. Resonating frequency	$f_r = \dfrac{1}{2\pi\sqrt{LC}}$

3.	Quality factor	$Q = \dfrac{\omega_r L}{R}$ $= \dfrac{1}{\omega_r RC}$ $Q = \dfrac{1}{R}\sqrt{\dfrac{L}{C}}$
4.	Reactancy type	Above f_r : Inductive At f_r : Resistive Below f_r : Capacitive
5.	Impedance	$Z_r = R$ at resonance $Z = R[1 + jQ\delta(2-\delta)]$ ... Near f_r $\delta = \dfrac{f - f_r}{f_r}$
6.	Voltage or current at resonance	$V_L = Q \cdot V$ $V_L = Q \cdot V$
7.	Frequencies of maximum voltage (V_L and V_C)	$f_L = \dfrac{f_r}{\sqrt{1 - \dfrac{R^2 C}{2L}}}$ $f_L > f_r$ $f_C = f_r \sqrt{1 - \dfrac{R^2 C}{2L}}$ $f_C < f_r$
8.	Bandwidth	$BW = \dfrac{R}{2\pi L} = \dfrac{f_r}{Q}$ BW match $= \dfrac{2 f_r}{Q}$

2.5 NUMERICALS ON SERIES RLC CIRCUIT

Ex. 2.1: A series R-L-C circuit consist of R = 10 Ω, L = 10 mH and C = 10 nF. Find:
(i) Resonant frequency
(ii) Quality factor at resonance
(iii) Bandwidth

Sol.: Given: R = 10 Ω, L = 10 mH and C = 10 nF.
To find: f_r, Q, BW.

(i) Resonating frequency:

$$f_r = \frac{1}{2\pi \sqrt{LC}}$$

$$= \frac{1}{2\pi \sqrt{10 \times 10^{-3} \times 10 \times 10^{-9}}}$$

$$\boxed{f_r = 15.915 \text{ kHz}}$$

(ii) Quality factor:

$$Q = \frac{\omega L}{R}$$

$$= \frac{2 \times \pi \times 15.915 \times 10^3 \times 10 \times 10^{-3}}{10}$$

$$\boxed{Q = 100}$$

(iii) Bandwidth Δf:

$$\Delta f = \frac{R}{2\pi L}$$

$$= \frac{10}{2 \times \pi \times 10 \times 10^{-3}}$$

$$\boxed{\Delta f = 159.154 \text{ Hz}}$$

Ans.:
$$\boxed{\begin{array}{l} f_r = 15.915 \text{ kHz} \\ Q = 100 \\ \Delta f = 159.154 \text{ Hz} \end{array}}$$

In the above numerical, Q can alternatively be calculated using

$$Q = \frac{1}{R}\sqrt{\frac{L}{C}}$$

$$= \frac{1}{10}\sqrt{\frac{10 \times 10^{-3}}{10 \times 10^{-9}}}$$

$$= 100$$

$$Q = \frac{1}{\omega_r RC}$$

$$= \frac{1}{2 \times \pi \times 15.915 \times 10^3 \times 10 \times 10 \times 10^{-9}}$$

$$Q = 100$$

Thus, Q can be calculated using any of the above used methods.

Ex. 2.2: A circuit contains resistance of 200 Ω, a capacitance of 100 pF and inductance of 100 μH in series. Find fall in the current if the generator frequency is increased by 20 kHz above resonance of the circuit. (Generator has 50 Ω internal resistance with 10 V open circuit voltage). Also calculate the voltage across L and C at frequency of resonance. Find the maximum current in the circuit.

Sol.: Given: $R = 200\ \Omega$, $C = 100$ pF, $L = 100$ μH, $R_g = 50\ \Omega$, $V_{OC} = 10$ V.

To find: I at f_r
I at $(f_r + 20\ \text{kH})$
V_L, V_C

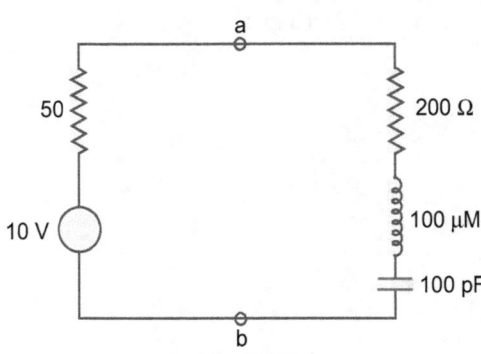

Fig. 2.15

$V_{OC} = 10$ V i.e. supply voltage = 10 V

(i) Resonating frequency:

$$f_r = \frac{1}{2\pi\sqrt{LC}}$$

$$= \frac{1}{2\pi\sqrt{100 \times 10^{-12} \times 100 \times 10^{-6}}}$$

$\boxed{f_r = 1.591\ \text{MHz}}$

(ii) Current at resonating frequency:

$$I_r = \frac{V}{R} \quad (R = 200 + 50 = 250\ \Omega)$$

$$I_r = \frac{10}{250} = 0.04\ \text{A}$$

$\boxed{I_r = 0.04\ \text{A}}$

(iii) Figure of merit i.e. Quality factor Q:

$$Q = \frac{\omega_r L}{R}$$

$$= \frac{2\pi \times 1.59 \times 10^6 \times 100 \times 10^{-6}}{250}$$

$\boxed{Q = 4}$

(iv) Voltage across L and C at resonance:

$$V_L = jQV$$
$$= j \times 4 \times 10$$
$$= j\,40\ V$$
$$= \boxed{40 \angle 90°\ V}$$

$$V_C = -jQV$$
$$= -j \times 4 \times 10$$
$$= -j\,40\ V$$
$$= \boxed{40 \angle -90°\ V}$$

(Recollect that Q in case of series RLC is a magnificent factor and circuit is voltage amplifier with V_L and $V_C > V$).

(v) Impedance of circuit 20 kHz above resonant.

Let us find δ $f = 1.591 \times 10^6 + 20 \times 10^3$

$$\delta = \frac{f - f_r}{f_r}$$
$$= \frac{20\ K}{1591\ K}$$
$$= 0.01257$$

$$Z_1 = R[1 + jQ\,\delta\,(2-\delta)]$$
$$Z_1 = 250[1 + j4\,(0.01257)\,(2)]$$
$$\boxed{Z_1 = 251.25\ \angle 57°\ \Omega}$$

I at 20 kHz above $f_r = \dfrac{V}{Z_1} = 0.0399 \angle -5.7°$.

$$\boxed{I = 0.0399 \angle -5.7°\ A}$$

i.e. voltage leads current. This is obvious as the impedance of the circuit is inductive above the resonant frequency.

Ans.:

$$\begin{aligned}
f_r &= 1.591\ \text{MHz} \\
I_r &= 0.04\ °A \\
V_L &= 40 \angle 90°\ V \\
V_C &= 40 \angle -90°\ V \\
I_{r+20K} &= 0.0399 \angle -5.7°A
\end{aligned}$$

Unit II | 2.31

Ex. 2.3: A series resonant circuit is in resonance at 8×10^6 Hz and it has coil of 35 µH and 10 Ω resistor.

(i) Find the current at resonance.
(ii) The value of the required capacitor.
(iii) Find the impedance at frequency of 8.1 MHz.
(iv) Find current at this frequency, applied voltage is sinusoidal 100 V_{rms}.

Sol.: Given: V = 100 V_{rms}, f_r = 8×10^6 Hz, L = 35 µH, R = 10 Ω.
To find: I_r, C, Z at 8.1 MHz, I at 8.1 MHz.

(i) Current at resonance:

$$I_r = \frac{V}{R}$$

$$= \frac{100}{10} = 10 \text{ A}$$

$$\boxed{I_r = 10 \text{ A}}$$

(ii) Value of required capacitor:

$$f_r = \frac{1}{2\pi}\sqrt{\frac{1}{LC}}$$

$$8 \times 10^6 = \frac{1}{2\pi}\sqrt{\frac{1}{35 \times 10^{-6} \times C}}$$

$$\boxed{C = 11.3 \text{ pF}}$$

(iii) Impedance at frequency 8.1 MHz.:

Let us find

$$\delta = \frac{f - f_r}{f_r} = 0.0125$$

$$Q = \frac{\omega L}{R}$$

$$= \frac{2\pi \times 8 \times 10^6 \times 35 \times 10^{-6}}{10} = 176$$

$$Z = R[1 + jQ\delta(2 - \delta)]$$

$$Z = 10[1 + j(176 \times 0.0125)(2 - 0.0125)]$$

$$\boxed{Z = 10 + j\,43.72 \text{ Ω at 8.1 MHz}}$$

(iv) Current at f = 8.1 MHz:

$$I = \frac{V}{Z} = \frac{100}{10 + j\,43.72}$$

$$\boxed{I = 2.23 \angle -77.11° \text{A at 8.1 MHz}}$$

The negative angle indicates current I is lagging voltage. Above f_r, the impedance is inductive as seen in (ii) and so voltage leads currents.

Ans.:

$$I_r = 10 \text{ A}$$
$$C = 11.3 \text{ pf}$$
$$\text{At } 8.1 \text{ MHz}, Z = 10 + j\, 43.72 \text{ }\Omega$$
$$\text{At } 8.1 \text{ MHz}, I = 2.23 \angle -77.11$$

Ex. 2.4: For a series RLC circuit
(i) Find the resonant frequency (ω_0)
(ii) Quality factor at resonance (Q_0)
(iii) Two half power frequencies (ω_1 and ω_2)
(iv) Bandwidth ($\Delta\omega$).

Assume circuit consists of R = 100 Ω, L = 100 mH and C = 10 nF. The applied voltage across the circuit is 100 V_{rms}.

Sol.: Given: R = 100 Ω, L = 100 mH, C = 10 nF, V = 100 V_{rms}.
To Find: ω_r, Q_r, ω_1 and ω_2

(i) Resonant frequency ω_r:

$$\omega_r = \frac{1}{\sqrt{LC}}$$

$$= \frac{1}{\sqrt{100 \times 10^{-3} \times 10 \times 10^{-9}}}$$

$$\omega_r = 31.6227 \text{ k rad/sec.}$$

(ii) Quality factor:

$$Q_r = \frac{\omega_r L}{R}$$

$$= \frac{31.6227 \times 100 \times 10^{-3}}{100}$$

$$Q_r = 31.6227$$

(iii) Bandwidth $\Delta\omega$:

$$\Delta\omega = \frac{R}{L} = \frac{100}{100 \times 10^{-3}}$$

$$\Delta\omega = 1000 \text{ rad/sec.}$$

(iv) Half power frequencies:
Upper half power frequency
∵ ω_2 is above ω_r

$$\omega_2 = \omega_0 + \frac{\Delta\omega}{2}$$

$$= 31.6227 \times 10^3 + \frac{1000}{2}$$

$$\omega_2 = 32.1227 \text{ k rad/sec.}$$

Lower half power frequency ω_1 is below ω_r

$$\therefore \quad \omega_1 = \omega_0 - \frac{\Delta\omega}{2}$$

$$= 31.6227 \times 10^3 - \frac{1000}{2}$$

$$\omega_1 = 31.1227 \text{ k rad/sec.}$$

Ans.:

ω_r :	31.6227 k rad/sec.
Q_r :	31.6227
$\Delta\omega$:	1000 rad/sec.
ω_1 :	31.1227 k rad/sec.
ω_2 :	32.1227 k rad/sec.

Ex. 2.5: A series circuit of negligible resistance and coil of 120 µH with 18 Ω resistance is resonated at 1 MHz. The circuit is driven by a generator of 1 V, 1 MHz frequency with $R_g = 0\Omega$.

(i) What will be the voltage across capacitor at resonance?

(ii) What current will flow at resonance and 10 kHz above resonance?

Sol.: Given: L = 120 µH, R = 18 Ω, f_r = 1 MHz, V = 1 V, f_r = 1 MHz.

To find: V_C, I_r, I at 10 kHz above f_r, BW = ?

(i) Quality factor:

$$Q = \frac{\omega_r L}{R}$$

$$= \frac{2 \times \pi \times 10^6 \times 120 \times 10^{-6}}{18}$$

$$\boxed{Q = 41.888}$$

(ii) Voltage across the capacitor:

$$V_C = -jQV$$
$$= -j(41.88)(1)$$
$$V_C = -j41.88$$
$$\boxed{V_C = 41.88 \angle -90° \text{ V}}$$

(iii) Current at resonance:

$$I_r = \frac{V}{R} = \frac{1}{18}$$
$$= 55.55 \text{ mA}$$
$$\boxed{I_r = 55.55 \text{ mA}}$$

(iv) Current at 10 kHz above f_r:

We will have to calculate impedance.
So let us find δ

$$\delta = \frac{f - f_r}{f_r}$$

$$= \frac{10 \times 10^3}{1 \times 10^6} = 0.01$$

$$Z = R\left[1 + jQ\delta(2 - \delta)\right]$$
$$Z = 18\left[1 + j\,41.888\,(0.01)(2 - 0.01)\right]$$
$$Z = 18\left[1 + j\,0.8335\right]$$
$$\boxed{Z = (18 + j\,15.003)\,\Omega}$$

$$\text{Current} = \frac{V}{Z}$$

$$= \frac{1}{18 + j\,15.003}$$

$$= \frac{1}{23.43\,\angle\,39.31°}$$

$$\boxed{I = 0.04267\,\angle -39.81°\,A}$$

(v) Bandwidth is given by

$$\Delta f = \frac{R}{2\pi L}$$

$$= \frac{18}{2\pi \times 120 \times 10^{-6}}$$

$$\boxed{\Delta f = 23.873\ \text{kHz}}$$

Ans.:

$$V_C = 41.888\,\angle -90°\,V$$
$$I_r = 55.55\ \text{mA}$$
$$\text{at 10 kHz above } f_r,\ I = 0.04267\,\angle -39.81$$
$$\Delta f = 23.873$$

Ex. 2.6: A 20 Ω resistor is connected in series with an inductor, a capacitor and an ammeter across 25 V variable frequency supply when frequency is 400 Hz the current in maximum of 0.5°A and the potential difference across capacitor is 150 V. Find:

(i) Capacitance of the capacitor
(ii) Resistance and inductance.

Sol.: Given: R = 20 Ω, V = 25 V, I_r = 0.5 A, f_r = 400 Hz, V_C = 150 V.
To find: C, R_L, L.

(i) Capacitance value:
- At 400 Hz, current is maximum, therefore the frequency f = 400 Hz is actually resonating f.
- At f = f_r, $V_C = X_C \cdot I_r$.
- At 400 Hz, $X_C = \dfrac{1}{\omega_r C}$

$$\dfrac{V_C}{I_r} = \dfrac{1}{\omega_r C}$$

$$\dfrac{150}{0.5} = \dfrac{1}{2\pi \times 400 \times C}$$

$$\boxed{C = 1.325 \ \mu f}$$

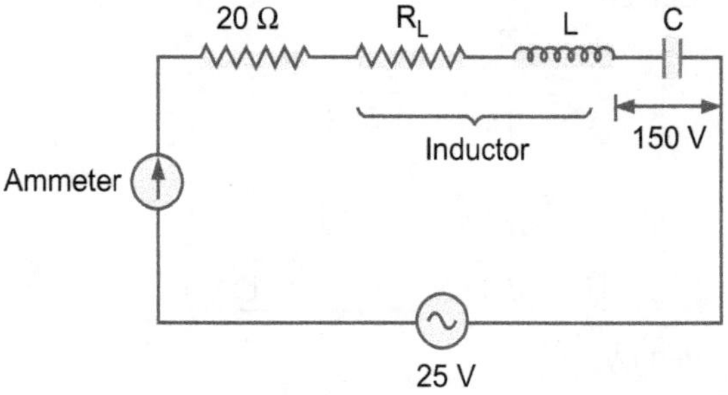

Fig. 2.16

(ii) Inductor value: At f = f_r,

$$X_L = X_C$$

$$\omega_r L = \dfrac{1}{\omega_r C}$$

$$2\pi \times 400 \times L = \dfrac{1}{2 \times \pi \times 400 \times 1.325 \times 10^{-6}}$$

$$\boxed{L = 0.119 \ H}$$

(iii) Resistance of inductor:

$$I_r = \dfrac{V}{R}$$

∴ $0.5 = \dfrac{25}{R}$

C = 20.2642 μF

$R = \dfrac{25}{0.5}$

R = 50 Ω

This R is actually 20 + R_L

∴ $\boxed{R_L = 30\ \Omega}$

Ans.:

$$\boxed{\begin{array}{l} C = 1.325\ \mu F \\ L = 0.119\ H \\ R_L = 30\ \Omega \end{array}}$$

Ex. 2.7: A resistor and a capacitor are in series with a variable inductor. When this circuit is connected to 200 V, 50 Hz supply, 0.314 A is the maximum current obtained. At the instant $V_C = 300$ V. Find the circuit components.

Sol.: Given: V = 200 V, F = 50 Hz, I_r = 0.314 A, V_C = 300 V.

To find: R, L, C.

(i) To find the resistance:

$$I_r = \frac{V}{R}$$

$$0.314 = \frac{200}{R}$$

$$\boxed{R = 636.95\ \Omega}$$

(ii) To find the capacitor value:

$$V_C = Q\,V$$
$$300 = Q\,200$$
$$Q = 1.5$$

$$Q = \frac{1}{\omega_r R C}$$

$$1.5 = \frac{1}{2\pi \times 50 \times 636.59 \times C}$$

$$\boxed{C = 3.3\ \mu F}$$

(iii) To find inductor value:

$$Q = \frac{\omega_r L}{R}$$

$$1.5 = \frac{2 \times \pi \times 50 \times L}{636.59}$$

$$\boxed{L = 3.041\ H}$$

Ans.:

$$\boxed{\begin{array}{l} R = 636.95\ \Omega \\ L = 3.041\ H \\ C = 3.3\ \mu F \end{array}}$$

Ex. 2.8: A circuit consisting of a resistance of 4 Ω and inductor of 0.5 H and a variable capacitor all in series connected across 100 V, 50 Hz supply. At resonance calculate:
(i) Capacitor
(ii) Voltage across inductor
(iii) Q factor
(iv) Current in the circuit
(v) Find current at 100 Hz.

Sol.: Given: R = 4Ω, L = 0.5 H, V = 100 V, f_r = 50 Hz.
To find: C, Q, V_L, I_r, I at 100 Hz.

(i) Capacitor:

$$f_r = \frac{1}{2\pi\sqrt{LC}}$$

$$50 = \frac{1}{2\pi\sqrt{0.5 \times C}}$$

$$\boxed{C = 20.2642\ \mu F}$$

(ii) Q factor:

$$Q = \frac{\omega_r L}{R}$$

$$= \frac{2 \times \pi \times 50 \times 0.5}{4}$$

$$\boxed{Q = 39.27}$$

(iii) Voltage across inductor:

$$V_L = jQV$$
$$V_L = j\,39.27 \times 100$$
$$\boxed{V_L = j\,3.927\ kV}$$

(iv) Current at resonance:

$$I = \frac{V}{R} = \frac{100}{4}$$

$$\boxed{I = 25\ A}$$

(v) Current at f = 100 Hz:
Let us first calculate Z and δ

$$\delta = \frac{f - f_r}{f_r}$$

$$= \frac{50}{50} = 1$$

$$Z = R[1 + jQ\delta(2-\delta)]$$
$$Z = 4[1 + j39.27]$$
$$Z = 4j\,157.08\,\Omega$$

$$\therefore \quad I = \frac{V}{Z} = \frac{100}{4 + j157.08}$$

$$I = \frac{100\angle 0}{157.13\angle 88.5}$$

$$\boxed{I = 0.636\angle -88.5\,A}$$

∴ Impedance above f_r is unductive. Therefore, voltage leads I.

Ans.:

$$\boxed{\begin{array}{rl} C & = 20.2642\,\mu F \\ Q & = 39.27 \\ V_L & = j\,3.927\,kV \\ I_r & = 25\,A \\ I\text{ at }100\,Hz & = 0.636\angle -88.5°\,A \end{array}}$$

Ex. 2.9: A circuit consisting of 5 Ω, an inductor of 0.4 H and a variable capacitor is connected across 230 V, 50 Hz supply. At resonance calculate:
(i) Capacitance
(ii) Voltage across inductor
(iii) Current in the circuit.

Sol.: Given: R = 5 Ω, L = 0.4 H, V = 230 V, f = 50 Hz.
To calculate: C, V_L, I_r.

(i) To calculate C:

$$f_r = \frac{1}{2\pi\sqrt{LC}}$$

$$50 = \frac{1}{2\times\pi\sqrt{0.4\times C}}$$

$$\boxed{C = 25.33\,\mu F}$$

(ii) Quality factor:

$$Q = \frac{\omega_r L}{R}$$

$$= \frac{2\pi \times 50 \times 0.4}{5}$$

$$\boxed{Q = 25.1327}$$

(iii) Voltage across inductor at resonance:

$$V_L = jQV$$
$$V_L = j\, 25.1327 \times 230$$
$$\boxed{V_L = j\, 5.78\text{ kV} = 5.78 \angle 90° \text{ V}}$$

(iv) Current at resonance:

$$I_r = \frac{V}{R} = \frac{230}{5}$$
$$\boxed{I_r = 46 \text{ A}}$$

Ans.:

$$\boxed{\begin{array}{l} C = 25.33 \text{ μF} \\ Q = 25.1327 \\ V_L = 5.78 \angle 90° \\ I_o = 46 \text{ A} \end{array}}$$

Ex. 2.10: A current in series resonant circuit is maximum at 3 kHz and it is 5 amperes. If the coil is of 0.05 mH and R = 5 Ω, then calculate the value of 'C' to get the resonance. What will be the value of 'V'? Draw the phasor diagram of the circuit at resonance.

Sol.: Given: $f_r = 3$ kHz, $I_r = 5$A, L = 0.05 mH, R = 5Ω.

To calculate: C, V, phasor diagrams.

(i) To calculate C:

Current is maximum at 3 kHz

∴
$$f_r = 3 \text{ kHz}$$
$$f_r = \frac{1}{2\pi \sqrt{LC}}$$
$$3 \times 10^3 = \frac{1}{2\pi \sqrt{0.05 \times 10^{-3} \times C}}$$
$$\boxed{C = 56.2895 \text{ μF}}$$

(ii) Value V:

$$I_r = \frac{V}{R}$$
$$5 = \frac{V}{5}$$
$$\boxed{V = 25 \text{ V}}$$

(iii) Phasor diagram at resonance:

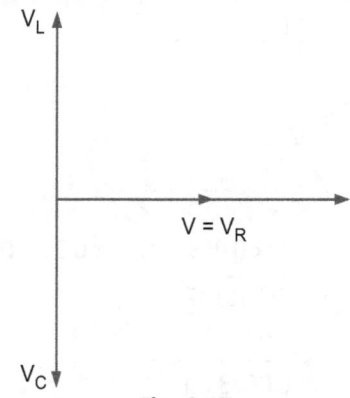

Fig. 2.17

Ans.:
$$\boxed{\begin{array}{l} C = 56.28\ \mu F \\ V = 25\ V \end{array}}$$

Ex. 2.11: A capacitor of 400 pF is in series with a coil is resonant at 1 MHz. The half power frequency is 0.9 MHz. Specify values of R and L. Also find second half power frequency.

Sol.: Given: $C = 400$ pF, $f_r = 1$ MHz, $f_1 = 0.9$ MHz.
To calculate: R and L, f_2.

(i) To calculate L:
$$f_r = \frac{1}{2\pi\sqrt{LC}}$$
$$1 \times 10^6 = \frac{1}{2\pi\sqrt{400 \times 10^{-12} \times L}}$$
$$\boxed{L = 0.0633\ mH}$$

(ii) To calculate f_2:
Given: $f = 0.9$ MHz is less than f_r.
∴ It is lower half power frequency.
$$f_1 = f_r - \frac{\Delta f}{2}$$
∴
$$\frac{\Delta f}{2} = 1\ MHz - 0.9\ MHz = 0.1\ MHz$$

Upper power frequency (f_2)
$$f_2 = f_r + \frac{\Delta f}{2}$$
$$f_2 = 1 + 0.1$$
$$\boxed{f_2 = 1.1\ MHz}$$

(iii) To calculate resistance R:

$$BW = \frac{R}{2\pi L}$$

$$(f_2 - f_1) = \frac{R}{2\pi L}$$

$$(1.1 - 0.9) \text{ MHz} = \frac{R}{2 \times \pi \times 0.063 \times 10^{-3}}$$

$$R = 2\pi \times 0.063 \times 10^{-3} \times 0.2 \times 10^6$$

$$\boxed{R = 79.5451 \ \Omega}$$

Ans.:

L	=	0.0633 mH
f_2	=	1.1 MHz
R	=	79.5451 Ω

Ex. 2.12: In an RLC series circuit shown in Fig. 2.18.
Determine:
(i) The necessary value of capacitor.
(ii) The supply voltage to produce a voltage of 5 V across the capacitance if resonance frequency is 5 kHz.
(iii) The frequency of resonance if the capacitance is made $\frac{1}{2}$ of that in (i). Also find Q of the new circuit.

Sol.: Given: R = 6.28 Ω, L = 20 mH, f_r = 5 kHz, V_C = 5 V

To calculate: V_{in}, Q and f_r if C = $\frac{1}{2}$ V.

(i) To calculate capacitance value:

$$f_r = \frac{1}{2\pi \sqrt{LC}}$$

$$5 \times 10^3 = \frac{1}{2\pi \sqrt{20 \times 10^{-3} \times C}}$$

$$\boxed{C = 0.0507 \ \mu F}$$

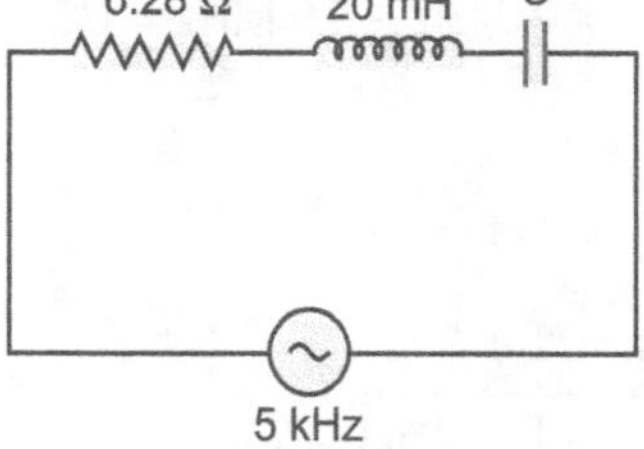

Fig. 2.18

(ii) To calculate supply voltage V:

At f_r

$$V_C = V \cdot Q$$

$$5 = V \left(\frac{1}{\omega_r RC} \right)$$

$$5 = V \left(\frac{1}{2 \times \pi \times 5 \times 10^3 \times 6.28 \times 0.05 \times 10^{-6}} \right)$$

$$\boxed{V = 0.05 \text{ V}}$$

(iii) To calculate f_r if $C' = \frac{1}{2} C$:

$$f_r' = \frac{1}{2\pi \sqrt{LC'}}$$

$$f_r' = \frac{1}{2\pi \sqrt{L \frac{C}{2}}}$$

$$f_r' = \sqrt{2} \frac{1}{2\pi \sqrt{LC}}$$

$$f_r' = \sqrt{2} \, f_r$$

$$f_r' = \sqrt{2} \, (5 \times 10^3)$$

$$\boxed{f_r' = 7071 \text{ Hz}}$$

(iv) Q' of new circuit:

$$Q' = \frac{\omega_r L}{R}$$

$$Q' = \frac{2 \times \pi \times f_r \times L}{R}$$

$$Q' = \frac{2 \times \pi \times 7071 \times 20 \times 10^{-3}}{6.28}$$

$$\boxed{Q' = 141.4}$$

Ans.:

$$\boxed{\begin{aligned} C &= 0.0507 \ \mu F \\ V &= 0.05 \text{ V} \\ \text{New } f_r &= 7071 \text{ Hz} \\ \text{New } Q &= 141.4 \end{aligned}}$$

Ex. 2.13: For the circuit shown in Fig. 2.19, $R_1 = 0.5\,\Omega$, $R_2 = 1.5\,\Omega$, $R_3 = 0.5\,\Omega$, $C_1 = 6\,\mu F$, $C_2 = 12\,\mu F$, $L_1 = 25\,mH$ and $L_2 = 15\,mH$.

Determine:
(i) The frequency of resonance.
(ii) Q of the circuit.
(iii) Q of the coil 1 and coil 2 individually.

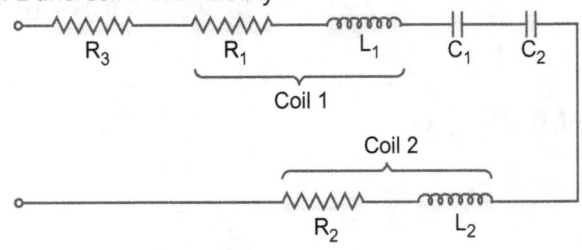

Fig. 2.19

Sol.: Given: $R_1 = 0.5\,\Omega$ $R_2 = 1.5\,\Omega$ $R_3 = 0.5\,\Omega$
$C_1 = 6\,\mu F$ $C_2 = 12\,\mu F$ $L_1 = 25\,mH$
$L_2 = 15\,mH$

To calculate: f_r, Q, $Q_{coil\ 1}$, $Q_{coil\ 2}$

(i) To calculate f_r:

$$\text{Total inductance} = L_1 + L_2$$
$$= 25 + 15$$
$$= 40\,mH$$

$$\text{Total capacitance} = \frac{C_1 \cdot C_2}{C_1 + C_2}$$
$$= \frac{6 \times 12}{18}$$
$$= 4\,\mu F$$

$$f_r = \frac{1}{2\pi\sqrt{LC}}$$

$$f_r = \frac{1}{2\pi\sqrt{40 \times 10^{-3} \times 4 \times 10^{-6}}}$$

$$\boxed{f_r = 397.88\,Hz}$$

(ii) To calculate Q of the circuit:

$$Q = \frac{\omega L_{eq}}{R_{eq}}$$

$$L_{eq} = L_1 + L_2$$
$$= 40\,mH$$

$$R_{eq} = R_1 + R_2 + R_3$$
$$= 2.5 \ \Omega$$

$$\therefore \quad Q = \frac{2\pi f_r \ L_{eq}}{R_{eq}}$$

$$Q = \frac{2\pi \times 397.88 \times 40 \times 10^{-3}}{2.5}$$

$$\boxed{Q = 40}$$

(iii) Q of individual coil:

$$Q_{coil\ 1} = \frac{\omega_r L_1}{R_1}$$
$$= \frac{2\pi f_r \times 25 \times 10^{-3}}{0.5}$$
$$\boxed{Q_{coil\ 1} = 125}$$

$$Q_{coil\ 2} = \frac{\omega_r L_2}{R_2}$$
$$= \frac{2\pi f_r \times 15 \times 10^{-3}}{1.5}$$
$$\boxed{Q_{coil\ 2} = 25}$$

Ans.:

$$\begin{array}{l} f_r = 397.88 \text{ Hz} \\ \text{Q of the circuit} = 40 \\ \text{Q of coil 1} = 125 \\ \text{Q of coil 2} = 25 \end{array}$$

Ex. 2.14: Show that the value of capacitance for maximum voltage across the capacitor in case of series resonance circuit with capacitor tunning is given by

$$C = \frac{L}{R^2 + X_L^2}$$

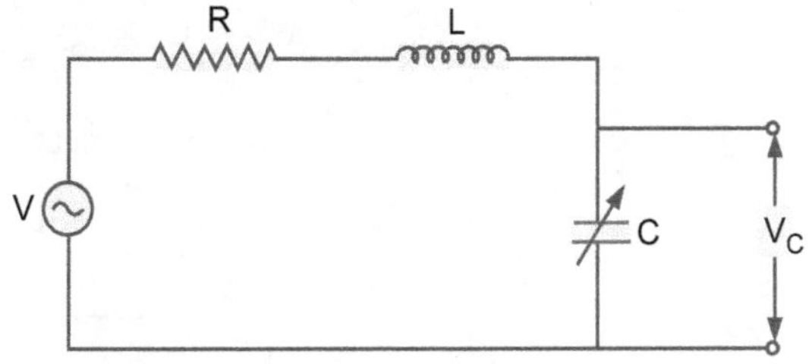

Fig. 2.20

Sol.: To prove: $C = \dfrac{L}{R^2 + X_L^2}$ for maximum V_C

The voltage across the capacitor V_C, will be maximum when the current through it is maximum.

$$|V_C| = \left|I \times \dfrac{1}{\omega C}\right|$$

$$V_C = \left|\dfrac{V}{R + j\omega L - \dfrac{j}{\omega C}}\right| \times \dfrac{1}{\omega C}$$

$$V_C = \dfrac{V}{\left[\sqrt{R^2 + \left(\omega L - \dfrac{1}{\omega C}\right)^2}\,\omega C\right]}$$

$$V_C = \dfrac{V}{\omega C \sqrt{\left(R^2 + \omega^2 L^2 - \dfrac{2L}{C} + \dfrac{1}{\omega^2 C^2}\right)}}$$

$$V_C = \dfrac{V}{\sqrt{R^2 \omega^2 C^2 + \omega^4 L^2 C^2 - 2L\omega^2 C + 1}}$$

For V_C to be maximum, when capacitor C is variable; differentiating V_C w.r.t. C and equating it to zero, we have

$$\dfrac{d}{dC} E_C = V\left[\dfrac{-1}{2} \times \dfrac{2R^2 C\omega^2 + 2L^2 C\omega^4 - 2L\omega^2}{(R^2 C^2 \omega^2 + L^2 C^2 \omega^4 - 2LC\omega^2 + 1)^{3/2}}\right]$$

$$= 0$$

$\therefore \quad \dfrac{-1}{2}(2R^2 C\omega^2 + 2L^2 C\omega^4 - 2L\omega^2) = 0$

$$CR^2 + CL^2\omega^2 - 2L = 0$$

$$C = \dfrac{L}{R^2 + L^2 \omega^2}$$

Since, $\quad X_L = \omega L$

$$\boxed{C = \dfrac{L}{R^2 + X_L^2}}$$

Hence, the proof.

2.6 PARALLEL RESONATING CIRCUIT

Consider circuit shown in Fig. 2.21.

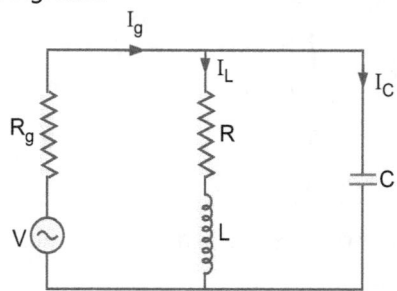

Fig. 2.21: A parallel resonating circuit

- We have consider R_g i.e. the internal generator resistance in this circuit. Moreover, the capacitor is connected in parallel to an inductor and it is assumed to be a lossless element and hence its resistance is negligible. R in this case is the sum of the resistance of inductor and any other load resistance connected externally.
- This circuit is connected to the voltage source of V volts and generator resistance R_g ohms.
- It is also called as an antiresonating circuit.

2.6.1 Antiresonating Frequency

The admittance of the capacitive branch of the circuit is
$$Y_C = j\omega C$$
and that of the inductive branch is
$$Y_L = \frac{1}{R + j\omega L} = \frac{R - j\omega L}{R^2 + \omega^2 L^2}$$

Thus, Y i.e. total admittance
$$Y = Y_C + Y_L$$
$$Y = \frac{R - j\omega L}{R^2 + \omega^2 L^2} + j\omega C$$
$$Y = \frac{R}{R^2 + \omega^2 L^2} - j\left[\frac{\omega L}{R^2 + \omega^2 L^2} - \omega C\right]$$

- For antiresonance, the circuit must have unity power factor, therefore the j term must be zero. So setting the reactive term equal to zero at ω_{ar} i.e. antiresonant frequency.

∴ At $\quad \omega = \omega_{ar}$

$$\frac{\omega_{ar} L}{R^2 + \omega_{ar}^2 L^2} - \omega_{ar} C = 0$$

$$\boxed{R^2 + \omega_{ar}^2 L^2 = \frac{L}{C}} \qquad \ldots (2.21)$$

This equation will be used in Section 2.5.3.

$$\omega_{ar}^2 = \left(\frac{L}{C} - R^2\right)\frac{1}{L^2}$$

$$\omega_{ar}^2 = \left(\frac{1}{LC} - \frac{R^2}{L^2}\right)$$

$$\boxed{f_{ar} = \frac{1}{2\pi}\sqrt{\frac{1}{LC} - \frac{R^2}{L^2}}} \quad \ldots (2.22)$$

f_{ar}, gives the frequency of resonance in a parallel R_{LC} circuit.

$$f_{ar} = \frac{1}{2\pi}\sqrt{\frac{1}{LC}}\sqrt{1 - \frac{1}{Q^2}}$$

$$\boxed{f_{ar} = f_r\sqrt{1 - \frac{1}{Q^2}}} \quad \ldots (2.23)$$

$$\boxed{\omega_{ar}^2 LC = 1 - \frac{1}{Q^2}} \quad \ldots (2.24)$$

which can be written as

$$\omega_{ar} L = \frac{1}{\omega_{ar} C}\left(1 - \frac{1}{Q^2}\right)$$

to give

$$\boxed{X_L = X_C\left(1 - \frac{1}{Q^2}\right)} \quad \ldots (2.25)$$

Equation 2.23 gives the expression for the antiresonating frequency. Equations 2.23, 2.24, 2.25 are the modified versions and need careful understanding.

Comments on Equations 2.21, 2.22, 2.23 and 2.24.

1. In series resonant circuit,

$$f_r = \frac{1}{2\pi\sqrt{LC}}$$

and thus resonance was possible for all the values of resistance present. In contrast to this, as clear from equation 2.22 in an antiresonant circuit, resonance is possible only when $\frac{1}{LC} > \frac{R^2}{L^2}$.

i.e. Resonance is impossible for all the values of R that makes

$$\frac{R^2}{L^2} > \frac{1}{LC}$$

This is clear from equation 2.22.

2. Equation 2.23 indicates that the antiresonant frequency, differs from that of a series resonant circuit with the same circuit elements only by the factor $\sqrt{1-\dfrac{1}{Q^2}}$.

   If Q > 10 then error < 10% and $f_{ar} = f_r$.

   Another point indicated by equation 2.23 is that it shows the antiresonance is impossible for circuits with values of Q less than unity.

3. Equations 2.24 and 2.25 shows another interesting fact. We define resonance as a condition of a circuit when $X_L = X_C$ and unity power factor is achieved. But in an antiresonant circuit at f_{ar} the reactances of inductive and capacitive branches are not quite equal as they were incase of series resonating circuit.

2.6.2 Reactance Curves

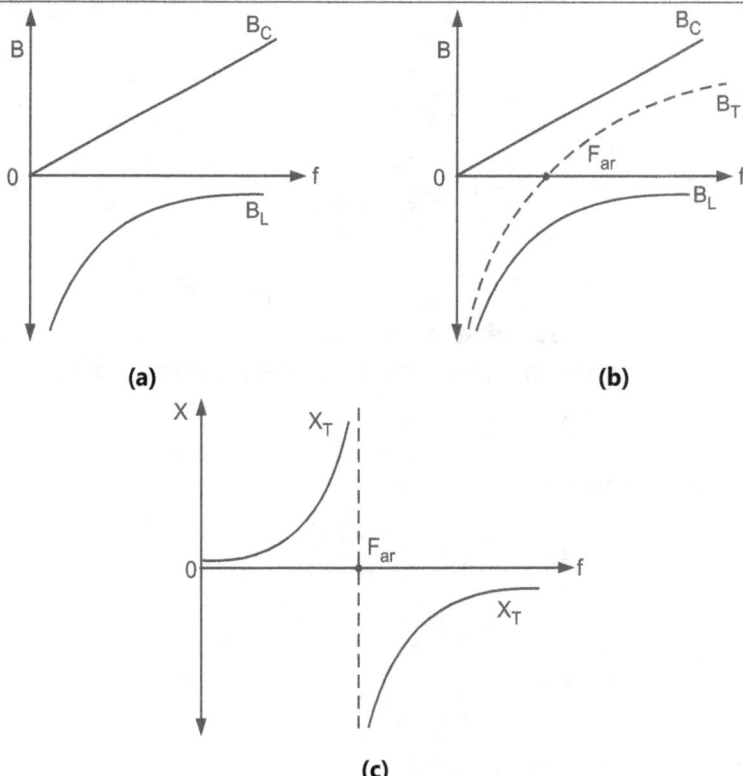

Fig. 2.22: (a) Suspectance Vs Frequency plot for L and C, (b) Total Suspectance B_T Vs Frequency, (c) X_T plotted as reciprocal of B_T

- Inductive reactance is a linear positive function of frequency and is plotted as a straight line through origin. Capacitive reactance similarly, is plotted as a negative hyperbola the reason being it is an inverse negative function of frequency.

- In case of parallel resonating circuit we plot the susceptances, thus inductive susceptance is plotted as hyperbolic negative and capacitive susceptance is plotted as a linear positive plot.
- These plots are shown in Fig. 2.22 (a) and (b). Fig. 2.22 (c) shows the plot of total reactance X_T plotted as a reciprocal of total susceptance. Thus, at antiresonating frequency f_{ar}, susceptance B_T was zero and so X_T is therefore infinity. Below f_{ar}, B_T is capacitive and thus X_T is inductive. Similarly X_T is capacitive above f_{ar}. Even this is very contradictory to the reactance plot of series resonance.

2.6.3 Impedance of Parallel Resonance Circuit

The admittance of the capacitive branch of the circuit is
$$Y_C = j\omega C$$
Similarly,
$$Y_L = \frac{1}{R + j\omega L}$$
$$= \frac{R - j\omega L}{R^2 + \omega^2 L^2}$$

∴ Total admittance Y is
$$Y = \frac{R - j\omega L}{R^2 + \omega^2 L^2} + j\omega C$$

∴ $$Y = \frac{R}{R^2 + \omega^2 L^2} - j\left(\frac{\omega L}{R^2 + \omega^2 L^2} - \omega C\right)$$

(a) Impedance at antiresonating frequency:

With the condition of unity power factor imposed, admittance at f_{ar} is
$$Y_{ar} = \frac{R}{R^2 + \omega_{ar}^2 L^2}$$

∴ Antiresonant impedance is

∴ $$Z_{ar} = R_{ar} = \frac{R^2 + \omega_{ar}^2 L^2}{R}$$

$$Z_{ar} = R + \frac{\omega_{ar}^2 L^2}{R}$$

$$\boxed{Z_{ar} = R\left(1 + Q_{war}^2\right)} \qquad \ldots (2.26)$$

For the circuit with very high value of Q.
$$\boxed{Z_{ar} = R \cdot Q_{ar}^2} \qquad \ldots (2.27) \text{ high Q values}$$

This equation gives Z_{ar} in terms of Q_{ar}. Recollect equation 2.21 which we saw in Section 2.5.1. The equation is
$$R^2 + \omega_{ar}^2 L = \frac{L}{C}$$

Using this result in the equation

$$Z_{ar} = R + \frac{\omega_{ar}^2 L^2}{R}$$

i.e.
$$Z_{ar} = \frac{R^2 + \omega_{ar}^2 L^2}{R}$$

Gives,
$$\boxed{Z_{ar} = \frac{L}{CR}} \qquad \ldots(2.28)$$

This equation gives the expression for Z_{ar} in terms of circuit components.

(b) The impedance of parallel resonant circuit near resonance:

The impedance of parallel resonant circuit at any frequency is given by,

$$Z = (R + j\omega L) \parallel \left(\frac{1}{j\omega C}\right)$$

$$Z = \frac{(R + j\omega L) \times \frac{1}{(j\omega C)}}{R + j\omega L + \frac{1}{j\omega C}}$$

$$Z = \frac{R\left(1 + \frac{j\omega L}{R}\right)\left(\frac{1}{j\omega C}\right)}{R\left[1 + \frac{j\omega L}{R}\left(1 - \frac{1}{\omega^2 LC}\right)\right]}$$

$$Z = \frac{R\left(1 + \frac{j\omega L}{R}\right)\left(\frac{1}{j\omega C}\right)}{R\left[1 + \frac{j\omega L}{R}\left(1 - \frac{1}{\omega^2 LC}\right)\right]}$$

$$Z = \frac{\frac{L}{RC} + \frac{1}{j\omega C}}{1 + \frac{j\omega L}{R}\left(1 - \frac{1}{\omega^2 LC}\right)} \qquad \ldots (2.29)$$

Above equation gives general expression for the impedance of a parallel resonant circuit at any frequency ω.

Let δ be the fractional deviation

$$\delta = \frac{f - f_{ar}}{f_{ar}}$$

$$= \frac{\omega - \omega_{ar}}{\omega_{ar}} = \frac{\omega}{\omega_{ar}} - 1$$

$$\boxed{(1 + \delta) = \frac{\omega}{\omega_{ar}}} \quad \text{or} \quad \boxed{\frac{\omega_{ar}}{\omega} = \frac{1}{(1 + \delta)}}$$

Now let us consider the terms in the denominator of equation 2.29.

$$\frac{\omega L}{R} = \frac{\omega_{ar} L}{R} \cdot \frac{\omega}{\omega_{ar}} = Q(1+\delta)$$

$$\frac{1}{\omega^2 LC} = \frac{\omega_{ar}^2}{\omega^2} \times \frac{1}{\omega_{ar}^2 LC}$$

$$= \frac{1}{(1+\delta)^2} \qquad \ldots \text{when Q is high } \omega_{ar}^2 LC = 1$$

Substituting these values in equation 2.29.

$$Z = \frac{\dfrac{L}{CR}\left(1 + \dfrac{R}{j\omega L}\right)}{1 + j\dfrac{\omega L}{R}\left(1 - \dfrac{1}{\omega^2 LC}\right)}$$

$$Z = \frac{L}{CR} \cdot \frac{1 - j\dfrac{1}{Q_0(1+\delta)}}{1 + jQ(1+\delta)\left[1 + \dfrac{1}{(1+\delta)^2}\right]}$$

$$Z = \frac{L}{CR} \cdot \frac{1 - j\dfrac{1}{Q(1+\delta)}}{1 + jQ\left[\dfrac{1 + \delta^2 + 2\delta - 1}{(1+\delta)}\right]}$$

$$Z = \frac{L}{CR} \cdot \frac{1 - j\dfrac{1}{Q(1+\delta)}}{1 + jQ\delta\dfrac{(2+\delta)}{(1+\delta)}} \qquad \ldots (2.30)$$

At antiresonating frequency

$$Z_{ar} = \frac{L}{CR}$$

and $\delta \ll 1$. Therefore, neglecting it.
Substituting in equation 2.30.

$$Z = Z_{ar} \frac{1 - j\dfrac{1}{Q}}{1 + jQ\delta \cdot 2}$$

$\dfrac{1}{Q}$ is $\ll 1$. Therefore, neglecting it.

$$\boxed{Z = \frac{Z_{ar}}{1 + j2\delta Q}} \qquad \ldots (2.31)$$

Equation (2.31) gives the value of impedance near resonance.

2.6.4 Currents in Antiresonant Circuits

At antiresonance, the power delivered by the generator to the circuit of Fig. 2.21.
$$P = I_g^2 R_{ar}$$
Power dissipated in the parallel circuit assuming negligible capacitor losses is
$$P = I_L^2 R$$
This power is equal to the power supplied by the generator, since there are no other power dissipating elements in the circuit.

∴ Input power = Delivered power
$$I_g^2 R_{ar} = I_L^2 R$$
$$\frac{I_g^2}{I_L^2} = \frac{R}{R_{ar}}$$

Now, $R_{ar} = \dfrac{L}{CR}$

$$\frac{I_g^2}{I_L^2} = \frac{R}{\frac{L}{CR}}$$

$$\frac{I_g^2}{I_L^2} = \frac{CR^2}{L}$$

$$I_L^2 = \frac{L}{CR^2} I_g^2$$

As $Q = \dfrac{\omega L}{R} = \dfrac{1}{R}\sqrt{\dfrac{L}{C}}$ .... $\omega_{ar} = \dfrac{1}{\sqrt{LC}}$

$$I_L^2 = Q^2 I_g^2$$

$$\boxed{I_L = Q I_g} \qquad \ldots (2.32)$$

At antiresonance:

Now current flowing through the capacitor is given by
$$I_C = \frac{V}{X_C} = \frac{V}{\left(\dfrac{1}{\omega_{ar}C}\right)}$$

$$I_C = \omega_{ar} C \cdot V$$
$$I_C = \omega_{ar} C [I_g \times Z_{ar}]$$
$$I_C = \omega_{ar} C I_g \left(\frac{L}{CR}\right)$$
$$I_C = \left(\frac{\omega_{ar} L}{R}\right) I_g$$

$$\boxed{I_C = Q I_g} \qquad \ldots (2.33)$$

Equations (2.32) and (2.33) show that at f_{ar}, the currents through the inductor and the capacitor are amplified by a factor Q.
- Recollect the equation (2.22), which we saw in Section 2.5.1.
  At antiresonance,
  $$X_L = X_C \left(1 - \frac{1}{Q^2}\right)$$
  i.e. the reactances of inductive and capacitive branches are not quite equal to units power factor.
- The current will always depend on reactance. So if reactances are not equal, the currents will obviously not be equal.
  At antiresonance
  $$\frac{I_C}{I_L} = \sqrt{1 - \frac{1}{Q^2}}$$
  This is the ratio of magnitude of the currents in the capacitive branch to the inductive branch at unity power factor.
- The two currents are thus not equal if the resistance is appreciable, approaching equality as R is decreased.
- Higher the value of Q, the higher will I_C and I_L be and I_g will be low.
- At infinite Q, currents I_C and I_L will be infinite and I_g will be zero.

2.6.5 Bandwidth of Antiresonant Circuit
- We have already defined bandwidth for resonating circuits.
- Let us derive equation for bandwidth of a parallel resonant circuit shown in Fig. 2.23 (a).

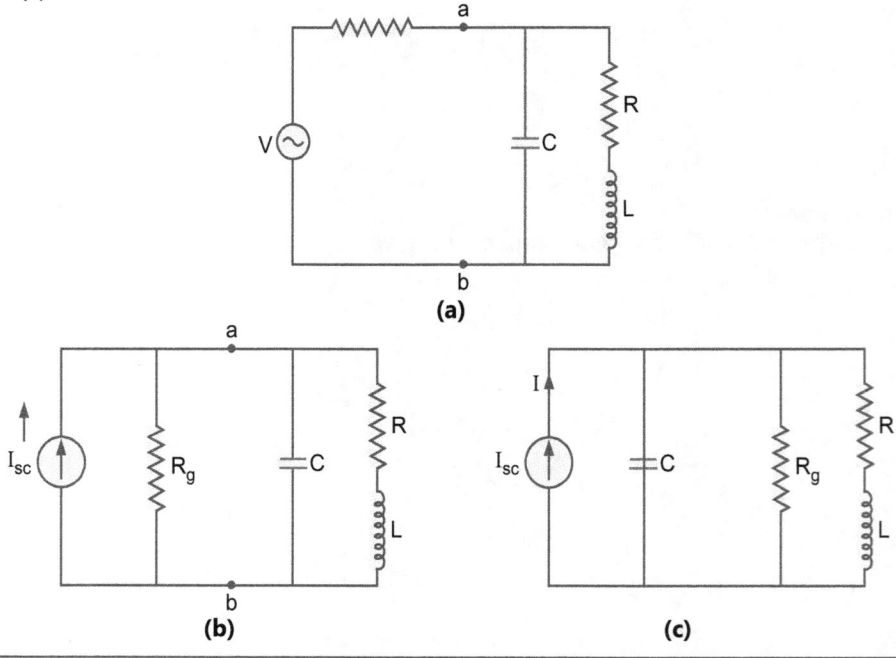

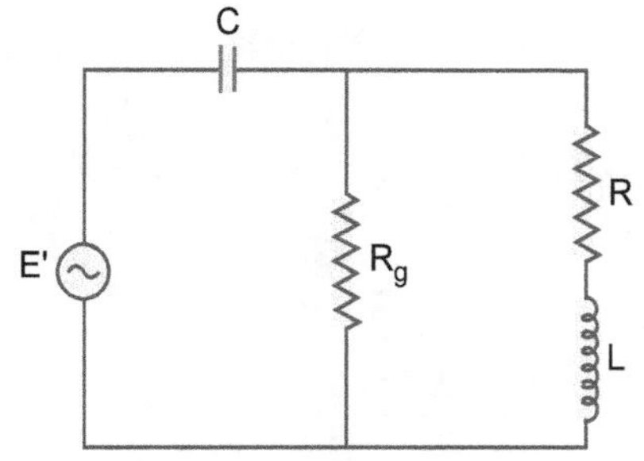

(d)

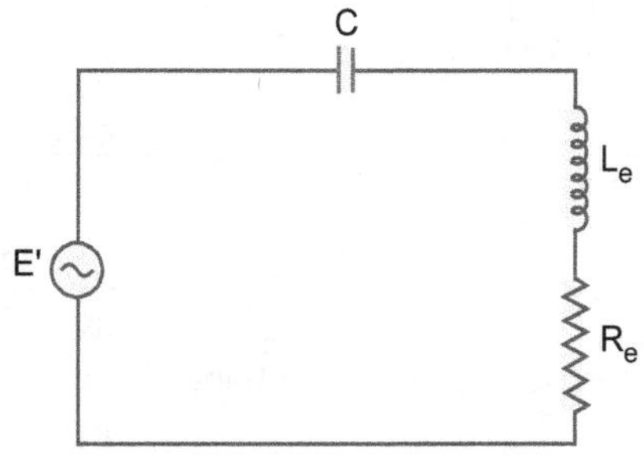

(d)

Fig. 2.23 (a) Parallel RLC circuit connected to a generator of internal resistance R_g
(b), (c), (d) Successive steps in reduction of (a) to (e)
(e) Series RLC equivalent of a

- Using voltage source transformation the circuit in Fig. 2.23 (a) is transformed to one in Fig. 2.23 (b). Since, all the branches are now in parallel we can interchange the positions of R_g and C. Using current source transformation circuit in Fig. 2.23 (c) can be drawn as in Fig. 2.23 (d). Finally, Fig. 2.23 (e) shows an equivalent of series RLC circuit the parallel RLC circuit in Fig. 2.23 (a) where

$$(R_e + X_{Le}) = R_g \parallel (X_L + R)$$

- Now, in the equivalent series RLC circuit capacitor C is the internal impedance of a new generator E'.
- Let us now analyse Fig. 2.23 (e) where we have,

$$Z_e = R_e + L_e = R_g \parallel (L + R)$$

$$Z_e = R_g \parallel (j\omega L + R)$$

$$Z_e = \frac{R_g \times (j\omega L + R)}{R_g + R + j\omega L}$$

After rationalizing,

$$Z_e = \frac{R_g (j\omega L + R)(R_g + R - j\omega L)}{(R_g + R + j\omega L)(R_g + R - j\omega L)}$$

$$Z_e = \frac{(j\omega L\, R_g + R_g R)(R_g + R - j\omega L)}{(R_g + R)^2 + \omega^2 L^2}$$

$$Z_e = \frac{R_g^2 R + R_g R^2 - j\omega L\, R_g R + j\omega L\, R_g^2 + j\omega L\, R_g R + \omega^2 L_g^2}{(R_g + R)^2 + \omega^2 L^2}$$

$$Z_e = \frac{R_g^2 R + R_g R^2 + j\omega L\, R_g^2 + \omega^2 L^2 R_g}{(R_g + R)^2 + \omega^2 L^2}$$

$$Z_e = (R_e + X_{Le}) = \frac{R_g^2 R + R_g R^2 + R_g \omega^2 L^2 + j\omega L\, R_g^2}{(R_g + R)^2 + \omega^2 L^2}$$

Form which we have,

$$R_e = \frac{R_g^2 R + R_g R^2 + R_g \omega^2 L^2}{(R_g + R)^2 + \omega^2 L^2}$$

$$\omega L_e = \frac{\omega L R_g^2}{(R_g + R)^2 + \omega^2 L^2}$$

It has been shown that bandwidth of a series resonant circuit is given as

$$BW = \frac{f_r}{Q}$$

The parallel RLC circuit is proved to be equivalent to a series resonant circuit.

$$\therefore \quad BW \text{ of parallel RLC circuit} = \frac{f_{ar}}{Q}$$

where, $\quad Q$ must be $= \dfrac{\omega L_e}{R_e}$

$\therefore \quad$ Bandwidth (BW) $= \Delta f$

$$= f_2 - f_1$$

$$\Delta f = \frac{f_{ar}}{Q}$$

$$\Delta f = \frac{f_{ar}}{\dfrac{\omega L_e}{R_e}}$$

$$\Delta f = f_{ar} \cdot \frac{R_e}{\omega L_e}$$

$$\Delta f = \left(\frac{R_g R^2 + R R_g^2 + R_g \omega^2 L^2}{\omega L R_g^2}\right) f_{ar}$$

$$\Delta f = \left(\frac{R}{\omega L} + \frac{R_g(R^2 + \omega^2 L^2)}{\omega L R_g^2}\right) f_{ar}$$

$$\Delta f = \left[\frac{1}{Q} + \frac{R^2\left(1 + \dfrac{\omega^2 L^2}{R^2}\right)}{\omega L R_g}\right] f_{ar}$$

$$\Delta f = \left[\frac{1}{Q} + \frac{R^2}{\omega L R_g}\left(\frac{R_{ar}}{R}\right)\right] f_{ar}$$

$\qquad\qquad\qquad\qquad\qquad\qquad\ldots$ equation (2.27) is section 2.6.3

$$Z_{ar} = R(1 + Q^2)$$

$$\Delta f = \left[\frac{1}{Q} + \frac{R \cdot R_{ar}}{\omega L R_g}\right] f_{ar}$$

$$\boxed{\Delta f = \frac{f_{ar}}{Q}\left[1 + \frac{R_{ar}}{R_g}\right]} \qquad \ldots(2.34)$$

- If it is desired to match the impedances, as to obtain the greatest possible power delivery from generator to load, then $R_g = R_{ar}$.

  ∴ Bandwidth for matched condition will be

  $$\Delta f = \frac{2}{Q} f_{ar} \qquad \text{...(2.35)}$$

- Above equation (2.34), can be modified slightly to explain the factors effecting bandwidth.

  We have $\qquad \Delta f = \frac{f_{ar}}{Q}\left(1 + \frac{R_{ar}}{R_g}\right)$

  But $\qquad R_{ar} = \frac{L}{CR}$

  $$\Delta f = \frac{f_{ar}}{Q}\left(1 + \frac{L}{CR\, R_g}\right) \qquad \text{... (2.36)}$$

Equations (2.34), (2.35) and (2.36) are the expressions of BW in terms of Q, R_{ar} and R_g and must be closely understood so need further clarification.

Comments on Bandwidth and Selectivity:

1. Equation (2.34) shows that as seen in series RLC circuit, even in parallel circuit the bandwidth is inversely proportional to the Q of the original parallel circuit modified by a factor dependent on R_g.

   Q of original parallel circuit $= \dfrac{\omega L}{R}$

   Q of equivalent series RLC circuit $= \dfrac{\omega L_e}{R_e}$

2. Equation 2.34, also shows that for smaller bandwidth or greater selectivity of the antiresonant circuit a generator of a very high internal resistance R_g, should be used. Thus, in case of parallel RLC circuit R_g must be of a very high value. This is indicated in Fig. 2.24.

3. Equation 2.35, indicates that for a matched conditions $R_g = R_{ar}$ [to have maximum power transfer]. Since, R_g must be high for high selectivity R_{ar} must also be very high for maximum power transfer in the circuit.

4. Equation 2.36, shows that L must be small and C must be large for designing a circuit with high frequency selectivity i.e. circuit with less bandwidth. But doing this will lower the value of Z_{ar} and R_{ar}.

   ∵ $\qquad Z_{ar} = R_{ar} = \dfrac{L}{CR}$

   Lowering the value of R_{ar} is highly undesirable if maximum power is needed to be transferred. So the designer must go for some engineering compromise between selectivity and maximum power to be transferred in a parallel resonating circuit.

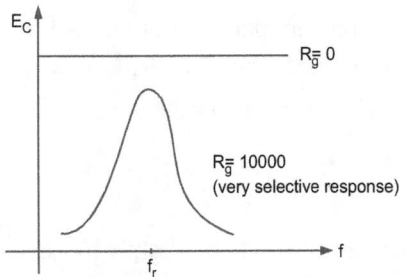

Fig. 2.24: Frequency response indicating effect of internal resistance R_g

2.6.6 General Case: Resistance present in both the Branches

Let the capacitor be lossy hence there will be resistances in both the branches as shown in Fig. 2.25.

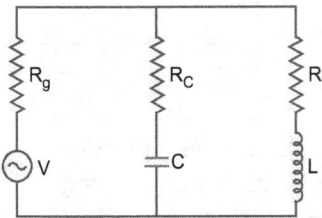

Fig. 2.25: Antiresonant circuit with resistance in both the branches

In this case, admittance Y_L of an inductive branch is

$$Y_L = \frac{1}{R_1 + j\omega L}$$

$$Y_L = \frac{R_1 - j\omega L}{R_1^2 + \omega^2 L^2}$$

Similarly, admittance Y_C of a capacitive branch is

$$Y_C = \frac{1}{R_2 - \dfrac{j}{\omega C}}$$

$$Y_C = \frac{R_2 + \dfrac{j}{\omega C}}{R_2^2 + \dfrac{1}{\omega^2 C^2}}$$

Total admittance $Y_T = Y_C + Y_L$

$$Y_T = \frac{R_1 - j\omega L}{R_1^2 + \omega^2 L^2} + \frac{R_2 + \dfrac{j}{\omega C}}{R_2^2 + \dfrac{1}{\omega^2 C^2}}$$

$$Y_T = \frac{R_1}{R_1^2 + \omega^2 L^2} + \frac{R_2}{R_2^2 + \dfrac{1}{\omega^2 C^2}} - j\left(\frac{\omega L}{R_1^2 + \omega^2 L^2} - \frac{\dfrac{1}{\omega C}}{R_2^2 + \dfrac{1}{\omega^2 C^2}}\right) \quad \ldots(4.37)$$

For antiresonant condition, unity power factor must be achieved. Therefore, the reactive term must be zero, thus at $\omega = \omega_{ar}$.

$$\omega_{ar} L \left[R_2^2 + \frac{1}{\omega_{ar}^2 C^2} \right] - \frac{1}{\omega_{ar} C} \left[R_1^2 + \omega_{ar}^2 L^2 \right] = 0$$

$$\omega_{ar} L R_2^2 + \frac{L}{\omega_{ar} C^2} = \frac{R_1^2}{\omega_{ar} C} + \frac{\omega_{ar} L^2}{C}$$

$$\omega_{ar}^2 R_2^2 C^2 L + L = R_1^2 C + \omega_{ar}^2 L^2 C$$

$$\omega_{ar}^2 LC \left(R_2^2 C - L \right) = C R_1^2 - L$$

$$\omega_{ar}^2 = \frac{1}{LC} \left[\frac{C R_1^2 - L}{R_2^2 C - L} \right]$$

$$\boxed{f_{ar} = \frac{1}{2\pi} \sqrt{\frac{1}{LC} \left(\frac{L - R_1^2 C}{L - R_2^2 C} \right)}} \qquad \ldots (2.38)$$

- Equation 2.38 gives the expression for f_{ar} when resistance is present in both the branches of the antiresonant circuit.
- If $R_2 = 0$, then the circuit will be same as in Fig. 2.37, and f_{ar} will be

$$f_{ar} = \frac{1}{2\pi} \sqrt{\frac{1}{LC} \left(1 - R_1^2 \frac{C}{L} \right)}$$

which is same as the one derived earlier.

(a) Antiresonance at all Frequencies:

- If two resistances R_1 and R_2 are equal and is $\sqrt{\frac{L}{C}}$

i.e. $\qquad R_1 = R_2 = \sqrt{\frac{L}{C}}$

Then the reactance associated with J terms in above Y_T equation 2.37, is

$$\frac{\omega L}{R_1^2 + \omega^2 L^2} - \frac{\frac{1}{\omega C}}{R_2^2 + \frac{1}{\omega^2 C^2}} = \frac{\omega L}{\frac{L}{C} + \omega^2 L^2} - \frac{\frac{1}{\omega C}}{\frac{L}{C} + \frac{1}{\omega^2 C^2}}$$

$$= \frac{\omega C}{1 + \omega^2 CL} - \frac{\omega C}{1 + \omega^2 CL} = 0$$

Thus, the reactance term is zero. The total admittance will be given by

$$Y_T = \frac{\sqrt{\frac{L}{C}}}{\frac{L}{C}} + \omega^2 L^2 + \frac{\sqrt{\frac{L}{C}}}{\frac{L}{C} + \frac{1}{\omega^2 C^2}}$$

$$Y_T = \frac{\sqrt{\frac{L}{C}} \times C}{L(1 + \omega^2 LC)} + \frac{\sqrt{\frac{L}{C}} \times \omega^2 C^2}{C(1 + \omega^2 LC)}$$

$$Y_T = \sqrt{\frac{L}{C}}$$

The impedance $= \dfrac{1}{Y_T} = \sqrt{\dfrac{L}{C}} = R_1 = R_2$.

Thus, at all the frequencies impedance of the parallel circuit is

$$\boxed{Z = \sqrt{\frac{L}{C}}}$$

when $\qquad R_1 = R_2 = \sqrt{\dfrac{L}{C}}$

So we say, the circuit is antiresonant at all the frequencies and thus the circuit is purely resistance (unity power factor) at all the frequencies.

(b) Variable Phase Angle Circuit:

Consider the circuit as shown in Fig. 2.26.

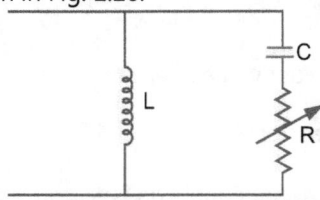

Fig. 2.26: Variable phase and constant impedance circuit

Impedance of the circuit is

$$Z = j\omega L \parallel \left(R - \frac{j}{\omega C}\right)$$

$$Z = \frac{j\omega L \cdot \left(R - \dfrac{j}{\omega C}\right)}{j\omega L + R - \dfrac{j}{\omega C}}$$

If at a given frequency ω,

$$\omega L = \frac{2}{\omega C}$$

Then,

$$Z = \frac{j\left(\frac{2}{\omega C}\right)\left(R - \frac{j}{\omega C}\right)}{R + \frac{2j}{\omega C} - \frac{j}{\omega C}}$$

$$Z = \frac{2}{\omega C} \angle 90° - 2\tan^{-1}\left(\frac{1}{\omega RC}\right)$$

As R is varied then the impedance magnitude $\left(\frac{2}{\omega C}\right)$ is constant but phase angle varies from $+30°$ at $R = \infty$ to $-90°$ at $R = 0$.

2.6.7 Applications of Parallel RCL Circuit

1. Parallel RLC circuit or an antiresonant circuit is used to achieve impedance transformation.

Impedance transformation is necessary to match the resistances of the generator and load in all the applications for the maximum power transfer. To mention a few applications, where impedance transform is required are radio transmitters and common emitter amplifier.

When a radio transmitter having output impedance of the order of few kilo ohms is coupled with an antenna having very small resistance (75 Ω – typical value) there is a mismatch, hence maximum power cannot be transferred.

Parallel resonant circuit offer a purely resistive impedance at antiresonance. At antiresonance

$$Z_{ar} = \frac{L}{CR_L}$$

R_L is negligible

$$Z_{ar} = \frac{L}{C}$$

∴ Thus, Z_{ar} depends on ratio $\frac{L}{C}$, so by varying the ratio $\frac{L}{C}$, the value of Z_{ar} can be varied.

2. Currents through the inductor and a capacitor are Q times the supplied current at antiresonance

$$I_L = Q I$$
$$I_C = Q I$$

Antiresonant circuit can be used as current amplifier.

2.6.8 Summary of Parallel Resonant Circuit

The characteristics of a parallel resonance are given as:
1. At antiresonance, the input impedance is maximum or the input admittance is minimum.
2. An antiresonance, circuit is purely resistive and hence the power factor is unity. Current is minimum at f_{ar}
3. The circuit is capacitive for frequencies above f_{ar}, (i.e. $f > f_{ar}$). It is inductive for frequency below f_{ar} (i.e. $f < f_{ar}$).

4. At antiresonance, parallel RLC circuit acts as a current amplifier where $I_L = QI$ and $I_C = QI$.
5. Quality factor is given as:
$$Q = \frac{R}{\omega_{ar} L} = \omega_{ar} CR$$
6. The resonant frequency is given
$$f_{ar} = \frac{1}{2\pi}\sqrt{\frac{1}{LC} - \frac{R^2}{L^2}} = f_r \sqrt{\frac{1-1}{Q^2}}$$
Antiresonance is possible when $\frac{1}{LC} > \frac{R^2}{L^2}$.
7. Rg, generator resistance must be very high for high selectivity in the parallel RLC circuit.
8. Bandwidth $= \frac{f_{ar}}{a}\left[1 + \frac{Z_{ar}}{Rg}\right]$. $f_{ar} = \sqrt{f_1 f_2}$
9. $f_{ar} = \sqrt{f_1 f_2}$ above f_1 and f_2 are half power frequencies and f_{ar} is geometric mean of f_1 and f_2.

2.6.9 Important Formulae

	Parallel RLC Circuit
1. Diagram	Fig.
2. Resonating frequency	$f_{ar} = \frac{1}{2\pi}\sqrt{\frac{1}{LC} - \frac{R^2}{L^2}}$ $f_{ar} = f_r\sqrt{1 - \frac{1}{Q^2}}$
3. Quality factor	$Q = \frac{\omega_{ar} L}{C}$ $Q = \frac{1}{\omega_{ar} CR}$
4. Reactancy type	Above f_{ar} : Capacitive At f_{ar} : Resistive Below f_{ar} : Inductive

5. Impedance	$Z_{ar} = \dfrac{L}{CR_L}$
	$= R(1 + Q^2)$ ... at F_{ar}
	$Z = \dfrac{Z_{ar}}{1 + j2\delta Q}$ ...near f_{ar}
6. Voltage or current at resonance	$I_C = Q \cdot I$ $I_L = Q \cdot I$
7. Bandwidth	$BW = \dfrac{f_{ar}}{Q}\left[1 + \dfrac{R_{ar}}{R_g}\right]$ $R_{ar} = Z_{ar}$

2.7 NUMERICALS ON PARALLEL RESONANT CIRCUITS

Ex. 2.15: Find the bandwidth of the antiresonant circuit with the following conditions:

(i) Q of the circuits inductive branch is 100.

(ii) Frequency of unity power factors is 1 MHz.

(iii) Value of inductance = 100 µH.

(iv) Internal resistance of generator is 10 kΩ.

Sol.: Given: Q of inductive branch = 100, f_r = 1 MHz, L = 100 µH, R_g = 10 kΩ.

To calculate: BW =

To calculate bandwidth

$$BW = \dfrac{f_{ar}}{Q}\left[1 + \dfrac{Z_{ar}}{R_g}\right]$$

$$= f_{ar}\left[1 + \dfrac{1}{CR_L \cdot R_g}\right]$$

Let us calculate BW. We need to calculate C, R_L.

(i) To calculate capacitance value:

$$f_{ar} = \dfrac{1}{2\pi\sqrt{LC}}\sqrt{1 - \dfrac{1}{Q^2}}$$

$$1 \times 10^6 = \dfrac{1}{2\pi\sqrt{100 \times 10^{-6}}\sqrt{C}}\sqrt{1 - \dfrac{1}{100^2}}$$

$$C = \dfrac{1}{(2\pi)^2(100 \times 10^{-6})(1 \times 10^6)^2}\sqrt{1 - \dfrac{1}{100^2}}$$

$$\boxed{C = 0.2533 \text{ nF}}$$

(ii) To calculate value of R_L:

$$Q = \frac{\omega_r L}{R}$$

$$\therefore \quad 100 = \frac{2 \times \pi \times 1 \times 10^6 \times 100 \times 10^{-6}}{R}$$

$$\boxed{R = 6.2831 \ \Omega}$$

(iii) To calculate Z_{ar}:

$$Z_{ar} = \frac{L}{CR_L} = \frac{100 \times 10^{-6}}{0.2533 \times 10^{-9} \times 6.2831} = 62.833 \ k\Omega$$

$$\boxed{Z_{ar} = 62.833 \ k\Omega}$$

(iv) To calculate bandwidth:

$$BW = \frac{f_{ar}}{Q}\left[1 + \frac{Z_{ar}}{R_g}\right]$$

$$BW = \frac{1 \times 10^6}{100}\left[1 + \frac{62.833 \times 10^3}{10 \times 10^3}\right]$$

$$\boxed{BW = 72.833 \ kHz}$$

Ans.:

$$\boxed{BW = 72.833 \ kHz}$$

In this example, Z_{ar} can alternatively be calculated using $Z_{ar} = R_L (1 + Q^2) = 6.2831 \ (1 + 100^2) = 62.83 \ k\Omega$. So no need to calculate value of C.

Ex. 2.16: For a parallel resonant circuit:
(i) Specify the value of the circuit capacitor.
(ii) Calculate the resistance of the circuit at parallel resonance.
(iii) What is the absolute bandwidth of the resonant circuit?
(iv) What is the bandwidth of the circuit when it is matched with the generator impedance?

Assume Q = 75, L = 120 µH and the resonating frequency of 1 MHz.

Sol.: Given: L = 120 µH, Q = 75, f_{ar} = 1 × 10⁶ Hz.

To calculate: C, R_L, Z_{ar}, BW, BW when $R_g = Z_{ar}$.

(i) To calculate value of capacitor:

$$f_{ar} = \frac{1}{2\pi\sqrt{LC}}\sqrt{1 + \frac{1}{Q^2}}$$

$$1 \times 10^6 = \frac{1}{2\pi\sqrt{120 \times 10^{-6}}\sqrt{C}}\sqrt{1 - \frac{1}{75^2}}$$

$$C = \frac{1}{(2\pi \times 1 \times 10^6)^2 (120 \times 10^{-6})}\left[1 - \frac{1}{75^2}\right]$$

$$\boxed{C = 208.9 \ pF}$$

(ii) Resistance of coil, R_{coil}:

$$Q = \frac{\omega_{ar} L}{R}$$

$$75 = \frac{2 \times \pi \times 1 \times 10^6 \times 120 \times 10^{-6}}{R}$$

$$\boxed{R_L = 10.05 \; \Omega}$$

(iii) The resistance of circuit at resonance:

i.e. Z_{ar} or R_{ar}

$$Z_{ar} = \frac{1}{CR_L}$$

or

$$Z_{ar} = R_L (1 + Q^2)$$

$$Z_{ar} = \frac{120 \times 10^{-6}}{(208.9 \times 10^{-12})(10.05)}$$

$$\boxed{Z_{ar} = 57.157 \; k\Omega}$$

(iv) Absolute bandwidth is given by:

$$BW = \frac{f_{ar}}{Q} = \frac{1 \times 10^6}{75}$$

$$\boxed{BW = 13.33 \; k\Omega}$$

(v) When it is matched condition $R_g = Z_{ar}$:

$\therefore \quad BW = \frac{f_{ar}}{Q}\left[1 + \frac{Z_{ar}}{R_g}\right]$

$\therefore \quad BW = 2\frac{f_{ar}}{Q}$

$\qquad \qquad = 26.66 \; k\Omega$

$$\boxed{BW = 26.66 \; k\Omega}$$

Ans.:

$$\boxed{\begin{aligned} C &= 208.9 \; pF \\ R_L &= 10.05 \; \Omega \\ Z_{ar} &= 57.157 \; k\Omega \\ BW &= 13.33 \; k\Omega \\ BW &= 26.66 \; k\Omega \\ &\text{when matched condition} \end{aligned}}$$

Ex. 2.17: In the circuit shown in Fig. 2.27 the inductance of 0.1 H having Q factor of 5 is in parallel with capacitor. Determine the value of capacitance and coil resistance at resonant frequency of 500 rad/sec.

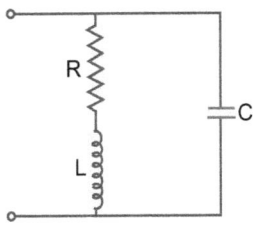

Fig. 2.27

Sol.: Given: f_r = 500 rad/sec., L = 0.1 H, Q = 5.

(i) To calculate R_L:

$$Q = \frac{\omega_{ar} L}{R}$$

$$5 = \frac{500 \times 0.1}{R}$$

$$\boxed{R_L = 10 \, \Omega}$$

(ii) To calculate value of capacitance:

$$f_{ar} = \frac{1}{2\pi} \sqrt{\frac{1}{LC} - \frac{R_L^2}{L^2}}$$

$$\omega_{ar}^2 = \left(\frac{1}{LC} - \frac{R_L^2}{L^2}\right)$$

$$500^2 = \frac{1}{(0.1) C} - \frac{10^2}{(0.1)^2}$$

$$\frac{1}{0.1 \, C} = 250000 + 10000$$

$$C = 38.46 \times 10^{-6} \, F$$

$$\boxed{C = 38.46 \, \mu F}$$

Ans.:

$$\boxed{\begin{array}{l} R_L = 10 \, \Omega \\ C = 38.46 \, \mu F \end{array}}$$

Ex. 2.18: A parallel resonant circuit has a coil of 150 µH with Q of 60 and resonated at 1 MHz.
  (i) Specify the value of required capacitor.
  (ii) What is the circuit impedance at resonance?
  (iii) What is the resistance of inductor?
  (iv) If Q is reduced to 4 by adding additional series resistance, then how much resistance is needed?

Sol.: Given: L = 150 μH, Q = 60, f_{ar} = 1 MHz.

To calculate C, R_L, Z_{ar}, New Q, New f_{ar}.

(i) The value of capacitance:

$$f_{ar} = \frac{1}{2\pi\sqrt{LC}}\sqrt{1 - \frac{1}{Q^2}}$$

$$1 \times 10^6 = \frac{1}{2\pi\sqrt{150 \times 10^{-6}}\sqrt{C}}\sqrt{1 - \frac{1}{60^2}}$$

$$C = \frac{1}{(2\pi \times 1 \times 10^6)^2 \cdot (150 \times 10^{-6})}\left[1 - \frac{1}{3600}\right]$$

$$C = 168.821 \times 10^{-12} \text{ F}$$

$$\boxed{C = 168.82 \text{ pF}}$$

(ii) The resistance of coil:

$$Q = \frac{\omega_{ar} L}{R_L}$$

$$60 = \frac{2\pi \times 1 \times 10^6 \times 150 \times 10^{-6}}{R_L}$$

$$\boxed{R_L = 15.7 \ \Omega}$$

(iii) The impedance of the parallel circuit:

$$Z_{ar} = \frac{L}{C R_L} = \frac{150 \times 10^{-6}}{168.82 \times 10^{-12} \times 15.7}$$

$$\boxed{Z_{ar} = 56.593 \text{ k}\Omega}$$

(iv) New quality factor can be expressed in terms of additional resistance:

$$Q' = \frac{\omega'_{ar} L}{(R_L + R')}$$

We will thus, need to calculate ω'_{ar}.

∴

$$f'_{ar} = \frac{1}{2\pi\sqrt{LC}}\sqrt{1 - \frac{1}{Q^2}}$$

$$f'_{ar} = \frac{1}{2\pi\sqrt{150 \times 10^{-6} \times 168.82 \times 10^{-12}}}\sqrt{1 - \frac{1}{4^2}}$$

$$\boxed{f'_{ar} = 968.385 \text{ kHz}}$$

∴

$$Q' = \frac{\omega'_{ar} L}{(R_L + R')}$$

where R' is the additional resistance to be added.

$$(R_L + R') = \frac{2\pi f'_{ar} L}{Q'}$$

$$(15.7 + R') = \frac{2\pi \times 968.385 \times 10^3}{4}$$

$$\boxed{R' = 212.417 \, \Omega}$$

Ans.:

C = 168.82 pF
R_L = 15.7 Ω
Z_{ar} = 56.593 kΩ
R' = 212.47 Ω

Ex. 2.19: Two impedances $Z_1 = 20 + 10j$ and $Z_2 = 10 - 30j$ are connected in parallel and this combination is connected in series with $Z_3 = 30 + Xj$. Find the value of X which will produce resonance.

Sol.:

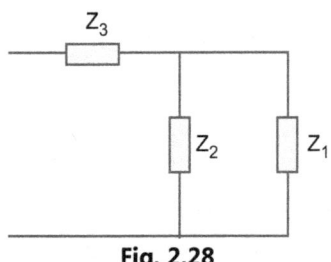

Fig. 2.28

Given:
$Z_1 = 20 + 10j$
$Z_2 = 10 - 30j$
$Z_3 = 30 + Xj$

To calculate X:
(i) To find the total impedance:

$$Z_T = Z_3 + (Z_1 \| Z_2) = Z_3 + \frac{Z_1 Z_2}{Z_1 + Z_2}$$

$$Z = Z_3 + \frac{Z_1 Z_2}{Z_1 + Z_2}$$

$$Z = (30 + jX) + \frac{(20 + j10)(10 - j30)}{(20 + j10) + (10 - j30)}$$

$$Z = 30 + jX + \frac{200 + j100 + j600 + 300}{30 - j20}$$

$$Z = 30 + jX + \frac{500 - j500}{30 - j20}$$

$$Z = 30 + jX + \frac{[500(1-j)][30+j20]}{30^2 + 20^2}$$

$$Z = 30 + jX + \frac{500}{1300}[30 + j20 - 30j + 20]$$

$$Z = 30 + jX + \frac{5}{13}[50 - j10]$$

$$Z = 30 + \frac{250}{13} + j\left[X - \frac{50}{13}\right]$$

To circuit will resonate, if imaginary part is zero.

$$\therefore \quad X - \frac{50}{13} = 0$$

$$X = \frac{50}{13}$$

$$\boxed{X = 3.846 \, \Omega}$$

Ans.:

$$X = 3.846 \, \Omega$$

Ex. 2.20: From the basics obtain the expression for the resonance frequency in the circuit shown in Fig. 2.29.

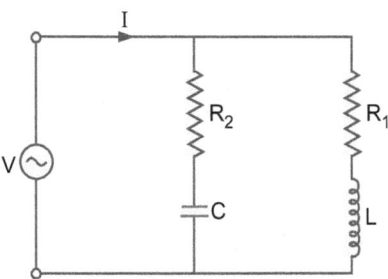

Fig. 2.29

Sol.: The two branches connected in parallel will produce resonance when the resultant current through combination i.e. I, is in phase with voltage V. The condition of parallel resonance is that the impedance of the parallel combination is purely resistive.

The admittance of branch containing:

L is:

$$Y_L = \frac{1}{R_1 + j\omega L}$$

$$= \frac{R_1 - j\omega L}{(R_1 + j\omega L)(R_1 - j\omega L)}$$

$$Y_L = \frac{R_1 - jX_l}{R_1^2 + X_L^2}$$

where, $\quad X_L = \omega L$

The admittance of branch containing C is

$$Y_C = \frac{1}{R_2 - \frac{j}{\omega C}} = \frac{R_2 + jX_C}{R_2^2 + X_C^2}$$

Total admittance Y is given by

$$Y = Y_L + Y_C$$

$$Y = \frac{R_1 + jX_C}{R_1^2 + X_L^2} + \frac{R_2 + jX_C}{R_2^2 + X_C^2}$$

$$Y = \left(\frac{R_1}{R_1^2 + X_L^2} + \frac{R_2}{R_2^2 + X_C^2}\right) + \left(\frac{X_C}{R_2^2 + X_C^2} - \frac{X_L}{R_1^2 + X_L^2}\right)$$

At resonance, we have unity power factor is zero condition

$$\therefore \quad \frac{X_C}{R_2^2 + X_C^2} - \frac{X_L}{R_1^2 + X_L^2} = 0$$

$$\frac{X_C}{R_2^2 + X_C^2} = \frac{X_L}{R_1^2 + X_L^2}$$

$$\frac{\frac{1}{\omega_{ar} C}}{R_2^2 + \left(\frac{1}{\omega_{ar} C}\right)^2} = \frac{\omega_{ar} L}{R_1^2 + \omega_{ar}^2 L^2}$$

$$\therefore \quad R_1^2 + \omega_{ar}^2 L^2 = \omega_{ar}^2 LC \left(R_2^2 + \frac{1}{\omega_{ar}^2 C^2}\right)$$

$$R_1^2 + \omega_{ar}^2 L^2 = \omega_{ar}^2 LC R_2^2 + \frac{L}{C}$$

$$\omega_{ar}^2 (L^2 - LC R_2^2) = \frac{L}{C} - R_1^2$$

$$(LC) \omega_{ar}^2 = \frac{\frac{L}{C} + R_1^2}{\frac{L}{C} - R_2^2}$$

$$\boxed{\omega_{ar} = \frac{1}{\sqrt{LC}} \left[\sqrt{\frac{R_1^2 - \frac{L}{C}}{R_2^2 - \frac{L}{C}}}\right]}$$

$$\boxed{f_{ar} = \frac{1}{2\pi\sqrt{LC}} \sqrt{\frac{R_1^2 - \frac{L}{C}}{R_2^2 - \frac{L}{C}}}}$$

where, f_{ar} : Antiresonating frequency
R_1 : Ohmic resistance of coil
R_2 : Leakage and dielectric loss resistance of capacitor

Ex. 2.21: In the circuit of Fig. 2.30 calculate resonant frequency (ω_{ar}). If R_1 is increased what is the maximum value of R_1 for which there is a resonant frequency?

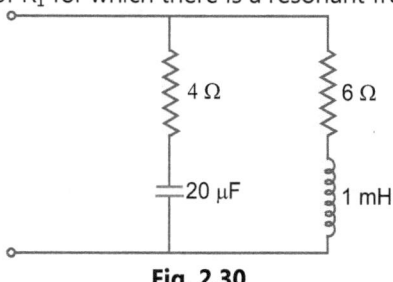

Fig. 2.30

Sol.: $R_2 = R_L = 6\,\Omega$, $R_1 = R_C = 4\,\Omega$, $L = 1$ mH, $C = 20$ μF.
To calculate: ω_{ar} and maximum value of R_L

(i) To calculate ω_{ar}:

In case when resistance is present in both the branches:

$$\omega_{ar} = \frac{1}{\sqrt{LC}} \sqrt{\frac{R_L^2 - \frac{L}{C}}{R_C^2 - \frac{L}{C}}} = \frac{1}{\sqrt{1 \times 10^{-3} \times 20 \times 10^{-6}}} \sqrt{\frac{6^2 - \frac{1 \times 10^{-3}}{20 \times 10^{-6}}}{4^2 - \frac{1 \times 10^{-3}}{20 \times 10^{-6}}}}$$

$$= \frac{1}{\sqrt{20 \times 10^{-9}}} \sqrt{\frac{36 - 50}{16 - 50}}$$

$$\boxed{\omega_{ar} = 2911.62 \text{ rad/sec.}}$$

(ii) To calculate $R_{1\,(max)}$ i.e. R_C maximum:

$$\omega_{ar} = \frac{1}{\sqrt{LC}} \sqrt{\frac{R_L^2 - \frac{L}{C}}{R_C^2 - \frac{L}{C}}}$$

So if $R_C^2 = \frac{L}{C}$, then denominator = 0 and $\omega_{ar} = \infty$

Therefore, maximum value should be selected as follows:

$$R_C = R_1 = \sqrt{\frac{L}{C}}$$

$$R_C = R_1 = \sqrt{\frac{10^{-3}}{20 \times 10^{-6}}}$$

$$R_C = \sqrt{50}$$

$$R_C = 7.071\,\Omega$$

At this value of R_C, $f_{ar} = \infty$.

∴ Maximum value of R_C must be less than 7

∴ $\boxed{R_{C\,(max)} < 7}$

Ans.:

$$\omega_{ar} = 2911.62 \text{ rad/sec.}$$
$$\text{Maximum value } R_C = 7\,\Omega$$

Ex. 2.22: Find exact resonant frequency of the network shown in Fig. 2.31. Also find 'Q_0' at that frequency.

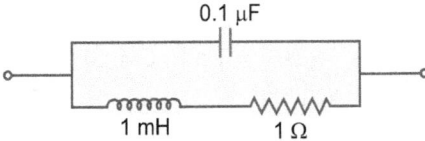

Fig. 2.31

Sol.: Given: C = 0.1 µF, L = 1 mH, R = 10 Ω. To calculate f_{ar}, Q.

(i) **To calculate f_{ar}:**

$$f_{ar} = \frac{1}{2\pi}\sqrt{\frac{1}{LC} - \frac{R^2 L}{L^2}}$$

$$= \frac{1}{2\pi}\sqrt{\frac{1}{1\times 10^{-3} \times 0.1 \times 10^{-6}} - \frac{10\times 10\times 1\times 10^{-3}}{(1\times 10^{-3})^2}}$$

$$\boxed{f_{ar} = 15.835 \text{ kHz}}$$

(ii) **To calculate Q:**

$$Q = \frac{\omega_{ar} L}{R}$$

$$Q = \frac{2\times\pi\times 15.83\times 10^3 \times 1\times 10^{-3}}{10}$$

$$Q = 9.95$$

$$\boxed{Q \approx 10}$$

Ans.:

$$f_{ar} = 15.83 \text{ kHz}$$
$$Q = 10$$

Ex. 2.23: Find 'R_L' for resonance circuit of Fig. 2.32. Comment on R_L obtained.

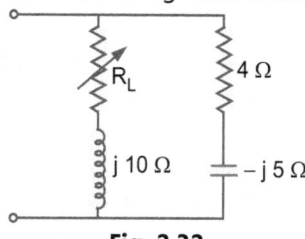

Fig. 2.32

Sol.: For the resonance, the susceptance in admittance must be zero.

$$Y = \frac{1}{R + j10} + \frac{1}{4 - j5}$$

$$Y = \frac{R - j10}{R^2 + 100} + \frac{4 + j5}{(4)^2 + 5^2}$$

$$Y = \frac{R - j10}{R^2 + 100} + \frac{4 + j5}{41}$$

$$Y = \left[\frac{R}{R^2 + 100} + \frac{4}{41}\right] + j\left[\frac{5}{41} - \frac{10}{R^2 + 100}\right]$$

Susceptance part must be zero.

$$\frac{5}{41} - \frac{10}{R^2 + 100} = 0$$

$$\frac{5}{41} = \frac{10}{R^2 + 100}$$

$$5R^2 + 500 = 410$$

$$R^2 = -\frac{90}{5} = -18$$

Ans.:

$$\boxed{R = \sqrt{18}\ \Omega}$$

Thus, for resonance, value of R is negative i.e. R is imaginary. This clearly shows that in the circuit, resonance is impossible for positive values of R.

Ex. 2.24: Find the value of 'L' for which the circuit in Fig. 2.33 is resonant at a frequency of $\omega_0 = 1000$ rad/sec.

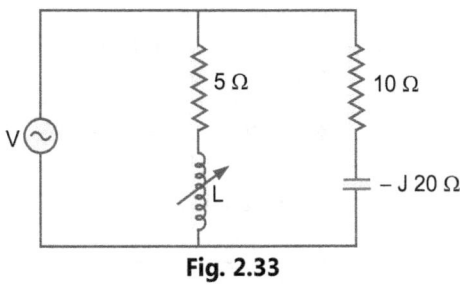

Fig. 2.33

Sol.: Given: $R_L = 5$, $R_C = 10$, $C = -j20\ \Omega$.

To calculate:

Let the reactance offered by the inductance is jX_L. Then the total admittance of parallel resonant circuit looking from source side is given by

$$Y_T = Y_L + Y_C$$

$$Y_T = \frac{1}{5 + jX_L} + \frac{1}{10 - j20}$$

$$Y_T = \frac{5 - jX_L}{5^2 + X_L^2} + \frac{10 + j20}{10^2 + 20^2}$$

$$Y_T = \frac{5}{25 + X_L^2} - \frac{jX_L}{25 + X_L^2} + \frac{10}{500} + \frac{j20}{500}$$

$$Y_T = \left[\frac{5}{25 + X_L^2} + \frac{10}{500}\right] + j\left[\frac{20}{500} - \frac{X_L}{25 + X_L^2}\right]$$

To have resonance, the imaginary term must be zero. Hence, to obtain the condition of resonance, equate susceptance to zero.

$$\frac{20}{500} - \frac{X_L}{25 + X_L^2} = 0$$

$$\frac{X_L}{25 + X_L^2} = \frac{1}{25}$$

$$X_L^2 - 25 X_L + 25 = 0$$

Solving quadratic equation for X_L,

$$X_L = \frac{+25 \pm \sqrt{25^2 - 4 \times 25 \times 1}}{2}$$

$$X_L = \frac{25 \pm \sqrt{0.525}}{2}$$

$$X_L = \frac{25 \pm 22.9128}{2}$$

$$X_L = 23.9564\ \Omega$$

or $\quad X_L = 1.0436$

But $\quad X_L = \omega L$

∴ $\quad \omega L = 23.9564\ \Omega$ or 1.0436

$\quad \omega = 1000$ rad/sec.

∴ $\boxed{L = 23.9564\ \text{mH or } 1.0436\ \text{mH}}$

Ans.:

$$\boxed{\text{Value of } L = 23.9564\ \text{mH or } 1.0436\ \text{mH}}$$

Ex. 2.25: A parallel resonant circuit has fixed 'C' and variable 'L'. The 'Q' of inductor is 5 and it is constant. Find the value of L and C for a circuit independence of 100 + j0 at f = 1.5 MHz. What is the bandwidth?

Sol.: Given: Q = 5, f_{ar} = 1.5 MHz, Z_{ar} = 100 + j0.

To calculate L, C, BW.

(i) To calculate R_L:

$$Z_{ar} = R(1 + Q^2) = R_Q^2$$
$$100 = R_L \cdot 25$$
$$\boxed{R_L = 4\,\Omega}$$

(ii) To calculate L:

$$Q = \frac{\omega_{ar} L}{R}$$
$$5 = \frac{2 \times \pi \times f_{ar} \times L}{4}$$
$$L = \frac{20}{2 \times \pi \times 1.5 \times 10^6}$$
$$\boxed{L = 2.122\ \mu H}$$

(iii) To calculate C:

$$f_{ar} = \frac{1}{2\pi\sqrt{LC}} \sqrt{1 - \frac{1}{Q^2}}$$
$$1.5 \times 10^6 = \frac{1}{2\pi\sqrt{2.122 \times 10^{-6} \times C}} \sqrt{1 - \frac{1}{5^2}}$$
$$\boxed{C = 5.0931\ nF}$$

(iv) To calculate BW:

$$BW = \frac{f_{ar}}{Q} = \frac{1.5 \times 10^6}{5}$$
$$\boxed{BW = 300\ kHz}$$

Ans.:

$$\begin{aligned} R_L &= 4\,\Omega \\ L &= 2.122\ \mu H \\ C &= 5.0931\ nF \\ BW &= 300\ kHz \end{aligned}$$

Ex. 2.26: A parallel resonant circuit has coil of 100 mH with Q = 50. It is resonant at 0.7 MHz.

Find:
(i) Value of capacitor
(ii) Resistance in series with coil.
(iii) Circuit impedance at resonance.

Sol.: Given: L = 100 mH, Q = 50, f_{ar} = 0.7 MHz.

To calculate: C =?, R_S =?, Z_{ar} =?

(i) To calculate the capacitor value:

$$f_{ar} = \frac{1}{2\pi\sqrt{LC}} \sqrt{1 - \frac{1}{Q^2}}$$

$$0.7 \times 10^6 = \frac{1}{2\pi\sqrt{100 \times 10^{-3} \times C}} \sqrt{1 - \frac{1}{50^2}}$$

$$C = 5.1684 \times 10^{-13} \text{ F}$$

$$\boxed{C = 0.5168 \text{ pF}}$$

(ii) To calculate R_L:

$$Q = \frac{\omega_{ar} L}{R}$$

$$50 = \frac{2 \times \pi \times 0.7 \times 10^6 \times 100 \times 10^{-3}}{R}$$

$$\boxed{R = 8.796 \text{ k}\Omega}$$

(iii) Circuit impedance at resonance:

$$Z_{ar} = \frac{L}{CR_L} = \frac{100 \times 10^{-3}}{0.5168 \times 10^{-12} \times 8.796 \times 10^3}$$

$$\boxed{Z_{ar} = 21.998 \text{ M}\Omega}$$

Ans.:

$$\boxed{\begin{array}{rcl} C &=& 0.5168 \text{ pF} \\ r &=& 8.796 \text{ k}\Omega \\ Z_{ar} &=& 21.99 \text{ M}\Omega \end{array}}$$

Ex. 2.27: A parallel resonant circuit has fixed 'C' and variable 'L'. The Q of inductor is 4 and constant. Find the values of 'L' and 'C' of a circuit impedance of 1000 + j0.0 at f_{ar} = 2.4 MHz. What is the bandwidth?

Sol.: Given: Q = 4, Z_{ar} = 1000 + j0 Ω, f_{ar} = 2.4 MHz.
To calculate: BW, L, C.

(i) To calculate value of L:

$$Z_{ar} = R_L(1 + Q^2)$$
$$1000 = R_L(1 + 4^2)$$
$$R_L = \frac{1000}{17} = 58.82\,\Omega$$

Now, Z_{ar} can also be expressed as

$$Z_{ar} = \frac{L}{CR_L}$$
$$1000 = \frac{L}{C \times 58.82}$$
$$\boxed{\frac{L}{C} = 58.82 \times 10^3} \quad \ldots(1)$$

Resonating frequency,

$$f_{ar} = \frac{1}{2\pi LC}\sqrt{1 - \frac{1}{Q^2}}$$
$$2.4 \times 10^6 = \frac{1}{2\pi LC}\sqrt{1 - \frac{1}{16}}$$
$$LC = \frac{15}{4 \times \pi \times 2.4 \times 10^6 \times (2.4 \times 10^6)^2}$$
$$\boxed{LC = 4.1227 \times 10^{-15}} \quad \ldots(2)$$

Using (1) and (2)

$$L\left(\frac{L}{58.82 \times 10^3}\right) = 4.1227 \times 10^{-15}$$
$$L^2 = 2.425 \times 10^{-10}$$
$$\boxed{L = 15.57\,\mu H}$$

(ii) To calculate value of C:

$$LC = 4.1227 \times 10^{-15}$$
$$C = \frac{4.1227 \times 10^{-15}}{L}$$
$$\boxed{C = 0.264\,nF}$$

(iii) To calculate the bandwidth:

$$\Delta f = \frac{f_{ar}}{Q}$$
$$= \frac{2.4 \times 10^6}{4}$$
$$\Delta f = 0.6 \times 10^6\,Hz$$
$$\boxed{BW = 0.6\,MHz}$$

Ans.:

$$L = 15.57 \, \mu H$$
$$C = 0.264 \, nF$$
$$\Delta F = 0.6 \, MHz$$

Ex. 2.28: Find exact resonant frequency in the network shown. Also find Z_{in} at that frequency.

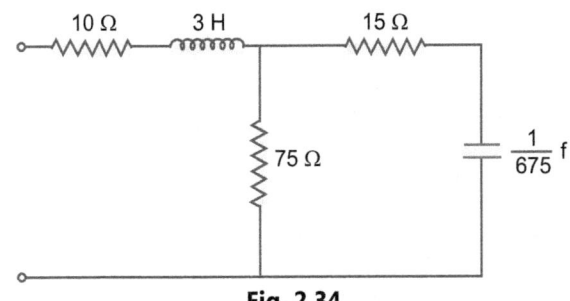

Fig. 2.34

Sol.: Given:
$$Z_1 = 75 \, \Omega$$
$$Z_2 = 15 - \frac{j\omega}{\frac{1}{625}}$$
$$Z_3 = 10 + j3\omega \quad \therefore X_L = \omega L = 3\omega$$

Total impedance can be written as:

$$Z = Z_3 + (Z_1 \| Z_2) = Z_3 + \frac{Z_1 Z_2}{Z_1 + Z_2}$$

$$= (10 + j3\omega) + \frac{75 \times \left(15 - j\frac{625}{\omega}\right)}{75 + \left(15 - j\frac{625}{\omega}\right)}$$

$$= (10 + j3\omega) + \frac{1125\,\omega - j\,50625}{90\,\omega - j\,625}$$

$$= (10 + j3\omega) + \frac{75\,\omega - 3375\,j}{6\omega - 45\,j}$$

$$= 10 + j3\omega + \left(\frac{75\,\omega - j3375}{6\omega - j45}\right)\left(\frac{6\omega + j45}{6\omega + j45}\right)$$

$$= 10 + j3\omega + \frac{450\,\omega - 1425\,j\omega + 15.1875}{\omega^2 6^2 + 45^2}$$

$$Z = \frac{360\,\omega^2 + 20250 + 108\,j\omega^3 + 450\,\omega - 14625\,j\omega + 151875}{36\,\omega^2 + 2025}$$

$$Z = \frac{360\,\omega^2 + 20250 + 450\,\omega + 151875}{36\,\omega^2 + 2025} + j\left(\frac{108\,\omega^3 - 14625\,\omega}{36\,\omega^2 + 2025}\right)$$

At resonating frequency, imaginary part is zero

$$\frac{108\omega^3 - 14625\omega}{36\omega^2 + 2025} = 0$$

$$108\omega^2 = 14625\omega$$
$$108\omega^2 = 14625$$
$$\omega^2 = 135.4$$
$$\omega = 11.6 \text{ Hz}$$

$$\boxed{f_{ar} = 1.8 \text{ Hz}}$$

At antiresonance, imaginary part is zero.

$$Z_{in} = \frac{360\omega^2 + 20250 + 450(\omega) + 151875}{36\omega^2 + 2025}$$

Substituting $\omega = 11.6$

$Z_{in} = 32.86 \; \Omega$

Ans.:

$$f_{ar} = 1.8 \text{ Hz}$$
$$Z_{in} = 34.86 \; \Omega$$

2.8 COMPARISON OF SERIES AND PARALLEL RESONATING CIRCUITS

	Series Resonating	Parallel Resonant
1.	Fig. (a)	Fig. (b)
2.	In series resonating circuit, resonance is possible at all values of R.	In parallel, resonating is possible only when $\frac{1}{LC} > \frac{R^2}{L^2}$.
3.	Series resonating circuit acts as a voltage amplified at f_r.	Parallel resonating circuit acts a current amplifier at f_{ar}.
4.	R_g must be for high selectivity.	R_g must be high for high selectivity.
5.	At $f > f_r$ – Circuit is inductive $f = f_r$ – Resistive $f < f_r$ – Capacitive	$f > f_{ar}$ – circuit is capacitive $f = f_{ar}$ – resistive $f < f_r$ – inductive
6.	At f_r: Impedance is minimum. Admittance is maximum. Current is maximum.	5. At f_{ar}: Impedance is maximum. Admittance is minimum. Current is minimum.

Important Formulae in Series and Parallel Resonating Circuit

		Series RLC Circuit	Parallel RLC Circuit
1.	Diagram	*Fig.* (Series RLC: V source with R, L, C in series)	*Fig.* (Parallel RLC: V source with R, L in one branch and C in parallel)
2.	Resonating frequency	$f_o = \dfrac{1}{2\pi\sqrt{LC}}$	$f_{ar} = \dfrac{1}{2\pi}\sqrt{\dfrac{1}{LC} - \dfrac{R^2}{L^2}}$ $f_{ar} = f_o\sqrt{1 - \dfrac{1}{Q^2}}$
3.	Quality factor	$Q = \dfrac{\omega_r L}{C} = \dfrac{1}{\omega_r RC}$ $Q = \dfrac{1}{R}\sqrt{\dfrac{L}{C}}$	$Q = \dfrac{\omega_{ar} L}{C}$ $Q = \dfrac{1}{\omega_{ar} CR}$
4.	Reactancy type	Above f_o : Inductive At f_o : Resistive Below f_o : Capacitive	Above f_{ar} : Capacitive At f_{ar} : Resistive Below f_{ar} : Inductive
5.	Impedance	$Z_r = R$ at resonance $Z = R[1 + jQ\delta(2-\delta)]$ ... Near f_r $\delta = \dfrac{f - f_r}{f_r}$	$Z_{ar} = \dfrac{L}{CR_L}$ $= R(1 + Q^2)$ ... at F_{ar} $Z = \dfrac{Z_{ar}}{1 + j2\delta Q}$ ...near f_{ar}
6.	Voltage or current at resonance	$V_L = Q \cdot V$ $V_L = Q \cdot V$	$I_C = Q \cdot I$ $I_L = Q \cdot I$
7.	Frequencies of maximum voltage (V_L and V_C)	$f_L = \dfrac{f_r}{\sqrt{1 - \dfrac{R^2 C}{2L}}}$ $f_L > f_o$ $f_C = f_o\sqrt{1 - \dfrac{R^2 C}{2L}}$ $f_C < f_o$	
8.	Bandwidth	$BW = \dfrac{R}{2\pi L} = \dfrac{f_r}{Q}$ $BW\ \text{match} = \dfrac{2 f_r}{Q}$	$BW = \dfrac{f_{ar}}{Q}\left[1 + \dfrac{R_{ar}}{R_g}\right]$, $R_{ar} = Z_{ar}$ $BW = \dfrac{f_{ar}}{Q_o}\left[1 + \dfrac{Z_{ar}}{R_g}\right]$

EXERCISE

1. Define and explain the figure of merit (Q) of an inductor and a capacitor on what factor does Q depend.
2. Draw reactance curve characteristics for series and a parallel resonant circuit illustrating condition of circuit at different frequencies.
3. Series resonant circuit acts a voltage amplifier. Justify.
4. The voltage across L and C at resonance is not the maximum voltage that can appear across it. Justify and derive the expression for frequency at which the voltage across L and C are maximum.
5. Derive the expression for an impedance of a series resonant circuit in terms of Q and δ.
6. Derive the expression for bandwidth of series resonating circuit and prove that resonant frequency is geometric mean of two half power frequencies.
7. Explain the effect of quality factor Q on the selectivity and the bandwidth of a series and a parallel resonating circuit.
8. Explain the effect of the generator resistance R_g on the bandwidth and the selectivity of a series and a parallel resonating circuit.
9. Obtain an expression of the frequency of resonance of a series and a parallel resonating circuit.
10. Parallel resonant circuit is a current amplifier justify.
11. Derive the expression for the bandwidth of an antiresonant circuit.
12. Give important properties and applications of series and parallel resonant circuits.
13. Two impedances $Z_1 = a + Jb$ and $Z_2 = C - Jd$ are connected in
    (a) series
    (b) parallel.

    Determine the condition of resonance in each case.
14. A series RLC circuit consists of a resistance R = 10 Ω, inductance L = 0.2 H and capacitance C = 0.2 μF. Calculate the frequency of resonance. A 10 volts sinusoidal voltage at the frequency of resonance is applied across the circuit. Draw the phasor diagram showing the value of each phasor. Also calculate values (i) current and (ii) voltage across R, C and L and draw the phasor diagram when 10 volt 850 Hz voltage is applied to the circuit.

    Ans.: V_r = 10 V

      V_C = 10^3 V

      V_L = 10^3 V

      I = 76.15 mA

15. A series RLC circuit consists of a resistance R = 20 Ω, inductance L = 0.01 H and capacitance C = 0.04 μF. Calculate the frequency of resonance. If a 10 volts voltage of frequency equal to the frequency of resonance is applied to this circuit, calculate the values of voltages V_C and V_L across C and L respectively. Find the frequencies at which these voltages V_C and V_L are maximum.

Ans.: F_r = 7960 Hz
   V_L = 250 V
   V_C = 250 V
   f_C = 7955 Hz
   f_L = 7960 Hz

16. A coil of R = 10 Ω, L = 0.5 H is connected in series with a capacitor. The current is maximum when f = 50 Hz. A second capacitor is connected in parallel with this circuit. What capacitance must it have so that the combination acts like a non-inductive resistor at 100 Hz. Calculate the total current supplied in each case if the applied voltage is 220 V.

Ans.:   I = 39.55 mA

■■■

Unit III

TWO PORT NETWORK PARAMETER

Contents ...

3.1 Introduction
    3.1.1 Four Terminal Network
    3.1.2 Port
    3.1.3 One Port Network
    3.1.4 Two Port Network
    3.1.5 Multiport Network
3.2 Characterization of Two Port Network
3.3 Open Circuit Impedance or Z-parameter
    3.3.1 Condition for Reciprocity and Symmetry
3.4 Short-Circuit Admittance of Y-parameters
    3.4.1 Condition for Symmetry and Reciprocity
3.5 Transmission or ABCD Parameters
    3.5.1 Condition for Symmetry and Reciprocity
3.6 Hybrid Parameters or h-parameters
    3.6.1 Condition for Symmetry and Reciprocity
3.7 Interrelationships between the Parameters
    3.7.1 Z-parameter in Terms of Other Parameters
    Exercise

3.1 INTRODUCTION

A network containing two pairs of terminals is called as two port network. One of them is input port other one is output port. In total there are 4 variables. Taking two variables as independent and expressing other two variables in terms of these independent variables gives rise to six types of parameters. In this chapter we are going to study only 4 types of parameters viz z-parameter, y-parameter. H-parameter and ABCD parameters in detail. No detailed study is carried out about inverse transmission parameters and g-parameters.

Parameters of a network represents characteristic of that particular network. For example, H-parameters are extensively used to define characteristic of a transistor such as its input impedance, output impedance. Reverse voltage gain, current gain etc. By knowing parameter we can judge suitability of a particular network to some applications. Thus parameters represents electrical characteristic (quality) of a particular network.

In addition to defining various types of parameters, and calculation of parameters of various network, effect on parameters, when various networks are inter-connected is also studied in this chapter. Also characteristic of gyrator, transformer and negative impedance converters is studied.

3.1.1 Four-Terminal Network

Every network has some external terminals. One for entry and other for exit.

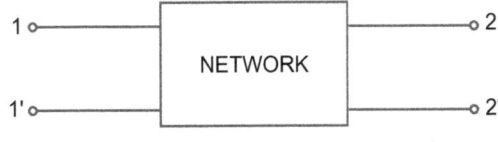

Fig. 3.1

A network having four such terminals is called as four terminal network.

3.1.2 Port

A pair of terminals at which an electrical signal may enter or leave a network is called as a port.

3.1.3 One Port Network

A network having only one pair of terminals is called as one port network.

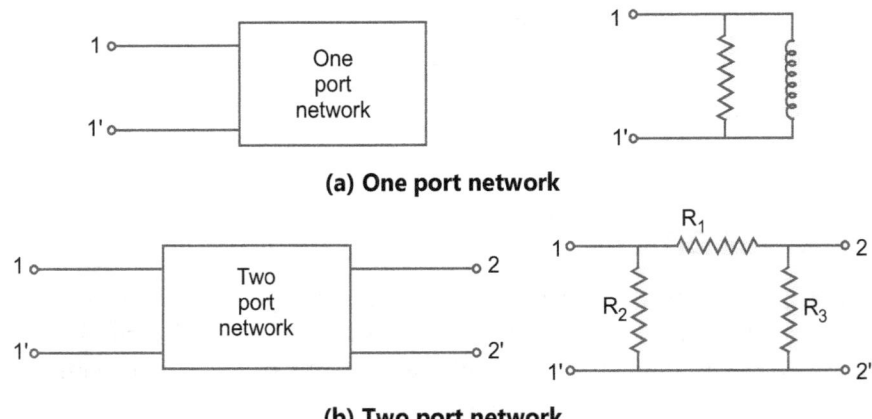

(a) One port network

(b) Two port network

Fig. 3.2

3.1.4 Two Port Network

A network having two pairs of terminals is called as two port network.

By analogy with transmission networks, one of the port (normally the port labelled with 1-1') is called as **input port**. While the other (labelled as 2-2') is called as **output port**.

3.1.5 Multiport Network

A network having multiple such ports is called as multiport network.

e.g.

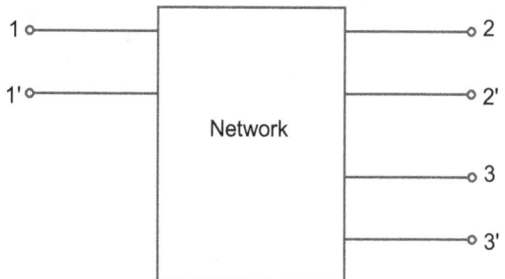

Fig. 3.3: 6-Terminal three port network

3.2 CHARACTERIZATION OF TWO PORT NETWORK

In the two port networks as shown in Fig. 3.4, we see four variables identified - two voltages (V_1 and V_2) and two currents (I_1 and I_2).

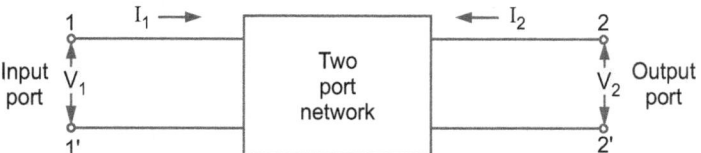

Fig. 3.4: Two port network

Here we assume that -
- There are other voltages and currents that might be identified inside the box. But they are not considered here for analysis.
- The box showing two port network is perfectly **linear** and **time invariant.**
- Only dependent sources may be present inside the box, no independent source is allowed.
- The direction of currents I_1 and I_2 is inside as shown in Fig. 3.4.

Here we assume that the variables V_1 and I_1 at input port and V_2 and I_2 at output port are transformed quantities. In order to describe the relationships among the port voltages and currents, as many linear equations are required as there are ports.

Thus, for a two port network, two linear equations are required among the four variables.

Out of the four variables - two are **independent** variables and remaining two are **dependent** i.e. by specifying any two we can calculate remaining two.

Here there are six possible ways of selecting two independent variables out of four variables.

These six combinations and their different network parameters names are indicated in the Table 3.1.

Table 3.1

Network Parameter	Variable Dependent	Variable Independent	Equation giving dependent variable
Open-circuit impedance (Z)	V_1, V_2	I_1, I_2	$\begin{bmatrix} V_1 \\ V_2 \end{bmatrix} = \begin{bmatrix} Z_{11} & Z_{12} \\ Z_{21} & Z_{22} \end{bmatrix} \begin{bmatrix} I_1 \\ I_2 \end{bmatrix}$
Short-circuit admittance (Y)	I_1, I_2	V_1, V_2	$\begin{bmatrix} I_1 \\ I_2 \end{bmatrix} = \begin{bmatrix} Y_{11} & Y_{12} \\ Y_{21} & Y_{22} \end{bmatrix} \begin{bmatrix} V_1 \\ V_2 \end{bmatrix}$
Transmission parameters (T) (A, B, C, D)	V_1, I_1	V_2, I_2	$\begin{bmatrix} V_1 \\ I_1 \end{bmatrix} = \begin{bmatrix} A & B \\ C & D \end{bmatrix} \begin{bmatrix} V_2 \\ -I_2 \end{bmatrix}$
Hybrid parameter (h)	V_1, I_2	V_2, I_1	$\begin{bmatrix} V_1 \\ I_2 \end{bmatrix} = \begin{bmatrix} h_{11} & h_{12} \\ h_{21} & h_{22} \end{bmatrix} \begin{bmatrix} I_1 \\ V_2 \end{bmatrix}$
Inverse transmission (T') (A', B', C', D')	V_2, I_2	V_1, I_1	$\begin{bmatrix} V_2 \\ I_2 \end{bmatrix} = \begin{bmatrix} A' & B' \\ C' & D' \end{bmatrix} \begin{bmatrix} V_1 \\ -I_1 \end{bmatrix}$
Inverse hybrid (g)	I_1, V_2	V_1, I_2	$\begin{bmatrix} I_1 \\ V_2 \end{bmatrix} = \begin{bmatrix} g_{11} & g_{12} \\ g_{21} & g_{22} \end{bmatrix} \begin{bmatrix} V_1 \\ I_2 \end{bmatrix}$

3.3 OPEN CIRCUIT IMPEDANCE OR Z-PARAMETER

In Z-parameter, voltages V_1 and V_2 are expressed in terms of current of I_1 and I_2.

$$(V_1, V_2) = f(I_1, I_2)$$

$$[V] = [Z][I]$$

$$\begin{bmatrix} V_1 \\ V_2 \end{bmatrix} = \begin{bmatrix} Z_{11} & Z_{12} \\ Z_{21} & Z_{22} \end{bmatrix} \begin{bmatrix} I_1 \\ I_2 \end{bmatrix}$$

∴ Z-parameter equations are

$$\left. \begin{array}{l} V_1 = Z_{11} I_1 + Z_{12} I_2 \\ V_2 = Z_{21} I_1 + Z_{22} I_2 \end{array} \right\} \qquad \ldots (3.1)$$

To calculate the values of Z_{11}, Z_{12}, Z_{21} and Z_{22}, we have to make either $I_1 = 0$ or $I_2 = 0$. Thus we will get,

(i) When $I_2 = 0$, output is open circuited,

$$Z_{11} = \left[\frac{V_1}{I_1}\right]_{I_2 = 0} \quad \ldots (a)$$

$$Z_{21} = \left[\frac{V_2}{I_1}\right]_{I_2 = 0} \quad \ldots (b)$$

(ii) When $I_1 = 0$, input is open circuited,

$$Z_{12} = \left[\frac{V_1}{I_2}\right]_{I_1 = 0} \quad \ldots (c)$$

$$Z_{22} = \left[\frac{V_2}{I_2}\right]_{I_1 = 0} \quad \ldots (d)$$

where, Z_{11} = Open circuit during point impedance
Z_{22} = Open circuit output impedance
Z_{12} = Open circuit forward transfer impedance
Z_{21} = Open circuit reverse transfer impedance

As per the conditions, $I_1 = 0$ or $I_2 = 0$ implies open circuit at port 1 or port 2. These parameters are called as **open-circuit parameters.**

The equivalent circuit for Z-parameters is as shown in Fig. 3.5.

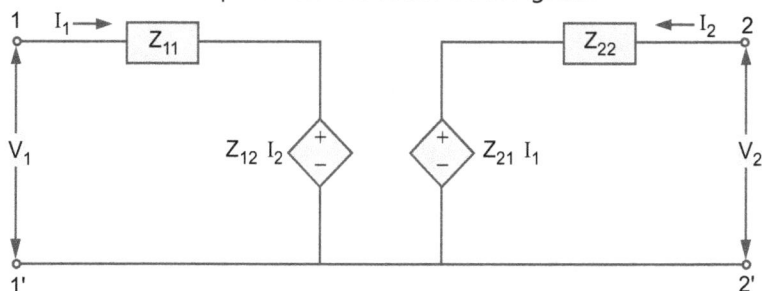

Fig. 3.5: Equivalent two port network in terms of Z-parameters

3.3.1 Condition for Reciprocity and Symmetry

(A) Symmetry condition:

The network is said to be symmetrical if impedance measured from one port with other port open circuit is equal to the impedance measured at other port with first port open circuited.

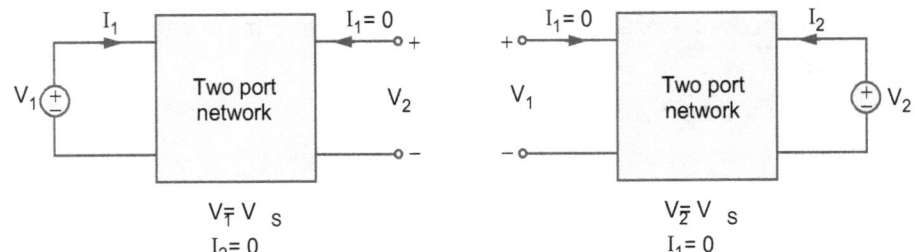

Fig. 3.6

To prove the condition of symmetry, let us consider,

Case I:
$$\left.\begin{array}{c}V_1 = V_s \\ I_2 = 0\end{array}\right\} \quad \ldots (a)$$

From equation (3.1),
$$V_1 = Z_{11} I_1 + Z_{12} I_2$$
$$V_2 = Z_{21} I_1 + Z_{22} I_2$$

Putting equation (a) in equation (3.1),
$$V_s = Z_{11} I_1$$

∴
$$\boxed{Z_{11} = \frac{V_s}{I_1}} \quad \ldots (b)$$

Case II:
$$\left.\begin{array}{c}V_2 = V_s \\ I_1 = 0\end{array}\right\} \quad \ldots (c)$$

Putting equation (c) in equation (3.1),
$$V_s = Z_{22} I_2$$

∴
$$\boxed{Z_{22} = \frac{V_s}{I_2}} \quad \ldots (d)$$

As per symmetry condition,

$$\text{Input impedance} = \text{Output impedance}$$

$$\frac{V_s}{I_1} = \frac{V_s}{I_2}$$

∴
$$\boxed{Z_{11} = Z_{22}} \quad \ldots (3.2)$$

is the condition for symmetry.

(B) Reciprocity Condition:

A network is said to be reciprocal, if the ratio of voltage at one port to the current at other port is same to the ratio, if position of voltage and current are interchanged.

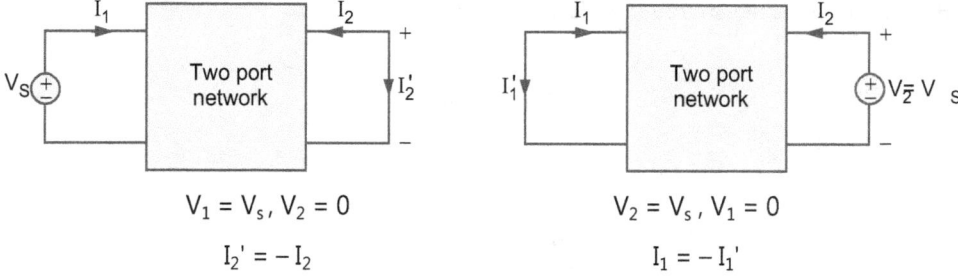

$V_1 = V_s, V_2 = 0$ $V_2 = V_s, V_1 = 0$
$I_2' = -I_2$ $I_1 = -I_1'$

Fig. 3.7

For reciprocal network, $\boxed{\dfrac{V_s}{I_1} = \dfrac{V_s}{I_2}}$ ... (e)

For Z-parameter:

Case I: $V_1 = V_s, V_2 = 0$

$I_2 = -I_2'$

Putting these values in equation (3.1),

$$V_s = Z_{11} I_1 + Z_{12}(-I_2') \quad \ldots (f)$$

and $\quad 0 = Z_{21} I_1 + Z_{22}(-I_2')$

$\therefore \quad Z_{21} I_1 = Z_{22} I_2'$

$\therefore \quad I_1 = \dfrac{Z_{22}}{Z_{21}} \cdot I_2' \quad \ldots (g)$

Putting in equation (f),

$$V_s = Z_{11}\left(\dfrac{Z_{22}}{Z_{21}}\right) I_2' - Z_{12}(I_2')$$

$$V_s = \dfrac{Z_{11} Z_{22}}{Z_{21}} \cdot I_2' - Z_{12} I_2'$$

$$= I_2' \left(\dfrac{Z_{11} Z_{22} - Z_{12} Z_{21}}{Z_{21}}\right)$$

$$\boxed{\dfrac{V_s}{I_2'} = \left(\dfrac{Z_{11} Z_{22} - Z_{12} Z_{21}}{Z_{21}}\right)} \quad \ldots (h)$$

Case II: $\quad V_2 = V_s, V_1 = 0$

$$I_1 = -I_1'$$

Putting these values in equation (3.1),

$$0 = Z_{11}(-I_1') + Z_{12} I_2 \quad \ldots (i)$$
$$V_s = Z_{21}(-I_1') + Z_{22} I_2 \quad \ldots (j)$$

From equation (i),

$$\boxed{I_2 = \frac{Z_{11}}{Z_{12}} \cdot I_1'} \quad \ldots (k)$$

Putting in equation (j),

$$V_s = Z_{21}(-I_1') + Z_{22}\left(\frac{Z_{11}}{Z_{12}}\right) I_1'$$

$$\therefore \quad \boxed{\frac{V_s}{I_1'} = \frac{Z_{11} Z_{22} - Z_{12} Z_{21}}{Z_{12}}} \quad \ldots (l)$$

From reciprocity condition,

$$\frac{V_s}{I_2'} = \frac{V_s}{I_1'}$$

$$\therefore \quad \frac{Z_{11} Z_{22} - Z_{12} Z_{21}}{Z_{21}} = \frac{Z_{11} Z_{22} - Z_{12} Z_{21}}{Z_{12}}$$

$$\therefore \quad \boxed{Z_{21} = Z_{12}} \quad \ldots (3.3)$$

is the condition for reciprocity.

Ex. 3.1: Find the Z-parameters of the network shown in Fig. 3.8 and draw its equivalent circuit.

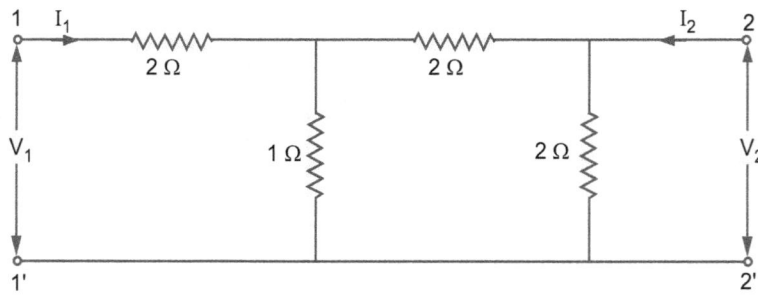

Fig. 3.8 (a)

Sol.: From definitions,

(a) $I_2 = 0$

Output terminals 2 - 2' open circuit.

∴ $Z_{11} = \left[\dfrac{V_1}{I_1}\right]_{I_2 = 0}$ and $Z_{21} = \left[\dfrac{V_2}{I_1}\right]_{I_2 = 0}$

Let us consider that a V_1 volt source is applied as input to 1 - 1'.

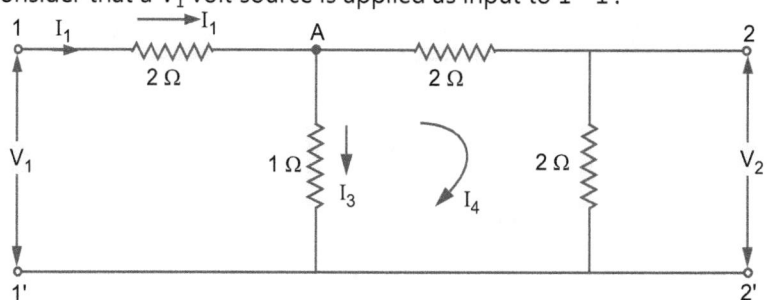

Fig. 3.8 (b)

By applying KCL at point A,

$$I_1 = I_3 + I_4$$

By current divider rule,

$$I_4 = \left(\dfrac{1}{1+4}\right) I_1$$

∴ $\boxed{I_4 = \dfrac{1}{5} I_1}$ ... (a)

and $I_3 = \dfrac{4}{(1+4)} I_1$

∴ $\boxed{I_3 = \dfrac{4}{5} I_1}$ ... (b)

But $I_4 = \dfrac{V_2}{2}$

∴ Putting into equation (a),

$$\dfrac{V_2}{2} = \dfrac{I_1}{5}$$

∴ $\dfrac{V_2}{I_1} = \dfrac{2}{5}$

∴ $Z_{21} = \left[\dfrac{V_2}{I_1}\right]_{I_2 = 0} = \dfrac{2}{5} \Omega$

∴ $\boxed{Z_{21} = \dfrac{2}{5}} \Omega$

Now by applying KVL to input loop,

$$\therefore \quad -2I_1 - I_3 + V_1 = 0$$

$$\therefore \quad V_1 = 2I_1 + I_3$$

But, $\quad I_3 = \dfrac{4}{5} I_1$

From equation (3.13 b)

$$\therefore \quad V_1 = 2I_1 + \dfrac{4}{5} I_1$$

$$V_1 = I_1 \left(2 + \dfrac{4}{5}\right)$$

$$\dfrac{V_1}{I_1} = \dfrac{14}{5}$$

$$\therefore \quad \boxed{Z_{11} = \dfrac{14}{5}\,\Omega}$$

(b) Now make $\quad I_1 = 0$

Input terminals 1 - 1' open circuit.

$$\therefore \quad Z_{12} = \left[\dfrac{V_1}{I_2}\right]_{I_1 = 0}$$

$$Z_{22} = \left[\dfrac{V_2}{I_2}\right]_{I_1 = 0}$$

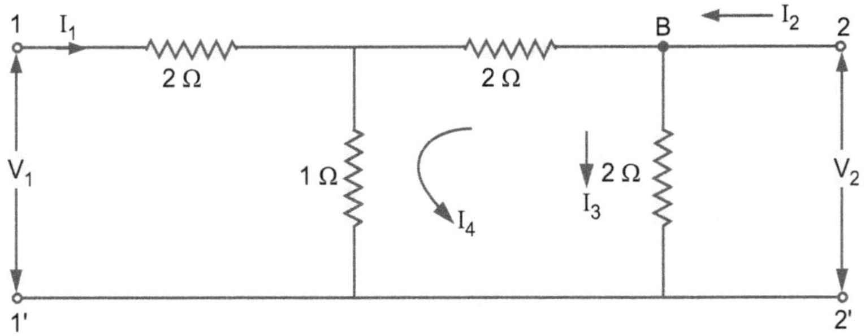

Fig. 3.8 (c)

By KCL at point B, $\quad I_2 = I_3 + I_4$

By current divider rule, $\quad I_4 = \dfrac{2 I_2}{(2 + 3)}$

$$I_4 = \dfrac{2}{5} I_2 \qquad \ldots (c)$$

and
$$I_3 = \frac{3 \times I_2}{(3+2)}$$
$$I_3 = \frac{3}{5} I_2 \quad \ldots (d)$$

But
$$I_4 = \frac{V_1}{1}$$
$$I_4 = V_1$$

∴
$$V_1 = \frac{2}{5} I_2 \quad \ldots \text{From equation (c)}$$
$$\frac{V_1}{I_2} = \frac{2}{5}$$

∴
$$\boxed{Z_{12} = \frac{2}{5} \Omega}$$

By applying KVL to output side,
$$V_2 = 2 I_3$$
$$= 2 \times \frac{3}{5} I_2 \quad \ldots \text{From equation (d)}$$

∴
$$\frac{V_2}{I_2} = \frac{6}{5} \Omega$$

∴
$$\boxed{Z_{22} = \frac{6}{5} \Omega}$$

∴ Z-parameters are:
$$[Z] = \begin{bmatrix} \frac{14}{5} & \frac{2}{5} \\ \frac{2}{5} & \frac{6}{5} \end{bmatrix} \Omega$$

Equivalent circuit for Z-parameters is

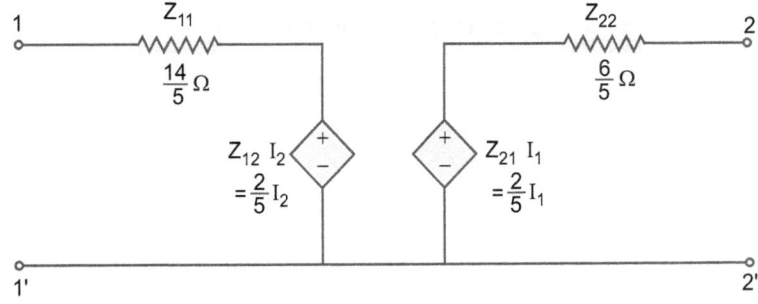

Fig. 3.8 (d)

3.4 SHORT-CIRCUIT ADMITTANCE OR Y-PARAMETERS

In Y-parameter, currents I_1 and I_2 are expressed in terms of voltage V_1 and V_2.

$$(I_1, I_2) = f(V_1, V_2)$$
$$[I] = [Y][V]$$

or

$$\begin{bmatrix} I_1 \\ I_2 \end{bmatrix} = \begin{bmatrix} Y_{11} & Y_{12} \\ Y_{21} & Y_{22} \end{bmatrix} \begin{bmatrix} V_1 \\ V_2 \end{bmatrix}$$

Y-parameter equation is

$$\left. \begin{array}{l} I_1 = Y_1 V_1 + Y_{12} V_2 \\ I_2 = Y_{21} V_1 + Y_{22} V_2 \end{array} \right\} \quad \ldots (3.4)$$

To calculate Y_{11}, Y_{12}, Y_{21} and Y_{22}, we have to make either $V_1 = 0$ or $V_2 = 0$

Case I: $V_2 = 0$, i.e. output is short-circuited.

(i) Driving point admittance,
$$Y_{11} = \left[\frac{I_1}{V_1}\right]_{V_2 = 0}$$

(ii) Forward transfer admittance,
$$Y_{21} = \left[\frac{I_2}{V_1}\right]_{V_2 = 0}$$

Case II: $V_1 = 0$ i.e. input is short circuited.

(iii) Output driving point admittance,
$$Y_{22} = \left[\frac{I_2}{V_2}\right]_{V_1 = 0}$$

(iv) Reverse transfer admittance:
$$Y_{12} = \left[\frac{I_1}{V_2}\right]_{V_1 = 0}$$

As $V_1 = 0$ or $V_2 = 0$, input or output are short circuited. Hence it is called as **short circuit admittance parameters**.

The equivalent circuit for Y-parameter is shown in Fig. 3.9.

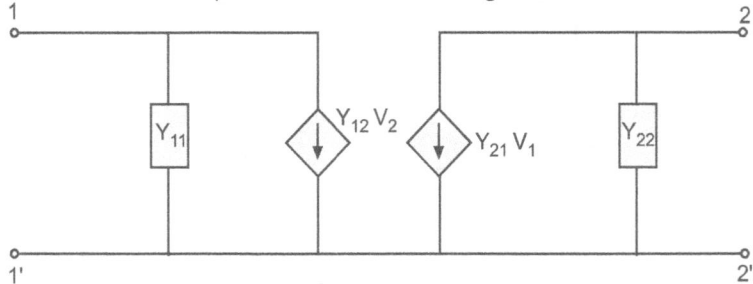

Fig. 3.9: Y-Parameters equivalent circuit

3.4.1 Condition for Symmetry and Reciprocity

(A) Symmetry Condition:

Similar to Z-parameters, Refer Fig. 3.6.

Case I: $\quad V_1 = V_s$
$\quad I_2 = 0$

From equation (3.14),

$$I_1 = Y_{11} V_s + Y_{12} V_2 \quad \ldots (a)$$
$$0 = Y_{21} V_s + Y_{22} V_2 \quad \ldots (b)$$

$$\therefore V_2 = -\frac{Y_{21}}{Y_{22}} V_s$$

Putting in equation (3.15 a),

$$I_1 = Y_{11} V_s + Y_{12} \left(-\frac{Y_{21}}{Y_{22}}\right) V_s$$

$$I_1 = V_s \left[Y_{11} - \frac{Y_{12} Y_{21}}{Y_{22}}\right]$$

$$\boxed{\frac{V_s}{I_1} = \frac{Y_{22}}{Y_{11} Y_{22} - Y_{12} Y_{21}}} \quad \ldots (c)$$

Case II: $\quad V_2 = V_s$
and $\quad I_1 = 0$

$\therefore$ From equation (3.4),

$$0 = Y_{11} V_1 + Y_{12} V_s \quad \ldots (d)$$
$$I_2 = Y_{21} V_1 + Y_{22} V_s \quad \ldots (e)$$

$$V_1 = -\frac{Y_{12}}{Y_{11}} \cdot V_s$$

Putting in equation (e),

$$I_2 = Y_{21} \left(-\frac{Y_{12}}{Y_{11}}\right) V_s + Y_{22} V_s$$

$$I_2 = V_s \left[-\frac{Y_{21} Y_{12}}{Y_{11}} + Y_{22}\right]$$

$$\boxed{\frac{V_s}{I_2} = \frac{Y_{11}}{Y_{11} Y_{22} - Y_{21} Y_{12}}} \quad \ldots (f)$$

But by symmetry condition,

$$\frac{V_s}{I_1} = \frac{V_s}{I_2}$$

$$\frac{Y_{22}}{Y_{11} Y_{22} - Y_{21} Y_{12}} = \frac{Y_{11}}{Y_{11} Y_{22} - Y_{21} Y_{12}}$$

$$\therefore \boxed{Y_{22} = Y_{11}} \quad \ldots (3.5)$$

That is the condition for symmetry.

Ex. 3.2: Find y-parameters for the 'T' network shown. Is this a symmetrical and reciprocal network?

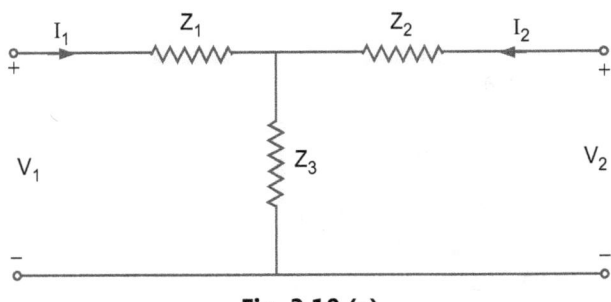

Fig. 3.10 (a)

Sol.: Step I: With $V_2 = 0$ we have,

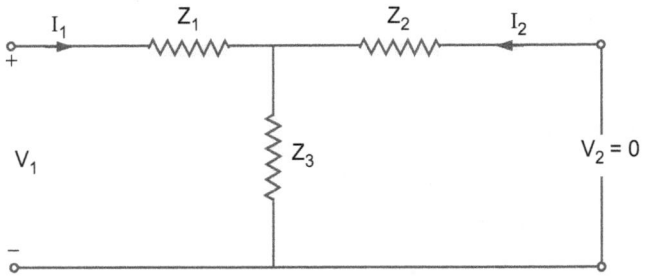

Fig. 3.10 (b)

$$I_1 = \frac{I_1}{Z_1 + \frac{Z_2 Z_3}{Z_2 + Z_3}} = \frac{V_1 (Z_2 + Z_3)}{Z_1 Z_2 + Z_2 Z_3 + Z_3 Z_1}$$

$$\therefore Y_{11} = \frac{I_1}{V_1} = \frac{Z_2 + Z_3}{Z_1 Z_2 + Z_2 Z_3 + Z_3 Z_1} \quad \ldots (a)$$

$$I_2 = -I_1 \times \frac{Z_3}{Z_2 + Z_3}$$

$$= -\frac{Z_3 V_1}{Z_1 Z_2 + Z_2 Z_3 + Z_3 Z_1} \quad \ldots (b)$$

Step II: With $V_1 = 0$.

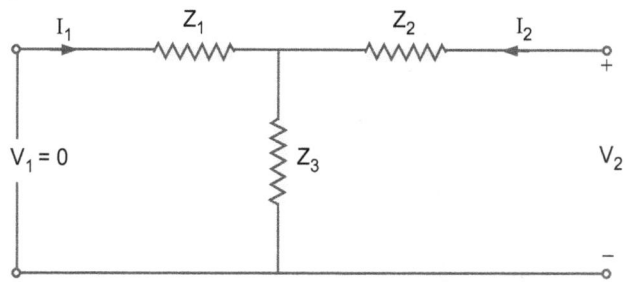

Fig. 3.10 (c)

$$I_2 = \frac{V_2}{Z_2 + \dfrac{Z_1 Z_3}{Z_1 + Z_3}} = \frac{(Z_1 + Z_3) V_2}{(Z_1 Z_3 + Z_1 Z_2 + Z_2 Z_3)}$$

$$Y_{22} = \frac{I_2}{V_2} = \frac{Z_1 + Z_3}{Z_1 Z_3 + Z_1 Z_2 + Z_2 Z_3} \quad \ldots \text{(c)}$$

$$I_1 = -I_2 \times \frac{Z_3}{Z_1 + Z_3} = \frac{Z_3 V_2}{Z_1 Z_3 + Z_2 Z_3 + Z_1 Z_2}$$

$\therefore \qquad Y_{12} = \dfrac{I_1}{V_2} = -\dfrac{Z_3}{Z_1 Z_3 + Z_2 Z_3 + Z_1 Z_2} \quad \ldots \text{(d)}$

Since $Y_{11} \ne Y_{22}$ network is not symmetrical

$Y_{12} = Y_{21}$ network is reciprocal.

(B) Reciprocity Condition:

Similar to Z-parameters,

Case I: $\qquad V_1 = V_s, V_2 = 0$

$\qquad\qquad\qquad I_2 = -I_2'$

Putting these values in equation (3.4),

$\qquad\qquad I_1 = Y_{11} V_s + 0$

$\qquad -I_2' = Y_{21} V_s + 0$

$\qquad\qquad I_1 = Y_{11} V_s$

and $\qquad \boxed{\dfrac{V_s}{I_2'} = \dfrac{-1}{Y_{21}}} \quad \ldots \text{(a)}$

Case II: $\qquad V_2 = V_s, V_1 = 0$

$\qquad\qquad\qquad I_1 = -I_1'$

Putting in equation (3.14),

$$-I_1' = Y_{12} V_s$$
$$I_2 = Y_{21} V_s$$

$$\boxed{\frac{V_s}{I_1'} = \frac{-1}{Y_{12}}} \quad \ldots \text{(b)}$$

But by reciprocity condition,

$$\frac{V_s}{I_2'} = \frac{V_s}{I_1'}$$

$\therefore \quad Y_{21} = Y_{12}$ or $\boxed{Y_{12} = Y_{21}}$ ... (3.6)

This is the condition for reciprocity.

3.5 TRANSMISSION OR ABCD PARAMETERS

In transmission or ABCD or chain parameters, voltage V_1 and current I_1 at input port is expressed in terms of voltage V_2 and current I_2 at output port.

$$V_1 = f(V_2, -I_2)$$
$$I_1 = f(V_2, -I_2)$$

Transmission parameters are generally used in the analysis of power transmission line, the input port is called as sending end and the output port is receiving end.

Here variable used is $-I_2$ instead of I_2. Negative sign indicates that current I_2 is considered outward i.e. leaving port 2 - 2'.

In matrix form,

$$\begin{bmatrix} V_1 \\ I_1 \end{bmatrix} = \begin{bmatrix} A & B \\ C & D \end{bmatrix} \begin{bmatrix} V_2 \\ -I_2 \end{bmatrix} \quad \ldots \text{(3.7)}$$

$\therefore$ ABCD parameter equations are

$$\left.\begin{array}{l} V_1 = AV_2 + B(-I_2) \\ I_1 = CV_2 + D(-I_2) \end{array}\right\} \quad \ldots \text{(3.8)}$$

$\therefore$ To calculate ABCD parameters, we have to make either $V_2 = 0$ or $I_2 = 0$.

Case I: $I_2 = 0$ i.e. output port 2 - 2' is open circuited.

(i) $\qquad A = \left[\dfrac{V_1}{V_2}\right]_{I_2 = 0}$

i.e. the reverse voltage ratio with receiving i.e. output port open circuited.

(ii) $$C = \left[\frac{I_1}{V_2}\right]_{I_2=0}$$

i.e. transfer admittance.

Case II: $V_2 = 0$ i.e. output or receiving end is short-circuited.

(iii) $$B = \left[\frac{V_1}{-I_2}\right]_{V_2=0}$$

i.e. transfer impedance with output short-circuited.

(iv) $$D = \left[\frac{I_1}{-I_2}\right]_{V_2=0}$$

i.e. reverse current ratio.

3.5.1 Condition for Symmetry and Reciprocity

(A) Symmetry Condition:

Similar to Z-parameters, refer Fig. 3.6.

Case I: $\quad V_1 = V_s, I_2 = 0$

From equation (3.7),

$$V_s = AV_2 \quad \ldots (a)$$

$$I_1 = CV_2 \quad \ldots (b)$$

$$\therefore \quad V_2 = \frac{I_1}{C}$$

Putting in equation (a), we get

$$V_s = \frac{A}{C} I_1$$

$$\therefore \quad \frac{V_s}{I_1} = \frac{A}{C} \quad \ldots (c)$$

Case II: $\quad V_2 = V_s, I_1 = 0$

Putting in equation (3.7),

$$V_1 = AV_s + B(-I_2)$$

$$0 = CV_s + D(-I_2)$$

$$\therefore \quad CV_s = DI_2$$

$$\therefore \quad \frac{V_s}{I_2} = \frac{D}{C} \quad \ldots (d)$$

But from symmetry condition,
$$\frac{V_s}{I_1} = \frac{V_s}{I_2}$$
$$\therefore \quad \frac{A}{C} = \frac{D}{C}$$
$$\therefore \quad \boxed{A = D} \qquad \ldots (3.9)$$

Symmetry condition.

(B) Reciprocity Condition:

Similar to Z-parameters,

Case I: $\quad V_1 = V_s, V_2 = 0$
and $\quad I_2' = I_2$

From equation (3.7),
$$V_s = B I_2'$$
$$\therefore \quad \frac{V_s}{I_2'} = B \qquad \ldots (e)$$

Case II: $\quad V_2 = V_s, V_1 = 0$ and $I_1' = -I_1$

$\therefore$ Equation (3.7) becomes,
$$0 = AV_s + B(-I_2) \qquad \ldots (f)$$
$$-I_1' = CV_s + D(-I_2) \qquad \ldots (g)$$

$\therefore$ From equation (f), we get
$$I_2 = \frac{A}{B} \cdot V_s$$

Putting this in equation (g) gives
$$-I_1' = CV_s + D\left(-\frac{A}{B} \cdot V_s\right)$$
$$-I_1' = V_s\left(C - \frac{AD}{B}\right)$$
$$-I_1' = V_s\left(\frac{BC - AD}{B}\right)$$
$$\frac{V_s}{I_1'} = \frac{B}{AD - BC}$$

$\therefore$ From reciprocity condition,
$$\frac{V_s}{I_1'} = \frac{V_s}{I_2'}$$
$$\frac{B}{AD - BC} = B$$
$\therefore \quad \boxed{AD - BC = 1} \qquad \ldots (3.10)$ Condition of reciprocity

Ex. 3.3: Find ABCD parameters for the given R-C network.

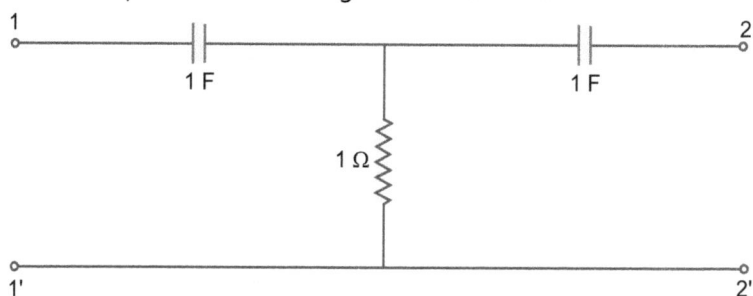

Fig. 3.11

Sol.: ABCD parameter equations are

$$V_1 = AV_2 + B(-I_2)$$
$$I_1 = CV_2 + D(-I_2)$$

Case I: $I_2 = 0$ i.e. output is open circuited.

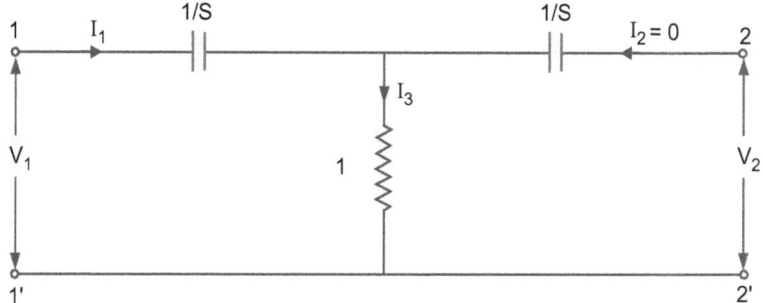

Fig. 3.11 (a): S-domain representation

∴ $$I_1 = \frac{V_1}{1 + \frac{1}{S}} = V_1 \cdot \frac{S}{S+1}$$

But, $$V_2 = I_1 \times 1\,\Omega$$

∴ $$A = \left[\frac{V_1}{V_2}\right]_{I_2 = 0} = \frac{\frac{s+1}{s} \cdot I_1}{I_1}$$

∴ $$\boxed{A = \frac{s+1}{s}}$$

and $$C = \left[\frac{I_1}{V_2}\right]_{I_2 = 0} = 1$$

∴ $$\boxed{C = 1}$$

Case II: $V_2 = 0$ i.e. output is short-circuited.

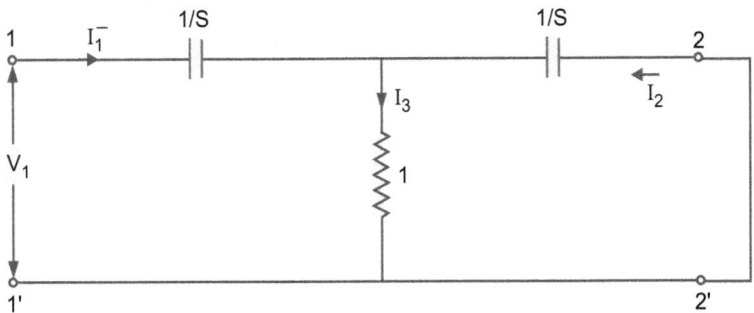

Fig. 3.11 (b)

$$V_2 = 0$$

$$\therefore I_3 = -I_2 \cdot \frac{1}{S}$$

$$I_1 = I_3 - I_2$$

$$= -\frac{I_2}{S} - I_2$$

$$I_1 = -I_2 \left[\frac{s+1}{s}\right]$$

$$\therefore D = \left[-\frac{I_1}{I_2}\right]_{V_2=0}$$

$$\therefore \boxed{D = \frac{s+1}{s}}$$

Now, $V_1 = I_1 \cdot \frac{1}{S} + I_3 = -I_2 \cdot \frac{s+1}{s^2} - I_2 \cdot \frac{1}{s}$

$$= -I_2 \left[\frac{2s+1}{s^2}\right]$$

$$\therefore B = \left[-\frac{V_1}{I_2}\right]_{V_2=0}$$

$$\therefore \boxed{B = \frac{2s+1}{s^2}}$$

$\therefore$ ABCD parameters are

$$[T] = \begin{bmatrix} \dfrac{s+1}{s} & \dfrac{2s+1}{s^2} \\ 1 & \dfrac{s+1}{s} \end{bmatrix}$$

3.6 HYBRID PARAMETERS OR H-PARAMETERS

The hybrid or h-parameters are used in constructing models of transistors. The parameter of transistor cannot be measured by short-circuit admittance or open circuit impedance parameter individually. Therefore, the combination of both short-circuit admittance and open-circuit impedance is called as hybrid or h-parameter.

In h-parameters, voltage at input port V_1 and the current of the output port I_2, are expressed in terms of the current at the input port I_1 and voltage at output port V_2.

$$(V_1, I_2) = f(I_1, V_2)$$

or

$$V_1 = f(I_1, V_2)$$

$$I_2 = f(I_1, V_2)$$

In matrix form,

$$\begin{bmatrix} V_1 \\ I_2 \end{bmatrix} = \begin{bmatrix} h_{11} & h_{12} \\ -h_{21} & h_{22} \end{bmatrix} \begin{bmatrix} I_1 \\ V_2 \end{bmatrix} \qquad \ldots (3.11)$$

h-parameter equations are

$$\left.\begin{array}{l} V_1 = h_{11} I_1 + h_{12} V_2 \\ I_2 = h_{21} I_1 + h_{22} V_2 \end{array}\right\} \qquad \ldots (3.12)$$

To calculate h-parameters,

Case I: $V_2 = 0$ i.e. output is short-circuited.

$$\therefore \qquad h_{11} = \left[\frac{V_1}{I_1}\right]_{V_2 = 0}$$

which is input impedance with output short-circuited.

$$h_{21} = \left[\frac{I_2}{I_1}\right]_{V_2 = 0}$$

which is forward current gain.

Case II: $I_1 = 0$

$$h_{12} = \left[\frac{V_1}{V_2}\right]_{I_1 = 0}$$

Which is reverse voltage gain with input open-circuited.

$$h_{22} = \left[\frac{I_2}{V_2}\right]_{I_1 = 0}$$

Which is output admittance (℧).

The equivalent circuit for h-parameters are shown in Fig. 3.12.

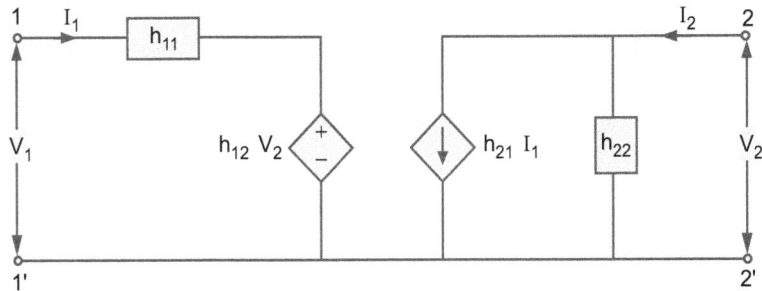

Fig. 3.12: h-parameters equivalent circuit

3.6.1 Condition for Symmetry and Reciprocity

(A) Symmetry Condition:

Similar to Z-parameters. Refer to Fig. 3.3.

Case I: $\quad V_1 = V_s, I_2 = 0$

From equation (3.15),

$$V_s = h_{11} I_1 + h_{12} V_2 \quad \ldots \text{(a)}$$

and

$$0 = h_{21} I_1 + h_{22} V_2 \quad \ldots \text{(b)}$$

$\therefore \quad -h_{22} V_2 = h_{21} I_1$

$$V_2 = -\frac{h_{21}}{h_{22}} \cdot I_1$$

Substituting value of V_2 in equation 3.21 (a) gives

$$V_s = h_{11} I_1 + h_{12} \left[\frac{-h_{21}}{h_{22}} \right] I_1$$

$$V_s = \left[h_{11} - \frac{h_{12} h_{21}}{h_{22}} \right] I_1$$

$$\frac{V_s}{I_1} = \frac{h_{11} h_{22} - h_{12} h_{21}}{h_{22}} \quad \ldots \text{(c)}$$

Case II: $\quad V_2 = V_s$ and $I_1 = 0$

$$V_1 = h_{12} V_s \quad \ldots \text{(d)}$$

$$I_2 = h_{22} V_s \quad \ldots \text{(e)}$$

$$\frac{V_s}{I_2} = \frac{1}{h_{22}} \quad \ldots \text{(f)}$$

From symmetry condition,

$$\frac{V_s}{I_1} = \frac{V_s}{I_2}$$

$$\frac{h_{11} h_{22} - h_{12} h_{21}}{h_{22}} = \frac{1}{h_{22}}$$

$$\therefore \boxed{h_{11} h_{22} - h_{12} h_{21} = 1} \qquad \text{... (3.13)}$$

which is condition of symmetry.

(B) Reciprocity Condition:

Similar to Z-parameter.

Case I: $\quad V_1 = V_s, V_2 = 0$

and $\quad I_2' = -I_2$

From equation (3.10),

$$V_s = h_{11} I_1 \qquad \text{... (g)}$$

and $\quad -I_2' = h_{21} I_1$

$$\therefore \quad I_1 = \frac{-1}{h_{21}} \cdot I_2'$$

Putting in equation (g), we get

$$V_s = \frac{-h_{11}}{h_{21}} \cdot I_2'$$

$$\therefore \quad \frac{V_s}{I_2'} = \frac{-h_{11}}{h_{21}} \qquad \text{... (h)}$$

Case II: $\quad V_2 = V_s, V_1 = 0$

$\quad I_1' = -I_1$

Putting in equation (3.10),

$$0 = -h_{11} I_1' + h_{12} V_s \qquad \text{... (i)}$$

and $\quad I_2 = -h_{21} I_1' + h_{22} V_s \qquad \text{... (j)}$

$$\therefore \quad I_1' = \frac{h_{12}}{h_{11}} V_s$$

$$\therefore \quad \frac{V_s}{I_1'} = \frac{h_{11}}{h_{12}} \qquad \text{... (k)}$$

By reciprocity condition,

$$\frac{V_s}{I_2'} = \frac{V_s}{I_1'}$$

$$-\frac{h_{11}}{h_{21}} = \frac{h_{11}}{h_{12}}$$

∴ $\boxed{h_{12} = -h_{21}}$ ... (3.14)

Reciprocity condition for h-parameters.

Ex. 3.4: The hybrid parameters of the network shown in Fig. 3.13 are $h_{11} = 2\,\Omega$, $h_{12} = 4$, $h_{21} = -5$, $h_{22} = 2\,\mho$.

Determine the supply voltage V_s if the power dissipated in the load resistor $R_L = 4\,\Omega$ is 25 W and $R_s = 2\,\Omega$.

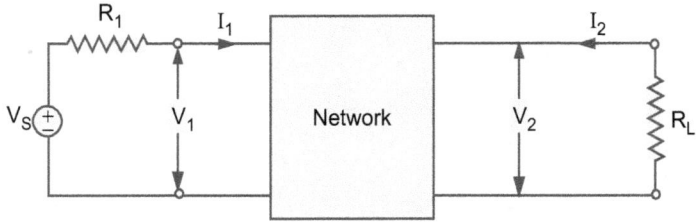

Fig. 3.13

The h-parameter equations are

$$V_1 = 2 I_1 + 4 V_2$$
$$I_2 = -5 I_1 + 2 V_2$$

Now power dissipated in R_L is

$$P_L = \frac{V_2^2}{R_L} = 25 \text{ watts}$$

∴ $V_2 = 10$ V

But $V_2 = -I_2 R_L$

∴ $I_2 = -2.5$ A

Putting these values in h-parameter equation,

$$V_1 = 2 I_1 + 40$$

and $-2.5 = -5 I_1 + 20$

Solving these two equations,

$$I_1 = 4.5 \text{ A}$$
and
$$V_1 = 49 \text{ V}$$

Since,
$$I_1 = \frac{V_s - V_1}{2}$$

$$4.5 = \frac{V_s - 49}{2}$$

$$9 = V_s - 49$$

$$\therefore V_s = 58 \text{ V}$$

∴ The supply voltage is $V_s = 58$ V

3.7 INTERRELATIONSHIPS BETWEEN THE PARAMETERS

Uptil now, we have studied four different parameters. Each has its own utility and is suited for certain specific application. But, we often find it necessary to convert from one set of parameters to another. Through simple mathematical manipulation, it is possible to convert from any one set to any of the remaining set.

3.7.1 Z-Parameter in Terms of Other Parameters

Let us first rewrite the equations of Z-parameters.

$$\left.\begin{array}{l} V_1 = Z_{11} I_1 + Z_{12} I_2 \\ V_2 = Z_{21} I_1 + Z_{22} I_2 \end{array}\right\} \quad \ldots \text{(a)}$$

(A) Z-Parameters in Terms of Y-Parameters

Now equations for Y-parameters are

$$\left.\begin{array}{l} I_1 = Y_{11} V_1 + Y_{12} V_2 \\ I_2 = Y_{21} V_1 + Y_{22} V_2 \end{array}\right\} \quad \ldots \text{(b)}$$

i.e.
$$\begin{bmatrix} I_1 \\ I_2 \end{bmatrix} = \begin{bmatrix} Y_{11} & Y_{12} \\ Y_{21} & Y_{22} \end{bmatrix} \begin{bmatrix} V_1 \\ V_2 \end{bmatrix}$$

Let us solve this equation simultaneously for V_1 and V_2 from (b)

By Cramer's rule,
$$V_1 = \frac{\begin{vmatrix} I_1 & Y_{12} \\ I_2 & Y_{22} \end{vmatrix}}{\begin{vmatrix} Y_{11} & Y_{12} \\ Y_{21} & Y_{22} \end{vmatrix}} = \frac{Y_{22} I_1 - Y_{12} I_2}{Y_{11} Y_{22} - Y_{12} Y_{21}}$$

$$V_1 = \frac{Y_{22}}{Y_{11} Y_{22} - Y_{12} Y_{21}} I_1 - \frac{Y_{12}}{Y_{11} Y_{22} - Y_{12} Y_{21}} I_2$$

Let
$$Dy = Y_{11}Y_{22} - Y_{12}Y_{21}$$

$$V_1 = \frac{Y_{22}}{Dy}I_1 - \frac{Y_{12}}{Dy}I_2 \quad \ldots (c)$$

and
$$V_2 = \frac{\begin{vmatrix} Y_{11} & I_1 \\ Y_{21} & I_2 \end{vmatrix}}{\begin{vmatrix} Y_{11} & Y_{12} \\ Y_{21} & Y_{22} \end{vmatrix}} = \frac{Y_{11}I_2 - y_{21}I_1}{Y_{11}Y_{22} - Y_{12}Y_{21}}$$

$$\therefore V_2 = \frac{Y_{11}}{Dy}I_2 - \frac{Y_{21}}{Dy}I_1$$

$$V_2 = \frac{-Y_{21}}{Dy}I_1 + \frac{Y_{11}}{Dy}I_2 \quad \ldots (d)$$

Comparing equations (c) and (d) with Z-parameter equations, we get

$$Z_{11} = \frac{Y_{22}}{Dy}, \; Z_{12} = \frac{-Y_{12}}{Dy}$$

$$Z_{21} = \frac{-Y_{21}}{Dy}, \; Z_{22} = \frac{Y_{11}}{Dy}$$

$$[Z] = \begin{bmatrix} \frac{Y_{22}}{Dy} & \frac{-Y_{12}}{Dy} \\ \frac{-Y_{21}}{Dy} & \frac{Y_{11}}{Dy} \end{bmatrix} \quad \ldots (3.15)$$

Thus Z-parameters matrix is obtained by inverse of y-parameters matrix. Similarly it can be proved that y-parameters matrix is obtained by inverse of z-parameters matrix.

(B) Z-Parameters in Terms of h-Parameters

The h-parameter equations are

$$V_1 = h_{11}I_1 + h_{12}V_2 \quad \ldots (e)$$
$$I_2 = h_{21}I_1 + h_{22}V_2 \quad \ldots (f)$$

$$\therefore h_{22}V_2 = I_2 - h_{21}I_2$$

$$V_2 = \frac{1}{h_{22}}I_2 - \frac{h_{21}}{h_{22}}I_1$$

$$V_2 = \frac{-h_{21}}{h_{22}}I_1 + \frac{1}{h_{22}}I_2 \quad \ldots (g)$$

Putting this value in equation (e), we get

$$V_1 = h_{11} I_1 + h_{12} \left[\frac{1}{h_{22}} I_2 - \frac{h_{21}}{h_{22}} I_1 \right]$$

$$V_1 = h_{11} I_1 + \frac{h_{12}}{h_{22}} I_2 - \frac{h_{12} h_{21}}{h_{22}} I_1$$

$$V_1 = \left[h_{11} - \frac{h_{12} h_{21}}{h_{22}} \right] I_1 + \frac{h_{12}}{h_{22}} I_2$$

$$V_1 = \frac{h_{11} h_{22} - h_{12} h_{21}}{h_{22}} I_1 + \frac{h_{12}}{h_{22}} I_2 \qquad \ldots \text{(h)}$$

Comparing this equation with Z-parameter equation,

$$\boxed{Z_{11} = \frac{h_{11} h_{22} - h_{12} h_{21}}{h_{22}}} \qquad \boxed{Z_{12} = \frac{h_{12}}{h_{22}}}$$

Comparing equation (g) with Z-parameter equation.

$$\boxed{Z_{21} = -\frac{h_{21}}{h_{22}} \quad \text{and} \quad Z_{22} = \frac{1}{h_{22}}}$$

$$\therefore \qquad [Z] = \begin{bmatrix} \dfrac{Dh}{h_{22}} & \dfrac{h_{12}}{h_{22}} \\ \dfrac{-h_{21}}{h_{22}} & \dfrac{1}{h_{22}} \end{bmatrix} \qquad \ldots \text{(3.16)}$$

(C) Z-Parameters in Terms of ABCD Parameters

ABCD parameter equations are

$$V_1 = AV_2 + B(-I_2) \qquad \ldots \text{(i)}$$
$$I_1 = CV_2 + D(-I_2) \qquad \ldots \text{(j)}$$

From equation (j), we get,

$$CV_2 = I_1 + DI_2$$

$$V_2 = \left(\frac{1}{C}\right) I_1 + \left(\frac{D}{C}\right) I_2 \qquad \ldots \text{(к)}$$

Comparing equation with Z-parameter equation,

$$\boxed{Z_{21} = \frac{1}{C}} \qquad \boxed{Z_{22} = \frac{D}{C}}$$

Putting value of V_2 in equation (j), we get

$$V_1 = A \left[\frac{1}{C} I_1 + \frac{D}{C} I_2 \right] + B(-I_2)$$

$$V_1 = \frac{A}{C} I_1 + \frac{AD}{C} I_2 - BI_2$$

$$V_1 = \frac{A}{C} I_1 + \left[\frac{AD}{C} - B\right] I_2$$

$$V_1 = \frac{A}{C} I_1 + \frac{AD - BC}{C} I_2 \quad \ldots (l)$$

Comparing with Z-parameter equation,

$$\boxed{Z_{11} = \frac{A}{C}} \quad \boxed{Z_{12} = \frac{AD - BC}{C}}$$

$$\therefore \quad [Z] = \begin{bmatrix} \frac{A}{C} & \frac{AD-BC}{C} \\ \frac{1}{C} & \frac{D}{C} \end{bmatrix} \quad \ldots (3.17)$$

In similar manner, we can express any one parameter in terms of remaining other parameters.

Table 3.2 gives the summary of all relationships between different sets of parameters. In this table matrices placed in each rows are equivalent. The equivalent table involves determinants Dz, Dy, Dh, ΔT, etc. where

$$Dz = Z_{11} Z_{22} - Z_{12} Z_{21}$$
$$Dy = Y_{11} Y_{22} - Y_{12} Y_{21}$$
$$Dh = h_{11} h_{22} - h_{12} h_{21}$$
$$\Delta T = AD - BC, \text{ etc.}$$

Table 3.2: Table for interrelationship between parameters

[Z]	[Y]	[T]	[h]
$\begin{bmatrix} Z_{11} & Z_{12} \\ Z_{21} & Z_{22} \end{bmatrix}$	$\begin{bmatrix} \frac{Y_{22}}{Dy} & \frac{-Y_{12}}{Dy} \\ \frac{-Y_{21}}{Dy} & \frac{Y_{11}}{Dy} \end{bmatrix}$	$\begin{bmatrix} \frac{A}{C} & \frac{DT}{C} \\ \frac{1}{C} & \frac{D}{C} \end{bmatrix}$	$\begin{bmatrix} \frac{Dh}{h_{22}} & \frac{h_{12}}{h_{22}} \\ \frac{-h_{21}}{h_{22}} & \frac{1}{h_{22}} \end{bmatrix}$
$\begin{bmatrix} \frac{Z_{22}}{Dz} & \frac{-Z_{12}}{Dz} \\ \frac{-Z_{21}}{Dz} & \frac{Z_{11}}{Dz} \end{bmatrix}$	$\begin{bmatrix} Y_{11} & Y_{12} \\ Y_{21} & Y_{22} \end{bmatrix}$	$\begin{bmatrix} \frac{D}{B} & \frac{-DT}{B} \\ \frac{-1}{B} & \frac{A}{B} \end{bmatrix}$	$\begin{bmatrix} \frac{1}{h_{11}} & \frac{-h_{12}}{h_{11}} \\ \frac{h_{21}}{h_{11}} & \frac{Dh}{h_{11}} \end{bmatrix}$
$\begin{bmatrix} \frac{Z_{11}}{Z_{21}} & \frac{Dz}{Z_{21}} \\ \frac{1}{Z_{21}} & \frac{Z_{22}}{Z_{21}} \end{bmatrix}$	$\begin{bmatrix} \frac{-Y_{22}}{Y_{21}} & \frac{-1}{Y_{21}} \\ \frac{-Dy}{Y_{21}} & \frac{-Y_{11}}{Y_{21}} \end{bmatrix}$	$\begin{bmatrix} A & B \\ C & D \end{bmatrix}$	$\begin{bmatrix} \frac{-Dh}{h_{21}} & \frac{-h_{11}}{h_{21}} \\ \frac{-h_{22}}{h_{21}} & \frac{-1}{h_{21}} \end{bmatrix}$
$\begin{bmatrix} \frac{Dz}{Z_{22}} & \frac{Z_{21}}{Z_{22}} \\ \frac{-Z_{21}}{Z_{22}} & \frac{1}{Z_{22}} \end{bmatrix}$	$\begin{bmatrix} \frac{1}{Y_{11}} & \frac{-Y_{12}}{Y_{11}} \\ \frac{Y_{21}}{Y_{11}} & \frac{Dy}{Y_{11}} \end{bmatrix}$	$\begin{bmatrix} \frac{B}{D} & \frac{DT}{D} \\ \frac{-1}{D} & \frac{C}{D} \end{bmatrix}$	$\begin{bmatrix} h_{11} & h_{12} \\ h_{21} & h_{22} \end{bmatrix}$

Table 3.3 gives the summary for condition of symmetry and reciprocity for different parameters.

Table 3.3: Condition for symmetry and reciprocity

Parameter	Condition of symmetry	Condition of reciprocity
[Z]	$Z_{11} = Z_{22}$	$Z_{12} = Z_{21}$
[Y]	$Y_{11} = Y_{22}$	$Y_{12} = Y_{21}$
{ABCD} or [T]	$A = D$	$AD - BC = 1$
[h]	$h_{11} h_{22} - h_{12} h_{21} = 1$	$h_{12} = -h_{21}$

EXERCISE

1. Define open circuit impedance parameters. Obtain the equivalent circuit in terms of Z-parameters.
2. Define short circuit admittance parameters. Obtain the equivalent circuit in terms of Y-parameters.
3. Define hybrid parameters. Obtain the equivalent circuit in terms of h-parameters. Explain why h-parameters are used for transistors.
4. Define Transmission (ABCD) parameters. Explain why ABCD parameters are also known as T-parameters.
5. Establish the relationship between Z and Y parameters.
6. What is the symmetrical network reciprocal network? Give relationship between parameters for symmetrical and reciprocal network.
7. Show that when two or more networks are cascaded, then their overall T-parameters is the multiplication of T-parameter matrix of individual networks.
8. Show that when two networks are series-series connected, then overall Z-parameter matrix is the addition of Z-parameters of the individual networks.
9. For the network shown below obtain Z and h parameters.

Fig. 3.14: Circuit for Q.9

10. Show that for the network given, following equation holds good.

$$\begin{bmatrix} V_2 \\ I_2 \end{bmatrix} = \begin{bmatrix} 1.5 & 6.5 \\ 0.25 & 1.25 \end{bmatrix} \begin{bmatrix} V_1 \\ -I_1 \end{bmatrix}$$

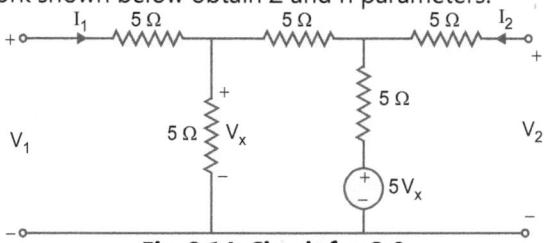

Fig. 3.15: Circuit for Q.10

11. Determine $\dfrac{V_2}{I}$ in terms of R_1, R_2 and Z-parameters of network.

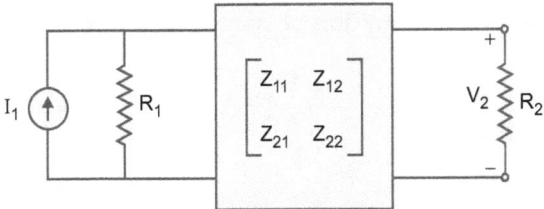

Fig. 3.16: Circuit for Q.11

12. Find Z and Y parameters.

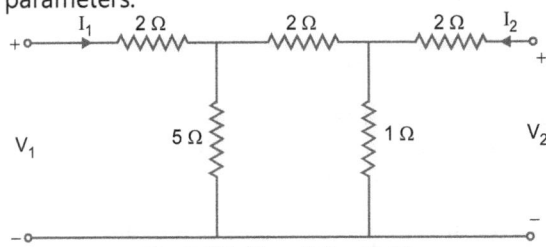

Fig 3.17: Circuit for Q.12

13. Show that ABCD parameters of the network is

$$\begin{bmatrix} A & B \\ C & D \end{bmatrix} = \begin{bmatrix} \left(\dfrac{1+s^2}{s^2}\right) & \left(\dfrac{1+2s^2}{s^3}\right) \\ \dfrac{1}{s} & \left(\dfrac{s^2+1}{s^2}\right) \end{bmatrix}$$

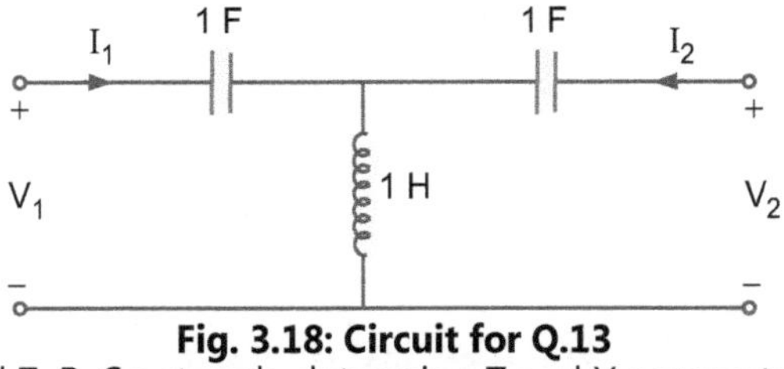

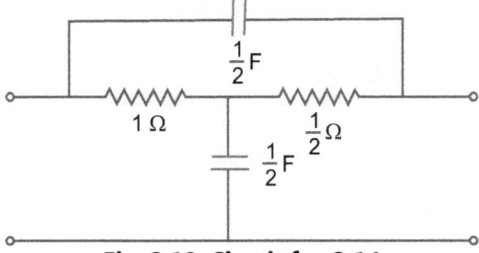

Fig. 3.18: Circuit for Q.13

14. For the bridged T, R-C network, determine Z and Y parameters.

Fig. 3.19: Circuit for Q.14

16. What is a network function? Explain various types of network functions for a one port network and a two port network.

Unit IV

ATTENUATORS AND FILTERS

Contents ...

(A) ATTENUATORS

- 4.1 Attenuator
    - 4.1.1 Introduction
    - 4.1.2 Relation in between Neper and Decibel
    - 4.1.3 Types of Attenuators
    - 4.1.4 Symmetrical Lattice Type Attenuator
    - 4.1.5 Symmetrical T Type Attenuator
    - 4.1.6 Symmetrical π Type Attenuator
- 4.2 Summary of Attenuators
- 4.3 Solved Numericals on Attenuators

(B) FILTERS

- 4.4 Introduction
- 4.5 Passive Filters
    - 4.5.1 Basic Definitions
    - 4.5.2 Classification of Passive Filters
    - 4.5.3 Ideal and Practical Filter
- 4.6 Filter Fundamentals
    - 4.6.1 Logical Thinking
    - 4.6.2 Mathematical Analysis
    - 4.6.3 Summary
- 4.7 Constant K Prototype filters
- 4.8 Constant K Low Pass Filters
    - 4.8.1 Operation
    - 4.8.2 Design Impedance
    - 4.8.3 Reactance Curves
    - 4.8.4 Design Equations
    - 4.8.5 α, β in a LPF
    - 4.8.6 Z_o in a LPF
    - 4.8.7 Summary
- 4.9 Solved Numericals on LPF

4.10 Constant k High Pass Filters
    4.10.1 Operation
    4.10.2 Design Impedance
    4.10.3 Reactance Curve
    4.10.4 Design Equations
    4.10.5 α, β in HPF
    4.10.6 Z_o in a HPF
    4.10.7 Summary
4.11 Solved Numericals on HPF
4.12 Constant k Band Pass Filters
    4.12.1 Logical thinking
    4.12.2 Operation
    4.12.3 Design Impedance
    4.12.4 Reactance Curves
    4.12.5 Design Equations
    4.12.6 α, β, Z_o in BPF
    4.12.7 Summary
4.13 Solved Numericals on Band Pass Filter
4.14 Constant k Band Stop Filter
    4.14.1 Logical thinking
    4.14.2 Operation
    4.14.3 Design impedance
    4.14.4 Reactance curves
    4.14.5 Design equations
    4.14.6 α, β, Z_o in a BSF
    4.14.7 Summary
4.15 Solved Numericals on BSF
4.16 Summary of all the constant k type filters
4.17 Disadvantages of constant k filters
    4.17.1 Solution
4.18 m derived filters
    4.18.1 m derived T section
    4.18.2 m derived π section

4.19 m derived Lowpass Filter
    4.19.1 Operation
    4.19.2 Reactance Curves
    4.19.3 f_∞ and f_c in m-LPF
    4.19.4 Derivations
    4.19.5 π Section m-LPF

4.20 m derived High Pass Filter
    4.20.1 Operation
    4.20.2 Reactance Curves
    4.20.3 f_∞ and f_c in mHPF
    4.20.4 Derivations
    4.20.5 π section m-HPF

4.21 Summary of m derived Filters

4.22 Solved Numericals on m derived Filters

4.23 Disadvantages of m derived Filters

4.24 Termination with m derived Half Sections
    4.24.1 Necessity of m derived Half Section
    4.24.2 m Derived half (L) Section (T type)
    4.24.3 m derived half (L) Section (π type)
    4.24.4 Characteristics Impedance of a m derived Half Section
    4.24.5 Terminating of T and a π Section Filter

4.25 Summary of Terminating Half Section

4.26 Composite Filter

4.27 Solved Numericals on Composite Filter

4.28 Summary of all the Formulae's in Filter
    4.28.1 Prototype Filters
    4.28.2 m-derived Filters
    4.28.3 Terminating Half Sections
    Exercise

(A) ATTENUATORS

4.1 ATTENUATORS

4.1.1 Introduction

An attenuator is a two port network which reduces the voltage, current or power between its properly terminated input and output ports by known amount. An attenuator is purely resistive network and its propagation constant is real. The attenuation is independent of frequency. It may be symmetrical or asymmetrical. An attenuator of constant attenuation is called "pad". Ladder attenuators provide fixed attenuation in two or more steps.

4.1.2 Relation in between Neper and Decibel

The attenuation is expressed either in decibels (dBs) or neper units.

Consider several four terminal (two port) networks in cascade as shown in Fig. 4.1.

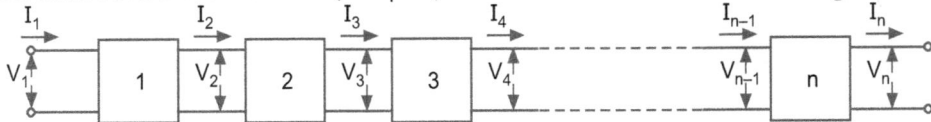

Fig. 4.1

Let the input and output image impedances or the ratios of voltage to current at input and output of the network are equal.

Then the magnitude ratios of the input to output currents or input to output voltages may be written as:

$$\left|\frac{I_1}{I_2}\right| = \left|\frac{V_1}{V_2}\right|$$

For the cascaded n networks,

$$\left|\frac{V_1}{V_n}\right| = e^a, \left|\frac{V_1}{V_2}\right| \times \left|\frac{V_2}{V_3}\right| \times \ldots \times \left|\frac{V_{n-1}}{V_n}\right|$$

Let,

$$\left|\frac{V_1}{V_2}\right| = e^a, \left|\frac{V_2}{V_3}\right| = e^b, \ldots \times \left|\frac{V_{n-1}}{V_n}\right| = e^n$$

Hence,

$$\left|\frac{V_1}{V_2}\right| = e^a \times e^b \times \ldots \times e^n$$

$$= e^{a+b+\ldots+n}$$

i.e.

$$\ln\left|\frac{V_1}{V_n}\right| = a + b + \ldots + n$$

The logarithm of the current and voltage ratio for all the networks in cascade is sum of various exponents.

Let,
$$\left|\frac{V_1}{V_2}\right| = \left|\frac{I_1}{I_2}\right| = e^{\alpha}$$

$\therefore \quad \alpha \text{ nepers} = \ln\left|\frac{V_1}{V_2}\right| = \ln\left|\frac{I_1}{I_2}\right|$

Two voltages or currents differ by one neper when one of them is e times as large as other.

Ratio of input to output power may also be expressed as

$$\frac{P_1}{P_2} = e^{2N} \quad \ldots (a)$$

The bel is defined as the logarithm of a power ratio,

$$\text{Number of bels} = \log\frac{P_1}{P_2}$$

$$\text{Attenuation in dB} = 10\log\frac{P_1}{P_2} = 20\log\frac{V_1}{V_2} = 20\log\frac{I_1}{I_2}$$

$\therefore \quad \dfrac{P_1}{P_2} = \text{Antilog}_{10}\left|\dfrac{d}{10}\right| \quad \ldots (b)$

Equating equations (a) and (b)

$$e^{2N} = \text{Antilog}\left|\frac{d}{10}\right|$$

Taking logarithm of both sides,

$$\log e^{2N} = \log \text{Antilog}\left|\frac{d}{10}\right|$$

$\therefore \quad 2N = \dfrac{dB}{10}\log_e 10$

$\therefore \quad N = \dfrac{dB}{20}(2.3025)$

$$dB = \frac{20}{2.3025}N$$

$$= 8.686\, N$$

$\therefore \quad \boxed{1 \text{ Neper} = 8.686 \text{ dB}} \quad \ldots (4.1)$

and $\quad 1\, dB = \dfrac{1}{8.686}\text{ neper}$

$\boxed{1\, dB = 0.115 \text{ neper}} \quad \ldots (4.2)$

In general, attenuation is expressed in decibel as

$$D = 10\log_{10}\left|\frac{P_{in}}{P_{out}}\right|$$

Attenuation can also be expressed in terms of Nepers as

$$D = 20 \log_{10} \sqrt{\frac{P_{in}}{P_{out}}}$$

$$D = 20 \log_{10} N$$

$$\boxed{N = \text{Antilog}_{10} \left| \frac{D}{20} \right|} \quad \ldots (4.3)$$

4.1.3 Types of Attenuators

Attenuators are classified on the basis of:
1. Type of network   2. Type of attenuation

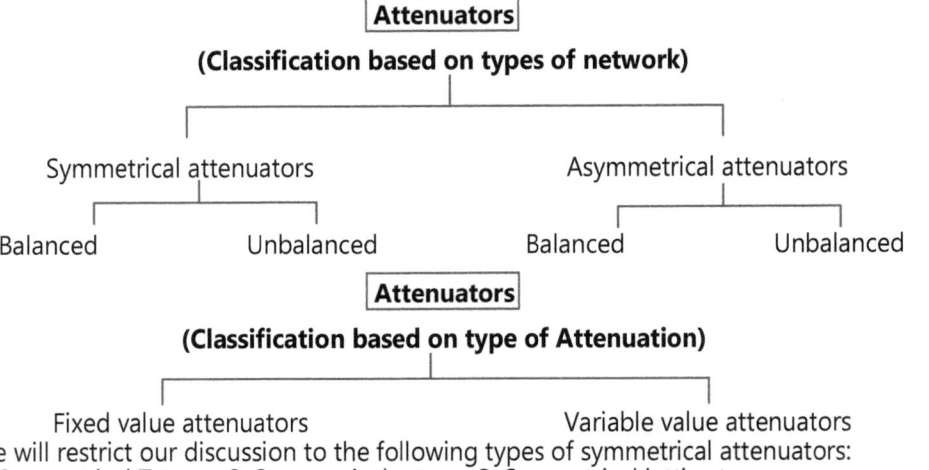

We will restrict our discussion to the following types of symmetrical attenuators:
1. Symmetrical T type   2. Symmetrical π type   3. Symmetrical lattice type

4.1.4 Symmetrical Lattice Attenuator

A symmetrical resistance lattice can be converted into an equivalent T, π or bridged T resistance network using the bisection theorem.

Consider lattice attenuator as shown in Fig. 4.2 (a). This simplified version redrawn as shown in Fig. 4.2 (b).

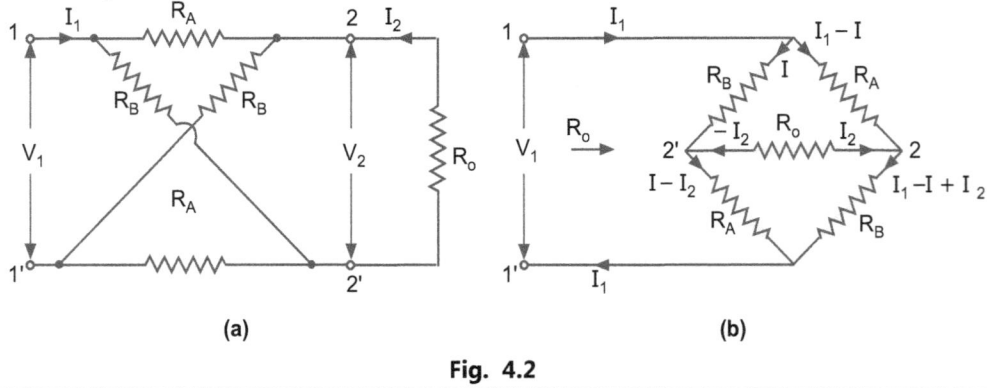

Fig. 4.2

Determine short circuit and open circuit impedances from Fig. 4.4 (b).

$\therefore \quad Z_{SC} = (R_A \| R_B) + (R_A \| R_B)$

$\qquad = 2 \dfrac{R_A R_B}{R_A + R_B}$ ... (a)

$\quad Z_{OC} = (R_A + R_B) \| (R_A + R_B)$

$\qquad = \dfrac{R_A + R_B}{2}$ ... (b)

Therefore, characteristic impedance R_o at lattice attenuator is

$\quad Z_0 = R_o = \sqrt{Z_{OC} Z_{SC}}$ from (1), (2)

$\qquad = \sqrt{R_A R_B}$

The input impedance at terminal 1, 1' is R_o, when the network is terminated at terminal 2, 2' by the impedance R_o.

Applying KVL, to the loop $1 - 2 - 2' - 1'$.

$\quad V_1 = I_1 R_o = (I_1 - I) R_A - I_2 R_o + (I - I_2) R_A$

$\quad I_1 R_o = (I_1 - I_2) R_A - I_2 R_o$

$\quad I_1 (R_o - R_A) = -I_2 (R_o + R_A)$

$\therefore \quad \dfrac{I_1}{-I_2} = \dfrac{R_o + R_A}{R_o - R_A} = \dfrac{1 + \dfrac{R_A}{R_o}}{1 - \dfrac{R_A}{R_o}}$

$\therefore \quad e^{\alpha} = \dfrac{I_1}{-I_2} = \dfrac{1 + \sqrt{\dfrac{R_A}{R_B}}}{1 - \sqrt{\dfrac{R_A}{R_B}}}$

$\therefore$ Propagation constant $N = \alpha = \ln \left[\dfrac{1 + \sqrt{\dfrac{R_A}{R_B}}}{1 - \sqrt{\dfrac{R_A}{R_B}}} \right]$

$\quad N = \dfrac{V_1}{V_2} = \dfrac{I_1}{-I_2} = e^{\alpha}$

$\qquad = \dfrac{1 + \sqrt{\dfrac{R_A}{R_B}}}{1 - \sqrt{\dfrac{R_A}{R_B}}}$

Substitute $R_o = \sqrt{R_A R_B}$

$\therefore \quad N = \dfrac{1 + \dfrac{R_A}{R_o}}{1 - \dfrac{R_A}{R_o}}$

or $\boxed{R_A = R_o \left(\dfrac{N-1}{N+1}\right)}$ ... (4.4)

$\boxed{R_B = R_o \left(\dfrac{N+1}{N-1}\right)}$ ... (4.5)

where, $N = \text{Antilog}_{10}\left(\dfrac{dB}{20}\right)$

These are design equations for the lattice attenuator.

4.1.5 Symmetry T-type Attenuator

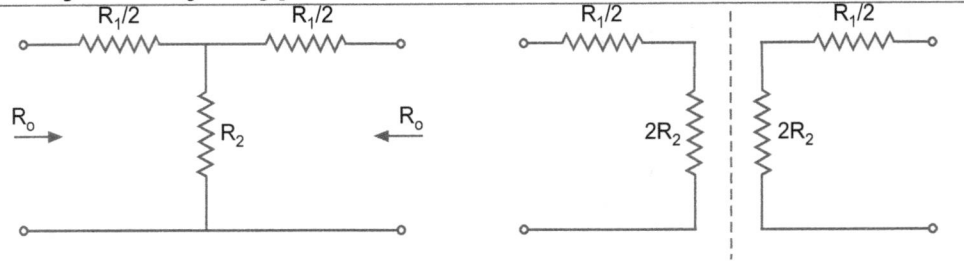

(a) T type attenuator (b) Bisection of T network

Fig. 4.3

For the half section shown in Fig. 4.2 (b),

$R_{SC} = \dfrac{R_1}{R_2} = R_A$

$R_{OC} = \dfrac{R_1}{2} + 2R_2 = R_B$

Hence,

$R_1 = 2R_A$ ... (a)

$R_2 = \dfrac{R_B - R_A}{2}$ ... (b)

Substituting equations (a) and (b) in equations (4.4) and (4.5)

$R_1 = 2R_A$

$R_1 = 2R_o \left(\dfrac{N-1}{N+1}\right)$

$\boxed{\dfrac{R_1}{2} = R_o \left(\dfrac{N-1}{N+1}\right)}$ ... (4.6)

$$R_2 = \frac{R_o}{2}\left[\frac{N+1}{N-1} - \frac{N-1}{N+1}\right]$$

$$\boxed{R_2 = R_o \frac{2N}{N^2-1}} \qquad \ldots(4.7)$$

4.1.6 π-type Attenuator

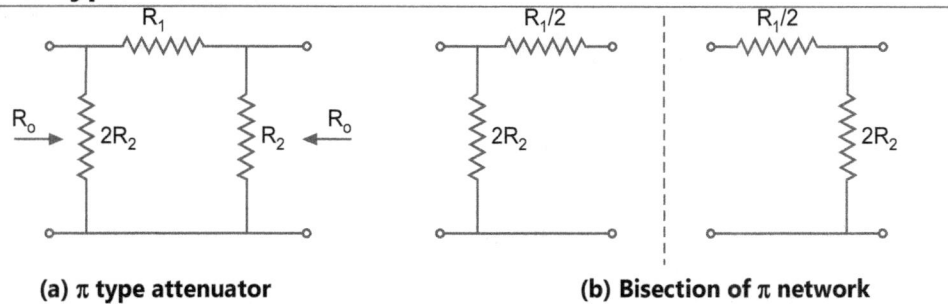

(a) π type attenuator (b) Bisection of π network

Fig. 4.4

For half section of π type attenuator:

$$R_{SC} = \frac{R_1}{2} \parallel 2R_2$$

$$= \frac{2 \times \frac{R_1 R_2}{2}}{\frac{R_1}{2} + 2R_2}$$

$$R_{SC} = \frac{R_1 R_2}{\frac{R_1}{2} + 2R_2} = R_A$$

$$R_A = \frac{R_1 R_2}{\frac{R_1}{2} + 2R_2} \qquad \ldots(a)$$

$$R_{OC} = 2R_2 = R_B$$

$$R_2 = \frac{R_B}{2} \qquad \ldots(b)$$

Substituting equation 4.5 in equation (b)

$$R_2 = \frac{R_o}{2}\left(\frac{N-1}{N+1}\right)$$

∴ $$\boxed{2R_2 = R_o\left(\frac{N+1}{N-1}\right)} \qquad \ldots(4.8)$$

Substituting in equation 4.4 in equation (a)

$$R_A = \frac{R_1 \left(\frac{R_B}{2}\right)}{\frac{R_1}{2} + R_B}$$

$$R_A R_B + \frac{R_1 R_A}{2} = \frac{R_1 R_B}{2}$$

$$R_A R_B = \frac{R_1}{2}(R_B - R_A)$$

∴ $$R_1 = \frac{2 R_A R_B}{R_B - R_A}$$

$$= \frac{2 R_0^2}{R_0 \left[\left(\frac{N+1}{N-1}\right) - \left(\frac{N-1}{N+2}\right)\right]}$$

$$\boxed{R_1 = R_0 \left(\frac{N^2 - 1}{2N}\right)} \qquad \ldots (4.9)$$

4.2 SUMMARY OF ATTENUATORS

Symmetrical T Type Attenuator	(circuit: $R_1/2$ series arms, R_2 shunt)	$N = \text{Antilog}\left(\frac{D}{20}\right)$ $\frac{R_1}{2} = R_o \left(\frac{N-1}{N+1}\right)$ $R_2 = R_o \left(\frac{2N}{N^2 - 1}\right)$
Symmetrical π Type Attenuator	(circuit: R_1 series, $2R_2$ shunts)	$N = \text{Antilog}\left(\frac{D}{20}\right)$ $R_1 = R_o \left(\frac{N^2 - 1}{2N}\right)$ $2R_2 = R_o \left(\frac{N+1}{N-1}\right)$

contd. ...

Symmetrical Lattice Type Attenuator	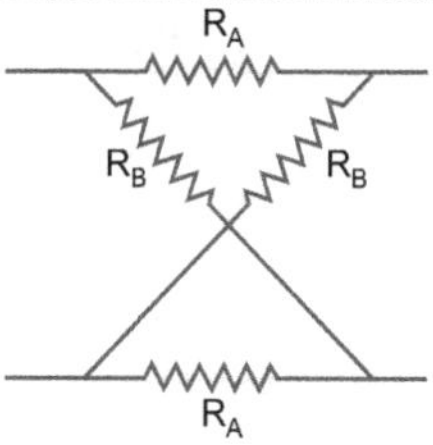 ![lattice diagram]	$N = \text{Antilog}\left(\dfrac{D}{20}\right)$ $R_A = R_0\left(\dfrac{N-1}{N+1}\right)$ $R_B = R_0\left(\dfrac{N+1}{N-1}\right)$
Bridged T Type Attenuator	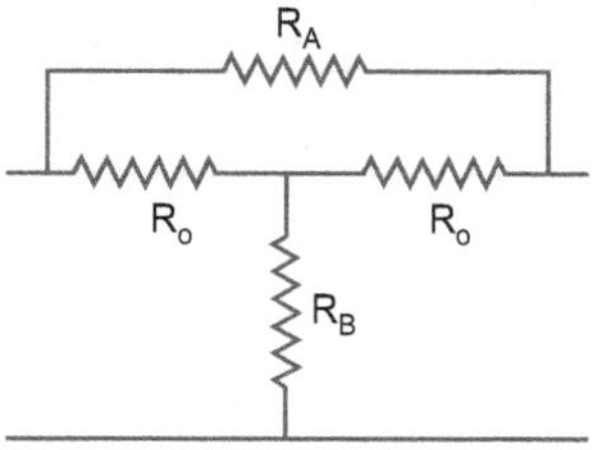 ![bridged T diagram]	$N = \text{Antilog}\left(\dfrac{D}{20}\right)$ $R_A = R_0(N-1)$ $R_B = \dfrac{R_0}{N-1}$

Fig. 4.5

4.3 SOLVED NUMERICAL ON ATTENUATORS

Ex. 4.1: Design T type attenuator to provide attenuation of 20 dB and working into characteristics impedance of 600 Ω.

Sol.:

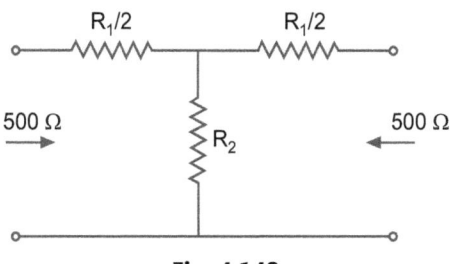

Fig. 4.142

$$N = \text{Antilog}\frac{D}{20} = 10$$

$$\frac{R_1}{2} = R_0\left(\frac{N-1}{N+1}\right)$$

$$= 600\left(\frac{9}{11}\right)$$

$$= 490.9 \ \Omega$$

$$R_2 = R_0\frac{2N}{N^2-1}$$

$$= 600 \times \frac{20}{99}$$

$$= 121.21 \ \Omega$$

Ex. 4.2: Design π type attenuator to provide attenuation of 10 dB and working into characteristic impedance of 600 Ω.

Sol.:

$$N = \text{Antilog}\frac{D}{20}$$
$$= 3.16$$

$$R_1 = R_o \frac{N^2 - 1}{2N}$$
$$= 600 \times \frac{[(3.16)^2 - 1]}{2 \times 3.16}$$
$$= 853.06 \ \Omega$$

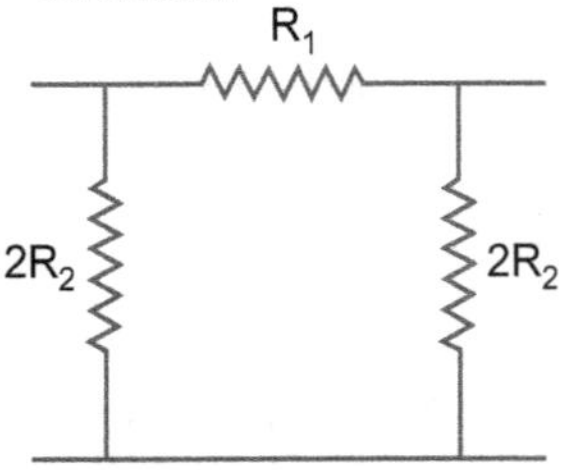

Fig. 4.7

$$2R_2 = R_o \left(\frac{N+1}{N-1}\right)$$
$$= 600 \left(\frac{4.16}{2.16}\right)$$
$$= 1.155 \ k\Omega$$

Ex. 4.3: An attenuator is composed of symmetrical T section having series arm of 175 Ω each and shunt arm of 350 Ω. Find the characteristic impedance and attenuation (in dBs).

Sol.:

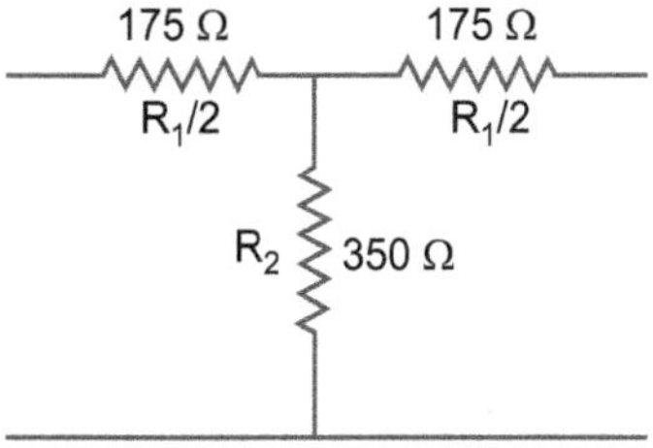

Fig. 4.8

$$\frac{R_1}{2} = R_o \left(\frac{N-1}{N+1}\right)$$
$$= 175 \qquad \qquad \ldots (1)$$

$$R_2 = R_o \frac{2N}{N^2 - 1}$$
$$= 350 \qquad \qquad \ldots (2)$$

Taking ratios of equations (1) and (2)

$$\frac{(N-1)(N^2-1)}{(N+1)2N} = \frac{1}{2}$$

$$\frac{(N-1)^2}{2N} = \frac{1}{2}$$

$$N^2 - 2N + 1 = N$$

$$\therefore \quad N^2 - 3N + 1 = 0$$

$$N = \frac{3 \pm \sqrt{9-4}}{2} = \frac{3 \pm 2.236}{2} = 2.618 \text{ or } 0.382$$

Since, N is greater than 1 choose N = 2.618.

$$N = \text{Antilog} \frac{D}{20}$$

$$\therefore \quad D = 20 \log N = 8.36 \text{ dB}$$

Substituting value of N in equation (1),

$$R_o \left(\frac{2.618-1}{2.618+1}\right) = 175$$

$$\therefore \quad \text{Characteristic impedance } R_o = 175 \times \left(\frac{3.618}{1.618}\right) = 391.316 \, \Omega$$

Ex. 4.4: An attenuator is composed of symmetrical π section having a series arm of 275 Ω and each shunt arm of 450 Ω. Calculate:
(1) The characteristic impedance of the network.
(2) Attenuation provided by each section.
Sol.:

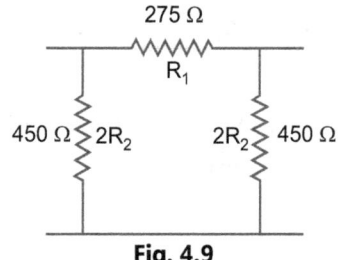

Fig. 4.9

$$R_1 = R_o \frac{N^2-1}{2N} = 275 \, \Omega \quad \ldots (1)$$

$$2R_2 = R_o \left(\frac{N+1}{N-1}\right) = 450 \, \Omega \quad \ldots (2)$$

Divide equation (1) by equation (2),

$$\therefore \quad \frac{(N^2-1)}{2n} \frac{(N-1)}{(N+1)} = \frac{275}{450}$$

$$\therefore \quad \frac{(N-1)^2}{2N} = \frac{275}{450}$$

$$N^2 - 2N + 1 = 1.222 \, N$$

$$\therefore \quad N^2 - 3.222\,N + 1 = 0$$

$$\therefore \quad N = \frac{3.222 \pm \sqrt{(3.222)^2 - 4}}{2} = \frac{3.222 \pm 2.526}{2}$$

$$= 2.874 \text{ or } 0.348$$

$$\therefore \quad D = 20 \log N = 20 \log 2.874 = 9.17 \text{ dBs}$$

Substituting in equation (1),

$$275 = R_o \left(\frac{7.259}{5.748}\right)$$

$$\therefore \quad R_o = 217.75 \ \Omega$$

Ex. 4.5: Design bridged T attenuator working into 600 Ω to provide 20 dB attenuation.

Sol.: $N = \text{Antilog}\left(\dfrac{D}{20}\right) = \text{Antilog}\left(\dfrac{20}{20}\right) = 10$

Using design equation,

$$R_A = R_o (N - 1) = 600 (10 - 1) = 5400 \ \Omega$$

$$R_B = \frac{R_o}{N - 1} = \frac{600}{10 - 1} = 66.657 \ \Omega$$

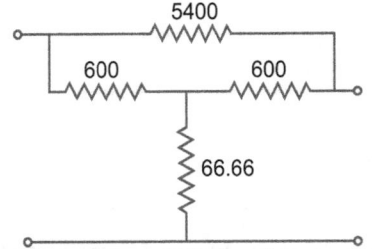

Fig. 4.10: Bridged T Type Attenuator

Ex. 4.6: Determine the components of bridged T attenuator which will give an attenuation of 30 dB and working with the characteristic resistance of 600 Ω.

Sol.: $N = \text{Antilog}\left(\dfrac{D}{20}\right) = \text{Antilog}\left(\dfrac{30}{20}\right) = 31.6227$

Using design equations,

$$R_A = R_o (N - 1) = 600 (31.6277 - 1)$$

$$\boxed{R_A = 18.3736 \ k\Omega}$$

$$R_B = \frac{R_o}{N - 1} = \frac{600}{31.6277 - 1}$$

$$\boxed{R_B = 19.5933 \ \Omega}$$

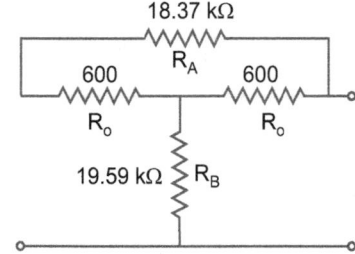

Fig. 4.11: Bridged T Attenuator

(B) FILTERS

4.4 INTRODUCTION

- Concept of "Filters" is very common in our day-to-day life. We use filters at many places. e.g. Paper filter is used to remove unwanted constituents such as suspended particles in water.

  Example: Breathing masks (Filters) are used when driving in a very polluted city, etc.

- These are all the examples of mechanical filters. Similarly electrical filters do exists and are used to remove unwanted constituents such as noise or some frequency band from a electrical signal.

- An electronic filter is an electronic circuit which performs signal processing functions, specifically to remove unwanted frequency components from the signal to enhance the wanted ones or both.

- An electronic filter may also be sometimes used in circuits with sinusoidal sources of constant frequency. Ex. L, C, LC filters used for ripple rejection in the various power supplies, just after the rectifier circuits. Filter are very commonly used in telephones, TV, radioreceivers and almost in every electronic circuit. Any electronic filters can roughly be classified as under:

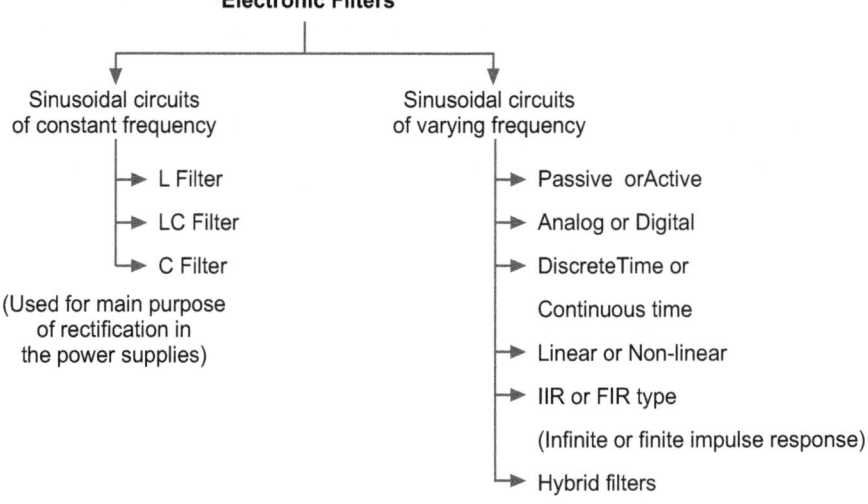

Fig. 4.12: Classification of Electronic Filters

In this chapter we will concentrate only on PASSIVE filters and analyse the effect on the o/p voltage due to the variation in the source frequency.

4.5 PASSIVE FILTERS

- Passive filters are the oldest forms of the electronic filters, which incorporates passive devices like resistors, capacitors and inductors.
- A passive filter does not have any active components like transistors or op-amps.
- Thus the output signal in case of passive filters can never have more power or amplitude than the applied that signal.
- Moreover use of inductors in the passive filters, make the circuit bulky and costly.
- The only advantage of using passive circuits is that they do not require additional power supplies for their operation.

  [op/amps need V_{cc}, V_{ee} supply for their operation. Even transistors have to be biased by V_{cc}, I_B etc. before their operation].

4.5.1 Basic Definitions

Let us now understand the basic terms associated with any filter circuit.

(a) Frequency Response:

- Filter networks are designed to separate different. Frequency bands available in an alternating input signal. Thus, when analyzing the filter network, we actually analyse the effect on voltage and current in different frequency bands, due to variation in the source frequency.
- That means we learn the response of the filter circuit (in terms of voltage, gain or current) to the changing i/p frequency. This is called as the frequency response of the circuit.

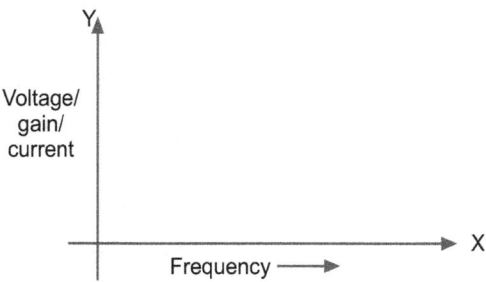

Fig. 4.13: Frequency Response: Plot of frequency Vs. Circuit parameter

- And the analysis of this behaviour is called as frequency response analysis.

(b) Cut-off Frequency:

- Speaking in terms of network filters, the cut-off frequency can loosely be defined as the frequency can loosely be defined as the frequency after which the circuit will show change in its behaviour and the response. It is the frequency which indicates the change in the band (pass band to stop band or vice versa) of the filter, thus separates the bands.
- It is actually the frequency at which the voltage gain equals 0.707 of its maximum value.
- This cut-off frequency is also referred to as the half power frequency because the load power is half of its maximum value at the this frequency.
- The output power is half of the maximum at the cut-off frequencies because:

    When the voltage gain is 0.707 of the maximum value, the output voltage is 0.707 of the maximum value. Now power = $\dfrac{(\text{Voltage})^2}{\text{Resistance}}$.

    So, when you square 0.707 we have 0.5 and so load power is half of its maximum value at the cut-off frequencies.
- Depending on the type of filter, the circuit may have one or two cut-off frequencies.
- Cut-off frequency is also referred as corner frequency.

(c) Pass Band:

- We have kept on defining a filter as the circuit which freely passes the desired band of the frequencies, while suppresses other band of frequencies. [Frequency discriminators].
- But in reality filters are not actually or physically separating the frequencies. It is the output voltage or current of the filter which prominently differs at different frequencies, thus enabling us to separate them.
- Thus, the pass band is defined as the range of frequencies for which the filter circuit responses to the input signal giving an considerable. Voltage at the output.
- In short it may be defined as the range of frequencies over which attenuation by the filter is zero, or the range of frequencies over which signals are passed from the input to the output.

(d) Stop Band or Attenuation Band:

- As the name indicates, a stop band can similarly be defined as the range of frequencies over which the filter circuit does not respond to the i/p signal giving almost no voltage at the output.
- In short it may be defined as the range of frequencies over which attenuation by the filter is infinite, or the range of frequencies over which the signals are blocked from input to the output.
- Depending on the type of the filter, the circuit may have one or two pass and stop bands.

Practically, we have one more band existing in the response of the filter circuit i.e. Transition Band. We will see this when discussing the ideal and practical filter.

4.5.2 Classification of Passive Filters

There are different types of filters existing in the electronics world. They are:

1. Low Pass Filter
2. High Pass Filter
3. Band Pass Filter
4. Band Stop Filter
5. All Pass Filter

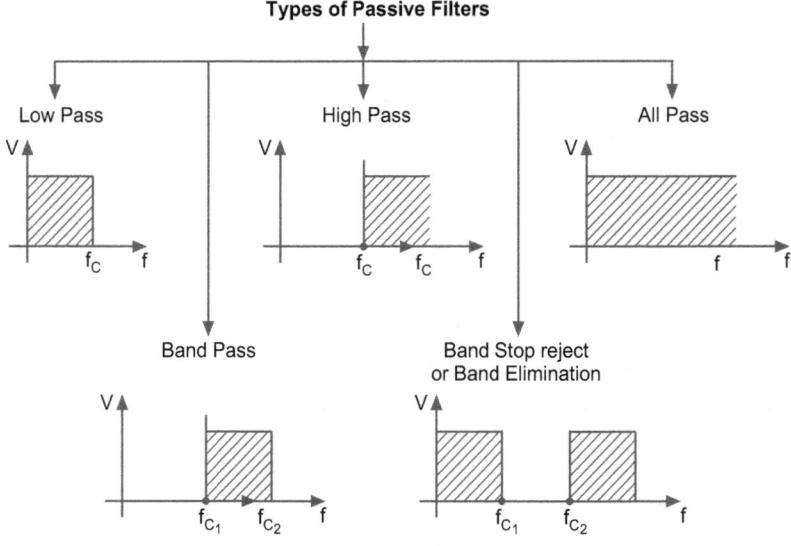

Fig. 4.14: Types of Passive Filters

1. **Low Pass Filter:**
   A low pass filter is a circuit which responses to all the frequencies below the cut-off (f_c) frequency which attenuates or blocks the frequencies higher than the cut-off frequency. Thus, we say that low frequency signals are passed from input to the output with ideally zero and practically less attenuation. Signals falling in the band of frequencies ($0 < f < f_c$) have their magnitude ideally equal to the signal and are known as passband. Input voltage outside this band ($f_c < f < \infty$) of frequencies have their magnitude attenuated by the circuit. This band of frequencies is known as **stop band**.

   Table 4.1: Low Pass Filter
   A filter that passes the frequencies lower than the cut-off frequency

Band	Frequency Range	O/P Voltage Ideal	Ideal Attenuation
Pass Band	$0 < f \leq f_c$	$V_{out} = V_{in}$	0
Stop Band	$f_c < f \leq \infty$	$V_{out} = 0$	∞

2. **High Pass Filter:**
   - A High pass filter is a circuit which responses to all the frequencies above the cut-off (f_c). Frequency which attenuates or blocks the frequencies lower than the cut-off frequency.
   - Thus, we Say that high frequency signals are passed from input to the output with ideally zero and practically less attenuation.
   - Signals falling in this band of frequencies ($f_c < f$) have their magnitude ideally equal to the input signal and are known as **pass band**.
   - Input voltage outside this band of frequencies ($0 < f < f_c$) have their magnitudes attenuated by the circuit. This band of frequencies is known as **stop band**.

3. **Band Pass Filter:**
   - A Band pass filter responses only to a particular band of frequencies and blocks the frequencies higher and lower than the desired hand.
   - It is a circuit with two cut-off frequencies f_L and f_H and has two stop hands.
   - The frequencies below f_L and above f_H are completely attenuated.
   - Only the frequencies between f_L and f_H are passed to the output.
   - This band of frequencies where ($f_L \leq f \leq f_H$) V_{out} is ideally equal to V_{in} is called as **pass band**.
   - The two bands of frequencies ($f < f_L$ and $f > f_H$) i.e. below the lower cut-off and above the higher cut-off are **stop band** frequencies.

4. **Band Stop Filter:**
   - A Band stop filter rejects or blocks a particular band of frequencies and passes all the frequencies higher and lower than this band.
   - It is a circuit with two cut-off frequencies f_L and f_H and it has two pass bands.
   - The frequencies between f_L and f_H are completely blocked or attenuated by the circuit and the frequencies less than f_L and higher than f_H are passed to the output.

- These band of frequencies where in ideally $V_{out} = V_{in}$ [$f \leq f_L$ and $f \geq f_H$] is **stop band** frequency. [$V_{out} = 0$].
- This filter is also called as **Band Stop** or **elimination** filter.

5. **All Pass Filter:**
   - All pass filter is a circuit with no stop band and has only a pass band. Because of it passes all the frequencies between zero and infinity.
   - It is strange that it still has to be called as filter. Since it zero attenuation for all the frequencies.
   - The reason it is so called is because of the effect it has on the phase of the signals passing thorough it.
   - This filter is useful when we want to produce a certain amount of phases shift for the signal being filtered without changing the amplitude.

We will however restrict our discussion and scope of analysis to only first four types of filters namely LPF, HPF, BPF, BSF. So let just summarise them:

Filter	Band	Frequency Range	Ideal output voltage	Ideal Attenuation	Ideal frequency Responses
Low Pass	Pass Stop	$0 < f \leq f_c$ $f_c < f < \infty$	$V_{out} = V_{in}$ $V_{out} = 0$	0 ∞	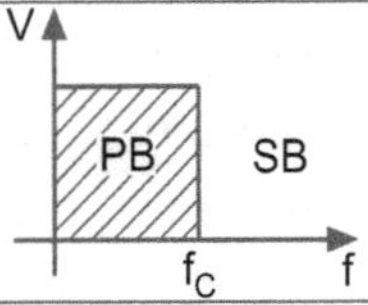
High Pass	Pass Stop	$f \leq f_c < \infty$ $0 < f < f_c$	$V_{out} = V_{in}$ $V_{out} = 0$	0 ∞	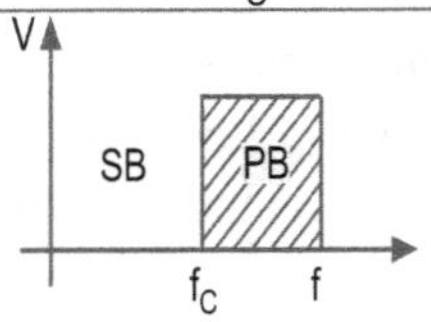
Band Pass	Pass Stop Stop	$f_L < f \leq f_H$ $0 < f < f_L$ $f_H < f < \infty$	$V_{out} = V_{in}$ $V_{out} = 0$ $V_{out} = 0$	0 ∞ ∞	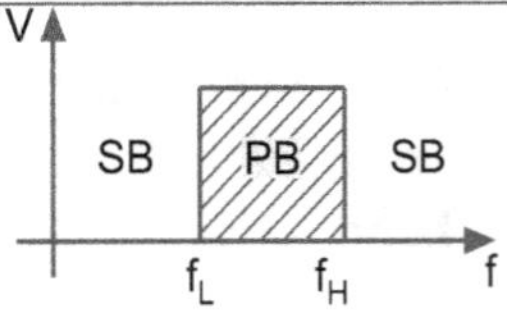
Band Stop	Pass Pass Stop	$0 < f < f_L$ $f_H < f < \infty$ $f_L < f < f_H$	$V_{out} = V_{in}$ $V_{out} = 0$ $V_{out} = 0$	0 0 ∞	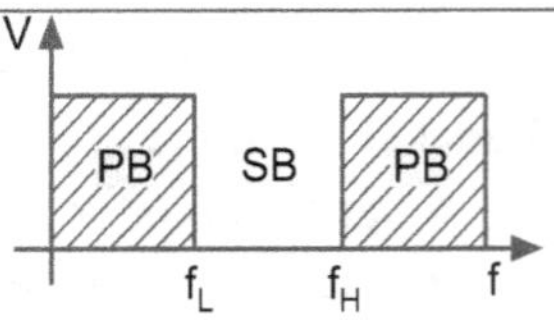

PB: Pass Band, SB: Stop Band

Fig. 4.15: Summary of Passive Filter

Low Pass : Passes the frequencies lower than the f_C.
High Pass : Passes the frequencies higher than the f_C.
Band Pass : Passes a band of frequencies between f_L and f_H.
Band Stop : Stops / Rejects a band of frequencies between f_L and f_H.

We have discussed one way of classifying the passive filters i.e. based on their functionality. Now each of these filters can be further classified as follows:

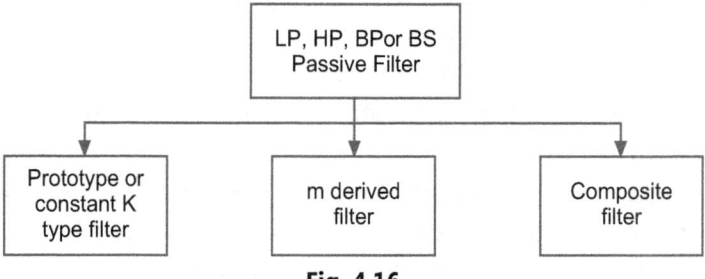

Fig. 4.16

We will be covering each of this type of filter in this chapter but at a later stage.

4.5.3 Ideal and a Practical Filter

You must have noticed that it all the discussions we had, there were always some terms like ideal and practical, may be related to voltages at the output or to the values of attenuation or frequency responses.

Now, let us understand these terms, considering an example.

Assume that you are on the sixth floor of a building and you want to reach the ground floor. Now this movement should ideally take absolutely no time. But practically even if you use an elevator with highest speed and latest technology it will still take some time (may be in ms) to reach the ground floor. So we need to understand that there is always some time elapsed in the change over of the states. No change can be sudden or instant. It will always take some time. That is the reason even the clock signal which ideally is drawn as in Fig. 4.17 (a) will in actual (practically) be as shown in Fig. 4.17 (b)

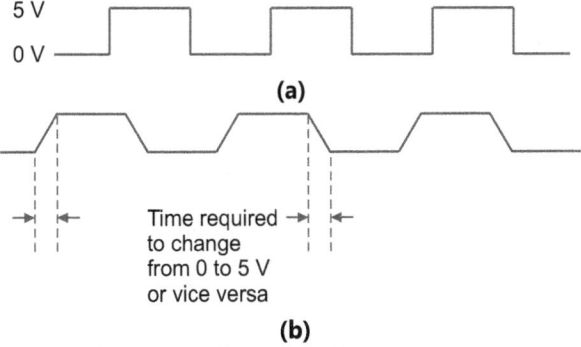

Fig. 4.17: Ideal and Practical Clock

- Now let us relate this concept with the filters.
  A filter circuit has two bands, pass band and stop band, following each other.

	Attenuation	V_{out}
Pass band	0	V_{in}
Stop band	∞	0

- Thus, it must now be clear that when the band changes from pass band to stop band, attenuation changes from 0 to ∞ and V_{out} change from V_{in} to 0.
- So this change over cannot be instant or sudden, as expected ideally. Practically it is gradual and takes time.
- As will be discussed in the point of filter fundamentals, filter is made up of reactive elements like inductors and capacitors, which oppose the change in current and voltage respectively. So change of voltage and current from 0 to maximum value cannot be instant.
- So an ideal frequency response, say for low pass filter is as shown in Fig. 4.18 (a) and a practical frequency curve would be as in Fig. 4.18 (b).

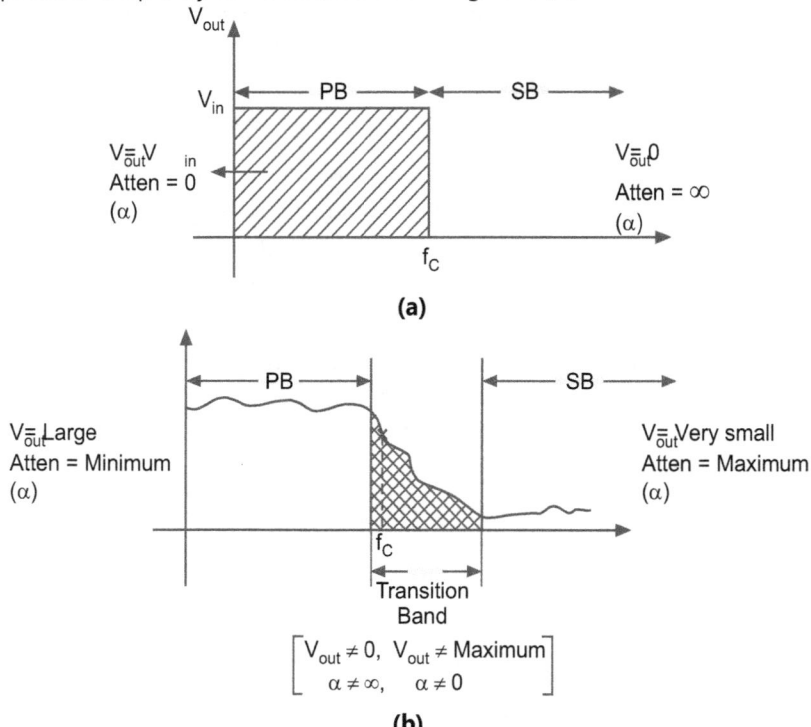

Fig. 4.18: Ideal and Practical Frequency Response (LPF)

- As seen in the diagram, the roll-off region between the pass band and the stop band, where V_{out} is neither zero nor equal to V_{in} and even the attenuation is neither infinity nor-zero, is called as transition band.
- This transition band does not exist in the ideal response for a filter. It is sometimes called a **brick wall response**, because the right edge of the rectangle looks like a brick wall.

Summary:

Ideal frequency curves or response of any filter differ from the practical response in three ways:

	Ideal Filter Response	**Practical Filter Response**
1.	Attenuation α is zero in pass band infinite in stop band	Attenuation α is minimum is pass band maximum in stop band
2.	Output voltage is equal to V_{in} in pass band 0 is stop band	Output voltage is maximum (≠ V_{in}) in PB very less (≠ 0) in SB
3.	There exists no transition band in ideal response (vertical transition)	There exists a transition band in practical response.

4.6 FILTER FUNDAMENTALS

- We have discussed about the pass and the stop bands which every filter must have.
- Let us now discuss about the:
- Type of component [R, L or C] required to build any filter circuit.
- Necessary conditions which these components should satisfy so that filter operates in both bands.
- Frequency range of these bands.

    Filters are realized using symmetrical T or π sections as shown in Fig. 4.19.

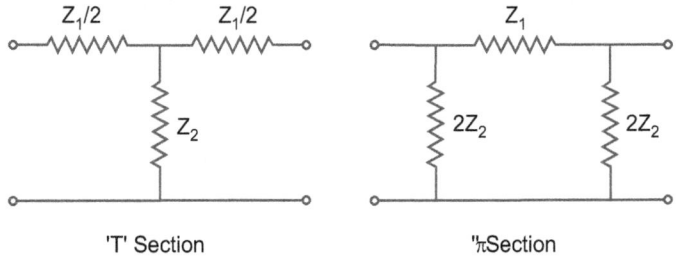

Fig. 4.19: Symmetrical T and π Sections

- Now, as we are discussing passive filters in this chapter, so obviously we have to choose between R, L and C as the values of Z_1 and Z_2.
- So the possible combinations would be having a filter circuit consisting of

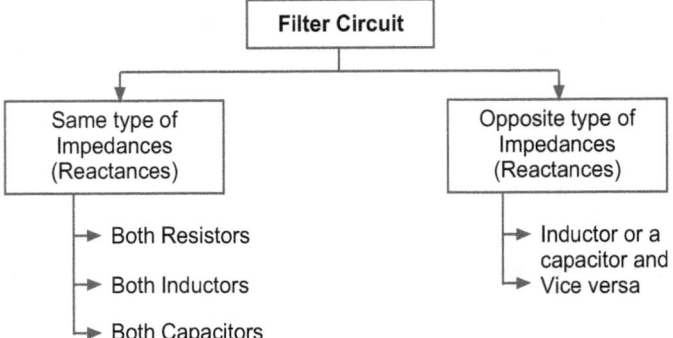

Fig. 4.20

- Before giving mathematical treatment or any analysis of all these possibilities, to reach a conclusion about the combination of Z_1 and Z_2, let us just logically think about the possible combination.

4.6.1 Logical Thinking

- Passive implementations of linear filters are based on combinations of the passive components resistors (R), Inductors (L) and Capacitors (C).
- This filter must have a pass and a stop band at high or low frequency depending on the type of the filter.
- So, naturally you must have the filter circuit components conducting at low and high frequencies.
- Possibility of having Z_1 and Z_2 both as resistors must be completely ruled out because the response of any filter depends on the frequency. So the component used to build filter must be frequency dependent. Resistors on their own have no frequency selective properties. Nor do their value depend on frequency. So we cannot have this frequency independent component to build a frequency dependent circuit.
- Now let us think about the components which are dependent on frequency. Reactances of inductor and a capacitor depend on frequency. Their behaviour can be summarized as:

		High Frequency	Low Frequency
Inductors ($j\omega L$)	Reactance (αf)	Very high	Very low
	Operation	Block signal	Pass signal
Capacitors $\left(\dfrac{1}{j\omega c}\right)$	Reactance $\left(\alpha \dfrac{1}{f}\right)$	Very low	Very high
	Operation	Pass signal	Block signal

- So now, with a conclusion of using L and C as the Z_1 and Z_2 components let us again think of the same possibility i.e. selecting Z_1 and Z_2 both as 'L' or selecting Z_1 and Z_2 both as 'C'. [Same type of reactance].
- If we build a filter with only inductors i.e. Z_1 and Z_2 both as inductors, then as clear from the summary table above, we will have a filter which will pass the lower frequencies and will block the higher frequencies.
- So with this combination a filter will always have a passband at lower freuqnices and a stop band at higher frequencies. Thus making it impossible to have pass band at higher frequencies which is desired for High pass and Band pass filters.
- The same will be the case if Z_1 and Z_2 both are capacitors. With this combination you will end up with a filter having a stop band at lower frequencies and pass band at higher frequencies, thus leaving no scope to design and low pass or a band stop filter, in which pass band is required at low frequencies as well.

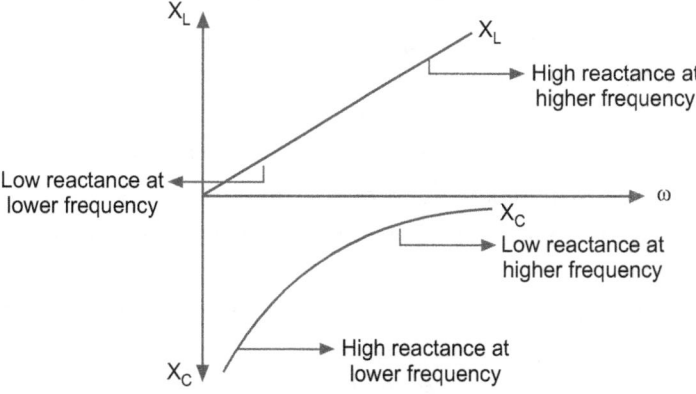

Fig. 4.21: Reactance Curves of L and C

- So we just cannot have a filter circuit having

    Z_1 and Z_2 both as Resistors

    Z_1 and Z_2 both as Capacitor

    Z_1 and Z_2 both as Inductor
- So the only choice we are left when selecting frequency dependent components for filters is having Z_1 and Z_2 as opposite type of reactances.
- So any filter can be build using Z_1 and Z_2 as L and C. With this combination we will have one component, inductor for filter circuit conducting (passing the signal) at lower frequency and one component, capacitor conducting at high frequency.
- So with the various combinations of L and C we can design any time of filter.
- Now, let us mathematically understand and also verify the necessity of having Z_1 and Z_2 as opposite type of reactances.

4.6.2 Mathematical Analysis

- Before we start with mathematical analysis let us revise the hyperbolic trigonometry without going into any details.
- Hyperbolic functions simply the writing of certain exponential relations and knowledge of their limits is useful.
- sinh, cosh, tanh are the hyperbolic functions that are normally used.
- The values of these functions at the limits $\mu = 0$, $\mu = \infty$ are

Table 4.2

Hyperbolic Function	$\mu = 0$	$\mu = \infty$
sinh μ	0	∞
cosh μ	1	∞
tanh μ	0	1

For complex angles, where $\mu = a + jb$, the expressions are:

$$\sinh(a + jb) = \sinh a \cosh jb + \cosh a \sinh jb$$
$$= \sinh a \cos b + j \cosh a \sin b$$

We will need these theory as we move into deeper filter fundamentals.

- A filter is made up of symmetrical T or π sections.
- The propagation constant 'γ' (gama) is one important property of the symmetrical networks.
- This property is a function of frequency and so can supply the information on the ability of the filter to perform as desired.

$$\gamma = \alpha + j\beta$$

γ is imaginary	$\alpha = 0$	$I_{out} = I_{in}$	No attenuation only phase shift (Pass Band)
γ is real and positive	$\alpha \neq 0$ $\alpha = +$ ve value	$I_{out} < I_{in}$	Attenuation occurred Attenuation/Stop band

$$\sinh \frac{\gamma}{2} = \sqrt{\frac{Z_1}{4Z_2}} \qquad \ldots(a)$$

$$\sinh \frac{\gamma}{2} = \sinh \left(\frac{\alpha}{2} + j\frac{\beta}{2}\right)$$

$$\sinh \frac{\gamma}{2} = \sinh \frac{\alpha}{2} \cos \frac{\beta}{2} + j \cosh \frac{\alpha}{2} \cdot \sin \frac{\beta}{2} \qquad \ldots(b)$$

A filter must have both the bands irrespective of the type of filter, both i.e. a pass and a stop band will exist in it. So for constructing a filter circuit γ must accordingly have both imaginary as well as real and positive values.

Case I: Z_1 and Z_2 Are the same type of reactance

- Let us start our analysis thinking that Z_1 and Z_2 can be same type of reactances.

    If Z_1 and Z_2 both are:

    (i) Resistors

    then, $\quad \dfrac{Z_1}{4Z_2} = \dfrac{R_1}{4R_2} = $ Real and positive ratio

    (ii) Inductors

    then, $\quad \dfrac{Z_1}{4Z_2} = \dfrac{j\omega L_1}{j\omega L_2} = $ Real and positive ratio

    (iii) Capacitors

    then, $\quad \dfrac{Z_1}{4Z_2} = \dfrac{\frac{1}{j\omega C_1}}{\frac{1}{j\omega C_2}} = $ Real and positive ratio

Thus, in any case, when Z_1 and Z_2 are of the same type,

$$\left|\dfrac{Z_1}{4Z_2}\right| > 0 \quad \text{Real and a positive ratio}$$

∴ $\sinh \dfrac{\gamma}{2}$ must be real and positive.

∴ From equation (b)

(i) $\sinh \dfrac{\alpha}{2} \cos \dfrac{\beta}{2} = \sqrt{\dfrac{Z_1}{4Z_2}}$

(ii) $\cosh \dfrac{\alpha}{2} \sin \dfrac{\beta}{2} = 0$

...must be simultaneously satisfied

From equation (ii)

$\sin \dfrac{\beta}{2} = 0 \quad \ldots \because \cosh \dfrac{\alpha}{2} \neq 0$ minimum value of cosh is '1'

∴ $\boxed{\beta = n\pi}$ ... (4.10)

If $\quad \sin \dfrac{\beta}{2} = 0$

then $\quad \cos \dfrac{\beta}{2} = 1 \quad \ldots \because \sin^2 x + \cos^2 x = 1$

So equation (i) becomes

$$\sinh\frac{\alpha}{2} = \sqrt{\frac{Z_1}{4Z_2}}$$

$$\boxed{\alpha = 2\sinh^{-1}\sqrt{\frac{Z_1}{4Z_2}}} \qquad \ldots(4.11)$$

Thus if the reactances are of the same type then γ will always be positive and thus only and only a stop band will exists in such a filter circuit.

Case II: Z_1 and Z_2 are opposite type of reactances

When Z_1 and Z_2 are L and C, then

If $Z_1 = L$ and $Z_2 = C$ $\quad \dfrac{Z_1}{4Z_2} = \dfrac{j\omega L}{\dfrac{1}{j\omega C}} = j^2\omega^2 LC = -\omega^2 LC$

OR

If $Z_1 = C$ and $Z_2 = L$ $\quad \dfrac{Z_1}{4Z_2} = \dfrac{\dfrac{1}{j\omega C}}{j\omega L} = \dfrac{1}{j^2\omega^2 LC} = -\dfrac{1}{\omega^2 LC}$

So, $\dfrac{Z_1}{4Z_2}$ is negative.

∴ $\sinh\dfrac{\gamma}{2}$ must be negative.

So, from equation (b)

(i) $\sinh\dfrac{\alpha}{2}\cos\dfrac{\beta}{2} = 0$

(ii) $\cosh\dfrac{\alpha}{2}\sin\dfrac{\beta}{2} = \sqrt{\dfrac{Z_1}{4Z_2}}$

...must be simultaneously satisfied

Let us start with two condition possible in (a) part.

$\sinh\dfrac{\alpha}{2} = 0$ and $\cos\dfrac{\beta}{2} = 0$

Condition I:

$$\sinh\frac{\alpha}{2} = 0$$

∴ $\boxed{\alpha = 0} \qquad \ldots(4.12)$

(i) and (ii) must be simultaneously satisfied.

If as per (a), $\alpha = 0$, then $\cosh\frac{\alpha}{2}$ in (b) will be '1' ($\cosh 0 = 1$).

$\therefore \quad \beta \neq 0$

$\therefore \quad \sin\frac{\beta}{2} = \sqrt{\frac{Z_1}{4Z_2}}$

$$\boxed{\beta = 2\sin^{-1}\sqrt{\frac{Z_1}{4Z_2}}} \quad \ldots(4.13)$$

Condition II:

If $\quad \cos\frac{\beta}{2} = 0$

$\therefore \quad \sin\frac{\beta}{2} = 1 \qquad (\because \cos^2 A + \sin^2 A = 1)$

$$\boxed{\beta = (2n-1)\pi} \quad \ldots(4.14)$$

(i) and (ii) must be simultaneously satisfied, so if as per equation (i)

$$\sin\frac{\beta}{2} = 1$$

then, as per (ii)

$$\cosh\frac{\alpha}{2} = \sqrt{\frac{Z_1}{4Z_2}}$$

$$\boxed{\alpha = 2\cosh^{-1}\sqrt{\frac{Z_1}{4Z_2}}} \quad \ldots(4.15)$$

Condition I Leads to a passband or region of zero attenuation.

$$\alpha = 0$$

$$\beta = 2\sin^{-1}\sqrt{\frac{Z_1}{4Z_2}}$$

The band is limited by the upper limit of sine, so it is required that

$$-1 < \frac{Z_1}{4Z_2} < 0$$

Thus, the cut-off frequencies would be

$\frac{Z_1}{4Z_2} = 0 \quad$ or $\quad \boxed{Z_1 = 0} \qquad \ldots(4.16)$

$\frac{Z_1}{4Z_2} = 1 \quad$ or $\quad \boxed{Z_1 = -4Z_2} \qquad \ldots(4.17)$

To conclude, let us understand that the pass band ($\alpha = 0$) for a filter circuit with the reactances of different type would exist when

$$\frac{Z_1}{4Z_2} = 0 \text{ to } -1$$

i.e. between, $Z_1 = 0$ and $Z_1 = -4Z_2$

The phase angle in this band would be

$$\boxed{\beta = 2 \sin^{-1} \sqrt{\frac{Z_1}{4Z_2}}}$$

Condition II Leads to a stop band or an attenuation band ($\alpha \neq 0$)

$$\boxed{\alpha = 2 \cosh^{-1} \sqrt{\frac{Z_1}{4Z_2}}}$$

Even this band will naturally be limited by the upper limit of cosh. As this upper limit for cosh is ∞ we would say,

$$\frac{Z_1}{4Z_2} < -1$$

4.6.3 Summary

- Thus finally we conclude that when Z_1 and Z_2 are selected to be of opposite types. Filter can operate in pass band as well as in stop band.
- The cut-off frequencies will occur when

$$\boxed{\begin{array}{l} Z_1 = 0 \\ Z_1 = -4Z_2 \end{array}}$$

$\frac{Z_1}{4Z_2} =$	$+\infty$ to 0	0 to -1	-1 to $-\infty$
Reactance type	Same	Opposite	Opposite
Band	Stop	Pass	Stop
α	$2 \sinh^{-1} \sqrt{\frac{Z_1}{4Z_2}}$	0	$2 \cosh^{-1} \sqrt{\frac{Z_1}{4Z_2}}$
β	π	$2 \sin^{-1} \sqrt{\frac{Z_1}{4Z_2}}$	π

The complete discussion of filter fundamentals can be explained using a simple diagram shown in Fig. 4.22.

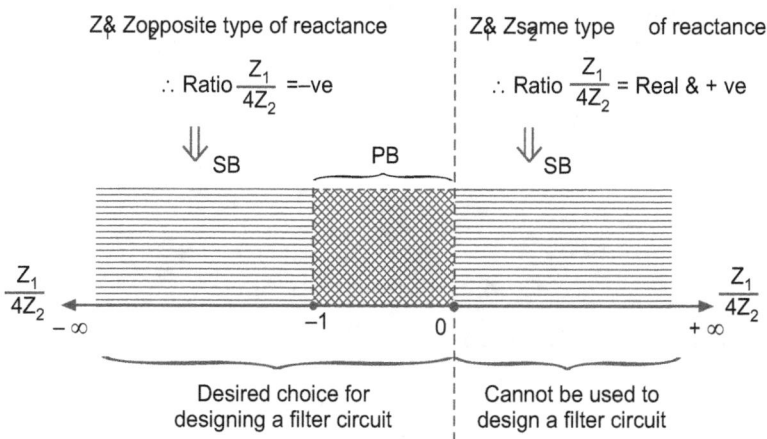

Fig. 4.22

4.7 CONSTANT k / PROTOTYPE FILTERS

- Z_1 and Z_2 of a filter circuit are opposite type of reactance's than,
$$Z_1 \cdot Z_2 = R_K^2$$
where k is a constant and it is independent of frequency. It is also called as a design impedance.

  Ex.: $Z_1 = j\omega L$ $Z_2 = -\dfrac{j}{\omega C}$

  then,
  $$Z_1 Z_2 = \dfrac{L}{C} = R_K^2$$

- Networks or filter sections for which this relation holds are called as **constant k filters**.
- These filters, either of T or π configuration are also known as **prototype** because more complex filters can be derived from them.

4.8 CONSTANT k LOW PASS FILTER

- A lowpass filter will ideally pass all the frequencies lower than (below) the cut-off frequencies. It will block the frequencies higher than the cut-off frequencies.
- We use inductor in the series arm and a capacitor in a shunt arm to achieve this kind of frequency response.
- (L) $\dfrac{Z_1}{2} + \dfrac{Z_1}{2} = Z_1$ series arm

  (C) $\dfrac{Z_2}{2} \| \dfrac{Z_2}{2} = Z_2$ shunt arm

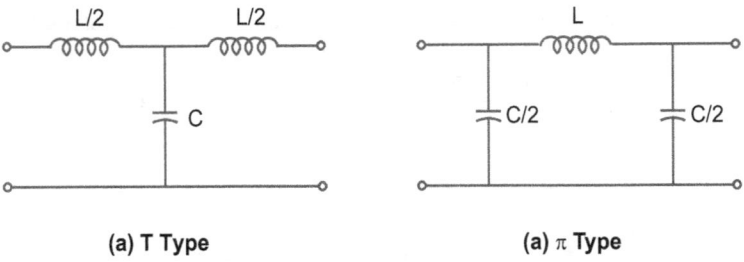

(a) T Type   (a) π Type

Fig. 4.23: Constant k LP filters

4.8.1 Operation of a Constant k LPF

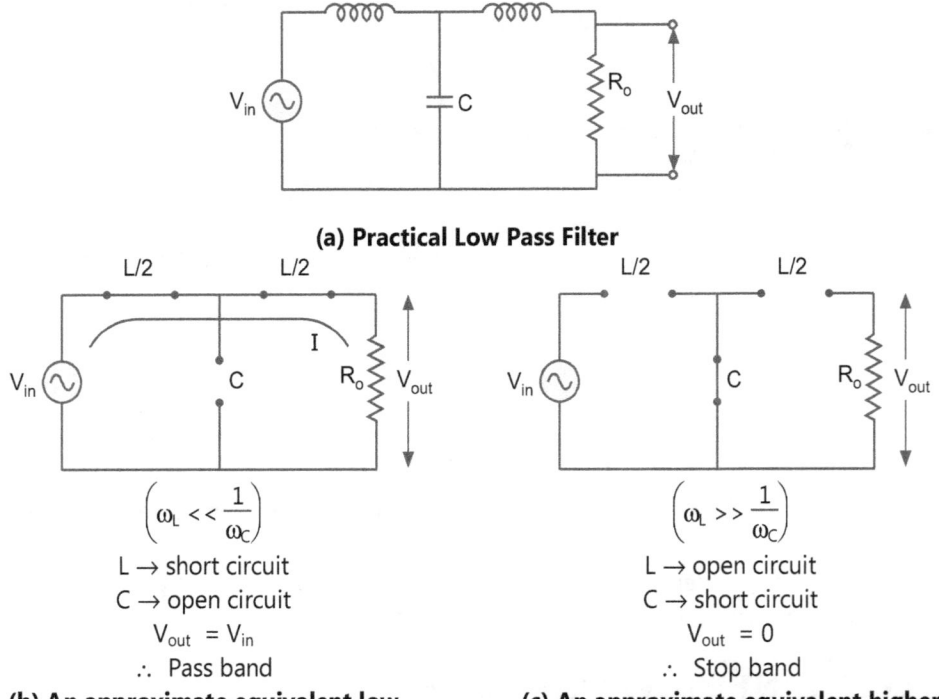

(a) Practical Low Pass Filter

(b) An approximate equivalent low frequency   (c) An approximate equivalent higher frequency

Fig. 4.24: Operation of a low pass filter

- Though resistors on their own have no frequency selective property, they are still added and used in all the practical circuits [to the inductors and capacitors to determine the time constant of the circuit].
- At low frequencies the reactance (ωL) of an indicator is small when compared to reactance $\dfrac{1}{\omega C}$ of a capacitor and so effectively, L functions as a short circuit and passes input signal to the output and C functions as a open circuit.

- For low frequencies output voltage V_o taken across the resistance R is almost equal to the input sinusoidal voltage. This is pass band of the circuit.
- At higher frequencies, the reactance ωL of inductors starts increasing and becomes much larger than the reactance of a capacitor.

$$\omega L \gg \frac{1}{\omega C}$$

So, it is acts as open circuit and no current flows through the circuit. Therefore, V_{out} gradually decreases and ultimately becomes zero. This is the stop band of the circuit.

4.8.2 Design Impedance of a Constant k LPF

In low pass filters
Total series impedance

$$Z_1 = j\omega L$$

Shunt impedance

$$Z_2 = \frac{-j}{\omega C}$$

$$Z_1 Z_2 = j\omega L \times \frac{-j}{\omega C}$$

$$Z_1 Z_2 = \frac{L}{C} = R^2$$

$$\boxed{R_k = \sqrt{\frac{L}{C}}} \qquad \ldots(4.18)$$

4.8.3 Reactance Curves and Cut-off Frequency of a Constant k LPF

- The reactances of Z_1 (inductor) and Z_2 (capacitor) will vary as shown in Fig. 4.65 (a).
- The curve representing $-4Z_2$ is draw and is compared with the curve for Z_1.
- Recollect that the pass band starts at a frequency at which $Z_1 = 0$ and runs to a frequency at which $Z_1 = -4Z_2$.
- It is clear from reactance curve that as ideally expected, pass band starts from $f = 0$ and continues till $f = f_c$. Frequencies
- All frequencies above f_c lie in the stop band.
- Thus, the network is called as a low pass filter.
- $Z_1 = 0$ and $Z_1 = -4Z_2$ determine the cut-off frequencies.

$$Z_1 = -4Z_2 \qquad \text{This is the condition at cut-off frequency}$$

$$j\omega L = -4\left(\frac{-j}{\omega C}\right)$$

$$\omega^2 LC = 4 \qquad \qquad \therefore \omega = \omega_c$$

$$4\pi^2 f_c LC = 4$$

$$\boxed{f_c = \frac{1}{\pi\sqrt{LC}}} \qquad \text{Higher cut-off frequency} \ldots (4.19)$$

Cut-off frequency of LPF is sometimes called as f_H.

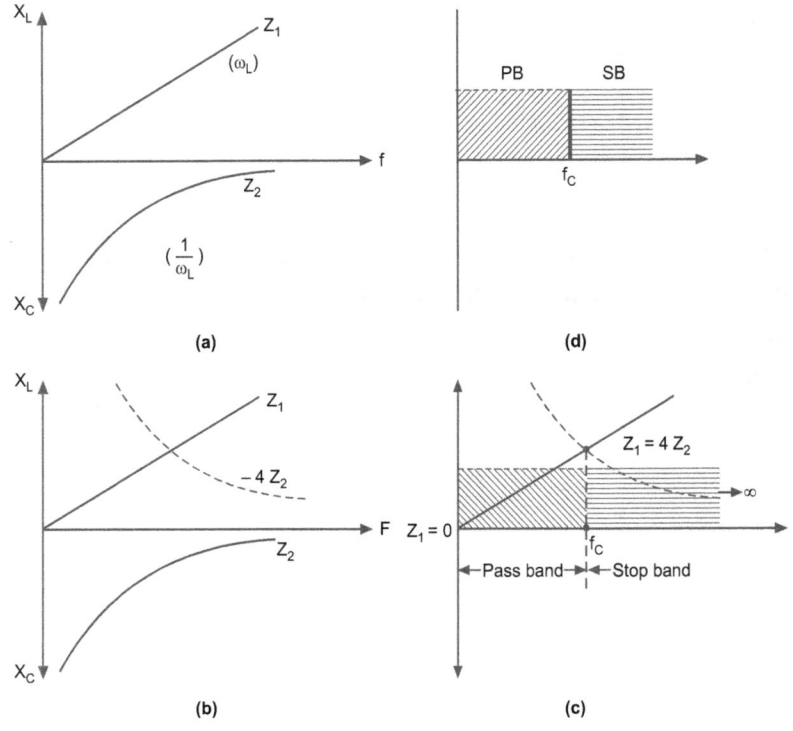

Fig. 4.25: Reactance curves for LPF

4.8.4 Design Equations of Constant K LPF

If the cut-off frequencies and the design impedance R_K for a filter are given we can design the filter components.

We have

$$f_C = \frac{1}{\pi\sqrt{LC}}$$

$$R_K = \sqrt{\frac{L}{C}}$$

Multiplying both the equations

$$f_C \cdot R_K = \frac{1}{\pi\sqrt{LC}} \times \sqrt{\frac{L}{C}}$$

$$f_C \cdot R_K = \frac{1}{\pi C}$$

$$\boxed{C = \frac{1}{\pi f_C R_K}} \qquad \ldots(4.20)$$

Dividing equation of R_K by f_C

$$\frac{R_K}{f_C} = \sqrt{\frac{L}{C}} / \frac{1}{\pi\sqrt{LC}}$$

$$\frac{R_K}{f_C} = \sqrt{\frac{L}{C}} \times \pi\sqrt{LC}$$

$$\boxed{L = \frac{R_K}{\pi f_C}}$$ ...(4.21)

These equations are called as design equations for prototype or constant K LPF.

4.8.5 Attenuation Constant and Phase Shift of a Constant K LPF

Recall the summary of the filter fundamentals.

β is pass band is

$$\beta = 2\sin^{-1}\sqrt{\frac{Z_1}{4Z_2}}$$

$$\beta = 2\sin^{-1}\sqrt{\frac{\omega L}{4 \cdot \frac{1}{\omega C}}}$$

$$\beta = 2\sin^{-1}\sqrt{\frac{\omega^2 LC}{4}}$$

$$\beta = 2\sin^{-1}\sqrt{\frac{\omega^2}{\omega_c^2}} \qquad \omega_c = \frac{4}{LC}$$

At $f = 0$, $\beta = 0$

At $f = f_C$ $\beta = 0$

Thus, $$\boxed{\beta = 2\sin^{-1}\left(\frac{f}{f_C}\right)}$$ ...(4.22)

As the frequency increases from 0 to f_C, β also increases from 0 to π radian.

β is stop band is $\boxed{\beta = \pi}$ radians. ...(4.23)

Attenuation of a constant K LPF.

α in pass band is

$\boxed{\alpha = 0}$ ...(4.24)

Recall the filter fundamentals

$$\alpha = 2\cosh^{-1}\sqrt{\frac{Z_1}{4Z_2}}$$

$$\alpha = 2\cosh^{-1}\sqrt{\frac{j\omega L}{4\frac{1}{\omega C}}}$$

$$\boxed{\alpha = 2\cosh^{-1}\left(\frac{f}{f_C}\right)} \qquad \ldots (4.25)$$

In stop band as frequency f increases above f_C, α also increases.

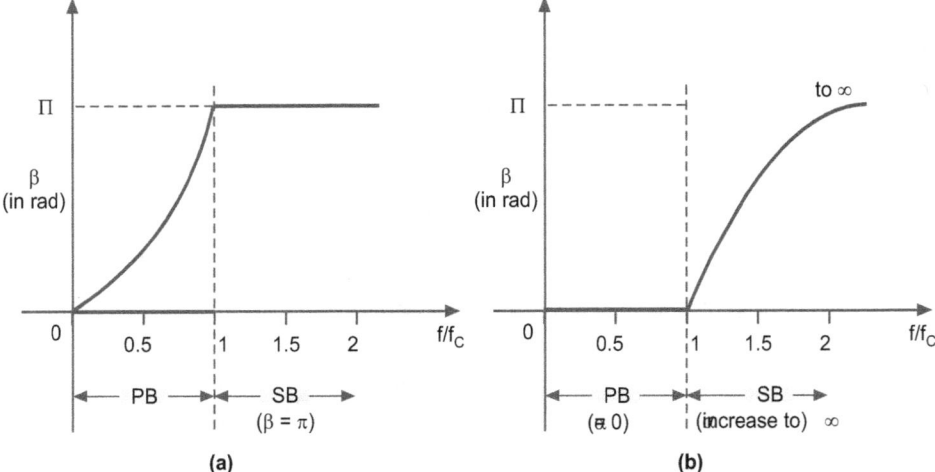

Fig. 4.26: Variation of (a) phase angle β and (b) attenuation α of a constant k LPF with frequency

4.8.6 Characteristics Impedance of Constant k LPF

- Any filter circuit is made up of symmetrical T or π type networks.
- Z_o, characteristics impedance is an important property of symmetrical network.

The characteristics impedance, of symmetrical T and π networks is given by,

$$Z_{OT} = \sqrt{\frac{Z_1^2}{4} + Z_1 Z_2}$$

$$Z_{O\pi} = \frac{Z_1 Z_2}{Z_{OT}}$$

Now, in case of LPF

$$Z_1 = j\omega L$$

$$Z_1 Z_2 = \frac{L}{C} = R_K^2$$

∴
$$Z_{OT} = \sqrt{\frac{(+j\omega L)^2}{4} + \frac{L}{C}} = \sqrt{\frac{-\omega^2 L^2}{4} + \frac{L}{C}}$$

$$= \sqrt{\frac{L}{C}} \sqrt{1 - \frac{\omega^2 LC}{4}}$$

$$Z_{OT} = \sqrt{\frac{L}{C}} \sqrt{1 - \frac{\omega^2}{\omega_c^2}} \qquad \omega_c = \frac{2}{\sqrt{LC}}$$

$$\boxed{Z_{OT} = R_K \sqrt{1 - \left(\frac{f}{f_c}\right)^2}} \qquad R_K = \sqrt{\frac{L}{C}} \qquad \dots (4.26)$$

$$\boxed{Z_{0\pi} = \frac{R_K}{\sqrt{1 - \left(\frac{f}{f_c}\right)^2}}} \qquad \dots (4.27)$$

Thus, for a T type LPF
when f = 0, $Z_{OT} = R_K$
f = f_C, $Z_{OT} = 0$

i.e. in T LPF as frequency increases from f to f_C Z_{OT} decreases from R_K to zero.
And, for a π type LPF
when f = 0, $Z_{0\pi} = R_K$
f = f_C, $Z_{0\pi} = \infty$

Similarly, here in π type LPF, when frequency increases from f = 0 and f = f_C, $Z_{0\pi}$ increases from R_K to ∞.

Characteristics impedance Z_0	Nature	Variation of Z_0 between frequencies		
		f = 0	to	f = f_c
Z_{OT}	Decreases	R_K	to	Zero
$Z_{0\pi}$	Increases	R_K	to	Infinity

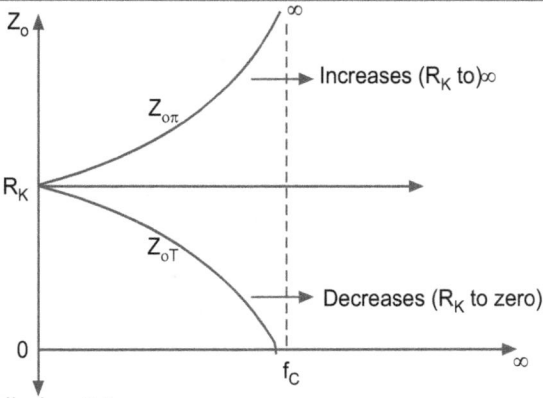

(f_C is sometimes called as F_H)

Fig. 4.27

4.8.7 Summary of Constant k LPF

Filter → Parameter ↓	LPF
Circuit diagram	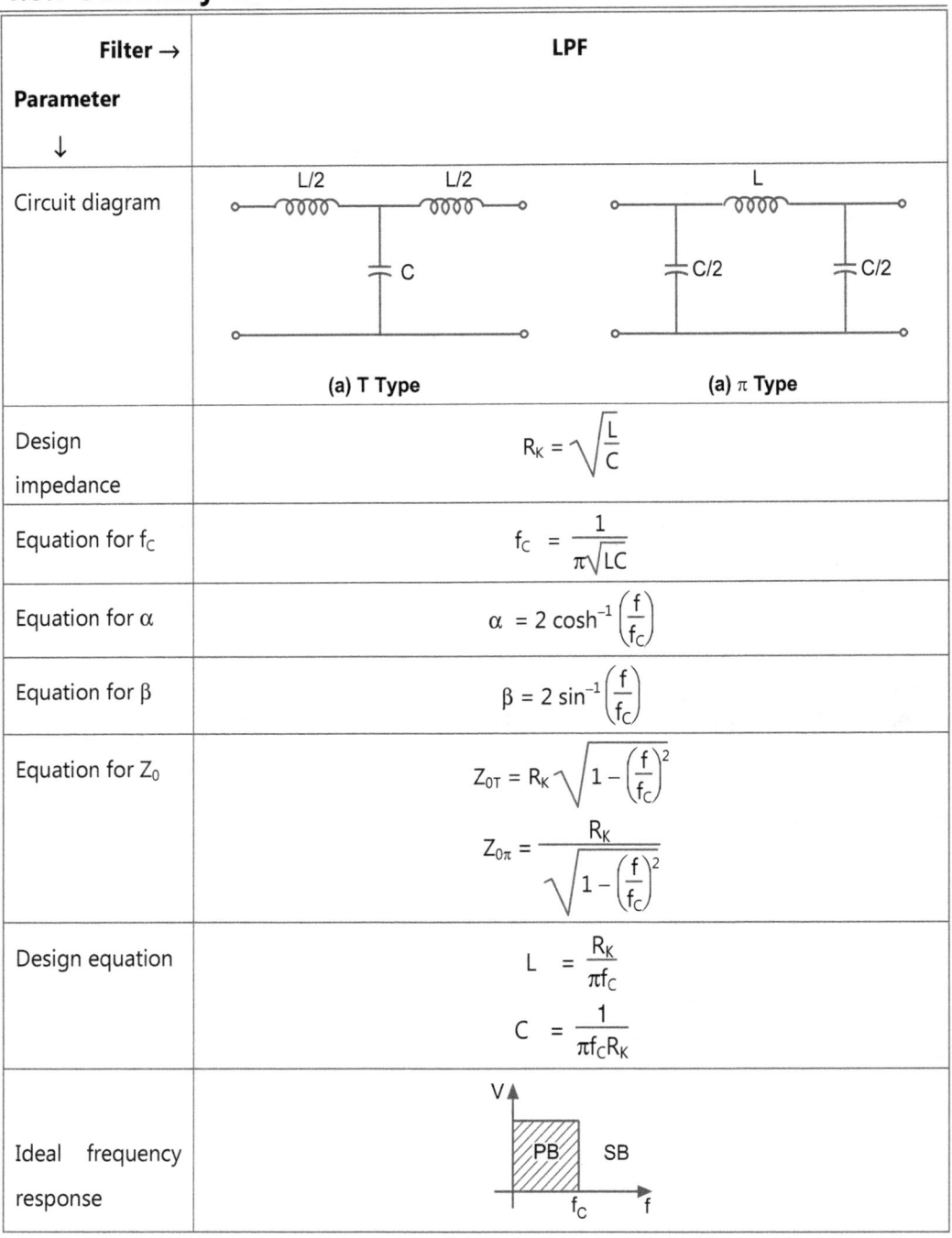 (a) T Type (a) π Type
Design impedance	$R_K = \sqrt{\dfrac{L}{C}}$
Equation for f_C	$f_C = \dfrac{1}{\pi\sqrt{LC}}$
Equation for α	$\alpha = 2\cosh^{-1}\left(\dfrac{f}{f_C}\right)$
Equation for β	$\beta = 2\sin^{-1}\left(\dfrac{f}{f_C}\right)$
Equation for Z_0	$Z_{0T} = R_K\sqrt{1-\left(\dfrac{f}{f_C}\right)^2}$ $Z_{0\pi} = \dfrac{R_K}{\sqrt{1-\left(\dfrac{f}{f_C}\right)^2}}$
Design equation	$L = \dfrac{R_K}{\pi f_C}$ $C = \dfrac{1}{\pi f_C R_K}$
Ideal frequency response	

Fig. 4.68

4.9 SOLVED NUMERICALS ON CONSTANT k LPF

Ex. 4.7: Design a constant K π section LPF to be terminated into 600 Ω and having a cut-off frequency of 3 kHz.

Determine:
(i) The frequency at which filter offers at attenuation of 17.37 dB.
(ii) Attenuation of 6 kHz.
(iii) Characteristics impedance and a phase constant at 2 kHz.

Given R_k = 600 Ω
             f_C = 3 kHz

To calculate:
(i) Filter elements
(ii) Frequency at which α = 17.372 dB
(iii) Attenuation at f = 6 kHz
(iv) Z_0 and β at f = 2 kHz.

Sol.: Given: R_k = 600 Ω
                        f_C = 3 kHz

(i) To calculate filter elements, design equations of LPF

$$L = \frac{R_0}{\pi f_C}$$

$$= \frac{600}{\pi \times 3 \times 10^3}$$

$$\boxed{L = 63.66 \text{ mH}}$$

$$C = \frac{1}{\pi f_C R_0}$$

$$= \frac{1}{\pi \times 3 \times 10^3 \times 600}$$

$$\boxed{C = 0.176 \text{ µF}}$$

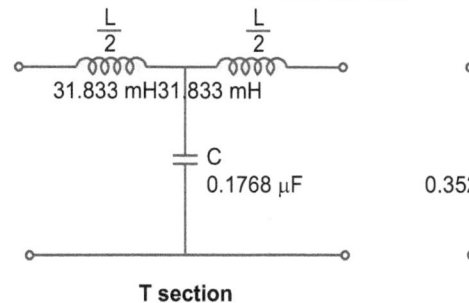
T section

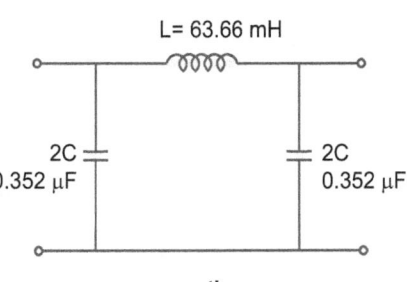
π section

Fig. 4.28

(ii) To calculate frequency at which $\alpha = 17.372$ dB

Let us express α in nepers

Attenuation in Nepers = $0.1151 \times$ Attenuation in dB
= 0.1151×17.372
= 1.9995 Nepers

For a prototype LPF

$$\alpha = 2 \cosh^{-1}\left(\frac{f}{f_C}\right)$$

$$1.995 = 2 \cosh^{-1}\left(\frac{f}{3000}\right)$$

$$\cosh\left(\frac{1.995}{2}\right) = \frac{f}{3000}$$

$$\boxed{f = 4.628 \text{ kHz}}$$

(iii) To calculate attenuation at $f = 6$ kHz.

∵ 6 kHz lies in stop band,

$$\alpha = 2 \cosh^{-1}\left(\frac{f}{f_C}\right)$$

$$\alpha = 2 \cosh^{-1}\left(\frac{6 \times 10^3}{3 \times 10^3}\right)$$

$$\alpha = 2.633 \text{ Nepers}$$

Attenuation in Neper = $0.1151 \times$ Attenuation in dB

∴ $\boxed{\alpha = 22.87 \text{ dB at } f = 6 \text{ kHz}}$

(iv) To calculate Z_0 and β at 2 kHz

$$Z_0 = R_k \sqrt{1 - \left(\frac{f}{f_C}\right)^2}$$

$$= 600 \sqrt{1 - \left(\frac{2 \times 10^3}{3 \times 10^3}\right)^2}$$

$$\boxed{Z_0 = 447.213 \, \Omega \text{ at } f = 2 \text{ kHz}}$$

2 kHz lies in pass band, therefore the phase constant β in pass band is given by

$$\beta = 2 \sin^{-1}\left(\frac{f}{f_C}\right)$$

$$\beta = 2 \sin^{-1}\left(\frac{2 \times 10^3}{3 \times 10^3}\right)$$

$$\beta = 1.4594^C \text{ or}$$

$$\boxed{\beta = 83.62°} \text{ at } f = 2 \text{ kHz}$$

Ans.:

> Filter elements $L = 63.66$ mH
> $C = 0.1768$ μF
> Frequency at which $\alpha = 17.372$ dB
> $= 4.628$ kHz
> α at $f = 6$ kHz is 2.633 Neper
> Z_0 at 2 kHz $= 447.213\ \Omega$
> β at 2 kHz $= 83.62°$

Ex. 4.8: Design a constant K LPF with $f_C = 1$ kHz and $R_0 = 600\ \Omega$. At what frequency α will be 10 dB ?

Given:
$$f_C = 1 \text{ kHz}$$
$$R_K = 600\ \Omega$$

To calculate (i) L, C (filter elements), (ii) Frequency at which $\alpha = 10$ dB.

Sol.: (i) To calculate filter elements using the design equations derived for constant K LPF.

$$L = \frac{R_K}{\pi f_C} = \frac{600}{\pi \times 1 \times 10^3}$$

$$\boxed{L = 190.98 \text{ mH}}$$

$$C = \frac{1}{\pi f_C R_K} = \frac{1}{\pi \times 1 \times 10^3 \times 600}$$

$$\boxed{LC = 0.5305 \text{ μF}}$$

(ii) T and π sections

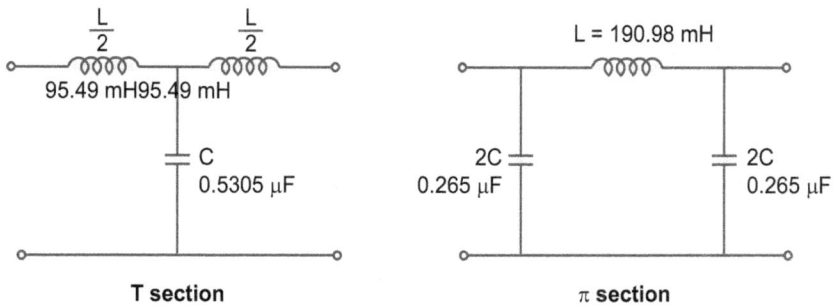

T section   π section

Fig. 4.29

(iii) Frequency at which $\alpha = 10$ dB

$$\alpha = 2 \cosh^{-1}\left(\frac{f_C}{f}\right)$$

Attenuation in nepers = $0.1151 \times \alpha$ in dB
$$= 0.1151 \times 10$$
$$\alpha = 1.151 \text{ Nepers}$$
$$\alpha = 2\cosh^{-1}\left(\frac{f}{f_c}\right)$$
$$1.151 = 2\cosh^{-1}\left(\frac{f}{1000}\right)$$
$$\cosh\left(\frac{1.151}{2}\right) = \frac{f}{1000}$$
$$\boxed{f = 1.17 \text{ K}}$$

Ans.:

L	= 190.98 mH
C	= 0.5305 µF
Freq. (α = 10 dB)	= 1.18 K

Ex. 4.9: Each of two series elements of T type LPF consists of an inductor of 60 mH and shunt element of 0.2 µF capacitor. Calculate cut-off frequency and design impedance at 1 kHz. Also find ratio of phase difference between the input and the output voltages of the filter at 1 kHz and 5 kHz.

Given:
$$\frac{L}{2} = 60 \text{ mH}$$
$$C = 0.2 \text{ µF}$$

To calculate:
(i) R_K and f_C = ?
(ii) Z_0 at 1 kHz = ?
(iii) β at 1 kHz = ? and 5 kHz = ?

Sol.: Each series element of T section is 60 mH.

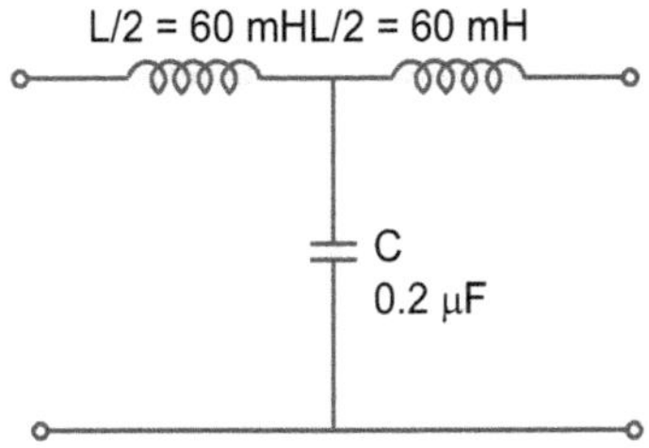

L/2 = 60 mH   L/2 = 60 mH

C
0.2 µF

Fig. 4.30

∴ $L = 2 \times 60 = 120$ mH

(i) To calculate cut-off frequency f_C

$$f_C = \frac{1}{\pi\sqrt{LC}}$$

$$= \frac{1}{\pi\sqrt{120 \times 10^{-3} \times 0.2 \times 10^{-6}}}$$

$$\boxed{f_C = 2.054 \text{ kHz}}$$

(ii) Design impedance

$$R_K = \sqrt{\frac{L}{C}} = \sqrt{\frac{120 \times 10^{-3}}{0.2 \times 10^{-6}}}$$

$$\boxed{R_K = 774.59 \ \Omega}$$

(iii) Z_{OT} at 1 kHz

$$Z_{OT} = R_0 \sqrt{1 - \left(\frac{f}{f_C}\right)^2}$$

$$= 774.59 \sqrt{1 - \left(\frac{1 \times 10^3}{2.054 \times 10^3}\right)^2}$$

$$\boxed{Z_{OT} = 676.59 \ \Omega} \text{ at 1 kHz}$$

(iv) β at 1 kHz

$$\beta = 2 \sin^{-1}\left(\frac{f}{f_C}\right)$$

$$= 2 \sin^{-1}\left(\frac{1 \times 10^3}{2.054 \times 10^3}\right)$$

$$\boxed{\beta = 58.26°} \text{ at 1 kHz}$$

(v) β at 5 kHz

$$\beta = 2 \sin^{-1}\left(\frac{f}{f_C}\right)$$

For a LPF, when f_C = 2.05 kHz.
5 kHz lies in stop band. Therefore, β in stop band is 180° or π^C.

$$\boxed{\beta = 180°} \text{ at 5 kHz}$$

Ans.:

f_C	= 2.054 kHz	
R_K	= 774.59 Ω	
Z_{OT}	= 676.59 Ω	at 1 kHz
β	= 58.26°	at 1 kHz
β	= 180°	at 5 kHz

Ex. 4.10: At what frequency will prototype T section LPF having a cut-off frequency f_C have an attenuation of 20 dB.

Given:
$$\alpha \text{ in neper} = 0.1151 \times \alpha \text{ in dB}$$
$$= 0.1151 \times 20$$
$$\alpha = 2.302 \text{ neper}$$

For a LPF,
$$\alpha = 2 \cosh^{-1}\left(\frac{f}{f_C}\right)$$
$$2.302 = 2 \cosh^{-1}\left(\frac{f}{f_C}\right)$$
$$\frac{f}{f_C} = \cosh(1.151)$$
$$\therefore \quad \frac{f}{f_C} = 1.7388$$
$$\boxed{f = 1.7388 \, f_C}$$

Ans.:
$$\boxed{\alpha = 20 \text{ dB at } f = 1.7388 \, f_C}$$

Ex. 4.11: A prototype LPF has a cut-off frequency of 5 kHz and is terminated into matched impedance of 600 Ω. Calculate the element values of filter. Also find attenuation in dB and phase shift in degree at a frequency of 8 kHz.

Given:
$$f_C = 5 \text{ kHz}$$
$$R_K = 600 \, \Omega$$

To calculate:
(i) Filter elements,
(ii) α at 8 kHz,
(iii) β at 8 kHz.

Sol.: (i) To calculate filter elements using design equations for prototype LPF

$$L = \frac{R_K}{\pi f_C}$$
$$= \frac{600}{\pi \times 5 \times 10^3}$$
$$\boxed{L = 38.1971 \text{ mH}}$$

$$C = \frac{1}{\pi f_C R_K}$$
$$= \frac{1}{\pi \times 5 \times 10^3 \times 600}$$
$$\boxed{C = 0.1061 \, \mu F}$$

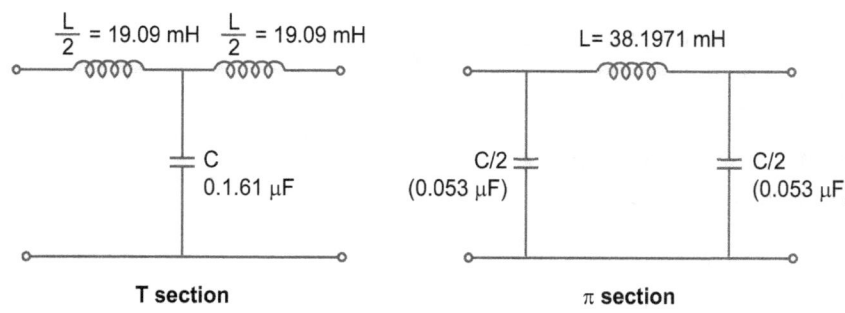

T section   π section

Fig. 4.31

(ii) Attenuation at 8 kHz.
For a low pass filter,

$$\alpha \text{ (in N)} = 2\cosh^{-1}\left(\frac{f}{f_c}\right) = 2\cosh^{-1}\left(\frac{8 \times 10^3}{5 \times 10^3}\right)$$

α = 2.0939 N at 8 kHz

But α in db = 8.686 in × α in N
= 8.686 × 2.0939

$\boxed{\alpha = 18.1879 \text{ dB at 8 kHz}}$

(iii) β at 8 kHz.
For a LPF with f_C = 5 kHz, 8 kHz lies in stop band.

∴ Phase shift at 8 kHz = 180°

$\boxed{\beta = \pi^c}$

Ans.:

$\boxed{\begin{array}{rl} L &= 38.1971 \text{ mH} \\ C &= 0.1061 \text{ μF} \\ \alpha &= 18.1879 \text{ dB at 8 kHz} \\ \beta &= 180° \quad \text{at 8 kHz} \end{array}}$

Ex. 4.12: Each of the series arm of a symmetrical low pass filter consists of an inductor of 18 mH having negligible resistance while shunt arm is a 0.1 μF capacitor. Calculate value of characteristics impedance α, β and Z_0 at frequency 1 kHz and 8 kHz. Comment on the result.

Given: $\frac{L}{2}$ = 18 mH   ∴ L = 36 mH

C = 0.1 μF

To calculate: (i) Z_0 at 1 kHz
(ii) Z_0 at 8 kHz.

Sol.: For a prototype low pass filter

$$Z_0 = R_K \sqrt{1 - \frac{f}{f_C}}$$

We will have to calculate f_C and R_K.

(i) To calculate f_C,

$$f_C = \frac{1}{\pi \sqrt{LC}}$$

$$f_C = \frac{1}{\pi \sqrt{36 \times 10^{-3} \times 0.1 \times 10^{-6}}}$$

$$\boxed{f_C = 5.305 \text{ kHz}}$$

(ii) To calculate R_0

$$R_K = \sqrt{\frac{L}{C}}$$

$$R_K = \sqrt{\frac{36 \times 10^{-3}}{0.1 \times 10^{-6}}}$$

$$\boxed{R_K = 600 \, \Omega}$$

(iii) To calculate Z_0 at $f = 1$ kHz

$$Z_0 = R_0 \sqrt{1 - \left(\frac{f}{f_C}\right)^2}$$

$$Z_0 = 600 \sqrt{1 - \frac{1 \times 10^3}{5.3 \times 10^3}}$$

$$\boxed{Z_0 = 589.24 \, \Omega} \text{ at 1 kHz}$$

(iv) To calculate Z_0 at $f = 8$ kHz.

$$Z_0 = R_0 \sqrt{1 - \left(\frac{f}{f_C}\right)^2}$$

$$Z_0 = 600 \sqrt{1 - \left(\frac{8 \times 10^3}{5.9 \times 10^3}\right)}$$

$$\boxed{Z_0 = j\,677.25 \, \Omega}$$

Comments:

f	$f_C = 5.3$ K	Band	Z_0
1 kHz	Below f_C	Pass band	589.24 Ω Real Resistive
8 kHz	Above f_C	Stop band	j 677.25 Ω Purely Reactive

Ans.

f_C cut-off frequency : 5.3 kHz
R_K : 600 Ω
At $f = 1$ kHz Z_0 : 589.24 Ω
At $f = 8$ kHz Z_0 : $j\,677.25$ Ω

Ex. 4.13: A prototype low pass filter is designed using L = 79.57 mH and C = 0.3183 μF. Calculate the cut-off frequency and the design impedance of the LPF. Also draw the corresponding T and π sections. State the exact difference between both the sections.

Given:
$$L = 79.57 \text{ mH}$$
$$C = 0.3183 \text{ μF}$$

To calculate: (i) f_C
(ii) R_K

Sol.: (i) To calculate cut-off frequency f_C

$$f_C = \frac{1}{\pi\sqrt{LC}}$$

$$f_C = \frac{1}{\pi\sqrt{79.57 \times 10^{-3} \times 0.3188 \times 10^{-6}}}$$

$$f_C = 2000 \text{ Hz}$$

$$\boxed{f_C = 2 \text{ kHz}}$$

(ii) To calculate R_K.

$$R_K = \pi \cdot f_C \cdot L$$

$$R_K = \pi \times 2000 \times 10^3 \times 79.57 \times 10^{-3}$$

$$\boxed{R_K = 500 \text{ Ω}}$$

You will get the same value of R_K using any of these formula

$$R_K = \frac{1}{\pi f_C C}$$

$$= \frac{1}{\pi \times 2000 \times 10^3 \times 0.3183 \times 10^{-6}}$$

$$\boxed{R_K = 500 \text{ Ω}}$$

$$R_K = \sqrt{\frac{L}{C}}$$

$$R_K = \sqrt{\frac{79.57 \times 10^{-3}}{0.3183 \times 10^{-6}}}$$

$$\boxed{R_K = 500 \text{ Ω}}$$

(iii) To design corresponding T and π Section we need to find $\frac{L}{2}$ and 2C.

$$\frac{L}{2} = \frac{79.57}{2} = \boxed{39.78 \text{ mH}}$$

$$\frac{C}{2} = \frac{0.3183}{2} = \boxed{0.1591 \text{ μF}}$$

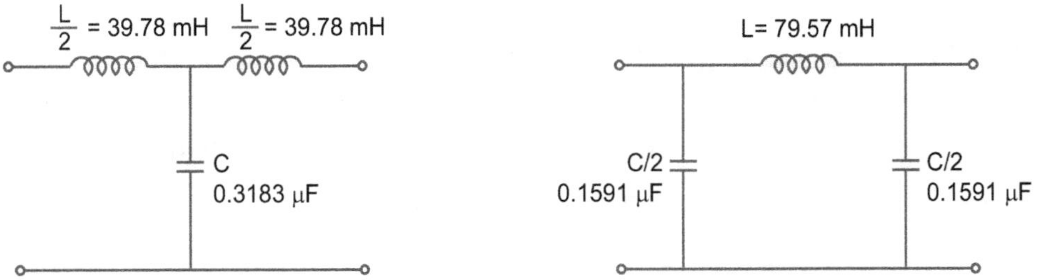

T section
(a)

π section
(b)

Fig. 4.32

Each section has a cut-off frequency of 2 kHz and design impedance of 500 Ω.

The difference in both the sections namely T and π sections is the way, the characteristics impedance varies with frequency and is shown in Fig. 4.32 (c).

$$Z_{0T} = R_K \sqrt{1 - \left(\frac{f}{f_c}\right)^2}$$

$$Z_{0\pi} = \frac{R_K}{\sqrt{1 - \left(\frac{f}{f_c}\right)^2}}$$

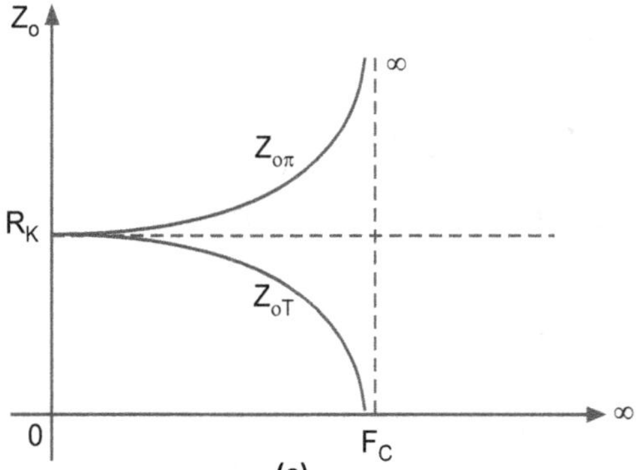

Fig. 4.32 (c)

4.10 CONSTANT k HIGH PASS FILTER

- A High Pass Filter would ideally pass all the frequencies higher than the cut-off frequencies and will block the frequencies lower than the cut-off frequencies.
- We use capacitor in a series arm and a inductor in a shunt arm to achieve this characteristics.

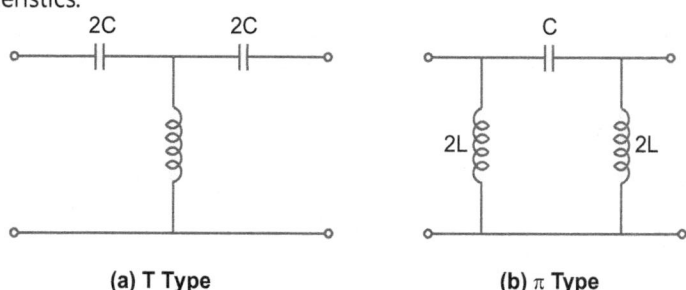

(a) T Type (b) π Type

Fig. 4.33: Constant k HP Filters

4.10.1 Operation of a Constant k HPF

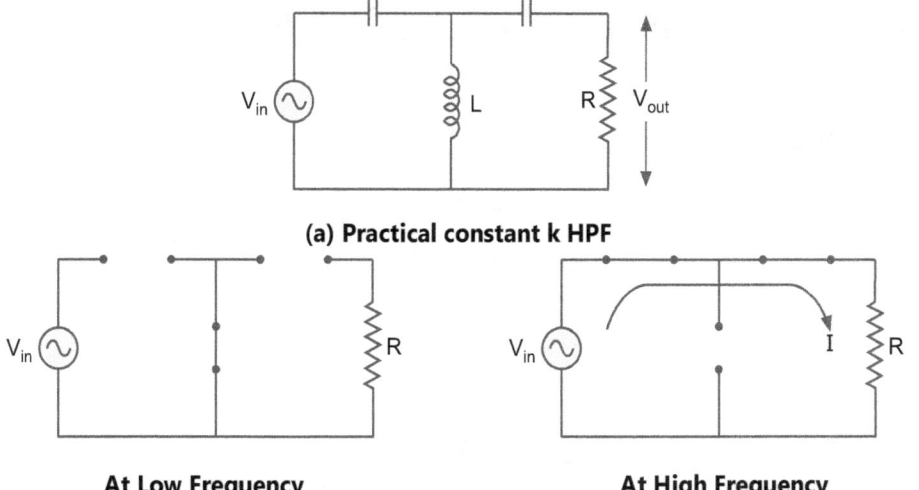

(a) Practical constant k HPF

At Low Frequency

$\omega L << \dfrac{1}{\omega C}$

Inductor → short circuit
Capacitor → open circuit
$V_{out} = 0$
∴ Stop band

At High Frequency

$\omega L >> \dfrac{1}{\omega C}$

Inductor → open
Capacitor → short
$V_{out} = V_{in}$
∴ Pass band

(b) An approximate equivalent at low frequencies

(c) An approximate equivalent at higher frequency

Fig. 4.34: Operation of Constant K HPF

- Though resistors on their own have no frequency selective property, they are still added and used in practical filters to determine the time constant of the circuit.
- At low frequencies the reactance of an inductor (ωL) will be very small, when compared to the reactance $\frac{1}{\omega C}$ of a capacitor. So effectively L functions as a short circuit and the input signal receives a path to ground. Thus, no signal reaches the output and it is completely blocked by the capacitor. Circuit is in stop band.
- But at higher frequencies the reactance $\frac{1}{\omega C}$ of a capacitor will be too less thus making it function almost like a short circuit and making inductor function as open circuit and giving a path to the input signal to reach output.
- Thus, at higher freqenices,

$$\omega L >> \frac{1}{\omega C}$$

and V_{out} is almost equal to V_{in}. The circuit operates in pass band.

4.10.2 Design Impedance of a constant k HPF

In a high pass filter

Total series impedance $Z_1 = \frac{-j}{\omega C}$

shunt impedance $Z_2 = j\omega L$

$\therefore \quad Z_1 Z_2 = j\omega L \times \frac{-j}{\omega C}$

$Z_1 Z_2 = \frac{L}{C} = R_K^2$

$$\boxed{R_K = \sqrt{\frac{L}{C}}} \quad \ldots (4.28)$$

...[This is similar to one derived for LPF]

4.10.3 Reactance Curves and Cut-off frequency of a Constant K HPF

- The reactance's of Z_1 (capacitor) and Z_2 (inductor) will vary as shown in Fig. 4.35 (a). The curve representing $-4Z_2$ is drawn and is compared with the curve for Z_1.
- Recollect that the pass band lies between the frequencies where $Z_1 = 0$ and $Z_1 = -4Z_2$.
- It is clear from the reactance curve that $Z_1 = 0$ at infinite frequency. As ideally expected, pass band starts from f_C, the frequency where $Z_1 = -4Z_2$ and continues till the frequency where $Z_1 = 0$ i.e. infinity.

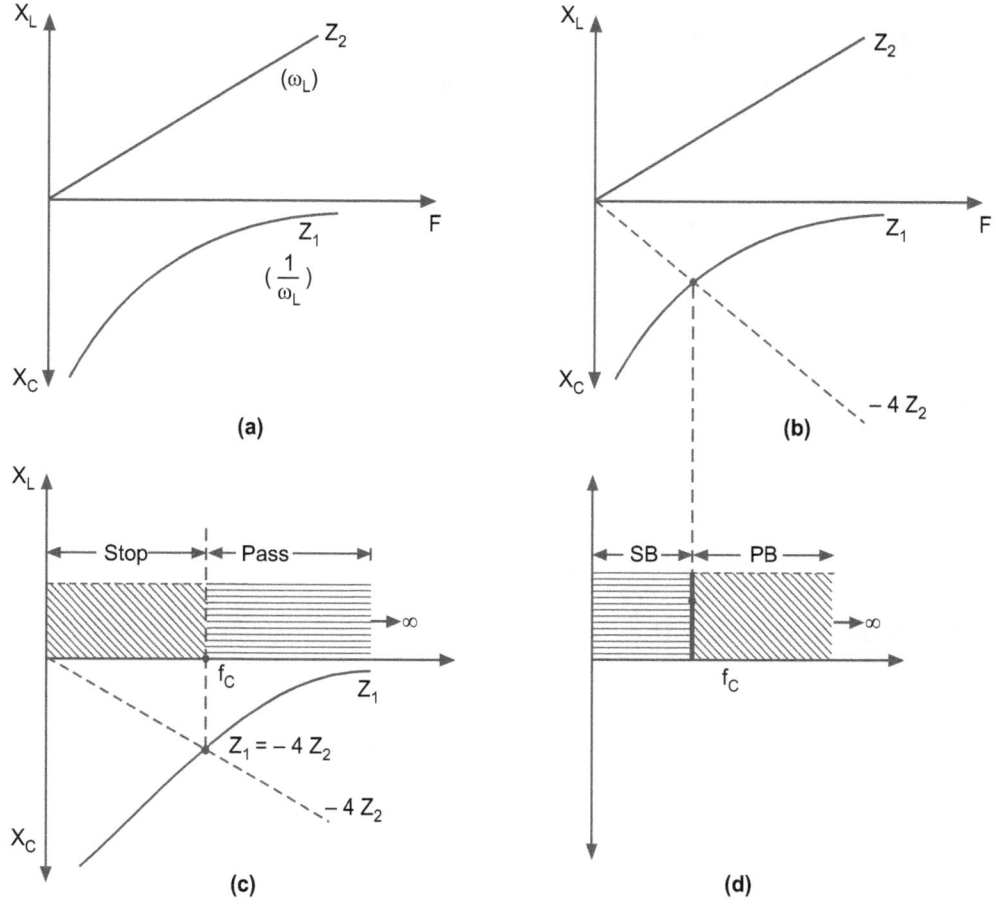

Fig. 4.35: Reactance curves

- All the frequencies above f_C lie in the pass band.
- Thus, the network is called as a high pass filter.
- Conditions $Z_1 = 0$ and $Z_1 = -4Z_2$ determine the cut-off frequency.

$$Z_1 = -4Z_2 \quad \ldots \text{This is the condition at cut-off frequency}$$

$$\frac{-j}{\omega_c C} = -4j\omega_c L$$

$$\omega_c^2 LC = \frac{1}{4} \quad \therefore \omega = \omega_c$$

$$\boxed{f_C = \frac{1}{4\pi\sqrt{LC}}} \quad \ldots (4.29)$$

Cut-off frequency of HPF is sometimes called as f_L lower cut-of frequency.

4.10.4 Design Equations of Constant k HPF

If the cut-off frequencies and the design impedance R_K for a filter are given we can design the filter components.

We have,

$$f_C = \frac{1}{4\pi\sqrt{LC}}$$

$$R_K = \sqrt{\frac{L}{C}}$$

Multiplying both the equations

$$f_C \cdot R_K = \frac{1}{4\pi\sqrt{LC}} \times \sqrt{\frac{L}{C}}$$

$$f_C \cdot R_K = \frac{1}{4\pi\sqrt{C}\cdot\sqrt{C}}$$

$$\boxed{C = \frac{1}{4\pi f_C R_K}} \qquad \ldots (4.30)$$

Dividing equation of R_K by f_C

$$\frac{R_K}{f_C} = \sqrt{\frac{L}{C}} \Big/ \frac{1}{4\pi\sqrt{LC}}$$

$$\frac{R_K}{f_C} = \sqrt{\frac{L}{C}} \times 4\pi\sqrt{LC}$$

$$\frac{R_K}{f_C} = 4\pi L$$

$$\boxed{L = \frac{R_K}{4\pi f_C}} \qquad \ldots(4.31)$$

These equations are called as design equations for prototype or constant k HPF.

4.10.5 Attenuation Constant and Phase Shift of a Constant k HPF

Recall the summary of the filter.

β in stop band is π. As will be clear later, in this case β will be $-\pi$.

In stop band

$$\boxed{\beta = -\pi} \qquad \ldots (4.32)$$

In pass band,

$$\beta = 2\sin^{-1}\sqrt{\frac{Z_1}{4Z_2}}$$

$$= 2\sin^{-1}\sqrt{\frac{\frac{-j}{\omega C}}{4j\omega L}}$$

$$= 2\sin^{-1}\sqrt{\frac{-1}{4\omega^2 LC}}$$

$$= 2\sin^{-1}\frac{-j}{2\omega\sqrt{LC}}$$

$$\beta = 2\sin^{-1}\frac{-j}{2\omega\sqrt{LC}}$$

$$\beta = 2\sin^{-1}\frac{-j}{2\omega \times \frac{1}{4\pi f_C}} \quad \ldots f_C = \frac{1}{4\pi\sqrt{LC}}$$

$$\boxed{\beta = 2\sin^{-1}-j\left(\frac{f_c}{f}\right) \text{ radians}} \qquad \ldots (4.33)$$

Thus, phase angle β will be negative. As the frequency f increases from f_C to ∞, the band of frequencies will be pass band, so β will decrease from − π to zero.

Attenuation of a constant K HPF

α in pass band is zero.

$$\boxed{\alpha = 0} \qquad \ldots(4.34)$$

Recall the filter fundamentals

$$\alpha = 2\cosh^{-1}\sqrt{\frac{Z_1}{4Z_2}}$$

$$\boxed{\alpha = 2\cosh^{-1}-j\left(\frac{f_c}{f}\right) \text{ Nepers}} \qquad \ldots (4.35)$$

Thus, in stop band attenuation α decreases from ∞ at f = 0 to zero at f = f_C.

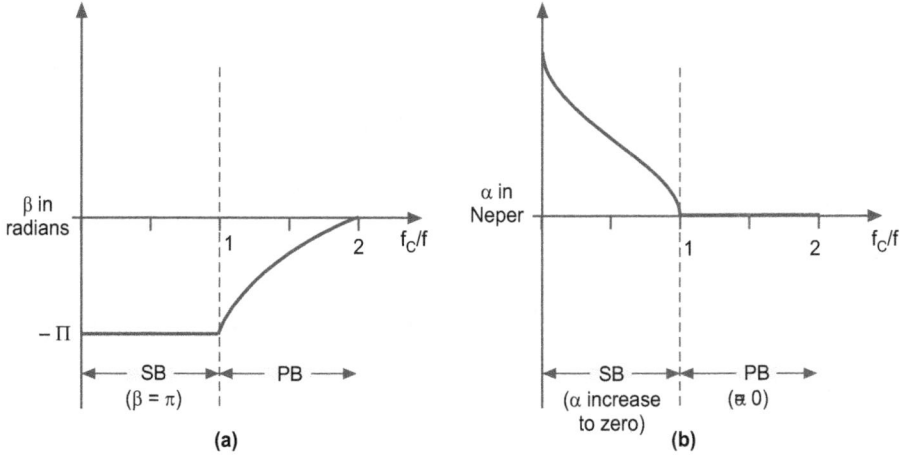

Fig. 4.36: Variation of (a) phase angle and (b) attenuation α

4.10.6 Characteristics Impedance of Constant k HPF

- Z_0, characteristics impedance is an important property of symmetrical network.
- Z_0 of a symmetrical T and π network is given by,

$$Z_{OT} = \sqrt{\frac{Z_1^2}{4} + Z_1 Z_2}$$

$$Z_{0\pi} = \frac{Z_1 Z_2}{Z_{OT}}$$

In case of HPF,

$$Z_1 = \frac{-j}{\omega C}$$

$$Z_2 = j\omega L$$

$$Z_1 Z_2 = \frac{L}{C} = R_K^2$$

$$Z_{OT} = \sqrt{\frac{\left(\frac{-j}{\omega C}\right)^2}{4} + \frac{L}{C}}$$

$$Z_{OT} = \sqrt{\frac{L}{C}} \sqrt{1 - \frac{1}{4\omega^2 LC}}$$

$$Z_{OT} = R_K \sqrt{1 - \frac{1}{4\omega^2 LC}}$$

$$\boxed{Z_{OT} = R_K \sqrt{1 - \left(\frac{f_C}{f}\right)^2}} \quad \ldots f_C = \frac{1}{4\pi \sqrt{LC}} \quad \ldots(4.36)$$

$$\boxed{Z_{0\pi} = \frac{R_K}{\sqrt{1 - \left(\frac{f_C}{f}\right)^2}}} \quad \ldots (4.37)$$

Thus, for a T type HPF
when
$\quad$ f = f_C $\quad\quad$ Z_{OT} = 0
$\quad$ f = ∞ $\quad\quad$ Z_{OT} = R_K

As frequency f increases from f_C to ∞ in pass band, Z_{OT} also increases from 0 to R_K.
Similarly, for a π type HPF
when,
$\quad$ f = f_C $\quad\quad$ $Z_{0\pi}$ = ∞
$\quad$ f = ∞ $\quad\quad$ $Z_{0\pi}$ = R_K

Characteristics impedance	Nature	Variation of Z_0 between frequencies
Z_{OT}	Increases	zero to R_K
$Z_{O\pi}$	Decreases	Infinity to R_K

Table 4.3

Note that this behaviour is exactly opposite to the behaviour of Z_0 in a LPF.

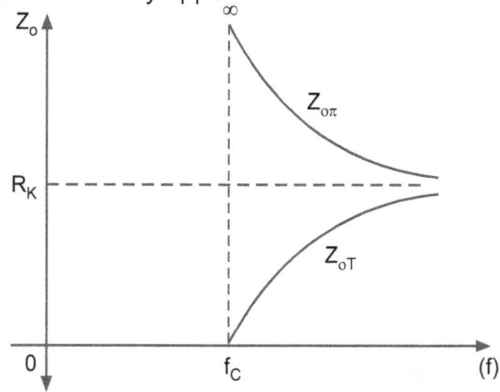

Fig. 4.37: Variation of characteristics impedance with frequency

4.10.7 Summary of Constant k HPF

Filter → / Parameter ↓	HPF
Circuit diagram	(a) T Type — 2C, 2C series capacitors with L shunt inductor; (b) π Type — C series capacitor with 2L shunt inductors on both sides
Design impedance	$R_K = \sqrt{\dfrac{L}{C}}$
Equation for f_C	$f_L = \dfrac{1}{4\pi\sqrt{LC}}$
Equation for α	$\alpha = 2\cosh^{-1}\left(\dfrac{f_C}{f}\right)$
Equation for β	$\beta = 2\sin^{-1}\left(\dfrac{f_C}{f}\right)$

Equation for Z_0	$Z_{OT} = R_K \sqrt{1 - \left(\dfrac{f}{f_C}\right)^2}$ $Z_{0\pi} = \dfrac{R_K}{\sqrt{1 - \left(\dfrac{f}{f_C}\right)^2}}$
Design equation	$L = \dfrac{R_K}{4\pi f_C}$ $C = \dfrac{1}{4\pi f_C R_K}$
Ideal frequency response	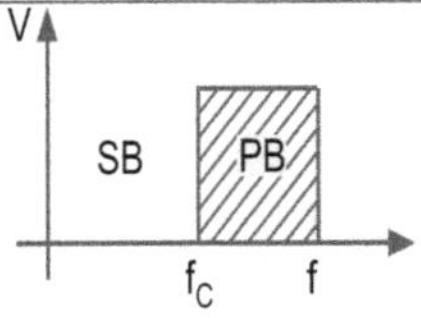 (graph: V vs f, SB below f_C, PB above f_C)

Fig. 4.38

4.11 SOLVED NUMERICALS ON CONSTANT k HPF

Ex. 4.14: A prototype HPF has cut-off frequency of 10 kHz and design impedance of 600 Ω. Find element values of L and C. Also find attenuation in dB and phase shift in degrees at a frequency of 8 kHz.

Given: (i) f_C = 10 kHz
(ii) R_K = 600 Ω

To calculate:
(i) Filter elements
(ii) α at 8 kHz
(iii) β at 8 kHz

Sol.: (i) To calculate filter elements L and C

$$L = \dfrac{R_K}{4\pi f_C}$$
$$= \dfrac{600}{4\pi \times 10 \times 10^3}$$

$\boxed{L = 4.77 \text{ mH}}$

$$C = \dfrac{1}{4\pi f_C R_K}$$
$$= \dfrac{1}{4\pi \times 10 \times 10^3 \times 600}$$

$\boxed{C = 13.26 \text{ nF}}$

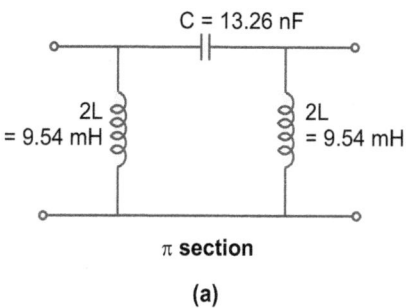
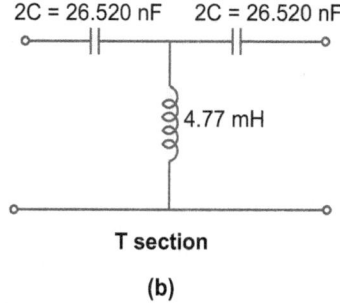

π section   T section
(a)   (b)

Fig. 4.39

(ii) To calculate α At 8 kHz. For a HPF of prototype type, attenuation is given

$$\alpha = 2\cosh^{-1}\left(\frac{f_c}{f}\right)$$

$$= 2\cosh^{-1}\left(\frac{10 \times 10^3}{8 \times 10^3}\right)$$

$$\boxed{\alpha = 1.3862\ N}\ \text{at 8 kHz}$$

α in dB = 8.68 × α in Neper
= 8.68 × 1.3862

$$\boxed{\alpha\ \text{in dB} = 12.04\ \text{dB}}\ \text{at 8 Hz}$$

(iii) β at 8 kHz.

For a high pass filter, with f_c = 10 kHz, f = 8 kHz lies in stop band.

∴ Phase shift in stop band is π^c or 180°.

$$\boxed{\beta = 180°}\ \text{at 8 kHz}$$

Ans.

$$\boxed{\begin{aligned} L &= 4.77\ \text{mH} \\ C &= 13.26\ \text{nF} \\ \alpha &= 12.04\ \text{dB at 8 kHz} \\ \beta &= 180°\ \ \ \ \text{at 8 kHz} \end{aligned}}$$

Ex. 4.15: Design a constant K π section high pass filter to have a design impedance of 600 Ω. The filter must have attenuation of 8.11 dB at 4.5 kHz. For the above design filter calculate phase angle in degrees at f = 5.5 kHz.

Given: R_K = 600 Ω

                α = 8.11 d_B at 4.5 kHz

To calculate:
$$L = ?$$
$$C = ?$$
$$\beta = ? \quad \text{at} \quad f = 5.5 \text{ kHz}$$

Sol.: (i) To calculate f_C, we have
$$\alpha = 2 \cosh^{-1}\left(\frac{f}{f_C}\right)$$
$$\alpha \text{ in dB} = 8.6866 \times \alpha \text{ in neper}$$
$$8.11 = 8.6866 \times \alpha$$
$$\boxed{\alpha = 0.933 \text{ nepers}}$$

$\therefore$
$$0.933 = 2 \cosh^{-1}\left(\frac{4.5 \times 10^3}{f_C}\right)$$
$$\boxed{f_C = 5 \text{ kHz}}$$

(ii) To calculate L and C
$$L = \frac{R_K}{4\pi f_C} = \frac{600}{4 \times \pi \times 5 \times 10^3}$$
$$\boxed{L = 9.55 \text{ mH}}$$

$$C = \frac{1}{4\pi f_C \cdot R_K} = \frac{1}{600 \times 4 \times \pi \times 5 \times 10^3}$$
$$\boxed{C = 0.0265 \text{ µF}}$$

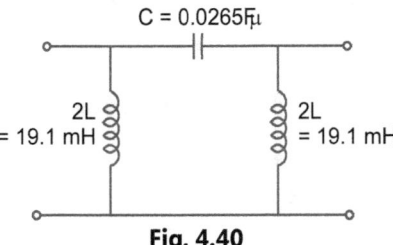

Fig. 4.40

(iii) To calculate phase angle β
$$\beta = 2 \sin^{-1}\left(\frac{f_C}{f}\right)$$
$$\beta = 2 \sin^{-1}\left(\frac{5 \times 10^3}{5.5 \times 10^3}\right)$$
$$\boxed{\beta = 130.76°}$$

Ans.:

$$\boxed{\begin{array}{l} f_C = 5 \text{ kHz} \\ L = 9.55 \text{ mH} \\ C = 0.0265 \text{ µF} \\ \beta = 130.76° \text{ at } 5.5 \text{ kHz} \end{array}}$$

Ex. 4.16: Design a HPF, T and π section to work into impedance 500 Ω and have a cut-off frequency of 1 kHz. For this filter calculate the phase angle 'β' at frequency 1.5 kHz and attenuation 'α' in neper at frequency of 0.9 kHz.

Given: $R_K = 500\ \Omega$
$f_C = 1$ kHz

To calculate:
β at 1.5 kHz
α at 0.9 kHz

(i) To calculate L and C

$$L = \frac{R_K}{4\pi f_C}$$

$$L = \frac{500}{4 \times \pi \times 1 \times 10^3}$$

$$\boxed{L = 39.78\ mH}$$

$$C = \frac{1}{(4\pi f_C)\ R_K}$$

$$C = \frac{1}{4 \times \pi \times 1 \times 10^3 \times 500}$$

$$\boxed{C = 0.159\ \mu F}$$

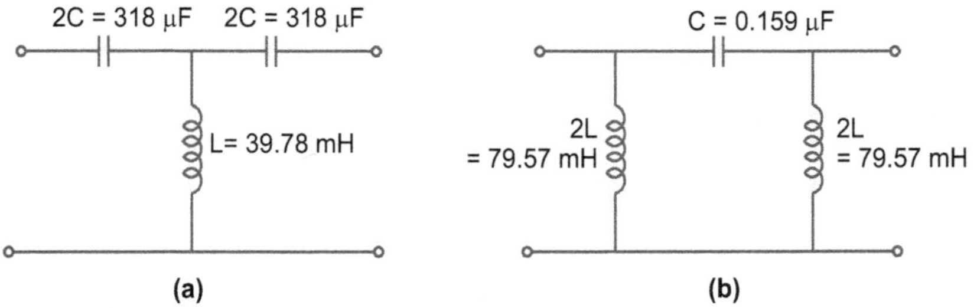

Fig. 4.41

(a) 2C = 318 μF, 2C = 318 μF, L = 39.78 mH

(b) 2L = 79.57 mH, 2L = 79.57 mH, C = 0.159 μF

(ii) To calculate β at f = 1.5 kHz.
In HPF, phase constant β is given by

$$\beta = 2\sin^{-1}\left(\frac{f_C}{f}\right)$$

$$\beta = 2\sin^{-1}\left(\frac{1 \times 10^3}{1.5 \times 10^3}\right)$$

$$\boxed{\beta = -83.62°}\ \text{at}\ 1.5\ kHz$$

Variation of β with frequency is discussed and it varies from $-\pi^c$ to 0.
Thus this is proven in this example.
∴ 1.5 kHz lies in pass band and β is negative.

(iii) To calculate α at f = 0.9 kHz

$$\alpha = 2 \cosh^{-1}\left(\frac{f_c}{f}\right)$$

$$\alpha = 2 \cosh^{-1}\left(\frac{1 \times 10^3}{0.9 \times 10^3}\right)$$

$$\boxed{\alpha = 0.9342 \text{ N}}$$

Ans.:

$$\boxed{\begin{array}{l} L = 39.788 \text{ mH} \\ C = 0.159 \text{ }\mu\text{F} \\ \beta = -83.62° \quad \text{at} \quad 1.5 \text{ kHz} \\ \alpha = 0.9342 \text{ N} \quad \text{at} \quad 0.9 \text{ kHz} \end{array}}$$

Ex. 4.26: A prototype high pass filter has a cut-off frequency of 10 kHz and terminal impedance of 600 Ω. Calculate the element value of L and C.

Given: $R_K = 600$ Ω
$f_C = 10$ kHz

To calculate: (i) L
(ii) C

Sol.: (i) To calculate value of L

$$L = \frac{R_K}{4\pi f_C} = \frac{600}{4\pi \times 10 \times 10^3}$$

$$\boxed{L = 4.774 \text{ mH}}$$

(ii) To calculate value of C

$$C = \frac{1}{4\pi f_C R_K}$$

$$C = \frac{1}{4\pi \times 10 \times 10^3 \times 600}$$

$$\boxed{C = 0.0132 \text{ }\mu\text{F}}$$

(iii) T and π sections of HPF

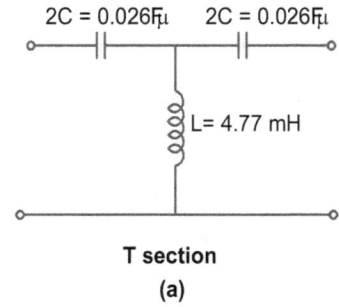

T section
(a)

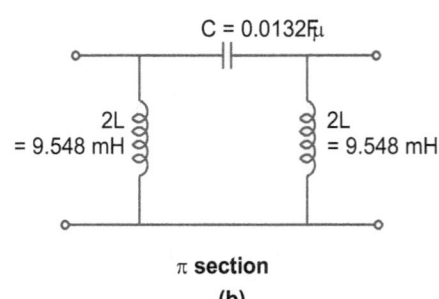

π section
(b)

Fig. 4.42

4.12 CONSTANT k BAND PASS FILTERS

- The filter that passes the voltages in a band of frequencies and blocks or attenuates the frequencies outside this band of frequencies is known as a band pass filter.
- Such a band pass filter is obtained by connecting low pass filter section in cascade with high pass filter section, provided that the cut-off frequency of a low pass filter section must be selected higher than that of the high pass filter section.

4.12.1 Logical Thinking

Let us recollect the frequency responses of a low pass filter and a high pass filter.

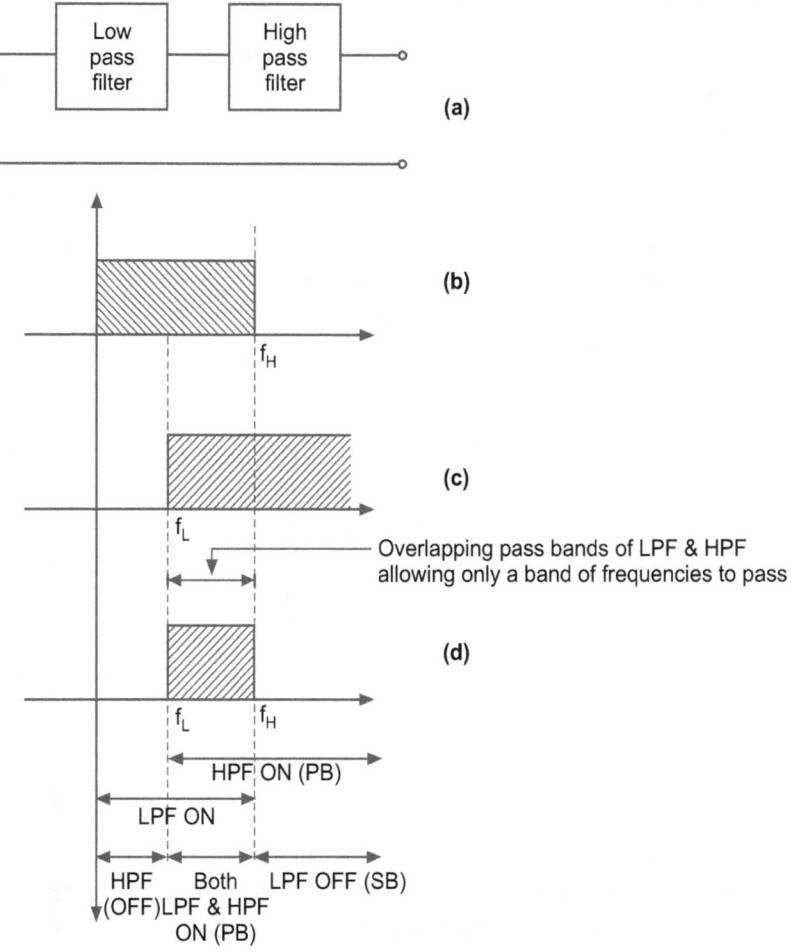

Fig. 4.43: Frequency responses of (a) LPF (b) HPF (c) BPF

- Now let us assume LPF and a HPF as switch S_1 and S_2. And let us connect these switches in series.
- Switch in ON indicates pass band and OFF position of switch indicates stop band.

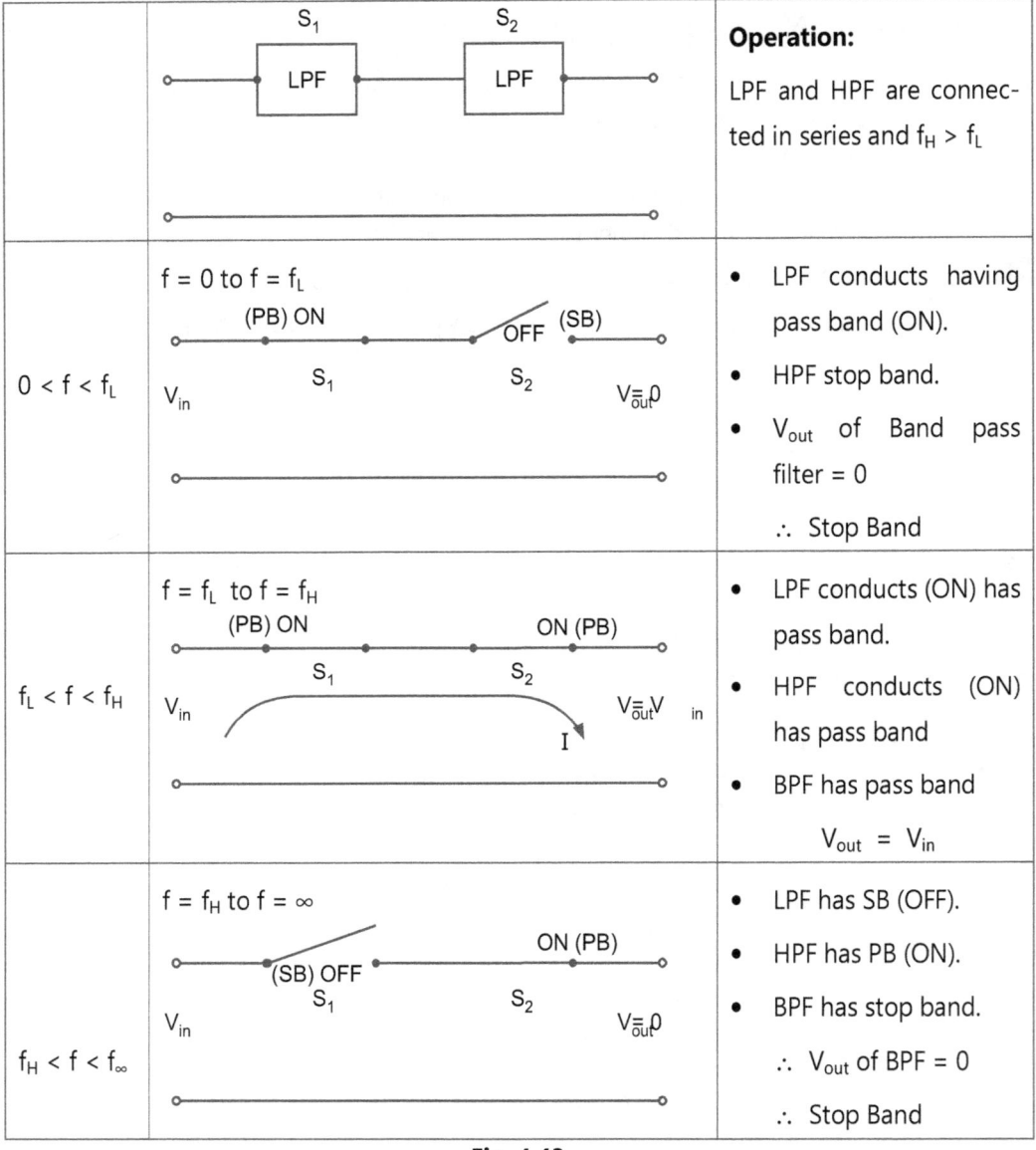

Fig. 4.43

- It must now be very clear that why is its mandatory to have cut-off frequency of LPF higher than the cut-off frequency of HPF. The overlapping pass bands of the LPF and HPF allows only a band of frequencies to pass, giving a pass band for BPF and having a stop band on both the sides of the pass band.
- Although a cascade connection of a LPF and a HPF, as shown in Fig. 4.44 would function appropriately as a band pass filter, it is always more economical to combine the low and high pass functions into a single filter section.

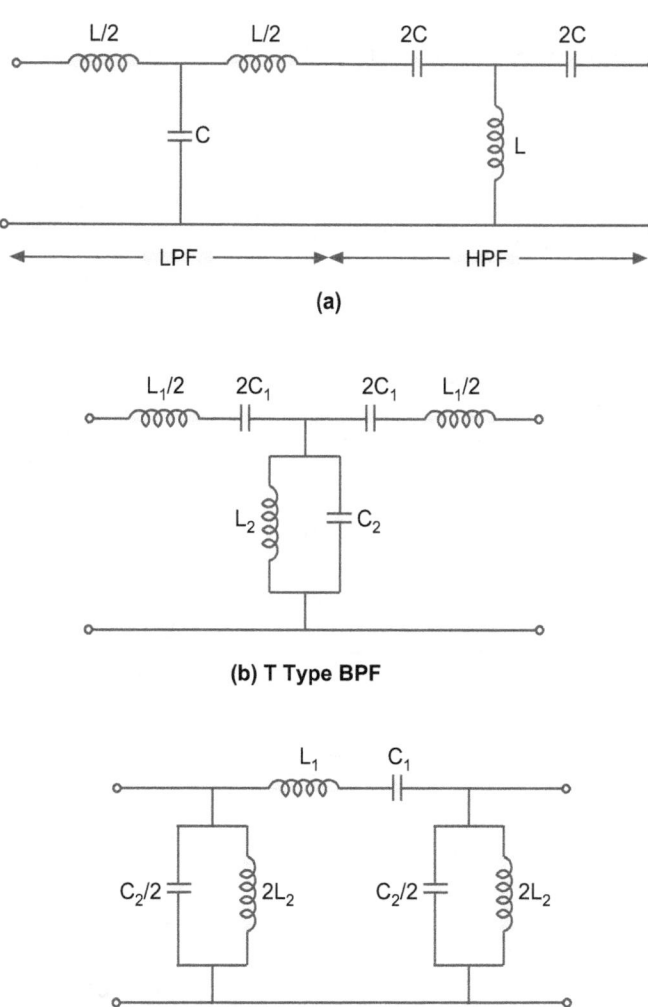

Fig. 4.44 (a) Cascade connection of LPF and BPF to form BPF

(b) A single 'T' Type BPF Section

(c) A single 'π' Type BPF Section

- The series arm of the single T and π type BPF section is actually a series resonant circuit while the shunt arm contains a parallel resonant circuit.
- Thus BPF is actually a circuit with series resonant series arm and an antiresonant shunt arm.

4.12.2 Operation of a Constant k BPF

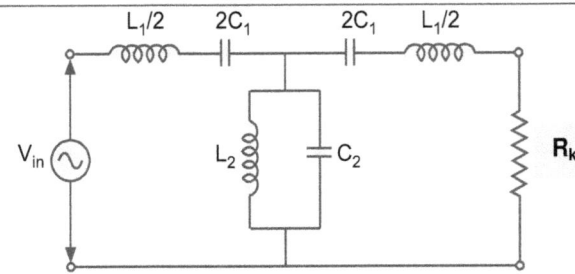

(a) Practical Band Pass Filter

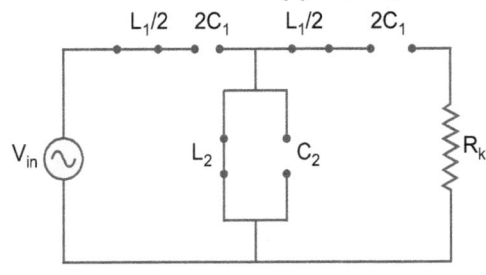

An approximate equivalent at low frequency (below f_1)
$0 < f < f_1$
L → Short circuit
C → Open circuit
$V_{out} = 0$
[Stop band of BPF]

(b)

An approximate equivalent at high frequency (above f_2)
$f_2 < f < \infty$
L → Open circuit
C → Short circuit
$V_{out} = 0$
[Stop band of BPF]

(c)

Fig. 4.45

- As already discussed earlier, though resistors on their own have no frequency selective property, they are still added and used in all the practical circuits to determine the time constant of the circuit.
- For all the frequencies till f_1, i.e. lower cut-off frequency of BPF, the circuit operates in stop band giving V_{out} = 0V. LPF and HPF are in series. So far lower frequencies through LPF is operating in pass band, HPF actually is having its stop band therefore giving V_{out} = 0 V.
- Similarly at higher frequencies, i.e. frequency greater than f_2, the circuit operates in stop band giving V_{out} = 0V. LPF and HPF are in series. So for higher frequencies through HPF is operating in pass band. LPF actually is having its sop band therefore giving V_{out} = 0V.

- In the frequencies between f_1 and f_2 the band pass filter operates in pass band, giving $V_{out} = V_{in}$. Both, LPF and HPF having cut-off frequencies (f_H) f_2 and $f_1(f_L)$ respectively, operate in pass band region.
- These overlapping pass bands of LPF and HPF allow the corresponding BPF to operate in pass band, thus allowing only a band of frequencies to pass giving $V_{out} = V_{in}$.

4.12.3 Design Impedance of a Constant k BPF

In a BPF,
Total series arm impedance Z_1 is

$$Z_1 = j\omega L_1 + \left(\frac{-j}{\omega C_1}\right)$$

$$Z_1 = j\left[\frac{\omega^2 L_1 C_1 - 1}{\omega C_1}\right]$$

Total shunt arm impedance Z_2 is

$$Z_2 = j\omega L_2 \parallel \left(\frac{-j}{\omega C_2}\right)$$

$$Z_2 = \frac{j\omega L_2 \times \frac{-j}{\omega C_2}}{j\omega L_2 - \frac{j}{\omega C_2}}$$

$$Z_2 = \frac{\frac{L_2}{C_2}}{j\frac{(\omega^2 L_2 C_2 - 1)}{\omega C_2}}$$

$$Z_2 = \frac{-j\omega L_2}{\omega^2 L_2 C_2 - 1}$$

Now design impedance $R_K = \sqrt{Z_1 Z_2}$.

$$R_K = \sqrt{Z_1 Z_2}$$

$$R_K^2 = j\left[\frac{\omega^2 L_1 C_1 - 1}{\omega C_1}\right] \times \frac{-j\omega L_2}{\omega^2 C_2 C_L - 1}$$

$$R_K^2 = \frac{L_2}{C_1} \qquad \ldots L_2 C_2 = L_1 C_1$$

$$R_K^2 = \frac{L_1}{C_2}$$

$$\boxed{R_K = \sqrt{\frac{L_2}{C_1}} = \sqrt{\frac{L_1}{C_2}}} \qquad \ldots (4.38)$$

$L_2 C_2 = L_1 C_1$ is another condition which must be satisfied by the filter elements of BPF. It is preassumed to the reason will be clear in the very next section of reactance curves.

4.12.4 Reactance Curves and Expression for cut-off Frequency of a constant K BPF

- BPF is made up of series and a shunt resonating circuit.
- Before we directly plot the graphs and curves of BPF, let us first revise the reactance plots of series and shunt resonating circuits.

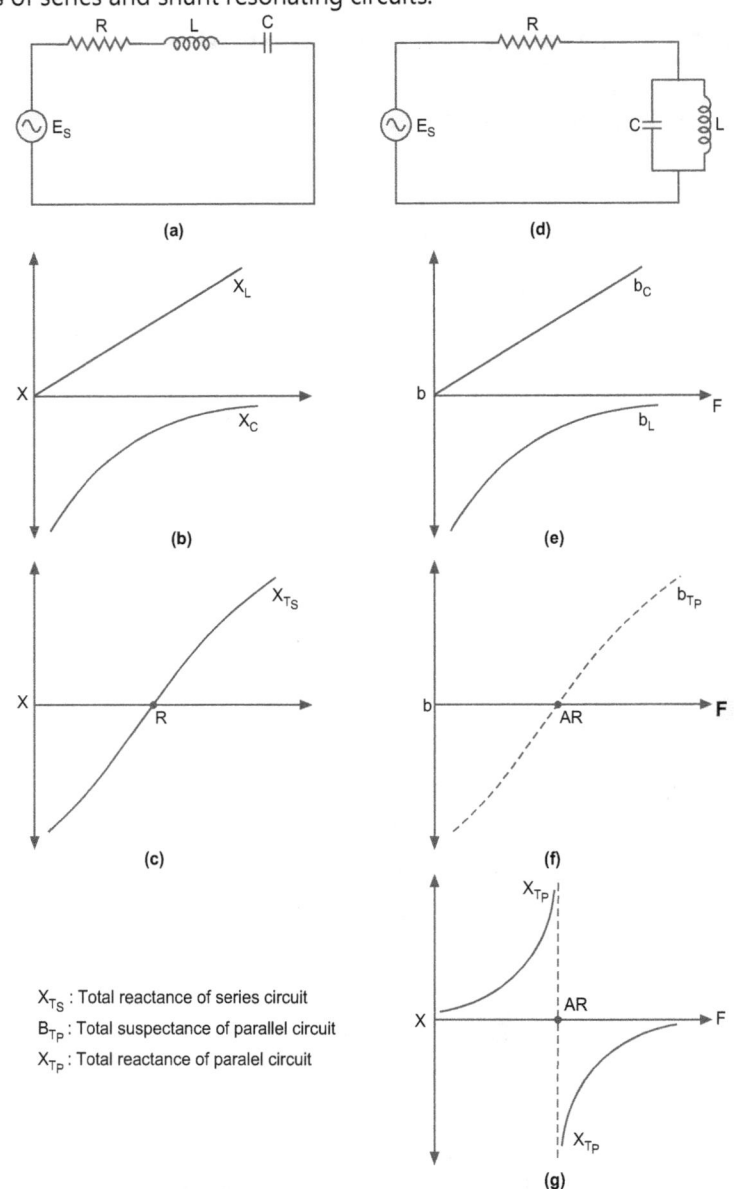

X_{TS} : Total reactance of series circuit
B_{TP} : Total suspectance of parallel circuit
X_{TP} : Total reactance of paralel circuit

Fig. 4.46: Circuit diagram and reactance curves of
a, b, c: Series Resonance
d, e, f, g: Parallel Resonance

- Let us understand these plots.

Table 4.4

Series Resonance	X_L: Inductive Reactance	Linear positive
	X_C: Capacitive Reactance	Hyperbolic negative
Shunt Resonance	b_L: Inductive Susceptance	Hyperbolic negative
	b_C: Capacitive Susceptance	Linear positive

The reciprocal of a positive linear relation is a negative hyperbola.

Series Resonance:
- Curves X_L and X_C in Fig. 4.46 (b) are the reactance plots of inductor and a capacitor.
- These curves are added algebraically as would be the case for the series resonant circuit to give the curve labelled X_{TS} in Fig. 4.46 (c).
- X_T gives the circuit performance as a frequency function.
- Point R is the resonant point showing zero reactance at that point.
- Series resonant circuit has capacitive reactance below the resonating frequency and inductive reactance at the frequencies above the resonanting frequency.

Parallel Resonance:
- Curves b_C and b_L in Fig. 4.46 (e) are the susceptance plots of inductor and a capacitor.
- These curves are added algebraically as would be the case for the parallel resonant circuit to give the curve labeled b_T in Fig. 4.46 (f).
- The reciprocal of b_{TP} is taken and plotted as x_{TP} in Fig. 4.46 (g) giving a curve of reactance Vs frequency for the parallel resonant circuit.
- At point "AR", b_{TP} is zero, so its reciprocal x_{TP} at that point will obviously theoretically go to infinity as shown in Fig. 4.46 (g).
- b_{TP} below point "AR" is capacitive and it is inductive above point "AR". So, x_{TP} i.e. reciprocal of b_{TP} is naturally inductive below "AR" and capacitive above AR.
- So Fig. 4.46 (c) and (g) are the final reactance plots of our interest.
- Fig. 4.47 (c) shows an existence of an additional stop band between two pass bands, which should not be the case, when compared with ideal response of BPF as shown in Fig. 4.47 (d).
- Fig. 4.47 (c) needs a through explanation which will help us in understanding a very important condition for BPF.
- Before understanding Fig. 4.47 (c) let us quickly revise the concepts we learned in section 4.19 i.e. filter fundamentals.

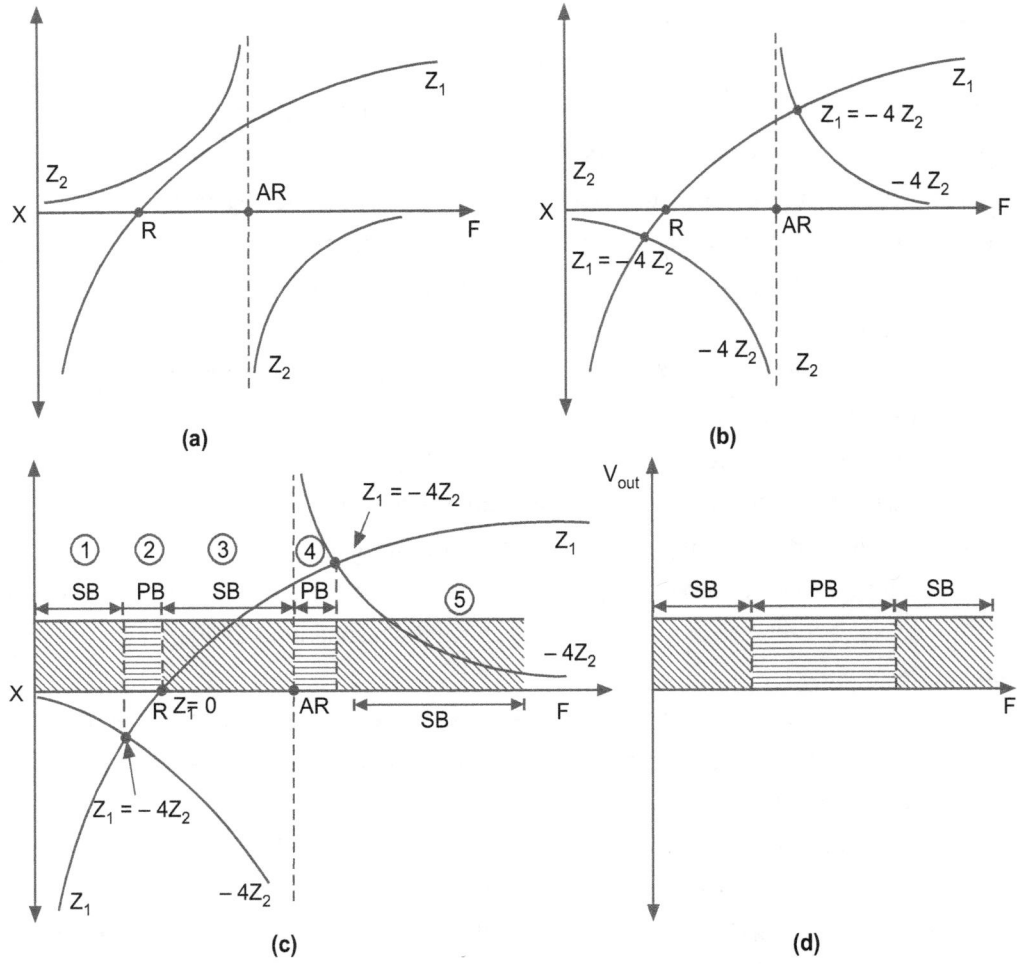

Fig. 4.47: Reactance curves

For a Filter circuit:
- Pass Band exists between Frequency $Z_1 = 0$ and $Z_1 = -4Z_2$.
- Stop Band exists between Frequency at which $Z_1 = -4Z_2$ and $-\infty$.
- And the most important concept Z_1 and Z_2 must always be opposite types of reactances.

• Concentrate on Fig. 4.47 (c).
- Band 1 is a stop band existing between the frequency at which $Z_1 = -4Z_2$ and $Z_1 = \infty$. This matches the ideal Frequency curve of BPF.
- Band 2 is a pass band existing between frequencies at which $Z_1 = 0$ and $Z_1 = -4Z_2$. Even this band matches the ideal Frequency curve of BPF.
- Band 3 is marked as a stop band, irrespective of the fact that it is seen to be starting from $Z_1 = 0$. Now this stop Band should not have existed at all. And if at

all existed should actually be considered as pass band [we know pass band exists between $Z_1 = 0$ and $Z_1 = -4Z_2$]. But the reason, that the circuit will definitely be in stop band for this slot is that, in this slot Z_1 and Z_2 are going to be the reactances of same type. See Fig. 4.47 (a). For the frequencies between the points R and AR, Z_1 and Z_2 are the reactances of same type. And so for the reactances of same type we are bound to get a stop band.

 o This is the reason for having the undesired stop band between the points R and AR.

- Now if a smooth operation of BPF is expected we must eliminate the existence of undesirable stop band in between the points R and AR on the frequency axis.
- Point R is actually the resonating frequency of series arm and point AR is the antiresonating frequency of the shunt arm.
- If the points 'R' and 'AR' overlap on the frequency axis, the undesirable stop band in between these points will not exists at all.
- Now making these points (R and AR) overlap means practically making the antiresonant frequency of the shunt arm to correspond to the resonant frequency of the series arm.

    i.e. $\quad\quad\quad\quad\quad\quad f_r = f_{ar}$

- Let us see the reactance curves when R = AR. i.e. $f_r = f_{ar}$

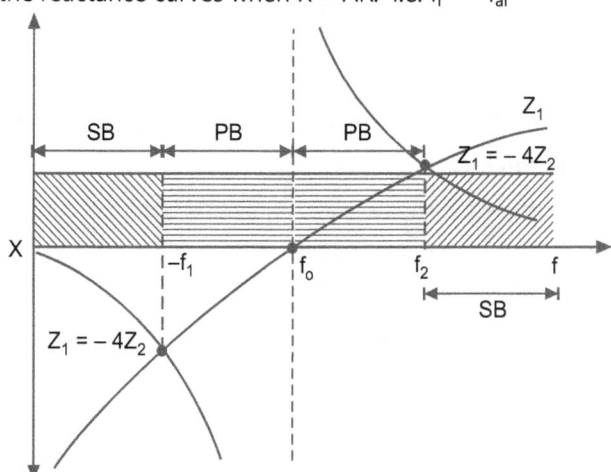

Fig. 4.48: Reactance curves for the band pass network when the resonant and antiresonant frequencies are equal

- Thus, when $f_r = f_{ar}$, the circuit behaves as expected for a BPF. We do not have any step band in between or do we have two different pass bands.
- Let us now derive the condition required for the filter elements (L_1, L_2, C_1, C_2) inorder to have $f_r = f_{ar}$.

$$f_r = \cfrac{1}{2\pi\sqrt{\cfrac{L_1}{2} \cdot 2C_1}}$$

$$= \cfrac{1}{2\pi\sqrt{L_1 C_1}}$$

$\therefore \quad \omega_0 = \omega_r = \cfrac{1}{\sqrt{L_1 C_1}}$

$$f_{ar} = \cfrac{1}{2\pi\sqrt{\cfrac{L_1}{2} \cdot 2C_1}}$$

$$= \cfrac{1}{2\pi\sqrt{L_2 C_2}}$$

$\therefore \quad \omega_0 = w_{ar} = \cfrac{1}{\sqrt{L_2 C_2}}$

$$\omega_0^2 L_1 C_1 = \omega_0^2 L_2 C_2 = 1 \qquad \ldots (a)$$

We must have

$$f_0 = f_r = f_{ar}$$

$$\cfrac{1}{2\pi\sqrt{L_1 C_1}} = \cfrac{1}{2\pi\sqrt{L_2 C_2}}$$

$$\boxed{L_1 C_1 = L_2 C_2} \qquad \ldots(4.39)$$

This is the required condition for the filter elements in order to have $f_r = f_{ar}$.

Derivation of Cut-off Frequency

- BPF has two cut-off frequencies as seen earlier. At both the cut-off frequencies

$$Z_1 = -4Z_2$$

Multiplying by Z_1 gives

$$Z_1^2 = -4Z_1 Z_2$$
$$Z_1^2 = -4 R_K^2$$
$$= +4j^2 R_K^2$$

$\therefore \qquad Z_1 = \pm 2j R_K$

Z_1 at lower cut-off frequency (f_1)

$$= -Z_1 \text{ at upper cut-off frequency } f_2$$

– ve sign in this equation (2), indicates that nature of Z_1 at f_1 and f_2 will be opposite.

$\therefore \quad Z_1$ at f_1 = opposite of Z_1 at f_2.

Below f_0, Z_1 is capacitive. So at lower cut-off frequency, f_1 capacitive reactance of Z_1 series resonating, is dominating. So naturally circuit

at f_1
$$Z_1 = \frac{1}{\omega_1 C_1} - \omega_1 L_1 \quad \ldots \left(\frac{1}{\omega_1 C_1} >> \omega_1 L_1\right) \quad \ldots \text{(b)}$$

Similarly, above f_0, Z_1 is inductive. So at higher cut-off frequency f_2, inductive reactance of Z_1 (series resonating circuit) is dominating,. So naturally

at f_2
$$Z_1 = \omega_2 L_1 - \frac{1}{\omega_2 C_1} \quad \ldots \left(\omega_2 L_1 >> \frac{1}{\omega_2 C_1}\right) \quad \ldots \text{(c)}$$

We had, Z_1 at f_1 $= -Z_1$ at f_2

$$\therefore \quad \frac{1}{\omega_1 C_1} - \omega_1 L_1 = \omega_2 L_1 - \frac{1}{\omega_2 C_1}$$

[writing – ve sign in the above equation is deliberately avoided because it has been taken care off when we wrote the equation (b) and (c) which are already opposite of each other].

$$\therefore \quad \frac{1}{\omega_1 C_1} - \omega_1 L_1 = \omega_2 L_1 - \frac{1}{\omega_2 C_1}$$

$$\frac{1 - \omega_1^2 L_1 C_1}{\omega_1 C_1} = \frac{\omega_2^2 L C_1 - 1}{\omega_2 C_1}$$

$$1 - \omega_1^2 L_1 C_1 = \frac{\omega_1 C_1}{\omega_2 C_1}\left[\omega_2^2 L_1 C_1 - 1\right]$$

From equation (a),
$$L_1 C_1 = \frac{1}{\omega_0^2}$$

$$1 - \frac{\omega_1^2}{\omega_0^2} = \frac{\omega_1}{\omega_2}\left[\frac{\omega_2^2}{\omega_0^2} - 1\right]$$

$$1 - \frac{f_1^2}{f_0^2} = \frac{f_1}{f_2}\left[\frac{f_2^2}{f_0^2} - 1\right]$$

$$f_2\left(f_0^2 - f_1^2\right) = f_1\left(f_2^2 - f_0^2\right)$$

$$f_2 f_0^2 - f_2 f_1^2 = f_1 f_2^2 - f_1 f_0^2$$

$$f_2 f_0^2 + f_1 f_0^2 = f_1 f_2^2 - f_2 f_1^2$$

$$f_0^2 (f_1 + f_2) = f_1 f_2 (f_1 + f_2)$$

$$f_0^2 = f_1 f_2$$

$$\boxed{f_0 = \sqrt{f_1 f_2}} \quad \ldots (4.40)$$

Equation (4.75) indicates that frequency of resonance of the individual arms is a geometric mean of two cut-off frequencies.

4.12.5 Design Equations for a Constant k BPF

Recollect the equations (b) and (c) of section 4.12.4.
We have,
At lower cut-off frequency

$$j\omega_1 L_1 - \frac{j}{\omega_1 C_1} = -j\, 2\, R_K$$

$$\omega_1 L_1 - \frac{1}{\omega_1 C_1} = -2\, R_K$$

$$\omega_1^2 L_1 C_1 - 1 = -2\, R_K\, \omega_1 C_1$$

$$1 - \omega_1^2 L_1 C_1 = +2\, R_K\, \omega_1 C_1$$

$$1 - \frac{\omega_1^2}{\omega_0^2} = 2\, \omega_1 C_1 \cdot R_K \qquad \dots \omega_0 = \frac{1}{\sqrt{L_1 C_1}}$$

$$1 - \frac{f_1^2}{f_0^2} = 4\pi\, f_1 C_1 R_K$$

$$1 - \frac{f_1^2}{f_1 f_2} = 4\pi\, f_1 C_1 R_K \qquad \dots f_0 = \sqrt{f_1 f_2}$$

$$1 - \frac{f_1}{f_2} = 4\pi\, R_K f_1 C_1$$

$$\frac{f_2 - f_1}{f_2} = 4\pi\, R_K f_1 C_1$$

$$\boxed{C_1 = \frac{f_2 - f_1}{4\pi\, R_K f_1 f_2}} \qquad \dots (4.41)$$

Now, for constant K BPF,

$$\omega_0 = \frac{1}{\sqrt{L_1 C_1}}$$

$$\omega_0^2 = \frac{1}{(\sqrt{L_1 C_1})^2} \qquad \therefore L_1 = \frac{1}{C_1 \omega_0^2}$$

Substituting value of C_1 and $\omega_0 = 2\pi f_0$

$$L_1 = \frac{1}{\frac{f_2 - f_1}{4\pi R_K f_1 f_2} \times 4\pi^2 f_0^2}$$

Substituting value of $f_0^2 = f_1 f_2$

$$L_1 = \frac{1}{\frac{f_2 - f_1}{4\pi R_K f_1 f_2} \times 4\pi^2 f_1 f_2} \qquad \boxed{L_1 = \frac{R_K}{\pi (f_2 - f_1)}} \quad \dots (4.42)$$

We have already derived ...

that
$$R_K^1 = \sqrt{\frac{L_2}{C_1}} = \sqrt{\frac{L_1}{C_1}}$$
$$R_K^2 = \frac{L_2}{C_1} = \frac{L_1}{C_2}$$

which gives
$$L_2 = R_K^2 C_1 \quad \text{and} \quad C_2 = \frac{L_1}{R_K^2}$$

Substituting values of C_1 and L_1 in above equation

$$L_2 = \frac{R_K^2 (f_2 - f_1)}{4\pi R_K f_1 f_2} \qquad C_2 = \frac{R_K}{R_K^2 \pi (f_2 - f_1)}$$

$$\boxed{L_2 = \frac{R_K (f_2 - f_1)}{4\pi f_1 f_2}} \quad ...(4.78) \qquad \boxed{C_2 = \frac{1}{\pi R_K (f_2 - f_1)}} \quad ...(4.43)$$

Above equations are called the design equations of a constant K BPF.

4.12.6 Attenuation Constant, Phase Shift and Characteristics Impedance of a Constant K BPF

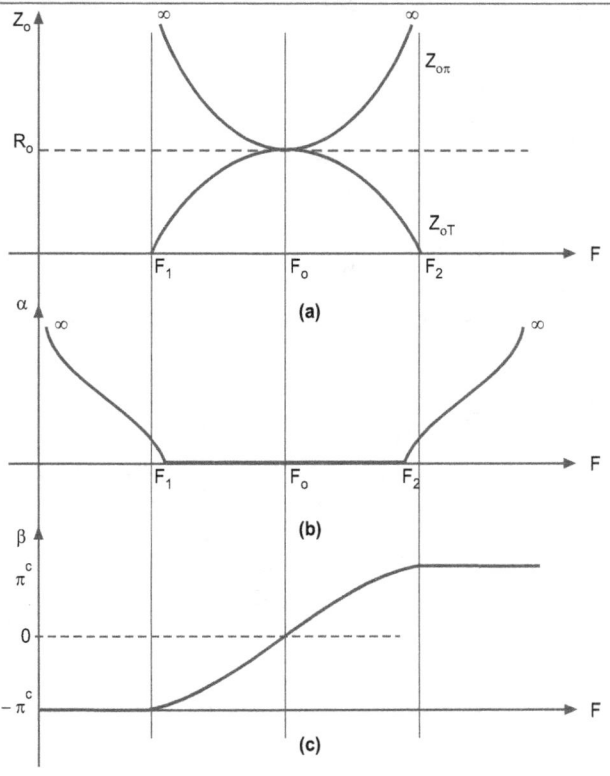

Fig. 4.49

4.12.7 Summary of Constant k BPF

Filter → Parameter ↓	BPF
Circuit diagram	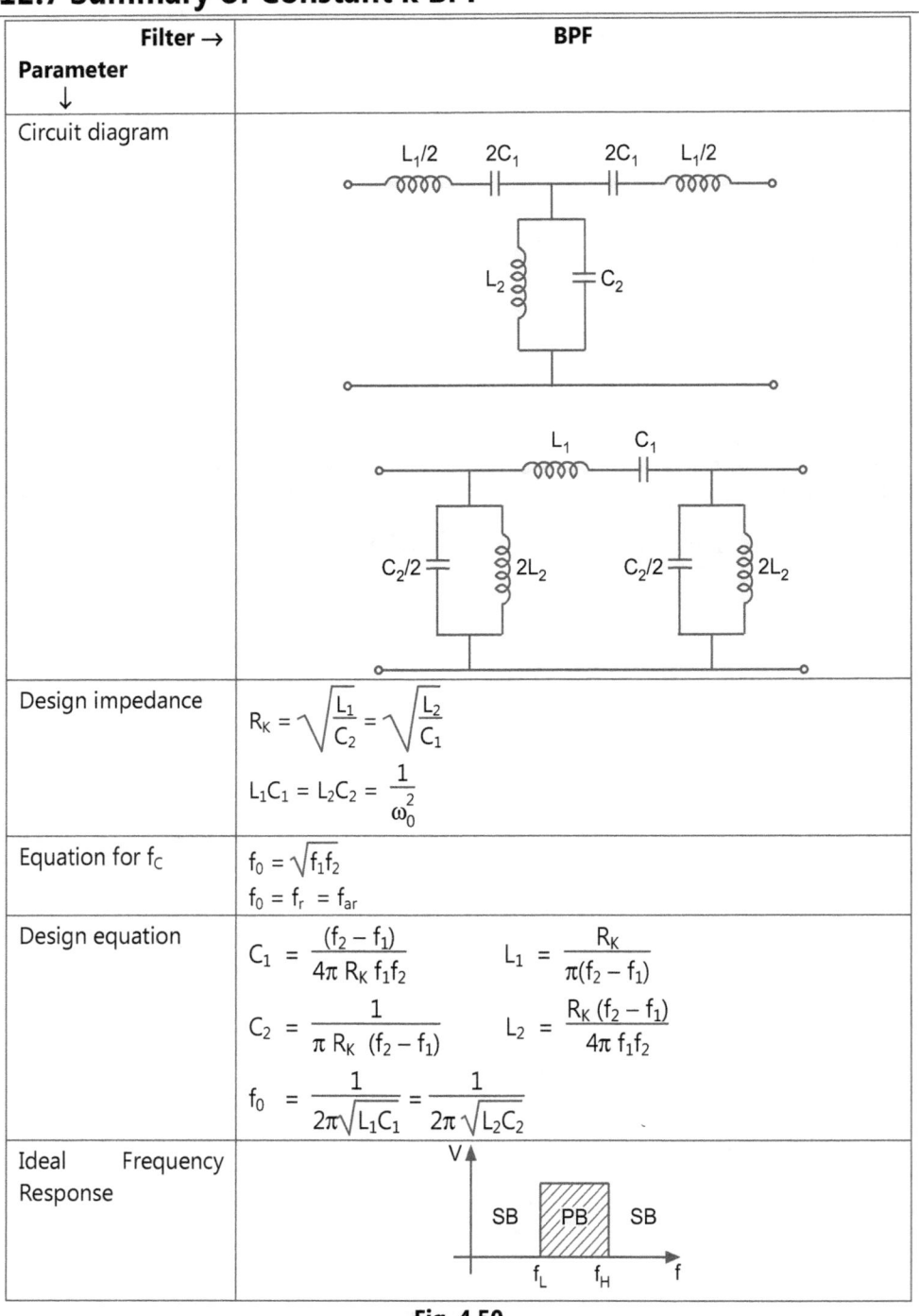
Design impedance	$R_K = \sqrt{\dfrac{L_1}{C_2}} = \sqrt{\dfrac{L_2}{C_1}}$ $L_1 C_1 = L_2 C_2 = \dfrac{1}{\omega_0^2}$
Equation for f_c	$f_0 = \sqrt{f_1 f_2}$ $f_0 = f_r = f_{ar}$
Design equation	$C_1 = \dfrac{(f_2 - f_1)}{4\pi R_K f_1 f_2}$ $L_1 = \dfrac{R_K}{\pi (f_2 - f_1)}$ $C_2 = \dfrac{1}{\pi R_K (f_2 - f_1)}$ $L_2 = \dfrac{R_K (f_2 - f_1)}{4\pi f_1 f_2}$ $f_0 = \dfrac{1}{2\pi \sqrt{L_1 C_1}} = \dfrac{1}{2\pi \sqrt{L_2 C_2}}$
Ideal Frequency Response	(SB / PB / SB vs f, with f_L, f_H)

Fig. 4.50

4.13 Solved Numericals on Constant k Band Pass Filters

Ex. 4.18: Find the element value of L and C for a prototype band pass filter terminated with 500 Ω and cut-off frequency of 1 kHz and 5 kHz.

Given: R_K = 500 Ω
f_1 = 1 kHz
f_2 = 5 kHz

To calculate: (i) L_1, C_1
(ii) L_2, C_2

Sol.:

$$L_1 = \frac{R_K}{\pi(f_2 - f_1)}$$

$$= \frac{500}{\pi(5000 - 1000)}$$

$\boxed{L_1 = 39.788 \text{ mH}}$

$$C_1 = \frac{(f_2 - f_1)}{(4\pi f_1 f_2) R_K}$$

$$= \frac{5000 - 1000}{4\pi \, 1 \times 5 \times 10^3 \times 10^3 \times 500}$$

$\boxed{C_1 = 0.1273 \text{ μF}}$

$$L_2 = \frac{(f_2 - f_1) R_K}{4\pi f_1 f_2}$$

$$= \frac{(5000 - 1000)(500)}{4\pi \times 5 \times 10^3 \times 1 \times 10^3}$$

$\boxed{L_2 = 31.83 \text{ mH}}$

$$C_2 = \frac{1}{\pi(f_2 - f_1) R_K}$$

$$= \frac{1}{\pi(5 \times 10^3 - 1 \times 10^3) \, 500}$$

$\boxed{C_2 = 0.159 \text{ μF}}$

Ans.:

L_1 = 39.788 mH
L_2 = 31.83 mH
C_1 = 0.1273 μF
C_2 = 0.159 μF

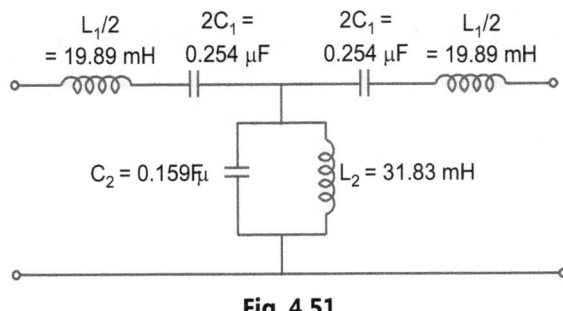

Fig. 4.51

Ex. 4.19: In a constant K bandpass filter, the ratio of the shunt arm capacitance to the total series arm capacitance is 100: 1. The frequency of resonance of both the arm is 1000 Hz. Calculate the bandwidth of the filter.

Sol.: Given total series arm capacitance

$$C_1 = \frac{f_2 - f_1}{4\pi R_0 f_1 f_2}$$

Total shunt arm capacitance = C_2

$$C_2 = \frac{1}{\pi R_0 (f_2 - f_1)}$$

The ratio of C_2, C_1 is = 100 : 1.

$$\frac{C_2}{C_1} = \frac{100}{1} = \frac{1}{\pi R_0 (f_2 - f_1)} \times \frac{4\pi R_0 f_1 f_2}{(f_2 - f_1)}$$

$$100 = \frac{4 f_1 f_2}{(f_2 - f_1)^2}$$

$$(f_2 - f_1)^2 = \frac{4 f_1 f_2}{100}$$

But

$$f_1 f_2 = f_0^2$$

$$(f_2 - f_1)^2 = \frac{4}{100} \times f_0^2$$

Taking square roots

$$f_2 - f_1 = \frac{2}{10} \times f_0$$

$$f_0 = \text{Resonance frequency}$$
$$= 1000 \text{ Hz}$$

∴

$$(f_2 - f_1) = \frac{2}{10} \times 1000$$

$$\boxed{f_2 - f_1 = 200 \text{ Hz}}$$

Ans.:

$$\boxed{\text{Bandwidth} = 200 \text{ Hz}}$$

Ex. 4.20: The series arm Z_1 of a filter consists of 0.5 μF capacitor in series with an inductor of 0.35 H. If $R_0 = 500\ \Omega$ determine the elements in the shunt arm. Also calculate frequency of resonance f_0 and pass band frequencies f_1 and f_2.

Sol.: As the series arm consists of induction in series with capacitor, it is a band pass filter.

∴ Shunt arm will have an inductor and a capacitor connected in parallel.

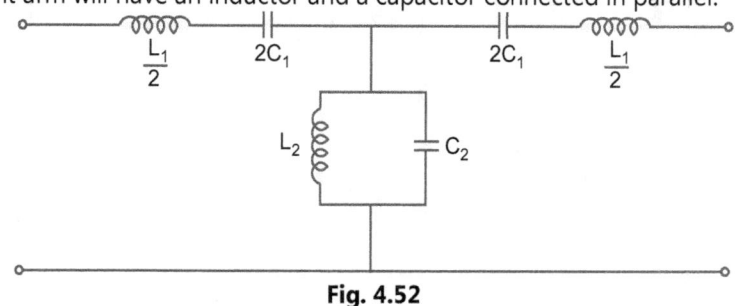

Fig. 4.52

1. To calculate L_2 and C_2:

$$\frac{L_2}{C_1} = \frac{L_1}{C_2} = R^2 = Z_1 Z_2$$

∴ $L_2 = C_1 R_K^2 = 0.5 \times 10^{-6} \times 500^2$

$$\boxed{L_2 = 125\ \text{mH}}$$

$$C_2 = \frac{L_1}{R_K^2} = \frac{0.35}{500^2} = 1.4\ \mu F$$

$$\boxed{C_2 = 1.4\ \mu F}$$

2. To calculate the frequency of resonance f_0:

$$f_0 = \frac{1}{2\pi \sqrt{L_1 C_1}}$$

$$= \frac{1}{2\pi \sqrt{0.35 \times 0.5 \times 10^{-6}}}$$

$$\boxed{f_0 = 380.453\ \text{Hz}}$$

3. To calculate pass band frequencies f_1 and f_2:

∴ $L_1 = \dfrac{R_K}{\pi (f_2 - f_1)}$

$f_2 - f_1 = \dfrac{R_K}{L_1 \cdot \pi}$

$= \dfrac{500}{\pi \cdot 0.35}$

$f_2 - f_1 = 454.73\ \text{Hz}$ ...(1)

But
$$f_0 = \sqrt{f_1 f_2}$$
$$f_0^2 = f_1 f_2 = (380.45)^2$$
$$f_1 = \frac{144.744 \times 10^3}{f_2} \quad \ldots (2)$$

Substituting value of 2 in 1.

$$f_2 - \frac{144.744 \times 10^3}{f_2} = 454.73$$

$$f_2^2 - 454.73\, f_2 - 144.744 \times 10^3 = 0$$

$$f_2 = \frac{-(-454.73) \pm \sqrt{-454.73^2 - 4 \times 1 \times (-144.7 \times 10^3)}}{2(1)}$$

$$= \frac{454.73 \pm 886.43}{2}$$

$$\boxed{f_2 = 670.58 \text{ Hz}}$$

Substituting in equation (1)

$$f_1 = f_2 - 454.73$$
$$\boxed{f_1 = 215.85}$$

Ans.:

Shunt arm elements L_2	= 125 mH
C_2	= 1.4 µF
Resonant frequency f_0	= 380 Hz
Pass band frequency f_1	= 215.85 Hz
f_2	= 670.58 Hz

4.14 CONSTANT k BAND STOP FILTERS

- The filter that blocks or attenuates the frequencies in between two cut-off frequencies f_1 and f_2 and passes all the frequencies below f_1 and above f_2.

  f_1 : Lower cut-off frequency (f_L)
  f_2 : Higher cut-off frequency also called as f_H.

- Thus, in BSF all the frequencies between f_L and f_H are attenuated and all the frequencies outside this range are passed.
- Such a band stop filter is obtained by connecting low pass filter section in parallel with a high pass filter provided that the cut-off frequency of a low pass filter section must be selected lower than that of high pass filter section.

4.14.1 Logical Thinking

- Let us recollect the frequency responses of a low pass filter and a high pass filter.

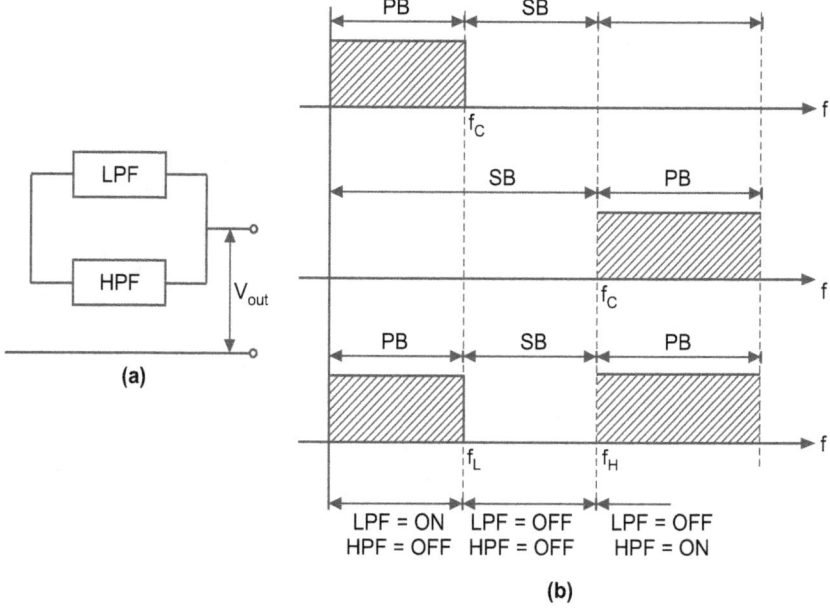

Fig. 4.53

- Now let us assume LPF and a HPF as switch S_1 and S_2. And let us connect these switches in parallel.
- ON position of a switch indicates a pass band of the filter and an OFF switch indicates a stop band.

	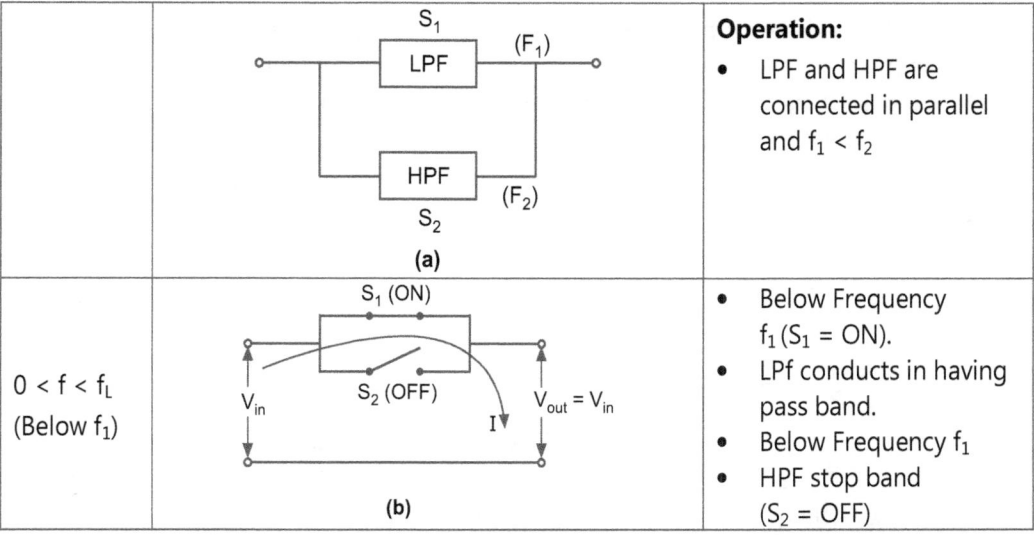 (a)	**Operation:** • LPF and HPF are connected in parallel and $f_1 < f_2$
$0 < f < f_L$ (Below f_1)	(b)	• Below Frequency f_1 (S_1 = ON). • LPf conducts in having pass band. • Below Frequency f_1 • HPF stop band (S_2 = OFF)

	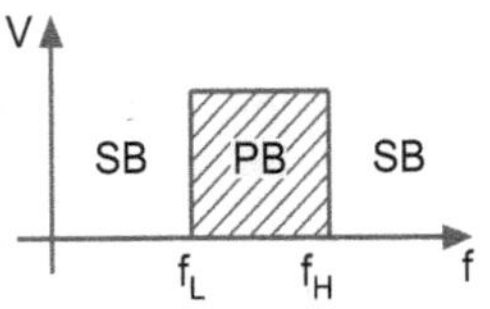 (V axis graph with SB, PB, SB regions at f_L, f_H)	• V_{out} of BSF = V_{in} ∴ Pass band
$f_1 < f < f_2$ (Between f_1 and f_2)	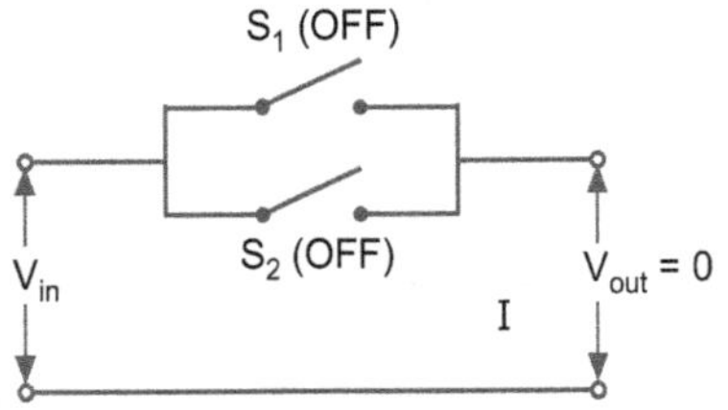 S_1 (OFF), S_2 (OFF), V_{in}, $V_{out} = 0$ (c)	• LPF stop band (S_1 = OFF) • HPF also has stop band (S_2 = OFF) • V_{out} of BSF = Zero ∴ Stop Band
$f_2 < f < f_\infty$ (Above f_2)	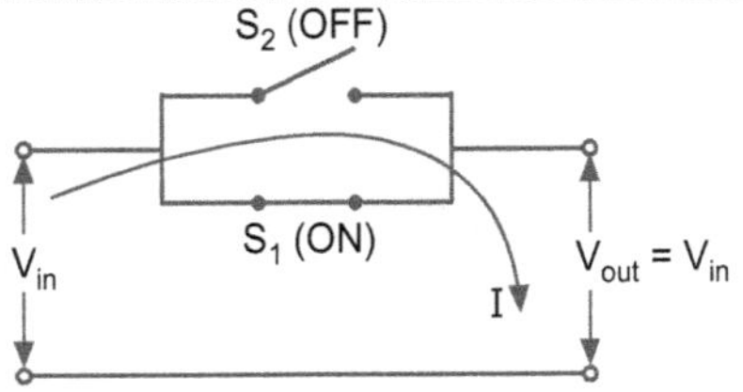 S_2 (OFF), S_1 (ON), V_{in}, $V_{out} = V_{in}$ (d)	• Above f_2 • LPF is stop band S_1 = OFF • Above f_2, HPF is in pass band S_2 = ON ∴ V_{out} of BSF = V_{in} ∴ Pass band

Fig. 4.54

- It must now be very clear that why it is mandatory to have cut-off frequency of LPF lower than the cut-off frequency of HPF.
- The overlapping stop bands of the LPF and HPF allows a band of frequencies to be blocked and having a pass band on the both the sides of the stop band.
- Although a parallel connection of a LPF and a HPF would function appropriately as a Band stop filter, it is always very economical to combine the low and high pass functions into a single filter function.

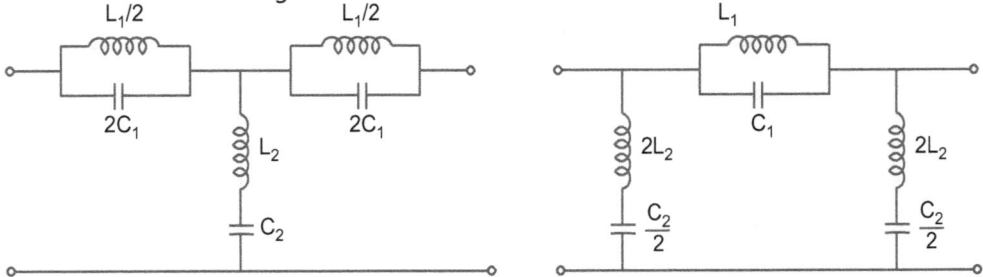

Fig. 4.55: (a) T Type of BSF (b) π Type of BSF

- Like a BPF, even a BSF is actually a circuit with an antiresonant series arm and a shunt arm consisting of series resonating circuit.

- As we have derived for a Band pass filter, similarly even for a Band stop filter, the series and shunt arms are made antiresonant and resonant at the same frequency f_0.
  i.e.
  $$f_r = f_{ar} = f_0$$
  f_r = Resonating frequency [shunt arm of BSF]
  f_{ar} = Anti resonating frequency [series arm of BSF]
- So if in a prototype BS filter series and shunt arms are made to have same series and antiresonant frequency f_0 then we have

$$f_0 = \frac{1}{2\pi \sqrt{\frac{L_1}{2} \cdot 2C_1}} = \frac{1}{2\pi \sqrt{L_2 C_2}}$$

$$\omega_0^2 = \frac{1}{L_1 C_1} = \frac{1}{L_2 C_2}$$

∴ Like in BPF, $\boxed{L_1 C_1 = L_2 C_2}$ ... (4.44)

4.14.2 Operation of a Constant k BSF

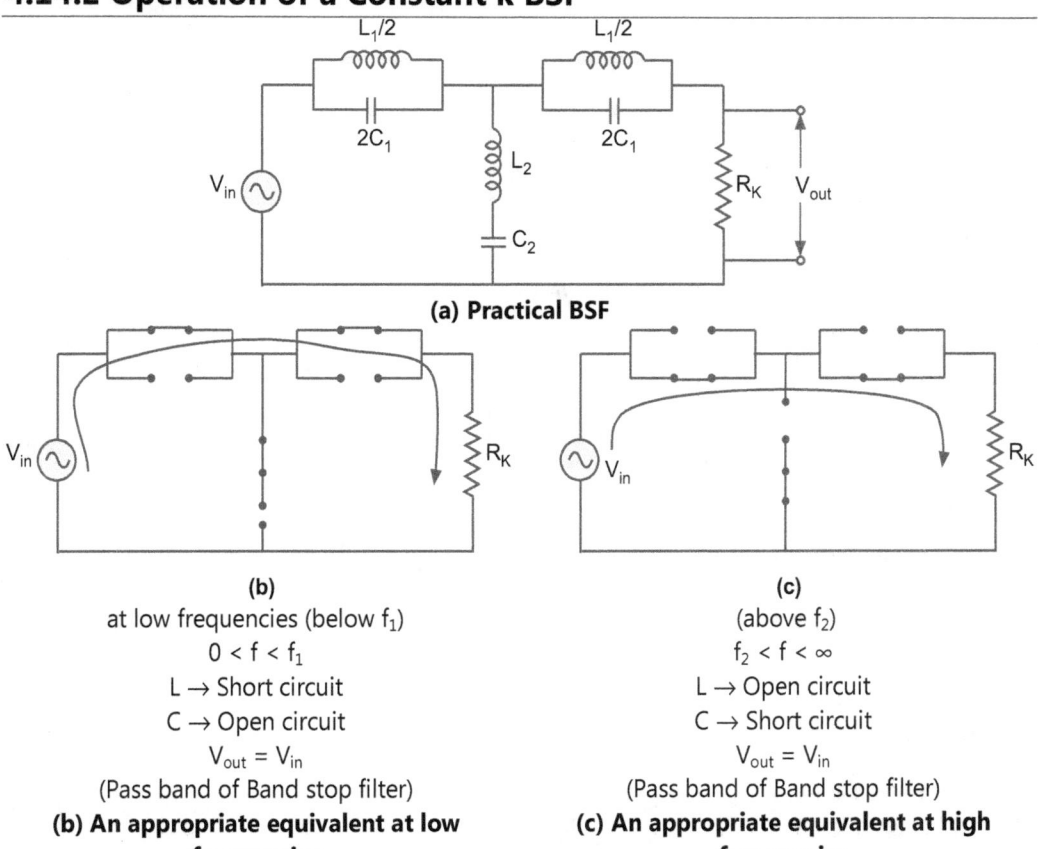

(a) Practical BSF

(b)
at low frequencies (below f_1)
$0 < f < f_1$
L → Short circuit
C → Open circuit
$V_{out} = V_{in}$
(Pass band of Band stop filter)
(b) An appropriate equivalent at low frequencies

(c)
(above f_2)
$f_2 < f < \infty$
L → Open circuit
C → Short circuit
$V_{out} = V_{in}$
(Pass band of Band stop filter)
(c) An appropriate equivalent at high frequencies

Fig. 4.56

- As already discussed earlier, though resistors can their own have no frequency selective property, they are still added and used in all the practical circuits to determine the time constant of the circuit.
- For all the frequencies till f_1, i.e. cut-off frequency of low pass filter, the circuit operates in pass band giving $V_{out} = V_{in}$. LPF and HPF are in parallel, so for lower frequencies though HPF is operating in stop band, LPF has its PB giving $V_{out} = V_{in}$.
- Similarly at higher frequencies, inductor acts as open circuit and capacitor acts as a short circuit. So even in this case current completes the path through capacitor making V_{in} available across the resistance. Thus, here the BSF is actually operating in the pass band of HPF.
- At frequencies between f_1 and f_2 ideally a stop band is expected. Practically the output is very small. The build BSF is said to operate in stop band.

4.12.3 Design Impedance of a Constant k BSF

In a BSF, total series arm is

$$Z_1 = j\omega L_1 \parallel \left(\frac{-j}{\omega C_1}\right)$$

$$Z_1 = \frac{j\omega L_1 \times \frac{-j}{\omega C_1}}{j\omega L_1 - \frac{j}{\omega C_1}}$$

$$Z_1 = \frac{\omega L_1}{j(\omega^2 L_1 C_1 - 1)} \quad \ldots(a)$$

Similarly, total shunt arm is

$$Z_2 = j\omega L_2 - \frac{j}{\omega C_2}$$

$$Z_2 = j\left(\omega L_2 - \frac{1}{\omega C_2}\right)$$

$$Z_2 = +j\left(\frac{\omega^2 L_2 C_2 - 1}{\omega C_2}\right) \quad \ldots(b)$$

Now, $R_K^2 = Z_1 Z_2$

$$\therefore \quad Z_1 Z_2 = \frac{\omega L_1}{j(\omega^2 L_1 C_1 - 1)} \times \frac{+j(\omega^2 L_2 C_2 - 1)}{\omega C_2}$$

From (2), i.e. $L_1 C_1 = L_2 C_2$

$$\therefore \quad Z_1 Z_2 = \frac{L_1}{C_2} = \frac{L_2}{C_1} = R_K^2$$

Thus, $R_K^2 = Z_1 Z_2$

$$\boxed{R_K^2 = \frac{L_2}{C_1} = \frac{L_1}{C_2}} \quad \ldots (4.45)$$

which is real and a constant. Hence above sections are a constant k filters.

4.14.4 Reactance Curves and Cut-off Frequency of BSF

As was already clear to us, the series and the shunt arm of the constant K BS filter are actually antiresonant and resonant circuits.

So we will reproduce the same reactance curves of series and parallel resonating circuits which we revised in the last section.

Z_1 : parallel resonating circuit
Z_2 : series resonating circuit

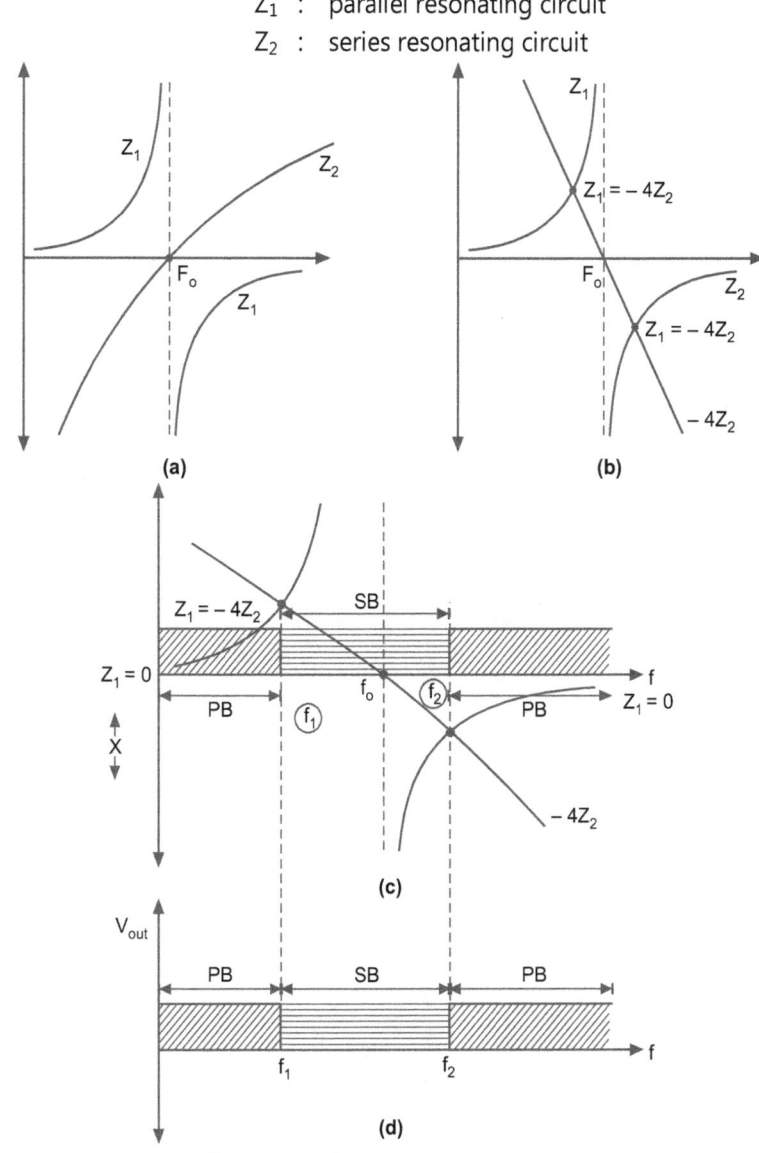

Fig. 4.57: a, b, c: Reactance curves
d: Ideal frequency curve

At both the cut-off frequencies
$$Z_1 = -4Z_2$$
Multiplying the equation by Z_1
$$Z_1^2 = -4Z_1Z_2$$
$$Z_1^2 = -4R_K^2$$
$$= +j^2 4R_K^2$$

$\therefore$ $\boxed{Z_1 = \pm j2R_K}$ ... (4.46)

This is also very clear from Fig. 4.56 (c).

Z_1 at lower cut-off frequency f_1 is equal and opposite to Z_1 at higher cut-off frequency f_2. [Z_1 is inductive at f_1 and capacitive at f_2].

From equation 'a' in Section 4.2.7.4 we already have,

$$Z_1 = \frac{\omega L_1}{j(\omega^2 L_1 C_1 - 1)}$$

$$Z_1 = \frac{j\omega L_1}{(1 - \omega^2 L_1 C_1)}$$

This value of Z_1 is equal and opposite at two different cut-off frequencies f_1 and f_2, therefore can be written as:

$$\frac{\omega_1 L_1}{1 - \omega_1^2 L_1 C_1} = -\frac{\omega_2 L_1}{1 - \omega_2^2 L_1 C_1}$$

$$\omega_1 L_1 (1 - \omega_2^2 L_1 C_1) = \omega_2 L_1 (\omega_1^2 L_1 C_1 - 1)$$

$$1 - \omega_2^2 L_1 C_1 = \frac{\omega_2}{\omega_1}(\omega_1^2 L_1 C_1 - 1)$$

We know that

$\therefore$ $$L_1 C_1 = \frac{1}{\omega_0^2}$$

$$\omega_0^2 = \frac{1}{L_1 C_1}$$

$\therefore$ $$1 - \frac{\omega_2^2}{\omega_0^2} = \frac{\omega_2}{\omega_1}\left(\frac{\omega_1^2}{\omega_0^2} - 1\right)$$

$$1 - \frac{f_2^2}{f_0^2} = \frac{f_2}{f_1}\left(\frac{f_1^2}{f_0^2} - 1\right)$$

$$\frac{f_0^2 - f_2^2}{f_0^2} = \frac{f_2}{f_1}\left(\frac{f_1^2 - f_0^2}{f_0^2}\right)$$

$$f_1 f_0^2 - f_1 f_2^2 = f_2 f_1^2 - f_2 f_0^2$$

$$f_1 f_0^2 - f_2 f_0^2 = f_2 f_1^2 - f_1 f_2^2$$

$$f_0^2 (f_1 + f_2) = f_1 f_2 (f_1 + f_2)$$

$$f_0^2 = f_1 f_2$$

$$\boxed{f_0 = \sqrt{f_1 f_2}} \qquad \ldots (4.47)$$

This result matches the one derived for BPF. The frequency of resonance of the individual arms is the geometric mean of two cut-off frequencies.

4.14.5 Design Equations of a Constant k BSF

From equation 4.46 and eq. (a) in Section 4.14.3.

$$Z_1 = \pm j\, 2 R_K$$

$$Z_1 = \frac{j\omega L_1}{(1 - \omega^2 L_1 C_1)}$$

At frequency f_1, Z_1 is inductive.

$\therefore$

$$Z_1 = +j\, 2 R_K$$

$$\frac{j\omega_1 L_1}{(1 - \omega_1^2 L_1 C_1)} = j\, 2 R_K$$

$$\frac{\omega_1 L_1}{1 - \omega^2 L_1 C_1} = j\, 2 R_K \qquad \ldots \quad \omega_0^2 = \frac{1}{L_1 C_1}$$

$$\omega_0^2 = \omega_1 \omega_2$$

$$\omega_1 L_1 = 2 R_K \left(1 - \frac{\omega_1^2}{\omega_0^2}\right)$$

$$\omega_1 L_1 = 2 R_K \left(1 - \frac{\omega_1^2}{\omega_1 \omega_2}\right)$$

$$\omega_1 L_1 = 2 R_K \left(\frac{\omega_1 \omega_2 - \omega_1^2}{\omega_1 \omega_2}\right)$$

$$L_1 = 2 R_K \left(\frac{\omega_2 - \omega_1}{\omega_1 \omega_2}\right)$$

$$L_1 = \frac{2 R_K}{2\pi} \left(\frac{f_2 - f_1}{f_1 f_2}\right)$$

$$\boxed{L_1 = \frac{R_K (f_2 - f_1)}{\pi f_1 f_2}} \qquad \ldots (4.84)$$

For constant k BSF

$$\omega_0 = \frac{1}{\sqrt{L_1 C_1}}$$

$$\omega_0^2 = \frac{1}{L_1 C_1}$$

$$C_1 = \frac{1}{L_1 \omega_0^2}$$

Substituting value of L_1 and $\omega_0 = 2\pi f_0$

$$C_1 = \frac{1}{\frac{R_K (f_2 - f_1)}{\pi f_1 f_2} \times 4\pi^2 f_0^2}$$

$$\boxed{C_1 = \frac{1}{4\pi R_K (f_2 - f_1)}} \qquad \ldots(4.48)$$

We have already derived in equation (4.81).

$$R_K = \sqrt{\frac{L_2}{C_1}} = \sqrt{\frac{L_1}{C_2}}$$

$$R_K^2 = \frac{L_2}{C_1} = \frac{L_1}{C_2}$$

which gives

$$L_2 = R_K^2 C_1$$

and $\qquad C_2 = \dfrac{L_1}{R_K^2}$

Substituting values of C_1 and L_1

$$\boxed{L_2 = \frac{R_K}{4\pi(f_2 - f_1)}} \qquad \ldots(4.49)$$

$$\boxed{C_2 = \frac{(f_2 - f_1)}{\pi R_K (f_1 f_2)}} \qquad \ldots(4.50)$$

Equations (4.47 to 4.48) are the design equations for BSF.

4.14.6 Attenuation Constant, Phase Shift and Characteristics Impedance of a Constant k BSF

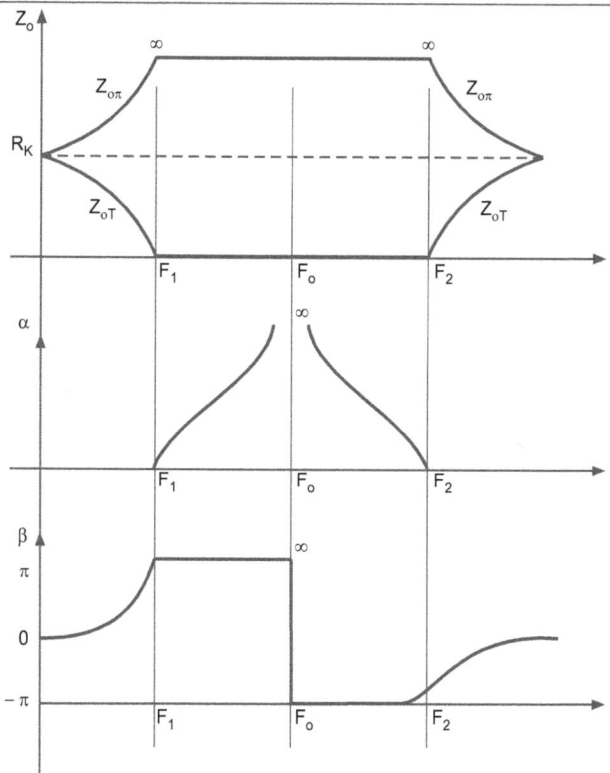

Fig. 4.58: Variation of α, β, Z_0 for BPF

4.14.7 Summary of Constant k BPF

Filter → Parameter ↓	BSF
Circuit diagram	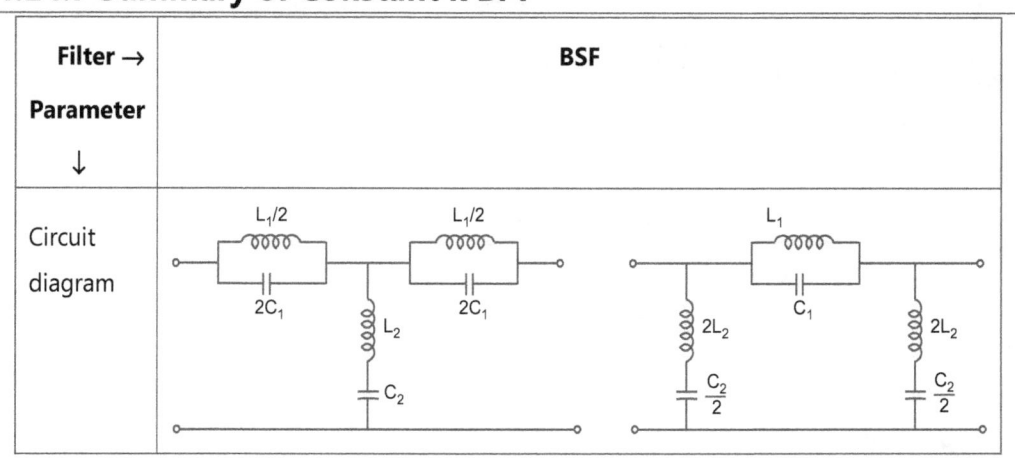

contd. ...

Design impedance	$R_K = \sqrt{\dfrac{L_1}{C_2}} = \sqrt{\dfrac{L_2}{C_1}}$ $L_1 C_1 = L_2 C_2 = \dfrac{1}{\omega_0^2}$
Equation for f_c	$f_0 = \sqrt{f_1 f_2}$ $f_0 = f_r = f_{ar}$
Design equation	$C_1 = \dfrac{1}{4\pi R_K (f_2 - f_1)}$ $L_1 = \dfrac{R_K (f_2 - f_1)}{\pi f_1 f_2}$ $C_2 = \dfrac{(f_2 - f_1)}{\pi R_K (f_1 f_2)}$ $L_2 = \dfrac{R_K}{4\pi (f_2 - f_1)}$ $f_0 = \dfrac{1}{2\pi \sqrt{L_1 C_1}} = \dfrac{1}{2\pi \sqrt{L_2 C_2}}$
Ideal Frequency Response	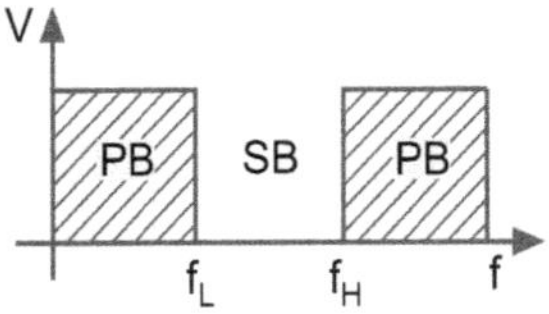 V ↑ PB SB PB f_L f_H f

Fig. 4.59

4.15 SOLVED NUMERICALS ON CONSTANT k BSF

Ex. 4.21: Compute the values of elements of a constant k band elimination or band stop filter so as to meet the following requirements.

(i) Cut-off frequencies: 350 kHz and 400 kHz.

(ii) Characteristics impedance: 300 Ω.

Given: f_1 = 350 kHz

             f_2 = 400 kHz

             R_K = 300 Ω

To calculate: L_1, L_2, C_1, C_2.

Sol.:

$$L_1 = \frac{R(f_2 - f_1)}{\pi f_1 f_2}$$

$$= \frac{300(400 - 350)}{\pi \cdot 350 \cdot 400}$$

$$\boxed{L_1 = 34 \ \mu H}$$

$$C_1 = \frac{1}{4\pi R_K (f_2 - f_1)} = \frac{1}{4 \times \pi \times 300(400 - 350) \times 10^3}$$

$$\boxed{C_1 = 5.3 \ nF}$$

$$L_2 = \frac{R_K}{4\pi (f_2 - f_1)} = \frac{800}{4\pi (400 - 350) \times 10^3}$$

$$\boxed{L_2 = 0.48 \ mH}$$

$$C_2 = \frac{(f_2 - f_1)}{4\pi R_K f_1 \cdot f_2} = \frac{(400 - 350) \times 10^3}{4\pi \cdot 300 \cdot 400 \cdot 350 \cdot 10^6}$$

$$\boxed{C_2 = 0.38 \ nF}$$

The component values can also be calculated using the formula as under:

$$C_2 = \frac{1}{\pi R_K} \left[\frac{f_2 - f_1}{f_1 f_2} \right]$$

$$= \frac{1}{\pi \cdot 300} \left[\frac{400 - 350}{350 \cdot 400} \right] \frac{10^3}{10^6}$$

$$\boxed{C_2 = 0.38 \ nF}$$

$$L_2 = \frac{R_K}{4\pi (f_2 - f_1)}$$

$$= \frac{300}{4\pi (400 - 350) \times 10^3}$$

$$\boxed{L_2 = 0.48 \ mH}$$

$$L_1 = R_K^2 \cdot C_2$$
$$= 300^2 \times 0.38 \times 10^{-9}$$

$$\boxed{L_1 = 34 \ \mu H}$$

$$C_1 = \frac{L_2}{R_K^2}$$

$$= \frac{0.48 \times 10^{-7}}{(300)^2}$$

$$\boxed{C_1 = 5.3 \ nF}$$

T and π Sections of BSF are

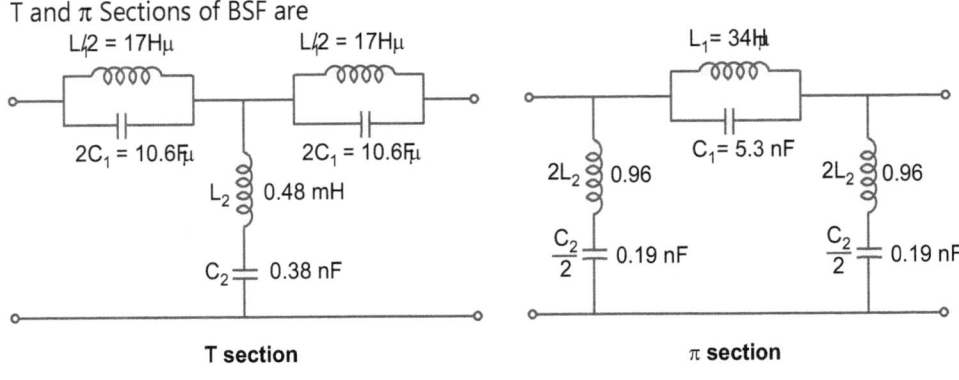

T section   π section

Fig. 4.60

Ex. 4.22: In a constant K band stop filter, the ratio of the shunt indicator to series capacitor is 100 : 1. Calculate the ratio of the series inductor to shunt capacitance. Also calculate the value of design impedance. Find the frequency of resonance of both the arm if the bandwidth is 500 Hz and ratio of $\dfrac{L_1}{L_2}$ is 152.

Given: $\dfrac{L_2}{L_1} = \dfrac{100}{1}$, $(f_2 - f_1)$ = BW = 500 Hz

$$\dfrac{L_1}{L_2} = \dfrac{152}{1}$$

To calculate:

(i) $\dfrac{L_1}{C_2}$ (ii) R_K (iii) f_0

Sol.: (i) To calculate $\dfrac{L_1}{C_2}$ and R_K.

We know that

$$\dfrac{L_2}{C_1} = \dfrac{L_1}{C_2} = R_K^2$$

∴ $\boxed{\begin{array}{l}\dfrac{L_1}{C_2} = 100 \\ R_K = 10\end{array}}$

(ii) To calculate f_0

$$\dfrac{L_1}{L_2} = 152$$

$$\dfrac{\dfrac{R_K (f_2 - f_1)}{\pi f_1 f_2}}{\dfrac{R_K}{4\pi (f_2 - f_1)}} = 152$$

$$\frac{R_K(f_2-f_1)}{\pi f_1 f_2} \times \frac{4\pi(f_2-f_1)}{R_K} = 152$$

$$4(f_2-f_1)^2 = 152\, f_1 f_2$$

$$(f_2-f_1)^2 = 38\, f_1 f_2$$

$$\frac{500 \times 500}{38} = f_1 f_2$$

But $\quad f_0^2 = f_1 f_2$

$$\frac{500 \times 500}{38} = f_0^2$$

$$f_0 = \frac{500}{\sqrt{38}}$$

$$\boxed{f_0 = 80.1}$$

Ans.:

$$\boxed{\begin{aligned} \frac{L_1}{C_2} &= 100 \\ R_K &= 10 \\ f_0 &= 80\ \text{Hz} \end{aligned}}$$

4.16 SUMMARY OF ALL THE CONSTANTS k PROTOTYPE FILTERS

Filter → Parameter ↓	LPF	HPF
Circuit diagram	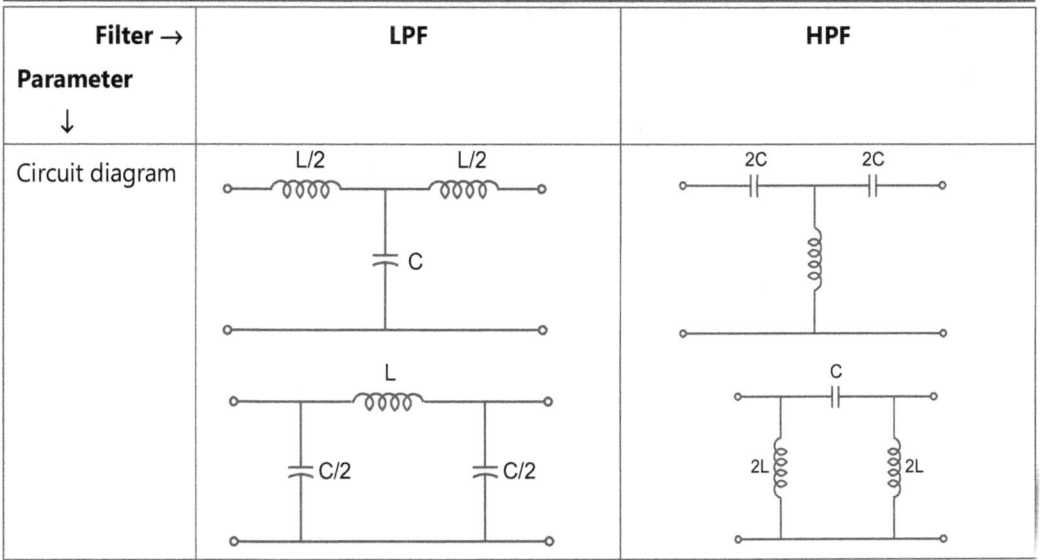	

contd. ...

Design impedance	$R_K = \sqrt{\dfrac{L}{C}}$	$R_K = \sqrt{\dfrac{L}{C}}$
Equation for f_C	$f_C = \dfrac{1}{\pi\sqrt{LC}}$	$f_L = \dfrac{1}{4\pi\sqrt{LC}}$
Equation for α	$\alpha = 2\cosh^{-1}\left(\dfrac{f}{f_C}\right)$	$\alpha = 2\cosh^{-1}\left(\dfrac{f_C}{f}\right)$
Equation for β	$\beta = 2\sin^{-1}\left(\dfrac{f}{f_C}\right)$	$\beta = 2\sin^{-1}\left(\dfrac{f_C}{f}\right)$
Equation for Z_0	$Z_{0T} = R_K\sqrt{1-\left(\dfrac{f}{f_C}\right)^2}$ $Z_{0\pi} = \dfrac{R_K}{\sqrt{1-\left(\dfrac{f}{f_C}\right)^2}}$	$Z_{0T} = R_K\sqrt{1-\left(\dfrac{f}{f_C}\right)^2}$ $Z_{0\pi} = \dfrac{R_K}{\sqrt{1-\left(\dfrac{f}{f_C}\right)^2}}$
Design equation	$L = \dfrac{R_K}{\pi f_C}$ $C = \dfrac{1}{\pi f_C R_K}$	$L = \dfrac{R_K}{4\pi f_C}$ $C = \dfrac{1}{4\pi f_C R_K}$
Ideal frequency response	PB | SB at f_C	SB | PB at f_C

Fig. 4.61 (a)

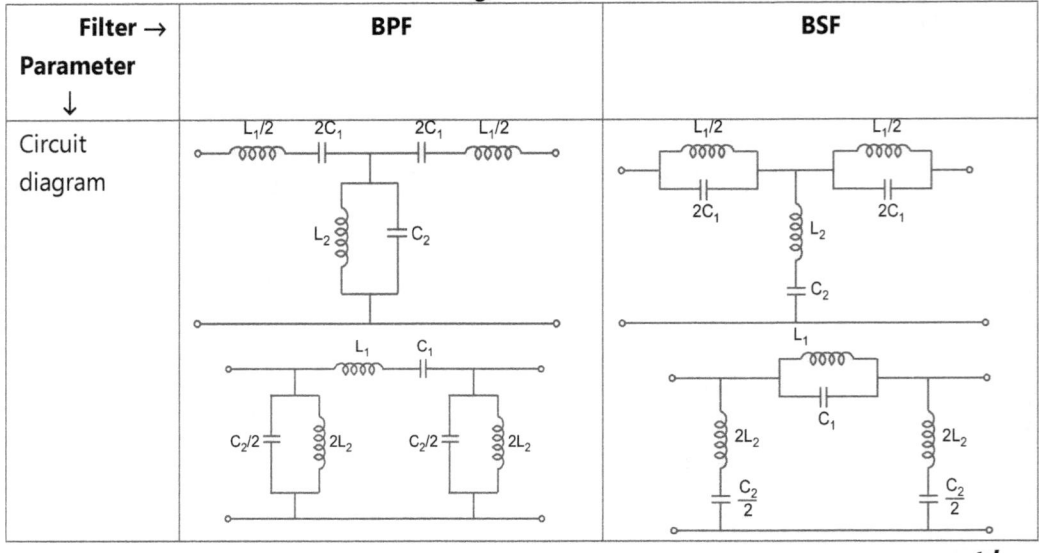

Filter → Parameter ↓	BPF	BSF
Circuit diagram	(see figure)	(see figure)

contd. ...

Design impedance	$R_K = \sqrt{\dfrac{L_1}{C_2}} = \sqrt{\dfrac{L_2}{C_1}}$ $L_1 C_1 = L_2 C_2 = \dfrac{1}{\omega_0^2}$	$R_K = \sqrt{\dfrac{L_1}{C_2}} = \sqrt{\dfrac{L_2}{C_1}}$ $L_1 C_1 = L_2 C_2 = \dfrac{1}{\omega_0^2}$
Equation for f_C	$f_0 = \sqrt{f_1 f_2}$ $f_0 = f_r = f_{ar}$	$f_0 = \sqrt{f_1 f_2}$ $f_0 = f_r = f_{ar}$
Design equation	$C_1 = \dfrac{(f_2 - f_1)}{4\pi R_K f_1 f_2}$ $L_1 = \dfrac{R_K}{\pi(f_2 - f_1)}$ $C_2 = \dfrac{1}{\pi R_K (f_2 - f_1)}$ $L_2 = \dfrac{R_K (f_2 - f_1)}{4\pi f_1 f_2}$ $f_0 = \dfrac{1}{2\pi \sqrt{L_1 C_1}}$ $= \dfrac{1}{2\pi \sqrt{L_2 C_2}}$	$C_1 = \dfrac{1}{4\pi R_K (f_2 - f_1)}$ $L_1 = \dfrac{R_K (f_2 - f_1)}{\pi f_1 f_2}$ $C_2 = \dfrac{(f_2 - f_1)}{\pi R_K (f_1 f_2)}$ $L_2 = \dfrac{R_K}{4\pi (f_2 - f_1)}$ $f_0 = \dfrac{1}{2\pi \sqrt{L_1 C_1}} = \dfrac{1}{2\pi \sqrt{L_2 C_2}}$
Ideal Frequency Response	SB / PB / SB with f_L, f_H	PB / SB / PB with f_L, f_H

Fig. 4.61 (b)

4.17 DISADVANTAGES OF CONSTANT k PROTOTYPE FILTERS

So far we have studied prototype or constant K type filters. We have also seen the variation of attenuation constant α and characteristic impedance Z_0 with frequency. The disadvantages of a prototype constant k filters are very clear from the plotted curves.

1. Characteristics Impedances Z_{0T} and $Z_{0\pi}$ do not remain constant in pass band. It varies for all the filters between R_K i.e. the design impedance and ∞ throughout the pass band. Because of this there will be mismatch between the load (which is fixed) and a filter section. So a satisfactory impedance match is not possible and therefore the output of the filter does not remain constant in pass band as is ideally expected.

2. It is ideally expected that the attenuation α must be ∞ in stop band and zero in pass band. But practically attenuation α does not change instantly or rapidly from ∞ to 0 as the filter changes the operation from stop to pass band or vice versa. Practically,

due to the finite resistances in the components used, attenuation changes gradually as the operating band of filter changes. Due to this disadvantage frequencies just outside the pass band are not appreciably attenuated w.r.t. frequencies just inside the pass band. Thus, making it difficult to separate the pass band and stop band.

4.17.1 Solution

In the cases, where an impedance match is not important, the attenuation may be built up near cut-off by cascading or connecting a number of constant k sections in series.

Example, if two sections of the same type are connected in cascade, the attenuation in the attenuation band gets doubled giving much sharper cut-off characteristics than the obtained using only one section i.e. two sections with α = 20 db for each when cascaded will give α = 20 db, which is higher than individual α values of each section.

Thus, with this modification, attenuation in stop band is seen to have increased, but due to this cascade connection, attenuation is pass band will also increase, which should ideally be zero, Thus making a rounded off α curve at the cut-off frequency in pass band.

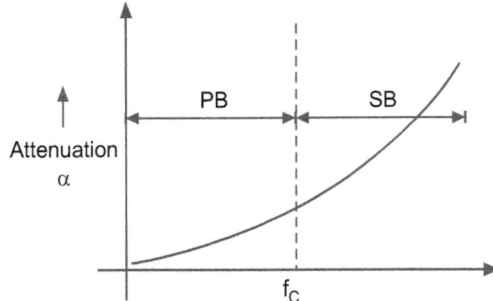

Fig. 4.62: Variation of α with frequency in a cascade connection of a prototype LPF

So the proposed solution is definitely not a wise solution as it is not overcoming any of disadvantages completely and we therefore need to design a completely new section.

4.18 'm' DERIVED FILTERS

- We need to completely eliminate the disadvantages of constant k or prototype section by designing a new section.
- For effective and appropriate working of the constant k section, the proposed new section must same satisfy the following conditions.
- The new section must have cut-off frequency as that of the constant k. Filter but different attenuation characteristics i.e. rapid rise in α at cut-off frequencies in stop band.
- The new section must have the same value of characteristic impedance Z_0 as that of prototype section at all the frequencies so that both the sections have identical pass bands.

- Such a filter section that satisfies all the above requirements is known as m-derived filter section. It is so called because the new section is actually derived from the original prototype, section with a slight modification.
- We have discussed T and π sections of LPF, HPF, BPF and BSF. On the similar grounds, we have m derived T and m derived π sections for each of the constant k filter.
- We will discuss m derived LPF and HPF in this chapter.

4.18.1 m Derived T Section

- A prototype T section is shown in Fig. 4.63 (a). Let the new section constructed from the prototype section be as shown Fig. 4.63 (b).

    1. Let this new section have the series arm impedance modified to $m\dfrac{Z_1}{2}$ where m is a constant. The shunt arm impedance also changes to some other value Z_2'.
    2. As will be clear later these two sections are connected in series.
    3. As already discussed, for satisfactory matching of several such types of sections in series, it is necessary that Z_0 of all be identical at all the points in the pass band. So Z_0 of both these sections must be equal $\dfrac{Z_2}{n}$.

- Now for Fig. 4.63 (a).

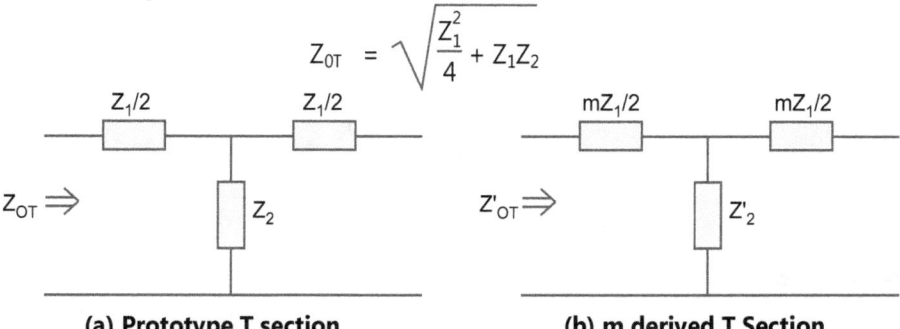

(a) Prototype T section   (b) m derived T Section

Fig. 4.63

Similarly for m derived section i.e. Fig. 4.63 (b).

$$Z'_{OT} = \sqrt{\left(\dfrac{mZ_1}{2}\right)^2 + mZ_1 Z'_2}$$

To maintain same Z_0 we must have

$$Z_{OT} = Z'_{OT}$$

$$\sqrt{\dfrac{Z_1^2}{4} + Z_1 Z_2} = \sqrt{\dfrac{m^2 Z_1^2}{4} + mZ_1 Z'_2}$$

$$\frac{Z_1^2}{4} + Z_1 Z_2 = \frac{m^2 Z_1^2}{4} + m Z_1 Z_2'$$

$$m Z_1 Z_2' = \frac{Z_1^2}{4}[1 - m^2] + Z_1 Z_2$$

$$\boxed{Z_2' = \left(\frac{1-m^2}{4m}\right) Z_1 + \frac{Z_2}{m}} \qquad \ldots(4.51)$$

- Thus, impedance Z_2' i.e. shunt arm of m derived section consists of two impedances in series.
- These two impedances are:
  $\left(\dfrac{1-m^2}{4m}\right) Z_1$ and $\left(\dfrac{Z_2}{m}\right)$ connected in series.
- Note that the value of m can range from 0 to 1, when m = 1 the prototype and the m derived sections are identical.

  (Substitute m = 1 in equation (4.51) and you will get $Z_2' = Z_2$)

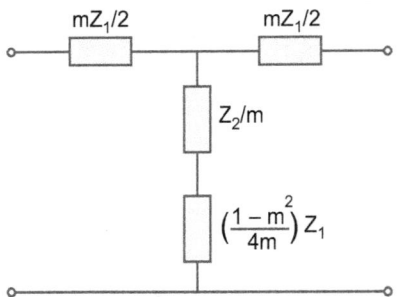

Fig. 4.64: m derived T section

4.18.2 m Derived π Section

- A prototype π section is shown in Fig. 4.65 (a). Let the new section constructed from the prototype section be as shown in Fig. 4.65 (b).
- Let this new section have the series arm Z_L' and the shunt impedance modified to $\dfrac{2Z_2}{m}$.
- As will be clear in the later part of the chapter, the prototype and m derived sections are connected in series.
- For satisfactory matching of several such type of sections in series it is very necessary that Z_0 of all the sections be identical at all points in the pass band. So Z_0 of both the sections must be equal.

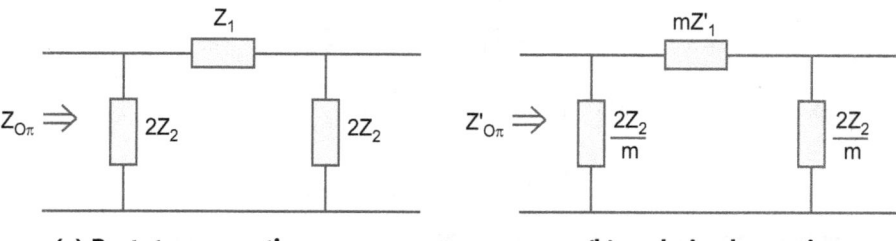

(a) Prototype π section (b) m derived π section

Fig. 4.65

$$Z_{O\pi} = \frac{Z_1 Z_2}{\sqrt{\frac{Z_1^2}{4} + Z_1 Z_2}}$$

Similarly for the m derived section of Fig. 4.107 (b).

$$Z'_{O\pi} = \frac{Z'_1 \frac{Z_2}{m}}{\sqrt{\frac{(Z'_1)^2}{4} + Z'_1 \frac{Z_2}{m}}}$$

To maintain same Z_0 we must have

$$Z_{O\pi} = Z'_{O\pi}$$

$$\frac{Z_1 Z_2}{\sqrt{\frac{Z_1^2}{4} + Z_1 Z_2}} = \frac{Z'_1 \frac{Z_2}{m}}{\sqrt{\frac{(Z'_1)^2}{4} + Z'_1 \frac{Z_2}{m}}}$$

$$\frac{Z_1^2}{\frac{Z_1^2}{4} + Z_1 Z_2} = \frac{\left(\frac{Z'_1}{m}\right)^2}{\frac{{Z'_1}^2}{4} + \frac{Z'_1 Z_2}{m}}$$

$$\frac{Z_1^2 {Z'_1}^2}{4} + \frac{Z_1^2 Z'_1 Z_2}{m} = \frac{{Z'_1}^2 Z_1^2}{4m^2} + Z_1 Z_2 \frac{{Z'_1}^2}{m^2}$$

Multiplying throughout by $4m^2$.

$$m^2 Z_1^2 {Z'_1}^2 + 4m Z_1^2 Z'_1 Z_2 = Z_1^2 {Z'_1}^2 + 4 Z_1 {Z'_1}^2 Z_2$$

dividing through by Z'_1.

$$m^2 Z_1^2 Z_1' + 4m Z_1^2 Z_2 = Z_1^2 Z_1' + 4 Z_1 Z_1' Z_2$$

$$Z_1' \left[m^2 Z_1^2 - Z_1^2 - 4Z_1 Z_2 \right] = -4m Z_1^2 Z_2$$

$$Z_1' = \frac{4 m Z_1^2 Z_2}{Z_1^2 + 4 Z_1 Z_2 - m^2 Z_1^2}$$

Multiplying numerator and denominator by m.

$$Z_1' = \frac{4 m^2 Z_1^2 Z_2}{m Z_1^2 + 4 m Z_1 Z_2 - m^3 Z_1^2}$$

$$Z_1' = \frac{4 m^2 Z_1^2 Z_2}{4 m Z_1 Z_2 + m Z_1^2 (1 - m^2)}$$

$$Z_1' = \frac{(4 m Z_2)(m Z_1^2)}{4 m Z_1 Z_2 + m Z_1^2 (1 - m^2)}$$

$$Z_1' = \frac{\left(\dfrac{4 m Z_2}{1 - m^2}\right) m Z_1}{\dfrac{4 m Z_2}{1 - m^2} + m Z_1}$$

$$\boxed{Z_1' = \left(\frac{4 m Z_2}{1 - m^2}\right) \parallel m Z_1} \qquad \ldots (4.52)$$

- Thus, importance Z_1' i.e. series arm of m derived section consists of two impedances in parallel.
- Z_1' is a parallel combination of $m Z_1$ and $\dfrac{4 m Z_2}{1 - m^2}$.
- Note that similar to m derived T section, even in this case value of m can range from 0 to 1. When m = 1 the prototype and the m derived sections are identical.

(Substitute m = 1 in equation (4.52) and we will have $Z_1' = Z_1$).

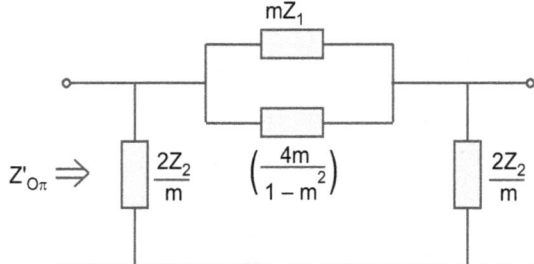

Fig. 4.66: m derived π sections

m derived T and π sections can be now designed for any of the constant k, filters, i.e. LPF, HPF, BSF and BPF. But here we will restrict our scope of discussion to m derived LPF and HPF.

4.19 m DERIVED LOW PASS FILTER

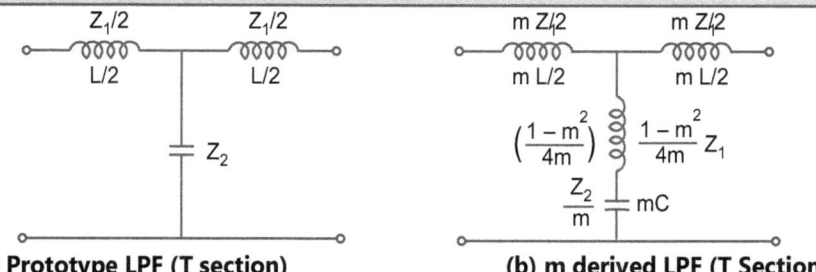

(a) Prototype LPF (T section)   (b) m derived LPF (T Section)

Fig. 4.67

- In the very last section we have seen that Z_2' in case of m derived section is a series combination of two impedances.

$$\frac{1-m^2}{4m} Z_1 \quad \text{and} \quad \frac{Z_2}{m}$$

- **Note:** When an impedance of a condenser is divided by m then its capacitance must be multiplied by m.
- Now let us clearly understand that how such a small modification in the circuit will give us infinite attenuation near cut-off frequency or how do we get zero output voltage near f_c in case of m derived LPF.

4.19.1 Operation of m derived LPF

- As is clear from the Fig. 4.67 (b) shunt arm of m derived section is a series resonant circuit. [L in series with C].
- In a series resonant circuit i.e. in a circuit when inductive and capacitive reactances are in series the reactances cancel each other at resonant frequency.
- So, at this resonant frequency, the shunt arm appears as a short circuit on the network.
- As shown in Fig. 4.68 the short circuit provides ground path to the input signal, thereby making V_{out} = 0V and thus attenuation is very high [as ideally expected] at this resonant frequency.
- This frequency of infinite or very high attenuation is called f_∞.

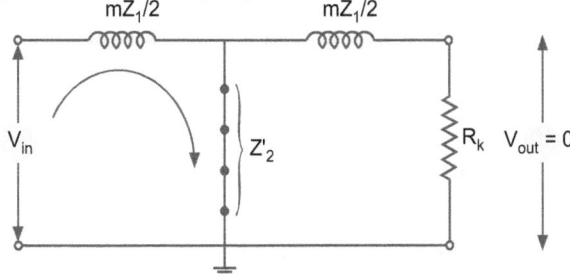

Fig. 4.68: An Approximate Model of m Derived LPF at f_∞, Where Shunt Arm Appears as Short circuit bypassing The Load

4.19.2 Reactance Curves

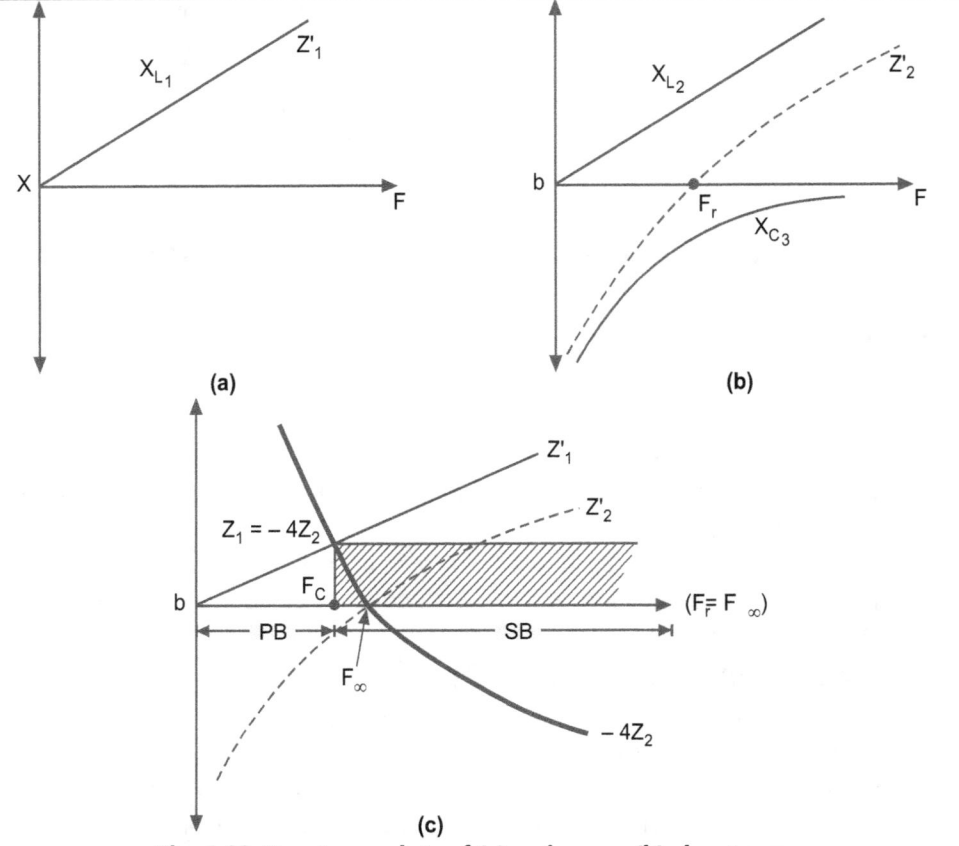

Fig. 4.69: Reactance plots of (a) series arm (b) shunt arm (c) reactance curve indicating PB and SB of m derived

Here,

$$Z_1' = \text{series arm having inductor } L_1$$

$$Z_2' = \text{shunt arm having inductor } L_2 \text{ capacitor C}$$

- Fig. 4.69 (a) is a plot of x_L against f. Fig. 4.69 (b) shows the plot of the individual components L_2 and C and also plot of Z_2' as a series resonating circuit.
- 'f_r' in Fig. 4.69 (b) is a resonating frequency at which $X_{L2} = X_C$.
  i.e. Reactances of inductor and capacitor present in the shunt arm of the m derived filter are equal, thus making it act as a short circuit at f_r.
- Fig. 4.69 (c) shows the reactance curves of Z_1' and Z_2' to indicate a pass band between the frequencies of which $Z_1' = -4Z_2'$ and $Z_1' = 0$.

- f_C and f_r are shown. f_r as discussed earlier is nothing but f_∞ i.e. the frequency at which shunt arm will act as short circuit making $V_{out} = 0$.
- **Note:** f_C and f_∞ are two different frequencies close to each other. This observation needs an explanation.

4.19.3 f_∞ and f_C in m derived LPF

- We have designed m derived filters with an objective to have very high attenuation at cut-off frequency (f_C).
- To achieve this, a inductor is added in shunt arm making it function as series resonant circuit resonating at frequency f_∞ (i.e. f_r).
- At this frequency, f_∞, $V_{out} = 0$ and thus attenuation is very very high.
- Ideally we want this operation, this behaviour at f_C i.e. cut-off frequency.
- Practically we achieve it to f_∞ and not at f_C. f_∞ can be chosen arbitrarily close to f_C so the α near f_C is made high.
- We might end up thinking that why is f_∞ not made same as f_C.
- There are two reasons justifying that f_∞ and f_C can never be the same frequencies. $f_\infty \neq f_C$. And f_∞ will always and always be higher than f_C, in case of m derived LPF.

    1. At f_C we must have $Z_1' = -4 Z_2'$.

        AT f_∞ we must have $Z_2' = 0$.

        It is impossible to achieve or satisfy both these conditions at very same frequency. So f_C can never be equal to f_∞. They have to be two different frequencies.

    2. Below f_C, Z_2' is capacitive.

        Below f_∞, Z_2' is capacitive

        Above f_∞, Z_2' is inductive.

        So, if f_∞ is below f_C than these conditions will not be met. So f_∞ is always higher than f_C.

4.19.4 Derivations of f_∞ and m for a m derived LPF

The shunt arm of m derived LPF (T section) resonates of frequency f_∞ (f_r).

$$f_r = \frac{1}{2\pi\sqrt{LC}} \quad \ldots \text{expression for } f_r \text{ series reasonance}$$

Here,
$$f_\infty = \frac{1}{2\pi\sqrt{\left(\frac{1-m^2}{4m}\right)L\,(mC)}}$$

$$f_\infty = \frac{1}{\pi\sqrt{(1-m^2)\,LC}} \quad \ldots \text{(a)}$$

But, for a low pass filter
$$f_C = \frac{1}{\pi\sqrt{LC}} \quad \ldots \text{(b)}$$

∴ Substituting equation (b) in (a)

$$\boxed{f_\infty = \frac{f_C}{\sqrt{(1-m^2)}}} \quad \ldots (4.53)$$

Simplifying equation (4.90) we have
$$\sqrt{1-m^2} = \frac{f_C}{f_\infty}$$

$$1 - m^2 = \left(\frac{f_C}{f_\infty}\right)^2$$

$$\boxed{m = \sqrt{1 - \left(\frac{f_C}{f_\infty}\right)^2}} \quad \ldots (4.54)$$

This equation determines the value of m to be used for a particular f_∞.

4.19.5 π-Section

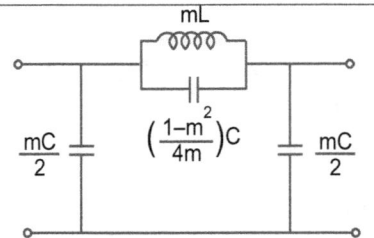

Fig. 4.70: m derived LPF π Section

4.20 m DERIVED HIGH PASS FILTER

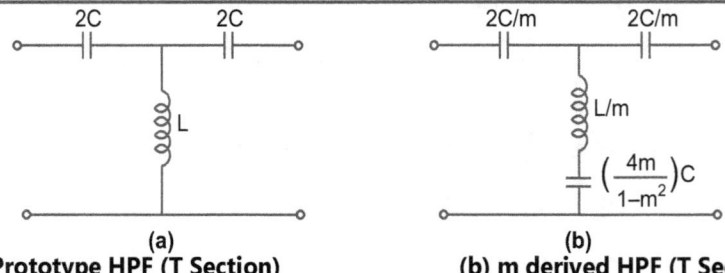

(a) Prototype HPF (T Section)   (b) m derived HPF (T Section)

Fig. 4.71

- Z_2' in case of m derived section in a series combination of two impedances.

$$\frac{1-m^2}{4m} Z_1 \text{ and } \frac{Z_2}{m}$$

Here Z_1 is a capacitor (C)

Here Z_2 is an inductor (L)

∴ Z_2' is $\frac{L}{M}$ in series with $\frac{4m}{1-m^2}$ C.

- Note: When a impedance of a condenser is divided by m then its capacitance should be multiplied by m.

4.20.1 Operation

- It is clear From the Fig. 4.71 (b) shunt arm of m derived section is a series resonant circuit [L in series with C].
- In a series resonant circuit i.e. in a circuit when inductive and capacitive reactances are in series the reactances can cell each other at resonant frequency.
- So at this resonant frequency, the shunt arm appears as a short circuit on the network.
- As shown in Fig. 4.72, this short circuit provides ground path to the input signal thereby making V_{out} = 0V and thus the attenuation is very very high [as ideally expected] at this resonant frequency.
- This frequency of infinite or very high attenuation is called f_∞.

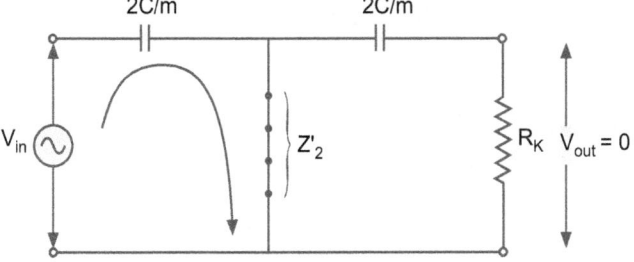

Fig. 4.72: An approximate model at f_∞,

where shunt arm appears as short circuit (bypassing the load)

4.20.2 Reactance Curves

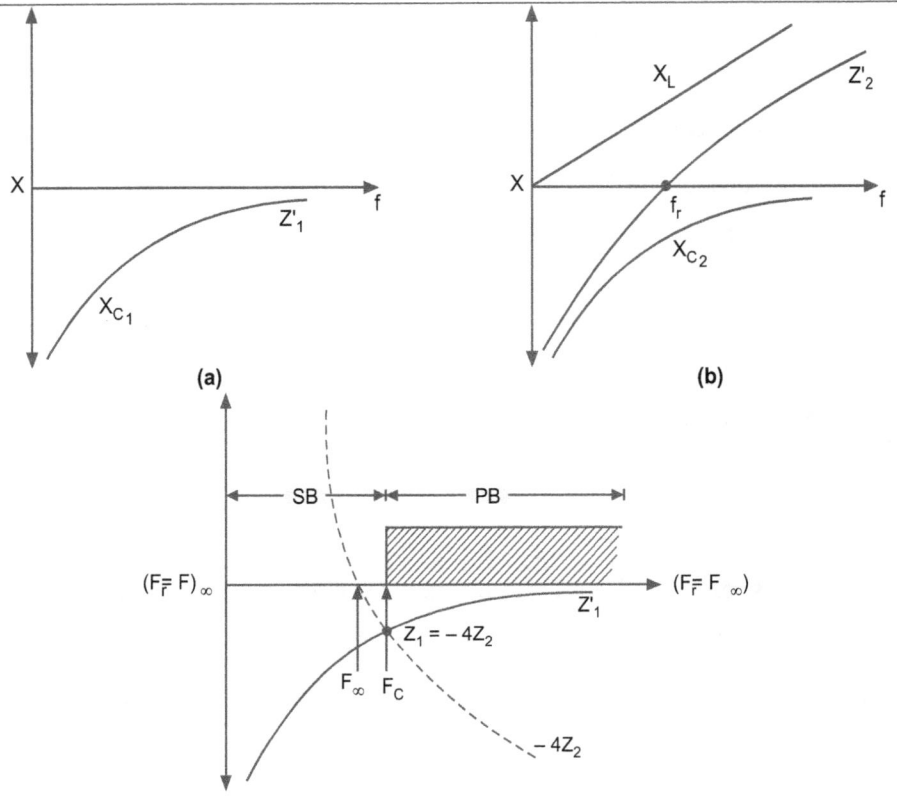

(c)
Fig. 4.73: Reactance plots of (a) series arm (b) shunt arm (c) reactance curve indicate PB, SB

Here, Z_1' = Series arm having capacitor (C_1)

Z_2' = Shunt arm having inductor (L), capacitor (C_2)

- Fig. 4.73 (a) is a plot of X_{C_1} against f and 4.73 (b) shows the plot of the individual components L and C_2 and also plot of Z_2' as a series resonating circuit.
- f_r is Fig. 4.73 (b) is a resonating frequency at which
$$X_L = X_{C_2}$$
i.e. reactances of inductor and capacitor present in the shunt arm of m derived filter are equal, thus making it act as a short circuit at f_r.
- Fig. 4.73 (c) shows the reactance curves of Z_1' and Z_2' to indicate a pass band between the frequencies at which $Z_1' = -4Z_2'$ and $Z_1' = 0$.

- f_r and f_∞ are indicated. f_r as already discussed is nothing but f_∞, i.e. the frequency at which shunt arm will act as short circuit making $V_{out} = 0$.
- f_C and f_∞ are two different frequencies close to each other.

4.20.3 f_∞ and f_C in m derived HPF

1. At f_C, we must have

$$Z_1' = -4Z_2'$$

At f_∞, we must have

$$Z_2' = 0$$

2. It is impossible to achieve or satisfy both these conditions at very same frequency. So f_C can never be equal to f_∞. They have to be two different frequencies.

   Above f_C Z_2' is inductive

   Below f_∞ Z_2' is capacitive

   Above f_∞ Z_2' is inductive

   So, if f_∞ is shifted above f_C, than these conditions will not be satisfied. So f_∞ is always lower than f_C.

4.20.4 Derivations of f_∞ and m

The shunt arm of m-derived HPF (T section) resonates at frequency f_∞ i.e. f_r.

$$f_\infty = \frac{1}{2\pi \sqrt{\left(\frac{L}{m}\right)\left(\frac{4m}{1-m^2}\right)C}}$$

$$f_\infty = \frac{1}{2\pi \sqrt{\frac{4LC}{(1-m^2)}}}$$

Substituting value of f_C in the equation for f_∞.

$$\boxed{f_\infty = f_C \sqrt{(1-m^2)}} \qquad \ldots (4.55)$$

Simplifying equation (4.92)

$$\frac{f_\infty}{f_C} = \sqrt{1-m^2}$$

$$\left(\frac{f_\infty}{f_C}\right)^2 = 1 - m^2$$

$$m^2 = 1 - \left(\frac{f_\infty}{f_C}\right)^2$$

$$\boxed{m = \sqrt{1 - \left(\frac{f_\infty}{f_C}\right)^2}} \qquad \ldots (4.56)$$

This equation determines the value of m to be used for a particular f_∞.

4.20.5 π Section

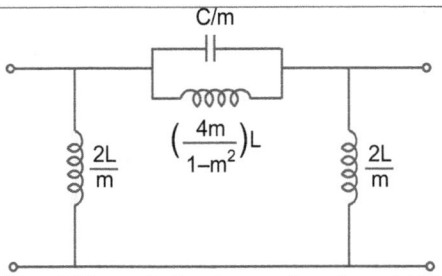

Fig. 4.74: m derived π section for a HPF

4.21 SUMMARY OF M DERIVED FILTERS

	m-derived LPF	m derived HPF
T section filter	mZ₁/2 — mZ₁/2 series arms with mL/2 each; shunt: $\left(\frac{1-m^2}{4m}\right)Z_1$, $\frac{Z_2}{m} = mC$	Series: 2C/m — 2C/m; shunt L/m in series with $\left(\frac{4m}{1-m^2}\right)C$
π section filter	Series: mL with $\left(\frac{1-m^2}{4m}\right)C$; shunt mC/2 each side	Series: C/m with $\left(\frac{4m}{1-m^2}\right)L$; shunt 2L/m each side
f_∞	$f_\infty = \dfrac{f_C}{\sqrt{1-m^2}}$	$f_\infty = f_C\sqrt{1-m^2}$
m	$m = \sqrt{1 - \left(\dfrac{f_C}{f_\infty}\right)^2}$	$m = \sqrt{1 - \left(\dfrac{f_\infty}{f_C}\right)^2}$
Relation in f_∞ and f_C	$f_\infty > f_C$	$f_\infty < f_C$

Fig. 4.73

4.22 SOLVED NUMERICALS ON m DERIVED FILTERS

Ex. 4.23: Design a m-derived low pas filter to match a line having characteristic impedance of 500 Ω and to pass signals upto 1 kHz with infinite attenuation at 1.2 kHz.

Sol.: Given $R_0 = 500$ Ω, $f_C = 1$ kHz, $f_\infty = 1.2$ kHz.

1. **Design of prototype low pass filter section (T Type)**

   Using design equations,

   $$L = \frac{R_0}{(\pi f_C)}$$

   $$L = \frac{500}{\pi \times 1000}$$

   $$\boxed{L = 159.155 \text{ mH}}$$

   $$C = \frac{1}{(\pi f_C) R_0}$$

   $$C = \frac{1}{(\pi \times 1000)(500)}$$

   $$\boxed{C = 0.6366 \text{ μF}}$$

   Thus, prototype low pass filter (T type) is as shown in the Fig. 4.76 (a).

   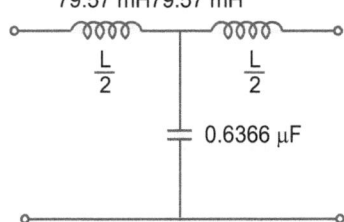

   Fig. 4.76 (a)

2. **Design of m-derived low pass filter:**

   The value of m is given by,

   $$m = \sqrt{1 - \left(\frac{f_C}{f_\infty}\right)^2}$$

   $$m = \sqrt{1 - \left(\frac{1000}{1200}\right)^2}$$

   $$\boxed{m = 0.552}$$

   The elements in the series and shunt arms of m-derived filter section are given by,

   $$\frac{mL}{2} = \frac{(0.5527)(159.155 \times 10^{-3})}{2}$$

   $$\boxed{\frac{mL}{2} = 43.976 \text{ mH}}$$

$$mC = (0.5527)(0.6366 \times 10^{-6})$$

$$\boxed{mL = 0.3518 \ \mu F}$$

$$\left(\frac{1-m^2}{4m}\right)L = \left[\frac{1-(0.5527)^2}{4(0.5527)}\right](159.133 \times 10^{-3})$$

$$\boxed{\left(\frac{1-m^2}{4m}\right)L = 50 \ mH}$$

Hence m-derived low pass filter is as shown in the Fig. 4.76 (b).

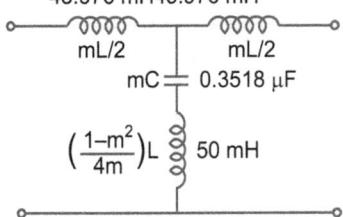

Fig. 4.76 (b): m-derived low pass filter T type section

Ex. 4.24: Design m-derived LPF having cut-off frequency of 5 kHz and impedance of 600 Ω. The frequency of infinite attenuation is 1.25 times the cut-off frequency.

Sol.: Given: $R_0 = 600 \ \Omega$, $f_C = 5$ kHz, $f_\infty = (1.25 \times 5) = 6.25$ kHz.

$$L = \frac{R_0}{\pi f_C} = \frac{600}{\pi \times 5 \times 10^3}$$

$$\boxed{L = 38.197 \ mH}$$

$$C = \frac{1}{(\pi f_C) R_0} = \frac{1}{\pi \times 5 \times 10^3 \times 600}$$

$$\boxed{C = 0.106 \ \mu F}$$

For m derived LPF m is given by,

$$m = \sqrt{1-\left(\frac{f_C}{f_\infty}\right)^2} = \sqrt{1-\left(\frac{5 \times 10^3}{6.25 \times 10^3}\right)^2}$$

$$\boxed{m = 0.6}$$

The actual values of components in series and shunt arms of m-derived filter are

$$\frac{mL}{2} = \frac{0.6 \times 38.197 \times 10^{-3}}{2}$$

$$\boxed{\frac{mL}{2} = 11.459 \ mH}$$

$$mC = 0.6 (0.106 \times 10^{-6})$$

$$\boxed{mC = 0.0636 \ \mu F}$$

$$\left(\frac{1-m^2}{4m}\right) L = \left(\frac{1-(0.6)^2}{4(0.6)}\right)(38.197 \times 10^{-3})$$

$$\boxed{\left(\frac{1-m^2}{4m}\right) L = 10.18 \text{ mH}}$$

∴ The low pass filter is as shown below.

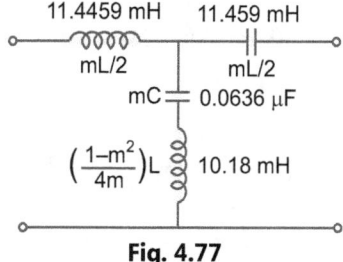

Fig. 4.77

Ex. 4.25: Design an m-derived lowpass T-section filter to have termination of 600 Ω resistance. The cut-off frequency is 1.8 kHz and finite attenuation occurs at 2 kHz.

Sol.: Given $R_0 = 600$ Ω, $f_C = 1.8$ kHz, $f_\infty = 2$ kHz

1. Design of prototype lowpass filter section:

Using design equations,

$$L = \frac{R_0}{\pi f_C} = \frac{600}{\pi \times 1.8 \times 10^3}$$

$$\boxed{L = 106.1 \text{ mH}}$$

$$C = \frac{1}{(\pi f_C) R_0} = \frac{1}{(\pi \times 1.8 \times 10^3 \times 600)}$$

$$\boxed{C = 0.2947 \text{ μF}}$$

Hence prototype T section is low pass filter is as shown in the Fig. 4.78 (a).

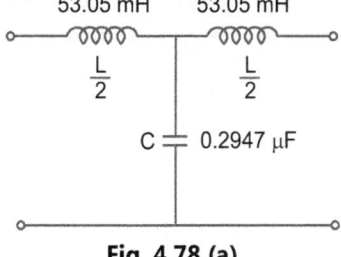

Fig. 4.78 (a)

2. Design of m-derived lowpass filter:

$$m = \sqrt{1-\left(\frac{f_C}{f_\infty}\right)^2} = \sqrt{1-\left(\frac{1800}{2000}\right)^2}$$

$$\boxed{m = 0.4358}$$

Thus the elements in series and shunt arms of m-derived sections are as follows:

$$\frac{mL}{2} = \frac{(0.4358)(106.1 \times 10^{-3})}{2}$$

$$\boxed{\frac{mL}{2} = 23.12 \text{ mH}}$$

$$mC = (0.4358)(0.2947 \times 10^{-6})$$

$$\boxed{mC = 0.1284 \ \mu F}$$

$$\left(\frac{1-m^2}{4m}\right)L = \left[\frac{1-(0.4358)^2}{4(0.4358)}\right] \times (106.1 \times 10^{-3})$$

$$\boxed{\left(\frac{1-m^2}{4m}\right)L = 49.305 \text{ mH}}$$

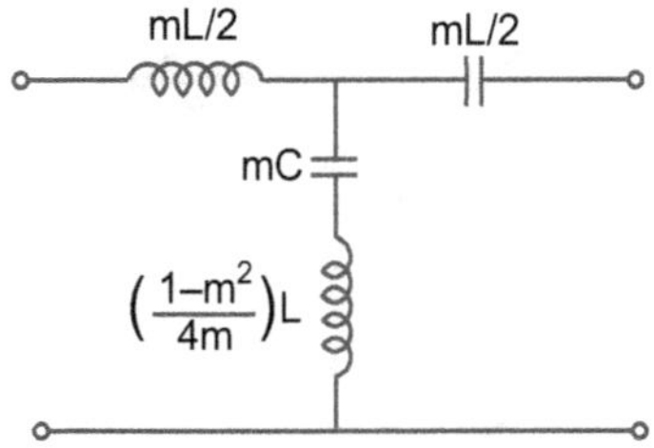

Fig. 4.78 (b)

Ex. 4.26: Design a composite high pass filter to operate into a load of 600 Ω and have a cut-off frequency of 1.2 kHz. The filter is to have one constant k-section and one m-derived section with an infinite attenuation at 1.1 kHz.

Sol.: Given $R_0 = 600 \ \Omega$, $f_C = 1.2$ kHz $= 1200$ Hz, $f_\infty = 1.1$ kHz $= 1100$ Hz.

1. **Design of constant – k high pass filter:**

   Using design equations, values of L and C are given by,

   $$L = \frac{R_0}{4\pi f_C} = \frac{600}{4 \times \pi \times 1200}$$

   $$\boxed{L = 39.788 \text{ mH}}$$

   $$C = \frac{1}{(4\pi f_C) R_0} = \frac{1}{4 \times \pi \times 1200 \times 600}$$

   $$\boxed{C = 0.11 \ \mu F}$$

   Hence constant-k type T-section of high pass filter is as shown in the Fig. 4.79 (a).

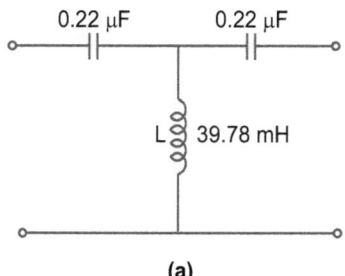

(a)
Fig. 4.79

2. **Design of m-derived high pass filter:**

$$m = \sqrt{1-\left(\frac{f_\infty}{f_c}\right)^2} = \sqrt{1-\left(\frac{1100}{1200}\right)^2} = 0.399 \approx$$

$$\boxed{m = 0.4}$$

Hence the elements of m-derived high pass filter are given by,

$$\frac{2C}{m} = \frac{2 \times 0.11 \times 10^{-6}}{0.4}$$

$$\boxed{\frac{2C}{m} = 0.55 \ \mu F}$$

$$\frac{L}{m} = \frac{39.788 \times 10^{-3}}{0.4}$$

$$\boxed{\frac{L}{m} = 99.47 \ mH}$$

$$\frac{4m}{1-m^2} C = \left[\frac{4 \times 0.4}{1-(0.4)^2}\right] \times 0.11 \times 10^{-6}$$

$$\boxed{\frac{4m}{1-m^2} C = 0.209 \ \mu F}$$

Hence m-derived high pass filter is shown in the Fig. 4.79 (b).

(b)
Fig. 4.79

Thus, the complete composite filter consisting one constant-k section and one m-derived section is as shown in the Fig. 4.79 (c).

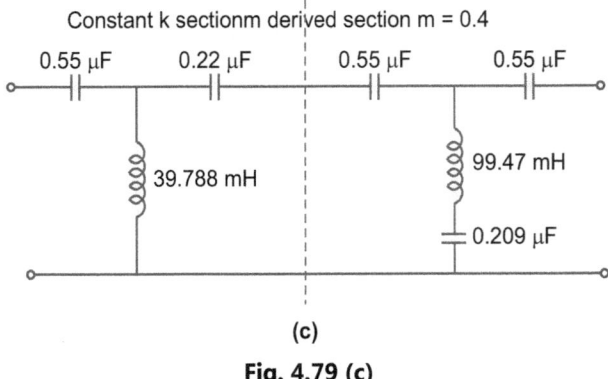

(c)

Fig. 4.79 (c)

4.23 DISADVANTAGES OF m DERIVED FILTER

- In constant k or prototype section, sharp rise in attenuation in the stop band was a limitation.
  i.e. In LPF, high α was needed in stop band after f_C.
  In HPF, high α was needed in stop band before f_C.
  and this was not achieved.
- So a m-derived. Filter was designed which gave very very high attenuation at frequency f_∞, very close but not equal to f_C.
- Thus, at f_∞ (which is located in stop band in LPF and HPF) the rise in the attenuation is very sharp.
- But the limitation is that this increase in α is only at f_∞. After f_∞ the value of α again decreases.
- Ideally α should be very large (infinite) throughout the stop band for any filter. But in the case of m derived filters the desired high attenuation is only at one frequency in stop band. It does not last for the entire stop band as actually expected and is clear. From Fig. 4.80.
- The reason for such a behaviour of ∝ is because of f_∞, the shunt arm of LPF and HPF acts as good as a short circuit. X_L cancels X_C at f_∞, which is the resonating frequency.
  But if we recollect the concepts of resonance, it is very clear that only at resonating frequency, $x_L = x_C$ i.e. only the resonance the total reactance is zero. In series resonance for any frequency above or below f_r, there is some reactance existing (may be inductive or capacitive respectively), so the output will not be completely zero. A finite voltage will appear across the load.
- The attenuation α is said to be infinite or very large only when V_{out} is zero. So, in case of m derived filter this is achieved only at f_∞, value of α drops for other frequencies in stop band.

- This happens to be a major limitation in m derived filters.
- However, this limitation can be overcomed by two ways:
    1. Use of composite filter (will be discussed in section 4.26).
    2. Use as many m derived sections as desired to:
        - Produce a high attenuation over the entire stop band.
        - Supress the signal components at only at some particular frequencies.

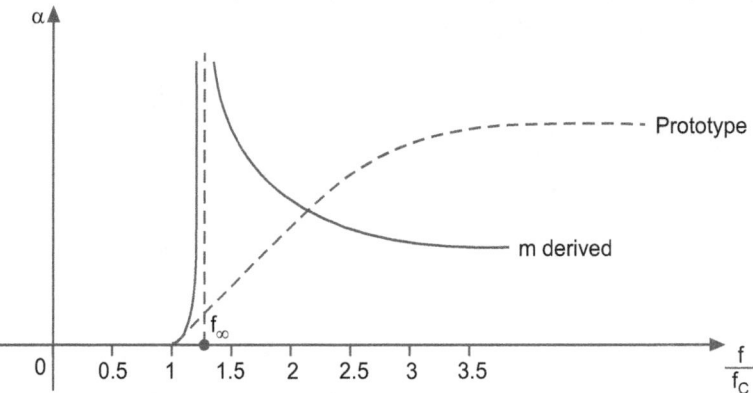

Fig. 4.80: Variation of α in prototype and m derived section

4.24 TERMINATION WITH m DERIVED HALF SECTIONS

4.24.1 Necessity of m-Derived Half Sections

- Let us revise the theorem of maximum power transfer, which was studied in chapter 1.
- "In an active network, maximum power transfer to the load takes place when the load impedance is equivalent to impedance of the network as viewed from the terminals of the load".
- In case of filter we occasionally have to cascade some T or π filter sections of constant k filters or of m derived or sometimes even a constant k with m derived filter (This will be discussed in the next section and this cascade connection has to be placed between the source and the load. So impedance matching at various points is a crucial requirement. For maximum power transfer.
- In chapter 5, reactance L sections were designed that would transform a given resistance to a more desired valued.
- But this L section will solve the problem of satisfactorily terminating a section or matching the impedance only at one particular frequency.
- Now, all the filters consists of frequency dependent components, whose reactances change with frequency.

- So, obviously in this case we will need a L-section, whose characteristics will change with frequency in such a way that filter is approximately matched to its load at all frequencies over the pass band.
- Zobel discovered m derived half sections which has the property of:
    (i) Constant impedance almost over the entire pass band (also explained in 4.24.4).
    (ii) Matching a T filter with a π filter and vice versa.

We have studied m derived filters of T and π type. They are reproduced here in Fig. 4.81 for reference.

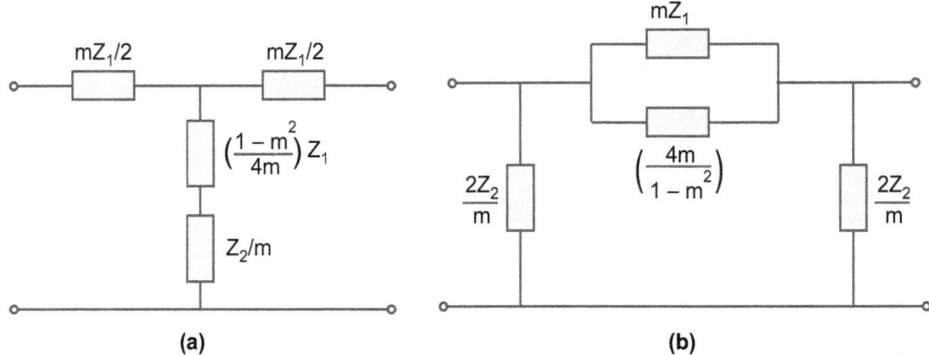

Fig. 4.81: m derived T and π type filters

4.24.2 m Derived Half Sections (T Type)

- Let us now analyse one of these types to verify the above stated properties.
- Consider the m derived T filter as shown in Fig. 4.82 (a). This 'T' type m derived filter can be split in two half sections i.e. m-derived half section as shown in Fig. 4.82 (a) and (b).
- These half sections are asymmetrical network. So let us start our analysis with the calculation of image impedances for a one of these half sections say Fig. 4.82 (b).

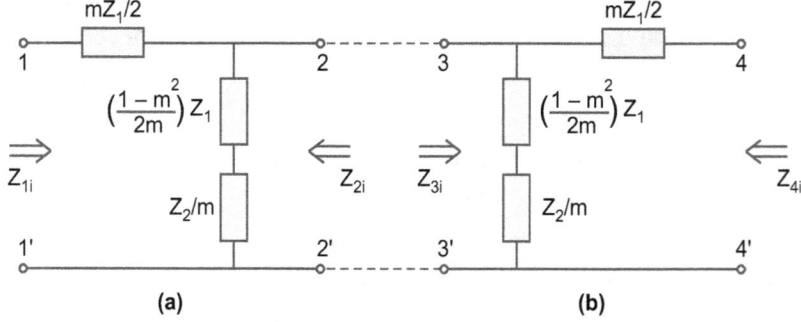

Fig. 4.82: m-derived half sections of a m-derived T section

- Image impedance at a port x is defined as:

$$Z_{xi} = \sqrt{Z_{xoc} Z_{xsc}}$$

- Now, let us find the image impedance at port 3-3'

$$Z_{3i} = \sqrt{Z_{3oc} Z_{3sc}}$$

- Open circuiting and short circuiting the terminal 4-4 of Fig. 4.82 (b) gives

$$Z_{30c} = \left(\frac{1-m^2}{2m}\right) Z_1 + \frac{2Z_2}{m}$$

$$Z_{3sc} = \left(\frac{mZ_1}{2}\right) \| \left[\left(\frac{1-m^2}{2m}\right) Z_1 + \frac{2Z_2}{m}\right]$$

$$= \frac{\left[\left(\frac{1-m^2}{2m}\right) Z_1 + \frac{2Z_2}{m}\right]\frac{mZ_1}{2}}{\left(\frac{1-m^2}{2m}\right) Z_1 + \frac{2Z_2}{m} + \frac{mZ_1}{2}}$$

Thus, equation $Z_{3i} = \sqrt{Z_{30z} \cdot Z_{3sc}}$ becomes

$$Z_{3i} = \sqrt{\left[\left(\frac{1-m^2}{2m}\right) Z_1 + \frac{2Z_2}{m}\right] \frac{\left[\left(\frac{1-m^2}{2m}\right) Z_1 + \frac{2Z_2}{m}\right]\frac{mZ_1}{2}}{\frac{1-m^2}{2m} Z_1 + \frac{2Z_2}{m} + \frac{mZ_1}{2}}}$$

$$Z_{3i} = \sqrt{\frac{\left[\left(\frac{1-m^2}{2m}\right) Z_1 + \frac{2Z_2}{m}\right]^2 \frac{mZ_1}{2}}{\left(\frac{1-m^2}{2m}\right) Z_1 + \frac{2Z_2}{m} + \frac{mZ_1}{2}}}$$

which on simplification gives

$$Z_{3i} = \left[1 + (1-m^2)\frac{Z_1}{4Z_2}\right] \sqrt{\frac{Z_1 Z_2}{1 + \frac{Z_1}{4Z_2}}}$$

$$\boxed{Z_{3i} = M \cdot Z_{0\pi}} \qquad \ldots (4.57)$$

where

$$Z_{0\pi} = \sqrt{\frac{Z_1 Z_2}{1 + \frac{Z_1}{4Z_2}}}$$

$$M = \left[1 - (1-m^2)\frac{Z_1}{4Z_2}\right]$$

Similarly, now let us find the image impedance at port 4–4'.

$$Z_{4i} = \sqrt{Z_{4oc} \cdot Z_{4sc}}$$

Open circuiting and short circuiting the terminal 3-3' of Fig. 4.82 (b) gives

$$Z_{4oc'} = \left(\frac{1-m^2}{2m}\right)Z_1 + \frac{2Z_2}{m} + \frac{mZ_1}{2}$$

$$Z_{4sc} = \frac{mZ_1}{2}$$

Equation $Z_{4i} = \sqrt{Z_{4oc} Z_{4sc}}$ becomes

$$Z_{4i} = \sqrt{\left[\left(\frac{1-m^2}{2m}\right)Z_1 + \frac{2Z_2}{m} + \frac{mZ_1}{2}\right]\left[\frac{mZ_1}{2}\right]}$$

$$Z_{4i} = \sqrt{Z_1 Z_2 + \frac{Z_1^2}{4} - \frac{Z_1^2 m^2}{4} + \frac{m^2 Z_2^2}{4}}$$

$$\boxed{Z_{4i} = \sqrt{\frac{Z_1^2}{4} + Z_1 Z_2} = Z_{0T}} \qquad \ldots(4.58)$$

It is very clear from equation (4.57) that the image impedance Z_{3i} is a function of $Z_{0\pi}$ modified by a factor M where,

$$M = 1 + (1 - m^2)\frac{Z_1}{4Z_2}$$

Similarly, equation (4.58) indicates that the image impedance at terminal 4-4' is equal to Z_{0T}, i.e. characteristics impedance of symmetrical T network.

Let us know discuss about the m derived half section in Fig. 4.82 (a).

$$Z_{1i} = \sqrt{Z_{1oc} \cdot Z_{25c}}$$

$$Z_{2i} = \sqrt{Z_{2oc} \cdot Z_{25c}}$$

Using the similar mathematical treatment and by the same reasoning, we have

$$\boxed{Z_{1i} = Z_{0T}} \qquad \ldots(4.59)$$

$$\boxed{Z_{2i} = M' Z_{0\pi}} \text{ i.e. modified } Z_{0\pi} \qquad \ldots(4.60)$$

where M' is a function of 'm'.

Fig. 4.74 compares a half section with m derived section and the difference is very clear.

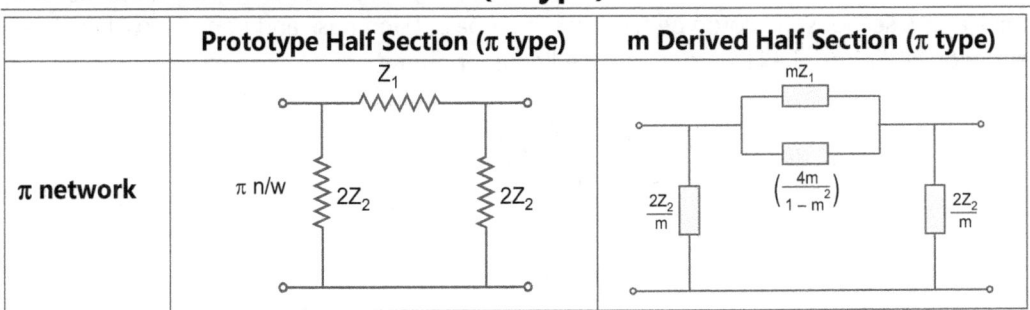

Prototype Half Section (T type)	m Derived Half Section (T type)
T n/w (circuit with $Z_1/2$, $Z_1/2$, Z_2)	(circuit with $mZ_1/2$, $mZ_1/2$, $\left(\frac{1-m^2}{4m}\right)Z_1$, Z_2/m)
(circuit with $mZ_1/2$, $2Z_2$, Z_{2i}, Z_{3i}, $2Z_2$, $mZ_1/2$)	(a) and (b) m derived half sections
Image impedances $Z_{1i} = Z_{0T}$ $Z_{2i} = Z_{0\pi}$ $Z_{3i} = Z_{0\pi}$ $Z_{4i} = Z_{0T}$	**Image impedances** $Z_{1i} = Z_{0T}$ $Z_{2i} = M' Z_{0\pi}$ $Z_{3i} = M Z_{0\pi}$ $Z_{4i} = Z_{0T}$ M and M' depend on 'm'.

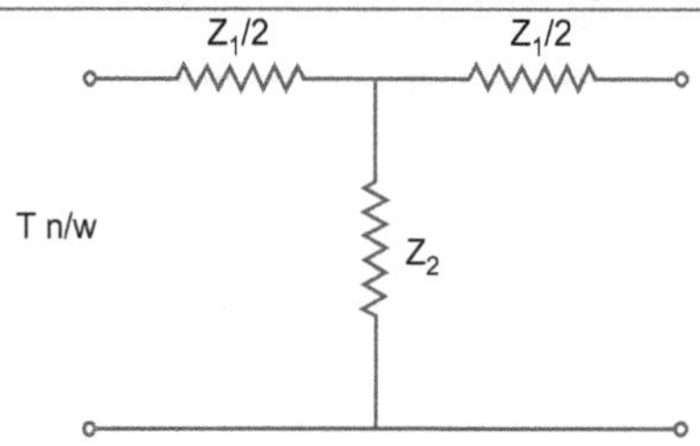

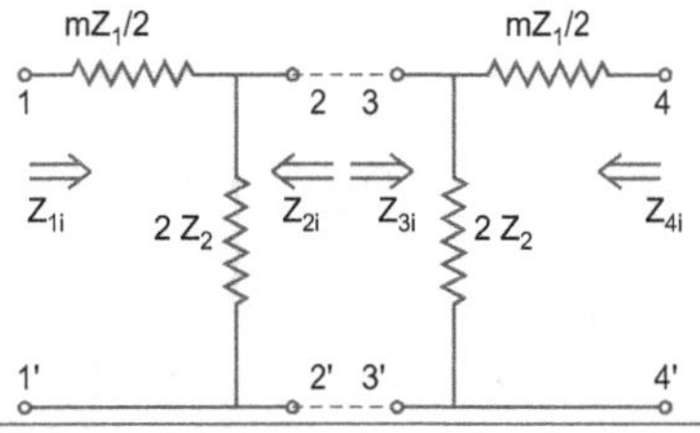

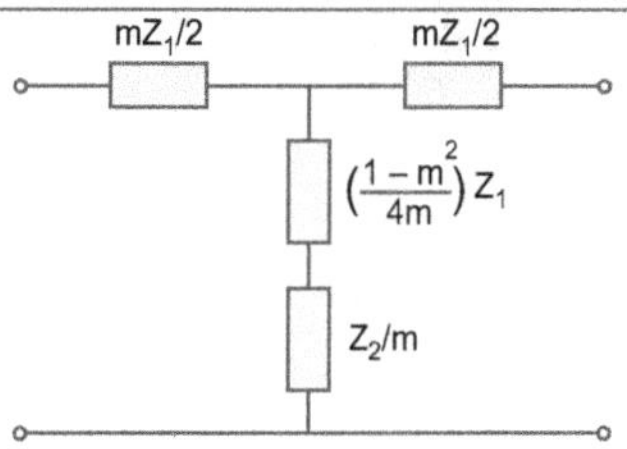

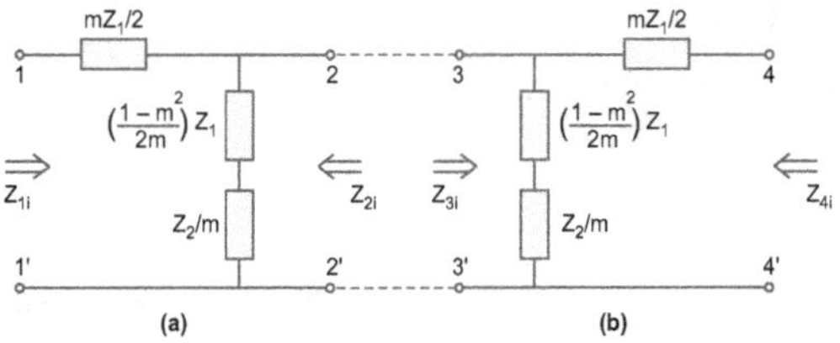

Fig. 4.83: Comparison of prototype half section with m derived half section

Image impedances at port 2-2' and 3-3' are both function of $Z_{0\pi}$ but modified values which depend on 'm' and thus has the possibility of variation of impedance with value of m. The image impedance at port 1-1' and 4-4' of the m derived half sections is equal to Z_{0T}. Thus, it can be used for matching the characteristic of a symmetrical T network.

4.24.3 m Derived Half Section (π Type)

	Prototype Half Section (π type)	m Derived Half Section (π type)
π network	π n/w (circuit with Z_1, $2Z_2$, $2Z_2$)	(circuit with mZ_1, $\left(\frac{4m}{1-m^2}\right)$, $\frac{2Z_2}{m}$, $\frac{2Z_2}{m}$)

contd. ...

	Half section of π network	Image impedances
Half section of π network	Half section of Z_{1i} π n/w ; (diagram with $Z_1/2$, $2Z_2$, $2Z_2$, $Z_1/2$, arrows showing Z_{2i}, Z_{3i}, Z_{4i})	$Z_{1i} = Z_{0\pi}$ $Z_{2i} = Z_{0T}$ $Z_{3i} = Z_{0T}$ $Z_{4i} = Z_{0\pi}$
	(m-derived diagram with $mZ_1/2$, $2Z_2/m$, $\left(\frac{2m}{1-m^2}\right)Z_2$, $\left(\frac{2m}{1-m^2}\right)Z_2$, $2Z_2/m$, $mZ_1/2$)	$Z_{1i} = Z_{0\pi}$ $Z_{2i} = M'_1 Z_{0T}$ $Z_{3i} = M''_1 Z_{0T}$ $Z_{4i} = Z_{0\pi}$ M and M' depend on the value of 'm'.

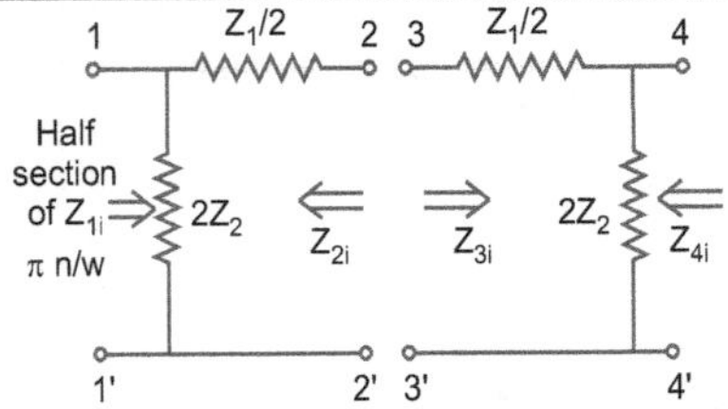

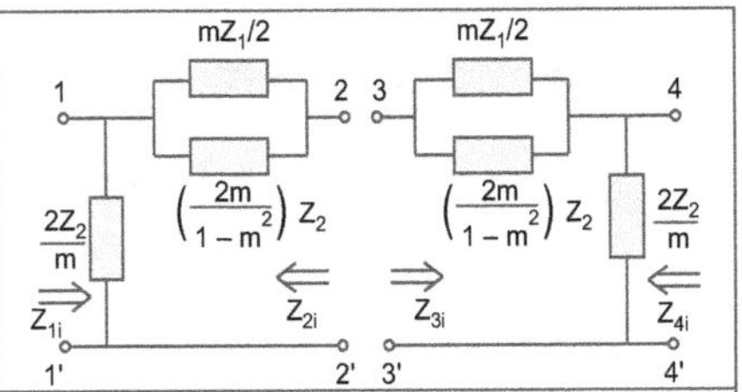

Fig. 4.84: Comparison of a Prototype and a m Derived Half Section

- Consider a m derived π filter of Fig. 4.81 (b). The image impedances of the m derived half sections can be derived in a very similar way to m derived half sections of a T network, derived in Section 4.24.2.
- These results are summarized in the comparison in above Fig. 4.84.
- All the explanations of section 4.24.2 are applicable to these derivations also. So, as clear from the comparison table, the image impedances Z_{1i} and Z_{4i} are equal to the characteristic impedance $Z_{0\pi}$ of a symmetrical π network and thus can be used for matching purpose.
- Image impedances Z_{2i} and Z_{3i} are both function of Z_{0T} but again modified by a factor which depends on m and thus to have possibility of variation of image impedance with value of m.

Thus, **m derived half sections** of m derived T and π network, also known as **terminating half sections** are normally added to the design of any filter to provide uniform termination and matching characteristics.

4.24.4 Characteristics Impedance of a m-Derived Half Section

We have derived the equations and also plotted the graphs of characteristics impedance for T and π sections of prototype low pass, high pass, band pass and band stop filter. These equation and plots of a LPF are reproduced here for our reference.

For a LPF

$$Z_{0T} = R_K \sqrt{1 - \left(\frac{f}{f_C}\right)^2}$$

$$Z_{0T} = \frac{R_K}{\sqrt{1 - \left(\frac{f}{f_C}\right)^2}}$$

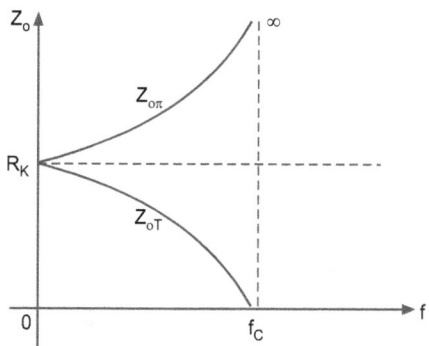

Fig. 4.85: Characteristics Impedance of a Prototype LPF

- As already discussed and also clear from Fig. 4.85, characteristics impedance of T and π section, Z_{0T} and $Z_{0\pi}$ varies between R_K and ∞. This applies to all the prototype filters.
- The curves show that the characteristic impedance of neither section T or π is sufficiently constant over the pass band that any load will give a satisfactory impedance match.
- One of the reason to design m derived half section was to eliminate this drawback.
- So, we derived the equations for the image impedances of m derived half section.
- As seen in Sections 4.24.2 and 4.24.3, image impedance Z_{2i} and Z_{3i} of both T and π type half sections, were function of $Z_{0\pi}$ and Z_{0T} respectively, modified by values M and M'.
- These values (M and M') are dependent on 'm'. The variation of these image impedances is plotted over the pass band for the several values of m.
- This variation of Z_{2i} and Z_{3i} of m derived half section over the pass band for various values of m is plotted in Fig. 4.86.

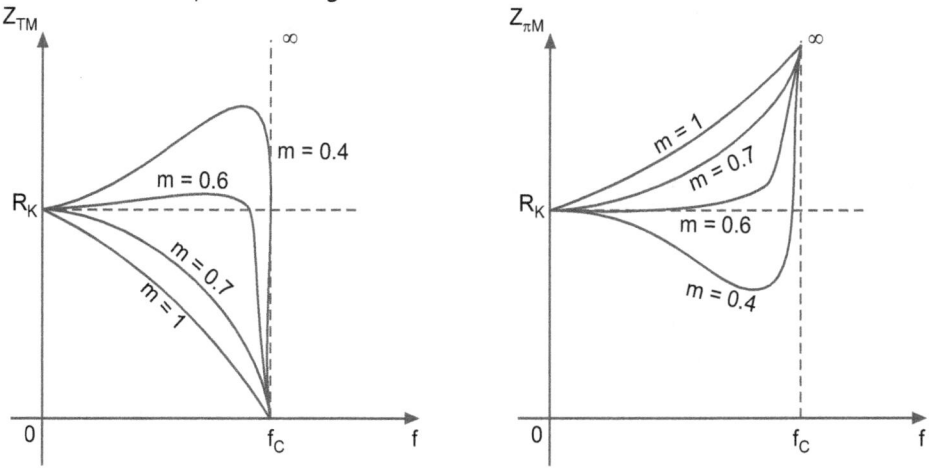

Fig. 4.86: Variation of Z_i of m Derived T and π Sections of a Prototype LPF

- It is observed that for m = 0.6, the image impedance equals the design impedance R_K over most of the pass band.
- The performed experiments say that, with m = 0.6 for a half section, a nearly constant value of $Z_i = R_K$ is obtained over 85 percentage of the pass band.
- Thus, impedance is constant in pass band and is equal to R_K i.e. design impedance. Therefore, a source impedance equal to R_K can be matched satisfactorily on an image basis at the corresponding terminal over most of the pass band.
- A similar variation with m can be developed for the high pass filter. Even in this case using m = 0.6, will give similarly satisfactory matching of impedances.
- So always, when m derived terminating half sections are used m must be equal to 0.6.
- These terminating half sections are also referred to as L section.
- **Note:** We have studied m derived filters which are used to obtain large attenuation and m derived half sections (terminating half sections) which are used for proper termination and matching. Value of m in m derived filters will depend on f_∞ i.e. frequency of infinite attenuation. We have also derived the formula for calculating the value of m in case of LPF and HPF. But value of m in m derived terminating half sections is fixed and will always be selected as 0.6. Let us not get confused in these two things.

4.24.5 Terminating a T and a π Section Filter Network

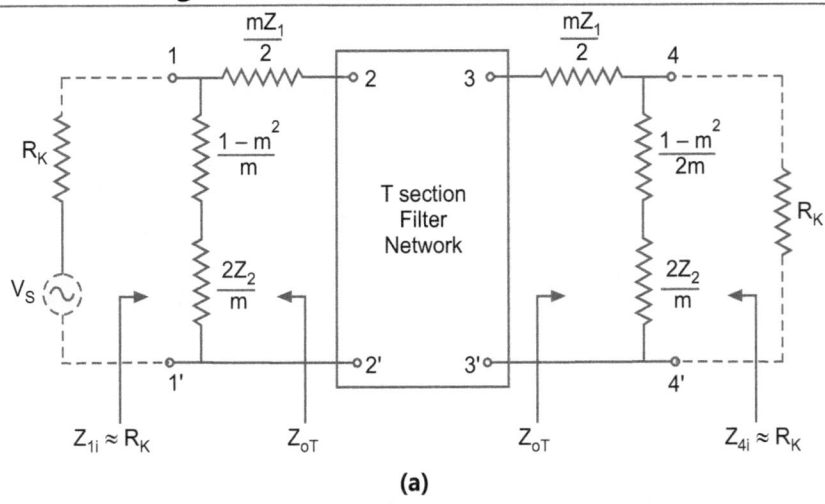

(a)

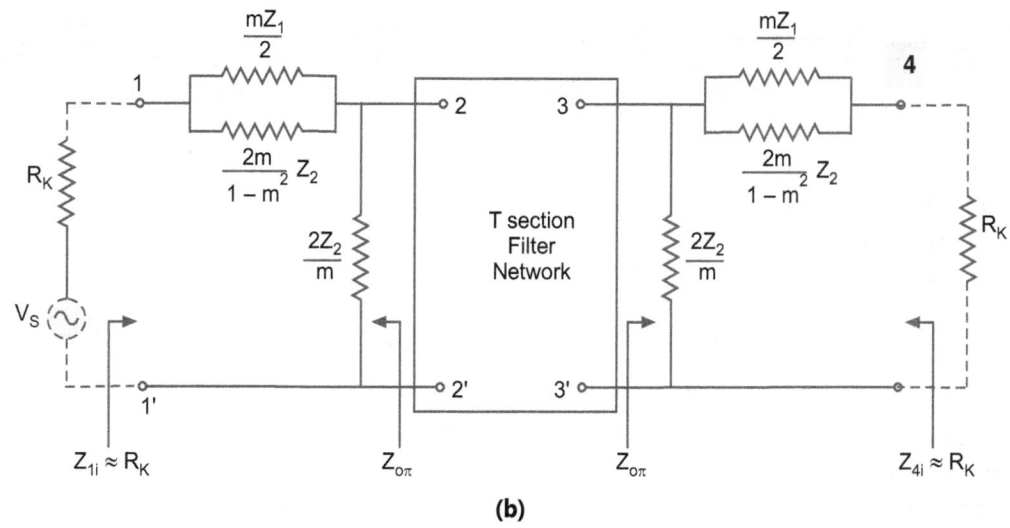

Fig. 4.87: Use of m Derived Terminating Half Sections [L Sections] to Terminate

(a) A T Section Filter

(b) A π Section Filter

Value of m should be 0.6

- Proper termination of any circuit is required to achieve maximum transfer of power.
- Fig. 4.87 (a) and (b) shows a general arrangement to use a m derived terminating half sections between the source and load.
- We have studied that image impedance at one of the terminals of these half section is almost constant and is equal to R_K and at another terminal impedance is = Z_{0T} or $Z_{0\pi}$.
- So, a generator of internal impedance R_K may be connected to the terminals 1-1' and a satisfactory image impedance match can be obtained over 85% of the pass band.
- Likewise, a load of value R_K may be connected to the 4-4 terminals.
- Prototype and m derived T or π sections, designed with design impedance R_K can be inserted between 2-2' and 3-3'.
- Maximum power will be transferred over atleast 85% of the pass band, because the overall characteristics impedance of the above discussed assembly will be almost constant with a satisfactory impedance match between all the connected sections.
- Thus, depending upon the designed filter section, an appropriate m derived half section with m = 0.6 must be used to achieve satisfactory impedance matching and thus transfer maximum power from source to the load.

4.25 SUMMARY OF m DERIVED TERMINATING HALF SECTIONS

	m derived T Section	m derived π Section
m derived Filter Section	Series arms: $mZ_1/2$ each; Shunt arm: $\left(\dfrac{1-m^2}{4m}\right)Z_1$ in series with Z_2/m	Shunt arm: mZ_1 in parallel with $\left(\dfrac{4m}{1-m^2}\right)$; Series arms: $2Z_2/m$ on each side
Terminating half Section (L Section)	(a) and (b) configurations with $mZ_1/2$, $\left(\dfrac{1-m^2}{2m}\right)Z_1$, Z_2/m; impedances $Z_{1i}, Z_{2i}, Z_{3i}, Z_{4i}$	$mZ_1/2$ series arms; shunt elements $\left(\dfrac{2m}{1-m^2}\right)Z_2$, $2Z_2/m$; impedances $Z_{1i}, Z_{2i}, Z_{3i}, Z_{4i}$
Image Impedance	$Z_{1i} = Z_{0T}$ $Z_{2i} = M' Z_{0\pi} \approx R_K$ (For m = 0.6) $Z_{3i} = M Z_{0\pi} \approx R_K$ (From m = 0.6) $Z_{4i} = Z_{0T}$	$Z_{1i} = Z_{0\pi}$ $Z_{2i} = M'_1 Z_{0T} \approx R_K$ (For m = 0.6) $Z_{3i} = M''_2 Z_{0T} \approx R_K$ (From m = 0.6) $Z_{4i} = Z_{0\pi}$

Fig. 4.88

4.26 COMPOSITE FILTER

- In this unit of filters, we started our discussion with prototype filters. We realized that the attenuation characteristics is not very sharp in the attenuation band as it is ideally expected. Due to this it was very difficult to distinguish the frequencies after and before cut-off frequency.

- So, to overcome this drawback in prototype filters, we designed m derived filters which gave very large attenuation at a frequency f_∞, very close to f_C. But even m derived filters had a limitation. It was observed that in the stop band though α is very high at f_∞, it drastically reduces after f_∞ in case of LPF and before f_∞ in case of HPF.

- Constant k or prototype filter is a good choice if high attenuation is needed in deeper stop band, at frequencies far away from f_0.

- Similarly a m-derived filter should be a preferable choice if very high attenuation is needed at a frequency close to f_c.

- But none of these filters are ideal filters because none of them give you high attenuation through out the stop band as ideally desired.
- So a wise choice is to use a prototype section in series with a m derived section. As indicated in Fig. 4.89. This assembly would definitely give appreciably high attenuation through out the stop band.
- Such a combination along with terminating half sections is called as a composite filter.

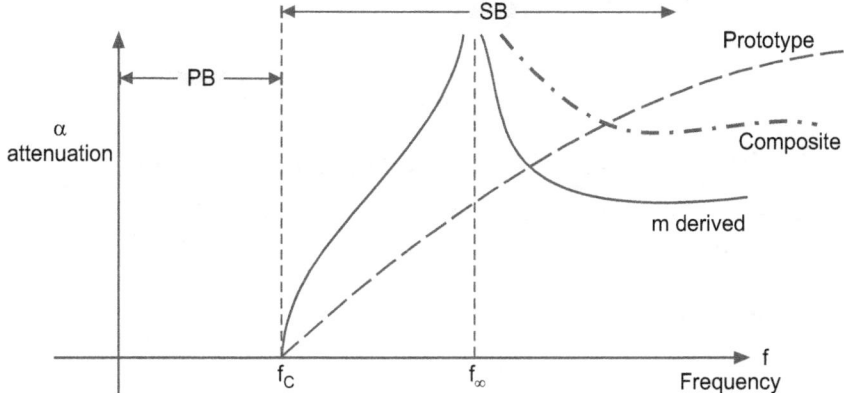

Fig. 4.89: Variation of α in Constant k, m Derived and Composite Filter

- Thus a general block schematic of the composite filter will have:
  1. One or more prototype sections.
  2. One or more m derived sections.
  3. Terminating half sections (with m = 0.6).
- Thus to summarize.

	Filter	Attenuation Near f_C	Attenuation after f_C
1.	Constant K	Very low	Very high
2.	m derived	Very high	Low
3.	Composite	High	High

- The block schematic of composite filter is shown in Fig. 4.90.

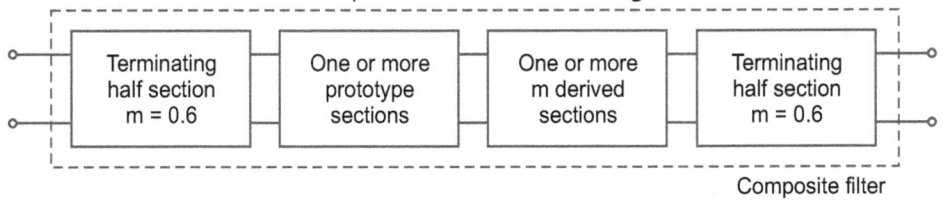

Fig. 4.90.: Block Schematic of the Composite Filter

- Terminating half sections with m = 0.6 are inserted to achieve proper impedance matching and constant characteristics impedance through out the pass band.
- If it is desired to have very large attenuation at few particular frequencies in the stop band, corresponding number of m derived filter section must be used in cascade with the desired value of f_∞.
- In cases, where an impedance match is not important, the attenuation may be built-up near cut-off by cascading or connecting a number of constant k prototype sections in series.
- Thus, the number of various sections in any composite filter would totally depend on the desired attenuation characteristics.
- In any case, design impedance R_K, the cut-off frequency f_C and infinite frequency f_∞ are some important design specification in a composite filter.

4.27 SOLVED NUMERICALS ON COMPOSITE FILTERS

Ex. 4.27: Design a composite low pass filter to work into 500 Ω resistance with cut-off at 1000 Hz. It should have very high attenuation at 1065, 1250 and ∞ kHz.

Given: f_C = 1000 Hz, $f_{\infty 1}$ = 1065, $f_{\infty 2}$ = 1250 Hz, $f_{\infty 3}$ = ∞, R_k = 500 Ω.

Sol.: (i) Prototype Section:

$$L = \frac{R_K}{\pi f_C}$$

$$= \frac{500}{\pi \times 1000}$$

$$L = 159 \text{ mH}$$

$$\boxed{\frac{L}{2} = 0.079 \text{ H}}$$

$$C = \frac{1}{\pi f_C R}$$

$$= \frac{1}{\pi \times 1000 \times 500}$$

$$\boxed{C = 0.636 \text{ μF}}$$

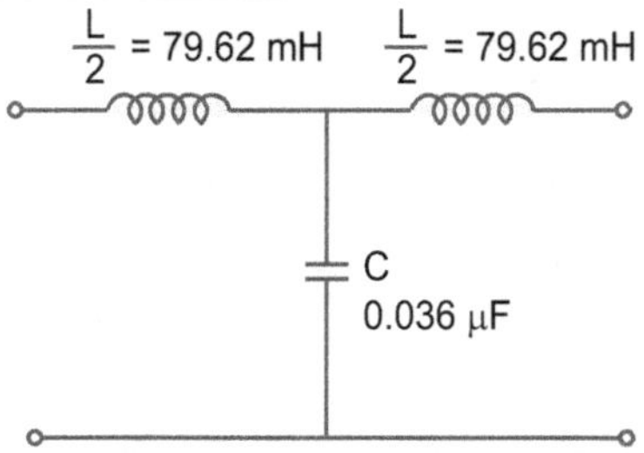

$\frac{L}{2}$ = 79.62 mH $\frac{L}{2}$ = 79.62 mH

C
0.036 μF

Fig. 4.91 (a)

(ii) m derived section

We know, $\quad m = \sqrt{1 - \left(\dfrac{f_c}{f_\infty}\right)^2}$

(a) For $\quad f_\infty = \infty$ (infinity) Hz

$\boxed{m = 1}$, which is nothing but the prototype as shown above in Fig. 4.133 (a)

(b) For $\quad f_\infty = 1065$ Hz

$$m = \sqrt{1 - \left(\dfrac{1000}{1065}\right)^2}$$

$\boxed{m = 0.344}$

$\left(\dfrac{1-m^2}{4m}\right) L = \left[\dfrac{1 - 0.344^2}{4 \times 0.344}\right] 159$

$\boxed{\left(\dfrac{1-m^2}{4m}\right) L = 101.9 \text{ mH}}$

$mC = 0.344 \times 0.636 \; \mu F$

$\boxed{mC = 0.219 \; \mu F}$

$\dfrac{mL}{2} = 0.344 \times \dfrac{0.0795}{2}$

$\boxed{\dfrac{mL}{2} = 0.0273 \text{ H}}$

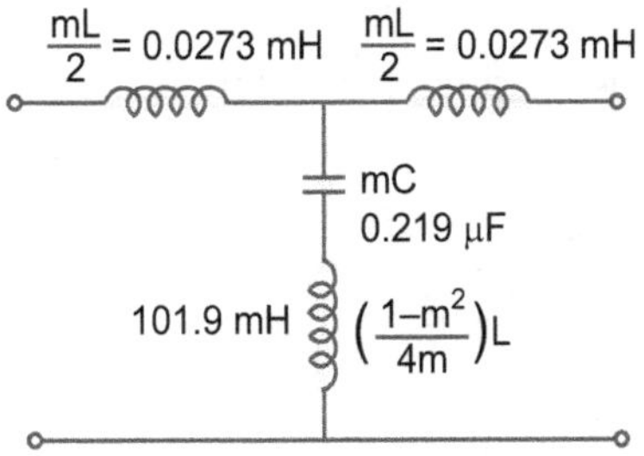

$\dfrac{mL}{2} = 0.0273$ mH $\quad \dfrac{mL}{2} = 0.0273$ mH

mC
0.219 μF

101.9 mH $\left(\dfrac{1-m^2}{4m}\right) L$

Fig. 4.91 (b)

(c) For $\quad f_\infty = 1250$ Hz

$$m = \sqrt{1 - \left(\dfrac{1000}{1250}\right)^2}$$

$\boxed{m = 0.6}$

Now since m = 0.6, this section can be used as a terminating half-section. Therefore series and shunt arms of the terminating sections are:

$$\frac{mL}{2} = 0.6 \times 0.0785$$

$$\boxed{\frac{mL}{2} = 0.0477 \text{ H}}$$

$$= \boxed{47.7 \text{ mH}}$$

$$\frac{mC}{2} = 0.6 \times \frac{0.6366}{2}$$

$$\boxed{\frac{mC}{2} = 0.1909 \text{ µF}}$$

$$\left(\frac{1-m^2}{2m}\right)L = \left[\frac{1-(0.6)^2}{2(0.6)}\right]0.1591$$

$$\boxed{\left(\frac{1-m^2}{2m}\right) = 84.8 \text{ H}}$$

Fig. 4.91 (c)

(iii) Composite filter: The designed constant k type, n-derived filter section and terminating half-sections are all connected in cascade to form a composite low pass filter.

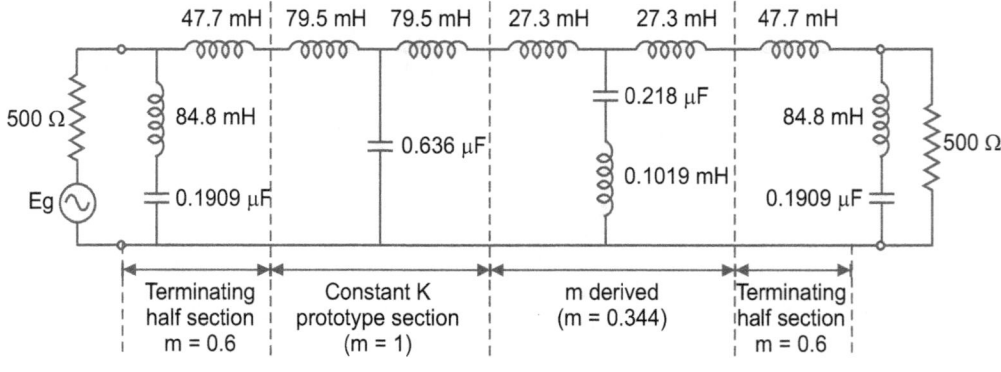

Fig. 4.91 (d)

The series inductors can be added to the circuit can be simplified to obtain equivalent composite filter as:

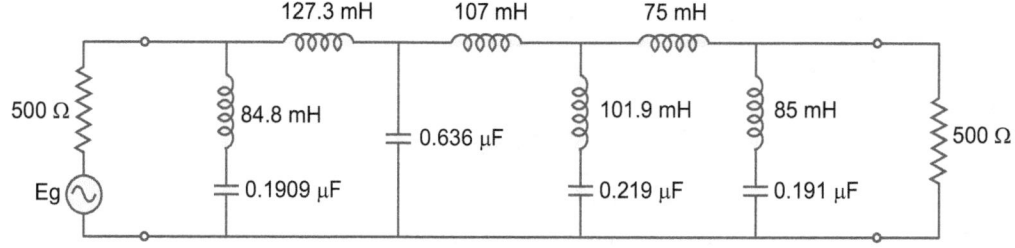

Fig. 4.91 (e)

Ex. 4.28: Design a composite high pass filter work into 1000 Ω resistance with cut-off frequency of 1000 Hz and with high attenuation of 800 Hz and 950 Hz.

Given:
$R_K = 1000\ \Omega$
$f_C = 1$ kHz
$f_{\infty 1} = 800$ Hz
$f_{\infty 2} = 950$ Hz

Sol.: (i) Design of prototype section

$$L = \frac{R_K}{4\pi f_C}$$

$$= \frac{1000}{4\pi \times 1000}$$

$$\boxed{L = 79\ \text{mH}}$$

$$C = \frac{1}{4\pi R_K f_C}$$

$$= \frac{1}{4\pi \times 1000 \times 1000}$$

$$\boxed{C = 0.0795\ \mu F}$$

$$\boxed{2C = 0.159\ \mu F}$$

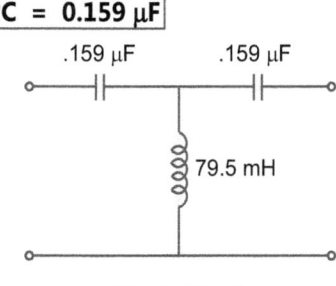

Fig. 4.92 (a)

(ii) Design of m derived section

We have $\quad m = \sqrt{1 - \left(\dfrac{f_\infty}{f_C}\right)^2}$

(a) $f_\infty = 800$ Hz

$$m = \sqrt{1 - \left(\dfrac{800}{1000}\right)^2}$$

$\boxed{m = 0.6}$

Thus, this can be used as a terminating half section. Therefore, the series and the shunt elements are:

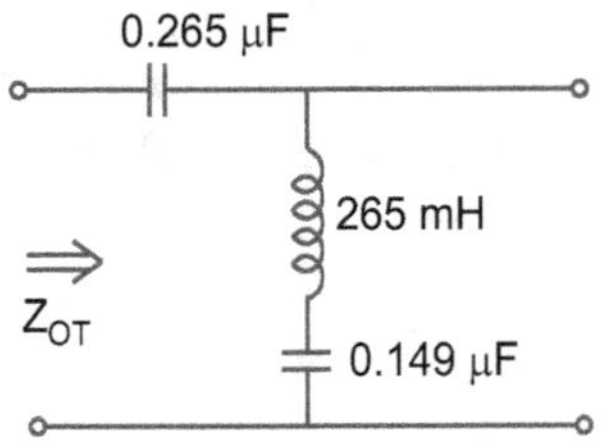

```
          0.265 μF
    o——————||——————•——————o
                   ⌇
         ⇒        ⌇ 265 mH
        Z_OT      ⌇
                   •———
                      ═ 0.149 μF
    o——————————————•——————o
```

Fig. 4.92 (b)

$\dfrac{2C}{m} = \dfrac{0.159}{0.6} = 0.265$ μF

$\dfrac{2L}{m} = \dfrac{79.5 \times 2}{0.6} = 265.0$ mH

$\left(\dfrac{2m}{1-m^2}\right) C = \dfrac{2 \times 0.6}{(1 - 0.36)} \times 0.0795 = 0.149$ μF

(b) $f_\infty = 950$ Hz

$$m = \sqrt{1 - \left(\dfrac{f_\infty}{f_C}\right)^2} = \sqrt{1 - \left(\dfrac{950}{1000}\right)^2}$$

$\boxed{m = 0.312}$

Components are:

$\dfrac{2C}{m} = \dfrac{2 \times 0.0795}{0.312}$

$\quad = \dfrac{0.159}{0.3} = 0.51$ μF

$\dfrac{L}{m} = \dfrac{0.0795}{0.312} = 25.5$ mH

$\left(\dfrac{4m}{1-m^2}\right) C = \left[\dfrac{4 \times 0.312}{1 - 0.097}\right] \times 0.0795 = 0.11$ μF

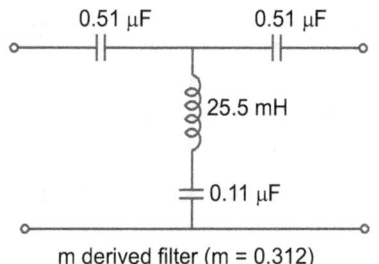

m derived filter (m = 0.312)

Fig. 4.92 (c)

(iii) Composite HPF is as shown in Fig. 4.92 (c).

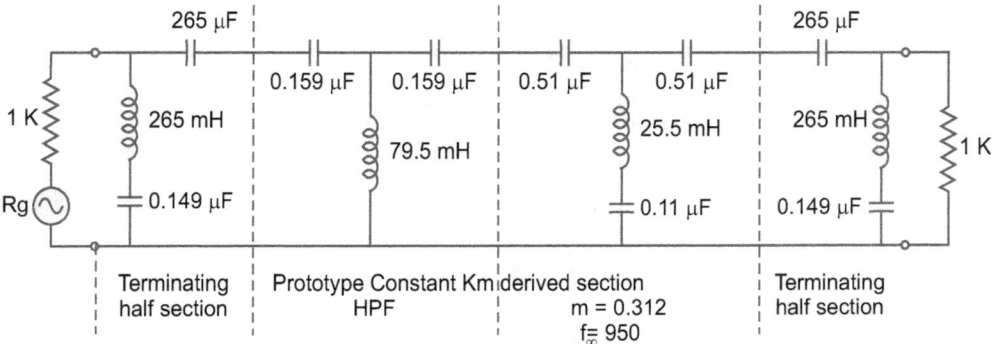

Fig. 4.92 (d)

The designed constant k type, m derived filter section and terminating half sections are all connected in cascade to form a composite high pass filter.

Capacitors in series can be combined and the simplified composite filter is as shown in Fig. 4.92 (e)

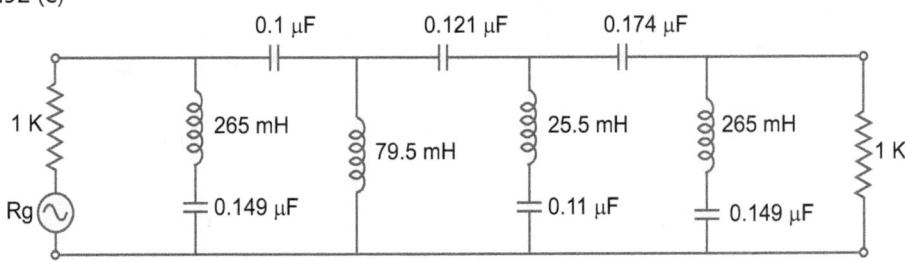

Fig. 4.92 (e)

Note: In both the above problems 4.27 and 4.28, at one of the frequency of high (infinite) attenuation m is equal to 0.6. Hence, this is used for the terminating half section. But in case if at infinite attenuation m ≠ 0.6 then m derived half-section is to be separately designed with m = 0.6.

Ex. 4.29: Design a High Pass Filter to satisfy the following conditions:
(i) Attenuation above 10.5 kHz is to be less than 6 dB.
(ii) Attenuation below 9.5 kHz is to be greater than 30 dB.
(iii) Input and Output impedance to be (600 + 50) Ω above 12 kHz, R_K = 600 Ω.

Sol.: Let us use a T section. Even π section can also be used. But finally the choice of section will depend upon the number of components required in each section. Cut-off frequency is selected to be 10 kHz which satisfies the first two conditions. Third condition can be satisfied by using two m = 0.6 terminating half sections.

Step I: Design of prototype section we have

$$f_C = 10 \text{ kHz}$$
$$R_K = 600 \text{ Ω}$$
$$L = \frac{R_K}{4\pi f_C}$$
$$= \frac{600}{4\pi \times 10^4}$$
$$\boxed{L = 3.77 \text{ mH}}$$
$$C = \frac{1}{4\pi f_C R_K}$$
$$= \frac{1}{4 \cdot \pi \cdot 600 \times 10^4}$$
$$C = 0.0133 \text{ μF}$$
$$\boxed{2C = 0.0266 \text{ μF}}$$

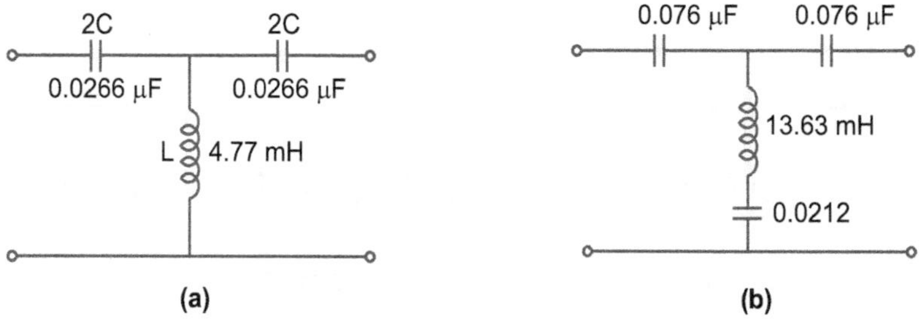

(a) 2C = 0.0266 μF, 2C = 0.0266 μF, L = 4.77 mH

(b) 0.076 μF, 0.076 μF, 13.63 mH, 0.0212

Fig. 4.93

Step II: Condition II requires that there should be a very sharp attenuation at 9.5 kHz. This corresponds to

$$m = \sqrt{1 - \left(\frac{f_\infty}{f_C}\right)^2}$$
$$= 0.35$$

Hence a m derived section with m = 0.35 as shown is to be used.

$$\frac{2C}{m} = 0.076 \, \mu F$$

$$\frac{L}{m} = 13.63 \, mH$$

$$\frac{4m\,C}{1-m^2} = \frac{4 \times 0.35 \times 0.0133}{1 - 0.35^2} = 0.0212$$

Step III: When m = 0.6 is used for the terminating half section, then the characteristics impedance will be between $\pm\, 0.9\, R_0$ i.e. between 550 Ω to 650 Ω. Hence half section with m = 0.6 is used to satisfy 3rd condition.

$$\frac{2C}{m} = \frac{0.0266}{0.6}$$

$$\boxed{\frac{2C}{m} = 0.0443 \, \mu F}$$

$$2\frac{L}{M} = \frac{4.77}{0.3} = 15.9 \, mH$$

$$2\frac{mC}{(1-m^2)} = \frac{2 \times 0.6 \times 0.0133}{0.64}$$

$$\boxed{2\frac{mC}{(1-m^2)} = 0.025 \, \mu F}$$

Fig. 4.93 (c)

Step IV: Composite filter. The designed constant K type, m derived filter section and terminating half sections are all connected in cascade to form a composite high pass filter.

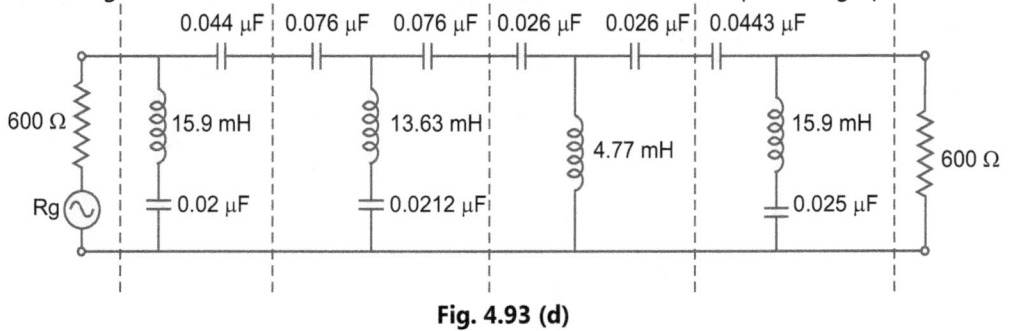

Fig. 4.93 (d)

Capacitors in series can be combined and the simplified composite filter is as shown in Fig. 4.93 (e)

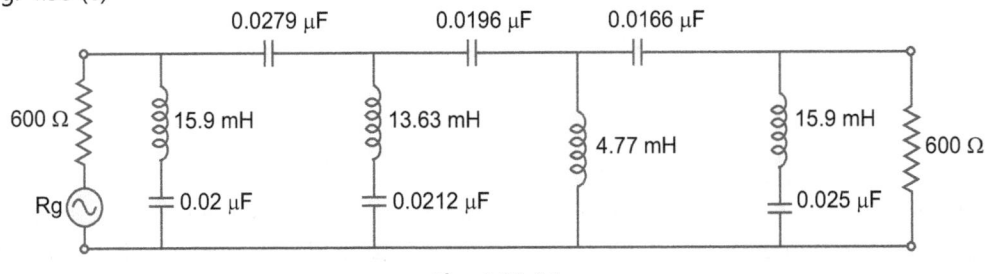

Fig. 4.93 (e)

Ex. 4.30: Design a composite π section pass filter to work into 600 Ω with cut-off frequency of 2 kHz and very high attenuation at 2.2 kHz. Terminating the filter properly.
Given: $R_K = 600\ \Omega$, $f_C = 2$ kHz, $f_\infty = 2.2$ kHz.

Sol.: Step I: Design of prototype filter

$$L = \frac{R_K}{\pi f_C} = \frac{600}{\pi \times 2 \times 1000}$$

$$\boxed{L = 95.5\ \text{mH}}$$

$$C = \frac{1}{\pi R_K f_C} = \frac{1}{\pi \times 600 \times 2 \times 100}$$

$$\boxed{C = 0.265\ \mu F}$$

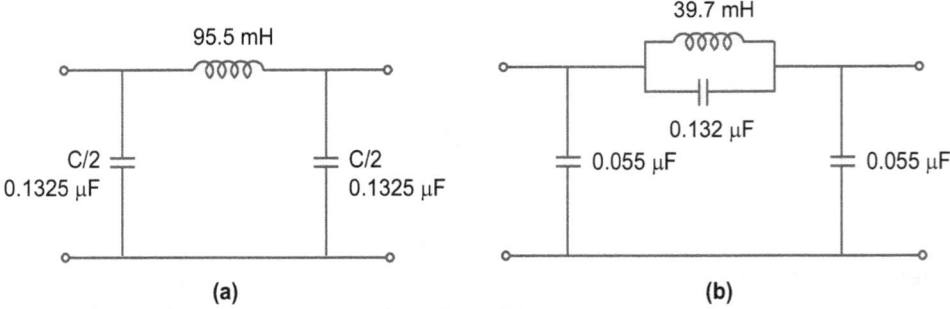

Fig. 4.94

Step II: Design of m derived filter

$$f_\infty = 2.2\ \text{kHz}$$

$$m = \sqrt{1 - \left(\frac{f_C}{f_\infty}\right)^2}$$

$$= \sqrt{1 - \left(\frac{2}{2.2}\right)^2}$$

$$\boxed{m = 0.416}$$

$$\left(\frac{1-m^2}{4m}\right)C = \left(\frac{1-0.1735}{4\times 0.416}\right)0.265$$
$$= 0.132\ \mu F$$
$$\frac{mC}{2} = \frac{0.416\times 0.265}{2}$$
$$= 0.055\ \mu F$$
$$mL = 0.416\times 95.5$$
$$= 39.7\ mH$$

Step III: Terminating half sections m = 0.6.
The elements in the terminating section
$$\frac{mL}{2} = \frac{(0.6)(95.5\times 10^{-3})}{2}$$
$$= 28.65\ mH$$
$$\left(\frac{1-m^2}{2m}\right)C = \left[\frac{1-(0.6)^2}{2\times 0.6}\right]0.265\times 10^{-6}$$
$$= 0.141\ \mu F$$
$$\frac{mC}{2} = \frac{0.6\times 0.265\times 10^{-6}}{2} = 0.0795\ \mu F$$

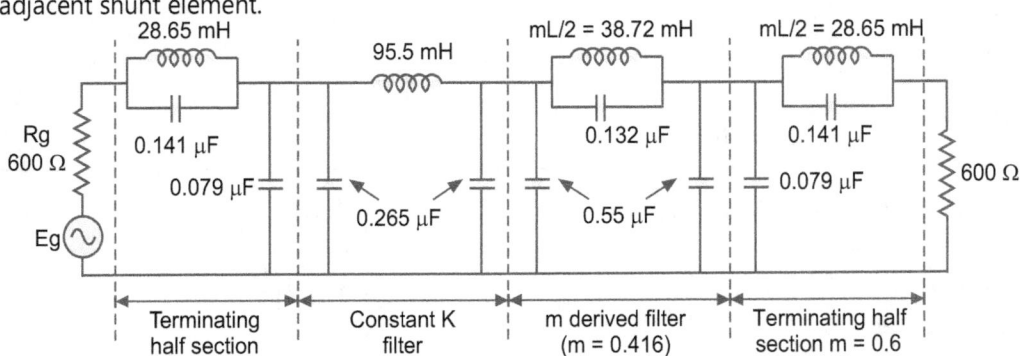

Fig. 4.94 (c)

Step IV: To design a composite filter: Composite filter can be obtained by cascading adjacent shunt element.

Fig. 4.94 (d)

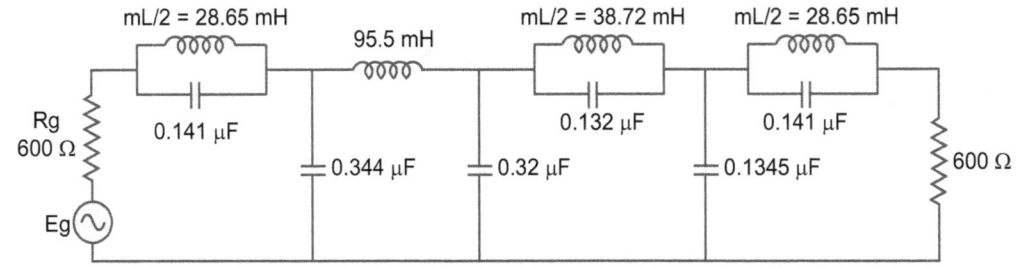

Fig. 4.94 (e)

4.28 SUMMARY OF FILTERS

4.28.1 Constant k Prototype Filters

Filter → Parameter ↓	LPF	HPF
Circuit diagram	(L/2 — L/2 series, C shunt); (L series, C/2 — C/2 shunt)	(2C — 2C series, L shunt); (C series, 2L — 2L shunt)
Design impedance	$R_K = \sqrt{\dfrac{L}{C}}$	$R_K = \sqrt{\dfrac{L}{C}}$
Equation for f_C	$f_C = \dfrac{1}{\pi\sqrt{LC}}$	$f_L = \dfrac{1}{4\pi\sqrt{LC}}$
Equation for α	$\alpha = 2\cosh^{-1}\left(\dfrac{f}{f_C}\right)$	$\alpha = 2\cosh^{-1}\left(\dfrac{f_C}{f}\right)$
Equation for β	$\beta = 2\sin^{-1}\left(\dfrac{f}{f_C}\right)$	$\beta = 2\sin^{-1}\left(\dfrac{f_C}{f}\right)$

... contd.

Equation for Z_0	$Z_{0T} = R_K \sqrt{1 - \left(\dfrac{f}{f_C}\right)^2}$ $Z_{0\pi} = \dfrac{R_K}{\sqrt{1 - \left(\dfrac{f}{f_C}\right)^2}}$	$Z_{0T} = R_K \sqrt{1 - \left(\dfrac{f}{f_C}\right)^2}$ $Z_{0\pi} = \dfrac{R_K}{\sqrt{1 - \left(\dfrac{f}{f_C}\right)^2}}$
Design equation	$L = \dfrac{R_K}{\pi f_C}$ $C = \dfrac{1}{\pi f_C R_K}$	$L = \dfrac{R_K}{4\pi f_C}$ $C = \dfrac{1}{4\pi f_C R_K}$
Ideal frequency response	PB at low f, SB at high f (cutoff f_C)	SB at low f, PB at high f (cutoff f_C)
Circuit diagram	T-section: series $L_1/2$, $2C_1$ — $2C_1$, $L_1/2$; shunt branch $L_2 \parallel C_2$. π-section: series L_1, C_1; shunt $C_2/2 \parallel 2L_2$ at each end.	T-section: series $L_1/2$ — $L_1/2$; shunt branch $2C_1 \parallel L_2$, with C_2 to ground. π-section: series $L_1 \parallel C_1$; shunt $2L_2$ in series with $C_2/2$ at each end.
Design impedance	$R_K = \sqrt{\dfrac{L_1}{C_2}} = \sqrt{\dfrac{L_2}{C_1}}$ $L_1 C_1 = L_2 C_2 = \dfrac{1}{\omega_0^2}$	$R_K = \sqrt{\dfrac{L_1}{C_2}} = \sqrt{\dfrac{L_2}{C_1}}$ $L_1 C_1 = L_2 C_2 = \dfrac{1}{\omega_0^2}$
Equation for f_C	$f_0 = \sqrt{f_1 f_2}$ $f_0 = f_r = f_{ar}$	$f_0 = \sqrt{f_1 f_2}$ $f_0 = f_r = f_{ar}$

... contd.

Design equation	$C_1 = \dfrac{(f_2 - f_1)}{4\pi R_K f_1 f_2}$ $L_1 = \dfrac{R_K}{\pi(f_2 - f_1)}$ $C_2 = \dfrac{1}{\pi R_K (f_2 - f_1)}$ $L_2 = \dfrac{R_K (f_2 - f_1)}{4\pi f_1 f_2}$ $f_0 = \dfrac{1}{2\pi\sqrt{L_1 C_1}} = \dfrac{1}{2\pi\sqrt{L_2 C_2}}$	$C_1 = \dfrac{1}{4\pi R_K (f_2 - f_1)}$ $L_1 = \dfrac{R_K (f_2 - f_1)}{\pi f_1 f_2}$ $C_2 = \dfrac{(f_2 - f_1)}{\pi R_K (f_1 f_2)}$ $L_2 = \dfrac{R_K}{4\pi (f_2 - f_1)}$ $f_0 = \dfrac{1}{2\pi\sqrt{L_1 C_1}} = \dfrac{1}{2\pi\sqrt{L_2 C_2}}$
Ideal Frequency Respnose	SB — PB — SB, f_L, f_H	PB — SB — PB, f_L, f_H

4.28.2 m Derived Filters

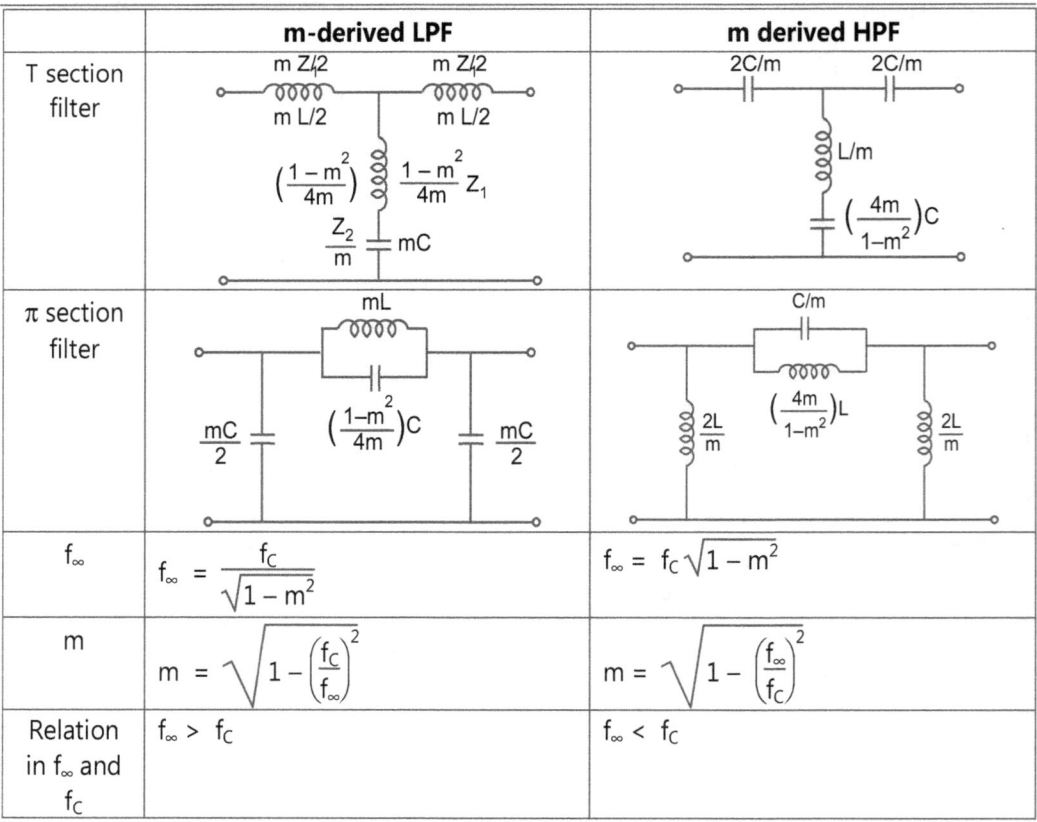

	m-derived LPF	m derived HPF
T section filter	$mL/2$, $mZ_1/2$ branches; shunt: $\left(\dfrac{1-m^2}{4m}\right) Z_1$, $\dfrac{Z_2}{m}$, mC	$2C/m$ series; shunt: L/m, $\left(\dfrac{4m}{1-m^2}\right) C$
π section filter	series: mL, $\left(\dfrac{1-m^2}{4m}\right) C$; shunt: $\dfrac{mC}{2}$, $\dfrac{mC}{2}$	series: C/m, $\left(\dfrac{4m}{1-m^2}\right) L$; shunt: $\dfrac{2L}{m}$, $\dfrac{2L}{m}$
f_∞	$f_\infty = \dfrac{f_C}{\sqrt{1-m^2}}$	$f_\infty = f_C \sqrt{1-m^2}$
m	$m = \sqrt{1 - \left(\dfrac{f_C}{f_\infty}\right)^2}$	$m = \sqrt{1 - \left(\dfrac{f_\infty}{f_C}\right)^2}$
Relation in f_∞ and f_C	$f_\infty > f_C$	$f_\infty < f_C$

4.28.3 m Derived Terminating Half Sections

	m derived T Section	m derived π Section
m derived Filter Section	Series arms: $mZ_1/2$, $mZ_1/2$; Shunt arm: $\left(\frac{1-m^2}{4m}\right)Z_1$ in series with Z_2/m	Shunt arms: $2Z_2/m$, $2Z_2/m$; Series arm: mZ_1 in parallel with $\left(\frac{4m}{1-m^2}\right)$
Termi-nating half Section (L Section)	(a) Series $mZ_1/2$, shunt $\left(\frac{1-m^2}{2m}\right)Z_1$ and Z_2/m; (b) shunt Z_2/m and $\left(\frac{1-m^2}{2m}\right)Z_1$, series $mZ_1/2$	Shunt $2Z_2/m$; series $mZ_1/2$ with $\left(\frac{2m}{1-m^2}\right)Z_2$; series $mZ_1/2$ with $\left(\frac{2m}{1-m^2}\right)Z_2$; shunt $2Z_2/m$
Image Impedance	$Z_{1i} = Z_{0T}$ $Z_{2i} = M'\, Z_{0\pi} \approx R_K$ (For m = 0.6) $Z_{3i} = M\, Z_{0\pi} \approx R_K$ (From m = 0.6) $Z_{4i} = Z_{0T}$	$Z_{1i} = Z_{0\pi}$ $Z_{2i} = M_1\, Z_{0T} \approx R_K$ (For m = 0.6) $Z_{3i} = M_2\, Z_{0T} \approx R_K$ (From m = 0.6) $Z_{4i} = Z_{0\pi}$

EXERCISE

1. Define characteristic impedance and propagation constant of a symmetrical network.
2. Define and explain the properties of an asymmetrical network.
3. For an symmetrical T and π network derive the expression for Z_{0T} and also show that $Z_{0T} = \sqrt{Z_{0C} \cdot Z_{SC}}$.
4. Define, explain and derive the formula for image and iterative impedances as applied to L section and Half sections.
5. Define: Cut-off frequency
   Pass band
   Stop band
   Transition band
   Design impedance
   of a filter.
6. What are the desirable characteristics of ideal filter ?
7. A filter circuit must have Z_1 and Z_2 as the opposite type of reactances. Justify.

8. Sketch reactance verses frequency curves of a low pass and a high pass constant k filter and obtain the expression for the cut-off frequency.
9. Sketch the reactance curves for a constant k T section and a π section of a F low and a high pass filter.
10. In a band pass filter resonating and an antiresonating frequency must be same. Justify with the help of reactance curves.
11. Prove that resonant frequency f_0 is the geometric mean of two cut-off frequencies f_1 and f_2.
12. What are the disadvantages of a prototype filter ? How are they corrected in the m derived filter ?
13. Why is a m derived half section used as terminating section in a filter ? Explain why is m = 0.6 used in terminating half sections.
14. Explain the disadvantages of a m derived filter. How are they corrected in a composite filter.
15. Define decibel and neper units. Derive the relation between these units.

■■■

Unit V

SYNTHESIS OF NETWORKS

Contents ...

5.1 Introduction
    5.1.1 Difference between Network Analysis and Network Synthesis
5.2 One Port and Two Port Synthesis
5.3 Causality and Stability
    5.3.1 Causality
    5.3.2 Stability
5.4 Hurwitz Polynomial
    5.4.1 Properties of Hurwitz Polynomial
    5.4.2 Testing of Hurwitz Polynomial
5.5 Problems on Hurwitz Polynomials
5.6 Positive Real Function (P.R.F.)
5.7 Testing of Driving Point Positive Real Functions
5.8 Problems on the Testing of Positive Real Functions
5.9 Elementary Synthesis Procedures (Concepts)
5.10 Introduction - Synthesis of One-Port Network
5.11 Synthesis of One-Port Network
    5.11.1 One-Port Functions (Driving Point Functions)
5.12 Basic Forms of Network
    5.12.1 Foster-I Form of Network
    5.12.2 Foster-II form of Network
    5.12.3 Cauer-I form of Network
    5.12.4 Cauer-II form of Network
5.13 Synthesis of Driving Point Functions of L-C Network
    5.13.1 Properties of L-C Driving Point Functions
    5.13.2 Synthesis of L-C Networks
5.14 Synthesis of Driving Point Functions of RC Network
    5.14.1 Properties of R-C Network Functions ($Z_{RC}(s)$ and $Y_{RC}(s)$)
    5.14.2 Synthesis (Realization) of R-C Networks

5.15 Synthesis of Driving Point Functions of R-L Network

    5.15.1 Properties of R-L Network Functions [$Z_{RL}(s)$ and $Y_{RL}(s)$]

    5.15.2 Synthesis or Realization of R-L Networks

5.16 Summary of L-C, R-C, R-L Network Synthesis

5.17 Synthesis of Driving Point Functions of R-L-C Network

    5.17.1 Properties of R-L-C Function

    5.17.2 Synthesis or Realization of a R-L-C Network

5.18 Additional Solved Problems on L-C, R-C, R-L and R-L-C Networks

Exercise

5.1 INTRODUCTION

This Unit covers the following topics:

- Difference between network analysis and network synthesis
- The concept of positive real functions (P.R.F.)
- Testing procedure for P.R.F. including Hurwitz polynomial
- Elementary synthesis procedures

5.1.1 Difference between Network Analysis and Network Synthesis

Electric network theory can be divided into two topics namely "Network Analysis" and "Network Synthesis".

To understand the difference between these two, let us consider an electric circuit consisting of excitation (input), response (output) and the network (containing R, L, C element). In the case of linear circuits, if any two of the three quantities that is, the network, the excitation and the response, are given then the third may be found.

The difference between these two is shown in Fig. 5.1.

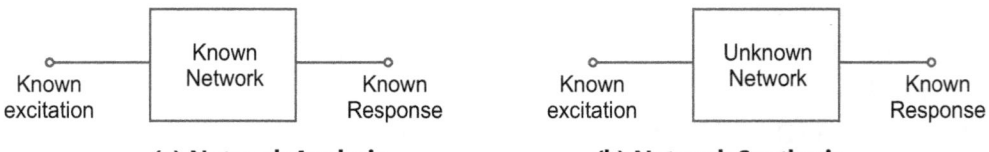

(a) Network Analysis   (b) Network Synthesis

Fig. 5.1: Comparison between Network Analysis and Synthesis

Difference between Network Analysis and Network Synthesis is given below.

No.	Network Analysis	Network Synthesis
1	Network and excitation are given. Response is to be determined.	Response and Excitation or a relation between the two in the form of a network function is given. Network that satisfies the given network function is to be synthesised.
2	It has a unique solution. Ex: If the response to be found, is current in a branch of the network, then the current must be the same irrespective of the method used to determine it.	The solution is not unique. We can create more than one type of networks that satisfy the given network function.
3	It always has a solution even if it is difficult to find.	Sometimes there may be no solution available.

The difference between these two is shown in Fig. 5.2.

5.2 ONE-PORT AND TWO-PORT SYNTHESIS

For a network having only one port as shown in Fig. 5.2, only the driving point function is defined.

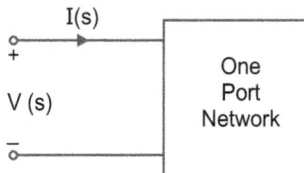

Fig. 5.2: One Port Network

Driving point impedance function $Z(s) = \dfrac{V(s)}{I(s)}$

Driving point admittance function $Y(s) = \dfrac{I(s)}{V(s)}$

Hence, to realize a one-port network, only $Z(s)$ and $Y(s)$ are to be specified. R-C, R-L, L-C or R-L-C networks can be realized as one-port networks.

When a network has two ports as shown in Fig. 5.3, both, the Driving point function and transfer function have to be defined.

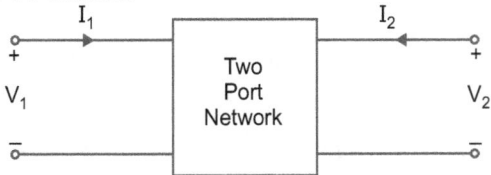

Fig. 5.3: Two Port Network

Driving point functions are

$$Z_{11}(s) = \frac{V_1(s)}{I_1(s)}$$

and

$$Z_{22}(s) = \frac{V_2(s)}{I_2(s)}$$

Transfer functions are -

Voltage ratio transfer function $\quad G_{21}(s) = \dfrac{V_2(s)}{V_1(s)}$

Current ratio transfer function $\quad \alpha_{21}(s) = \dfrac{I_2(s)}{I_1(s)}$

Transfer impedance function $\quad Z_{21}(s) = \dfrac{V_2(s)}{I_1(s)}$

Transfer admittance function $\quad Y_{21}(s) = \dfrac{-I_2(s)}{V_1(s)}$

Hence in order to realize two-port network functions we have to specify $Z_{11}(s)$ and $Z_{12}(s)$ OR $Y_{22}(s)$ and $Y_{12}(s)$ etc. **Synthesis of transfer functions is explained in Unit III.**

5.3 CAUSALITY AND STABILITY

Let us consider a network function F(s) which may be impedance, admittance or transfer function. To synthesis this function into a network containing R, L, C elements, it has to satisfy certain conditions. In this section, we explain two such conditions namely, causality and stability. Another condition of the function to be positive real function (P.R.F) will be explained in a later section.

5.3.1 Causality

Generally, we cannot get an output (response) without giving an input (excitation). Causality gives the relationship between the cause and the effect. Before excitation e(t) is applied at t = 0, if the response r(t) is zero in a network then it is said to be *a causal network*.

Impulse response h(t) of the network will determine whether a network is causal or non-causal. Since impulse response h(t) and network function F(s) are Laplace Transform pair i.e. $h(t) = L^{-1}[F(s)]$, in a causal network h(t) = 0 for t < 0. Thus, we have

$$\boxed{h(t) = 0 \text{ for } t < 0} \leftarrow \text{Causal network}$$
$$\boxed{h(t) \# 0 \text{ for } t < 0} \leftarrow \text{Non-causal network} \qquad \ldots (5.1)$$

Hence a network with impulse response of $h(t) = 2e^{-2t} u(t)$ is a *causal network*. This is because u(t) = 0 for t < 0 and hence h(t) = 0. However, a network with impulse response of $h(t) = 2e^{-2(t)}$ is not a causal network.

In some cases, an impulse response can be made causal by introducing a delay in it. Consider a function h(t) whose response is as shown in Fig. 5.4 (a) below. It is not causal as h(t) = 0 for t < 0. If we delay the function h(t) by a time T, the function becomes causal as shown in Fig. 5.4 (b).

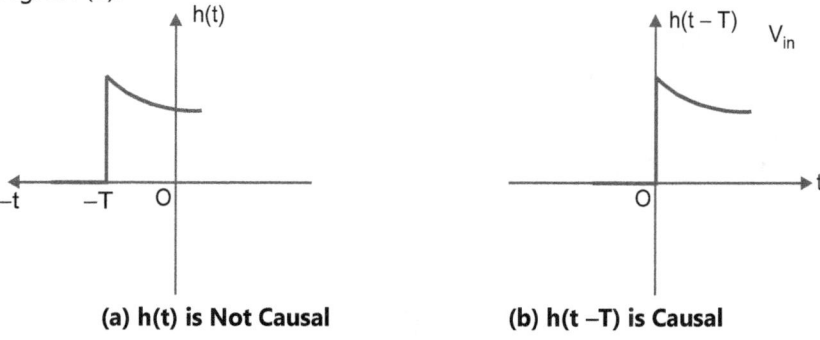

(a) h(t) is Not Causal   (b) h(t −T) is Causal

Fig. 5.4: Two-Port Network

We can only realize a causal function. For a function H(s) to be causal in frequency domain it must have a Fourier transform, and the square magnitude function $[H(j\omega)]^2$ must be integrable i.e.

$$\int_{-\infty}^{\infty} [H(j\omega)]^2 \, d\omega < \infty \qquad \ldots (5.2)$$

Note: Inductors and capacitors are energy storage elements that can store energy. If they have stored energy in them then the response r(t) will not be zero even when excitation e(f) = 0. In such a situation, the network becomes non-causal. Therefore, for an R-L-C circuit to be causal, the initial conditions must be zero.

5.3.2 Stability

A network is said to be stable if -
(a) It gives a bounded output for a bounded input.
(b) The output becomes zero if the input is reduced to zero.

Thus, if the excitation is e(t) and $|e(t)| < k_1$ for $0 \leq t < \infty$, then the output r(t) must satisfy the condition $|r(t)| < k_2$ for $0 \leq t < \infty$.

Where, k_1 and k_2 are real, positive and finite constants.

A network is stable if and only if its impulse response is absolutely integrable.

$$\int_0^{\infty} |h(\tau)| \, d\tau < \infty \quad \ldots \text{ for a stable system}$$

Above condition is satisfied only when impulse response h(t) approaches zero as $t \to \infty$ i.e.

$$\lim_{t \to \infty} h(t) = 0$$

Note: In general for a stable network the impulse response h(t) must be bounded for all t i.e. $|h(t)| < k$ for all $t \geq 0$, where k is a real, finite, positive constant.

5.4 HURWITZ POLYNOMIAL

A polynomial P(s) is said to be Hurwitz polynomial if it satisfies the following properties -

(a) The polynomial P(s) is real when 'S' is real.

(b) The roots of polynomial P(s) have real parts, which can be zero or negative.

In addition to the above basic properties, the Hurwitz polynomial has following additional properties.

5.4.1 Properties of Hurwitz Polynomial

Hurwitz polynomial P(s) can be formed by three types of factors.

Type of Root	Factor
Real root	(s + a) where 'a' is real and positive or zero.
Imaginary root	$(s^2 + b^2)$ where 'b' is real and positive.
Complex root	$[s^2 + 2Cs + d]$ where 'c' and 'd' are real and positive.

The general form of an nth order polynomial P(s) is given by:

$$P(s) = a_n s^n + a_{n-1} s^{n-1} + \ldots\ldots a_1 s + a_0 \quad \ldots (a)$$

where, $a_n, a_{n-1}, \ldots a_0$ are called coefficients.

The properties of P(s) to be Hurwitz are -

1. All coefficients a_i of s are real and positive i.e. $a_0, a_1, a_2, \ldots, a_n$ must be positive.

2. No power of 's' should be missing between the Highest degree term and lowest degree term of 's' unless all even terms OR all odd terms are missing.

   The polynomial is said to be 'even' if its consists of only even powers of 's'.

   For example, $p_1(s) = s^4 + 3s^2 + 5$ is an *even polynomial*.

   The polynomial is said to be *odd* if it consists of only odd powers of 's'.

   For example $p_2(s) = s^5 + 2s^3 + s$ is an *odd polynomial*.

3. If the polynomial is even or odd then all its roots must be lying on imaginary (jω) axis.
4. The polynomial can be expressed as a sum of even part m(s) and odd parts n(s). Thus P(s) = m(s) + n(s).
   For example, if $P(s) = s^5 + s^4 + 2s^3 + 3s^2 + s + 5$.
   Then $P(s) = (s^4 + 2s^2 + 5) + (s^5 + 2s^3 + s) = m(s) + n(s)$. Roots of m(s) and n(s) are lying on jω axis.
5. When the ratio of even to odd part of P(s) or odd to even part of P(s) is expressed in Continued Fraction Expansion (CFE), all the quotients terms must be real and positive.

   If $\quad \psi(s) = \dfrac{m(s)}{n(s)}$

   or $\quad \psi(s) = \dfrac{n(s)}{m(s)}$

   then CFE will give

   $$\psi(s) = q_1 s + \cfrac{1}{q_2 s + \cfrac{1}{q_3 s + \cfrac{1}{\cdots + \cfrac{1}{q_n s}}}}$$

   All the quotient terms $q_1, q_2, q_3, \ldots, q_n$ must be real and positive.

6. If CFE gives all positive quotients then the polynomial P(s) can be expressed as the product of two factors which are Hurwitz polynomials. Thus

   $$P(s) = p_1(s)\, x(s)$$

   where, $p_1(s)$ and $x(s)$ both are Hurtwiz polynomials.

7. If P(s) is even or odd polynomial then it is not possible to express P(s) in CFE form since n(s) or m(s) is absent and ψ(s) cannot be obtained. In such cases CFE of P(s) and its derivative p'(s) is obtained and this CFE should have all the quotients with positive and real value.

   For example, if $\quad P(s) = s^4 + 3s^2 + 2 \quad$ then $\quad p'(s) = 4s^3 + 6s$

   Now, CFE gives $\quad \psi(s) = \dfrac{p(s)}{p'(s)} \text{ or } \dfrac{p'(s)}{p(s)}$

5.4.2 Testing of Hurwitz Polynomial

There are two methods by which polynomial P(s) can be tested and it can be confirmed whether it is a Hurwitz polynomial or not. If it is Hurwitz *then all its roots will be lying in left half of the s-plane or on the imaginary axis. There will be no root in the right half of the s-plane.* These two methods are -
1. Continued Fraction Expansion (CFE).
2. Routh Array and Routh Hurwitz criterion.

Method I: Continued Fraction Expansion (Euclid's Algorithm)

Example $\quad P(s) = s^4 + s^3 + 5s^2 + 3s + 4$

Now separate the given polynomial into even part m(s) and odd part n(s)

$$\psi(s) = \frac{m(s)}{n(s)} = \alpha_1 s + \cfrac{1}{\alpha_2 s + \cfrac{1}{\alpha_3 s + 1}}$$

$$\vdots$$

$$\cfrac{1}{\alpha_n s}$$

This is called Euclid's algorithm. Necessary condition for F(s) to be a P.R.F. is that all 'α' coefficients should be positive and real.

In the given example, $\quad m(s) = s^4 + 5s^2 + 4$

$$n(s) = s^3 + 3s$$

$$\therefore \quad \psi(s) = \frac{s^4 + 5s^2 + 4}{s^3 + 3s}$$

$$s^3 + 3s \overline{)s^4 + 5s^2 + 4} \,(\, s$$
$$\underline{s^4 + 3s^2}$$
$$2s^2 + 4 \overline{)s^3 + 3s} \,(\, \tfrac{s}{2}$$
$$\underline{s^3 + 2s}$$
$$s\,)\,2s^2 + 4\,(\,2s$$
$$\underline{2s^2}$$
$$4\,)\,s\,(\,\tfrac{s}{4}$$
$$\underline{\tfrac{s}{00}}$$

Hence $\quad \psi(s) = s + \cfrac{1}{\cfrac{s}{2} + \cfrac{1}{2s + \cfrac{1}{\tfrac{s}{4}}}}$

Since all the coefficient are positive, the given polynomial F(s) is Hurwitz.

Method II: Routh Array and Routh Hurwitz criterion

Consider a polynomial

$$P(s) = b_0 s^6 + b_1 s^5 + b_2 s^4 + b_3 s^3 + b_4 s^2 + b_5 s + b_6$$

Now Routh Array is formed as given below.

s^6	b_0	b_2	b_4	b_6
s^5	b_1	b_3	b_5
s^4	c_0	c_2	c_4
s^3	d_1	d_3	0
s^2	e_0	e_2
s^1	f_1
s	f_0

where

$$c_0 = \frac{b_1 b_2 - b_0 b_3}{b_1} \qquad c_2 = \frac{b_1 b_4 - b_0 b_5}{b_1}$$

$$c_4 = \frac{b_1 b_6 - 0}{b_1}$$

$$d_1 = \frac{c_0 b_3 - b_1 c_2}{c_0} \qquad d_3 = \frac{c_0 b_5 - b_1 c_4}{c_0}$$

$$e_0 = \frac{c_2 d_1 - c_0 d_3}{d_1} \qquad e_2 = \frac{d_1 c_4 - 0}{d_1}$$

$$f_1 = \frac{e_0 d_3 - d_1 e_2}{e_0} \qquad g_0 = \frac{f_1 e_2 - 0}{f_1}$$

Hence for the polynomial P(s) to be Hurtwiz
1. There should not be any sign change in first column of the array.
2. All elements in the first column should be non-zero.

Now, in the given example

$$F(s) = s^4 + s^3 + 5s^2 + 3s + 4$$

Routh array is

s^4	1	5	4
s^3	1	3
s^2	2	4
s^1	1	0
s^0	4

Since all elements are real and positive, F(s) is strictly Hurwitz.

5.5 PROBLEMS ON HURWITZ POLYNOMIALS

Ex. 5.1: Test whether $p(s) = s^4 + 7s^3 + 6s^2 + 21s + 8$ is Hurwitz or not.

Sol.: Routh array is as given below. As all elements are positive and real, p(s) is Hurwitz.

s^4	1	6	8
s^3	7	21	
s^2	3	8	
s^1	$\frac{7}{3}$	0	
s^0	8		

Ex. 5.2: Test whether the given polynomial is Hurwitz or not.

Sol.: Routh array is given by

s^7	1	2	4	8
s^6	2	1	8	4
s^5	1.5	0	6	0
s^4	1	0	4	
s^3	0	0		

The array terminates (vanishes) prematurely. The polynomial obtained by the row just above is

$$P_1(s) = s^4 + 4 = (s^2 + 2s + 2)(s^2 - 2s + 2)$$

$(s^2 + 2s - 2)$ has two roots which are in the right half of the s-plane. Hence, the given function $p_1(s)$ is not Hurwitz.

Ex. 5.3: Test whether $s^5 + 8s^4 + 24s^3 + 28s^2 + 23s + 6$ is Hurwitz or not.

Sol.: Routh Array is given by

s^5	1	24	23
s^4	8	28	6
s^3	20.5	22.25	
s^2	19.317	6	
s^1	15.88	0	
s^0	6		

Since all elements in the first column are real and positive, the given polynomial is Hurwitz.

Ex. 5.4: Test whether $s^6 + 7s^4 + 14s^2 + 8$ is a Hurwitz polynomial or not.

Sol.: Routh-Hurwitz method

$$p(s) = s^6 + 7s^4 + 14s^2 + 8$$
$$p'(s) = 6s^5 + 28s^3 + 28s$$

Routh array is as given below. Since all elements in the first column are real and positive, the polynomial given is Hurwitz.

s^6	1	7	14	8
s^5	6	28	28	
s^4	$\dfrac{7}{3}$	9.33	8	
s^3	4	7.4		
s^2	5	8		
s^1	1			
s^0	8			

Ex. 5.5: Determine whether $F(s) = s^4 + s^3 + 2s^2 + 3s + 2$ is Hurwitz or not.

Sol.: Routh array is given by

s^4	1	2	2
s^3	1	3	
s^2	–1	2	
s^1	+ 5	0	
s^0	2		

Since there is a sign change in the first column of the array, the given function is not Hurwitz.

This is because $-s^2 + 2 = 0$ OR $s^2 = 2$.

This corresponds to two roots in the right half of the s-plane and hence, this is not Hurwitz.

Ex. 5.6: Determine whether $F(s) = s^3 + 2s^2 + 3s + 6$ is Hurwitz or not.

Sol.: Routh array is given by

s^3	1	3	
s^2	2	6	
s^1	0	0	← Vanishing row
s^1	4	0	
s^0	6	0	

Since all terms are real and positive, the given function is Hurwitz.

Note: Since there is a vanishing row,

$$F_1(s) = 2s^2 + 6 \text{ is the polynomial formed by the row just above the vanishing row.}$$

∴ $F_1'(s) = 4s$, now continue the array.

Ex. 5.7: Test whether the following polynomial is Hurwitz or not.
$$p(s) = s^7 + 3s^6 + 8s^5 + 15s^4 + 17s^3 + 12s^2 + 4s$$

Sol.: We have $p(s) = s[s^6 + 3s^5 + 8s^4 + 15s^3 + 17s^2 + 12s + 4]$

Now $p(s)$ has a zero at $s = 0$, which may be removed by forming $\dfrac{p(s)}{s}$ before testing starts.

Thus
$$\psi(s) = \dfrac{m(s)}{n(s)} = \dfrac{s^6 + 8s^4 + 17s^2 + 4}{3s^5 + 15s^3 + 12s} = \dfrac{p(s)}{s}$$

Continued fraction expansion (Euclid's algorithm gives)

$$3s^5 + 15s^3 + 12s \overline{\smash{)}\, s^6 + 8s^4 + 17s^2 + 4} \left(\dfrac{s}{3}\right.$$
$$\underline{s^6 + 5s^4 + 4s^2}$$

$$3s^4 + 13s^2 + 4 \overline{\smash{)}\, 3s^5 + 15s^3 + 12s}\, (s$$
$$\underline{3s^5 + 13s^3 + 4s}$$

$$2s^3 + 8s \overline{\smash{)}\, 3s^4 + 13s^2 + 4} \left(\dfrac{3}{2}s\right.$$
$$\underline{3s^4 + 12s^2}$$

$$s^2 + 4 \overline{\smash{)}\, 2s^3 + 8s}\, (2s$$
$$\underline{2s^3 + 8s}$$
$$0$$

Hence
$$\psi(s) = \dfrac{s}{3} + \cfrac{1}{s + \cfrac{1}{\cfrac{3}{2}s + \cfrac{1}{2s}}}$$

Since the coefficients of CFE $\left[\alpha_1 = \dfrac{1}{3},\, \alpha_2 = 1,\, = \dfrac{3}{2} \text{ and } \alpha_4 = 2\right]$ are all real and positive, the given polynomial is Hurwitz.

Ex. 5.8: Test whether $p(s) = 2s^6 + s^5 + 13s^4 + 6s^3 + 56s^2 + 25s + 25$ is Hurwitz or not.

Sol.: Then C.F.E. gives

$$\psi(s) = \dfrac{m(s)}{n(s)} = \dfrac{2s^6 + 13s^4 + 56s^2}{s^5 + 6s^3 + 25s}$$

$$= 2s + \cfrac{1}{s\left[\dfrac{s^4 + 6s^2 + 25}{s^4 + 6s^2 + 25}\right]}$$

Thus, the expansion terminates abruptly.

Now, $s^4 + 6s^2 + 25 = (s^2 + 2s + 5)(s^2 - 2s + 5)$
$= (s + 1 - j2)(s + 1 - j2)(s - 1 + j2)(s - 1 - j2)$

Since there are two roots which have a positive and real part, the given polynomial is not Hurwitz.

Ex. 5.9: Determine the range of k so that polynomial $p(s) = s^3 + 3s^2 + 2s + k$ is Hurwitz.

Sol.: Given $p(s) = s^3 + 3s^2 + 2s + k$

Routh Array is given by

s^3	1	2
s^2	3	k
s^1	$\frac{6-k}{3}$	0
s^0	k	

For p(s) to be Hurwitz, all terms in the first column of Array must be positive or real.

Thus, $k > 0$ and $\frac{6-k}{3} > 0$ or $6 > k$

Thus, range of k is $\boxed{0 < k < 6}$

5.6 POSITIVE REAL FUNCTION (P.R.F.)

Networks made up of elements which are LLFPB (Linear, Lumped, Finite, Passive, Bilateral) are rational and are in the form of quotient of polynomial in 's'. But all quotients of polynomial in 's' do not describe a network. A driving point function must satisfy a few requirements before it can be synthesised into a network. These requirements were first proposed in complete form by **Otto Brune** in 1931. Functions satisfying these requirements are called as **Brune's positive real functions** or **P.R.F.**

Consider a driving point impedance function expressed as a quotient of polynomials written in the form

$$Z(s) = \frac{p(s)}{q(s)}$$

$$= \frac{a_0 s^n + a_1 s^{n-1} + \ldots a_{n-1} s + a_n}{b_0 s^m + b_1 s^{m-1} + \ldots b_{m-1} s + b_m} \quad \ldots (5.3\text{ a})$$

where, 'n' is degree of numerator and 'm' is degree of denominator polynomial. These polynomial may be factored to identify poles and zeroes for Z(s).

$$Z(s) = \frac{a_0(s - z_1)(s - z_2) \ldots (s - z_n)}{b_0(s - p_1)(s - p_2) \ldots (s - p_n)} \quad \ldots (5.3\text{ b})$$

The necessity condition for both poles and zeros of driving-point functions is **that its real part must be negative or zero**. Poles and zeros must be in the left half of the s-plane (or on the imaginary axis). Also 'a' and 'b' coefficients of p(s) and q(s) in Equation (a) above must all be positive. The reason being that problems of terms like $(s + b_1)$ and $(s^2 + \alpha_1 s + \beta_1)$ result in a polynomial with positive coefficient.

If F(s) is the immittance (impedance or admittance (function), then F(s) is said to be a positive real function if it satisfies following conditions -

1. $\text{Re}[F(s)] \geq 0$ for $s \geq 0$.
2. F(s) is real when 's' is real. ... (5.4)

A number of important properties of P.R.F are summarized in Table 5.1 below. These conditions are necessary conditions but they are not sufficient conditions for a function to be a P.R.F.

Table 5.1: Necessary Conditions for Positive Real Functions

If $$F(s) = \frac{p(s)}{q(s)} = \frac{a_0 s^n + a_1 s^{n-1} + \dots a_{n-1} s + a_n}{b_0 s^m + b_1 s^{m-1} + \dots b_{m-1} s + b_m}$$

is the immittance function then it is a P.R.F if -

No.	Necessary Condition
1.	The coefficient of numerator and denominator polynomial in F(s) is real. This means- (a) F(s) is real when 's' is real. (b) Complex poles and zeroes of F(s) occur in conjugate pairs. (c) Scale factor $H = \frac{a_0}{b_0}$ is real and positive.
2.	Poles and zeros of F(s) have either negative or zero real parts.
3.	Poles of F(s) on the imaginary axis are simple and their residues are real and positive.
4.	The highest degree of numerator and denominator polynomial in F(s) differs at the most by "1" (unity). Thus, the number of finite poles and finite zeros of F(s) differs at the most by 1.
5.	Terms of lowest degree in numerator and denominator polynomial of F(s) may differ in degree at the most by "1" (unity). Hence F(s) has neither multiple poles nor zeros at the origin (s = 0).

Conditions as imposed by Equation (5.4) can be explained graphically as shown in Fig. 5.5.

When F(s) is expressed in polar form, we have

$$F(s) = H \frac{M_1 M_2 \dots M_n}{m_1 - m_2 \dots m_m} e^{j(\alpha_1 + \alpha_2 \dots - \beta_1 - \beta_2 \dots)}$$

where, 'α_k' is the angle of zero factor i.e. $s - Z_k = M_k e^{\alpha k}$

'β_k' is the angle of pole factor i.e. $s - P_k = m_k e^{j \beta k}$

Real part of F(s) is given by

$$\text{Re}[F(s)] = H \frac{M_1 M_2 \ldots M_n}{m_1 - m_2 \ldots m_m} \cos(\alpha_1 + \alpha_2 - \beta_1 - \beta_2 \ldots)$$

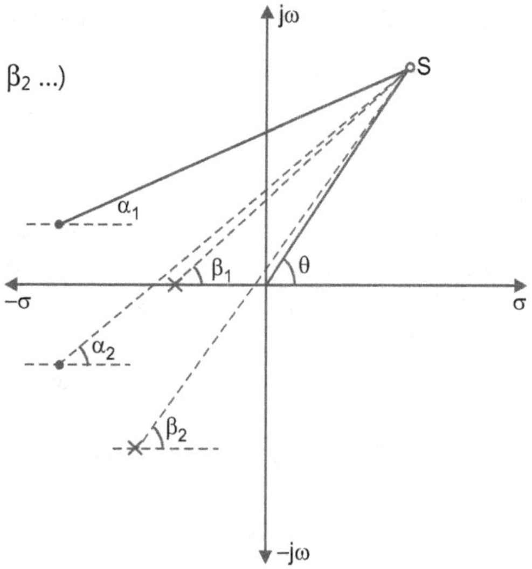

Fig. 5.5: Graphical Explanation for Equation (5.9)

For Re[F(s)] to be positive when 's' is positive, which is the first condition,

$$|\phi| = |\alpha_1 + \alpha_2 + \ldots \beta_1 - \beta_2 \ldots \beta_m| \leq \frac{\pi}{2}$$

If 'ϕ' is the argument (angle) of 'F(s)', then the second condition of F(s) to be real when 's' is real implies,

$$|\phi| = |\alpha_1 + \alpha_2 \ldots - \beta_1 - \beta_2 \ldots| \text{ must be} < '\phi'$$

Some Examples of P.F. Functions are given below.

(a) F(s) = R where 'R' is + ve and real, is a P.R.F. Here R is the resistance when F(s) is an impedance.

(b) F(s) = sL where 'L' is real and positive, is a P.R.F. Here 'L' is the inductance when F(s) is an impedance.

(c) $F(s) = \frac{1}{Cs}$ where 'C' is positive and real, is a P.R.F. Here 'C' is the capacitance when F(s) is an impedance function.

Thus, three basic passive impedance or admittances are P.R.F.

Followings are not P.R.F.

(a) $F(s) = 1 - s$

(b) $F(s) = \frac{(s^2 + 1)}{(s - 2s + 1)}$

(c) $F(s) = \frac{s^3 + 5s}{s^4 + 2s^2 + 1} = \frac{s[s^2 + 5]}{(s^2 + 1)^2}$ (there are multiple poles on the imaginary axis)

(d) $F(s) = 5 \frac{(s + 1)^2}{(s + 4)(s^2 - 2s + 10)}$ (there are two poles in the right half of the s-plane)

5.7 TESTING OF DRIVING POINT POSITIVE REAL FUNCTIONS

When one or more conditions given in Table 5.1 are not satisfied then the function under test is not a positive real function. However, a function can satisfy all the requirements as given in the table but still not be a positive real function. Hence, the conditions given in Table 5.1 are necessary conditions but not sufficient to ensure positive realness of a function. A complete test to establish positive real character of a given function requires a demonstration that ReF(s) $\geq$ 0 for all right-half plane values of 's'. This is a difficult task especially when F(s) is made up of a polynomial of degree greater than 2. There are some equivalent conditions that are better suited to a routine testing of functions. Thus, positive real character of a rational function may be tested by carrying out the following three steps (tests).

Test 1: There should be no poles and zeros of F(s) in the right half of the s-plane.

Note:
- In some textbooks only poles are tested, zeros are not tested.
- If a function has zeros in the right half of the s-plane, it will fail Test 3 because it cannot be positive real.
- Since Test 3 is more difficult to complete than Test 1, we recommend the testing of zeros as well.

Test 2: Poles of F(s) on the imaginary axis must be simple and the residues evaluated at these poles must be real and positive.

Test 3: It is required that Re F(jω) $\geq$ 0 for 0 $\leq \omega \leq \infty$.

Note: Testing in the complete range $-\infty < \omega < +\infty$ is not required since ReF(jω) is an even function.

If a function passes the above 3 tests then it is a positive real function. The test requirements are equivalent to the following conditions.

(a) ReF(s) $\geq$ 0 for Re s $\geq$ 0.
(b) F(s) s real for 's' real.

These two conditions may be used interchangeably to show that F(s) is positive and real.

Testing of above conditions:

Test 1: The roots of p(s) and q(s) must be in the left half of the s-plane. There are many tests available to determine the sign of real part of roots p(s) and q(s) without finding the roots. One of them is given **by Routh-Hurwitz criterion**.

Test 2: The residue at the imaginary axis poles of F(s) should be real and positive.

This test is carried out by doing PFE of F(s) and then checking the residue at the imaginary axis poles and this should be real and positive.

Graphical method can also be used to find the residue at the poles but this method is applicable to non-multiple poles only.

If F(s) has a pair of poles s = $\pm j\omega_0$ then PFE of F(s) gives

$$\frac{k_1}{s - j\omega_0} + \frac{k_1^*}{s + j\omega_0}.$$

Since residue of complex poles are themselves complex conjugate, $k_1 = k_1^*$ and should be positive, and also real. Thus we have

$$\frac{k_1}{s - j\omega_0} + \frac{k_1^*}{s + j\omega_0} = \frac{k_1}{s - j\omega_0} + \frac{k_1}{s + j\omega_0}$$

$$= \frac{2 k_1 \omega_0}{s^2 + \omega_0^2}$$

Test 3: $\text{Re}[F(j\omega)]$ must be positive and real for all 'ω'.

To compute $\text{Re}[F(j\omega)]$ from $F(s) = \dfrac{p(s)}{q(s)}$, first separate $p(s)$ and $q(s)$ into even and odd parts.

$$F(s) = \frac{p(s)}{q(s)} = \frac{m_1(s) + n_1(s)}{m_2(s) + n_2(s)}$$

$$= \frac{m_1 + n_1}{m_2 + n_2}$$

Now multiply by $\dfrac{q(-s)}{q(-s)}$ or $\dfrac{m_2 - n_2}{m_2 - n_2}$ to get

$$F(s) = \frac{p(s)\, q(-s)}{p(s)\, q(-s)}$$

$$= \frac{(m_1 m_2 - n_1 n_2) + (m_2 n_1 - m_1 n_2)}{m_2^2 - n_2^2} \quad \ldots \text{(a)}$$

Since the product of two even functions or odd functions is an even function while the product of an even and an odd function is odd, we have

Even part of $\qquad F(s) = E_v F(s)$

$$= \frac{m_1 m_2 - n_1 n_2}{m_2^2 - n_2^2} \quad \ldots \text{(b)}$$

Odd part of $\qquad F(s) = \text{Od}\, F(s)$

$$= \frac{m_2 n_1 - m_1 n_2}{m_2^2 - n_2^2} \quad \ldots \text{(c)}$$

Now substituting $s = j\omega$ is an even polynomial gives the real part of $F(s)$.
Substituting $s = j\omega$ in an odd polynomial gives the imaginary part of $F(s)$.

i.e.
$$\text{Ev}\, F(s) \big|_{s = j\omega} = \text{Re}\, F(j\omega)$$

$$\text{Od}\, F(s) \big|_{s = j\omega} = j\, \text{Im}\, F(j\omega)$$

We only have to test $\text{Re}\, F(j\omega) \geq 0$ for all the $w \geq 0$
However, for $s = j\omega$, $q(j\omega)$ and $q(-j\omega)$ are conjugate and this product is always positive.

$\therefore \qquad m_2^2 - n_2^2 \big|_{s = j\omega}$ is $+$ ve

Hence, for Ev F(jω) to be positive, it is necessary that
$$m_1m_2 - n_1n_2 \big|_{s=j\omega} = A(\omega^2)$$
should be positive and real for all $\omega \geq 0$.
This condition $A(\omega^2) \geq 0$ can be tested by one of the following methods.
(a) Find factor $A(\omega^2)$. The factor may contains terms like -
1. $(\omega^2 + \delta_1^2)$ where, δ_1 is always real and positive, and hence permitted.
2. Complex terms occurring in conjugate pairs like $(\omega^2 + d_2^2) \times (\omega^2 + d_3^2)$ are always positive and hence permitted.

However, this method may be difficult to use if the degree of polynomial in ω^2 is high because that will be difficult to factorise.
(b) Plot $A(\omega^2)$ over sufficiently large range of 'ω' to ensure that it is never negative.
(c) Make use of 'Sturm Test' to determine the presence of real zeros within the range $0 < \omega < \infty$.

Note that if $A(\omega^2) = k_0\omega^n + k_1\omega^{n-2} + k_2\omega^{n-4} + ...$, then k_0, k_1, k_2 etc. are real and positive and $A(\omega^2) \geq 0$ for all 'ω'.
But if $A(\omega^2)$ contains coefficient which are both positive and negative, then Sturm test can be performed to find if any zeros are in the range $0 < \omega < \infty$.

Table 5.2 gives a summary of the testing procedure for positive realness of $F(s) = \frac{p(s)}{q(s)}$.

Table 5.2: Summary of the Testing Procedure for Positive Realness of $F(s) = \frac{p(s)}{q(s)}$

Test for necessary conditions	1. All polynomial coefficients of p(s) and q(s) should be real and positive. 2. Highest degree of numerator and denominator polynomial should differ at the most by '1'. 3. Numerator and denominator terms of lowest degree should differ at the most by '1'. 4. Imaginary axis poles and zeros should be simple. There should be no multiple poles. 5. There should be no missing terms in the numerator and denominator polynomial unless all even or odd terms are missing.
Test for necessary and sufficient conditions	1. F(s) must not contain poles and zeros in the right half of the s-plane. For this both p(s) and q(s) must be Hurwitz polynomial. 2. Imaginary axis poles of F(s) must be simple and residue evaluated at these poles must be real and positive. 3. Re F(jω) $\geq$ 0 for $0 < \omega < \infty$. It is necessary and sufficient that $A(\omega^2) = m_1m_2 - n_1n_2\big|_{s=j\omega} \geq 0$ for all ω. Ensure this by factoring $A(\omega^2)$ or by Sturm test.

5.8 PROBLEMS ON THE TESTING OF POSITIVE REAL FUNCTIONS

Ex. 5.10: Test whether $F(s) = \dfrac{s^2 + 6s + 5}{s^2 + 9s + 14}$ is P.R.F.

Sol.: Since all the necessary conditions of Table 5.2 are satisfied, the function may be a P.R.F.

Now test for the necessary and sufficient conditions.

1. There must not be poles or zeros in the right half of the s-plane.

   $P(s) = s^2 + 6s + 5$ $\qquad\qquad q(s) = s^2 + 9s + 14$

s^2	1	5	s^2	1	14
s^1	6		s^1	9	
s^0	5		s^0	14	

   As both p(s), q(s) are Hurwitz, the first condition is satisfied.

2. Residue at imaginary axis poles must be real and positive.

   Since $\qquad\qquad q(s) = s^2 + 9s + 14$
   i.e. $\qquad\qquad q(s) = (s + 7)(s + 2)$

   and there are no poles on the imaginary axis, the condition is automatically satisfied.

3. $\qquad\qquad A(\omega^2) \geq 0$ for $0 < \omega < \infty$

   Now $\qquad A(\omega^2) = m_1 m_2 - n_1 n_2 \big|_{s = j\omega}$

   $A(\omega^2) = (s^2 + 5)(s^2 + 14) - 6s \times 9s \big|_{s = j\omega}$

   $= s^4 + 19s^2 + 70 - 54 s^2 \big|_{s = j\omega}$

   $= s^4 - 35 s^2 + 70 \big|_{j\omega} = \omega^4 + 35 \omega^2 + 70$

   This is positive for all $\omega > 0$. Hence, the given function is a P.R.F.

Ex. 5.11: Test whether $F(s) = \dfrac{s^2 + \frac{3}{4}s + \frac{3}{4}}{s^2 + s + 4}$ is P.R.F.

Sol.: Since all the necessary conditions of Table 5.2 are satisfied, the function may be a P.R.F. Now test for the necessary and sufficient conditions.

1. p(s) and q(s) must be Hurwitz

   $P(s) = s^2 + \dfrac{3}{4}s + \dfrac{3}{4}$ $\qquad\qquad q(s) = s^2 + s + 4$

s^2	1	$\frac{3}{4}$	s^2	1	4
s^1	$\frac{3}{4}$	0	s^1	1	
s^0	$\frac{3}{4}$		s^0	4	

   As both p(s) and q(s) are Hurwitz, there are no poles OR zeros in the right half of the s-plane.

2. There are no poles on the imaginary axis because

$$\phi(s) = s^2 + s + 4 = \left(s + 0.5 + j\frac{\sqrt{15}}{2}\right)\left(s + 0.5 - j\frac{\sqrt{15}}{2}\right)$$

The second condition is automatically satisfied.

3. Now $A(\omega^2) = m_1 m_2 - n_1 n_2 \big|_{s=j\omega}$

$$A(\omega^2) = \left(s^2 + \frac{3}{4}\right)(s^2 + 4) - \frac{3}{4}s^2 \Big|_{s=j\omega}$$

$$= s^4 + \frac{19}{4}s^2 + 3 - \frac{3}{4}s^2 \Big|_{s=j\omega} = [\omega^4 - 4\omega^2 + 3]$$

This is not positive for all $\omega > 0$. For example when $\omega = 1.5$

$$A(\omega^2) = (1.5)^4 - 4(1.5)^2 + 3$$
$$= 5.125 - 9 + 3 = -0.875$$

Hence, the given function is not a P.R.F.

Ex. 5.12: Determine whether $F(s) = \dfrac{s^2 + 1}{s^2 + 4s}$ is P.R.F.

Sol.: Since all the necessary conditions of Table 5.2 are satisfied, the function may be a P.R.F. Now test for the necessary and sufficient conditions.

1. p(s) and q(s) must be Hurwtiz

   Now $p(s) = s^2 + 1 = (s + j1)(s - j1)$
   $q(s) = s^3 + 4s = s[s^2 + 4]$
   $= s(s + j2)(s - j2)$

   Since there are no poles and zeros in the right half of the s-plane, the p(s) and q(s) are Hurwitz.

2. Residue at imaginary axis poles must be real and positive.

   Let us find the residue at the imaginary axis pole.

   $$F(s) = \frac{s^2 + 1}{s(s^2 + 4)}$$

   $$= \frac{A}{s} + \frac{B}{s + j2} + \frac{B^*}{(s - j2)}$$

   $$B = (s + j2) F(s)\big|_{s \to -j2}$$

   $$= \frac{(s^2 + 1)}{s(s - j2)}\bigg|_{s \to -j2}$$

   $$= \frac{(-4 + 1)}{-j2(-2j2)} = \frac{+3}{8}$$

   Also $B^* = B = \dfrac{3}{8}$ which is real and positive. Hence, the second condition is satisfied.

3. Now
$$A(\omega^2) = m_1m_2 - n_1n_2\big|_{s=j\omega}$$
$$= (s^2+1)\times 0 - 0\times(s^3+4s)\big|_{s=j\omega}$$
$$= 0 \text{ for all '}\omega\text{'}$$

Hence, all the conditions are satisfied. Therefore, the given function F(s) is a P.R.F.

Ex. 5.13: Test whether $F(s) = \dfrac{s^2+4}{s^3+3s^2+3s+1}$ is P.R.F.

Sol.: Since all the necessary conditions of Table 5.2 are satisfied, the given function F(s) may be a P.R.F.

Now test for the necessary and sufficient conditions.

1. p(s) and q(s) must be Hurwitz

$P(s) = s^2 + 4$

s^2	1	4
s	2	
s^0 ↓	4	

$q(s) = s^3 + 3s^2 + 3s + 1$

s^3	1	3
s^2	3	1
s^1	$\dfrac{8}{3}$	
s^0 ↓	1	

positive p(s) is Hurwtiz

all positive and real

∴ q(s) is Hurwitz

2. Residue at imaginary axis poles must be real and positive.

$$F(s) = \frac{s^2+4}{s^3+3s^2+3s+1} = \frac{s^2+4}{(s+1)(s^2+2s+1)} = \frac{s^2+4}{(s+1)^3}$$

As there are no poles on the imaginary axis, this condition is automatically satisfied.

3.
$$A(\omega^2) = m_1m_2 - n_1n_2\big|_{s=j\omega}$$

should be greater than zero for all 'w'.
$$A(\omega^2) = (s^2+4)(3s^2+1) - 0\times s^3 + 3s\big|_{s=j\omega}$$
$$= (3s^4 + 13s^2 + 4)\big|_{s=j\omega}$$
$$= (3\omega^4 - 13\omega^2 + 4)$$

$A(\omega^2)$ is not greater than zero for all 'ω'.

For example $\omega = 1$ A(1) = 3 − 13 + 4 = − 6 which is negative.

Hence, the given function is not a P.R.F.

Ex. 5.14: Test whether $F(s) = \dfrac{s^3 - 1}{4s^3 - 3s^2 - 1}$ is a positive real function.

Sol.: By inspection the function does not seem to be a P.R.F. But, by factoring the numerator and denominator polynomials there will be cancellation of common terms as given below:

$$F(s) = \dfrac{(s-1)(s^2 + s + 1)}{(s-1)(4s^2 + s + 1)}$$

$$= \dfrac{s^2 + s + 1}{(4s^2 + s + 1)} = \dfrac{p(s)}{q(s)}$$

As both p(s) and q(s) have complex roots in the left half of the s-plane, both these are Hurwitz polynomials. Hence the first condition is satisfied.

As there are no imaginary axis poles the second test is automatically satisfied.

Now
$$A(\omega^2) = m_1 m_2 - n_1 n_2 \big|_{s = j\omega}$$

$$= [(s^2 + 1)(4s^2 + 1) - s^2]_{s = j\omega}$$

$$= 4s^4 + 4s^2 + 1 \big|_{s = j\omega}$$

$$= 4\omega^4 - 4\omega^2 + 1$$

$$= (1 - 2\omega^2)^2$$

$A(\omega^2)$ being a perfect square it is always > 0 for all ω > 0. Thus, third test is also satisfied. Hence, the given function F(s) is a P.R.F.

Ex. 5.15: Test whether $F(s) = \dfrac{2s^4 + 7s^3 + 11s^2 + 12s + 4}{s^4 + 5s^3 + 9s^2 + 11s + 6}$ is a P.R.F.

Sol.: Since all the necessary conditions of Table 5.2 are satisfied, the given function may be a P.R.F.

Now test for the necessary and sufficient conditions.

1. p(s) and q(s) must be Hurwitz.

   $p(s) = 2s^4 + 7s^3 + 11s^2 + 12s + 4$ $q(s) = s^4 + 5s^3 + 9s^2 + 11s + 6$

s^4	2	11	4	s^4	1	9	6
s^3	7	12		s^3	5	11	
s^2	$\dfrac{53}{7}$	4		s^2	6.8	6	
s^1	8.3			s^1	6.58		
s^0	4			s^0			

   Thus, p(s) and q(s) both are Hurwitz.

2. Residue at the imaginary axis poles must be real and positive.
   Since $q(s) = s^4 + 5s^3 + qs^2 + 11s + 6 = (s + 1)(s + 3)(s^2 + s + 2)$, there are no imaginary axis poles and hence this condition is satisfied automatically.

3. Now test for $A(\omega^2)$.

$$A(\omega^2) = m_1(s) m_2(s) - n_1(s) n_2(s)\big|_{s=j\omega}$$
$$= (2s^4 + 11s^2 + 4)(s^4 + 9s^2 + 6) - (7s^3 + 12s)(5s^3 + 11s)$$
$$= (2s^8 + 29s^6 + 115s^4 + 24) - 35s^6 - 137s^4 - 132s^2$$
$$= 2\omega^8 + 6\omega^6 - 22s^4 + 30\omega^2 + 24$$

For all 'ω' $A(\omega^2) > 0$ hence the given function is a P.R.F.

Ex. 5.16: Test whether $F(s) = \dfrac{s^2 + s + 6}{s^2 + s + 1}$ is P.R.F.

Sol.: Since all the necessary conditions of Table 5.2 are satisfied, the given function may be a P.R.F.

Now test for the necessary and sufficient conditions.

1. $p(s)$ and $q(s)$ must be Hurwitz.

   $p(s) = s^2 + s + 6$ $q(s) = s^2 + s + 1$

s^2	1	6		s^2	1	14
s	1			s^1	1	
s^0	6			s^0	1	

   Thus, $p(s)$ and $q(s)$ are both Hurwitz.

2. Residue at the imaginary axis poles must be real and positive.

$$F(s) = \frac{s^2 + s + 6}{s^2 + s + 1}$$

$$= \frac{A}{\left(s - 0.5 + J\dfrac{\sqrt{3}}{2}\right)} + \frac{A^*}{\left(s - 0.5 + J\dfrac{\sqrt{3}}{2}\right)}$$

Since there are no imaginary axis poles, this condition is automatically satisfied.

3. $$A(\omega^2) = m_1(s) m_2(s) - n_1(s) n_2(s)\big|_{s=j\omega}$$
$$= (s^2 + 6)(s^2 + 1) - s^2\big|_{s=j\omega}$$
$$= (s^4 + 7s^2 + 6 - s^2)_{s=j\omega}$$
$$= (s^4 + 6s^2 + 6)_{s=j\omega}$$
$$= \omega^4 - 6\omega^2 + 6$$

for $\omega = 2$ $A(2^2) = 16 - 24 + 6$ is negative

Since this condition is not satisfied, the given function is not a P.R.F.

Ex. 5.17: Test whether $F(s) = \dfrac{s^3 + 6s^2 + 7s + 3}{s^2 + 2s + 1}$ is a P.R.F.

Sol.: Since all the necessary conditions of Table 5.2 are satisfied, the given function may be a P.R.F.

Now test for the necessary and sufficient conditions.

1. p(s) and q(s) must be Hurwitz

   $p(s) = s^3 + 6s^2 + 7s + 3$ $\qquad$ $q(s) = s^2 + 2s + 1$

s^3	1	7
s^2	6	3
s^1	6.5	
s^0	3	

s^2	1	1
s^1	2	
s^0	1	

   Thus, p(s) and q(s) both are Hurwitz.

2. Residue at the imaginary axis poles must be real and positive.

   As there are no poles on the imaginary axis, this condition is automatically satisfied.

3. $\qquad A(\omega^2) = m_1(s) m_2(s) - n_1(s) n_2 s \big|_{s=j\omega}$

   $= (6s^2 + 3)(s^2 + 1) - (s^3 + 7s) 2s \big|_{s=j\omega}$

   $= 6s^4 + 9s^2 + 3 - 2s^4 - 14s^2 \big|_{s=j\omega}$

   $= 4s^4 - 5s^2 + 3 \big|_{s=j\omega} = 4\omega^4 + 5\omega^2 + 3$

   $A(\omega^2) > 0$ for all 'ω'. Since all three conditions are satisfied, the given function is a P.R.F.

Ex. 5.18: Test whether $F(s) = \dfrac{s^2 + 1}{s^3 + 4s}$ is P.R.F.

Sol.: 1. p(s) and q(s) must be Hurwitz

   $$F(s) = \frac{(s+j1)(s-j1)}{s(s+j2)(s-j2)}$$

   Since there are no poles or zero in the right half of the s-plane, p(s) and q(s) is Hurwitz.

2. Residue at the imaginary axis poles must be real and positive.

   $$F(s) = \frac{A}{s} + \frac{B}{(s+j2)} + \frac{B^*}{(s-j2)}$$

   $$= \frac{s^2 + 1}{s(s^2 + 4)}$$

   $A = sF(s)\big|_{s \to 0} = \dfrac{1}{4}$

   $B = (s+j2) F(s)\big|_{s \to -j2}$

   $= \dfrac{(-4+1)}{-j2(-2j2)} = \dfrac{-3}{-8} = \dfrac{3}{8}$

   hence $\qquad B = B^* = \dfrac{3}{8}$

   Since imaginary axis poles have real and positive residue, the second condition is satisfied.

3.
$$A(\omega^2) = m_1(s)\, m_2(s) - n_1(s)\, n_2(s)\big|_{s=j\omega}$$
$$= (s^2 + 1) \times 0 - (s^3 + 4s) \times 0 = 0$$

Since $A(\omega^2) \geq 0$, the third condition is satisfied. Hence the given function is a P.R.F.

Ex. 5.19: Test whether $F(s) = \dfrac{s^3 + 10s^2 + 27s + 18}{s^2 + 7s + 11.25}$ is P.R.

Sol.: 1. p(s) and q(s) must be Hurwitz

$p(s) = s^3 + 10s^2 + 27s + 18$

s^3	1	27
s^2	10	18
s^1	25.2	
s^0	18	

$q(s) = s^2 + 7s + 11.25$

s^2	1	11.25
s^1	7	
s^0	11.25	

Hence p(s) and q(s) are Hurwitz.

2. Residue at the imaginary axis poles must be real and positive.

$$F(s) = \dfrac{s^3 + 10s^2 + 27s + 18}{s^2 + 7s + 11.25} = \dfrac{s^3 + 10s^2 + 27s + 18}{(s + 2.5)(s + 4.5)}$$

Since there are no imaginary axis poles, this condition is automatically satisfied.

3.
$$A(\omega^2) = m_1(s)\, m_2(s) - n_1(s)\, n_2(s)\big|_{s=j\omega}$$
$$= (10s^2 + 18)(s^2 + 11.25) - 9s^2 + 27s)\big|_{s=j\omega}$$
$$= 10s^4 + 130.5\, s^2 + 202.5 - 7s^4 - 189\, s^2\big|_{s=j\omega}$$
$$= 10\omega^4 - 130.5\, \omega^2 + 202.5 - 7\omega^4 + 189\, \omega^2$$
$$= 3\omega^2 + 58.5\, \omega^2 + 202.5$$

$A(\omega^2) > 0$ for all 'ω'. Hence, the given function is a P.R.F.

Ex. 5.20: Test whether $F(s) = \dfrac{s^4 + 3s^3 + s^2 + s + 2}{s^3 + s^2 + s + 1}$ is a P.R.F.

Sol.: Since all necessary conditions are satisfied, the function may be a P.R.F.

Now test for the necessary and sufficient conditions.

1. p(s) and q(s) must be Hurwitz.

$p(s) = s^4 + 3s^3 + s^2 + s + 2$

s^4	1	1	2
s^3	3	1	
s^2	$\dfrac{2}{3}$	2	
s^1	-8		
s^0	2		

$q(s) = s^3 + s^2 + s + 1$

s^3	1	1	
s^2	1	1	
s^1	0		vanishing row
s^1	2	0	
s^0	1	0	

Here q(s) is Hurwitz but p(s) is not Hurwitz, which indicates that there are zeros in the right half of the s-plane. Hence, the given function is not a P.R.F.

Ex. 5.21: Test whether $y(s) = \dfrac{2s^2 + s + 2}{s^2 + s + 2}$ is P.R.F.

Sol.: Since all necessary conditions are satisfied, the given function may be a P.R.F.

Now test for the necessary and sufficient conditions.

1. $p(s)$ and $q(s)$ must be Hurwitz

   $p(s) = 2s^2 + s + 2$ $\qquad\qquad$ $q(s) = s^2 + s + 2$

s^2	2	2
s^1	1	
s^0	2	

s^2	1	2
s^1	1	
s^0	2	

   $p(s)$ and $q(s)$ are Hurwitz.

2. Residue at the imaginary axis poles must be real and positive.

   Since $\qquad q(s) = s^2 + s + 2$

   $$= \left(s + 0.5 + \frac{j\sqrt{7}}{2}\right)\left(s + 0.5 - \frac{j\sqrt{7}}{2}\right)$$

   there are no imaginary axis poles, and this condition is automatically satisfied.

3. $A(\omega^2) = m_1(s)\, m_2(s) - n_1(s)\, n_2(s)\Big|_{s=j\omega}$

   $\qquad\quad = (2s^2 + 1)(s^2 + 2) - s^2\Big|_{s=j\omega}$

   $\qquad\quad = 2s^4 + 5s^2 + 2 - s^2\Big|_{s=j\omega}$

   $\qquad\quad = 2\omega^4 - 4\omega^2 + 2$

   $\qquad\quad = 2[\omega^4 - 2\omega^2 + 1]$

   $\qquad\quad = 2[\omega^2 - 1]^2$

   for all $\omega > 0$ this is +ve.

   Hence, the given function is a P.R.F.

Ex. 5.22: Show that for $F(s) = \dfrac{s + a}{s^2 + bs + c}$ to be a P.R.F necessary conditions are

1. $a, b, c \geq 0$
2. $b \geq a$

Sol.: By inspection, the necessary condition is that coefficient of numerator and denominator polynomial should be real and positive.

Hence, the condition (is) $a, b, c, \geq 0$.

Now by condition $\qquad A(\omega^2) \geq 0$ for $0 < \omega < \infty$

we have

$\qquad A(\omega^2) = a(s^2 + c) - bs^2 \Big|_{s=j\omega}$

$\qquad A(\omega^2) = s^2(a - b) + ac \Big|_{s=j\omega}$

∴ $\qquad A(\omega^2) = \omega^2(b - a) + ac$

From above it is obvious that
$$A(\omega^2) \geq 0 \text{ for } 0 < \omega < \infty \text{ only if } b \geq a$$
Hence the condition $b \geq a$ is essential

Note: With the above conditions
$$F(s) = \frac{s+2}{s^2 + 3s + 4} \text{ is a P.R.F.}$$
while
$$F(s) = \frac{s+4}{s^2 + 3s + 2} \text{ is not a P.R.F.}$$

Ex. 5.23: Assuming that coefficients a_1, b_1, a_0, b_0 are all real and positive constants, determine the condition for quadratic rational function $F(s) = \frac{s^2 + a_1 s + a_0}{s^2 + b_1 s + b_0}$ to be a P.R.F.

Sol.: Since the condition of $p(s)$ and $q(s)$ to be Hurwitz for a function to be P.R.F. is essential, a_0, b_0, a_1, b_1 must be real and positive.

Now condition $A(\omega^2) \geq 0$ for all 'w' gives
$$A(\omega^2) = m_1(s) m_2(s) - n_1(s) n_2(s) \big|_{s=j\omega}$$
$$= (s^2 + a_0)(s^2 + b_0) - a_1 b_1 s^2 \big|_{s=j\omega}$$
$$A(\omega^2) = s^4 + a_0 b_0 + s^2(s_0 + b_0) - a_1 b_1 \big|_{s=j\omega}$$
$$= a_0 b_0 + \omega^2 [+ a_1 b_1 - (a_0 + b_0)] + \omega^4$$

This should be $>$ for $0 < \omega < \infty$.
Factorising this
$$\omega_{1,2}^2 = -\frac{[+ a_1 b_1 - (a_0 + b_0)]}{2} \pm \sqrt{\frac{1}{2}[+a_1 b_1 - (a_0 + b_0)]^2 - 4 a_0 b_0}$$

Roots are not simple when quantity under radial sign is zero OR negative.
Thus the conditions are -

(i) $[+ a_1 b_1 - (a_0 + b_0)]^2 - 4 a_0 b_0 \leq 0$

(ii) $+ a_1 b_1 - (a_0 + b_0) \geq 0$.

This gives rise to the condition
$$a_1 b_1 \geq \left[\sqrt{a_0} - \sqrt{b_0}\right]^2$$

as a necessary and sufficient condition for the function to be a P.R.F.

For example $F(s) = \frac{s^2 + 3s + 25}{s^2 + 4s + 9}$ is a P.R.F because
$$a_1 b_1 = 3 \times 4 = 12 \text{ is } > \left[\sqrt{a_0} - \sqrt{b_0}\right]^2$$
$$\left[\sqrt{a_0} - \sqrt{b_0}\right]^2 = [5-3]^2 = 4$$

Ex. 5.24: Test whether the given $F(s)$ is a positive real function

Sol.: We have
$$F(s) = \frac{s^3 + 7s^2 + 15s + 9}{(s^4 + 6s^2 + 9)}$$
$$p(s) = s^3 + 7s^2 + 15s + 9$$
$$q(s) = s^4 + 6s^2 + 9$$

Since all the necessary conditions of Table 5.1 are satisfied, the given function may be a P.R.F.

Now we shall test for the necessary and sufficient conditions.

1. Both p(s) and q(s) must be Hurwitz.

   $p(s) = s^3 + 7s^2 + 15s + 9$ $q(s) = s^4 + 6s^2 + 9$
                                          $q'(s) = 4s^3 + 12s$

s^3	1	15
s^2	7	9
s^1	$\frac{96}{7}$	0
s^0	9	0

s^4	1	6	9
s^3	4	12	0
s^2	3	9	
	0	0	vanishing row
s	6	0	
s^0	9	0	

   p(s) is Hurwitz   q(s) is also Hurwitz

2. Residue at the imaginary axis poles must be real and positive.
   $q(s) = (s^4 + 6s^2 + 9) = (s^2 + 3)^2 = (s^2 + 3)= (s^2 + 3)(s^2 + 3)$
   As there are multiple poles at $s = \pm j3$ on the jω axis the given function is not a P.R.F. This can also be confirmed from the third test of $A(\omega)^2$.

3. $A(\omega^2) = m_1 m_2 - n_1 n_2 \big|_{s = j\omega}$
   $= (7s^2 + 9)(s^4 + 6s + 9) - 0 \times s^2 + 15s \big|_{s = j\omega}$
   $= 7s^6 + 51s^4 + 117s^2 + 81 \big|_{s = j\omega}$
   $= -7\omega^6 + 51\omega^4 - 117\omega^2 + 81$

   For $\omega = 2$ we have $A(\omega^2) = -19$
   Since $A(\omega^2) < 0$ for $\omega > 0$, the given function is not a P.R.F.

5.9 ELEMENTARY SYNTHESIS PROCEDURES (CONCEPTS)

Impedance and admittance of time invariant passive networks are P.R.Fs. Hence, addition of impedances of the two passive networks gives a function, which is also a P.R.F.

Thus, if $z_1(s)$ and $z_2(s)$ are P.R.Fs,
$$z(s) = z_1(s) + z_2(s) \text{ is a P.R.F.} \qquad \ldots (A)$$

Similarly, if $y_1(s)$ and $y_2(s)$ are P.R.Fs
$$y(s) = y_1(s) + y_2(s) \text{ is a P.R.F} \qquad \ldots (B)$$

This is shown in Fig. 5.6.

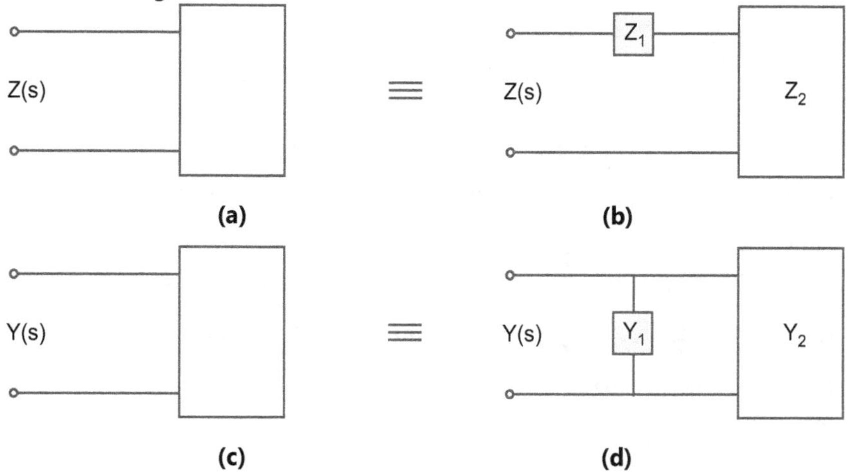

Fig. 5.6: Elementary Synthesis Concepts

There is a special terminology associated with the synthesis procedure.

From equation (A), solving for $z_2(s)$ gives $z_2(s) = z(s) - z_1(s)$.

Now $z_1(s)$ is said to be removed from $z(s)$ while forming the new function $z_2(s)$.

In other words, the network described by $z_1(s)$ is said to be removed from the network described by $z(s)$ while forming the new network described by $z_2(s)$.

If the removed network is associated with the pole or zero of the original network impedance then the pole or zero is said to be removed. The expression "Removal of pole at infinity" means poles at infinity of $z(s)$ do not appears in $z_2(s)$ since these have been removed in the formation of $z_1(s)$.

If the pole of impedance at infinity is associated with inductor, then the inductor is said to be removed from the network represented by $z(s)$ in order to form the new impedance $z_2(s)$.

Some basic removal operations are:

(a) Removal of a pole at infinity

Consider an impedance function $z(s)$ having a pole at infinity. This means the numerator polynomial is greater in degree than the denominator polynomial by "1" (unity).

i.e.
$$z(s) = \frac{a_{n+1} s^{n+1} + a_n s^n + ... + a_1 s + a_0}{b_n s^n + b_{n-1} s^{n-1} + ... b_1 s + b_0}$$

$$= Hs + \frac{c_n s^n + c_{n-1} s^{n-1} + ... c_1 s + c_0}{b_n s^n + b_n - 1 s^{n-1} + ... b_1 s + b_0}$$

where $H = \dfrac{a_{n+1}}{b_n}$ is constant

Let $z_1(s) = Hs$

Then $z_2(s) = \dfrac{C_n s^n + C_{n-1} s^{n-1} + \dots C_1 s + C_0}{b_n s^n + b_{n-1} s^{n-1} + \dots b_1 s + b_0} = z(s) - Hs$

is also a P.R.F.

$z_1(s) = Hs$ represents an inductor of value 'L' = H.

Hence, the removal of poles at infinity corresponds to the removal of inductor from the network as shown in Fig. 5.7 (a).

If the given function is an admittance function $y(s)$ then $y_1(s) = Hs$ corresponds to an admittance of capacitor $y_c(s) = sC$ and the network for $y_1(s)$ is a capacitor of value $C = H = \dfrac{a_n + 1}{b_n}$. This is illustrated in Fig. 5.7 (b).

(a) Removal of Inductor   (b) Removal of a Capacitor

Fig. 5.7: Network Interpretation of Removal of a Pole of Infinity (s = ∞)

(b) Removal of a pole at zero

If $z(s)$ has a pole at the origin then

$$z(s) = \dfrac{a_0 + a_1 s + \dots a_{n-1} s^{n-1} + a_n s^n}{b_0 + b_1 s + \dots b_m s^m}$$

This can be written as

$$z(s) = \dfrac{k_0}{s} + \dfrac{d_1 + d_2 s + \dots + d_n s^{n-1}}{b_1 + b_2 s + \dots b_m s^{m-1}}$$

$$= z_1(s) + z_2(s)$$

where, $k_0 = \dfrac{a_0}{b_0}$

Now $z_1(s) = \dfrac{k_0}{s}$ represents a capacitor of value $\dfrac{1}{k_0}$.

If the given function is an admittance function $y(s)$ then removal of $Y_1(s) = \dfrac{k_0}{s}$ corresponds to an inductor of value $\dfrac{1}{k_0}$.

This is as shown in Fig. 5.8.

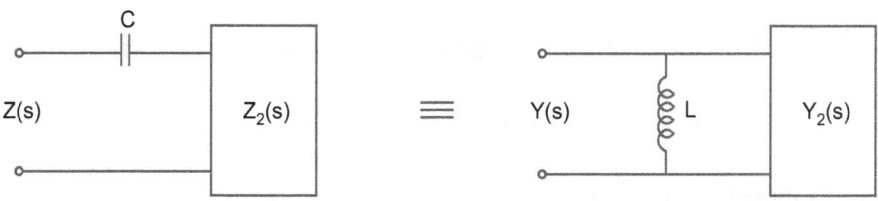

(a) Removal of Capacitor   (b) Removal of a Inductor

Fig. 5.8: Network Interpretation of Removal of a Pole at s = 0

Thus,
- Removal of a pole from impedance function z(s) at the origin corresponds to the removal of a capacitor
- Removal of a pole from admittance function y(s) at the origin corresponds to the removal of an inductor

(c) Removal of conjugate imaginary axis poles:

If $z(s)$ contains poles on imaginary axis say at $s = \pm j\omega_1$ then $z(s)$ has the factors $(s + j\omega_1)(s - j\omega_1)$ which is equal to $s^2 + \omega_1^2$ in the denominator.

Hence $z(s)$ may be written as

$$z(s) = \frac{p(s)}{(s^2 + \omega_1^2)\, q_1(s)}$$

PFE gives

$$z(s) = \frac{k_1}{(s + j\omega_1)} + \frac{k_1^*}{(s - j\omega_1)} + z_2(s) \qquad \ldots (5.5)$$

For a P.R.F,
- Imaginary axis poles must be conjugate
- They must have positive and real residues
- These must be equal

$\therefore \qquad k_1 = k_1^* \equiv k$ (real and positive)

Hence $z(s)$ becomes

$$z(s) = \frac{2k_1 s}{s^2 + \omega_1^2} + z_2(s)$$

Thus $\quad z_1(s) = \dfrac{2k_1 s}{s^2 + \omega_1^2}$

$$= \frac{1}{\dfrac{s}{2k_1} + \dfrac{\omega_1^2}{2k_1 s}} = \frac{1}{y_a + y_b} \qquad \ldots (5.6)$$

where, y_a = Admittance of a capacitor of $C_1 = \dfrac{1}{2k_1}$

y_b = Admittance of inductor of $L_1 = \dfrac{2k_1}{\omega_1^2}$

This is as shown in Fig. 5.9 (a).

If the given function is an admittance function y(s),

then $\quad y_1(s) = \dfrac{2k_1 s}{s^2 + \omega_1^2} = \dfrac{1}{z_a + z_b}$ ... (5.7)

$$= \dfrac{1}{\dfrac{s}{2k_1} + \dfrac{\omega_1^2}{2k_1 s}}$$

z_a = impedance of inductor $L_2 = \dfrac{1}{2k_1}$

z_b = impedance of capacitor of $C_2 = \dfrac{2k_1}{w_1^2}$

This is as shown in Fig. 5.9 (b).

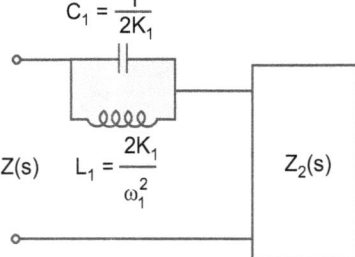
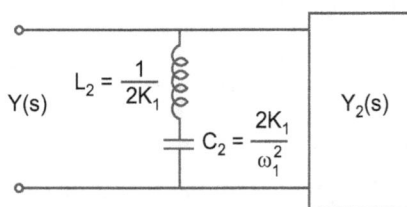

(a) Removal of a Parallel L-C Branch   (b) Removal of a Series L-C Branch

Fig. 5.9: Network interpretation of Removal of Conjugate Pole at $s = \pm j\omega_1$

Table 5.3 summarizes the above three pole removal operations.

Table 5.3: Removal of Poles

Location of pole at s =	If pole of impedance (serial element)	If pole of admittance (parallel element)
0	C	L
∞	L	C
$\pm j\omega_1$	L-C in parallel	L-C in series

(d) Removal of a constant:

If a real number R_1 is subtracted from z(s) such that

$\quad z_2(s) = z(s) - R_1$

OR $\quad z(s) = R_1 + z_2(s)$

Then R_1 represents a resistor.

If y(s) is admittance then removal of $y_1(s) = R_1$ represents a conductance of value R_1 (or a resistor of $\frac{1}{R_1}$ Ohms).

The operations just described can be applied repeatedly to an immittance function [z(s) or y(s)]. Thus, repeated removal of a pole at s = 0 or ∞ or ± $j\omega_1$ and removal of a constant is the basic concept of network synthesis of one-port networks.

Note: In addition to necessary and sufficient conditions already mentioned, the above synthesis procedure makes use of following important properties of P.R.F.

(a) If T(s) is P.R.F, then $\frac{1}{T(s)}$ is also P.R.F.

This property implies that if the driving point function z(s) is a P.R.F then its reciprocal $\frac{1}{z(s)}$ = y(s), which is the driving point admittance, is also a P.R.F.

(b) Sum of two P.R.Fs is also a P.R.F.

If two impedances are connected in series or two admittances are connected in parallel then the resultant impedance or admittance is also a P.R.F.

(c) The difference of two P.R.Fs is not necessarily a P.R.F.

5.10 INTRODUCTION - SYNTHESIS OF ONE-PORT NETWORK

In Unit I, we studied about the following topics.
- Various types of network functions
- Testing a function to for being a positive real function (P.R.F.).
- How a function that is ensured to be a P.R.F., can be realized into a network
- Basic concepts of network synthesis

In Unit II, we shall cover the following topics.
- Synthesis of given impedance or admittance function into the one-port network
- Properties of L-C immittance (admittance or impedance) function and realization of this function into Foster-I, Foster-II, Cauer-I and Cauer-II forms of network
- Properties of R-C impedance and admittance functions and realization of these functions into four canonical forms (Foster-I, Foster-II, Cauer-I and Cauer-II)
- R-L impedance and admittance functions and realization of these functions into four forms of network (Foster-I, Foster-II, Cauer-I and Cauer-II)
- Properties of one-port R-L-C driving point functions and their synthesis into a network by using Partial Fraction Expansion (PFE) and Continued Fraction Expansion (CFE))

5.11 SYNTHESIS OF ONE-PORT NETWORK

Since one-port network has only one input terminal pair (port) as shown in Fig. 5.10, the transfer function is not defined for this network, only the driving point function is defined.

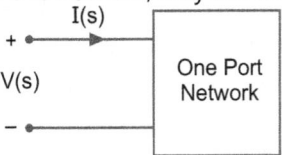

Fig. 5.10: One-Port Network Function

The two driving point functions of a one-port network are:

$$\text{Input impedance} = Z(s) = \frac{V(s)}{I(s)}$$

$$\text{Input admittance} = Y(s) = \frac{I(s)}{V(s)}$$

For a one-port network $Y(s) = \frac{1}{Z(s)}$ or vice versa.

5.11.1 One-Port Functions (Driving Point Functions)

While synthesizing one-port networks we are given only impedance function Z(s) or admittance function Y(s). These functions are the ratio of polynomials P(s) and Q(s). Obviously these functions must be P.R.F. Otherwise it is not possible to realize them into a network with positive real components. Properties of these functions depend upon the type of network. If the network contains only L-C elements, then both $Z_{LC}(s)$ and $Y_{LC}(s)$ have the same properties. If the network consists of R-C elements only, then $Z_{RC}(s)$ and $Y_{RC}(s)$ will have different properties. Properties of $Z_{RL}(s)$ are similar to those of $Y_{RC}(s)$ while the properties of $Z_{RC}(s)$ are similar to those of $Y_{RL}(s)$. The network containing R-L-C element will have different properties for the impedance $Z_{RLC}(s)$ and $Y_{RLC}(s)$.

Once the driving point function [Z(s) or Y(s)] is given, then before synthesising, it is very much essential to identify the type of network which the function is going to yield. This will be possible only if we know the properties of the functions of various network types.

5.12 BASIC FORMS OF NETWORK

Any given driving point function can be realized into four basic forms of networks
1. Foster-I
2. Foster-II
3. Cauer-I
4. Cauer-II

These four forms are known as *canonical (or simple)* forms since they are formed by minimum number of components.

The realized network will contain R, L and C elements. These three basic elements and their Laplace Transforms are shown in Table 5.13.

Table 5.4: Basic Elements and their Transforms

Element	Z(s)	Y(s)
Resistance (R)	R	$G = \frac{1}{R}$ = Conductance
Inductance (L)	sL	$\frac{1}{sL}$
Capacitance (C)	$\frac{1}{sC}$	sC

Now we shall explain each form of network realization.

5.12.1 Foster-I Form of Network

"This form of network is obtained by PFE of the impedance function Z(s)".

When this is done, the given function Z(s) can be represented as a sum of simpler impedance $Z_1(s)$, $Z_2(s)$, ... etc.

i.e. $\qquad Z(s) = Z_1(s) + Z_2(s) + ... + Z_n(s) \qquad ...(5.8)$

Based on the properties of P.R.F., since Z(s) is a P.R.F., $Z_1(s)$, $Z_2(s)$, ... etc. must also be P.R.F. When these simple functions are realized in the form of a network and all of them are connected in series, we get the Foster-I form.

The general form of Foster-I network corresponding to equation (5.8) is shown in Fig. 5.11 (a). The Foster-I form for L-C network is shown in Fig. 5.11 (b).

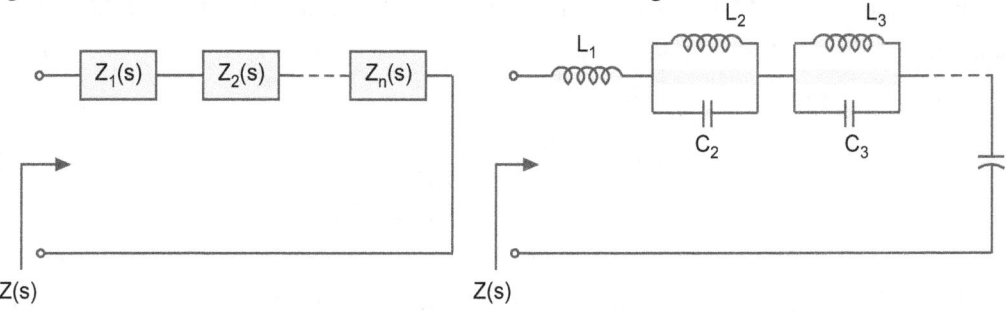

(a) General Form (b) L-C Network

Fig. 5.11: Foster-I Form of Network

5.12.2 Foster-II form of Network

"This form of network is obtained by PFE of the admittance function Y(s)".

When this is done, the given function Y(s) can be represented as a sum of simpler admittance $Y_1(s)$, $Y_2(s)$, ... etc.

i.e. $$Y(s) = Y_1(s) + Y_2(s) + ... + Y_n(s) \quad ...(5.9)$$

Based on the properties of P.R.F., since the given Y(s) is a P.R.F. $Y_1(s)$, $Y_2(s)$, ... etc. must also be P.R.F. When we realize these simple admittance functions in the form of a network and connect all of them in parallel, we get the Foster-II form.

The general form of Foster-II network corresponding to equation (5.9) is shown in Fig. 5.12 (a). Foster-II form of an L-C network is shown in Fig. 5.12 (b).

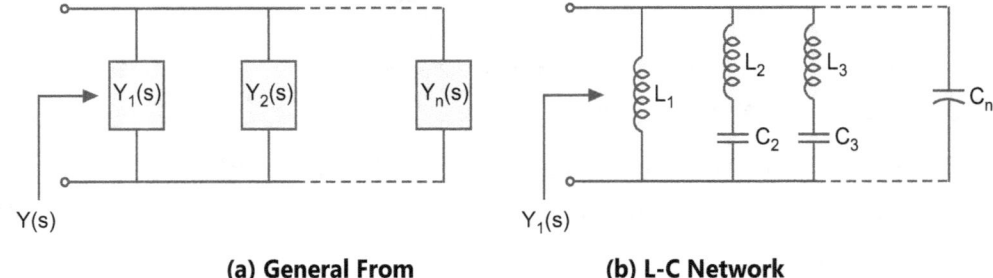

(a) General From   (b) L-C Network

Fig. 5.12: Foster-II Form of Network

5.12.3 Cauer-I form of Network

"This form of network is obtained by successive removal of a pole at s = ∞ from the function [Z(s) or Y(s)]". Alternatively, Cauer-I form of network is obtained by CFE of the driving point immittance [Z(s) or Y(s)] function.

Here, the numerator and the denominator are arranged in the *descending power of s* starting from the highest to lowest degree of s".

The CFE gives the general form as:

$$Z(s) = \underset{\text{(series)}}{Z_1(s)} + \cfrac{1}{\underset{\text{(shunt)}}{Y_2(s)} + \cfrac{1}{\underset{\text{(series)}}{Z_3(s) + ...}}} \quad ...(5.10)$$

The CFE gives the network in the form of a ladder. The general form of Cauer-I network corresponding to equation (5.10) is shown in Fig. 5.13 (a). The Cauer-I form of L-C network is shown in Fig. 5.4 (b). This network looks like a low-pass filter structure.

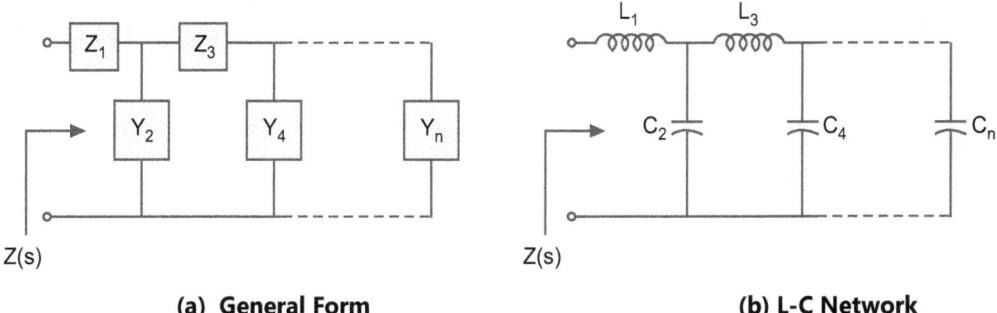

(a) General Form (b) L-C Network

Fig. 5.13: Cauer-I Form of Network

5.12.4 Cauer-II form of Network

"This form of network is obtained by successive removal of a pole origin (s = 0) from the function [Z(s) or Y(s)]". Alternatively Cauer-II form of network is obtained by CFE or driving point immittance [Z(s) or Y(s)] function.

Here, the numerator and the denominators are arranged in the *ascending power of s* starting from lowest to highest power of s".

The CFE gives the general form as :

$$Z(s) = \frac{Z_1(s)}{(\text{series})} + \cfrac{1}{\cfrac{Y_2(s)}{(\text{shunt})} + \cfrac{1}{\cfrac{Z_3(s)}{(\text{series})} + \cfrac{1}{Y_4(s)} + \cdots}} \qquad \ldots (5.11)$$

The CFE gives the network in the form of a ladder. The general form of Cauer-II network corresponding to equation (5.11) is shown in Fig. 5.14 (a). Cauer-II form of L-C network is shown in Fig. 5.14 (b). The *network looks like a high-pass filter circuit.*

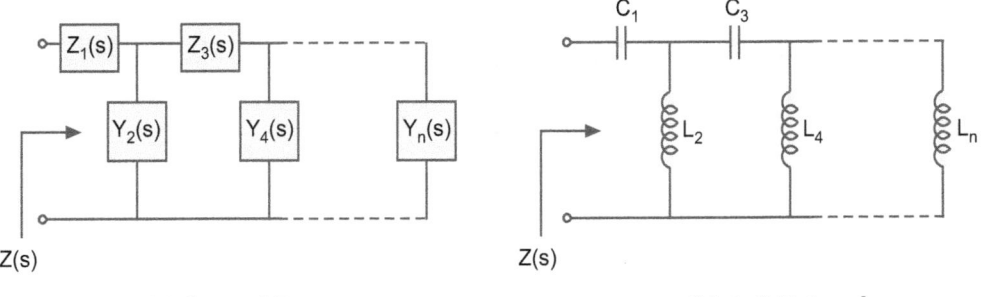

(a) General Form (b) L-C Network

Fig. 5.14: Cauer-II Form of Network

5.13 SYNTHESIS OF DRIVING POINT FUNCTIONS OF L-C NETWORK

Let us use the concepts studied in the last section to synthesise an L-C network. For this we need to know the properties of L-C network functions.

5.13.1 Properties of L-C Driving Point Functions

If a network contains only 'L' and 'C' elements then the network is called a reactance or lossless network.

The poles and zeros of the driving point *immittance function* [Y(s) or Z(s)] of L-C network must lie on the jω-axis only.

Since poles and zeros lie on the imaginary axis, the polynomial p(s) and q(s) of $F(s) \left[\text{where, } F(s) = \frac{p(s)}{q(s)} \right]$ must be either even or odd. Since the behaviour of immittance function of L-C network must approach that of an inductor or capacitor at s = 0 or s = ∞, we conclude that F(s) must have a zero or a pole at the origin, or at s = ∞. Further it can be shown that poles and zeros must alternate on imaginary axis to satisfy condition that residue at jω-axis poles must be real and positive. This imposes the condition that slopes of reactance function must be strictly positive for all frequencies. Fig. 5.15 shows a plot of reactance function as a function.

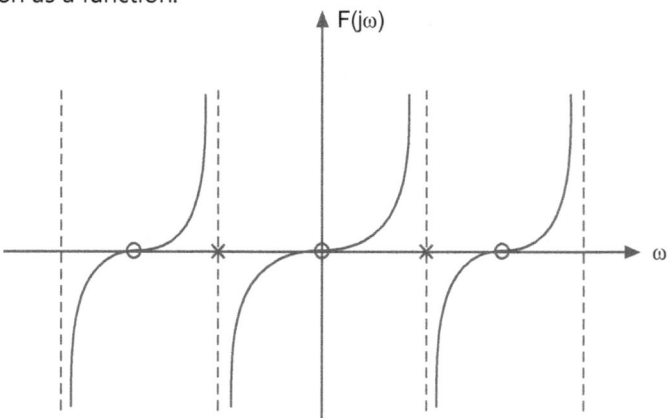

Fig. 5.15: Plot of Reactance Function V/s Frequency for L-C Network

Table 5.2 summarises the above properties of the driving point immittance functions for an L-C network.

Table 5.5: Properties of L-C Driving Point Immittance Function F(s)

No.	Properties of L-C Driving Point Immittance Function F(s)
1.	Poles and zeros are simple and must lie on imaginary (jω) axis.
2.	Poles and zeros must be interlacing.
3.	At the origin, there must be a pole or zero.
4.	At infinity, there must be a pole or zero.
5.	Re F (jω) = 0 for all 'ω'
6.	Slope of F(jω) against frequency (ω) must be strictly positive (Fig. 5.6)
7.	F(s) is ratio of even to odd polynomial OR odd to even polynomial.
8.	Residue at the imaginary axis poles must be real and positive.

Note:
- The poles or zeros of a network function are collectively called *'critical frequencies'*.
- Poles and zeros located at s = 0 and s = ∞ are called *"external critical frequencies"*.
- All other poles and zeros are called *'Internal critical frequencies'*.

5.13.2 Synthesis of L-C Networks

There are many methods by which we can realize a reactance network corresponding to the given immittance F(s). Here we will study only four basic forms - Foster-I, Foster-II, Cauer-I and Cauer-II forms. As mentioned earlier, these are also called canonical forms.

(1) Foster-I Form:

Foster-I form of L-C network is obtained by partial fraction expansion of Z(s) and identifying each term in the summation of impedance as a *simple network*. The form of the equation is

$$Z(s) = Z_1(s) + Z_2(s) + Z_3(s) + \ldots$$

which implies a series connection of simple networks.

In general, if F(s) is an L-C impedance function Z(s), then P.F.E. gives

$$F(s) = Z(s) = \frac{p(s)}{q(s)} = \frac{k_0}{s} + \sum_{i=1}^{n} \frac{2k_i s}{s^2 + \omega_i^2} + k_\infty s \qquad \ldots (5.12)$$

Where, k_0, k_i and k_∞ are residues of poles of Z(s) at the origin, at $j\omega_i$ and at '∞' respectively. These are calculated as below.

$$k_0 = sF(s)\big|_{s \to 0}$$

$$2k_i = \frac{s^2 + \omega_i^2}{s} z(s)\bigg|_{s \to -j\omega_i}$$

$$k_\infty = \frac{Z(s)}{s}\bigg|_{s \to \infty}$$

Elements represented by each term in Equation (5.12) are as shown below.

Impedance function	Element
$\dfrac{k_0}{s}$	$C_0 = \dfrac{1}{k_0}$
$\dfrac{2k_i s}{s^2 + \omega_i^2} = \dfrac{1}{\dfrac{s}{2k_i} + \dfrac{\omega_i^2}{2k_i s}}$	$\dfrac{2k_i}{\omega_i^2}$ and $\dfrac{1}{2k_i}$
$k_\infty s$	k_∞

The Equation (5.12) for Z(s) is written by assuming that there was a pole at the origin and a pole at infinity. *If Z(s) has no pole at the origin (and has a zero), then the first term in Equation (5.12) is missing, and the capacitor is not present in the network. Similarly if there is zero rather than pole at '∞' then $k_\infty \cdot s$, s is not present and inductor is not present in the circuit.*

The network represented by Equation (5.12) which is a Foster-I form of network, is shown in Fig. 5.16.

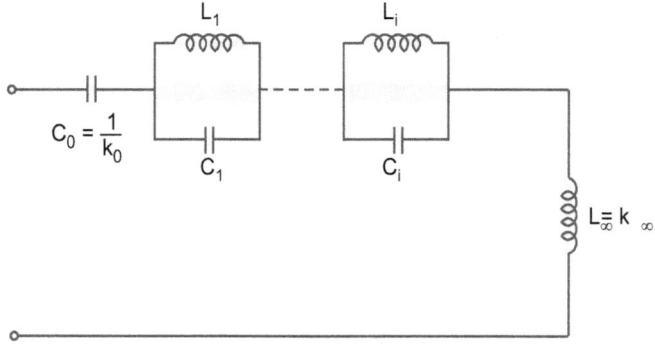

Fig. 5.16: Foster-I Form of L-C Network

(2) Foster-II Form:

Foster-II form of L-C network is obtained by partial fraction expansion of Y(s) and identifying each term in the summation of admittance as *a simple network*.

Form of the equation is

$$Y(s) = Y_1(s) + Y_2(s) + Y_3(s) + \ldots$$

which implies parallel connection of simple networks.

In general, if Y(s) is the admittance function then its partial fraction expansion is

$$Y(s) = \frac{k_0}{s} + \sum_{i=1}^{n} \frac{2k_i s}{s^2 + \omega_i^2} + k_\infty s \qquad \ldots (5.13)$$

Elements represented by each term in above equation are as shown below.

Admittance function	Element
$\dfrac{k_0}{s}$	$L_0 = \dfrac{1}{k_0}$
$\dfrac{2k_i s}{s^2 + \omega_i^2} = \dfrac{1}{\dfrac{s}{2k_i} + \dfrac{\omega_i^2}{2k_i s}}$	$C_i = \dfrac{2k_i}{\omega_i^2}$, $L_i = \dfrac{1}{2k_i}$
$k_\infty s$	k_∞

Foster-II form of the network represented by Equation (5.13) is as shown in Fig. 5.17.

If there is no pole at s = 0 then 'k_0' is absent. Hence the first element (inductor) is absent. If there is no pole at s = ∞ then $k_\infty \cdot s$ is absent. Hence the capacitor is not present.

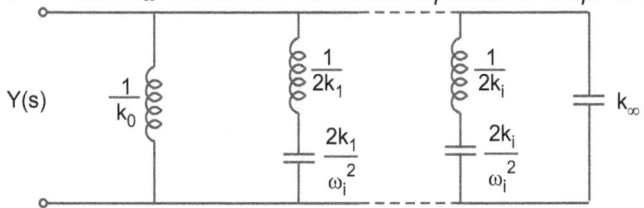

Fig. 5.17: Foster-II Form of L-C Network

Following example explains how to obtain Foster-I and Foster-II forms of network.

Ex. 5.25: Obtain Foster-I and Foster-II forms of network for the impedance function:

$$Z(s) = \frac{(s^2 + 1^2)(s^2 + 3^2)}{s(s^2 + 2^2)}$$

Sol.: Given function is L-C impedance function because all the poles are lying on 'jω' axis as shown in Fig. 5.18. It can be noted that poles and zeros are interlaced. And there is a pole at the origin and at infinity.

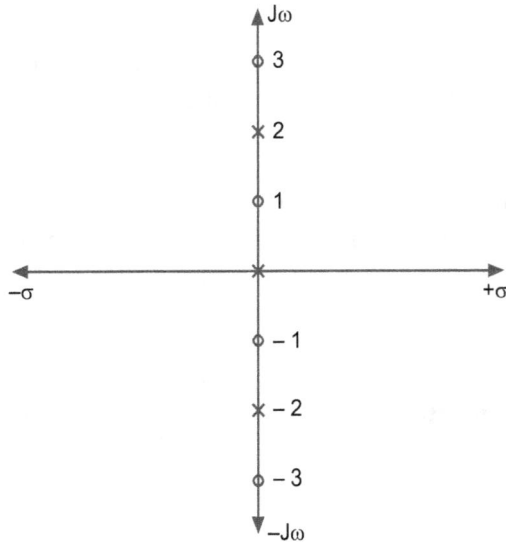

Fig. 5.18: Pole-Zero Location of Z(s)

Foster-I Form: Partial fraction expansion of Z(s) gives

$$Z(s) = \frac{(s^2+1)(s^2+3^2)}{s(s^2+2^2)} = \frac{k_0}{s} + \frac{2k_1 s}{(s^2+2^2)} + k_\infty s$$

$$k_0 = sZ(s)\Big|_{s \to 0} = \frac{1 \times 9}{4} = +\frac{9}{4}$$

$$2k_1 = \frac{(s^2+2^2)Z(s)}{s}\Big|_{s^2 \to -4}$$

$$= \frac{(-4+1)(-4+9)}{-4} = \frac{15}{4}$$

$$k_\infty = \frac{Z(s)}{s}\Big|_{s \to \infty}$$

$$= \frac{(s^2+1)(s^2+3^2)}{s^2(s^2+2^2)}\Big|_{s \to \infty}$$

$$= \frac{1 \times 1}{1} = 1$$

Hence, Z(s) can written as

$$Z(s) = \frac{9}{4s} + \frac{\frac{15}{4}s}{(s^2+2^2)} + s = \frac{1}{\frac{4}{9}s} + \frac{1}{\frac{4}{15}s + \frac{1}{\frac{15}{16s}}} + s$$

Foster-I form of network is as shown in Fig. 5.19.

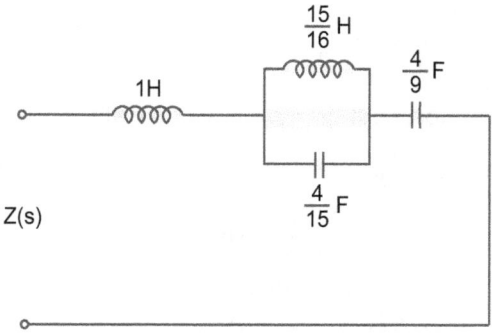

Fig. 5.19: Foster-I Form of L-C Network

Foster-II Form: This is obtained by partial fraction expansion of Y(s).

$$Y(s) = \frac{s(s^2 + 2^2)}{(s^2 + 1)(s^2 + 3^2)} = \frac{2k_1 s}{(s^2 + 1)} + \frac{2k_2 s}{(s^2 + 3^2)}$$

$$2k_1 = \left.\frac{(s^2 + 1)}{s} Z(s)\right|_{s^2 \to -1} = \frac{(-1 + 4)}{(-1 + 9)} = \frac{3}{8}$$

$$2k_2 = \left.\frac{(s^2 + 3^2)}{s} Z(s)\right|_{s^2 \to -9} = \frac{(-9 + 4)}{(-9 + 1)} = \frac{5}{8}$$

k_0 and k_∞ being zero, function Y(s) will be

$$Y(s) = \frac{\frac{3}{8}s}{s^2 + 1} + \frac{\frac{5}{8}s}{s^2 + 9} = \frac{1}{\frac{8}{3}s + \frac{1}{\frac{3}{8}s}} + \frac{1}{\frac{8}{5}s + \frac{1}{\frac{5}{72}s}}$$

Hence Foster-II form of the network is as shown in Fig. 5.20.

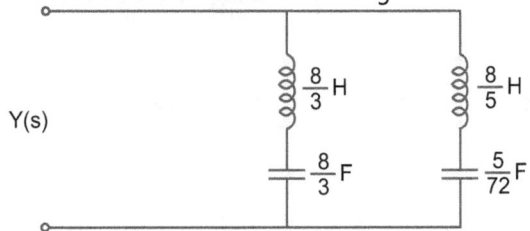

Fig. 5.20: Foster-II Form of L-C Network

(3) Cauer I Form:

Cauer-I form of the network is obtained by successive removal of a pole at infinity from the function [Z(s) or Y(s)].

Synthesis of this form of network is accomplished as shown in the following steps.

If $Z(s) = \frac{m(s)}{n(s)}$ where 'm' is of higher degree than 'n',

then removal of pole at infinity gives
$$Z_1(s) = \frac{m_1(s)}{n(s)} = Z(s) - H_1 s \text{ where } H_1 \text{ is inductor}$$

Now, $Z_1(s)$ has zero at infinity but $Y_1 = \frac{1}{Z_1}$ has a pole at infinity.

This pole can be removed as given below.
$$Y_2(s) = \frac{n_1(s)}{m_i(s)} = Y_1(s) - H_2 \cdot s, \qquad \text{where, } H_2 \text{ is capacitor.}$$

These two steps are equivalent to equations
$$Z(s) = L_1 s + Z_1(s)$$
and
$$\frac{1}{Z_1(s)} = Y_1(s) = C_2 s + Y_2(s)$$

This process is repeated in following pattern.
1. Remove a pole at infinity.
2. Invert the resultant function.
3. Remove a pole at infinity.

This gives following form to $Z(s)$.
$$Z(s) = L_1 s + \cfrac{1}{C_2 s + \cfrac{1}{L_3 s + \cfrac{1}{C_4 s}}} \qquad \ldots (5.14)$$

This form is similar to CFE used in Hurwitz criterion.

The general pattern is
$$Z(s) = Z_1 + \cfrac{1}{Y_2 + \cfrac{1}{Z_3 + \cfrac{1}{Y_4 + \cfrac{1}{Z_5}}}} \qquad \ldots (5.15)$$

Cauer-I form of the network as represented by Equation (5.14) and Equation (5.15), is as shown in Fig. 5.21.

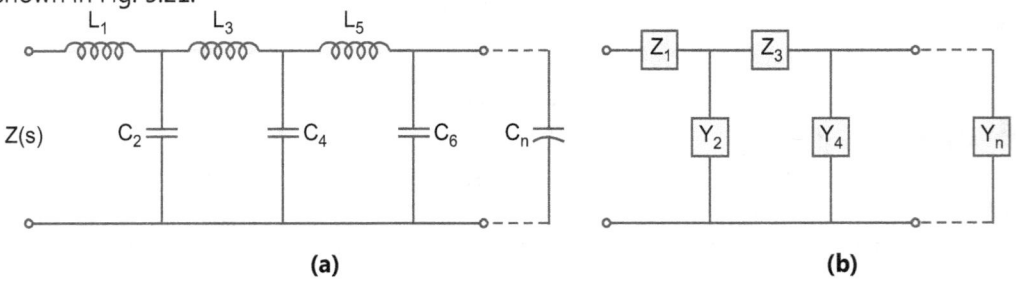

(a) (b)

Fig. 5.21: Cauer-I Form of L-C Network

Nature of the first element is fixed by the nature of Z(s) at infinity.
- *If Z(s) has a pole at infinity, then the first element is inductor.*
- *If Z(s) has a zero at infinity, then the first element is capacitor (C_2) and L_1 is not present.*

Similarly nature of the last element is fixed by the nature of Z(s) at the origin (s = 0).
- *If Z(s) has a pole at the origin, then the last element is capacitor.*
- *If Z(s) has a zero at the origin, then the last element is an inductor* (shunt capacitor is missing).

There are only two possible endings for Cauer-I form of the network and these are shown in Fig. 5.22.

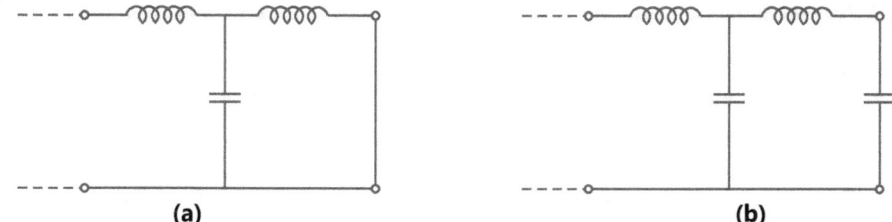

(a)   (b)

Fig. 5.22: Two Possible Endings for Cauer-I Form of Network

(4) Cauer-II Form:

Cauer-II form of the network is obtained by successive removal of a pole at the origin from the function [Z(s) or Y(s)].

Here impedance function Z(s) is expanded in CFE in terms of poles at the origin.

This process is repeated in following pattern until expansion is complete.
1. Remove a pole at the origin
2. Invert the resultant function
3. Remove a pole at the origin

Such expansion gives

$$Z(s) = \frac{1}{C_1 s} + \cfrac{1}{\cfrac{1}{L_2 s} + \cfrac{1}{\cfrac{1}{C_3 s} + \cfrac{1}{L_4 s} + \cdots}} \qquad \ldots (5.16)$$

Or

$$Z(s) = Z_1(s) + \cfrac{1}{Y_1(s) + \cfrac{1}{Z_3(3) + \cfrac{1}{Y_4(s)}}} \qquad \ldots (5.17)$$

General form of Cauer-II network is as shown in Fig. 5.23 (a).

The elements at beginning and at the end are fixed by the poles or zeros at s = 0 or s = ∞, which are called as external critical frequencies There are only two possible endings for Cauer-II form of the network and these are is shown in Fig. 5.23 (b).

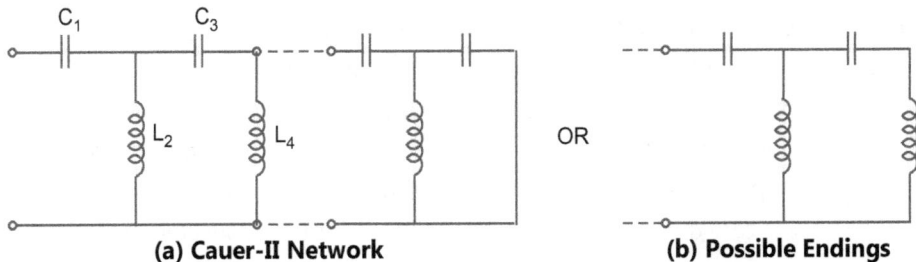

(a) Cauer-II Network (b) Possible Endings
Fig. 5.23: Cauer-II Form of L-C Network

Following example shows how to obtain Cauer-I and Cauer-II forms of network.

Ex. 5.26: Find Cauer-I and Cauer-II forms of network for $Z(s) = \dfrac{s^4 + 10s^2 + 9}{s^3 + 4s}$.

Sol.: Cauer-I Form: Method I: Removal of pole at '∞'

$Z(s)$ has a pole at infinity whose coefficient is $H = 1$. Hence when factor 's' is removed from $Z(s)$, the resulting function will be

$$Z_1(s) = \frac{s^4 + 10^2 + 9}{s^3 + 4s} - s = \frac{6s^2 + 9}{s^3 + 4s} = \frac{6s^2 + 9}{s(s^2 + 4)}$$

Thus $Z_1(s)$ has no pole at infinity but $Y_1(s) = \dfrac{1}{Z_1(s)}$ has a pole at infinity which may be removed by subtracting $\dfrac{s}{6}$ from $Y_1(s)$.

$$\therefore \quad Y_2(s) = \frac{s(s^2 + 4)}{6s^2 + 9} - \frac{s}{6}$$

$$= \frac{\frac{5}{2}s}{6s^2 + 9}$$

$Y_2(s)$ has no pole at '∞'. But $Z_2(s) = \dfrac{1}{Y_2(s)}$ has a pole at '∞' which is removed by subtracting $\dfrac{12}{5}s$. Thus

$$Z_3(s) = Z_2(s) - \frac{12}{5}s$$

$$= \frac{6s^2 + 9}{\frac{5}{2}s} - \frac{12}{5}s = \frac{18}{5s}$$

This function has a zero at infinity. But its reciprocal has a pole at infinity.

$$Y_4(s) = Y_3(s) - \frac{5}{18}s$$

$$= \frac{5}{18}s - \frac{s}{18}s = 0$$

The steps in this development are illustrated in Fig. 5.24.

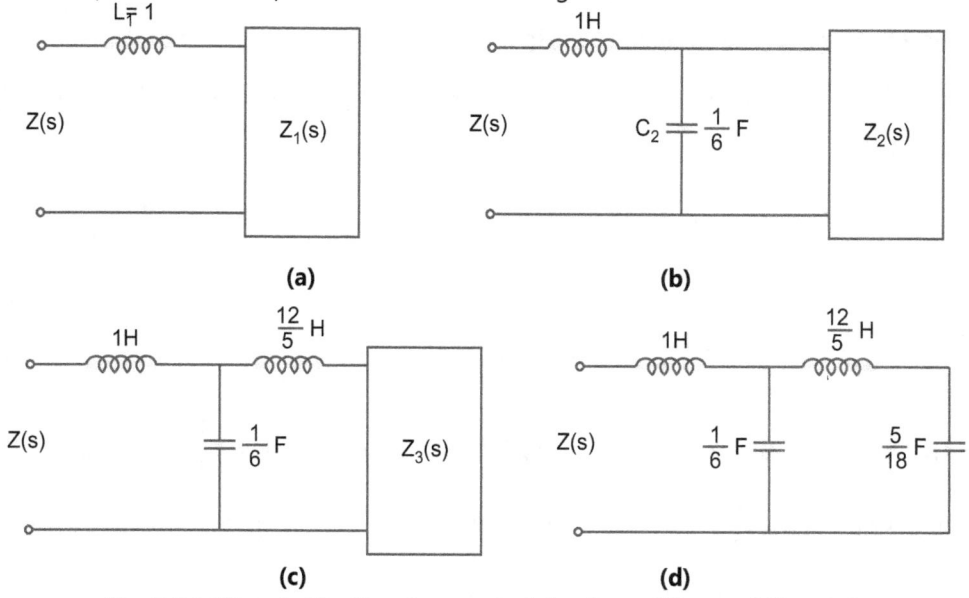

(a)
(b)
(c)
(d)

Fig. 5.24: Steps in the Development of the Cauer-I Form of Network

Method II: Continued Fraction Expansion (CFE) Method

Cauer-I form of the network is obtained by CFE about pole at '∞'. This is as shown below:

$$s^3 + 4s \overline{\big)\, s^4 + 10s^2 + 9} \,\big(\, s \leftarrow L_1 s \leftarrow Z_1(s) \text{ (series)}$$
$$\underline{s^4 + 4s^2}$$
$$6s^2 + 9 \overline{\big)\, s^3 + 4s} \,\big(\, \tfrac{s}{6} \leftarrow C_2 s \leftarrow Y_2(s) \text{ (shunt)}$$
$$\underline{s^3 + 1.5s}$$
$$\tfrac{5}{2} s \overline{\big)\, 6s^2 + 9} \,\big(\, \tfrac{12}{5} \leftarrow L_3 \cdot s \leftarrow Z_3(s) \text{ (series)}$$
$$\underline{6s^2}$$
$$9 \overline{\big)\, \tfrac{5}{2} s} \,\big(\, \tfrac{5}{18} s \leftarrow C_4 s \leftarrow Y_4(s) \text{ (shunt)}$$
$$\underline{\tfrac{5}{2} s}$$
$$00$$

Corresponding CFE is as shown below.

$$Z(s) = s + \cfrac{1}{\cfrac{s}{6} + \cfrac{1}{\cfrac{12}{5} s + \cfrac{1}{\cfrac{5}{18} s}}}$$

Cauer-II Form:

Method I: By removal of pole at the origin

Partial fraction expansion of Z(s) gives a terms of $\dfrac{9}{4s}$ which has a pole at the origin (s = 0).

Since Cauer-II form is obtained by removing a pole at the origin, removal of $\dfrac{9}{4s}$ from Z(s) gives

$$Z_1(s) = \dfrac{s^4 + 10s^2 + 9}{s^3 + 4s} - \dfrac{9}{4s} = \dfrac{s\left(s^2 + \dfrac{31}{4}\right)}{s^2 + 4}$$

This function has a zero at the origin. But its reciprocal $Y_1(s) = \dfrac{1}{Z_1(s)}$ has a pole at the origin with term $\dfrac{16}{31s}$ in its partial fraction expansion. Removing this form $Y_1(s)$ gives $Y_2(s)$.

$$Y_2(s) = \dfrac{s^2 + 4}{s\left(s^2 + \dfrac{31}{4}\right)} - \dfrac{16}{31s} = \dfrac{\dfrac{15}{31s}}{\left(s^2 + \dfrac{31}{4}\right)}$$

Above procedure is repeated by subtracting $\dfrac{961}{60s}$ from $Z_2(s) = \dfrac{1}{Y_2(s)}$ giving

$$Z_3(s) = \dfrac{\left(s^2 + \dfrac{31}{4}\right)}{\dfrac{15}{31}s} - \dfrac{961}{60s} = \dfrac{31}{15}s$$

Finally $\quad Y_3(s) = \dfrac{1}{Z_3(s)} = \dfrac{15}{31s}$

The steps carried out above are shown in Fig. 5.25.

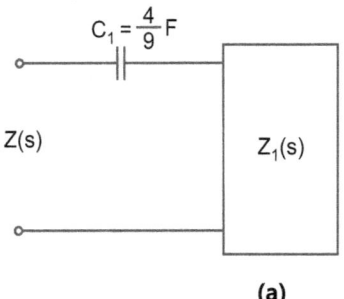
(a)

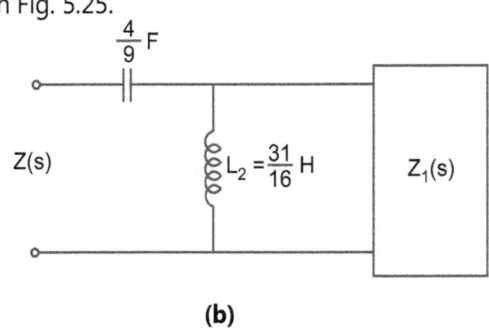
(b)

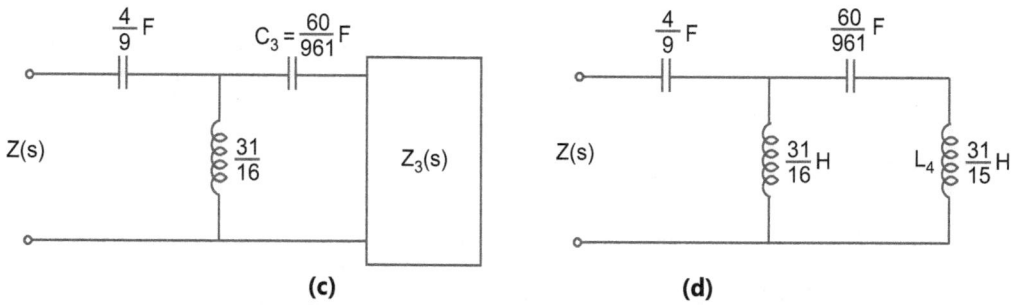

(c)   (d)

Fig. 5.25: Steps in Development of Cauer-II Form of Network

Method II: Continued Fraction Expansion (CFE) Method

Cauer-II form of the network is obtained by CFE about pole at the origin (s = 0).

$$4s + s^3 \overline{)9 + 10s^2 + s^4} \left(\frac{9}{4s} \leftarrow \frac{1}{C_1 s} \right.$$

$$\underline{9 + \frac{9}{4}s^2}$$

$$\frac{31}{4}s^2 + s^4 \overline{)4s + s^3} \left(\frac{16}{31\ s} \leftarrow \frac{1}{L_2 s} \right.$$

$$\underline{4s + \frac{16}{31}s^3}$$

$$\frac{15}{31}s^3 \overline{)\frac{31}{4}s^2 + s^4} \left(\frac{961}{60s} \leftarrow \frac{1}{C_3 s} \right.$$

$$\underline{\frac{31}{4}s^2}$$

$$s^4 \overline{)\frac{15}{31}s^3} \left(\frac{15}{31s} \leftarrow \frac{1}{L_4 s} \right.$$

$$\underline{\frac{15}{31}s^3}$$

$$00$$

Corresponding CFE is

$$Z(s) = \frac{9}{4s} + \cfrac{1}{\frac{16}{31s} + \cfrac{1}{\frac{961}{60s} + \cfrac{1}{\frac{15}{31s}}}}$$

Ex. 5.27: Synthesis the following impedance function in Cauer-II form.

$$Z(s) = \frac{s^3 + 2s}{s^4 + 4s^2 + 3}$$

Sol.:

$$Z(s) = \frac{s[s^2 + 2]}{(s^2 + 3)(s^2 + 1)} = \frac{s^3 + 2s}{s^4 + 4s^2 + 3}$$

By the properties given in Table 5.2, the given function is an L-C impedance function. Cauer-II form is obtained by *CFE about pole at the origin*. But since Z(s) has a zero, s = 0. Hence $Y(s) = \dfrac{1}{Z(s)} = \dfrac{s^4 + 4s^2 + 3}{s(s^2 + 2)}$ has a pole of the origin. Hence CFE of Y(s) is carried out. Referring Fig. 5.23, capacitor 'C_1' is absent.

$$2s + s^3 \overline{)\, 3 + 4s^2 + s^4} \left(\dfrac{3}{2s} \leftarrow \dfrac{1}{L_2 s} \leftarrow Y_2(s) \text{ (shunt)}\right.$$

$$\underline{3 + \dfrac{3}{2}s^2}$$

$$\dfrac{5}{2}s^2 \overline{)\, 2s + s^3} \left(\dfrac{4}{5s} \leftarrow \dfrac{1}{C_3 s} \leftarrow Z_3(s) \text{ (series)}\right.$$

$$\underline{2s + \dfrac{4}{5}s^3}$$

$$\dfrac{s^3}{5} \overline{)\, \dfrac{5}{2}s^2 + s^4} \left(\dfrac{25}{2s} \leftarrow \dfrac{1}{L_4 s} \leftarrow Y_4(s) \text{ (shunt)}\right.$$

$$\underline{\dfrac{5}{2}s^2}$$

$$s^4 \overline{)\, \dfrac{s^3}{5}} \left(\dfrac{1}{5s} \leftarrow \dfrac{1}{C_5 s} \leftarrow Z_5(s) \text{ (series)}\right.$$

$$\underline{\dfrac{s^3}{5}}$$
$$00$$

Hence Cauer-II form of the network is as shown in Fig. 5.17.

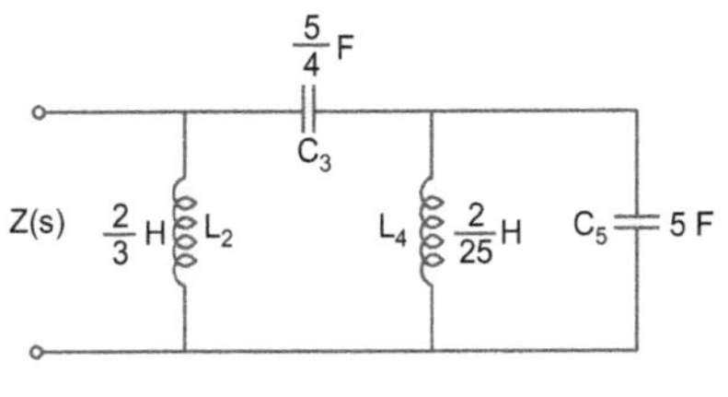

Fig. 5.26: Cauer-II form of Network for Ex. 5.27

Ex. 5.28: Synthesise the following network function in a realizable form.

$$Z(s) = \dfrac{6s^4 + 42s^2 + 48}{s^5 + 18s^3 + 48s}$$

Sol.: This is an L-C driving point impedance function having a pole at s = 0. This can be realized in Cauer-II form of the network as shown below.

Cauer-I Form:

It can be obtained as shown below.

$Z(s)$ does not have a pole at $s = \infty$ but $Y(s) = \dfrac{1}{Z(s)}$ has a pole at $s = \infty$. Hence, expand $Y(s)$ as a CFE about $s = \infty$.

where,
$$Y(s) = \dfrac{s^5 + 18s^3 + 48s}{6s^4 + 12s^2 + 48}$$

$$6s^4 + 42s^2 + 48 \,\overline{)\, s^5 + 18s^3 + 4s\,} \left(\dfrac{s}{6} \leftarrow C_2 s \leftarrow Y_2(s)\ \text{(shunt)} \right.$$

$$\underline{s^5 + 7s^3 + 8s}$$

$$11s^3 + 40s \,\overline{)\, 6s^4 + 42s^2 + 48 \,} \left(\dfrac{6}{11} s \leftarrow L_3 s \leftarrow Z_3(s)\ \text{(series)} \right.$$

$$\underline{6s^4 + \dfrac{240}{11} s^2}$$

$$\dfrac{222}{11} s^2 + 48 \,\overline{)\, 11s^3 + 40s \,} \left(\dfrac{121}{222} s \leftarrow C_4 s\ Y_4(s)\ \text{(shunt)} \right.$$

$$\underline{11s^3 + \dfrac{5808s}{222}}$$

$$\dfrac{3072}{222} s \,\overline{)\, \dfrac{222}{11} s^2 + 48 \,} \left(\dfrac{49284}{33792} s \leftarrow L_4 s \leftarrow Z_4(s)\ \text{(series)} \right.$$

$$\underline{\dfrac{222}{11} s^2}$$

$$48 \,\overline{)\, \dfrac{3072}{222} s \,} \left(\dfrac{127}{444} s \leftarrow C_5 s \leftarrow Y_5(s)\ \text{(shunt)} \right.$$

$$\underline{\dfrac{3072}{222} s}$$

$$00$$

Hence, Cauer-I form of the network is as shown in Fig. 5.27.

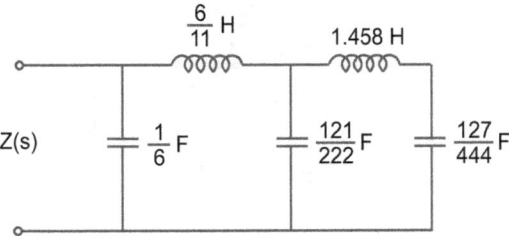

Fig. 5.27: Cauer-I Form of Network for Example. 5.28

Cauer-II Form:

$$48s + 18s^2 + s^5 \overline{\smash{\big)}\ 48 + 42s^2 + 6s^4} \left(\frac{1}{s} \leftarrow \frac{1}{C_1 s} \leftarrow Z_1(s) \text{ (series)} \right.$$

$$\underline{48 + 18s^2 + s^4}$$

$$24s^2 + 5s^4 \overline{\smash{\big)}\ 48s + 18s^3 + s^5} \left(\frac{2}{5} \leftarrow \frac{1}{L_2 s} \leftarrow Y_2(s) \text{ (shunt)} \right.$$

$$\underline{48s + 10s^3}$$

$$8s^3 + s^5 \overline{\smash{\big)}\ 24s^2 + 5s^4} \left(\frac{3}{s} \leftarrow \frac{1}{C_3 s} \leftarrow Z_3(s) \text{ (series)} \right.$$

$$\underline{24s^2 + 3s^4}$$

$$2s^4$$

Now the remainder is an impedance $Z_1(s) = \dfrac{2s^4}{8s^3 + s^5}$

Thus, $\quad Z_1(s) = \dfrac{1}{\dfrac{s}{2} + \dfrac{4}{s}} = \dfrac{1}{C_5 s + \dfrac{1}{L_4 s}} \leftarrow$ (series impedance)

Hence, $\quad Z(s) = \dfrac{1}{s} + \dfrac{1}{\dfrac{2}{5} + \dfrac{1}{\dfrac{3}{s} + \dfrac{1}{\dfrac{s}{2} + \dfrac{4}{s}}}}$

Hence, the realized network is as shown in Fig. 5.28.

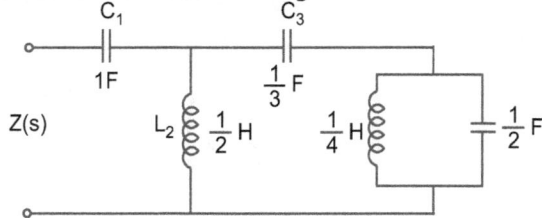

Fig. 5.28: Cauer-II Form of Network for Example. 5.28

Foster-I Form: This is obtained by partial fraction expansion of Z(s).

$$Z(s) = \frac{6s^4 + 42s^2 + 48}{s^5 + 18s^3 + 48s}$$

$$= \frac{6\,[s^2 + 5.56]\,[s^2 + 14.4]}{s\,[s^2 + 14.75]\,[s^2 + 3.26]}$$

$$= 1 \cdot \frac{k_0}{s} + \frac{2k_1 s}{(s^2 + 14.75)} + \frac{2k_2 s}{(s^2 + 3.26)}$$

$$k_0 = sZ(s)\Big|_{s \to 0} = \frac{6(5.56)(1.44)}{(14.75)(3.26)} = 1$$

$$2k_1 = \frac{(s^2 + 14.75)}{s} Z(s)\Big|_{s^2 \to -14.75}$$

$$= \frac{6(-9.19)(-11.5)}{(-14.75)(-11.5)} = 3.74$$

$$2k_2 = \frac{(s^2 + 3.26)}{s} Z(s)\Big|_{s^2 \to -3.26}$$

$$= \frac{6(2.3)(-1.82)}{(-3.26)(11.5)} = 0.68$$

Hence,
$$Z(s) = \frac{1}{s} + \frac{3.74s}{(s^2 + 14.75)} + \frac{0.68s}{(s^2 + 3.26)}$$

$$Z(s) = \frac{1}{s} + \frac{1}{\left(0.267s + \frac{3.94}{s}\right)} + \frac{1}{\left(1.47s + \frac{4.8}{s}\right)}$$

Hence, Foster-I form of the network is as shown in Fig. 5.29.

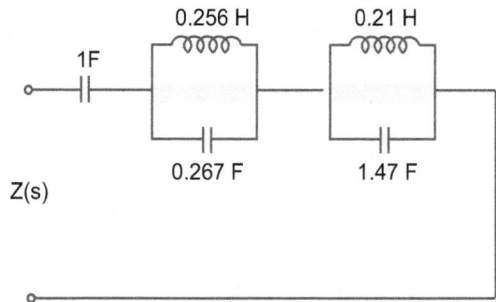

Fig. 5.29 (a): Foster-I Form of Network

Foster-II Form: This is obtained by partial fraction expansion of Y(s).

$$Y(S) = \frac{s[s^2 + 14.75][s^2 + 3.26]}{6[s^2 + 5.56][s^2 + 1.44]}$$

$$= \frac{k_0}{s} + \frac{2k_1 s}{[s^2 + 5.56]} + \frac{2k_2 s}{[s^2 + 1.44]} + k_\infty s$$

$$k_0 = sY(s)\Big|_{s \to 0} = 0$$

$$2k_1 = \frac{(s^2 + 5.56)}{s} Y(s)\Big|_{s^2 \to -5.56}$$

∴ $$2k_1 = \frac{[+9.19][-2.3]}{6[-4.21]} = 0.85$$

$$2k_2 = \frac{(s^2 + 1.44) Y(s)}{s}\bigg|_{s^2 = -1.44}$$

$$= \frac{(1.82)(13.31)}{(4.12) 6} = 0.98$$

$$k_\infty = \frac{Y(s)}{s}\bigg|_{s \to \infty} = \frac{s^2\left(1 + \frac{14.75}{s^2}\right) s^2\left(1 + \frac{3.26}{s^2}\right)}{6s^2\left[1 + \frac{5.56}{s^2}\right] \times s^2\left[1 + \frac{1.44}{s^2}\right]}$$

$$= \frac{1}{6} = 0.166$$

Hence,

$$Y(s) = \frac{0.85s}{(s^2 + 5.56)} + \frac{0.98s}{(s^2 + 1.44)} + 0.166s$$

$$= \frac{1}{1.18s + \frac{6.54}{s}} + \frac{1}{1.02s + \frac{1.47}{s}} + \frac{s}{6}$$

Hence Foster-II form of the network corresponding to Y(s) is as shown in Fig. 5.29 (b).

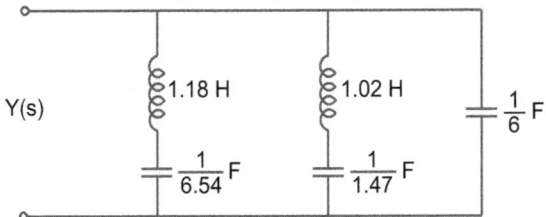

Fig. 5.29 (b): Foster-II Form of Network

Ex. 5.29: Input impedance of the network shown in Fig. 5.30 is $Z_{in} = \dfrac{2s^2 + 2}{s^3 + 2s^2 + 2s + 2}$.

If Z_0 is an L-C function,

(1) Find the expression for Z_0.

(2) Synthesise Z_0 in Foster-I form of the network.

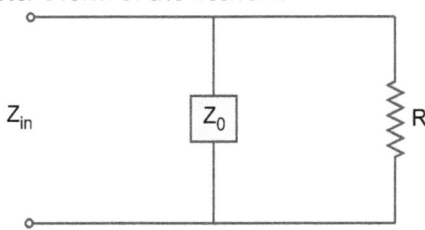

Fig. 5.30: Network given in Example. 5.29

Sol.: From the given network

$$Z_{in} = \cfrac{1}{G + \cfrac{1}{Z_0}} \quad \ldots (A)$$

Now the given $Z_{in} = \dfrac{2s^2 + 2}{s^3 + 2s^2 + 2s + 2}$ can be written as

$$Z_{in} = \cfrac{1}{1 + \cfrac{s^3 + 2s}{2s^2 + 2}} \quad \ldots (B)$$

Comparing (A) and (B) we get $G = R = 1$.

Hence $\quad Z_0 = \dfrac{2s^2 + 2}{s^3 + 2s} = \dfrac{2(s^2 + 1)}{s(s^2 + 2)}$

is the required expression for Z_0.

Partial fraction expansion of $Z_0(s)$ gives

$$Z_0(s) = \dfrac{2(s^2 + 1)}{s(s^2 + 2)}$$

$$= \dfrac{k_0}{s} + \dfrac{2k_1 s}{(s^2 + 2)} + k_\infty \cdot s$$

$$k_0 = sZ_0(s) \Big|_{s \to 0}$$

$$= \dfrac{2}{2} = 1$$

$$2k_1 = \dfrac{(s^2 + 2) Z_0(s)}{s} \Big|_{s^2 \to -2}$$

$$= \dfrac{2(-1)}{-2} = 1$$

$$k_\infty = \dfrac{Z_0(s)}{s} \Big|_{s \to \infty} = \dfrac{2s^2 \left[1 + \dfrac{1}{s^2}\right]}{s^4 \left[1 + \dfrac{2}{s^2}\right]} \Bigg|_{s \to \infty} = 0$$

Hence $Z_0(s)$ can be written as

$$Z_0(s) = \dfrac{1}{s} + \dfrac{s}{s^2 + 2} = \dfrac{1}{s} + \dfrac{1}{\left(s + \dfrac{2}{s}\right)}$$

Hence Foster-(I) form of the network is as shown in Fig. 5.31 (a). And, the given network can be expressed as shown in Fig. 5.31 (b).

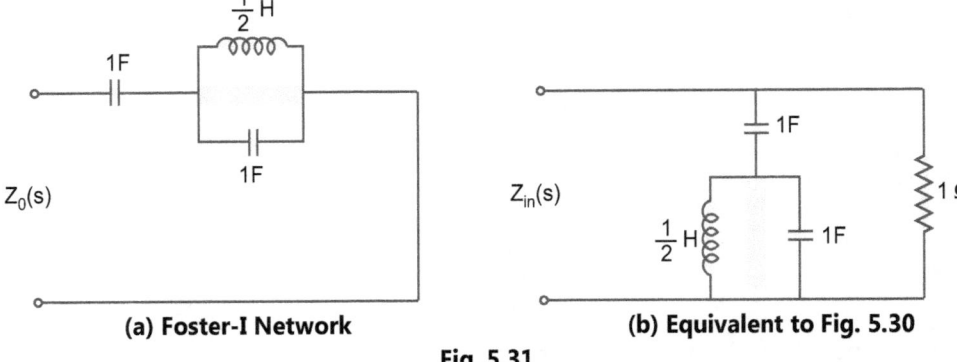

(a) Foster-I Network   (b) Equivalent to Fig. 5.30

Fig. 5.31

Ex. 5.30: Synthesise the following function in Foster-I and Cauer-I form of the network.

$$F(s) = \frac{s^6 + 5s^4 + 6.75s^2 + 2.25}{s^5 + 3s^3 + 2s}$$

Sol.: F(s) can be written as

$$F(s) = \frac{(s^2 + 0.5)(s^2 + 1.5)(s^2 + 3)}{s[s^2 + 1][s^2 + 2]}$$

Poles are at $s = 0, \pm j1, \pm j\sqrt{2}$.
Zeros are at $s = \pm j\sqrt{0.5}, \pm j\sqrt{1.5}, \pm j\sqrt{3}$.
As poles and zeros are interlaced on $j\omega$ axis, the function is an L-C impedance function.

Foster-I Form: Partial fraction expansion of F(s) gives

$$F(s) = \frac{k_0}{s} + \frac{2k_1 s}{(s^2 + 1)} + \frac{2k_2 s}{(s^2 + 2)} + k_\infty \cdot s$$

$$k_0 = sF(s)\Big|_{s \to 0}$$

$$= \frac{(0.5)(1.5)(3)}{1 \times 2}$$

$$= 1.125$$

$$2k_1 = \frac{(s^2 + 2)}{s} F(s)\Big|_{s^2 \to -2} = 0.5$$

$$2k_2 = \frac{s^2 + 2}{s} F(s)\Big|_{s^2 \to -2} = 0.375$$

$$k_\infty = \frac{F(s)}{s}\Big|_{s \to \infty} = 1.0$$

$$F(s) = \frac{1.125}{s} + \frac{0.5s}{s^2 + 1} + \frac{0.375s}{(s^2 + 2)} + s$$

$$= \frac{1.125}{s} + \frac{1}{2s + \frac{2}{s}} + \frac{1}{2.66s + \frac{5.33}{s}} + s$$

Hence, Foster-I form of the network is as shown in Fig. 5.32.

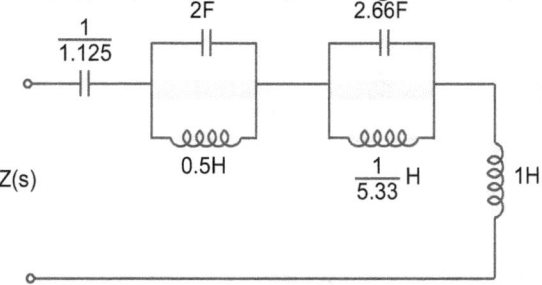

Fig. 5.32: Foster-I Form of Network

Cauer-I Form: This is obtained by removal of pole at s = ∞. This is done by CFE of Z(s).

$$s^5 + 3s^3 + 2s \overline{)s^6 + 5s^4 + 6.75s^2 + 2.25} \left(s \leftarrow L_1 s \right.$$

$$\underline{s^5 + 3s^4 + 2s^2}$$

$$2s^4 + 4.75s^2 + 2.25 \overline{)s^5 + 3s^3 + 2s} \left(\frac{s}{2} \leftarrow C_2 s \right.$$

$$\underline{s^5 + 2.37s^3 + 1.125s}$$

$$0.63s^3 + 0.875s \overline{)2s^4 + 4.75s^2 + 2.25} \left(3.17s \leftarrow L_3 s \right.$$

$$\underline{2s^4 + 2.77s^2}$$

$$2s^2 + 2.25 \overline{)0.63s^3 + 0.875s} \left(\frac{s}{3.17} \leftarrow C_4 s \right.$$

$$\underline{0.63s^3 + 0.71s}$$

$$0.165s \overline{)2s^2 + 2.25} \left(12.12 s \leftarrow L_5 s \right.$$

$$\underline{2s^2}$$

$$2.25 \overline{)0.165s} \left(\frac{s}{13.630} \leftarrow C_6 s \right.$$

$$\underline{0.165s}$$

$$00$$

Hence, Cauer-I form of the network is as shown in Fig. 5.33.

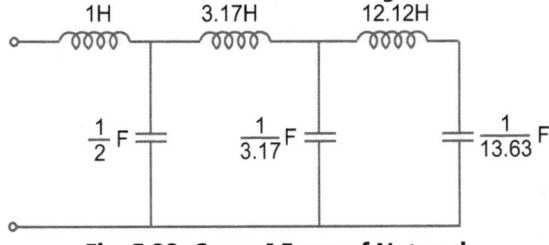

Fig. 5.33: Cauer-I Form of Network

5.14 SYNTHESIS OF DRIVING POINT FUNCTIONS OF RC NETWORK

R-C network consists of only resistors and capacitors as a circuit elements. The driving point impedance function $Z_{RC}(s)$ and driving point admittance function $Y_{RC}(s)$ have *some properties which are same* (or common). But *some other properties are different for them*. We shall start our discussion of R-C network synthesis by studying the properties of R-C network functions.

5.14.1 Properties of R-C Network Functions ($Z_{RC}(s)$ and $Y_{RC}(s)$)]

Fig. 5.34 shows simple series R-C and parallel R-C networks.

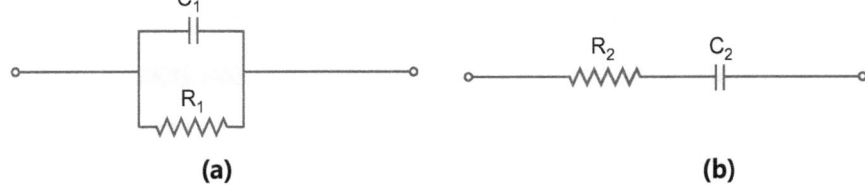

Fig. 5.34: Two Simple R-C Networks

For the parallel R-C network of Fig. 5.34 (a), we have

$$Z_1(s) = \frac{R_1 \times \frac{1}{C_1 s}}{R_1 + \frac{1}{C_1 s}}$$

$$= \frac{1}{C_1 \left[s + \frac{1}{R_1 C_1} \right]} \quad \ldots (5.18)$$

For series R-C network of Fig. 5.34 (b), we have

$$Y_1(s) = \frac{1}{R_2 + \frac{1}{sC_2}}$$

$$= \frac{s}{R_2 \left[s + \frac{1}{R_2 C_2} \right]} \quad \ldots (5.19)$$

A comparison of the above two equations shows, that both have poles on the negative real axis of the s-plane. The comparison also shows that $Z(s)$ and $\frac{Y(s)}{s}$, and not $Y(s)$, have the same form for these two particular networks. Properties of R-C impedance and R-C admittance are summarized in Table 5.6 and Table 5.7 respectively.

Table 5.6: Properties of R-C Driving Impedance Function $Z_{RC}(s)$

No.	Properties
1.	Poles and zeros of $Z_{RC}(s)$ are on the negative real axis of s-plane and are simple.
2.	Poles and zeros are interlaced.
3.	Critical frequency nearest to the origin is a pole. There can be a pole at the origin (this indicates a series capacitor). There cannot be a zero at the origin (this indicates an inductor).
4.	Highest critical frequency (critical frequency farthest from the origin) is a zero. This zero can be at infinity (this would indicate a shunt capacitor). There cannot be a pole at infinity (this indicates an inductor).
5.	Slope of $\dfrac{d Z_{RC}}{d\sigma}$ is strictly negative as shown in Fig. 5.35 (a).
6.	$Z_{RC}(0) > Z_{RC}(\infty)$ as shown in Fig. 5.35 (a).
7.	If $Z_{RC}(s) = \dfrac{p(s)}{q(s)}$ then the order of q(s) must be one greater than, or equal to, that of p(s).
8.	Residues at the poles of $Z_{RC}(s)$ are all positive and real.

Table 5.7: Properties of R-C Driving Point Admittance Function $Y_{RC}(s)$

No.	Properties
1.	Poles and zeros of $Y_{RC}(s)$ are all on the negative real axis of s-plane and are simple.
2.	Poles and zeros of $Y_{RC}(s)$ are interlaced.
3.	Lowest critical frequency (nearest to the origin) is zero and it can be at the origin. Therefore, there will be a pole at the origin.
4.	Lowest critical frequency (farthest from the origin) is a pole and this can be at infinity. There cannot be a zero at infinity.
5.	Slope of $\dfrac{dY_{RC}(s)}{d\sigma}$ is strictly positive as shown in Fig. 5.35 (b).
6.	If $Y_{RC}(s) = \dfrac{p(s)}{q(s)}$, then order of p(s) must be one greater than, or equal to, that of q(s).
7.	Residue at the poles of $Y_{RC}(s)$ are real and negative, while that of $\dfrac{Y_{RC}(s)}{s}$ are real and positive.
8.	$Y_{RC}(0) \leq Y_{RC}(\infty)$, as shown in Fig. 5.35 (b).

It can be shown that:

1. R-C admittance $Y_{RC}(s)$ and R-C admittance $Y_{LC}(s)$ are related by the following transformation.

$$Y_{RC}(s) = pY_{LC}(p)\Big|_{p^2 = s} \qquad \ldots (5.20)$$

2. R-C impedance $Z_{RC}(s)$ and L-C impedance $Z_{LC}(s)$ are related by the following transformation.

$$Z_{RC}(s) = \frac{1}{p} Z_{LC}(p)\Big|_{p^2 = s} \qquad \ldots (5.21)$$

Fig. 5.35 (a) and Fig. 5.35 (b) show the plots of R-C impedance and R-C admittance function respectively.

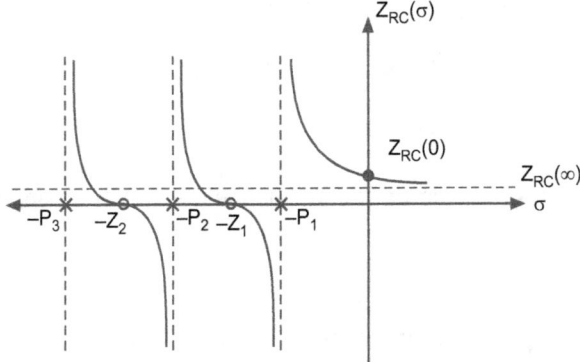

Fig. 5.35: (a) Plot of $Z_{RC}(\sigma)$ Against 'σ'

$$Z_{RC}(s) = \frac{k(s + Z_1)(s + Z_2)}{(s + p_1)(s + p_2)}$$

$$0 \leq p_1 < Z_1 < p_2 < Z_2 < P_3$$

Fig. 5.35 (b): Plot of $Y_{RC}(\sigma)$ against 'σ'

$$Y_{RC}(s) = \frac{k(s + Z_1)(s + Z_2)(s + Z_3)}{(s + p_1)(s + p_2)}$$

$$0 \leq Z_1 < P_1 < Z_2 < p_2 < Z_3$$

5.14.2 Synthesis (Realization) of R-C Networks

Just as in the case of reactance (L-C) functions, R-C functions can also be realized in 4 different ways. $Z_{RC}(s)$ can appear in one of the two forms shown below:

$$Z_{RC}(s) = \frac{H(s + \sigma_1)(s + \sigma_3)}{s(s + \sigma_2)} \quad \ldots (5.22)$$

Or
$$Z_{RC}(s) = \frac{H(s + \sigma_2)(s + \sigma_4)}{(s + \sigma_1)(s + \sigma_3)} \quad \ldots (5.23)$$

The four canonical forms of realization are:

(1) Foster-I Form:

This is obtained by the partial function expansion of $Z_{RC}(s)$. Thus

$$Z_{RC}(s) = \frac{k_0}{s} + \sum_{i=1}^{n} \frac{k_i}{(s + \sigma_i)} + k_\infty \quad \ldots (5.24)$$

where
$$k_0 = s\, Z_{RC}(s)\Big|_{s \to 0}$$

$$k_\infty = Z_{RC}(s)\Big|_{s \to \infty}$$

and
$$k_i = (s + \sigma_i)\, Z_{RC}(s)\Big|_{s \to \sigma_k}$$

Thus Equation (5.17) can be written as

$$Z_{RC}(s) = \frac{1}{\frac{s}{k_0}} + \sum_{i=1}^{n} \frac{1}{\frac{s}{k_i} + \frac{\sigma_i}{k_i}} + k_\infty \quad \ldots (5.25)$$

Foster-I form of the network corresponding to Equation (5.25) is shown in Fig. 5.36 (a).

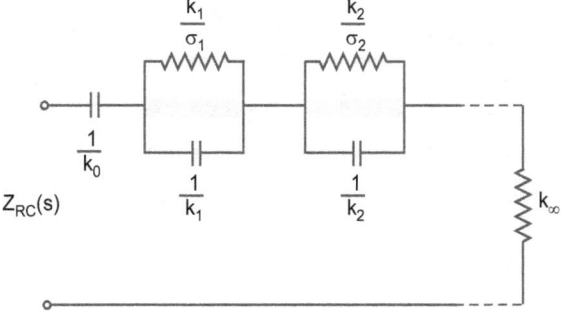

Fig. 5.36 (a): Foster-I Form of Network

(2) Foster-II Form:

Since $Y_{RC}(s) = \dfrac{1}{Z_{RC}(s)}$ has a negative residue at its pole, Foster-II form is obtained by expanding $\dfrac{Y_{RC}(s)}{s}$ as shown below.

$$\dfrac{Y_{RC}(s)}{s} = \dfrac{k_0}{s} + \sum_{i=1}^{n} \dfrac{k_i}{(s+\sigma_i)} + k_\infty \qquad \ldots (5.26)$$

Multiplying this equation by 's'

$$Y_{RC}(s) = k_0 + \sum_{i=1}^{n} \dfrac{k_i s}{(s+\sigma_i)} + k_\infty \cdot s$$

Or

$$Y_{RC}(s) = k_0 + \sum_{i=1}^{n} \dfrac{1}{\dfrac{1}{k_i} + \dfrac{\sigma_i}{k_i s}} + k_\infty \cdot s \qquad \ldots (5.27)$$

Foster-II form of the network corresponding to Equation (5.27) is shown in Fig. 5.37 (b).

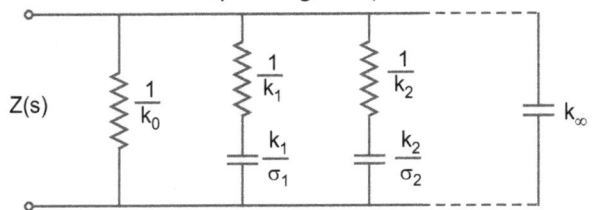

Fig. 5.37 (b): Foster-II Form of Network

First and the last elements in Foster R-C networks is shown in Table 5.8.

Table 5.8: First and Last Elements in Foster R-C Networks

Form	Behaviour of Z(s) at the origin	First element	Behaviour of Z(s) at infinity	Last element
Foster-I	Pole	C	Constant	R
	Constant	None	Zero	None
Foster-II	Constant	R	Zero	C
	Pole	None	Constant	None

Following example explains how to obtain Foster-I and Foster-II forms of a network.

Ex. 5.31: Find the Foster-I and Foster-II forms of the function $Z(s) = \dfrac{(s+1)(s+3)}{s(s+2)}$

Sol.: Foster-I Form: Partial fraction expansion of Z(s) gives

$$Z(s) = \dfrac{k_0}{s} + \dfrac{k_1}{(s+2)} + k_\infty$$

The residue is

$$k_0 = sZ(s)\Big|_{s \to 0} = \frac{1 \times 3}{2} = \frac{3}{2}$$

$$k_\infty = Z(s)\Big|_{s \to \infty} = \frac{s\left[1+\frac{1}{s}\right]s\left[1+\frac{3}{s}\right]}{s^2\left[1+\frac{2}{s}\right]}\Bigg|_{s \to \infty} = 1$$

$$k_1 = (s+2)Z(s)\Big|_{s \to -2} = \frac{(-1) \times (1)}{-2} = \frac{1}{2}$$

Hence,
$$Z(s) = \frac{3}{2s} + \frac{1}{2(s+2)} + 1$$

Hence, the Foster-I form of the network is as shown in Fig. 5.38 (a).

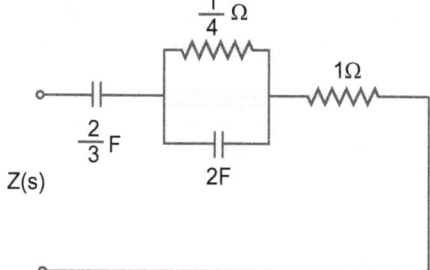

Fig. 5.38 (a): Foster-I Form of Network

Foster-II Form: This is obtained by partial fraction expansion of $\frac{Y(s)}{s}$.

$$\frac{Y(s)}{s} = \frac{(s+2)}{(s+1)(s+3)}$$

$$= \frac{k_1}{(s+1)} + \frac{k_2}{(s+3)}$$

$$k_1 = (s+1)\frac{Y(s)}{s}\Big|_{s \to -1} = \frac{1}{2}$$

$$k_2 = (s+3)\frac{Y(s)}{s}\Big|_{s \to -3} = \frac{(-1)}{(-2)} = \frac{1}{2}$$

Hence
$$\frac{Y(s)}{s} = \frac{\frac{1}{2}}{(s+1)} + \frac{\frac{1}{2}}{(s+3)}$$

∴
$$Y(s) = \frac{s/2}{(s+1)} + \frac{s/2}{(s+3)} = \frac{1}{\left(\frac{2}{s}+2\right)} + \frac{1}{\left(2+\frac{6}{s}\right)}$$

Hence Foster-II form of the network is as shown in Fig. 5.38 (b).

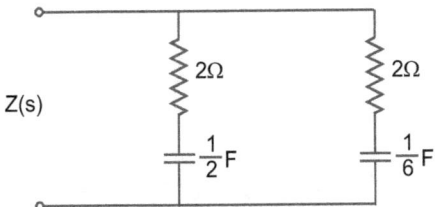

Fig. 5.38 (b): Foster-II Form of Network

(3) Cauer-I Form:

It is obtained by removal of a pole from the impedance function at $s = \infty$. This is same as CFE about infinity of an impedance function.

According to the property of R-C impedance function, maximum constant that can be removed is $Z_{RC}(\infty)$. Removal of this constant is equivalent to dividing the numerator by the denominator to eliminate the highest power of 's' in the numerator. If the impedance function has a zero at infinity, we can not remove the constant. [Hence first Resistor (β_1) is absent].

Reciprocal of impedance will have a pole at infinity, which is then removed as a capacitor. Then the process is repeated by removing constant from the impedance function and pole at '∞' from the admittance function. The CFE gives

$$Z(s) = \beta_1 + \cfrac{1}{\beta_2 s + \cfrac{1}{\beta_3 s + \cfrac{1}{\beta_4 s} + \cfrac{1}{\cdots}}} \qquad \ldots (5.28)$$

The corresponding Cauer-I form of the network is shown in Fig. 5.39.

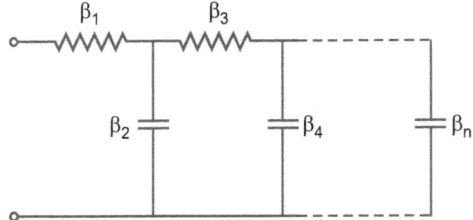

Fig. 5.39 : Cauer-I Form of R-C Network

(4) Cauer-II Form:

This is obtained by removal of a pole from the impedance function at the origin ($s = 0$). This is the same as CFE at the origin of impedance function.

If the given impedance function has a pole at the origin, it is removed as a capacitor (γ_1). Reciprocal of the remainder function has a minimum value at $s = 0$, which is removed as a constant of resistor (γ_2). If the original impedance function has no pole at the origin then the first capacitor is absent. The process is repeated with the removal of constant corresponding to resistor (γ_2).

CFE about the origin gives

$$Z(s) = \frac{1}{\gamma_1 s} + \cfrac{1}{\gamma_2 + \cfrac{1}{\gamma_2 s + \cfrac{1}{\gamma_4} + \ldots}}$$

The corresponding Cauer-II form of the network is shown in Fig. 5.40.

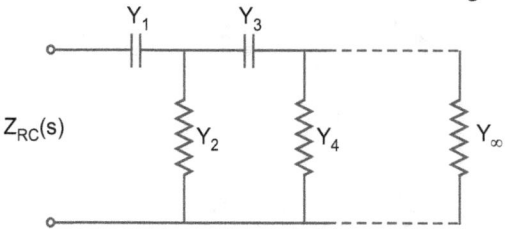

Fig. 5.40 : Cauer-II Form of R-C Network

Following examples illustrate the above procedure.

Ex. 5.32 : Obtain Cauer-I, Cauer-II forms of network for the function

$$Z(s) = \frac{(s+1)(s+3)}{s(s+2)}$$

Sol.: Cauer I Form:

Given
$$Z(s) = \frac{s^2 + 4s + 3}{s^2 + 2s}$$

CFE gives

$$s^2 + 2s \overline{)\, s^2 + 4s + 3\,} \bigl(1 \leftarrow R_1 \leftarrow \text{(series impedance)}$$
$$\underline{s^2 + 2s}$$

$$2s + 3 \overline{)\, s^2 + 2s\,} \bigl(\tfrac{s}{2} \leftarrow C_2 s \leftarrow Y_2(s) \text{ (shunt)}$$
$$\underline{s^2 + \tfrac{3}{2}s}$$

$$\tfrac{s}{2} \overline{)\, 2s + 3\,} \bigl(4 \leftarrow R_3 \leftarrow \text{(series impedance)}$$
$$\underline{2s}$$

$$3 \overline{)\, \tfrac{s}{2}\,} \bigl(\tfrac{s}{6} \leftarrow C_4 s \leftarrow Y_4(s) \text{ (shunt)}$$
$$\underline{\tfrac{s}{2}}$$
$$00$$

Hence, the Cauer-I form of the network is as shown in Fig. 5.41.

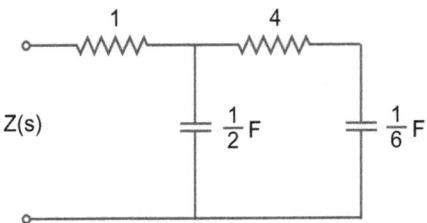

Fig. 5.41 : Cauer-I Form of Network

Cauer-II Form:

CFE about the origin gives

$$2s + s^2 \overline{) 3 + 4s + s^2} \left(\frac{3}{2s} \leftarrow \frac{1}{C_1 s} \leftarrow Z_1(s) \text{ (series)} \right.$$

$$\underline{3 + \frac{3}{2}s}$$

$$\frac{5}{2}s + s^2 \overline{) 2s + s^2} \left(\frac{4}{5} \leftarrow \frac{1}{R_2} \leftarrow Y_2 \text{ (shunt)} \right.$$

$$\underline{2s + \frac{4}{5}s^2}$$

$$\frac{s^2}{5} \overline{) \frac{5}{2}s + s^2} \left(\frac{25}{2s} \leftarrow \frac{1}{C_3 s} \leftarrow Z_3(s) \text{ (series)} \right.$$

$$\underline{\frac{5}{2}s}$$

$$s^2 \overline{) \frac{s^2}{5}} \left(\frac{1}{5} \leftarrow \frac{1}{R_4} \leftarrow Y_4 \text{ (shunt)} \right.$$

$$\underline{\frac{s^2}{5}}$$

$$0$$

Hence, the Cauer-II form of the network is as shown in Fig. 5.42.

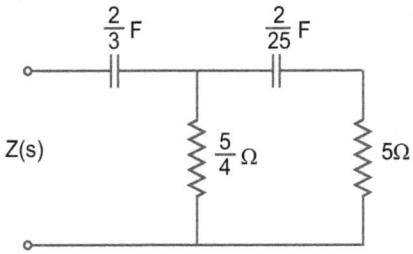

Fig. 5.42 : Cauer-II Form of Network

Ex. 5.33: A designer requires the network with following data :
(1) An impedance function has simple poles at – 2 and – 6.
(2) It has simple zeros at – 3 and – 7.
(3) Z(0) = 20 ohms.
Is it possible to Synthesise Z(s) as a passive network? If yes, then realize Z(s) in one Cauer and one foster form.

Sol.: With the given data, the impedance function is

$$Z(s) = \frac{k(s+3)(s+7)}{(s+2)(s+6)}.$$ Since it is given Z(0) = 20

We have, $Z(0) = 20 = \dfrac{k \times 3 \times 7}{2 \times 6}$ ∴ $k = \dfrac{80}{7}$

Hence $Z(s) = \dfrac{80}{7} \dfrac{(s+3)(s+7)}{(s+2)(s+6)}$

Since the residues at the poles are positive, (as shown below), this can be realized as a R-C network.

Foster-I Form: This is obtained by partial fraction expansion of Z(s).

$$Z(s) = \frac{80}{7}\left[\frac{(s+3)(s+7)}{(s+2)(s+6)}\right] = \frac{80}{7}\left[\frac{s^2+10s+21}{s^2+8s+12}\right]$$

$$= \frac{80}{7}\left[1 + \frac{2s+9}{(s+2)(s+6)}\right]$$

$$= \frac{80}{7}\left[1 + \frac{K_0}{(s+2)} + \frac{K_1}{(s+6)}\right]$$

$$= \frac{80}{7}\left[1 + \frac{5}{4(s+2)} + \frac{3}{4(s+6)}\right]$$

$$= \frac{80}{7} + \frac{1}{\frac{28s}{400} + \frac{56}{400}} + \frac{1}{\frac{28s}{240} + \frac{108}{240}}$$

The realized Foster-I form of the network is shown in Fig. 5.43.

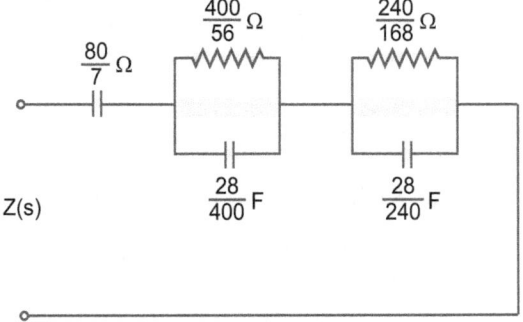

Fig. 5.43: Foster-I Form of Network

Cauer-I Form: This is obtained by CFE of Z(s).

$$Z(s) = \frac{80s^2 + 800s + 1680}{7s^2 + 56s + 84}$$

$$7s^2 + 56s + 84 \overline{\smash{\big)}\ 80s^2 + 800s + 1680} \left(\frac{80}{7} \leftarrow R_1 \leftarrow \text{(series impedance)} \right.$$

$$\underline{80s^2 + 640s + 960}$$

$$160s + 720 \overline{\smash{\big)}\ 7s^2 + 56s + 84} \left(\frac{7s}{160} \leftarrow C_2 s \leftarrow Y_2(s) \text{ (shunt)} \right.$$

$$\underline{7s^2 + \frac{63s}{20}}$$

$$\frac{49}{2}s + 84 \overline{\smash{\big)}\ 160s + 720} \left(\frac{320}{49} \leftarrow R_3 \leftarrow \text{(series impedance)} \right.$$

$$\underline{160 + 548.6}$$

$$171.4 \overline{\smash{\big)}\ \frac{49}{2}s + 84} \left(0.143\, s \leftarrow C_4 s \leftarrow Y_4(s) \text{ (shunt)} \right.$$

$$\underline{\frac{49}{2}s}$$

$$84 \overline{\smash{\big)}\ 171.4} \left(2.04 \leftarrow R_5 \leftarrow \text{(Series imp.)} \right.$$

$$\underline{171.4}$$

$$00$$

The realized Cauer-I form of the network is shown in Fig. 5.44.

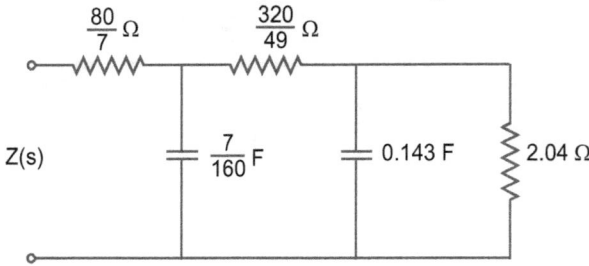

Fig. 5.44: Cauer-I Form of Network

Ex. 5.34: Synthesis $Z(s) = \dfrac{(s+1)(s+4)}{s(s+2)}$ in Cauer forms.

Sol.: $Z(s) = \dfrac{s^2 + 5s + 4}{s^2 + 2s}$ is a R-C impedance function.

Cauer-I Form: This is obtained by CFE about $s = \infty$.

$$s^2 + 2s \overline{\big)\, s^2 + 5s + 4} \,\big(\, 1 \leftarrow R_1 \text{ (series)}$$
$$\underline{s^2 + 2s}$$
$$3s + 4 \overline{\big)\, s^2 + 2s} \,\big(\, \frac{s}{3} \leftarrow C_2 s \leftarrow Y_2(s) \text{ (shunt)}$$
$$\underline{s^2 + \frac{4}{3}s}$$
$$\frac{2}{3}s \overline{\big)\, 3s + 4} \,\big(\, \frac{9}{2} \leftarrow R_3 \text{ (series)}$$
$$\underline{3s}$$
$$4 \overline{\big)\, \frac{2}{3}s} \,\big(\, \frac{s}{6} \leftarrow C_4 s \leftarrow Y_4(s) \text{ (shunt)}$$
$$\underline{\frac{2}{3}s}$$
$$00$$

The realized Cauer-I form of the network is shown in Fig. 5.45.

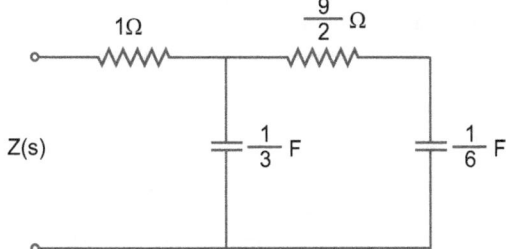

Fig. 5.45: Cauer-I Form of Network

Cauer-II Form: This is obtained by CFE about $s = 0$.

$$2s + s^2 \overline{\big)\, 4 + 5s + s^2} \,\big(\, \frac{2}{s} \leftarrow \frac{1}{C_1 s} \leftarrow Z_1(s) \text{ (series)}$$
$$\underline{4 + 2s}$$
$$3s + s^2 \overline{\big)\, 2s + s^2} \,\big(\, \frac{2}{3} \leftarrow \frac{1}{R} \leftarrow Y_2 \text{ (shunt admittance)}$$
$$\underline{2s + \frac{2}{3}s^2}$$
$$\frac{s^2}{3} \overline{\big)\, 3s + s^2} \,\big(\, \frac{9}{s} \leftarrow \frac{1}{C_3 s} \leftarrow Z_3(s) \text{ (series)}$$
$$\underline{3s}$$
$$s^2 \overline{\big)\, \frac{s^2}{3}} \,\big(\, \frac{1}{3} \leftarrow \frac{1}{R_4} \leftarrow Y_4 \text{ (shunt)}$$
$$\underline{\frac{s^2}{3}}$$
$$00$$

Hence, Cauer-II form of the network is as shown in Fig. 5.36.

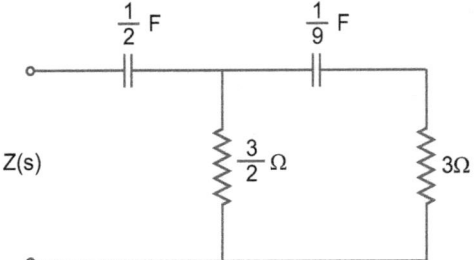

Fig. 5.46: Cauer-II Form of Network

Ex. 5.35: Synthesise the following function in one Foster and one Cauer form.

$$F(s) = \frac{s^3 + 9s^2 + 23s + 15}{s(s^3 + 12s^2 + 44s + 48)}$$

Sol.: Now,
$$F(s) = \frac{(s+1)(s+3)(s+5)}{s(s+2)(s+4)(s+6)}$$

As residue at the poles is real and positive, this is a R-C impedance function or R-L admittance function. Let us consider it as a R-C impedance function.

Foster-I Form:

This is obtained by partial fraction expansion of $F(s) = Z_{RC}(s)$

$$F(s) = Z_{RC}(s) = \frac{k_0}{s} + \frac{k_1}{(s+2)} + \frac{k_2}{(s+4)} + \frac{k_3}{(s+6)} = \frac{5}{16s} + \frac{3}{16(s+2)} + \frac{3}{16(s+4)} + \frac{5}{16(s+6)}$$

$$= \frac{5}{16s} + \frac{1}{\left(\frac{16}{3}s + \frac{32}{3}\right)} + \frac{1}{\left(\frac{16}{3}s + \frac{64}{3}\right)} + \frac{1}{\left(\frac{16s}{5} + \frac{96}{5}\right)}$$

Hence, Foster I form of the network is as shown in Fig. 5.47.

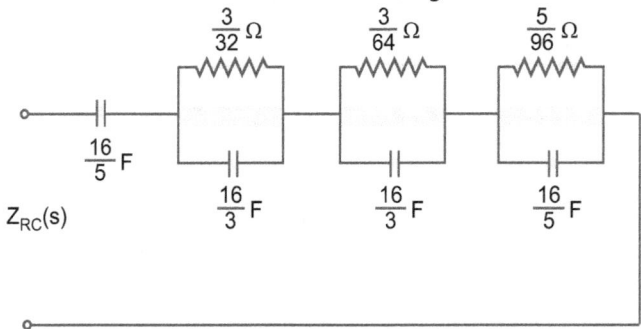

Fig. 5.47: Foster-I Form of Network

Cauer I Form: This is obtained by CFE of $F(s)$ about the pole at $s = \infty$.

$$Z(s) = \frac{s^3 + 9s^2 + 23s + 15}{s^4 + 12s^3 + 44s^2 + 48s}$$

CFE is as shown below. Since there is zero at s = ∞, we first invert the function and then carry out expansion.

$$s^3 + 9s^2 + 23s + 15 \overline{)\, s^4 + 12s^3 + 44s^2 + 48s} \, (s \leftarrow C_1 s$$
$$\underline{s^4 + 9s^3 + 23s^2 + 15s}$$
$$3s^2 + 21s^2 + 33s \overline{)\, s^3 + 9s^2 + 23s + 15} \, (\tfrac{1}{3} \leftarrow R_2$$
$$\underline{s^3 + 17s^2 + 11s}$$
$$2s^2 + 12s + 15 \overline{)\, 3s^3 + 21s^2 + 33s} \, (\tfrac{3}{2}s \leftarrow C_3 s$$
$$\underline{3s^3 + 18s^2 + 22.5s}$$
$$3s^2 + \tfrac{21}{2}s \overline{)\, 2s^2 + 12s + 15} \, (\tfrac{2}{3} \leftarrow R_4$$
$$\underline{2s^2 + 7s}$$
$$5s + 15 \overline{)\, 3s^2 + \tfrac{21}{2}s} \, (\tfrac{3}{2}s \leftarrow C_5 s$$
$$\underline{3s^2 + 9s}$$
$$\tfrac{3}{2}s \overline{)\, 5s + 15} \, (\tfrac{10}{3} \leftarrow R_6$$
$$\underline{5s}$$
$$15s \overline{)\, \tfrac{3}{2}s} \, (\tfrac{3}{30}s \leftarrow C_7 s$$

The realized Cauer-I form of the network is shown in Fig. 5.48.

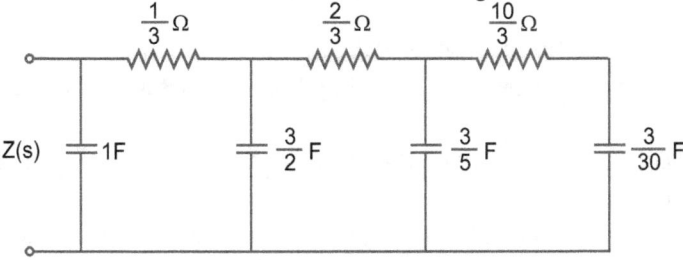

Fig. 5.48: Cauer-I Form of Network

5.15 SYNTHESIS OF DRIVING POINT FUNCTIONS OF R-L NETWORK

R-L network consists of only resistors and inductors as circuit elements. For the synthesis of R-L network, we first need to understand the properties of R-L network function.

5.15.1 Properties of R-L Network Functions [$Z_{RL}(s)$ and $Y_{RL}(s)$]

Admittance of an inductor is similar to the impedance of a capacitor (Or R-L admittance is considered to be dual of R-C impedance) and vice-versa.

i.e. $Z_{RC}(s) = Y_{RL}(s)$ ... (5.29)
             $Z_{RL}(s) = Y_{RC}(s)$

Thus, impedance expression for R-L case has the same form as admittance expression for a R-C case, and R-L admittance is similar to R-C impedance. Thus, any conclusion reached for R-C impedance applies to R-L admittance, and vice-versa.

Hence, the properties of R-L impedance $Z_{RL}(s)$ are the same as $Y_{RC}(s)$ and are given in Table 5.9. The properties of R-L admittance $Y_{RL}(s)$ are the same as $Z_{RC}(s)$ and are given in Table 5.10.

Table 5.9 : Properties of R-L Driving Point Impedance Function $Z_{RL}(s)$

No.	Properties
1.	Poles and zeros of $Z_{RL}(s)$ are all on negative real axis of s-plane and are simple.
2.	Poles and zeros of $Z_{RL}(s)$ are interlaced.
3.	Lowest critical frequency (near to origin) is zero and it can be at the origin. There cannot be a pole at the origin.
4.	Highest critical frequency (farthest from origin) is a pole and this can be at infinity. There cannot be a zero at infinity.
5.	Slope of $\dfrac{dZ_{RL}(s)}{d\sigma}$ is strictly positive as shown in Fig. 5.49 (b).
6.	If $Z_{RC}(s) = \dfrac{p(s)}{q(s)}$ then order of p(s) must be one greater or equal to that of q(s).
7.	Residue at the poles of $Z_{RC}(s)$ are real and negative while that of $\dfrac{Z_{RL}(s)}{s}$ are real and positive.
8.	$Z_{RL}(0) \leq Z_{RL}(\infty)$ as shown in Fig. 5.49 (b).

Table 5.10 : Properties of R-L Driving Point Admittance Function $Y_{RL}(s)$

No.	Properties
1.	Poles and zeros of $Y_{RL}(s)$ are on the negative real axis of s-plane and are simple.
2.	Poles and zeros are interlaced.
3.	Critical frequency nearest to the origin is a pole. There can be a pole at the origin (because it indicates a parallel inductor). But there cannot be zero at the origin as it indicates a capacitor.
4.	Highest critical frequency (critical frequency farthest from the origin is a zero. This zero can be at infinity (this would indicate an inductor). But there cannot be a pole at infinity (this indicates a capacitor)
5.	Slope of $\dfrac{dY_{RL}}{d\sigma}$ is strictly negative as shown in Fig. 5.49 (a).
6.	$Y_{RL}(0) > Y_{RL}(\infty)$, as shown in Fig. 5.49 (a).
7.	If $Y_{RL}(s) = \dfrac{p(s)}{q(s)}$ then the order of q(s) must be one greater than or equal to that of p(s).
8.	Residue at the poles of $Y_{RL}(s)$ are all positive and real.

Fig. 5.49 (a) and Fig. 5.49 (b) given below show the plot of R-L impedance and R-L admittance functions respectively.

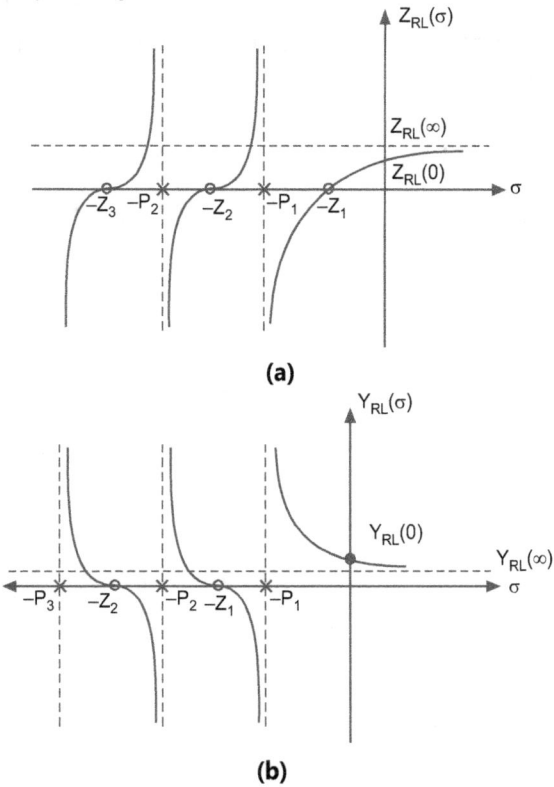

Fig. 5.49 : Plot of Z_{RL} and Y_{RL}

Hence, we can summarise the important points related to the networks which have only R-C or R-L elements, as given below.

Note:
1. If Z(s) is positive and real –
   - All its poles and zeros are located on the negative real axis of the s-plane,
   - Poles and zeros are interlaced
   - If the smallest and largest critical frequencies (external critical frequencies) are of opposite kinds (one pole and other zero) then Z(s) can be realized either as R-C network or R-L network, **but not both.**
2. Smallest critical frequency [s = 0] of Z(s)
   - If it is a pole, Z(s) can be realized as R-C network
   - If it is a zero, Z(s) can be realized as R-L network
3. R-C impedance function and R-L admittance function
   - R-C impedance function is realizable as R-L admittance function
   - R-C admittance function is realizable as an R-L impedance function

4. Removal of a pole
- Removal of a pole of Z(s) on the negative real axis gives a parallel R-C or R-L network
- Removal of a pole of Y(s) which is a zero of Z(s) on the negative real axis, gives a series R-C or R-L network.

In general, a function remaining after each removal operation will be positive real only if Z(s) satisfies the requirements of statement (1).

5.15.2 Synthesis or Realization of R-L Networks

R-L networks can be realized in four different forms namely Foster-I, Foster-II, Cauer-I and Cauer-II forms. To realize Foster-I form, we expand $\dfrac{Z_{RL}(s)}{s}$, while to realize Foster-II form, we expand $Y_{RL}(s)$ directly. Following examples explain the realization of R-L networks.

Ex. 5.36: Synthesise the following impedance function in Foster-I and Foster-II forms

$$Z(s) = \dfrac{2(s+1)(s+3)}{(s+2)(s+6)}$$

Sol.: Since this is an impedance function and residue at the poles are negative as shown below, this can be realized as a R-L network.

$$Z(s) = \dfrac{k_0}{(s+2)} + \dfrac{k_1}{(s+6)} = \dfrac{-\dfrac{1}{2}}{(s+2)} + \dfrac{-\dfrac{15}{2}}{(s+6)}$$

Since the residue of Z(s) is negative the given function is an R-L impedance function.

Foster-I Form: This is obtained by expanding $\dfrac{Z(s)}{s}$.

$$\dfrac{Z(s)}{s} = \dfrac{2(s+1)(s+3)}{s(s+2)(s+6)} = \dfrac{k_0}{s} + \dfrac{k_1}{(s+2)} + \dfrac{k_2}{(s+6)}$$

$$= \left[\dfrac{2 \times 3}{12s} + \dfrac{1}{(s+2)} \dfrac{(+2)(-1)(1)}{(-2) \times (4)} + \dfrac{1}{(s+6)} \dfrac{2(-5)(-3)}{-6 \times (-4)}\right]$$

$$= \left[\dfrac{1}{2s} + \dfrac{1}{4(s+2)} + \dfrac{5}{4(s+6)}\right]$$

$$Z(s) = \left[\dfrac{1}{2} + \dfrac{s}{(4s+8)} + \dfrac{5s}{4(s+6)}\right]$$

$$= \left[\dfrac{1}{2} + \dfrac{1}{\left[4 + \dfrac{4}{8}\right]} + \dfrac{1}{\left[\dfrac{4}{5} + \dfrac{24}{5s}\right]}\right]$$

Hence the required Foster-I form of the network is as shown in Fig. 5.50.

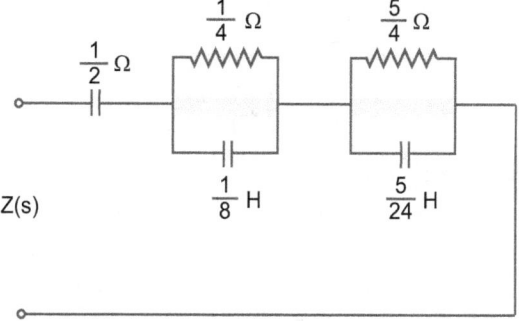

Fig. 5.50: Foster-I Form of Network

Foster-II Form: This is obtained by partial fraction expansion of Y(s).

$$Y(s) = \frac{(s+2)(s+6)}{2(s+1)(s+3)} = \frac{1}{2}\left[1 + \frac{4s+9}{(s+1)(s+3)}\right]$$

$$= \frac{1}{2}\left[1 + \frac{k_0}{(s+1)} + \frac{k_1}{(s+3)}\right] = \frac{1}{2}\left[1 + \frac{1}{2(s+1)} + \frac{3}{2(s+3)}\right]$$

$$= \frac{1}{2} + \frac{1}{(4s+4)} + \frac{1}{\left(\frac{4s}{3}+4\right)}$$

Hence Foster-II form of the network is as shown in Fig. 5.51.

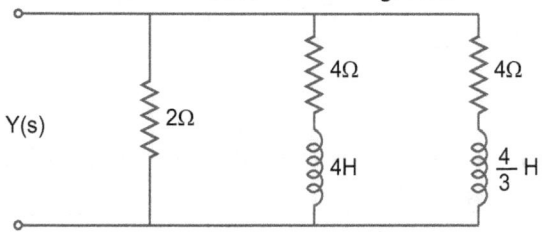

Fig. 5.51: Foster-II Form of Network

Ex. 5.37: State the properties of an R-L impedance function. Find out which of the following functions are R-L imp\x\to(−edance functions. Synthesise one of the functions in one Foster and one Cauer forms.

$$Z(s) = \frac{4(s+1)(s+3)}{s(s+2)} \qquad Z(s) = \frac{s(s+4)(s+8)}{(s+1)(s+6)}$$

$$Z(s) = \frac{(s+1)(s+4)}{s(s+2)} \qquad Z(s) = \frac{2(s+1)(s+3)}{(s+2)(s+6)}$$

Sol.: Properties of R-L impedance function are similar to those of R-C admittance $Y_{RC}(s)$ This is given in Table 5.9.

Residue at the poles of $Z_{RL}(s)$ must be negative.

(1) $$Z(s) = \frac{4(s+1)(s+3)}{s(s+2)}$$
$$= \frac{k_0}{s} + \frac{k_1}{(s+2)} = \frac{6}{s} + \frac{2}{(s+2)}$$

This is a **R-C impedance function**.

(2) $$Z(s) = \frac{s(s+4)(s+8)}{(s+1)(s+6)}$$
$$= \frac{s^3 + 12s^2 + 32s}{(s+1)(s+6)} = s + \frac{5s^2 + 26s}{(s+1)(s+6)}$$
$$= (s+5) - \frac{(11s+30)}{(s+1)(s+6)}$$

Since there is a zero at the origin, this is not a R-C function. Hence this is a **R-L impedance function**.

(3) $$Z(s) = \frac{(s+1)(s+4)}{s(s+2)} = 1 + \frac{3s+4}{s+(s+2)}$$
$$= 1 + \frac{k_0}{(s+2)} + \frac{k_1}{s} = 1 + \frac{1}{(s+2)} + \frac{2}{s}$$

This is a **R-C impedance function**.

(4) $$Z(s) = \frac{2(s+1)(s+3)}{(s+2)(s+6)}$$
$$= 2\left[1 - \frac{(4s+9)}{(s+2)(s+6)}\right]$$

Since the residues at the poles are negative, this function is a **R-L impedance function**.

We shall realize $Z(s) = \dfrac{s(s+4)(s+8)}{(s+1)(s+6)}$ in Foster-I and Cauer-I forms.

Foster-I Form: This is obtained by partial fraction expansion of $\dfrac{Z(s)}{s}$.

$$\frac{Z(s)}{s} = \frac{(s+4)(s+8)}{(s+1)(s+6)}$$
$$= 1 + \frac{5s+26}{(s+1)(s+6)}$$
$$= 1 + \frac{k_0}{(s+1)} + \frac{k_1}{(s+6)}$$
$$= 1 + \frac{\frac{21}{5}}{(s+1)} + \frac{\frac{4}{5}}{(s+6)}$$

Hence,
$$Z(s) = s + \frac{21s}{5(s+1)} + \frac{4s}{5(s+6)}$$
$$= s + \frac{1}{\left(\frac{5}{21} + \frac{5}{21s}\right)} + \frac{1}{\left(\frac{5}{4} + \frac{7.5}{s}\right)}$$

Hence, Foster-I form of the network is as shown in Fig. 5.52.

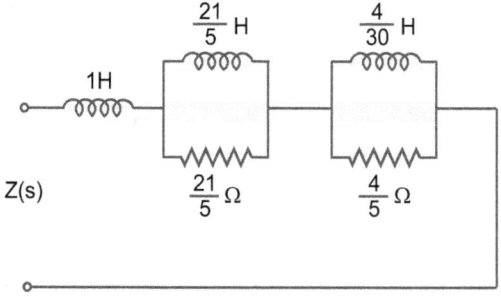

Fig. 5.52: Foster-I Form of Network

Cauer-I Form: This is obtained by CFE of Z(s) with respect to pole at '∞'.

$$Z(s) = \frac{s^3 + 12s^2 + 32s}{s^2 + 7s + 6} \text{ hence}$$

$$s^2 + 7s + 6 \overline{\smash{\big)}\, s^3 + 12s^2 + 32s} \,(s \leftarrow L_1 s$$
$$\underline{s^3 + 7s^2 + 6s}$$
$$5s^2 + 26s \overline{\smash{\big)}\, s^2 + 7s + 6} \,(\frac{1}{5} \leftarrow R_2$$
$$\underline{s^2 + \frac{26}{5}s}$$
$$\frac{9}{5}s + 6 \overline{\smash{\big)}\, 5s^2 + 26s} \,(\frac{25}{9}s \leftarrow L_3 s$$
$$\underline{5s^2 + \frac{50s}{3}}$$
$$\frac{28}{3}s \overline{\smash{\big)}\, \frac{9}{5}s + 6} \,(\frac{27}{140} \leftarrow R_4$$
$$\underline{\frac{9}{5}s}$$
$$6 \overline{\smash{\big)}\, \frac{28}{3}s} \,(\frac{28}{18}s \leftarrow L_5 s$$
$$\underline{\frac{28}{3}}$$
$$00$$

Hence Cauer-I form of the network is as shown in Fig. 5.53.

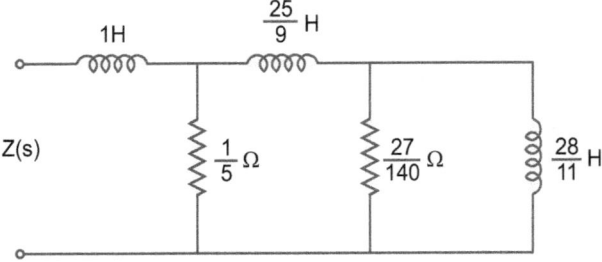

Fig. 5.53: Cauer-I Form of Network

Ex. 5.38: Synthesise $Z(s) = \dfrac{3(s+1)(s+4)}{(s+3)}$ using Cauer forms.

Sol.: Given function can be realized as R-L network, since it represents an R-L impedance function.

Foster-II Form: Expand $Y(s)$ directly.

$$Y(s) = \frac{(s+3)}{3(s+1)(s+4)} = \frac{k_0}{(s+1)} + \frac{k_1}{(s+4)} \quad \ldots (a)$$

$$k_0 = (s+1)Y(s)\Big|_{s \to -1} = \frac{(-1+3)}{3(-1+4)} = +\frac{2}{9}$$

$$k_1 = (s+4)Y(s)\Big|_{s \to -4} = \frac{(-4+3)}{3(-4+1)} = +\frac{1}{9}$$

Thus, $\quad Y(S) = \dfrac{2}{9(s+1)} + \dfrac{1}{9(s+4)} = \dfrac{1}{\left(\dfrac{9}{2}s+\dfrac{9}{2}\right)} + \dfrac{1}{(9s+36)}$

Foster-II form of the network corresponding to the above $Y(s)$ is shown in Fig. 5.54.

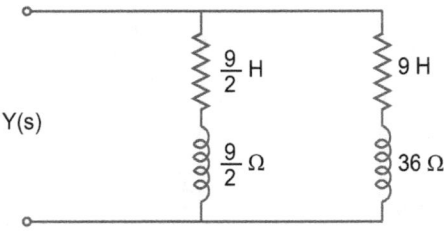

Fig. 5.54: Foster-II Form of Network

Cauer-I Form: $Z(s) = \dfrac{3s^2 + 15s + 12}{(s + 3)}$

Using CFE we get

$$s + 3 \overline{)\, 3s^2 + 15s + 12\,} \big(3s \leftarrow \text{series impedance } Z_1(s))$$
$$\underline{3s^2 + 9s}$$
$$6s + 12 \overline{)\, s + 3\,} \big(\tfrac{1}{6} \leftarrow Y_2(\text{shunt})$$
$$\underline{s + 2}$$
$$1 \overline{)\, 6s + 12\,} (6s \leftarrow Z_3(s))$$
$$\underline{6s}$$
$$12 \overline{)\, 1\,} (\tfrac{1}{12} \leftarrow Y_4$$
$$\underline{1}$$
$$00$$

The realized Cauer-I form of the network is shown in Fig. 5.55.

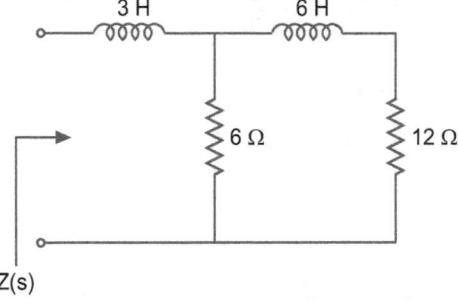

Fig. 5.55: Cauer-I Form of Network

Ex. 5.39: Realize the given impedance functions into all four canonical forms.

$$Z(s) = \dfrac{(s + 1)(s + 3)}{(s + 2)(s + 4)}$$

Sol.: Since poles and zeros are lying on the negative real axis and these are interlaced, and also, there is a zero nearest to the origin, the given function is a R-L impedance.

Foster-I Form: Expand $\dfrac{Z(s)}{s}$ by Partial Fraction Expansion (PFE)

$$\dfrac{Z(s)}{s} = \dfrac{(s + 1)(s + 3)}{s(s + 2)(s + 4)}$$
$$= \dfrac{k_0}{s} + \dfrac{k_1}{(s + 2)} + \dfrac{k_2}{(s + 4)}$$
$$= \dfrac{3/8}{s} + \dfrac{1/4}{(s + 2)} + \dfrac{3/8}{(s + 4)}$$

Hence,
$$Z(s) = \frac{3}{8} + \frac{s}{4(s+2)} + \frac{3s}{8(s+4)}$$
$$= \frac{1}{8/3} + \frac{1}{\left[4 + \frac{8}{s}\right]} + \frac{1}{\left[\frac{8}{3} + \frac{32}{35}\right]}$$

Thus, $Z(s) = Z_1(s) + Z_2(s) + Z_3(s)$

The Foster-I form of the network is shown in Fig. 5.56.

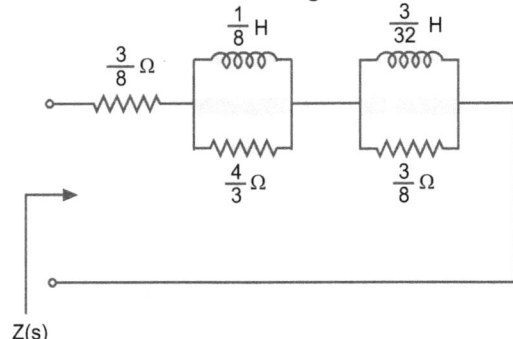

Fig. 5.56: Foster-I Form of Network

Foster-II Form: Expand $Y(s)$ by using PFE.

$$Y(s) = \frac{(s+2)(s+4)}{(s+1)(s+3)}$$

$$= k_\infty + \frac{k_0}{(s+1)} + \frac{k_1}{(s+3)}$$

$$k_\infty = Y(s)\bigg|_{s \to \infty} = \frac{\left(1+\frac{2}{s}\right)\left(1+\frac{4}{s}\right)}{\left(1+\frac{1}{s}\right)\left(1+\frac{3}{s}\right)}\bigg|_{s \to \infty} = 1$$

$$k_0 = (s+1)Y(s)\bigg|_{s \to -1} = \frac{(s+2)(s+4)}{(s+3)}\bigg|_{s \to -1} = +\frac{3}{2}$$

$$k_1 = (s+3)Y(s)\bigg|_{s \to -3} = \frac{(s+2)(s+4)}{(s+1)}\bigg|_{s \to -3} = +\frac{1}{2}$$

Thus, we can write $Y(s)$ as

$$Y(s) = 1 + \frac{\frac{3}{2}}{(s+1)} + \frac{\frac{1}{2}}{(s+3)}$$

$$= 1 + \frac{1}{\left(\frac{2s}{3} + \frac{2}{3}\right)} + \frac{1}{(2s+6)}$$

The Foster-II form of the network is shown in Fig. 5.57.

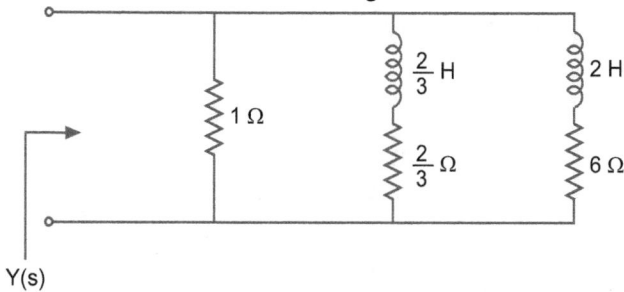

Fig. 5.57: Foster-II Form of Network

Cauer-I Form: This is obtained by CFE as shown below.

$$Z(s) = \frac{s^2 + 4s + 3}{(s^2 + 6s + 8)}$$

$$s^2 + 6s + 8 \overline{\smash{\big)}\, s^2 + 4s + 3} \,(\, 1$$
$$\underline{s^2 + 6s + 8}$$
$$-2s - 6 \overline{\smash{\big)}\, s^2 + 6s + 8} \,(\, -s/2$$

The quotients are negative because there is no pole near the origin (there is a zero near origin). Hence, we first invert and then continue to CFE.

$$s^2 + 4s + 3 \overline{\smash{\big)}\, s^2 + 6s + 8}\, (\, 1 \leftarrow Y_2$$
$$\underline{s^2 \pm 4s + 3}$$
$$\qquad 2s + 5 \overline{\smash{\big)}\, s^2 + 4s + 3}\, (\, \tfrac{s}{2} \leftarrow Z_3(s)$$
$$\qquad \underline{s^2 \pm \tfrac{5}{2}s}$$
$$\qquad\qquad \tfrac{3}{2}s + 3 \overline{\smash{\big)}\, 2s + 5}\, (\, \tfrac{4}{3} \leftarrow Y_4$$
$$\qquad\qquad \underline{2s \pm 4}$$
$$\qquad\qquad\qquad 1 \overline{\smash{\big)}\, \tfrac{3}{2}s + 3}\, (\, \tfrac{3}{2}s \leftarrow Z_5(s)$$
$$\qquad\qquad\qquad \underline{3/2\, s}$$
$$\qquad\qquad\qquad\qquad 3 \overline{\smash{\big)}\, 1}\, (\, 1/3 \leftarrow Y_6$$
$$\qquad\qquad\qquad\qquad \underline{1}$$
$$\qquad\qquad\qquad\qquad\, 00$$

The realized Cauer-I form of the network is shown in Fig. 5.58.

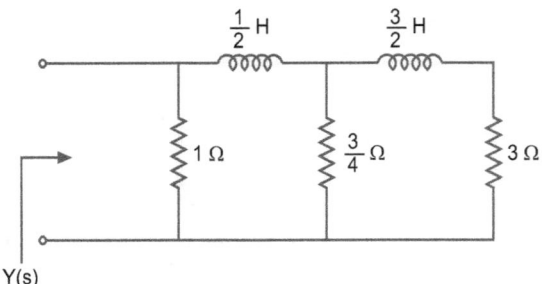

Fig. 5.58: Cauer-I Form of Network

Cauer-II Form: This is obtained by CFE as shown below.

$$8 + 6s + s^2 \overline{\smash{\big)}\, 3 + 4s + s^2} \left(\frac{3}{8} \leftarrow Z_1 \right.$$

$$\underline{3 \pm \frac{9}{4}s \pm \frac{3}{8}s^2}$$

$$\frac{7}{5}s + \frac{5}{8}s^2 \overline{\smash{\big)}\, 8 + 6s + s^2} \left(\frac{32}{7s} \leftarrow Y_2(s) \right)$$

$$\underline{8 + 160s}$$
$$-56$$

$$\frac{176}{56}s + s^2 \overline{\smash{\big)}\, \frac{7}{4}s + \frac{5}{8}s^2} \left(\frac{98}{176} \leftarrow Z_3 \right.$$

$$\underline{\frac{7}{4}s \pm \frac{98}{176}s^2}$$

$$\frac{12}{176}s^2 \overline{\smash{\big)}\, \frac{176}{56}s + s^2} \left(\frac{968}{21s} \leftarrow Y_4 \right.$$

$$\underline{\frac{176}{56}s}$$

$$s^2 \overline{\smash{\big)}\, \frac{12}{176}s^2} \left(\frac{12}{176} \leftarrow Z_5 \right.$$

$$\underline{\frac{12}{176}s^2}$$
$$00$$

The Cauer-II form of the network is shown in Fig. 5.59.

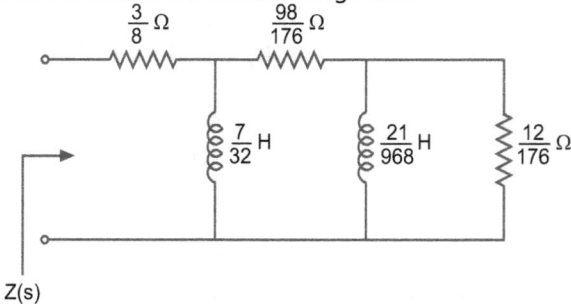

Fig. 5.59: Cauer-II Form of Network

5.16 SUMMARY OF L-C, R-C, R-L NETWORK SYNTHESIS

Table 5.11 summarises the synthesis procedure for one-port R-C, R-L and L-C networks.

Table 5.11: Summary of the Synthesis Procedure for ONE-PORT Networks

Network form	Procedure	Resulting L-C network. For R-C case replace L by R For R-L case replace C by R
Foster-I	Partial fraction expansion of Z(s)*	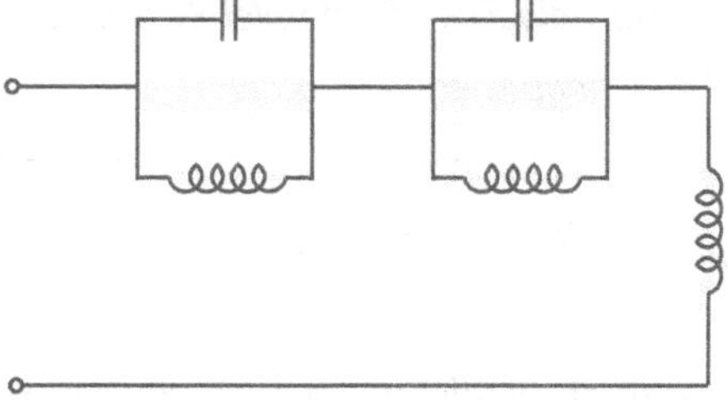 (a)
Foster-II	Partial fraction expansion of Y(s)+	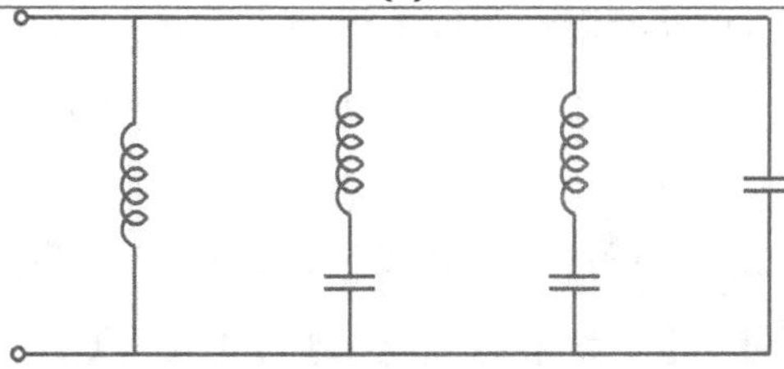 (b)
Cauer-I	Continued fraction expansion of Z(s) or Y(s) about infinity	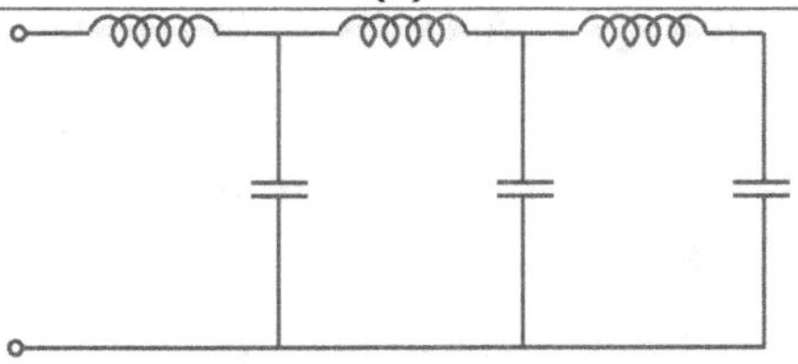 (c)
Cauer-II	Continued fraction expansion of Z(s) or Y(s) about zero	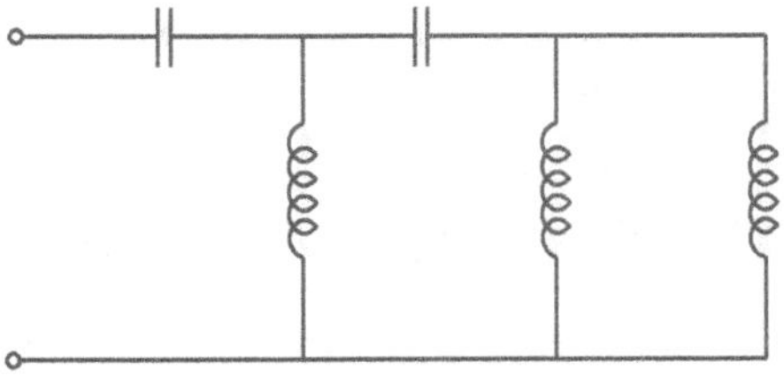 (d)

Fig. 5.60: One-port Synthesis Summary

* For R-L case, expand $\dfrac{Z(s)}{s}$ rather than Z(s).

\+ For R-C case, expand $\dfrac{Y(s)}{s}$ rather than Y(s).

> **Note:**
> The synthesis of one-port R-C, R-L and LC network can be concluded in terms of four canonical forms as follows -
> - R-C, R-L and LC networks can be realized in 4 canonical forms - Foster-I, Foster-II, Cauer-I and Cauer-II
> - These networks are completely equivalent. If all were enclosed within black box one cannot be distinguished from other.
> - No single canonical form can be called the best, preference of one form over another is due to practical considerations such as element size, cost and compensation for parasitic effects etc.
> - Synthesis of all 4 forms is simple and straight forward.
> - For the sake of comparison, it is advised that all 4 forms are found.
> - Canonical forms help in the realization of a network with minimum number of elements.

5.17 SYNTHESIS OF DRIVING POINT FUNCTIONS OF R-L-C NETWORK

5.17.1 Properties of R-L-C Function

An R-L-C circuit consists of resistors, inductors and capacitors as their circuit elements. The driving point functions [Z(s) or Y(s)] of the R-L-C circuit need not necessarily be P.R.F. But they have all their poles and zeros located in the left half of the s-plane. They can be located any where on the L-H s-plane. If they lie on negative real axis or on imaginary axis then they need not be overlaced (or alternate). Some times the partial fraction expansion (PFE) of Z(s) and $\frac{Z(s)}{s}$ or Y(s) and $\frac{Y(s)}{s}$, may both give negative coefficients in the case of R-L-C functions.

Since we know some of the properties of R-L-C function, we can now proceed with the synthesis of R-L-C driving point functions.

5.17.2 Synthesis or Realization of a R-L-C Network

Under certain conditions, R-L-C driving point functions can be synthesised by using either PFE OR CFE. But not all R-L-C functions can be synthesised like this. Generally speaking, if an R-L-C function can be synthesised in positive real form, then it must be a minimum function. Once the function is confirmed as a minimum function, it can be synthesised by using two simple methods given below.

(A) Partial Fraction Expansion (PFE) Method:

Following two examples will illustrate this method of synthesis.

Ex. 5.40: Synthesise $Z(s) = \dfrac{(s+2)(s+4)}{(s+1)(s+5)}$ into the form shown in Fig. 5.61.

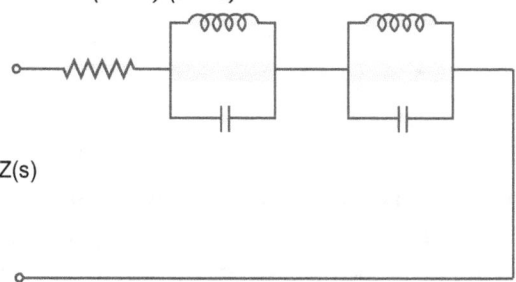

Fig. 5.61: Network form given in Ex. 5.40

Sol.:
$$Z(s) = \dfrac{s^2 + 6s + 8}{s^2 + 6s + 5}$$

$$= 1 + \dfrac{3}{(s+1)(s+5)} = 1 + \dfrac{k_0}{(s+1)} + \dfrac{k_1}{(s+5)}$$

If
$$Z_1(s) = \dfrac{k_0}{(s+1)} + \dfrac{k_1}{(s+5)} = \dfrac{3}{(s+1)(s+5)}$$

Then
$$k_0 = (s+1)\, F_1(s)\,\big|_{s \to -1} = \dfrac{-3}{4}$$

$$k_1 = (s+3)\, F_1(s)\,\big|_{s \to -3} = \dfrac{3}{4}$$

Hence,
$$Z(s) = 1 + \dfrac{3}{4(s+1)} - \dfrac{3}{4(s+5)}$$

Here residues are negative with term $(s + 5)$. Hence, it cannot be Synthesised into positive real form. Therefore, expand $\dfrac{Z(s)}{s}$ and then multiply the whole expansion by 's'.

$$\dfrac{Z(s)}{s} = \dfrac{(s+2)(s+4)}{s(s+1)(s+5)}$$

$$= \dfrac{k_0}{s} + \dfrac{k_1}{(s+1)} + \dfrac{k_2}{(s+5)} = \dfrac{8}{5s} - \dfrac{3}{4(s+1)} + \dfrac{3}{20(s+5)}$$

∴ $$Z(s) = \dfrac{8}{5} - \dfrac{\tfrac{3}{4}s}{(s+1)} + \dfrac{\tfrac{3}{20}s}{(s+5)} = \dfrac{8}{5} - \left[\dfrac{3}{4} - \dfrac{\tfrac{3}{4}}{(s+1)}\right] + \dfrac{3s}{20(s+5)}$$

$$= \dfrac{17}{20} + \dfrac{3}{4(s+1)} + \dfrac{3s}{20(s+5)} = \dfrac{17}{20} + \dfrac{1}{\left(\tfrac{4}{3}s + \tfrac{4}{3}\right)} + \dfrac{1}{\left(\tfrac{20}{3} + \tfrac{100}{3s}\right)}$$

Hence, the Synthesised network will be as shown in Fig. 5.62, which is Foster-I form.

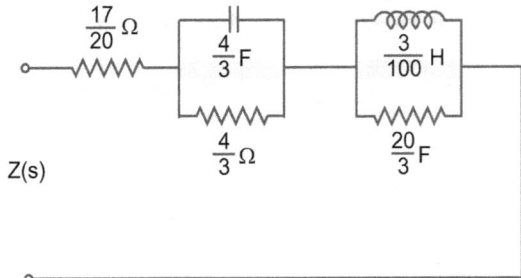

Fig. 5.62: Synthesised Network (Foster-I Form)

Note: In the given function Z(s) Poles and Zero are on the negative real axis. However, they do not alternate. Hence Z(s) is neither L-C or R-C function, nor R-L function. It is an R-L-C function.

Ex. 5.41: Synthesise the following admittance function using partial fraction expansion.

$$Y(s) = \frac{(s+2)(s+3)}{(s+1)(s+4)}$$

Sol.: In the above function poles and zeros are interlacing on negative real axis but do not alternate. Hence it neither R-C, R-L function nor L-C function. It is an R-L-C function.

Partial fraction expansion of Y(s) gives:

$$Y(s) = 1 + \frac{k_0}{(s+1)} + \frac{k_1}{(s+4)}$$

$$= 1 + \frac{\frac{2}{3}}{(s+1)} + \frac{\frac{-2}{3}}{(s+4)}$$

Thus, we see that there are negative residue with term (s + 4) in the expansion of Y(s) which will give components with negative value. Hence cannot be realized as a PRF.

Hence, Expand $\frac{Y(s)}{s}$ and then multiply whole expansion by 's'.

Thus, $\frac{Y(s)}{s} = \frac{(s+2)(s+3)}{s(s+1)(s+4)} = \frac{k_0}{s} + \frac{k_1}{(s+1)} + \frac{k_2}{(s+4)} = \frac{\frac{3}{2}}{s} - \frac{\frac{2}{3}}{s+1} + \frac{\frac{1}{6}}{s+4}$

Multiplying by 's' gives :

$$Y(s) = \frac{3}{2} - \frac{\frac{2}{3}s}{(s+1)} + \frac{\frac{s}{6}}{(s+4)} = \frac{3}{2} - \left[\frac{2}{3} - \frac{\frac{2}{3}}{(s+1)}\right] + \frac{s}{6(s+4)}$$

$$= \frac{5}{6} + \frac{2}{3(s+1)} + \frac{s}{6(s+4)} = \frac{5}{6} + \frac{1}{\frac{3}{2}s + \frac{3}{2}} + \frac{1}{6 + \frac{24}{s}}$$

Hence Foster-II network will be as shown in Fig. 5.63.

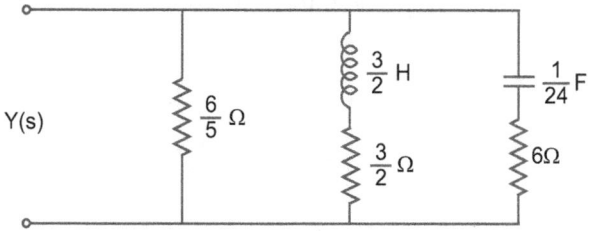

Fig. 5.63: Realized Network (Foster-II Form)

Thus, Foster forms of network are obtained by *partial fraction expansion of Z(s) or Y(s)*. Similarly, *CFE* will give Cauer form of the networks which is explained below.

(B) Continued Fraction Expansion (CFE) Method:

Following two examples will illustrate this method of R-L-C one-port synthesis.

Ex. 5.42: Expand the following impedance function by CFE.

$$Z(s) = \frac{s^2 + 2s + 2}{s^2 + s + 1}$$

Sol.: This function is neither L-C [Poles and Zeros are not on the imaginary axis] nor R-L [Poles and zeros are not on the negative real axis]. Hence the function is an R-L-C driving point impedance function.

$$
\begin{array}{r}
s^2 + s + 1 \overline{\smash{)}\, s^2 + 2s + 2} \, (1 \leftarrow Z \\
\underline{s^2 \pm s \pm 1} \\
s + 1 \overline{\smash{)}\, s^2 + s + 1} \, (s \leftarrow Y \\
\underline{s^2 \pm s} \\
1 \overline{\smash{)}\, s + 1} \, (s + 1 \leftarrow Z \\
\underline{s \pm 1} \\
00
\end{array}
$$

The network derived from the above expansion is shown in Fig. 5.64.

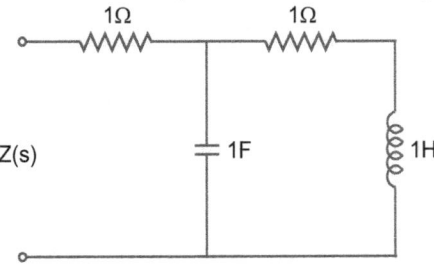

Fig. 5.64: Realized Network

It can be noted that the network realized is neither Cauer-I nor Cauer-II form of the network. It is a ladder network.

Ex. 5.43: Realize $Y(s) = \dfrac{s^2 + 5s + 6}{s^2 + 5s + 4}$ into the form shown in Fig. 5.65.

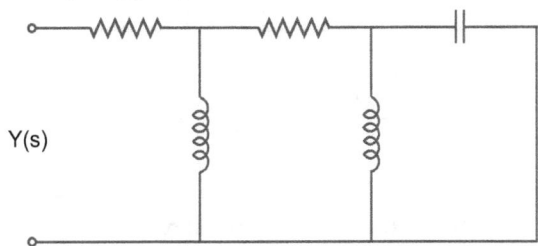

Fig. 5.65: Network form given in Ex. 5.43

Sol.: If we expand Y(s) directly by CFE, we will get negative quotients. Therefore, expand $Z(s) = \dfrac{1}{Y(s)}$ by CFE as given below.

$$6 + 5s + s^2 \overline{\smash{\big)}\, 4 + 5s + s^2} \left(\dfrac{3}{2} \leftarrow Z\right.$$

$$\underline{4 \pm \dfrac{10}{3}s \pm \dfrac{2}{3}s^2}$$

$$\dfrac{5}{3}s + \dfrac{s^2}{3} \overline{\smash{\big)}\, 6 + 5s + s^2} \left(\dfrac{18}{5s} \leftarrow Y\right.$$

$$\underline{6 + \dfrac{8}{5}s}$$

$$\dfrac{19}{5}s + s^2 \overline{\smash{\big)}\, \dfrac{s^2}{3} + \dfrac{s}{3}} \left(\dfrac{1}{3} \leftarrow Z\right.$$

$$\underline{\dfrac{s^2}{3} \pm \dfrac{19}{15}s}$$

$$\dfrac{6}{15}s \overline{\smash{\big)}\, \dfrac{19}{5}s + s^2} \left(\dfrac{19}{2} \leftarrow Y\right.$$

$$\underline{\dfrac{19}{5}s}$$

$$s^2 \overline{\smash{\big)}\, \dfrac{6}{15}s} \left(\dfrac{6}{15}s \leftarrow Z\right.$$

$$\underline{\dfrac{6}{15}s}$$

$$00$$

Please note that the division process giving the quotient of $\dfrac{1}{3}$ involves a reversal of the order of polynomial involved. This reversal of order is some time necessary in the case of R-L-C function, but not in the case of R-C, L-C and R-L functions.

Hence, the realized ladder network is as shown in Fig. 5.66.

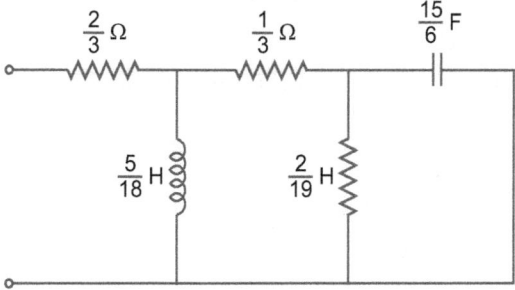

Fig. 5.66: Realized Ladder Network

R-L-C Synthesis can be summarized into following important points.
- R-L-C driving point function can be synthesized with use of ladder form and Foster form only under special conditions.
- If an R-L-C function can be synthesized as a positive real network, then it must be a *minimum function*.
- An impedance function with no poles on the imaginary axis is known as *"minimum reactance function"*.
- An admittance function with no poles on imaginary axis is called *"minimum susceptance function"*.
- An impedance function whose real part vanishes at some real frequency is known as *"minimum resistance function"*.
- An admittance function with its real part vanishing at some real frequency is known as *"minimum conductance function"*.
- A function which is simultaneously minimum reactance, susceptance, resistance and conductance is simply known as a *"minimum function"*.
- A minimum function is a special class of driving point impedance or admittance function which are P.R.F., and have the following properties -
  1. It has no poles and zeros on the imaginary axis of s-plane.
  2. It has a finite, real and positive value at $s = 0$ and $s = \infty$.
  3. It will have a real part which vanishes for at least one finite real frequency, ω_1 such that
     $$J(j\omega_1) = 0 \pm JX \text{ where } X \neq 0$$
- Once the function is tested to be a positive real function, then it can be realized as an R-L-C one-port network. For this *Brune's method* OR *Bott and Duffin method* can be used. These are quite complicated methods and are out of scope of this book.

5.18 ADDITIONAL SOLVED PROBLEMS ON L-C, R-C, R-L AND R-L-C NETWORKS

In this section we shall study some of the solved problems on various types of networks.

(A) Solved Problems on L-C Networks

Ex. 5.44: For the network shown in Fig. 5.67 find Y when

$$\frac{V_2}{V_0} = \frac{1}{2+Y} = \frac{s(s^2+3)}{2s^3+s^2+6s+1}$$

Synthesise Y as an L-C admittance.

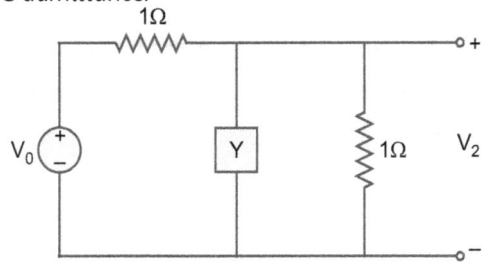

Fig. 5.67: Network form given in Ex. 5.54

Sol.: Total admittance = $Y_T = (Y+1)$

Total impedance = $Z_T = \dfrac{1}{Y_T} = \dfrac{1}{(Y+1)}$

$$V_2 = \frac{Z_T V_0}{Z_T + 1} \quad \text{hence} \quad \frac{V_2}{V_0} = \frac{1}{1+\dfrac{1}{Z_T}} = \frac{1}{1+Z_T}$$

Thus, $\quad \dfrac{V_2}{V_0} = \dfrac{1}{1+1+Y} = \dfrac{1}{2+Y}$ ... (a)

Given expression can be rewritten as:

$$\frac{V_2}{V_0} = \frac{(s^3+3s)}{(2s^3+6s)+(s^2+1)} = \frac{1}{2+\dfrac{s^2+1}{(s^3+3s)}}$$ ... (b)

Comparing (a) and (b) we have $Y = \dfrac{s^2+1}{(s^3+3s)}$

$$Y = \frac{s^2+1}{s(s^2+3)} = \left[\frac{K_0}{s} + \frac{2K_1 s}{(s^2+3)}\right]$$

$$K_0 = \frac{1}{3}, \quad 2K_1 = \frac{(-3+1)}{(-3)} = \frac{2}{3}$$

Thus, $\quad Y = \dfrac{1}{3s} + \dfrac{2}{3}\dfrac{s}{(s^2+3)}$

$$Y = \frac{1}{3s} + \frac{1}{\left(\dfrac{3}{2}s + \dfrac{9}{2s}\right)}$$

The L-C circuit that realizes Y is shown in Fig. 5.68.

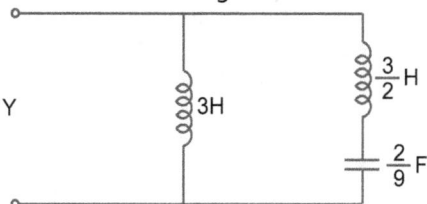

Fig. 5.68: Realized L-C Network

Ex. 5.45: Synthesise the L-C driving point impedance in the form shown in Fig. 5.69.

$$Z(s) = \frac{6s^4 + 42s^2 + 48}{s^5 + 18s^3 + 48s}$$

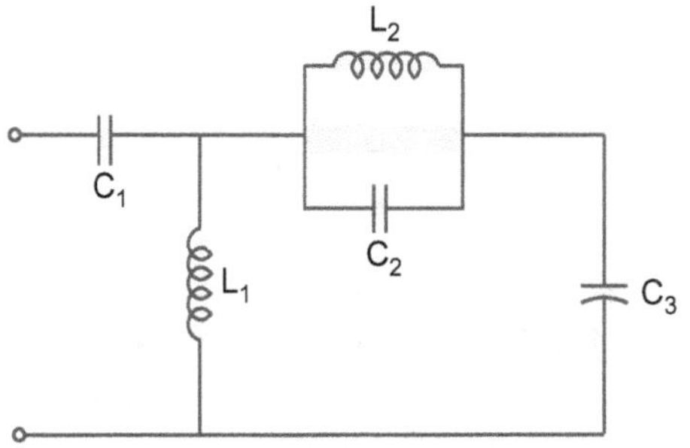

Fig. 5.69: Network form given in Ex. 5.45

Sol.:
$$Z(s) = \frac{6s^4 + 42s^2 + 48}{s(s^4 + 18s^2 + 48s)}$$

There is a pole at the origin (s = 0), which can be removed as a capacitor.

$$48s + 18s^3 + s^5 \overline{\smash{\big)}\ \begin{array}{c} 48 + 42s^2\ 6s^4 \\ 48 + 18s^2 + s^4 \end{array}} \quad \left(1/s \leftarrow \frac{1}{SC_1}\right)$$

$$24s^2 + 5s^4 \overline{\smash{\big)}\ \begin{array}{c} 48s + 18s^3 + s^5 \\ 48s + 105^3 \end{array}} \quad \left(\frac{2}{s} \leftarrow \frac{1}{SL_1}\right)$$

$$8s^3 + s^5$$

The remainder is $\quad Z_1(s) = \dfrac{24s^2 + 5s^4}{8s^2 + s^5} = \dfrac{5s^4 + 24s^2}{s^5 + 8s^3}$

This can be now expanded in the Foster I form to get elements L_2, C_2 and C_3

$$Z_1(s) = \frac{5s^4 + 24s^2}{s(s^4 + 8s^2)} = \frac{5s^2 + 24}{s(s^2 + 8)} = \frac{K_0}{s} + \frac{2K_1 s}{(s^2 + 8)}$$

$$K_0 = sZ_1(s)\bigg|_{s \to 0} = \frac{24}{8} = 3$$

$$2K_1 = \left(\frac{z^2+8}{s}\right)Z_1(s)\bigg|_{s^2 \to -8}$$

$$= \frac{-5 \times 8 = 24}{-8} = 2$$

Thus,
$$Z_1(s) = \frac{1}{3s} + \frac{2s}{s^2+8} = \frac{1}{3s} + \frac{1}{\left(\dfrac{s}{2}+\dfrac{4}{s}\right)}$$

Hence, the realized network is as shown in Fig. 5.60.

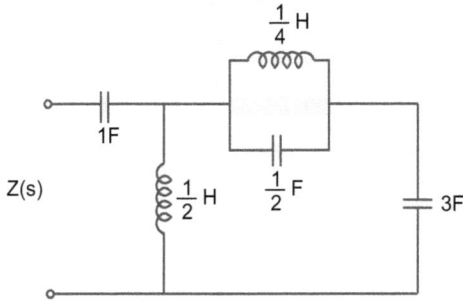

Fig. 5.70: The Realized Network

Ex. 5.46: Find the element values of a network having the same driving-point impedance as the network shown in Fig. 5.71, but with only three elements.

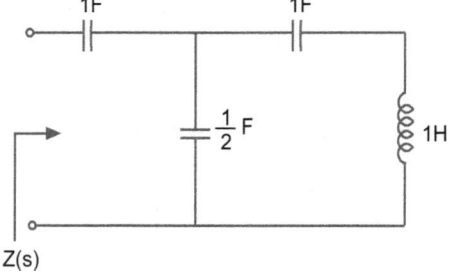

Fig. 5.71: Network given in Ex. 5.46

Sol.: The impedance $Z(s)$ of the network is given by

$$Z(s) = \frac{1}{s} + \frac{2}{s} \parallel \left(s + \frac{1}{s}\right) = \frac{1}{s} + \frac{2}{s} \parallel \left(\frac{s^2+1}{s}\right)$$

$$= \frac{1}{s} + \left[\frac{\dfrac{2}{s} \times \left(\dfrac{s^2+1}{s}\right)}{\dfrac{2}{s} + \left(\dfrac{s^2+1}{s}\right)}\right]$$

$$= \frac{1}{s} + \frac{2s^2+2}{s(s^2+3)}$$

$$= \frac{3s^2+5}{s(s^2+3)}$$

Z(s) can be expanded to get Foster I form, which will contain only three elements.

$$Z(s) = \frac{3s^2 + 5}{s(s^2 + 3)} = \frac{K_0}{s} + \frac{2K_1 s}{(s^2 + 3)}$$

$$K_0 = sZ(s)\Big|_{s \to 0} = \frac{5}{3}$$

$$2K_1 = (s^2 + 3) Z(s)\Big|_{s^2 \to -3} = \frac{-3 \times 3 - 5}{-3} = \frac{4}{3}$$

$$Z(s) = \frac{5}{3s} + \frac{4s}{3(s^2 + 3)} = \frac{5}{3s} + \frac{1}{\left(\frac{3s}{4} + \frac{9}{4s}\right)}$$

The realized network is shown in Fig. 5.72.

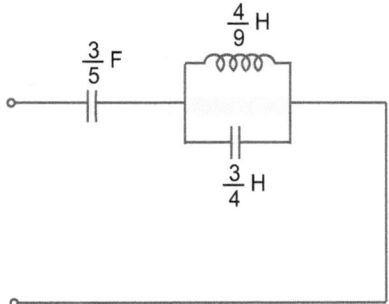

Fig. 5.72: The Realized Network

Ex. 5.47: Classify the following impedance functions in R-L, R-C and L-C functions, and state the reasons.

$$Z(s) = \frac{s^2 + 10s^2 + 9}{s^3 + 4s}; \quad Z(s) = \frac{2(s^2 + 4s + 3)}{s^2 + 8s + 12}$$

Sol.: (1) Function $Z(s) = \dfrac{s^4 + 10s^2 + 9}{s^3 + 4s} = \dfrac{(s^2 + 9)(s^2 + 1)}{s(s^2 + 4)}$

Hence $\quad Z(s) = \dfrac{(s^2 + 3^2)(s^2 + 1^2)}{s(s^2 + 2^2)}$

is an *L-C impedance function* because poles and zeros are lying on the imaginary (jω) axis and are interlaced. Also it satisfies all the properties as mentioned in Table 5.2.

(2) $\quad$ Function $Z(s) = \dfrac{2(s^2 + 4s + 3)}{s^2 + 8s + 12}$

$$= \frac{2(s + 3)(s + 1)}{(s + 6)(s + 2)}$$

This is a *R-L impedance function* because the residues at the poles of Z(s) are real and negative.

$$Z(s) = \frac{2(s+3)(s+1)}{(s+6)(s+2)} = \frac{k_0}{(s+6)} + \frac{k_1}{(s+2)}$$

$$= \frac{-7.5}{(s+6)} + \frac{-\frac{1}{2}}{(s+2)}$$

Also poles and zeros lies on negative real and are interlaced. Besides, it satisfies all the properties of Table 5.9.

Ex. 5.48: Synthesise the following function into Cauer-I and Cauer-II forms of networks

$$Z(s) = \frac{s(s^2+2)(s^2+5)}{(s^2+1)(s^2+3)}$$

Sol.: The given function is an L-C function since poles and zeros are lying on the imaginary axis and are interlaced. The function can be rewritten as

$$Z(s) = \frac{s[s^4 + 7s^2 + 10]}{[s^4 + 4s^2 + 3]} = \frac{s^5 + 7s^3 + 10s}{(s^4 + 4s^2 + 3)}$$

Cauer-I Form: This is obtained by removing the pole at $s = \infty$ from the function. It can be obtained by CFE method shown below.

$$s^4 + 4s^2 + 3 \overline{\smash{\big)}\, s^5 + 7s^3 + 10s} \,\big(s \leftarrow Z_1(s) \text{ (series)}$$
$$\underline{s^5 \pm 4s^3 + 3s}$$

$$3s^3 + 7s \overline{\smash{\big)}\, s^4 + 4s^2 + 3} \,\big(\frac{s}{3} \leftarrow Y_2(s) \text{ (shunt)}$$
$$\underline{s^4 + \frac{7}{3}s^2}$$

$$\frac{5}{3}s^2 + 3 \overline{\smash{\big)}\, 3s^3 + 7s} \,\big(\frac{9}{5}s \leftarrow Z_3(s)) \text{ (series)}$$
$$\underline{3s^3 + \frac{27}{5}s}$$

$$\frac{8}{5}s \overline{\smash{\big)}\, \frac{5}{3}s^2 + 3} \,\big(\frac{25}{24}s \leftarrow Y_4(s) \text{ (shunt)}$$
$$\underline{\frac{5}{3}s^2}$$

$$3 \overline{\smash{\big)}\, \frac{8}{5}s} \,\big(\frac{8}{15}s \leftarrow Z_5(s) \text{ (series)}$$
$$\underline{\frac{8}{5}s}$$
$$00$$

The Cauer-I form of the network realized is shown in Fig. 5.73.

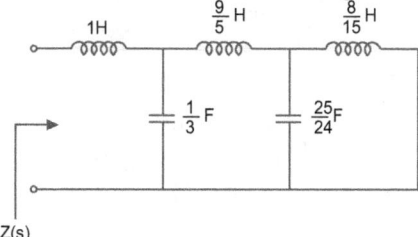

Fig. 5.73: Cauer-I Form of Network

Cauer-II Form: This is obtained by the removal of pole at the origin from the function. If can be obtained by CFE method shown below.

$$3 + 4s^2 + s^4 \overline{)\, 10s + 7s^3 + s^5 \,} \left(\frac{10}{3s} \right.$$

$$\underline{10s + \frac{40}{3}s^3 + \frac{10}{3}s^5}$$

$$-\frac{19}{3}s^3 - \frac{7}{3}s^5$$

Here the remainders are negative. Hence, start the CFE with inversion.

$$10s + 7s^3 + s^5 \overline{)\, 3 + 4s^2 + s^4 \,} \left(\frac{3}{10s} \leftarrow Y_2(s) \text{ (shunt)} \right.$$

$$3 + \frac{21}{10}s^2 + \frac{3}{10}s^4$$

$$\frac{10}{19}s^2 + \frac{7}{10}s^4 \overline{)\, 10s + 7s^3 + 5^3 \,} \left(\frac{100}{19s} \leftarrow Z_3(s) \text{ (series)} \right.$$

$$10s + \frac{70}{19}s^3$$

$$\frac{63}{19}s^3 + s^5 \overline{)\, \frac{19}{10}s^2 + \frac{7}{10}s^4 \,} \left(\frac{361}{630s} \leftarrow Y_4(s) \text{ (shunt)} \right.$$

$$\frac{19}{10}s^2 + \frac{361}{630}s^4$$

$$\frac{80}{630}s^4 \overline{)\, \frac{63}{19}s^3 + s^5 \,} \left(\frac{39690}{1520s} \leftarrow Z_5(s) \text{ (series)} \right.$$

$$\frac{63}{19}s^3$$

$$s^5 \overline{)\, \frac{80}{630}s^4 \,} \left(\frac{80}{630s} \leftarrow Z_6(s) \text{ (shunt)} \right.$$

$$\frac{80}{630}s^4$$

$$00$$

The realized Cauer-II network is shown in Fig. 5.74.

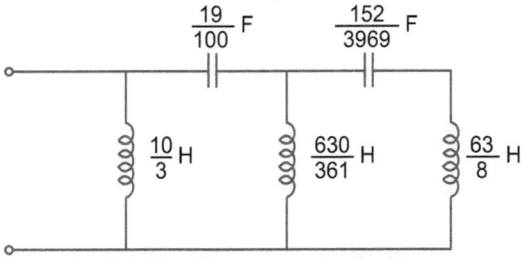

Fig. 5.74: Cauer-II Network

Ex. 5.49: Obtain the synthesis of $Z(s) = \dfrac{(s^2 + 1)(s^2 + 9)(s^2 + 25)}{s(s^2 + 4)(s^2 + 16)}$ using Foster-II form.

Sol.: Given function is an L-C impedance function. Foster-II form is obtained by PFE of $Y(s)$.

$$Y(s) = \dfrac{s(s^2 + 4)(s^2 + 16)}{(s^2 + 1)(s^2 + 9)(s^2 + 2s)} = \dfrac{2k_1 s}{(s^2 + 1)} + \dfrac{2k_2 s}{(s^2 + 9)} + \dfrac{2k_3 s}{(s^2 + 2s)}$$

$$2k_1 = \dfrac{(s^2 + 1)}{s} Y(s) \bigg|_{s^2 \to -1} = \dfrac{(s^2 + 4)(s^2 + 16)}{(s^2 + 9)(s^2 + 2s)} \bigg|_{s^2 \to -1} = \dfrac{3 \times 15}{8 \times 24} = \dfrac{15}{64}$$

$$2k_2 = \dfrac{(s^2 + 9)}{s} Y(s) \bigg|_{s^2 \to -9} = \dfrac{(s^2 + 4)(s^2 + 16)}{(s^2 + 1)(s^2 + 25)} \bigg|_{s^2 \to -9} = \dfrac{-5 \times 7}{-8 \times 16} = \dfrac{35}{128}$$

$$2k_3 = \dfrac{(s^2 + 25)}{s} Y(s) \bigg|_{s^2 \to -25} = \dfrac{(s^2 + 4)(s^2 + 16)}{(s^2 + 1)(s^2 + 9)} \bigg|_{s^2 \to -25}$$

$$= \dfrac{-21 \times -9}{-24 \times -16} = \dfrac{163}{128}$$

Thus $Y(s)$ can be written as:

$$Y(s) = \dfrac{15s}{64(s^2 + 1)} + \dfrac{35s}{128(s^2 + 9)} + \dfrac{63s}{128(s^2 + 25)}$$

$$= \dfrac{1}{\left[\dfrac{64}{15}s + \dfrac{64}{15s}\right]} + \dfrac{1}{\left[\dfrac{128}{35}s + \dfrac{1152}{35s}\right]} + \dfrac{1}{\left[\dfrac{128}{63}s + \dfrac{3200}{63s}\right]}$$

The realized Foster-II network is shown in Fig. 5.65.

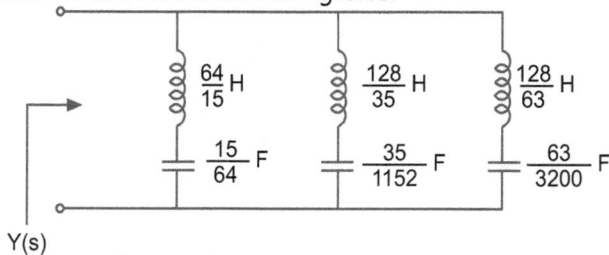

Fig. 5.75: Foster-II Form of Network

Ex. 5.50: Realize $Z(s) = \dfrac{s(s^2+2)(s^2+4)}{(s^2+1)(s^2+s)(s^2+5)}$ in first Cauer form.

Sol.: Given function is a L-C impedance function since poles and zeros are lying on jω-axis and are interlaced. The function may be written as

$$Z(s) = \dfrac{(s^5 + 6s^3 + 8s)}{(s^6 + 9s^4 + 23s^2 + 15)}$$

Since the first Cauer form (Cauer-I) is obtained by the removal of pole at $s = \infty$, and the given function I(s) has zero at $s = \infty$ [as $s \to \infty$ then $Z(\infty) = 0$], the expansion should start with Y(s). The first series inductor will be absent.
The CFE is a shown below.

$$s^5 + 6s^3 + 8s \overline{) s^6 + 9s^4 + 23s^2 + 15} \left(s \leftarrow Y_2(s) \text{ (shunt)} \right.$$
$$\underline{s^6 + 6s^4 + 8s^2}$$

$$3s^4 + 15s^2 + 15 \overline{) s^5 + 6s^3 + 8s} \left(\dfrac{s}{3} \leftarrow Z_3(s) \text{ (series)} \right.$$
$$\underline{s^5 + 5s^3 + 5s}$$

$$s^3 + 3s \overline{) 3s^4 + 15s^2 + 15} \left(3s \leftarrow Y_4(s) \text{ (shunt)} \right.$$
$$\underline{3s^4 + 9s^2}$$

$$6s^2 + 15 \overline{) s^3 + 3s} \left(\dfrac{s}{6} \leftarrow Z_5(s) \text{ (series)} \right.$$
$$\underline{s^3 + \dfrac{5}{2}s}$$

$$\dfrac{s}{2} \overline{) 6s^2 + 15} \left(12s \leftarrow Y_6(s) \text{ (shunt)} \right.$$
$$\underline{6s^2}$$

$$15 \overline{) \dfrac{s}{2}} \left(\dfrac{s}{30} \leftarrow Z_7(s) \text{ (series)} \right.$$
$$\underline{\dfrac{s}{2}}$$
$$00$$

The Cauer-I form that is realized, is shown in Fig. 5.76.

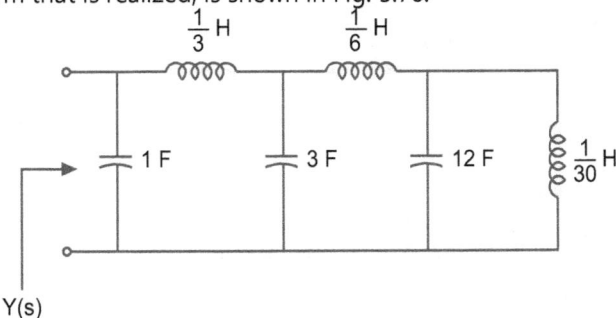

Fig. 5.76: Realized Cauer-I form

(B) Solved Examples on R-C Networks

Ex. 5.51: Synthesise the following functions in Foster-I and Foster-II forms.

$$F(s) = \frac{6(s+2)(s+4)}{s(s+3)}$$

Sol.: The function given is an R-C impedance function $Z_{RC}(s)$.

Foster-I Form: This is obtained by PFE of $Z_{RC}(s)$.

$$F(s) = Z_{RC}(s) = \frac{6(s+2)(s+4)}{s(s+3)}$$

$$= k_\infty + \frac{k_0}{s} + \frac{k_1}{(s+3)}$$

$$k_\infty = F(s)\Big|_{s \to \infty} = 6 \times 1 = +6$$

$$k_0 = sF(s)\Big|_{s \to 0}$$

$$= \frac{6 \times 2 \times 4}{3} = +16$$

$$k_1 = (s+3)F(s)\Big|_{s \to -3}$$

$$= \frac{6 \times (-3+2)(-3+4)}{-3} = +2$$

Thus the given function may be written as

$$Z_{RC}(s) = 6 + \frac{16}{s} + \frac{2}{(s+3)} = 6 + \frac{16}{s} + \frac{1}{\left(\frac{s}{2}+6\right)}$$

The realized Foster-I form is shown in Fig. 5.77.

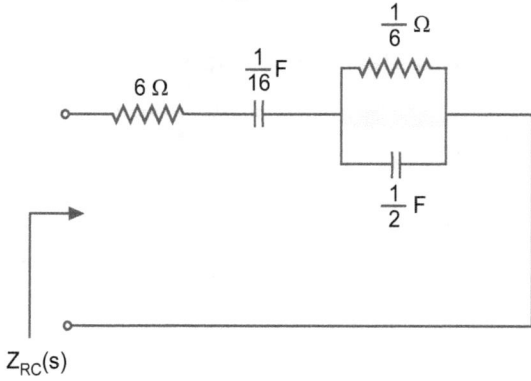

Fig. 5.77: Foster-I Form of Network

Foster-II Form: Obtained by PFE of function $\dfrac{Y_{RC}(s)}{s}$.

$$\dfrac{Y_{RC}(s)}{s} = \dfrac{2 \times s(s+2)}{6s(s+2)(s+4)} = \dfrac{(s+3)}{6(s+2)(s+4)} = \dfrac{k_1}{(s+2)} + \dfrac{k_2}{(s+4)}$$

$$k_1 = (s+2)\dfrac{Y_{RC}(s)}{s}\bigg|_{s \to -2} = \dfrac{1}{6} \times \dfrac{(-2+3)}{(-2+4)} = +\dfrac{1}{12}$$

$$k_2 = (s+4)\dfrac{Y_{RC}(s)}{s}\bigg|_{s \to -4} = \dfrac{1}{6} \times \dfrac{(-4+3)}{(-4+2)} = +\dfrac{1}{12}$$

Hence we have,

$$\dfrac{Y_{RC}(s)}{s} = \dfrac{1}{12(s+2)} + \dfrac{1}{12(s+4)}$$

$$Y_{RC}(s) = \dfrac{1}{12(s+2)} + \dfrac{s}{12(s+4)} = \dfrac{1}{\left(\dfrac{24}{s}+12\right)} + \dfrac{1}{\left(12+\dfrac{48}{s}\right)}$$

The realized Foster-II form of the network is shown in Fig. 5.78.

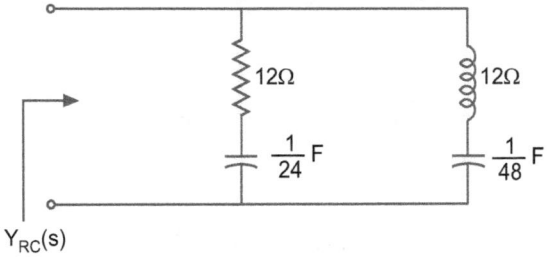

Fig. 5.78: Foster-II Form of Network

Ex. 5.52: Pole-zero diagram of an impedance function is as shown in Fig. 5.79. If $Z(-4) = \dfrac{3}{8}$ obtain the function and realize it in Cauer-I and Cauer-II forms.

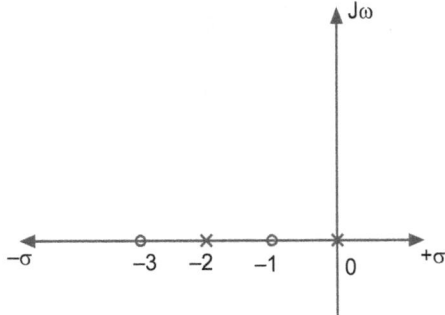

Fig. 5.79: Pole-Zero Diagram

Sol.: From the plot it is obvious that there are two zeros at $s = -1$ and $s = -3$ and two poles at $s = 0$ and $s = -2$. Thus, the function of the R-C impedance is given by -

$$Z(s) = \frac{k(s+2)(s+3)}{s(s+2)}$$

Also $\quad Z(-4) = \frac{3}{8} = \frac{k(-4+1)(-4+3)}{-4(-4+2)} = k \times \frac{3}{8}$

Hence we have $\boxed{k = +1}$

The impedance function is $Z(s) = \dfrac{(s+1)(s+3)}{s(s+2)} = \dfrac{s^2 + 4s + 3}{s^2 + 2s}$

Cauer-I Form: This is obtained by CFE as given below:

$$\begin{array}{r}
s^2 + 2s \overline{\smash{\big)}\, s^2 + 4s + 3} \,\big(\, 1 \leftarrow Z_1 \text{ (series)} \\
\underline{s^2 + 2s } \\
\end{array}$$

$$\begin{array}{r}
2s + 3 \overline{\smash{\big)}\, s^2 + 2s} \,\big(\, \dfrac{s}{2} \leftarrow Y_2(s) \text{ (shunt)} \\
\underline{s^2 + \dfrac{3}{2}s } \\
\end{array}$$

$$\begin{array}{r}
\dfrac{s}{2} \overline{\smash{\big)}\, 2s + 3} \,\big(\, 4 \leftarrow Z_3 \text{ (series)} \\
\underline{2s } \\
\end{array}$$

$$\begin{array}{r}
3 \overline{\smash{\big)}\, \dfrac{s}{2}} \,\big(\, \dfrac{s}{6} \leftarrow Y_4(s) \text{ (shunt)} \\
\underline{\dfrac{s}{2}} \\
00
\end{array}$$

The Cauer-I form obtained is shown in Fig. 5.80.

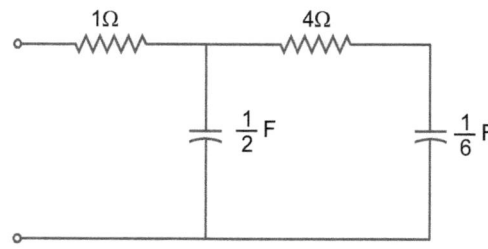

Fig. 5.80: Cauer-I Form of Network

Cauer-II Form: This is obtained by CFE as shown below.

$$2s + s^2 \overline{\smash{\big)}\, 3 + 4s + s^2} \left(\frac{3}{25} \leftarrow Z_1(s) \text{ (series)} \right.$$

$$\underline{3 + \frac{3}{2}s}$$

$$\frac{5}{2}s + s^2 \overline{\smash{\big)}\, 2s + s^2} \left(\frac{4}{5} \leftarrow Y_2 \text{ (shunt)} \right.$$

$$\underline{2s + \frac{4}{5}s^2}$$

$$\frac{s^2}{5} \overline{\smash{\big)}\, \frac{5}{2}s + s^2} \left(\frac{25}{2s} \leftarrow Z_3(s) \text{ (series)} \right.$$

$$\underline{\frac{5}{2}s}$$

$$s^2 \overline{\smash{\big)}\, \frac{s^2}{5}} \left(\frac{1}{5} \leftarrow Y_4 \text{ (shunt)} \right.$$

$$\underline{\frac{s^2}{5}}$$
$$00$$

The realized Cauer-II form is shown in Fig. 5.81.

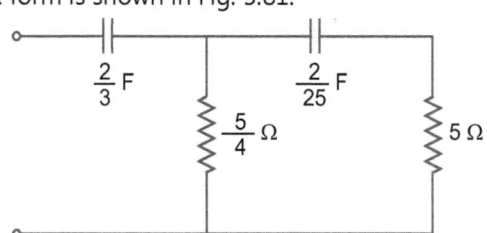

Fig. 5.81: Cauer-II Form of Network

Ex. 5.53: Synthesise $Y(s) = \dfrac{1 + 4s + 3s^2}{1 + 3s + 1.25s^2}$ in the form of Cauer-II network.

Sol.: Given Y(s) can be written as

$$Y(s) = \frac{3s^2 + 4s + 1}{1.25s^2 + 3s + 1} = \frac{(3s + 1)(s + 1)}{(1.25s + 0.5)(s + 2)}$$

$$= \frac{3\left(s + \frac{1}{3}\right)(s + 1)}{1.25(s + 0.4)(s + 2)} = 2.4 \frac{\left(s + \frac{1}{3}\right)(s + 1)}{(s + 0.4)(s + 2)}$$

Since critical frequency nearest to origin is zero and poles and zeros are interlaced on the negative real axis, the given function is an R-C admittance function.

The CFE to obtain Cauer-II form is as below.

$$1 + 3s + 1.25s^2 \overline{\smash{\big)}\, 1 + 4s + 3s^2} \; (1 \leftarrow Y_1(\text{shunt})$$

$$\underline{1 + 3s + 1.25s^2}$$

$$s + 1.75s^2 \overline{\smash{\big)}\, 1 + 3s + 1.25s^2} \; \left(\frac{1}{s} \leftarrow Z_2(s) \;(\text{series})\right.$$

$$\underline{1 + 1.75s}$$

$$1.25s + 1.25s^2 \overline{\smash{\big)}\, s + 1.75s^2} \; (0.8 \leftarrow Y_3$$

$$\underline{s + s^2}$$

$$0.75s^2 \overline{\smash{\big)}\, 1.25s + 1.25s^2} \; \left(\frac{1.66}{s} \leftarrow Z_4(s)\right.$$

$$\underline{1.25s}$$

$$1.25s^2 \overline{\smash{\big)}\, 0.75s^2} \; (0.6 \leftarrow Y_5$$

$$\underline{0.75s^2}$$

$$00$$

The realized network is shown in Fig. 5.82.

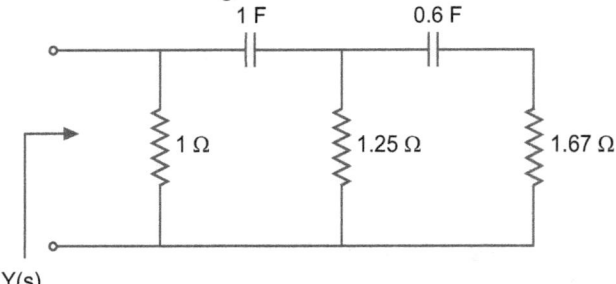

Fig. 5.82: Cauer-II Form of Network

Ex. 5.54: Realize the following admittance function into Cauer-I and Cauer-II forms

$$Y(s) = \frac{4s^2 + 6s}{(s+1)}$$

$$= \frac{4s\,(s+1.5)}{(s+1)}$$

Sol.: Given admittance function is an R-C admittance function since it satisfies all the properties of $Y_{RC}(s)$.

Cauer-I Form: CFE for Cauer-I form is as below. Since Y(s) has pole at s = ∞, start the division from Y(s).

$$s + 1 \overline{\smash{\big)}\, 4s^2 + 5s} \, \big(\, 4s \leftarrow Y_1(s) \text{ (series)}$$
$$\underline{4s^2 + 4s}$$
$$2s \overline{\smash{\big)}\, s + 1} \, \big(\, \tfrac{1}{2} \leftarrow Z_2 \text{ (shunt)}$$
$$\underline{s}$$
$$1 \overline{\smash{\big)}\, 25} \, \big(\, 2s \leftarrow Y_3(s) \text{ (series)}$$
$$\underline{25}$$
$$00$$

The realized Cauer-I network is shown in Fig. 5.83.

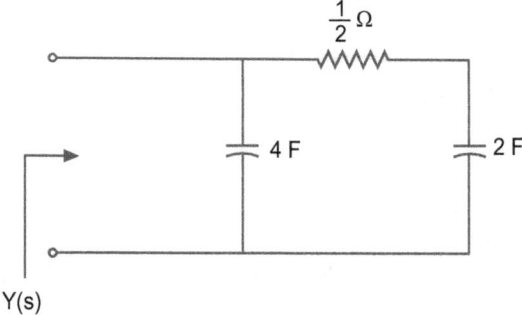

Y(s)

Fig. 5.83: Cauer-I Form of Network

Cauer-II Form: CFE for Cauer-II form is shown below. Since Z(s) has pole at the origin, start the division from Z(s).

We have, $\quad Z(s) = \dfrac{1}{Y(s)} = \dfrac{s+1}{(4s^2 + 6s)}$

$$6s + 4s^2 \overline{\smash{\big)}\, 1 + s} \, \big(\, \tfrac{1}{6s} \leftarrow Z_1(s) \text{ (series)}$$
$$\underline{1 + \tfrac{2}{3}s}$$
$$\tfrac{s}{3} \overline{\smash{\big)}\, 6s + 4s^2} \, \big(\, 18 \leftarrow Y_2(s) \text{ (shunt)}$$
$$\underline{6s}$$
$$4s^2 \overline{\smash{\big)}\, \tfrac{s}{3}} \, \big(\, \tfrac{1}{12s} \leftarrow Z_3(s) \text{ (series)}$$
$$\underline{\tfrac{s}{3}}$$
$$00$$

The realized Cauer-II network is shown in Fig. 5.84.

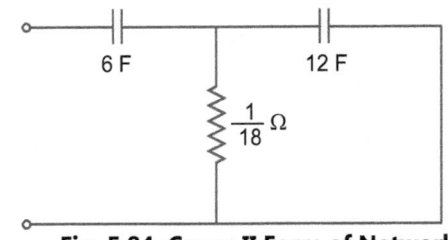

Fig. 5.84: Cauer-II Form of Network

Ex. 5.55: Synthesise the following function in Cauer-I form

$$Z(s) = \frac{(s^3 + 9s^2 + 23s + 15)}{s(s^3 + 12s^2 + 44s + 48)}$$

Sol.: CFE to obtain Cauer-I form is given below. Since there is no pole at the origin, there will be a pole at $s = \infty$ for $Y(s)$. Hence, start the division from $Y(s)$. First inductor (L_1) will remain absent.

$$Y(s) = \frac{(s^4 + 12s^3 + 44s^2 + 48s)}{(s^3 + 9s^2 + 23s + 15)}$$

$$s^3 + 9s^2 + 23s + 15 \,\overline{)\, s^4 + 12s^3 + 44s^2 + 48s} \,\bigl(\, s \leftarrow y_2(s)$$

$$\quad\quad s^4 + 9s^3 + 23s^2 + 15s$$

$$3s^3 + 21s^2 + 33s \,\overline{)\, s^3 + 9s^2 + 23s + 15} \,\bigl(\, \tfrac{1}{3} \leftarrow Z_3$$

$$\quad\quad s^3 + 7s^2 + 16s$$

$$2s^2 + 12s + 15 \,\overline{)\, 3s^3 + 21s^2 + 48s} \,\bigl(\, \tfrac{3}{2}s \leftarrow Y_4(s)$$

$$\quad\quad 3s^3 + 18s^2 + \tfrac{45}{2}s$$

$$3s^2 + \tfrac{21}{2}s \,\overline{)\, 2s^2 + 12s + 15} \,\bigl(\, \tfrac{2}{3} \leftarrow Z_4$$

$$\quad\quad 2s^2 + 7s$$

$$5s + 15 \,\overline{)\, 3s^2 + \tfrac{21}{2}s} \,\bigl(\, \tfrac{3}{5}s \leftarrow Y_5(s)$$

$$\quad\quad 3s^2 + 9s$$

$$\tfrac{3}{2}s \,\overline{)\, 5s + 15} \,\bigl(\, \tfrac{10}{3} \leftarrow Y_6$$

$$\quad\quad 5s + 0$$

$$15 \,\overline{)\, \tfrac{3}{2}s} \,\bigl(\, \tfrac{s}{10} \leftarrow Y_7(s)$$

$$\quad\quad \tfrac{3}{2}s$$

$$\quad\quad 00$$

The realized Cauer-I network is shown in Fig. 5.85.

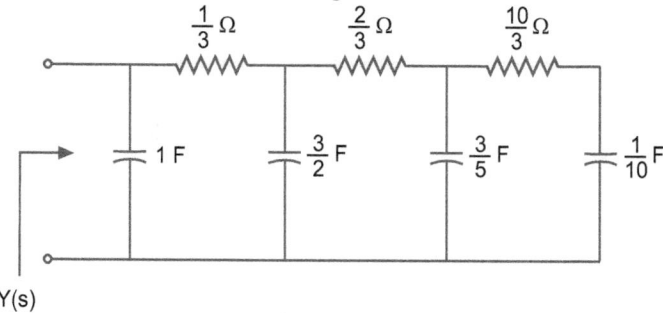

Fig. 5.85: Cauer-I Form of Network

Ex. 5.56: Realize the following function in Cauer-I form

$$Z(s) = \frac{k(s+3)(s+7)}{(s+2)(s+6)} \text{ and } Z(0) = 20.$$

Sol.: Putting $s = 0$ in the above equation we get

$$Z(0) = 20 = \frac{k \times 3 \times 7}{2 \times 6} \quad \text{Here } k = 11.423 = \frac{80}{7}$$

Thus, $\quad Z(s) = 11.423 \left[\dfrac{s^2 + 10s + 21}{s^2 + 8s + 12} \right]$

$$= \frac{11.423s^2 + 114.28s + 240}{s^2 + 8s + 12}$$

CEF for Cauer-I form is shown below.

$$s^2 + 8s + 12 \overline{\smash{\big)}\, 11.423s^2 + 114.28s + 240} \; (\; 11.423 \leftarrow Z_1$$
$$\underline{11.423s^2 + 91.43s + 137.14}$$

$$22.86s + 102.86 \overline{\smash{\big)}\, s^2 + 8s + 12} \; \left(\dfrac{s}{22.86} \leftarrow Y_2(s) \right.$$
$$\underline{s^2 + 4.5s}$$

$$3.5s + 12 \overline{\smash{\big)}\, 22.86s + 102.86} \; (\; 6.53 \leftarrow Z_3$$
$$\underline{22.86s + 78.36}$$

$$24.5 \overline{\smash{\big)}\, 3.5s + 12} \; (\; 0.142s \leftarrow Y_4(s)$$
$$\underline{3.5s}$$

$$12 \overline{\smash{\big)}\, 24.5} \; (\; 2.04 \leftarrow Z_4$$
$$\underline{24.5}$$
$$00$$

The realized Cauer-I network is shown in Fig. 5.86.

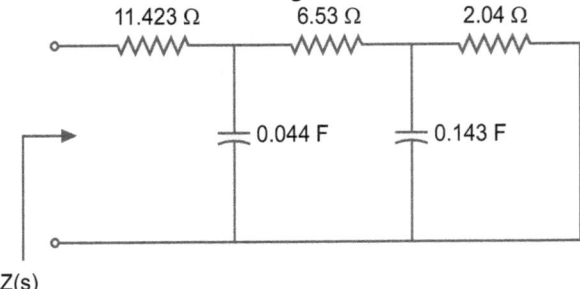

Fig. 5.86: Cauer-I Form of Network

(C) Solved Examples on R-L Network

Ex. 5.57: Synthesise the following function into Cauer-I and Cauer-II forms of network.

$$Y(s) = \frac{(s+2)(s+5)}{s(s+4)(s+6)}$$

Sol.: The given function is $Y(s) = \dfrac{s^2 + 7s + 10}{s^3 + 10s^2 + 24s}$

Cauer-I Form: CFE for removal of pole at $s = \infty$ gives

$$s^3 + 10s^2 + 24s \,\overline{\smash{\big)}\, s^2 + 7s + 10} \;\Big(\dfrac{1}{s}$$

$$\underline{s^2 + 10s + 24}$$
$$-3s - 14$$

It gives negative coefficient since there is no pole of Z(s) at $s = \infty$. Therefore, start the CFE from

$$Z(s) = \frac{s^3 + 10s^2 + 24s}{s^2 + 7s + 10}$$

$$s^2 + 7s + 10 \,\overline{\smash{\big)}\, s^3 + 10s^2 + 24s}\;(s \leftarrow Z_2(s)$$
$$\underline{s^3 + 7s^2 + 10s}$$
$$3s^2 + 14s \,\overline{\smash{\big)}\, s^2 + 7s + 10}\;\Big(\dfrac{1}{3} \leftarrow Y_3$$
$$\underline{s^2 + \dfrac{14}{3}s}$$
$$\dfrac{7}{3}s + 10 \,\overline{\smash{\big)}\, 3s^2 + 14s}\;\Big(\dfrac{9}{7}s \leftarrow Z_4(s)$$
$$\underline{3s^2 + \dfrac{90}{7}s}$$
$$\dfrac{8}{7}s \,\overline{\smash{\big)}\, \dfrac{7}{3}s + 10}\;\Big(\dfrac{49}{24} \leftarrow Y_5$$
$$\underline{\dfrac{7}{3}s}$$

... *contd.*

$$10 \overline{\smash{)}\tfrac{8}{7}s} \left(\tfrac{8}{70} s \leftarrow Z_6(s) \right.$$

$$\underline{\tfrac{8}{7}s}$$

$$00$$

The realized Cauer-I network is shown in Fig. 5.87 (a).

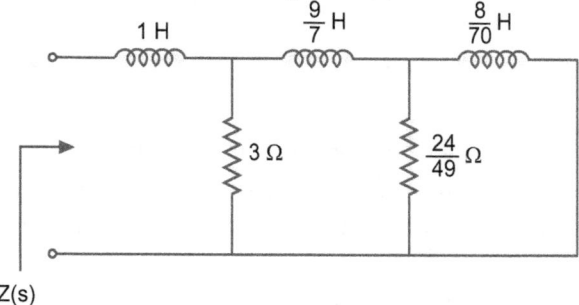

Fig. 5.87 (a): Cauer-I Form of Network

Cauer-II Form: Obtained by CFE about pole at the origin. Since Y(s) has a pole at s = 0 start the division from Y(s) only.

$$24s + 10s^2 + s^3 \overline{\smash{)}\, 10 + 7s + s^2} \left(\tfrac{5}{12s} \leftarrow Y_2(s) \right.$$

$$\underline{10 + \tfrac{25}{6}s + \tfrac{5}{12}s^2}$$

$$\tfrac{17}{6}s + \tfrac{7}{12}s^2 \overline{\smash{)}\, 24s + 10s^2 + s^3} \left(\tfrac{144}{17} \leftarrow R_3 \right.$$

$$\underline{24s + \tfrac{84}{17}s^2}$$

$$\tfrac{86}{17}s^2 + s^3 \overline{\smash{)}\, \tfrac{17}{6}s + \tfrac{7}{12}s^2} \left(\tfrac{289}{516s} \leftarrow Y_4(s) \right.$$

$$\underline{\tfrac{17}{6}s + \tfrac{289}{516}s^2}$$

$$\tfrac{12}{516}s^2 \overline{\smash{)}\, \tfrac{86}{17}s^2 + s^3} \left(\tfrac{3698}{17} \leftarrow R_5 \right.$$

$$\underline{\tfrac{86}{17}s^2}$$

$$s^3 \overline{\smash{)}\, \tfrac{12}{516}s^2} \left(\tfrac{12}{516s} \leftarrow Y_6(s) \right.$$

$$\underline{\tfrac{12}{516}s^2}$$

$$00$$

The realized Cauer-II network is shown in Fig. 5.87 (b).

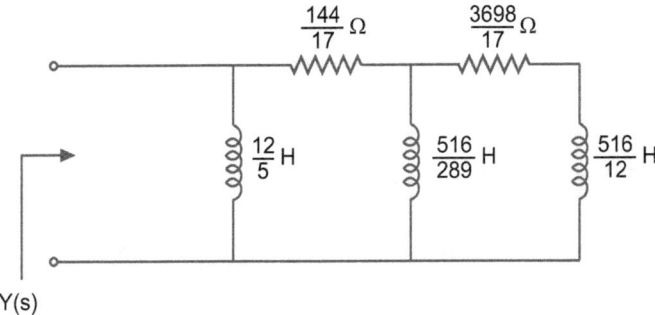

Y(s)

Fig. 5.87 (b): Cauer-II Form of Network

Ex. 5.58: Pole-zero diagrams of two networks are given below in Fig. 5.88. Choose the diagram that represents R-L impedance function and realize it in the Foster-I form.

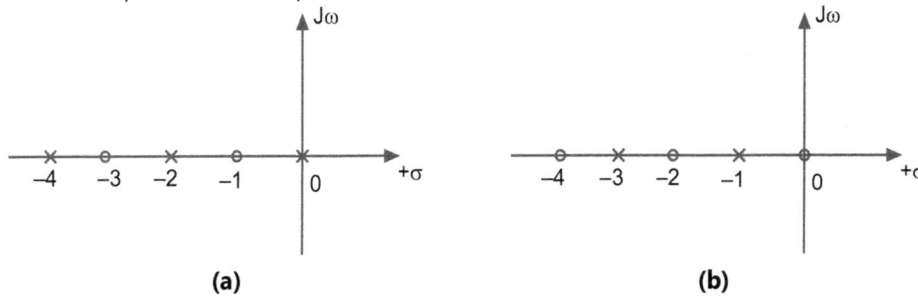

Fig. 5.88: Pole Zero Diagram

Sol.: Since R-L impedance $Z_{RL}(s)$ does not have a pole at $s = 0$. The plot of Fig. 5.88 (b) represents an R-L impedance function.

Thus, $Z(s) = Z_{RL}(s) = \dfrac{s(s+2)(s+4)}{(s+1)(s+3)}$

To get Foster-I form, expand $\dfrac{Z(s)}{s}$ for R-L network.

$$\dfrac{Z(s)}{s} = \dfrac{(s+2)(s+4)}{(s+1)(s+3)} = \dfrac{k_0}{(s+1)} + \dfrac{k_1}{(s+3)} + k_\infty$$

$$k_0 = (s+1)\dfrac{Z(s)}{s}\bigg|_{s \to -1} = \dfrac{(-1+2)(-1+4)}{(-1+3)} = +\dfrac{3}{2}$$

$$k_1 = (s+3)\dfrac{Z(s)}{s}\bigg|_{s \to -3} = \dfrac{(-3+2)(-3+4)}{(-3+1)} = +\dfrac{1}{2}$$

$$k_\infty = \dfrac{Z(s)}{s}\bigg|_{z \to \infty} = 1$$

Thus, the impedance function Z(s) is given as

$$Z(s) = s + \frac{3s}{2(s+1)} + \frac{s}{2(s+3)} = s + \frac{1}{\left(\frac{2}{3} + \frac{2}{3s}\right)} + \frac{1}{\left(2 + \frac{6}{s}\right)}$$

The realized Foster-I form of the network is shown in the Fig. 5.89.

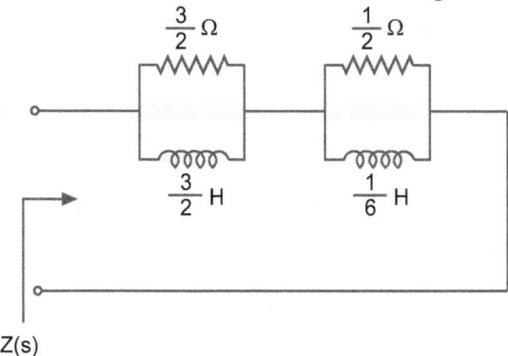

Fig. 5.89: Foster-I Form of Network

Ex. 5.59: An impedance function is given by

$$Z(s) = \frac{2(s+1)(s+3)}{(s+2)(s+4)}$$

Find R-L representation using Foster-I form.

Sol.: As there is a zero close to origin, the given function is an R-L impedance function $Z_{RL}(s)$. Expand $\frac{Z(s)}{s}$.

$$\frac{Z(s)}{s} = \frac{2(s+1)(s+3)}{s(s+2)(s+4)} = \frac{k_0}{s} + \frac{k_1}{(s+2)} + \frac{k_2}{(s+4)}$$

$$k_0 = s \cdot \frac{Z(s)}{s}\bigg|_{s \to 0} = \frac{2 \times 1 \times 3}{2 \times 4} = +\frac{3}{4}$$

$$k_1 = (s+2)\frac{Z(s)}{s}\bigg|_{s \to -2} = \frac{2 \times (-2+1)(-2+3)}{(-2+4)(-2)} = +\frac{1}{2}$$

$$k_2 = (s+4)\frac{Z(s)}{s}\bigg|_{s \to -4} = \frac{2 \times (-4+1)(-4+3)}{-4(-4+2)} = +\frac{3}{4}$$

Thus, $$Z(s) = \frac{3}{4} + \frac{s}{2(s+2)} + \frac{3s}{4(s+4)}$$

$$= \frac{3}{4} + \frac{1}{\left(2 + \frac{4}{5}\right)} + \frac{1}{\left(\frac{4}{3} + \frac{16}{3s}\right)}$$

The realized network is shown below in Fig. 5.90.

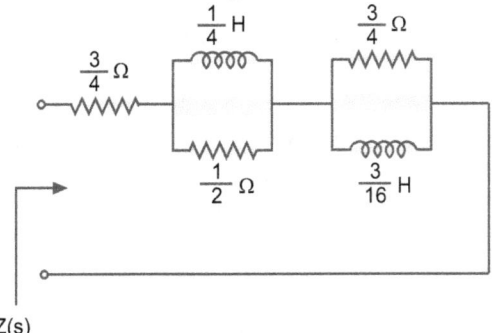

Fig. 5.90: Realized R-L Network

(D) Solved Examples on R-L-C Networks

Ex. 5.60: Synthesise the given function into a network

$$F(s) = \frac{2s^2 + 2s + 1}{s^3 + 2s^2 + s + 2}$$

Sol.: This function is neither L-C immittance nor R-C or R-L function.

$$F(s) = Z(s) = \frac{2s^2 + 2s + 1}{(s+2)(s^2+1)} = \frac{k_0}{(s+2)} + \frac{(k_1 s + k_2)}{(s^2+2)}$$

Equating the terms on both sides gives

$$s^2(k_0 + k_1) + s(k_1 + k_2) + 2(k_0 + k_2) = 2s^2 + 2s + 1$$

Hence, $\boxed{k_0 + k_1 = 2}$ $\boxed{k_1 + k_2 = 2}$ $\boxed{k_0 + 2k_2 = 1}$

But $k_0 = (s+2) Z(s) \big|_{s \to -2} = +1$

Thus, $\boxed{k_1 = 1}$ $\boxed{k_2 = 0}$

Thus given function can be written as

$$Z(s) = \frac{1}{(s+2)} + \frac{1}{(s^2+2)} = \frac{1}{(s+2)} + \frac{1}{(s+2/s)}$$

The realized R-L-C network in Foster-I form is shown in Fig. 5.91.

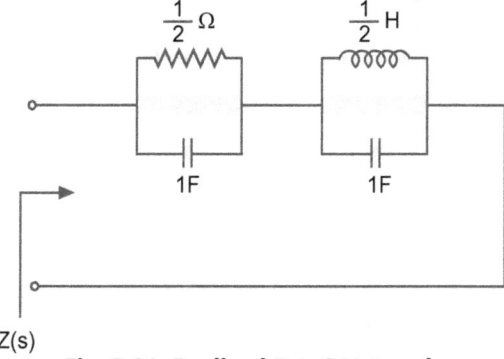

Fig. 5.91: Realized R-L-C Network

Ex. 5.61: For the circuit given in Fig. 5.92 (a), the system function $H(s) = \dfrac{V(s)}{I(s)}$ has poles as shown in Fig. 5.92 (b).

(1) Find the element values of R and C.
(2) If excitation i(t) is a pulse of unit height and duration 1 sec. find V(t) using convolution integral by other method.

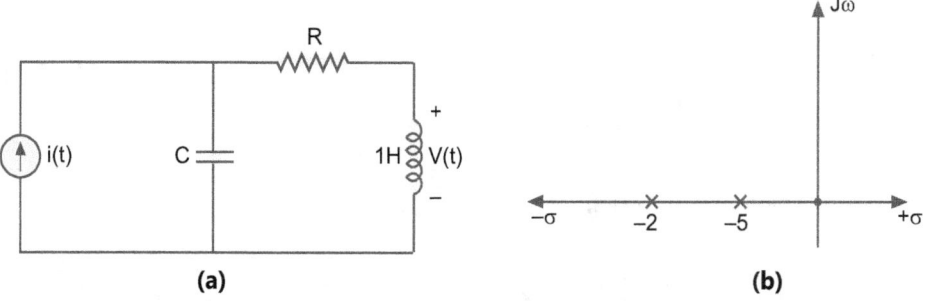

Fig. 5.92: Details given in Ex. 5.61

Sol.: (1) Laplace Transform of circuit is shown in Fig. 5.93.

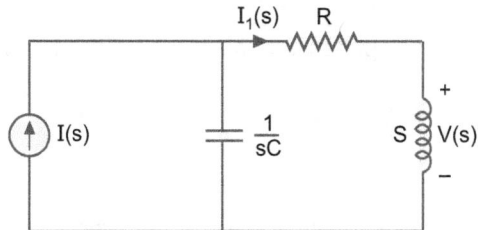

Fig. 5.93: Transformed Circuit

We have $\quad I_1(s) = \dfrac{I(s) \times \dfrac{1}{sC}}{R + s + \dfrac{1}{sC}}$

Or $\quad I_1(s) = I(s) \times \dfrac{1}{s^2C + RsC + 1}$

And $\quad V(s) = sI_1(s)$

$\quad = \dfrac{s \cdot I(s)}{(s^2C + RCs + 1)}$

Hence $\quad H(s) = \dfrac{V(s)}{I(s)}$

$\quad = \dfrac{s}{s^2C + RCs + 1} \quad \ldots \text{(A)}$

With the given pole-zero plot of Fig. 5.82 (b), we have

$$H(s) = \frac{s}{(s+2)(s+0.5)} = \frac{s}{s^2 + 2.5s + 1} \quad \ldots (B)$$

Comparing (A) and (B) we have

$C = 1F$ and $RC = 2.5$ hence $R = 2.5\,\Omega$

(2) Since excitation i(t) is a pulse of unit height, we have

$$i(t) = u(t) - u(t-1)$$

hence $\quad I(s) = \dfrac{1}{s}[1 - e^{-s}]$

Now by (B) $\quad H(s) = \dfrac{V(s)}{I(s)} = \dfrac{s}{s^2 + 2.5s + 1}$

$\therefore \quad V(s) = I(s) \cdot H(s) = \dfrac{1 - e^{-s}}{(s^2 + 2.5s + 1)}$

$$V(s) = (1 - e^{-s})\left[\frac{k_0}{(s+2)} + \frac{k_1}{(s+0.5)}\right] = (1 - e^{-s})\left[\frac{4}{3(s+2)} - \frac{1}{3(s+0.5)}\right]$$

$V(t) = L^{-1}[V(s)]$

$$V(t) = \frac{4}{3}e^{-2t} - \frac{1}{3}e^{-0.5t} - \frac{4}{3}e^{-2(t-1)}U(t-1) - \frac{1}{3}e^{-0.5(t-1)}U(t-1)$$

Ex. 5.62: The driving point impedance of a network with positive and real components is given by

$$Z(s) = \frac{6s^3 + 3s^2 + 3s + 1}{6s^3 + 3s}$$

Realize the structure of the network.

Sol.: As poles are lying on the imaginary axis while zeros are not on the imaginary axis, it is an R-L-C impedance function.

Using CFE we get

```
              6s³ + 3s ) 6s³ + 3s² + 3s + 1 ( 1 ← Z₁
                         6s³ + 3s
                         ─────────
                              3s² + 1 ) 6s³ + 5s ( 2s ← Y₂(s)
                                        6s³ + 2s
                                        ────────
                                             s ) 3s² + 1 ( 3s ← Z₃(s)
                                                 3s²
                                                 ────
                                                     1 ) s ( s ← Y₄(s)
                                                         s
                                                         ──
                                                         00
```

The realized network is shown in Fig. 5.94.

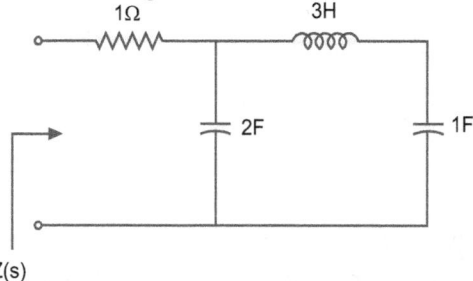

Fig. 5.94: R-L-C Network (Cauer-I Form)

Ex. 5.63: Impedance function of a network is given by
$$Z(s) = \frac{s^2 + 2s + 2}{(s^2 + s + 1)}$$
Synthesise this impedance into a network.

Sol.: The function given is an R-L-C impedance. It can be realized by using CFE as shown below.

$$
\begin{array}{r}
s^2+s+1 \overline{\smash{\big)}\ s^2+2s+2}\ \big(1 \leftarrow Z_1 \\
\underline{s^2+s+1} \\
(-)\ (-)\ (-)
\end{array}
$$

$$
\begin{array}{r}
s+1 \overline{\smash{\big)}\ s^2+s+1}\ \big(s \leftarrow Y_2(s) \\
\underline{s^2+s}
\end{array}
$$

$$
\begin{array}{r}
1 \overline{\smash{\big)}\ s+1}\ \big(s \leftarrow Z_3(s) \\
\underline{s}
\end{array}
$$

$$
\begin{array}{r}
1 \overline{\smash{\big)}\ 1}\ \big(1 \leftarrow Y_4 \\
\underline{1} \\
00
\end{array}
$$

The Cauer-I form of the realized R-L-C network is as shown in Fig. 5.95.

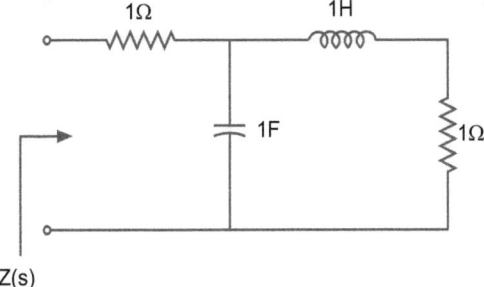

Fig. 5.95: Realized R-L-C Network

EXERCISE

1. Define the stability of a network. State and explain the conditions for stability of a network.
2. What is Hurwitz polynomial? Give the conditions for a function p(s) to be a Hurwitz polynomial.
3. Explain Routh-Hurwitz method for testing a polynomial to be Hurwitz.
4. State the necessary conditions for the transfer function of a network.
5. State the necessary conditions for the driving point function of a network.
6. What is a positive real function? State the necessary condition for a function to be P.R.F.
7. Give the necessary and sufficient conditions for a function to be P.R.F.
8. Explain the testing procedure for a function to be P.R.F.
9. Explain the following basic removal operation:
   (a) Removal of a pole at $s = \infty$ from the function.
   (b) Removal of a pole at $s = 0$ from the function.
   (c) Removal of a conjugate imaginary axis poles from a function.
10. Test whether the following polynomials are Hurwitz.
    (a) $s^4 + 9s^3 + 9s^2 + 24s + 20$
    (b) $s^6 + 3s^5 + 3s^4 + 3s^2 + 3s^2 + 3s + 2$
    (c) $s^5 + 5.5 s^4 + 9s^3 + 6.5s^2 + 8s + 6$
11. Test whether the following functions are P.R.F.
    (a) $\dfrac{s^4 + 2.5s^2 + 1}{s^5 + 4.5s^3 + 4.5s}$
    (b) $\dfrac{2s^2 + 2s + 4}{s^3 + s^2 + 2s + 2}$
    (c) $\dfrac{2s^2 + 3s + 5}{s^2 + 2s + 2}$
12. Explain with reasons, why the following functions are not P.R.F.
    (a) $\dfrac{(s^2 + 1)(s^2 + 2)}{s(s^2 + 3)}$
    (b) $\dfrac{s^3 + 6s^2 + 2s + 1}{s + 4}$
    (c) $\dfrac{s^2 + 2s + 1}{s^2}$
    (d) $\dfrac{s^2 + 7s^2 + 15s + 9}{s^4 + 6s^2 + 9}$

13. Test whether following polynomials are Hurwitz.
    (a) $s^4 + 9s^3 + 9s^2 + 24s + 20$
    (b) $s^5 + 5s^4 + 6s^3 + s^2 = 5s + 6$
    (c) $s^6 + 3s^5 + 3s^4 + 3s^3 + 3s^2 + 3s + 2$
    (d) $s^5 + 2s^4 + 5s^3 + 10s^2 + 9s + 18$
    (e) $s^5 + 17s^4 + 107s^3 + 307s^2 + 396s + 180$
    (f) $s^5 + 5.5s^4 + 9s^3 + 6.5s^2 + 8s + 6$

14. Test the following functions for positive realness
    (a) $\dfrac{s^2 + 4s + 3}{s^2 + 6s + 8}$
    (b) $\dfrac{s^4 + 2.5s^2 + 1}{s^5 + 4.5s^3 + 4.5s}$
    (c) $\dfrac{s^4 + 2s^3 + 8s^2 + s + 1}{s^4 + s^3 + 3s^2 + 2s + 1}$
    (d) $\dfrac{2s^2 + 3s + 5}{s^2 + 2s + 2}$
    (e) $\dfrac{2s^2 + 2s + 4}{s^3 + s^2 + 2s + 2}$
    (f) $\dfrac{s^4 + 2.5s^2 + 1}{s^5 + 4.5s^3 + 4.5s}$

15. Following functions are not positive real. Justify your answer with reasons.
    (a) $\dfrac{(s^2 + 1)(s^2 + 2)}{s(s^2 + 3)}$
    (b) $\dfrac{s^3 + 6s^2 + 2s + 1}{s + 4}$
    (c) $\dfrac{s^2 + 2s + 1}{s^2}$
    (d) $\dfrac{s^2 + 7s^2 + 15s + 9}{s^4 + 6s^2 + 9}$

16. Obtain the first and second Foster form of the L-C impedance function
    $$Z(s) = 78 \dfrac{s(s^2 + 2)(s^2 + 4)}{(s^2 + 1)(s^2 + 3)}$$

17. Obtain the Cauer-I and Cauer-II forms of network for the following functions.
    (a) $Z(s) = \dfrac{(s^2 + 1)(s^2 + 9)(s^2 + 25)}{s(s^2 + 4)(s^2 + 16)}$
    (b) $Z(s) = \dfrac{s(s^2 + 4)(s^2 + 36)}{(s^2 + 1)(s^2 + 25)(s^2 + 81)}$

18. Find two Foster networks meeting the specification
$$Z(s) = \frac{(s + 2.5)(s + 10)}{(s + 1)(s + 7.5)}$$

19. Synthesise first and second Cauer forms of the network for the impedance functions.

    (a) $Z(s) = \dfrac{2s + s^2}{3 + 4s + s^2}$

    (b) $Z(s) = \dfrac{s^2 + 7s + 4}{2s + 3s^2}$

20. An impedance function has simple poles at -1 and -4 and simple zeros at -2 and -5, and $Z(0) = 10\ \Omega$. Find four canonical networks with element values.

21. Find $Z(s)$ given:

    (a) Poles at -2 and 0

    (b) Zeros at -1 and -3

    (c) $Z(\infty) = 2$.

    Is it possible to Synthesise it? Give reasons. Hence find one Cauer and one Foster representation.

22. Classify following R-C immittances.

    (a) $\dfrac{s^2 + 10s^2 + 24s}{s^2 + 7s + 10}$

    (b) $\dfrac{s^2 + 10s + 24}{s^2 + 7s + 10}$

    (c) $\dfrac{s^2 + 3s + 1.25}{s^2 + 7.5s + 9s}$

    (d) $\dfrac{s^2 + 12s + 35}{s^3 + 15s^2 + 62s + 48}$

    Realize one of the impedance functions in four canonical forms.

www.ingramcontent.com/pod-product-compliance
Lightning Source LLC
Chambersburg PA
CBHW060503300426
44112CB00017B/2538